RENEWALS 458-4574
DATE DUE

D1737417

WITHDRAWN
UTSA LIBRARIES

ANTHONY EDEN AT THE FOREIGN OFFICE 1931-1938

Anthony Eden at the Foreign Office 1931-1938

A. R. PETERS

Gower

St. Martin's Press

New York

© Anthony R. Peters 1986

All rights reserved. No part of this publication may be reproduced, stored in a retrieval system, or transmitted in any form or by any means, electronic, mechanical, photocopying, recording or otherwise without the prior permission of Gower Publishing Company Limited and St Martin's Press, New York.

First published in Great Britain by
Gower Publishing Company Ltd
Gower House, Croft Road
Aldershot, Hampshire GU11 3HR
England

First published in the United States of America in 1986
All rights reserved. For information write:
Scholarly and Reference Division
St Martin's Press, Inc.
175 Fifth Avenue
New York, NY10010
USA

British Library Cataloguing in Publication Data

Peters, Anthony R.
    Anthony Eden at the Foreign Office, 1931–1938.
    1. Eden, Anthony — Career in international relations
    2. Great Britain — Foreign relations — 1910–1936
    3. Great Britain — Foreign relations — 1936–1945
    I. Title
    327.41'0092'4   DA578
    ISBN 0-566-05117-6

Library of Congress Cataloging-in-Publication Data

Peters, A.R.
    Anthony Eden at the Foreign Office, 1931–1938

    Bibliography: p.
    1. Eden, Anthony, Earl of Avon, 1897–
    2. Great Britain — Foreign relations — 1910–1936
    3. Great Britain — Foreign relations — 1936–1945
    4. Great Britain. Foreign Office — History — 20th Century
I. Title
DA566.9E28P47   1986   941.083'092'4 [B]   85-24994
ISBN 0-312-04236-1

ISBN 0-566-05117-6 Gower
ISBN 0-312-04236-1 St Martin's

Printed in Great Britain by
Blackmore Press, Longmead, Shaftesbury, Dorset

LIBRARY
The University of Texas
at San Antonio

Contents

Acknowledgements

A number of people must be acknowledged for their assistance in the preparation of this book. In particular I owe a great debt to Professor Paul Rolo whose guidance and encouragement were invaluable. In addition I must record my thanks to Robert Haigh and David Morris of Sheffield City Polytechnic. Without their support this book would not have been completed. The staff at the Public Record Office, Kew; the University of Cambridge Library; the University of Birmingham Library; and Churchill College Library, Cambridge, also rendered great assistance at various times in the production of the manuscript. The typing was undertaken by Mrs Ruth Barker with great patience from drafts that left much to be desired in terms of legibility.

For permission to reproduce material I thank: MacMillan Publishing Company (New York); Collins (London); the Royal Institute of International Affairs; and the Master and Fellows of Churchill College in the University of Cambridge. Extracts from Crown Copyright material in the Public Record Office are reproduced by permission of the Controller of Her Majesty's Stationery Office.

Finally this book is dedicated to Alison, Sarah and Laura with thanks for their patience and tolerance during the years in which the manuscript was in preparation.

A.R.P.
Sheffield, 1986

Preface

This work is based upon an examination of Anthony Eden's role at the Foreign Office in the period 1931–1938. It is not intended to be either a biography of Eden or a comprehensive analysis of the conduct of British foreign policy in the 1930s but rather is an interpretation of Eden's particular contribution to the making of foreign policy in this period.

An attempt to analyse Eden's role would be incomplete without an examination of his formative years. Chapter 1 briefly surveys his family background, education, war service and his early years within the House of Commons with the aim of establishing the influences which initially moulded his views on foreign policy. Subsequent chapters trace his rise within the Foreign Office from the position of Parliamentary Under-Secretary in August 1931 to his resignation of the post of Foreign Secretary in February 1938.

The text naturally concentrates upon the areas of policy-making in which Eden was most involved and, therefore, particular attention is paid to the Disarmament Conference, the Italo-Abyssinian war, the Rhineland crisis, the Spanish Civil War and, finally, the search for a European security agreement which was a constant theme throughout his term of office. The book looks not only at Eden's personal interpretation of the goals to be pursued but also the restrictions that surrounded and influenced his deliberations. In this context an examination is made of his relationship with officials at the Foreign Office and also his colleagues within the National Government. Attention is also devoted to the limitations imposed by popular expectations, political and military commitments and the ambitions of other nations.

On the basis of this evidence an attempt is made to assess Eden's views on the conduct of British foreign policy and to evaluate his contribution to, and influence upon, the course pursued by the British Government in the period 1931–1938.

1 The road to the Foreign Office

Robert Anthony Eden was the third son of Sir William Eden, 7th Baronet of West Auckland and 5th Baronet of Maryland. As befitted the son of a family that had held a 300-acre estate at Windlestone Hall near Bishop Auckland for over 300 years, Anthony was raised in a typically aristocratic mould.[1] At the age of eight he was despatched to preparatory school[2] and from then on his school holidays were divided between Windlestone in the winter and periods of residence at either the family's London home or on the continent in the summer.[3]

Although he was taught to ride and shoot at an early age and was later to distinguish himself as an oarsman of some merit, it was apparent that he was not a keen sportsman; in his memoirs Eden describes with evident distaste the periods of physical exercise that he and his younger brother, Nicholas, were subjected to by their governess.[4] It is interesting to note that Eden's subsequent recollections of Windlestone concentrate essentially on the splendour of the house, its grounds and the variety of characters who served the Eden family, with only passing references to his relationship with his brothers and sister and their activities.[5] The picture that emerges is of a rather shy, frail boy who, as with many of his contemporaries, had a much closer relationship with his governess than with either of his parents.[6] Eden's brother, Timothy, was later to testify graphically to their father's eccentricity and volatile temper which frightened and distanced him from his children.[7] Looking back on his childhood, Eden was later to note:

1

The idiosyncratic way of life my father led was nevertheless genuinely expressed, with intense originality and taste. As such it affected his children in various ways, Jack was impervious . . . Marjorie was amused and understanding and anyway the best-loved of his children. Timothy, solitary in age between the two groups of the family was, perhaps on that account, my mother's special care. Nicholas and I, though spared some of the impact in our younger years, were often rather bewildered by what was occasionally irrational behaviour.

'You are a typical Grey' my father used sometimes to say. I took this to mean a plodder of conventional ability and tolerable good looks, taking after my mother's family and not very exciting.[8]

It would appear that there was very little direct contact between father and son and it was only in the last years of Sir William's life that Anthony was able to approach his father without fear of rebuke, the bridge between them being provided by their love for Windlestone and, in particular, its grounds and Sir William's collection of paintings.[9]

Eden's mother, who was the daughter of Sir William Grey, a former Lieutenant-Governor of Bengal, was a celebrated Victorian beauty. Although Eden recorded with fondness his pride at the impact his mother made on her occasional visits to his preparatory school, it was evident that Sybil Eden was far more comfortable in the social circles of Edwardian society or in the committee rooms of her various charities than with four demanding young children.[10] For maternal comfort Anthony turned to his governess or to his elder sister, Marjorie, and subsequently noted of his mother:

I think my mother preferred the simpler relationship which existed between donor and recipient to the more complicated one between mother and child. No doubt she often found her children mystifying, wilful, or even ungrateful, though she was always conscientious about us.[11]

At the age of 13 Anthony followed his elder brother Timothy to Eton where, although he was a capable scholar, he achieved little distinction and later admitted that he 'never pretended to like school' and that his years at Eton 'were far from the happiest' in his life.[12] In part, perhaps, this can be explained by the unfortunate circumstances which surrounded his last twelve months at Eton. War was declared in August 1914 and while Eden drilled with the Eton College Officer Training Corps, news was received that his eldest brother John had been killed in action at Ypres. John was nine years Eden's senior and

2

had served with the Twelfth Lancers in South Africa and India.[13] The death of a figure that Anthony idolised was a severe blow which was compounded by the news that his brother, Timothy, and his uncle had fallen into German hands. The former had the misfortune to be in Germany at the time of the outbreak of hostilities and the latter had been shot down while serving with the Royal Flying Corps in France.[14] With the death of his father, in February 1915, it is not surprising that Eden had few happy memories of his last year at Eton.

His central goal was to enlist as soon as he reached the age of 18 and, although there was some speculation as to his joining the Grenadier Guards, a friend of the family, Lord Feversham, persuaded him to apply for the newly formed Durham platoon of the Yeoman Rifles which was to form part of the King's Royal Rifle Corps.[15] The following four years were a crucial period in the moulding of Eden's character. The callow youth who enlisted in 1915 returned in 1919 a self-confident and assertive man. He had been promoted to the rank of adjutant within a year and in 1918 was the youngest brigade-major in the British Army. During the course of the war he was engaged in action at Passchendaele, Ypres, Messines Ridge and the Somme, being awarded the Military Cross in June 1917 for braving enemy fire to rescue a member of his platoon. In addition to qualities of leadership he also displayed a remarkable capacity for organisational and administrative minutiae; it was this meticulous attention to detail which was to become the hallmark of his work in later years.[16] More significantly, however, the war claimed many of his close friends and a further brother, Nicholas, who was killed at the Battle of Jutland.[17] In his memoirs Eden expressed his frustration with the carnage wreaked by the war and his disaffection with the politicians who had allowed Europe to slide into conflict:

> In the Army I shared the soldier's antipathy towards politicians which was more widespread and sharper than in the Second World War.

> The fighting over, I was with my Brigade among the snows of the Ardennes for the long winter of 1918–19 and I took no close interest in the general election at home. Nor did I respond to a feeler that I should stand for a constituency in my home county of Durham.[18]

Although Eden could never be classed as a pacifist, the war certainly left him with the conviction that the generation of soldiers who had served in the trenches would in future recognise the advantages of negotiation and compromise as opposed to the futility of armed conflict in settling national rivalries.[19]

In 1919 Eden seemed destined to follow the family tradition of service to the State and eventually rejected the Army in favour of the Diplomatic Service. He had been advised by Sir George Clark, a former Ambassador to Turkey, that a grasp of foreign languages would be advantageous in such a career and accordingly elected to pick up the threads of his education by going to Christ Church, Oxford, to study oriental languages. While at Oxford Eden concentrated largely on his studies, taking little or no interest in university politics. His only prominent role at Oxford was President of the Uffizi Society, formed to discuss painters and painting.[20] Therefore it was, perhaps, surprising that on leaving Oxford with a first class degree Eden decided to plunge into politics and stand as Conservative candidate for Spennymoor at the General Election of 1922. This decision was, however, once again directed by the network of influential connections that surrounded the Eden family and particularly by the Marquess of Londonderry who offered to support Eden's nomination for the Conservative candidacy at Spennymoor.[21] This offer, made at a time when Eden was considering the direction which his career should take, proved to be a decisive turning-point in his life.

Although he was heavily defeated in what was overwhelmingly a working-class constituency,[22] the campaign had whetted his appetite for politics and in 1923 he was invited to stand as Conservative candidate for Leamington and Warwick. In this largely rural area, where his Labour opponent was the Countess of Warwick, Eden's war service and family background provided the perfect credentials for a young aspiring Conservative candidate, while his marriage to Beatrice Beckett, daughter of the Chairman of the *Yorkshire Post*, during the election campaign attracted further favourable publicity. Eden's brand of mild Conservatism, centring on a call for the exploitation of Empire markets to revive trade and reduce unemployment, was well received in a traditional Conservative stronghold and he won the seat with a majority of 5000, although the election saw the Conservative Party lose its overall majority in the House of Commons.[23]

Eden entered Westminster in January 1924, by his own admission 'earnest but only sketchily informed'.[24] Yet within a month he had risen to make his maiden speech. On 19 February he spoke in a debate in support of a resolution moved by Sir Samuel Hoare that Britain should maintain an Air Force 'of sufficient strength to give adequate protection against air attack by the strongest air force within striking distance of her shores'. In an outspoken attack on the Labour Government Eden declared:

It is a natural temptation to honourable Members opposite, some of whose views on defence were fairly well known during the years of the War, to adopt the attitude of that very useful animal the terrier and roll on their backs and wave their paws in the air with a pathetic expression. But that is not the line on which we can hope to insure this country against attack from the air.[25]

The blatantly aggressive nature of Eden's maiden speech was not well received and it was significant that the Liberal MP Wedgwood Benn, following Eden in the debate, pointedly did not congratulate the member for Warwick and Leamington on his first speech before the House of Commons.[26] Eden was, however, apparently undeterred and although he toned down his allusion to the pacifist sympathies of several senior Labour Ministers, he returned to the attack within a month in a speech which once again urged the need to develop a strong Air Force:

We have all to realize that in the next war co-ordination will be even more vital than it was in the last war, and unless I am mistaken, it is the Air Force that will prove the pivot point in this co-ordination.[27]

Although the tone of these pronouncements was, in general, contrary to the widespread support for disarmament and international conciliation that surrounded the establishment of the League of Nations in the immediate post-war era, Eden appreciated that he was essentially on safe ground. Conservative Party policy certainly envisaged an overall reduction in armament expenditure, but the Air Force had been identified as the one sector of the armed forces that should be allowed to expand.[28]

His first incursion into the field of foreign affairs was far more controversial. Speaking in support of the Treaty of Lausanne in April 1924[29] he urged that an attempt be made to overcome British hostility to the Government of Kemal Ataturk following its comprehensive victory over the Greeks in 1922:

The Turkish people have always had a strong sentiment of nationality . . . . It was nationalism that saved Turkey; it is nationalism that rules Turkey today.

I believe that it is our duty to foster and build upon such friendship as exists between this country and Turkey today.[30]

It was as a result of this plea for a sympathetic stance towards the rising tide of nationalism in the Middle East and Asia that Eden first laid claim to some form of specialisation in foreign affairs. Undoubtedly he felt that his studies at Oxford had given him an insight into the nature of Turkish nationalism which enabled him to discount the fears of many of his colleagues that the nationalist fervour was being manipulated by the Bolsheviks.[31] However, in December 1925 following the return of the Conservative Party to office, he was to be found expounding a far more orthodox line defending Baldwin's decision to accept the ruling made by the League of Nations on the extension of the British Mandate in Iraq:

> although we might perhaps be able to leave Iraq under normal circumstances, having discharged our obligations without any serious loss of prestige, I do say that no words, however strong, could exaggerate the harm which we should do to our reputation not only in Iraq, but throughout the East, if we were to scuttle, like flying curs, at the sight of our own shadow. Honourable Members know that if we pursued a course like that our name would be a jibe in the mouth of every tavern-lounger from Marakesh to Singapore. It might take centuries to recover our prestige.[32]

This stirring call to the defence of British overseas commitments was well in tune with the broad body of opinion within the Conservative Party and by this time Eden had already taken his first step on the ladder of promotion with his appointment as Parliamentary Private Secretary to Godfrey Locker-Lampson, Under-Secretary of State to the Home Office. The post gave Eden an invaluable insight into the workings of a major government department. Locker-Lampson later recalled of his young PPS that he was 'very ambitious, but in a good sense and as every young man ought to be'.[33] It was quickly apparent, though, that his interest did not lie in domestic politics and in the latter half of the year he took six months' leave of absence. Eden had already contributed several articles to the *Yorkshire Post*, probably as a result of his father-in-law's connection with the newspaper, and he seized the opportunity to represent the newspaper at the Imperial Press Conference in Melbourne. As a result of his journey to Australia which was, in effect, almost a leisurely world tour, he produced a book entitled *Places in the Sun*. As with many of his early speeches *Places in the Sun* indicated that Eden had little talent for the construction of elegant prose. It was significant, however, that Eden chose to approach Baldwin to write a foreword to the book and that the Prime Minister readily agreed.[34]

Given this decision to absent himself from Britain for six months, it was perhaps surprising that within a year he had received further promotion to the position of Parliamentary Private Secretary to the Foreign Secretary, Sir Austen Chamberlain.[35] Of this promotion one of Eden's biographers, Randolph Churchill, was subsequently to note:

Promotion in the main event went not by merit or outstanding abilities, but by solid devoted services to the party and the Government. Eden perceived correctly what was the correct ladder to climb and the method of climbing it . . . .[36]

This view has also been adopted by Sidney Aster:

> The competition was not keen and distinction which Eden possessed as opposed to brilliance was sufficient recommendation for advancement. Besides it was the attention to style in the form of his speeches and to detail in their substance which helped him on the road to advancement.[37]

There is certainly some truth in their line of reasoning in that Eden rarely strayed from the mainstream of Conservative orthodoxy but, as with his nomination for the Spennymoor parliamentary seat, chance and influential connections played a significant part in his rapid promotion. The element of chance in 1926 was provided by the decision of Chamberlain's PPS, Roger Lumley, to resign in order to participate in a British delegation due to depart for Australia.[38] The influential connection took the form of Locker-Lampson who had recently been transferred to the Foreign Office and was a close friend of the Foreign Secretary's, having at one time served as his Parliamentary Private Secretary. It would appear that it was Locker-Lampson who pressed Eden's candidature upon Chamberlain and propelled him, at the age of 29, into the inner circles of the Foreign Office.[39]

Within three years of entering Parliament, Eden had achieved rapid promotion in a rise that Harold Macmillan was later to describe as one of 'the most spectacular among the young men who entered Parliament just after the War'.[40] If, however, there was little to mark Eden out in terms of policy innovation from many of his contemporaries, there was never any doubt as to where his loyalties lay amongst the senior party figures. Throughout this period his unswerving loyalty to Stanley Baldwin was never in question. Indeed it is significant that, for a man who rarely indulged in personal attacks on his contemporaries in public, Eden was to become a vociferous critic in the House of Commons of Lord Beaverbrook and Lloyd George. Undoubtedly the fact that both of these parties, for various reasons, were waging campaigns against Baldwin's leadership was the root cause of Eden's outbursts.[41] In particular he was attracted by Baldwin's allusions to a nation united in the battle against poverty and oppression rather than divided on class lines. He was subsequently to write of Baldwin:

> It was his faith in the British people and his conviction that they should be led in no selfish spirit of class advantage, that drew

7

many of the younger men in his party toward him and held their loyalty.[42]

Yet if Baldwin was a fairly adept manipulator of domestic politics, Eden's infrequent sallies into this field were generally ill-defined and naive. In a speech delivered during the election campaign of 1929, he attempted to outline his thoughts on the economic problems confronting the nation and their solution:

> The Conservative objective . . . must be to spread the private ownership of property as widely as possible, to enable every worker to become a capitalist. The status of the worker in industry must be raised. This Socialism can never do. In order to achieve this the first task is to assist productive industry to a greater prosperity than rules today. We must be prepared to assist those who are at work, and there lies, incidentally, the greatest measure of help that we can give to those who are at present unemployed.[43]

Yet in terms of policy proposals he offered little more than an attempt to seek new markets for British goods and the advocation of 'schemes of co-partnership in industry' between management and workforce.[44] While outwardly co-partnership was an interesting concept, it was evident that he had little idea of how such a scheme would be implemented and of the forces within society and, indeed, his own party which would oppose a major redistribution of national wealth. In essence the scheme was indicative of a lack of perception and understanding of economics and class politics that was to characterise his infrequent intrusions into domestic affairs.[45]

It was in the field of foreign affairs that Eden was most at ease and in this area he served his apprenticeship under the tutelage of Sir Austen Chamberlain.[46] As a diplomat in the nineteenth-century mould, Chamberlain frowned upon Lloyd George's style of bold, adventurous diplomacy and was inherently suspicious of Ramsay MacDonald's campaign to raise the status of the League of Nations to that of an accepted forum for the reconciliation of international disputes. While Chamberlain was the first British Foreign Secretary to attend the meetings of the League of Nations on a regular basis, it was evident that he shared the scepticism evinced by many of his party colleagues as to the ability of the League of Nations to establish and enforce an international code of conduct. It was not, therefore, entirely unexpected when Chamberlain announced that the British Government would not endorse the Geneva Protocol.[47] This rejection of a scheme which had been carefully nurtured by his predecessor, MacDonald, was indicative of the Foreign Secretary's concept of

British security requirements which revolved around the maintenance of close links with the Dominions in the defence of global commitments and the establishment of a regional arrangement to solve the more immediate problem of European security.[48] Indeed it was to the European question that Chamberlain first turned. His initial aim was to find a formula that would guarantee the maintenance of the Franco-German frontiers and, therefore, placate French fears of a resurgent German nation. The priority given to the stabilisation of Franco-German relations was clearly outlined by the Foreign Secretary in the House of Commons in March 1925:

> All our greatest wars have been fought to prevent one great military power dominating Europe, and at the same time dominating the coast of the Channel and the ports of the Low Countries . . . . The issue is one which affects our security.[49]

This assertion had been a basic tenet of British policy for over a century but had been recently re-emphasised in a General Staff Memorandum of February 1925:

> The true strategic frontier of Great Britain is the Rhine; her security depends entirely upon the present frontiers of France, Belgium and Holland being maintained and remaining in friendly hands.

> Any line of policy which permitted Germany (with or without allies) first to swallow up France, and then to deal with Great Britain would be fatal strategically.[50]

In the same month Chamberlain had written to King George V:

> I believe that the key to the solution is to be found in allaying French fears, and that unless we find means to do this we may be confronted with a complete breakdown of our friendly relations with France and an exacerbation of her attitude towards Germany.[51]

Although Chamberlain preferred a purely Anglo-French security pact with which Germany and Belgium would be subsequently invited to associate, the desire not to offend German opinion led to the negotiation of the Locarno Pact which was initialled in October 1925. In essence British commitments were limited to Western Europe in the form of a guarantee to uphold the existing Franco-Belgian frontiers with Germany and the maintenance of the Rhineland as a demilitarised zone. Not only did the agreement satisfy the French demand for a positive British commitment to the defence of the status quo in Western Europe, but the accompanying agreement on the promotion of German candidature to the League of Nations represented a further step in the reintegration of Germany into the West-European community of nations.[52] Although, in presenting the agreement to the House of Commons, Chamberlain described it as a regional arrangement within the wider context of collective security, it was evident that the pact had clearly defined and limited goals and there was no intention of further expanding Britain's commitment to the cause of collective security.[53] In a letter to Lord Crewe, the Foreign Secretary outlined his reasons for preferring a regional agreement to an international settlement:

> I am firmly convinced that the true line of progress is to proceed from the particular to the general and not, as hitherto embodied in Covenant and Protocol, to reverse the process and attempt to eliminate the particular by the general. A form of guarantee which is so general that we undertake exactly the same obligations in defence shall I say, of the Polish Corridor (for which no British Government ever will or ever can risk the bones of a British Grenadier) as we extend to these international arrangements or conditions on which, as our history shows, our national existence depends, is a guarantee so wide and general that it carries no conviction whatever and gives no sense of security to those who are concerned in our action.[54]

In this sense, although the Foreign Secretary described the agreement before the House of Commons 'not as the end of appeasement and reconciliation, but as its beginning',[55] it was designed from the outset to fulfil the limited goal, outlined by the General Staff in February 1925, of stabilising Franco-German relations.[56] While this in itself was an achievement, the fact that the British Government never seriously examined its military capacity to fulfil its pledges under the Locarno agreement was indicative of a certain smug complacency which pervaded British foreign policy in this period. In the following three years the British Government displayed at times an almost ambivalent attitude to the issues of armament limitation and international co-operation. In many ways the conviction that the logic of Locarno had provided a secure anchorage for British interests was symbolised by the Committee of Imperial Defence endorsing the Ten Year Rule in July 1928.[57] Only in the field of European economic reconstruction was there any sense of urgency in the conduct of British foreign policy, while the Foreign Secretary showed little appetite for the wider issues of collective security and armament limitation. Not surprisingly, in view of the events of the following decade, subsequent commentators have questioned Chamberlain's direction of British foreign policy.[58] For example, N.H. Gibbs observed:

> there were unfortunately too many in Britain who allowed the pact's attractions as a gesture of friendship to Germany and reassurance to France to obscure the fact that such gestures might prove worthless, and even dangerous, unless Locarno was also seen as a positive move in the construction of a new European security system.[59]

In this light Chamberlain's judgement is certainly open to debate, but it has to be remembered that Eden was appointed to the post of Parliamentary Private Secretary in the summer of 1926 at a time when the Foreign Secretary's prestige was still high following the conclusion of the Locarno agreement.[60] It would seem that Eden had implicit faith in Chamberlain's ability and, indeed, had vigorously defended him in a House of Commons debate in March of the same year when the Foreign Secretary's less than wholehearted support for the German candidature to the League of Nations was under intense attack.[61] In discussing his relationship with Chamberlain, Eden later noted:

> Austen Chamberlain in appearance and sometimes in speech could be stiff and forbidding. This had nothing to do with the real man who was warm-hearted, considerate and generous. He was incapable of mean action and conscientious to a fault. I had the greatest affection for him and our friendship grew and lasted until his death.[62]

Undoubtedly Eden found little difficulty in identifying with Chamberlain's concept of statesmanship which was based firmly in the nineteenth-century Foreign Office mould.[63] In terms of the conduct and format of British policy, Eden appeared prepared to accept Chamberlain's distaste for open-ended international agreements and they were in agreement that the Locarno format of traditional alliance politics with limited obligations was the correct basis for the defence of British interests. They were also in accord in their appreciation of the importance of developing the relationship with the Dominions as a major factor in the maintenance of British global interests in both the economic and military spheres. In fact, advocation of the need to promote ties with the Dominions was one of the few areas where Eden's stance in the field of foreign affairs was clearly discernible in this period and this was due to the deep impression that had been made upon him during his journey through Canada, Australia, New

Zealand and Ceylon in 1925. The mood of growing independence and strength in these nations had convinced Eden that Britain's future prosperity and status could only be assured if developed in partnership with the emerging strength of the Dominions.[64]

Subsequent biographers have claimed that, as a result of Chamberlain's tutelage, by 1929 Eden's interpretation of the bases of British foreign policy had effectively crystallised.[65] For example, Sidney Aster has commented:

> He believed that good Anglo-French and Anglo-American relations were fundamental to the safety of Britain. He was a convinced sympathiser with the facts of national attitudes, such as French fears of war, or Turkish nationalism. He was not an old fashioned Imperialist, but held that the Empire was in itself a developing community for which Britain had a special responsibility. Finally, he believed that foreign policy must be conducted with patience after very thorough preparation in the Foreign Office.[66]

Except for the section relating to the role of the Dominions, Aster's comments are difficult to substantiate and in one area can be openly questioned. In fact, although Eden was later to claim that he identified the development of Anglo-American relations as a central pillar in the overall format of British foreign policy,[67] he had no hesitation in fully endorsing Chamberlain's negotiation of an Anglo-French armament agreement in 1928 without prior consultation with the USA. If the agreement had been accepted, it would have effectively undermined not only Anglo-American and Anglo-German relations but also the entire programme of naval limitation proposals sponsored by President Coolidge in 1927.[68] In this context it is difficult to see how Eden could possibly be presented as an advocate of close Anglo-American relations. This episode in itself, however, provides an interesting insight into the relationship between Eden and Chamberlain, for it is indicative of the fact that throughout his period of office Eden remained completely loyal to the policies formulated by the Foreign Secretary. In no sphere was this more apparent than in the role to be assigned to the League of Nations. One of the advantages of Eden's work with Chamberlain was that it afforded him the opportunity to travel with the Foreign Secretary to Geneva and observe, at first hand, both the formal machinery of the League of Nations and also the network of informal meetings that took place between the various Foreign Ministers. Eden later noted of this experience:

There was a formidable weight of world opinion behind this attempt to create an international order.

> The experiment might have appeared hazardous, but it aroused brave hopes for me also. It seemed an opportunity to escape from a balance of power, which had failed to keep the peace, to an international authority which might have the collective strength to do so.[69]

It was apparent that Chamberlain had little faith in the League and saw his visits to Geneva initially as an opportunity to hold private negotiations with his French and German counterparts Briand and Stresemann rather than any form of commitment to broadening the concept of collective security.[70] In this sense he remained rooted in the principles of traditional alliance diplomacy which sought to maintain a balance of power in Europe. Not surprisingly the Foreign Secretary had little hesitation in rejecting the Geneva Protocol in 1925. This decision was, however, roundly attacked by the Labour Party and certain elements within the Conservative Party who rallied around the figure of Lord Robert Cecil.[71] Whether or not Eden really viewed the potential of the League of Nations with optimism is open to conjecture, but he was in no doubt as to where his loyalties lay. In the House of Commons on 24 November 1927, following a particularly intense assault upon Chamberlain by Cecil, Eden not only denounced Cecil but also the entire rationale of the Geneva Protocol:

> I think we should refuse to bind ourselves, to tie our hands in directions where we cannot see what the future may hold for us. I do not believe we can maintain peace in Europe now by handing out a hotchpotch of pledges. I believe that the policy of 1925 is in the long run better and wiser than the policy of 1924.[72]

It would perhaps be unfair, however, to conclude from this that Eden was either completely submissive to Chamberlain or had few ideas of his own. In the first instance it was certainly not the place of a Parliamentary Private Secretary to oppose his chief publicly. However, while Eden might have wished to place more emphasis on the potential value of the League of Nations or Anglo-American relations, it would appear that he and Chamberlain were in broad agreement on the approach to be adopted to what they saw as the central issues in British foreign policy. This consensus was based on the need to co-ordinate policy with the Dominions on a global scale, and to a lesser extent the USA in the Far East, while the European question was to be tackled through the maintenance of close Anglo-French relations.

This relationship not only guaranteed the status quo in Western Europe but also sufficiently reassured France to allow the rebuilding of German economic power, which was seen as an important factor in preventing the spread of Bolshevism into Western Europe. In essence this stance was built on a determination to limit British military commitments to Europe in order to free resources for the defence of Britain's global interests. It could be contended, therefore, that Eden stood firmly in the centre ground of Conservative party-politics, within the ranks of those who sought to maintain Britain's pre-war role as a major international power, rejecting the alternatives presented by Cecil's promotion of the League of Nations or the isolationism espoused by those of the extreme right of the party.[73]

Eden's Conservatism was a mild brand which made him few enemies and opened the pathway to promotion. He later learned that Baldwin had intended to reward his loyalty and dependability with the post of Under-Secretary at the Foreign Office if the Conservatives had won the General Election of May 1929.[74] Although Eden held his parliamentary seat with a majority of 5460, it was the only occasion that he failed to gather over 50 per cent of the votes cast and through-out the country the Conservative Party was unable to secure an overall majority. For one whose star was in the ascendant the election result must have come as a severe blow. The defeat, however, did not shake his faith in the Party leadership and during the following two years, when Baldwin was subject to extensive criticism from within the Party ranks, Eden stood staunchly by him. The turning-point in the battle for the Party leadership was undoubtedly Duff Cooper's victory at the St George by-election in March 1931.[75] Following this success Eden noted on 12 March 1931:

> S.B. has got away with it again. He has won back from the edge of the precipice. I was of course delighted . . . .

> He is the only Statesman we possess. Unhappily we have too few who can recognise one, still fewer who will fight for one.[76]

This loyalty was rewarded when later in the same month Baldwin acknowledged Eden's standing within the Party in the field of foreign affairs by nominating him, along with Austen Chamberlain and Sir Samuel Hoare, to represent the Conservative Party on the three-party preparatory committee for the World Disarmament Conference. The committee was designated as a subcommittee of the Committee of Imperial Defence and was also attended by Ramsay MacDonald, Arthur Henderson and Lloyd George.[77] Although as the junior member of the Conservative delegation Eden's contribution to the meetings, held over a period of four months, was minimal, he obviously relished the opportunity to mix with such illustrious company.[78] He later recorded: 'This was my first taste of discussion at the Cabinet level and I liked it.'[79]

Opportunities to further Eden's career in the sphere of foreign affairs were, however, few and far between as the Labour Government conducted a largely moderate policy at which the Opposition could hardly take umbrage. Only in the hostility of the Conservative right wing to the improvement of Anglo-Soviet relations was there any indication of a major difference with the Government.[80] It was apparent to all in this period that foreign affairs were being increasingly eclipsed by the problems posed by the slide into economic recession. In one of his few noteworthy parliamentary speeches delivered at this time, on 29 June 1931, Eden once again returned to the topic of air defence and the need to counter the threat of aerial bombardment: 'There will be no heroes in a war where the safest place will be the front line, if there is one, and the most dangerous the houses of our civilian population.'[81]

Although the main thrust of the speech was concerned with the need to increase expenditure on air defence, it is interesting to note that Eden spoke in a gloomy manner of the 'sore spots of Europe' where 'the youngest generation is being trained up into military formations':

> The seeds of war psychology still exist in Europe. I even doubt whether during the last two years what is usually called the spirit of the League has grown in strength in Europe. On the contrary, the probability is that it has grown weaker. I do not wish to be alarmist, but I do not think that anyone who studies the European situation today can be otherwise than anxious about it. It seems to me that we can divide Europe for this purpose into two groups of nations. There is the group which is, if not dominated, at least influenced by fear, and the group which is dominated by impatience.[82]

Without any outward condemnation of Chamberlain's period of office, it was evident that Eden was disturbed by the international undercurrents generated by the growing world economic crisis which presented a problem that threatened not to respond to the traditional Foreign Office tenets of skilfully manipulated alliances and formal diplomacy. His immediate concern was the reappearance of aggressive German nationalism in the form of the National Socialist Party and there were equally ominous rumblings in the Far East.[83] While Eden certainly could not be counted amongst the internationalist sections of the Conservative Party and, indeed, had played little part in the

15

debates surrounding the Kellogg-Briand Pact and the Briand Plan, it is possible that his role on the preparatory committee for the Disarmament Conference had persuaded him there was a need to give greater emphasis to the cause of international collaboration and collective security.[84] There is a suggestion of a revision of his stance in relation to the role of the League of Nations when, in the debate surrounding Britain's acceptance of the Optional Clause for the compulsory arbitration of inter-nation disputes, Eden declared that these were times 'in the lives of nations and peoples when it is necessary to take risks, even grave risks, in the cause of world peace'. He could not, however, bring himself to endorse the Optional Clause as a major contribution to world peace:

> You cannot mechanise peace. Peace, if it comes, is maintained as the result of a feeling growing up among the nations of the world, and all that you have to do is to provide the instruments of interpretation.[85]

By accepting on the one hand the principle of international conciliation as a goal to be striven for while on the other hand rejecting it in its existing form, Eden remained firmly within the mainstream of Conservative party politics.[86] This loyalty was rewarded in August 1931 with his first ministerial post following the formation of the National Government.[87]

References

1   Eden provides a detailed account of his life up to the age of twenty years in Earl of Avon, *Another World 1897—1917* (London, 1976). Further material can be found in Sidney Aster, *Anthony Eden* (London, 1976), Dennis Bardens, *Portrait of a Statesman* (London, 1955), Lewis Broad, *Sir Anthony Eden* (London, 1955), Alan Campbell-Johnson, *Sir Anthony Eden* (London, 1955), Randolph Churchill, *The Rise and Fall of Sir Anthony Eden* (London, 1959), William Rees-Mogg, *Sir Anthony Eden* (London, 1956) and David Carlton, *Anthony Eden* (London, 1981).
2   Eden was first sent to the South Kensington Preparatory School but within a year had moved on to Sandroyd where he remained until going on to Eton, Rees-Mogg, p. 17.
3   The vast majority of the family's continental excursions were to France. See Avon, *Another World*, pp. 20—2.
4   Avon, p. 27.
5   Ibid., pp. 11—36.
6   Ibid., pp. 23—5.
7   Timothy Eden, *The Tribulations of a Baronet* (London, 1933).
8   Avon, p. 34.
9   For details of the relationship between Eden and his father see Avon, pp. 34—6 and pp. 55—9. In addition see Churchill, pp. 22—6 and Broad, pp. 18—20.

10   Avon, pp. 35—6.

11   Ibid., pp. 35—6. For further comments on the relationship between mother and son see Rees-Mogg, pp. 17—18 and Carlton, p. 12.

12   Avon, p. 48. Lord Vansittart was later to note that Eden 'had been at Eton, but the place had no magic for him as for me, and he never mentioned it'. Lord Vansittart, *The Mist Procession* (London, 1958), p. 429.

13   John Eden was killed in action on 17 October 1914. See Avon, pp. 51—2 and p. 59.

14   Ibid., pp. 54 and 59. Timothy Eden was released in 1916 and subsequently enlisted in the Yorkshire Light Infantry, Churchill, p. 21.

15   Avon, pp. 62—3.

16   For details of Eden's war service see Avon, pp. 62—150; Churchill, pp. 29—31; Campbell-Johnson, pp. 20—1; and Carlton, pp. 12—13.

17   Nicholas Eden was killed at the Battle of Jutland on 31 May 1916.

18   Earl of Avon, *The Eden Memoirs, Vol. 1 : Facing the Dictators* (London, 1962), p. 3.

19   Ibid., p. 4. It is interesting to note that Eden in 1934 was convinced that the fact that Hitler had served extensively in the front line during the war would provide a bridge based on their joint determination to prevent a repeat of such a conflict, see Avon, *Facing the Dictators*, p. 64.

20   Ibid., p. 4; Rees-Mogg, pp. 24—9; and Churchill, pp. 31—2.

21   In this case it would appear that the link between the Marquess of Londonderry and Sir William Eden, who both came from prominent families in the North East of England, was the central factor in the offer of the Conservative candidacy for Spennymoor, Carlton, p. 14 and Rees-Mogg, p. 30.

22   Eden polled only 7567 votes as opposed to the Labour candidate who totalled over 13,000 votes, Churchill, p. 37.

23   The seat at Warwick initially became vacant with the elevation of Sir Ernest Pollock to the House of Lords. The resulting by-election campaign was prolonged, however, when Baldwin decided to call a General Election which was held in December of 1923. Eden polled 16,337 votes to the Liberal candidate's 11,134. Eden held the seat until his retirement in 1957, Avon, *Facing the Dictators*, p. 4; Rees-Mogg, pp. 30—2; and Carlton, p. 14.

24   Avon, *Facing the Dictators*, p. 4.

25   *House of Commons* (hereafter cited as *H of C*), Debates, 5's, vol. 169, cols 1678—9, 19 February 1924.

26   *H of C*, Debs, 5's, vol. 169, cols 1679—80, 19 February 1924.

27   *H of C*, Debs, 5's, vol. 171, cols 729—31, 20 March 1924.

28   Although the Royal Air Force had been run down in the period following the cessation of hostilities in 1918, the Conservative Government of Bonar Law had accepted the need to rebuild the Air Force towards a target of 52 squadrons for Home Defence. For details see Michael Howard, *The Continental Commitment* (Harmondsworth, 1974), pp. 80—5 and N.H. Gibbs, *Grand Strategy, A History of the Second World War, United Kingdom Military Series, Vol. 1 : Rearmament Policy* (HMSO, 1976), pp. 44—50.

29   In the latter months of 1922, Mehemet VI had fled Turkey leaving Kemal Ataturk's nationalist forces unchallenged. At the Lausanne Conference of July 1923, Lord Curzon attempted to stabilise both Anglo-Turkish and Greco-Turkish relations with an agreement that Allied forces withdraw from the Straits and Eastern Thrace be returned to Turkey. While this appeared to be a significant victory for the Turkish national movement, Curzon had, in fact, achieved his goal of disengagement from the Greco-Turkish dispute with an undertaking that the Straits remain effectively neutralised and had also maintained British control of

the oil interests in Mosul. Not surprisingly, certain elements of the Conservative Party saw this as a retreat from Imperial commitments that was likely to undermine the position of British-sponsored rulers in the Middle and Near East. See C.L. Mowat, *Britain Between the Wars* (London, 1955), pp. 116–19 and pp. 156–7. See also H. Nicolson, *Curzon, The Last Phase, 1919–1925* (New York, 1939).

30   *H of C*, Debs, 5's, vol. 171, cols 2054–7, 1 April 1924.

31   There is no suggestion that Eden was in any sense pro-Bolshevik. During the election campaign of October 1924 Eden joined with the bulk of his colleagues in denouncing both the Anglo-Soviet treaties and, in particular, the logic of links with a country which he saw as innately hostile to the British Empire, Campbell-Johnson, pp. 33–4 and Churchill, pp. 44–5.

32   *H of C*, Debs, 5's, vol. 190, cols 2091–3, 21 December 1925.

33   Campbell-Johnson, p. 49.

34   Eden represented the *Yorkshire Post* at the Conference and in all was out of the country from July until December 1925. An account of his journey is given in Anthony Eden, *Places in the Sun* (London, 1926).

35   Eden was appointed as PPS to Chamberlain in July 1926.

36   Churchill, p. 47.

37   Aster, p. 16.

38   Avon, *Facing the Dictators*, pp. 6–7.

39   It might also have been significant that Eden had defended Chamberlain vigorously in the House of Commons in March 1926 when the Foreign Secretary was under attack as a result of his less than enthusiastic support for the League of Nations, *H of C*, Debs, 5's, vol. 193, cols 1105–9, 23 March 1926. For further discussion of the role of influential connections in Eden's promotion, see Campbell-Johnson, pp. 48–9 and Rees-Mogg, pp. 39–40.

40   Harold Macmillan, *Winds of Change* (London, 1966), p. 321.

41   For examples of the attacks launched by Eden on Beaverbrook and Lloyd George in the House of Commons in this period, see *H of C*, Debs, 5's, vol. 190, cols 1105–9, 23 March 1926; vol. 210, cols 2160–5, 24 November 1927; and vol. 189, cols 2088–94, 21 December 1925.

42   Avon, *Facing the Dictators*, p. 5. In addition see Broad, p. 28; Aster, p. 14; Campbell-Johnson, pp. 34–5; and Rees-Mogg, pp. 41–3.

43   Avon, *Facing the Dictators*, pp. 12–13.

44   Ibid., p. 13.

45   An example of Eden's naivety was his surprise that the Conservative Party's decision to take the duty off tea was not sufficient to win the female vote in 1929, Avon, *Facing the Dictators*, p. 11. A detailed account of the Baldwin administration's approach to the economic problems that confronted it can be found in K. Middlemas and J. Barnes, *Baldwin, A Biography* (London, 1969), pp. 212–316. See also R. Blake, *The Conservative Party from Peel to Chamberlain* (London, 1970), pp. 214–35.

46   Austen Chamberlain (1863–1937), Chancellor of the Exchequer 1903–5, Secretary of State for India 1915–17, Chancellor of the Exchequer 1919–21, Foreign Secretary 1924–9. For an analysis of his career see Sir Charles Petrie, *The Life and Letters of the Rt Hon. Sir Austen Chamberlain*, 2 vols (London, 1940).

47   The decision not to endorse the Geneva Protocol is covered in Middlemas and Barnes, pp. 342–9; Howard, pp. 197–9; and Campbell-Johnson, pp. 38–40. See also Petrie, *The Life and Letters of Sir Austen Chamberlain*, vol. 2, p. 250.

48   One of Chamberlain's first acts as Foreign Secretary was to emphasise the 'diplomatic unity of the British Empire'. See Sir Austen Chamberlain, *Peace in Our Time : Addresses on Europe and the Empire* (London, 1928), pp. 1–2.

49   *H of C*, Debs, 5's, vol. 182, col. 316, 24 March 1925.

50   Quoted in Gibbs, *Grand Strategy, Vol. 1*, p. 41.

51   Quoted from Sir H. Nicolson, *George V* (London, 1952), p. 407.

52   Middlemas and Barnes, pp. 350–62 and Martin Gilbert, *The Roots of Appeasement* (New York, 1966), pp. 117–25.

53   *H of C*, Debs, 5's, vol. 188, cols 431–2, 18 November 1925.

54   Quoted from Petrie, vol. 2, p. 258.

55   *H of C*, Debs, 5's, vol. 188, col. 420, 18 November 1925.

56   Quoted from Gibbs, *Grand Strategy, Vol. 1*, p. 41.

57   The decision to endorse the Ten Year Rule is discussed in Gibbs, *Grand Strategy, Vol. 1*, pp. 44–64 and Howard, pp. 89–91.

58   For examples see Gilbert, *The Roots of Appeasement*, pp. 117–25; Petrie, vol. 2, p. 294; and F.S. Northedge, *The Troubled Giant* (London, 1966), pp. 270–1.

59   Gibbs, *Grand Strategy, Vol. 1*, p. 44.

60   Broad, p. 32.

61   *H of C*, Debs, 5's, vol. 193, cols 1105–9, 23 March 1926.

62   Avon, *Facing the Dictators*, p. 7.

63   It has been argued that Chamberlain rejected Lloyd George's brand of leadership and worked assiduously to re-establish the nineteenth-century format of diplomacy based firmly on the influence and direction of the Foreign Office in the conduct of foreign relations. See Gordon A. Craig, 'The British Foreign Office from Grey to Austen Chamberlain' in G.A. Craig and F. Gilbert (eds), *The Diplomats 1919–1939, Vol. 1* (New York, 1963), pp. 15–48.

64   This view is clearly outlined in Eden, *Places in the Sun*, pp. 111–12. The importance of the Dominions also pervaded his thinking on domestic matters with the conviction that they provided the market for industrial goods and source of raw materials that was needed to resuscitate the economy, Campbell-Johnson, pp. 36–7.

65   Rees-Mogg, pp. 45–6.

66   Aster, p. 18.

67   Avon, *Facing the Dictators*, p. 87.

68   This episode is discussed by Carlton, pp. 24–6.

69   Avon, *Facing the Dictators*, p. 8.

70   Petrie, vol. 2, p. 250.

71   Lord Robert Cecil was Lord Privy Seal 1923, Chancellor of the Duchy of Lancaster 1924–7 and President of the League of Nations Union 1923–45. Gordon Craig has suggested that one of Chamberlain's first moves upon being appointed Foreign Secretary was to limit Cecil's influence as British delegate to the League of Nations. See Craig and Gilbert, vol. 1, pp. 15–22. Cecil resigned from the Cabinet in August 1927 in protest at the British Government's reluctance to consider a reduction in its armaments and subsequently became a focus for attacks on the Foreign Secretary, Carlton, pp. 22–4.

72   *H of C*, Debs, 5's, vol. 190, cols 2160–5, 24 November 1927.

73   It is interesting to note that in the House of Commons in November 1927, Eden advocated settlement of disputes by direct negotiation rather than League of Nations intervention and concluded that in terms of international agreement further progress 'will have to be made by regional pacts'. Britain with the Locarno agreement had 'gone as far as we are entitled to go. The Empire . . . would not be prepared to pledge its future more extensively'. Quoted from Campbell-Johnson, pp. 56–7.

74   Avon, *Facing the Dictators*, p. 11.

75   Middlemas and Barnes, pp. 598–601; and Blake, pp. 233–5.

76   Avon, *Facing the Dictators*, p. 14. This quote was an attack not only upon those within the party who doubted Baldwin's leadership, but also the press barons, Lord Beaverbrook and Viscount Rothermere, who orchestrated the attack on Baldwin. On several occasions Eden made no secret of his contempt for their attempts to depose Baldwin, see *H of C*, Debs, 5's, vol. 189, cols 2088—94, 21 December 1925 and Eden's letter to *The Times* of 6 October 1930.

77   Avon, *Facing the Dictators*, p. 14.

78   See Carlton, p. 27.

79   Avon, *Facing the Dictators*, p. 14.

80   See D. Carlton, *MacDonald versus Henderson : The Foreign Policy of the Second Labour Government* (London, 1970) and in particular the section on Anglo-Soviet relations, pp. 144—62. Also Campbell-Johnson, pp. 68—72.

81   *H of C*, Debs, 5's, vol. 254, cols 938—45, 29 June 1931.

82   Ibid., cols 938—45.

83   Avon, *Facing the Dictators*, p. 15.

84   For details of the Kellogg-Briand Pact and the Briand Plan, see F.P. Walters, *A History of the League of Nations* (London, 1969), pp. 384—7 and pp. 430—4.

85   Quoted from Campbell-Johnson, p. 69.

86   For a discussion of the debate surrounding the Optional Clause see Carlton, *MacDonald versus Henderson*, pp. 75—8.

87   Eden took up his position as Under-Secretary at the Foreign Office on 1 September 1931. Avon, *Facing the Dictators*, p. 19.

2 Apprenticeship
October 1931 — May 1934

In August 1931, following the resignation of the Labour Government, Anthony Eden gained his first ministerial post with his appointment as Parliamentary Under-Secretary of State to the Foreign Office.[1] The post of Foreign Secretary had been assigned to Lord Reading, the Liberal Leader in the House of Lords, in accordance with an agreement devised by Ramsay MacDonald to obtain Liberal support for the National Government. As Reading was also earmarked for the role of Government Leader in the House of Lords, the position of Parliamentary Under-Secretary and, therefore, spokesman for the Foreign Office in the House of Commons was of strategic importance. It would seem that the Prime Minister had his son, Malcolm MacDonald, in mind for the role but the combined pressure exerted by Stanley Baldwin and Sir Austen Chamberlain in support of Eden's case prevailed. While Eden went to the Foreign Office, Malcolm MacDonald accepted the post of Parliamentary Under-Secretary of State to the Dominions Office.[2] Although Lord Reading's biographer, H. Montgomery Hyde, has claimed that Sir Austen Chamberlain played the leading role in persuading the Foreign Secretary to appoint Eden, Anthony Eden himself had little doubt as to who had been the driving force behind his promotion.[3] In a letter to Stanley Baldwin dated 1 September 1931, Eden declared: 'It is never easy to say "thank you" without seeming either fulsome or insincere, but I think that you do know how very grateful I am for your kindness to me.'

Eden could not conceal his pleasure at returning to the Foreign Office: 'I saw Van this afternoon and it was a real joy to talk over the old work again; in truth I feel almost ashamed to be so happy at it, when there is so little national cause.'[4]

Sir Robert Vansittart, in *The Mist Procession*, later commented on Eden's appointment:

> As Parliamentary Under Secretary we acquired young Eden. We thought ourselves lucky and were sure that he was. He had had a little innings as Parliamentary Private Secretary to Austen and omitted nothing to deserve his promotion. His appearance went far to ensure that he would get what he wanted and that was a lot. He was ambitious, but not self-seeking, if by that we mean search for a self rarely found. Baldwin strongly recommended him to me; his mind was less capacious than his master's, but he used it to better advantage. Zealous, affable, intelligent, he had inherited from his father a temper mitigated by the restraints which careers impose on youth. He thus possessed early the makings of 'a good House of Commons Manner'. Desirous and deserving of praise, he avoided suspicions of brilliance or originality and pruned protrusions with sense. He said the right thing so often that he seemed incapable of saying anything else.[5]

Although Vansittart's assessment of Eden — written in retrospect over 20 years after the event — was probably coloured by later marked differences between the two on policy, it appears that, from the outset, the Permanent Under-Secretary found little in common with the young Eden whom he considered to be more concerned with serving his political mentors, and through them advancing his own cause, than contributing anything original to the field of foreign policy.[6] Certainly this suspicion and, at times, hostility to Eden's rapid rise was also felt by other leading figures of the period, one of whom, L.S. Amery, described Eden as a man 'who cheerfully voiced all the popular catchwords'.[7] For his part Anthony Eden was aware of the differences in personality and methods that separated him from the Permanent Under-Secretary. In his memoirs Eden remarked:

> The truth is that Vansittart was seldom an official giving cool and disinterested advice based on study and experience. He was himself a sincere, almost fanatical crusader and much more a Secretary of State in mentality than a permanent official.

> . . . his instinct was usually right, but his sense of the political methods that could be used was sometimes at fault.[8]

While the relationship between the two was never, therefore, intimate there was nothing to suggest that the element of personal distance between the two in any way hampered their working relationship within the Foreign Office during this early period in Eden's career. Indeed, in their common concern for Anglo-French relations, probably inherited on Eden's part from his apprenticeship under Sir Austen Chamberlain, the two men discovered a bond that was on several occasions to find them working closely in harness.

Eden's role as Foreign Office spokesman in the House of Commons was to be shortlived. In the General Election of October 1931 the National Government completely overwhelmed its opponents. At Warwick and Leamington Eden, without the opposition of a Liberal candidate, secured a majority of 29,000, while throughout the country the Parliamentary Opposition was reduced to a mere 56 seats. In the resulting Cabinet restructure the post of Foreign Secretary was assigned to Sir John Simon.

Simon was relatively inexperienced at ministerial level, having briefly served under Asquith as Home Secretary during the First World War and having also occupied the position of Attorney General.[9] Although one of the primary considerations in appointing Simon had been the need to court the support of certain elements of the Liberal Party that were moving away from their former insistence on the defence of free trade, there were few contemporary politicians who doubted the intellectual capacity of the incoming Foreign Secretary. However, several of Simon's colleagues were subsequently to express their exasperation at the reluctance of the Foreign Secretary to provide a decisive lead in the formulation of foreign policy after having methodically dissected the issues at stake. In *Facing the Dictators* Eden was later to write of Simon:

> Too penetrating a discernment and too frail a conviction encouraged confusion where there should have been a fixed intent. Simon could master a brief quicker than any man, but this is only part of the business of foreign affairs. His colleagues used to complain that he was more apt to turn to them for a policy than to champion his own.[10]

There is no evidence to suggest, however, that the relationship between Simon and Eden was soured from the outset and, indeed, the Foreign Secretary was later to record the value that he placed on Eden's 'comradeship' during his period of tenure at the Foreign Office.[11]

It can be contended that Sir John Simon has been harshly judged by Eden; in his defence it has to be noted that the direction of British foreign policy in this period was a particularly complex matter. In

September 1931 major hostilities had erupted in Manchuria which focused initially on a Sino-Japanese dispute as to the control of the South Manchurian Railway, but eventually led to the expansion of Japanese influence in the area with the establishment of the puppet state of Manchukuo in March 1932.[12] In that Japan appeared to have flagrantly seized Manchurian territory, the dispute seemed to represent a major challenge to the authority of the League of Nations, to whom China immediately turned for redress of its grievances. The seriousness of the situation was admitted by Lord Reading on 21 October 1931: 'A failure by the League to find some way round the difficulty would be nothing short of a calamity . . . and might imperil any hopes we may have of making progress in the more immediate field of Europe . . . .'[13]

There was, however, a considerable feeling, even amongst those who supported the League of Nations, that very little could be done to bring Japan to heel. The need for caution was emphasised by Viscount Cecil in a report from Geneva dated 19 October 1931. Cecil outlined the range of sanctions that could be implemented against Japan but concluded:

> Before . . . attempting to put into force any of these sanctions, it would be well to ascertain what position the United States would be likely to take up and as a preliminary it becomes essential that the United States should express its agreement with the terms of any settlement proposed to the parties on behalf of the Council.[14]

The same conclusion had been reached by the Foreign Office, except that they were in no doubt as to the stance that would be adopted by the USA. On 27 October 1931 Sir John Pratt, Chief Adviser to the Far Eastern Department, observed: 'America could never in any circumstances contemplate using other methods than that of moral suasion and the force of public opinion.'[15]

In this light Lord Reading's successor, Sir John Simon, appreciated that without assistance from Washington the implementation of sanctions against Japan would fall primarily on the shoulders of Britain and France and that neither nation was in a position to conduct a successful military campaign against Japan. Furthermore it was apparent that there would be little popular support in Britain for a war to restore Manchuria to Chinese sovereignty. In a Foreign Office minute dated 14 November 1931, Sir John Simon concluded:

> I am strongly opposed to any treatment of the question which will bring up the question of sanctions. We ought to co-operate in any course that will preserve the moral authority of the League

and a futile reference to Article 16 would surely have the opposite effect.[16]

This assertion fully reflected the stance adopted by the Cabinet on 11 November 1931.[17]

The position was, however, further complicated in January 1932 by the Japanese assault on the district of Chapei in Shanghai. Although there had been considerable sympathy for the seizure of the South Manchurian Railway given the extent of Japanese economic interests in Manchuria, the Chapei incident directly involved the British Government in that Britain was partly responsible for the defence of the International Settlement in Shanghai.[18] There is no evidence, however, to indicate that the Japanese action in Shanghai or the mounting evidence of the expansion of its military activities in Manchuria led the Cabinet to consider the possibility of a more active role to deter further Japanese aggression. The general air of impotence was expressed by Sir R. Vansittart in a memorandum dated 3 February 1932:

(2) We are incapable of checking Japan in any way if she really means business and has sized us up, as she certainly has done.
(3) Therefore, we must eventually be done for in the Far East unless
(4) The United States are eventually prepared to use force.
(5) It is universally assumed here that the United States will never use force.[19]

This assessment was underlined in the same week by a report from the Chiefs-of-Staff which concluded that, even if emergency measures were taken immediately, in the event of hostilities with Japan nothing could be done to prevent the bases of Singapore and Hong Kong falling before the British Fleet could reach the Far East.[20] It was not surprising, therefore, that after achieving a ceasefire in Shanghai in March 1932 the British Government rejected any suggestion of the application of economic or military sanctions against Japan and emphasised the need to consider the extent of Japan's legitimate economic interests with Manchuria, which the Chinese were obliged to respect.[21]

Anthony Eden's direct involvement in the Manchurian crisis was essentially confined to his role as Foreign Office spokesman within the House of Commons in the period September to November 1931 and his participation in the Cabinet Committee on the Far East. The Cabinet Committee was established on 2 February 1932 as a direct result of the spread of hostilities to Shanghai, but with a wider brief to consider the course of action to be taken by Britain at the League of Nations.[22] On this topic the Committee, which held its fifth and final meeting on 3 March 1932 following the announcement of a ceasefire in Shanghai, concluded 'that sanctions against Japan are out of the question and would not be supported in this country'.[23] This assertion was supported by the Cabinet on 9 March 1932 with the recommendation that sanctions be restricted to the mobilisation of world opinion against Japan.[24]

Although Eden was later to argue that had the League of Nations adopted a resolute approach to the Manchurian issue from the outset Japan might have been deterred from further aggression, there is no evidence that, at the time, he dissented from the viewpoint expressed by the Cabinet Committee on the Far East.[25] In fact it would appear that he fully supported its conclusions and had similarly endorsed memoranda by Sir John Pratt, Sir R. Vansittart and Sir V. Wellesley of the Foreign Office which emphasised the need for British policy to be determined by the realities of the situation in the Far East given that British interests would be most directly affected by the imposition of economic or military sanctions.[26] This point is re-inforced by Eden's comments of 6 September 1932 on a despatch from the British Ambassador in Tokyo. Noting that C.W. Orde, Head of the Far Eastern Department, had minuted that the only solution was to avoid involvement in sanctions, Eden minuted 'I agree' and added: 'We with vital interests at stake must continue to moderate the zeal of those with none.'[27] This remark undoubtedly was directed against the USA and particularly the US Secretary of State, Stimson, who sought to censure Japan by eliciting support for a movement to refuse recognition of the Japanese-sponsored regime in Manchuria.[28]

Eden's stance was entirely consistent with the approach that he had previously adopted towards the League of Nations, in that he had steadfastly denied that British foreign policy should be determined by decisions made at Geneva.[29] His view of Britain's obligations to the League of Nations was that of a limited commitment with no automatic obligation to become involved in disputes that were either of no primary relevance or perhaps contrary to British security interests. If the experience of working at Geneva was later to imbue him with a more optimistic view of the role of the League of Nations, it was certainly not evident in this early period of his career.

Although the Manchurian crises contrived to test the patience and endurance of the Foreign Office for over two years, as Eden was to admit to Baldwin after first-hand experience of the tangled web of diplomacy weaved around the crises at Geneva,[30] international attention during this period was largely focused on the proceedings of the Disarmament Conference which had opened at Geneva under the aegis of the League of Nations on 2 February 1932. As early as 8 April 1931 a Foreign Office memorandum presented to the Labour Foreign Secretary, Arthur Henderson, had noted that Germany was certain to demand equality of rights with the major European powers as a precondition for the acceptance of a comprehensive disarmament convention. The memorandum continued: 'They will doubtless be content with very much less but the fact remains that a good deal will have to be done for them in the direction of equality before we can hope to bring them into line . . . .'[31]

In essence it was recommended that Part V of the Treaty of Versailles, dealing with the prohibition of certain military weapons, the level of forces within Germany and the allied right to supervise these restrictions, would have to be replaced by a disarmament convention under which Germany would move towards equality with the major European states.[32] This conviction was supported by Simon, Stanley Baldwin and Ramsay MacDonald and was reflected in the Cabinet instructions to the British delegation to the Disarmament Conference. On 15 December 1931 the Cabinet concluded: 'Germany has a strong moral backing for her claim to the principle of equality.'[33]

However, given this point of departure, the Cabinet seemed primarily concerned to avoid any further European military commitments, despite the suggestion that only a comprehensive security agreement realistically offered a solution to the disarmament question and the specific issue of the reconciliation of German claims for equality of armaments with French insistence on guarantees of security.[34] This essentially negative approach to the Conference appears to have been based on the conviction that in the post-war era Britain had already taken considerable steps towards disarmament and that it was now time for the other major powers to indicate their good faith by forwarding proposals at Geneva. In March 1931 Ramsay MacDonald had chaired the three-party subcommittee of the Committee of Imperial Defence (CID) to examine British preparations for the Disarmament Conference.[35] MacDonald reported to the House of Commons on 29 June 1931 that the Committee recommended:

> Any further reduction of British armaments could only be undertaken as part of an international agreement containing comparable reductions by other powers, and after taking into account the particular obligations and dangers of each country.[36]

The decision to emphasise the steps taken by Britain towards disarmament was to form a major part of the Cabinet instructions to the British delegation to the Disarmament Conference, in the somewhat pious hope that it would encourage other states to make similar

27

sacrifices.[37] Therefore the British delegation arrived at Geneva with what the Chief Military delegate described as 'somewhat nebulous instructions upon the critical questions'.[38] Major-General A.C. Temperley observed:

> what should have been a very strong hand to play turned out to be the reverse. Other powers were frankly bored when we talked about the amount of disarmament that we had carried out and were quite unable to understand how we could have placed ourselves in such a weak position. They were certainly not disposed to help us retrieve it.[39]

The initial five months of the Conference, until its adjournment on 23 July 1932, revealed that national interests and rivalries were never far removed from the proceedings at Geneva. At no time was this more apparent than in the debate surrounding the proceedings of the Technical Commissions, which were ostensibly established in order to identify those weapons purely of an offensive nature with a view to their ultimate abolition.[40] Temperley recorded:

> The battles of 'offensive' and 'defensive' armaments in the Land, Naval and Air Commissions were all fought on somewhat similar lines. There was little pretence of objectivity. Each state tried to attach a 'defensive' label to the weapons or vessels suited to their own need and an 'offensive' one to those in which they were not interested or actively disliked.[41]

In this the British delegation were as guilty as any other in seeking to protect British interests, particularly in relation to the maintenance of British Naval superiority.[42] One member of the British delegation observing these manoeuvrings — Lord Robert Cecil — could only conclude:

> I gathered that the view of the Government was that Britain had done enough in arranging with United States and Japan for Naval limitation and were not inclined to take any initiative about land or air armaments.
>
> It was evident from what was said to me that some of the Government had little or no belief in international disarmament.[43]

In this assessment Cecil was fairly close to the truth for although Baldwin, MacDonald and Simon worked actively towards the goal of disarmament, the three Service Ministers were representative of an influential block within the Cabinet which opposed any further British concessions to disarmament.[44] Therefore the elongated debate over

28

weapon classification and the merits of qualitative and quantitative disarmament was largely overshadowed by a wider fear that national security might be sacrificed to an unknown end. It was an atmosphere that bred distrust amongst all those concerned, to the extent that each nation found objections to the various disarmament schemes raised at Geneva between February and July of 1932. Given this stalemate it was naturally the German delegation, having most to lose through the maintenance of the status quo, which registered its dissatisfaction with the proceedings. On 22 July 1932 the German representative, Nadolny, informed the General Commission of the Conference:

> Equality of rights is the fundamental principle upon which the League of Nations and the Community of States in general is founded.

> . . . collaboration is only possible if the subsequent work of the Conference is based on a clear and definite recognition of the equality of rights between nations.[45]

Although he was not an official member of the British delegation to the Conference, Eden had closely monitored the proceedings at Geneva. He was particularly concerned at the apparent British equivocation over air disarmament and expressed his view in a letter to Baldwin, dated 9 May 1932, outlining Simon's promotion of qualitative disarmament and the need to follow this initiative with a comprehensive set of proposals:

> It is therefore all the more necessary that our contribution towards air disarmament should not be a blank negative, nor even a paltry one, such an attitude would now stultify our earlier contribution and would make the English attitude appear incomprehensible to our friends and disingenuous to our critics. The species that is ever ready to cry 'Perfide Albion' is not extinct. By a negative attitude on bombing at this stage we should give it every latitude.

> Since we admit our present inferiority in the air any international limitation in that sphere must surely be to our advantage . . . I do hope, therefore, that our contribution in the air will at least embrace the prohibition of bombing and, if possible, the abolition of bombers as well.[46]

In addressing these observations to Baldwin, Eden was quite aware that he was preaching to the converted. In Cabinet, on 4 May 1932, Baldwin had advocated that the British proposals at Geneva be based on the abolition of all military aircraft.[47] The following week Baldwin expanded this proposal to include an offer to abolish submarines and greatly reduce the size of capital ships. Baldwin based his argument on the economy that would be made in national expenditure and the positive contribution that the proposals would make towards disarmament.[48] In relation to air disarmament the attempt to ban all military aircraft was also supported on strategic grounds by the Chief of the Imperial General Staff who, in a report to the Cabinet, concluded:

> From the broadest view of National Defence an effective total abolition of all naval and military air craft throughout the world cannot but be advantageous to this country as tending to restore to us the sea as our first line of defence and as removing the danger of air attack on London.[49]

However, there were others who did not support this view. On 11 May 1932 the Air Disarmament Subcommittee of the CID recommended to the Cabinet the rejection of the total abolition of bombing and suggested that instead a limit of 11,000 pounds (unloaded) should be proposed as a maximum weight for military aircraft.[50] This report echoed the conviction of the Secretary of State for Air, Lord Londonderry, who, in opposing any scheme incorporating the abolition of bombing, declared to the Cabinet: 'To give up bombing was to surrender what in the long run would prove our best defence.'[51] Such was the controversy surrounding the bombing debate that Ramsay MacDonald was forced to reassure King George V on 10 June 1932 'that there was no idea of committing this country to the abolition of the Air Force unless we were absolutely certain that other countries would do likewise'.[52]

While the domestic debate on disarmament policy continued unabated, events at Geneva had been further complicated on 22 June 1932 by a declaration by President Hoover broadly proposing that there should be a general reduction in armaments by one third, with the aim of retaining only defensive armaments.[53] This attempt to combine qualitative and quantitative disarmament essentially cut across the work that Simon had been promoting at Geneva which had been based purely on qualitative reductions, on the assumption that Britain had already undertaken quantitative reductions in its armaments. Although consideration of the Hoover proposals further extended the work of the Disarmament Conference and many considered that the President's move was little more than a manoeuvre in his forthcoming election campaign,[54] Baldwin, on 7 July 1932, had no option but to welcome the new initiative.[55] This move was motivated not only by the need to draw the USA into partnership in any prospective disarmament convention but also by the awareness of the need to maintain close links with the USA in view of the crucial on-going negotiations on reparations and war debts. The Foreign Secretary had forcibly made this point in Cabinet on 24 June 1932 and was supported by Neville Chamberlain, Chancellor of the Exchequer.[56] On 30 June 1932 Chamberlain informed the Cabinet 'that the Prime Minister was most anxious that nothing should be done which would in any way disturb the cordial relations which had been established by the British and American delegations at Geneva'.[57]

Although Baldwin accepted the Hoover proposals as a basis for discussion, in July 1932 a more immediate problem was presented by Germany's withdrawal from the Disarmament Conference. Britain had successfully played the role of mediator between Germany and France at the Lausanne Conference and it now seemed that this role would have to be repeated in finding a compromise which would satisfy France and also lure Germany back to Geneva.[58] Sir John Simon set the tone, on 15 September 1932, in a carefully worded statement that emphasised the need to respect existing treaty obligations but expressed the hope that a disarmament convention could be achieved which granted equality of status to all concerned.[59] Privately the Cabinet endorsed Simon's contention, made on 30 September 1932, that 'the possibility could not be ruled out that it might be unavoidable to agree to Germany possessing some of the weapons prohibited by the Treaty of Versailles'.[60]

The following month, with no sign of the Franco-German gulf diminishing, the Cabinet accepted the recommendation of the Prime Minister and Foreign Secretary that Britain promote an informal four power meeting at Geneva which would be preceded by a major initiative by the Foreign Secretary to engineer a compromise formula.[61] This Simon undertook in a speech before the House of Commons on 10 November 1932 in which he proposed that the disarmament sections of the Versailles Treaty be replaced by a disarmament convention granting Germany equality of status.[62] This broad formula was sufficient to draw Germany back to Geneva in December of 1932 when a compromise agreement was devised.[63] The agreement reaffirmed the dedication of the parties concerned not to resort to force to solve differences. Britain, France and Italy also declared formally that:

> one of the principles that should guide the Conference on Disarmament should be the grant to Germany, and to other powers disarmed by the treaty of equality of rights in a system which would provide security for all nations.[64]

Despite this success at the turn of the year, both MacDonald and

Simon were deeply pessimistic as to the future course of the Conference. Both ministers appreciated that the December agreement had only camouflaged the divisions still existing between Germany and France.[65] As the Conference prepared to reassemble, Sir John Simon reported to the Cabinet that:

> A new programme, firmly promoted and boldly pursued, was the sole hope, and only by doing our utmost to give the right lead ourselves could we escape the verdict, undeserved as it may be, that it was our own shortcomings which had caused the conference to fail.[66]

It was in this period that Anthony Eden began to move quickly into the spotlight. On 13 December 1932 MacDonald had pointed out that the British delegation at the Disarmament Conference was handicapped by the lack of a permanent delegate who did not have to divide his time between Geneva and ministerial duties in London.[67] It was decided that Eden, who had displayed a keen interest in the negotiations and had observed some of the proceedings at Geneva, should be formally attached to the British delegation.[68] This was an opportunity that Eden readily grasped. In October 1932 he had set out in a memorandum to the Foreign Secretary his thoughts on the future of the Conference. Eden argued that the collapse of the Conference would inevitably lead to political instability within Europe, caused by a Franco-German arms race. Such a situation would represent a severe blow to the League of Nations, while the USA would refuse any further involvement in the question of international security. He stressed the unfortunate consequences of the latter point in relation to British hopes for a relaxation of the American attitude on war debts and the forthcoming World Economic Conference. In this light Eden saw as the only course, a major British initiative involving the total abolition of all military aircraft, tanks and heavy guns. Furthermore he suggested a reduction in the size of capital ships, with Germany being allowed to build up to an agreed tonnage within the categories of ships to be retained. Eden concluded that if the scheme failed it would at least absolve Britain of any blame for the failure of the Conference.[69]

Thus in January 1933, as substitute Head of the British Delegation, Eden was to encounter at first hand the problems of guiding an international conference through such a sensitive topic as disarmament. His instructions from London were broadly to build on the Hoover proposals while concentrating essentially on qualitative disarmament and the principle of equality of status for Germany under any eventual agreement.[70]

However, Eden was soon to discover that the Conference was

heading rapidly towards an impasse. Indeed, with the replacement of Herriot by Daladier in Paris and Von Papen by Hitler in Berlin, the divergence between the German and French viewpoints appeared to have been extended. In January 1933 the French Foreign Minister, M. Paul-Boncour, outlined a plan designed to dismantle European long-service professional armies and, with the creation of an international force at the disposal of the League of Nations, to link security closely with a commitment to impose sanctions against an aggressor under Article 16 of the Covenant of the League of Nations.[71] Eden sympathised with French security fears for he was aware that the Foreign Office had received regular reports from the military attaché of the Berlin Embassy chronicling German infringements of the Versailles Treaty military provisions.[72] As early as 9 December 1931 Colonel Marshall Cornwall had reported:

> It has been said that a coach and horses can be driven through most treaties; it is certain that the Germans have driven something more formidable in the way of mechanical transport through the Treaty of Versailles.[73]

Eden was aware, however, that Germany would not accept an agreement on the basis of the Paul-Boncour plan, which would effectively dismantle the Reichswehr while ensuring French military superiority by virtue of the continued existence of extensive French forces in North Africa. Furthermore it was apparent that the British Cabinet would not accept the French demand that a disarmament agreement be supported by an automatic commitment to impose sanctions if the agreement was broken. The French scheme was, therefore, clearly unacceptable to both London and Berlin and Eden concluded that the point of attack had to be an attempt to reduce French security demands.[74] In a letter to Baldwin on 10 February 1933, Eden indicated that the best hope appeared to lie in continuing to push for air disarmament which, if achieved, might persuade the French to relax their demands in other spheres:

> This is the only sphere where the French do not tightly link disarmament with security. I do hope, therefore, that we shall be able to continue to press for total abolition of military and naval aircraft as the only real solution of the problem.[75]

It would seem that Eden was attempting to line up Cabinet support for an initiative on air disarmament.[76] It was well known that Baldwin was a particularly keen proponent of the abolition of bombing.[77] As recently as 10 November 1932 he had declared in the House of Commons:

I think it is well for the man in the street to realise that there is no power on earth that can protect him from being bombed. Whatever people tell him, the bomber will always get through . . . .[78]

Although Baldwin was sympathetic, he was bound by a Cabinet decision of 9 November 1932 to insist that Britain reserve the right to use military aircraft 'as are necessary for police purposes in outlying places'.[79] This decision was designed for application to the use of aircraft in areas such as Iraq and North-West India but Eden appreciated that its retention completely undermined any chance of the major powers accepting a British lead on air disarmament.[80] The problem was further compounded when the Ministerial Committee on Disarmament reaffirmed the above decision on the basis that it was impossible to control military aircraft without similar restrictions on civilian aircraft. In a report to the Cabinet the Committee concluded: 'Consequently the total abolition of military air forces is not practicable . . . .'[81]

Letters from Eden to Stanley Baldwin on 22 and 24 February 1933 indicate that Eden had rapidly been coming to the conclusion that the Conference could only be saved if presented with a comprehensive draft convention rather than continuing to pursue piecemeal agreements:

We shall work at producing a convention this weekend and I cannot help feeling that if the Cabinet regard it as in any way respectable we should make an attempt to get it through the conference.[82]

The result was the production of a draft convention limiting all European armies, except the Soviet Union, to 200,000 men on a short-term service basis.[83] Restrictions were to be imposed on gun calibres and the weight of airplanes and tanks. Air forces were to be restricted to 500 planes, although Germany was not to be allowed to build up to that level. Naval armaments were to continue to be regulated by the agreement reached in the Treaty of London. Finally the above measures were to be supervised by a permanent Disarmament Commission and infringement of the terms of the convention would be referred under the Pact of Paris to all signatory states for consultation as to possible action. It was really a compromise formula in every sense of the word, allowing Germany equality of land forces during the initial trial period of five years and also providing France with an element of disarmament supervision and potential collective action against an aggressor. The use of the Pact of Paris ensured that the USA would be involved in consultation if a breach of the agreement were to take place.[84]

The convention was produced primarily in co-operation with Sir Alexander Cadogan and Sir William Malkin, although Eden later paid tribute to the invaluable technical assistance that was supplied by Major-General Temperley.[85] He had already broached the scheme to Sir John Simon in a memorandum dated 24 February 1933 and he now personally delivered a copy of the draft convention to London.[86] Although the attention of the Cabinet at this time was largely pre-occupied with a proposed embargo on the sale of arms to China and Japan, Eden, with Baldwin's support, was able to present his case to the Cabinet Committee on Disarmament on 2 and 3 March 1933. The draft convention received a sympathetic hearing and it was decided that MacDonald and Simon would travel to Geneva with the option of presenting the proposals if they saw fit. This decision was un-doubtedly prompted by Eden's observation that, if not pre-empted, Arthur Henderson, the President of the Conference, was likely to present a set of proposals that would involve acceptance of sanctions against any party disregarding its commitments under a disarmament agreement.[87] There is no evidence to uphold Temperley's assertion that Eden received permission to waive the police bombing proviso if it proved a major obstacle to agreement and, indeed, the report of the Ministerial Committee on Disarmament, presented on 8 March 1933, maintained the need to uphold previous policy on the use of bombing for policing purposes.[88]

It appeared that MacDonald and Simon viewed their task with a distinct lack of optimism.[89] Following discussion with Daladier and Paul-Boncour in Paris, on 10 March 1933, in which the French had outlined their increasing concern at the militarisation of the German police and various other bodies such as the *Stahlheim*, MacDonald candidly admitted that it was not the time to attempt a major initiative.[90] This was a view that was supported by Baldwin and the Cabinet in a telegram to MacDonald at Geneva on 13 March 1933.[91] However, MacDonald eventually reversed his opinion and, in pre-senting the draft convention to the conference on 16 March 1933, over-rode Cabinet advice. Furthermore he accepted Eden's recom-mendation that he should not confine himself to generalities but outline the specific figures drawn up by the British delegation.[92] This decision seemed to have been motivated by two factors. Firstly the belief that his visit to Geneva had been so highly publicised that to return without making a major initiative would be an admission of defeat. This was a view that was certainly put squarely to MacDonald by Eden after their interview with the Italian delegate, Aloisi, on 14 March 1933. Secondly, while at Geneva, MacDonald received an invitation from Mussolini to visit Rome. It appeared that MacDonald considered the British draft convention might, at least, delay a breakdown of the Disarmament Conference while Britain, France and Italy worked actively to create the basis of an agreement that would be acceptable to all parties. Therefore the British Prime Minister was by no means pinning all his hopes on the convention and saw a greater chance of success as lying in the Rome negotiations rather than the proceedings at Geneva.[93]

The British draft convention was, in general, well received, although only Italy formally accepted its terms. After one week of discussion it was decided that the Conference would adjourn for one month to consider the convention. In retrospect both Eden and Temperley admitted that this was probably a mistake for when the Conference reconvened, the air of optimism had apparently evaporated.[94] During the following five months Eden shouldered the unenviable task of attempting to pilot the British draft convention through the Conference. The French Foreign Minister, Paul-Boncour, was adamant that France required further security guarantees, including effective measures for supervision of the convention and the denial of any element of German rearmament during an initial trial period.[95] Despite the conciliatory nature of Hitler's speech on 17 May 1933, Nadolny continued to press at Geneva for German rearmament up to the level of its European neighbours by the end of the first stage of the convention.[96] On 11 May 1933 Eden reported to the Foreign Secretary:

> I have now a definite impression what Germany really wants, rearmament, i.e. she demands to have weapons allowed to others. German delegate speaks of 'samples' without giving any indication as to numbers. I believe Germans have raised Reichswehr difficulty largely in order to secure more ardently desired concessions on material. I made it perfectly clear to German delegate that there could be no German rearmament.[97]

This was a view that was supported by the Foreign Secretary in Cabinet on 17 May 1933. Sir John Simon referred to the international climate as 'definitely disquieting in relation to the increasingly militant attitude adopted in Germany'.[98] It appeared that the Foreign Secretary held little confidence in the future prospects for progress at the Conference and, on 12 May 1933, instructed Eden to avoid any further discussion of disarmament details until Germany agreed to 'the principle of disarmament by stages and nothing that could really be described as rearmament by Germany'.[99]

The Conference appeared to be heading towards deadlock. Eden was prepared to concede to Germany an increased number in their quota of militarised police but could get no comparable concession from the Germans in exchange.[100] In a letter to Baldwin, Eden expressed his growing frustration:

> The Germans are exasperating and progress is very slow. One feels it is rather like a 1917 campaign in Flanders; we can only make such progress as we may in the mud between the pill boxes and leave the strong points to be attacked at the last — and, as in Flanders, the pill boxes are occupied by Germans![101]

A similar feeling of exasperation was noticeable in a memorandum drawn up by Temperley and forwarded to the Foreign Office by Cadogan on 10 May 1933. Temperley outlined the growing element of militarism in German society and urged Britain and France to: 'resolutely combine either to ensure its destruction or at least its confinement until the disease runs its course.'

Although the memorandum concluded that if the Disarmament Conference were to fail, Britain and France must warn Germany that they were prepared to enforce the Versailles settlement, in a later conversation with Sir John Simon, Temperley indicated that he would prefer a more forward policy, including the seizing of the Rhine bridgeheads as 'a hostage for good behaviour'.[102]

Eden, however, did not appear to endorse Temperley's conclusions and still retained the hope that he could succeed in his role of *rapporteur* between France and Germany. This hope was essentially based on the expectation that the USA would back the British initiative. On 16 May 1933 President Roosevelt openly declared his support for the British draft convention and, in addition, proposed the establishment of an international pact of non-aggression.[103] On 22 May 1933 Norman Davis, in a speech to the General Commission of the Disarmament Conference, stated that the USA was prepared 'to consult with other states in case of a threat to peace with a view to averting a conflict'. This in itself represented a significant advance on any previous commitment by the USA to the maintenance of international security but fell far short of the positive commitment sought by Eden. Not only did the USA reserve the right to decide for itself whether an act constituted a breach of the peace but also its support for the enforcement of collective security was confined to opposing any action which would undermine the collective efforts of other states.[104] Such a negative contribution indicated that the USA was still averse to any form of international commitment. Eden was forced to conclude that the USA was unlikely to adhere to the disarmament convention, and would even obstruct those sections which attempted to place on it any form of automatic obligation to participate in collective action against a state that transgressed the agreement.[105]

The problems faced by Eden were not confined to his negotiations with the major powers. On several occasions he was forced to report to the Foreign Office that the British position at Geneva was being severely undermined by the insistence of the three Service Ministers on the maintenance of a level of British armed forces that, in regard to tanks and aircraft, was actually in excess of existing strength.[106] In addition Londonderry was adamant on the need to retain the right to use bombing for police purposes.[107] In a letter to Baldwin dated 1 May 1933, Eden pointed out that if he were to proceed on the basis of estimates provided by the Air Ministry and the Dominions 'These figures will give the British Empire as a whole an Air Force nearly three times as large as that of any nation'.[108]

Not surprisingly, when the air chapter of the disarmament convention was discussed at Geneva on 27 May 1933, Eden reported that the 'reservation as to police bombing was universally condemned except by Iraqi and Persian delegates'.[109] The Cabinet decision to uphold the War Ministry and Air Ministry estimates effectively indicated that the British Government no longer held much faith in the proceedings at Geneva.[110] Eden tacitly admitted this when it was agreed that the Conference adjourn on 10 June 1933, without a decision on the British draft convention, to allow the delegates to move on to the World Economic Conference to be held in London.[111]

The Foreign Office had been predicting the failure of this session of the Disarmament Conference as early as 19 May 1933. A memorandum which was largely the work of Sir Robert Vansittart noted:

Extract 1

His Majesty's Government have been confronted at the Disarmament Conference during the last fifteen months with a peculiarly difficult and well nigh hopeless problem.

The memorandum contended that the stance adopted by His Majesty's Government had been based largely on the claim that Britain had already taken significant steps towards disarmament:

Extract 2

such an argument has little effect on other countries, it does not touch the root difficulties of disarmament, which are those of the French demand for security and the demand of Germany and other ex-enemy states for equality of status. It is these two problems which have always been present throughout fifteen months of discussion of world limitation and reduction of armaments. The second of them has progressively assumed greater and greater importance, and on its solution the very peace of Europe may depend, if, indeed, the attitude of Germany renders it soluble.[112]

The blame for the failure of the Conference was laid squarely at the feet of Germany and its demand for immediate equality of status which was unacceptable to both France and Britain.[113]

Anthony Eden later argued that the decision to adjourn for four weeks after only one week's discussion of the British draft convention effectively nullified the impetus and initiative given to the Conference by the British proposals.[114] More realistically, though, the proceedings at Geneva were overtaken by events elsewhere. Given the problems of getting agreement at Geneva which Eden described as 'like trying to force a bill through an international House of Commons with no whips and no government majority', the major European powers once again reverted to select and private negotiations.[115] Therefore MacDonald and Simon responded immediately to Mussolini's offer of informal discussions in Rome, in March 1933, which ultimately led to the conclusion of the Four Power Pact initialled by Britain, Italy, Germany and France on 7 June 1933.[116] While the centre of attention was focused for three months on negotiations for a European pact that merely reaffirmed the general dedication to eventual equality of status for Germany and an undertaking to uphold the Covenant of the League of Nations, the proceedings at Geneva were relegated to secondary importance.[117] Furthermore, as Simon noted, this resort to private negotiation severely undercut the confidence of the smaller states who suspected that the outcome would be 'a plot to dish the League of Nations'.[118]

With the decision to adjourn the Disarmament Conference on 10 June 1933, Eden was forced to concede that hope of any further progress at Geneva was remote. He admitted as much in a report to Sir John Simon in which he recommended that the Foreign Secretary organise a meeting of the major heads of state in order to seek a compromise that might revitalise the Conference.[119] The most important point appeared to be the maintenance of Anglo-French unity and, therefore, before approaching Germany it was necessary to ascertain how far France would be prepared to go in making concessions to Germany. On 8 June 1933 Eden met with Daladier and Norman Davis in Paris. It was soon clear that Daladier wanted a trial period of at least three years included in the disarmament convention, during which Germany would transform the Reichswehr to a short-service force while French disarmament would commence after the completion of the trial period.[120] The text of this discussion submitted to the Cabinet indicated that Eden sympathised with the French position:

> the importance the French attached to supervision was due to their conviction that Germany was rearming so much. Mr. Eden

thought that the French were confident that the evidence in this respect was so strong that when it came to light no-one could ask France to do very much in the way of disarmament.[121]

In meetings with Paul-Boncour on 26 June 1933 and with Arthur Henderson on 21 June 1933, Eden agreed that there was little point in reconvening the Conference until the Franco-German gulf was bridged.[122] He reported to the Cabinet in this vein on 26 July 1933 but his plea for further Anglo-French talks was ignored by MacDonald who feared that the French would insist upon further British commitments to European security.[123] It was, therefore, not until 19 September 1933 that Eden travelled to Paris to meet Daladier. The French Premier now wanted the trial period extended to four years, with a commitment to take positive action against any state which broke the convention.[124] Once again the road appeared barred when the Cabinet rejected the suggestion of Britain entering into any form of automatic commitment to implement sanctions.[125] It was agreed that Simon would travel to Paris to reinforce the British negotiating team, but he too found Daladier insistent on maintaining the terms outlined to Eden. In reply to the Premier's demand for sanctions Simon could only declare that 'public opinion in England would not support it'.[126] The deadlock appeared complete when, on 27 September 1933, Simon and Eden met Von Neurath at Geneva. The German Foreign Minister repeated the demand that Germany be permitted an unspecified number of samples of weapons, at present prohibited by the Versailles Treaty, during the first period of the disarmament convention.[127] A breakdown appeared imminent as Eden referred to what was likely to be 'the last days of the long-drawn agony of the Conference'.[128]

Eden was certainly moving towards the conviction that the German claims were unjustifiable and, therefore, welcomed Sir John Simon's statement to the Bureau of the Disarmament Conference, on 14 October 1933, advocating a trial period of four years during which Germany would not be permitted to rearm.[129] Hitler replied almost immediately that the proposal denied Germany equality of status and, therefore, Germany would be withdrawing from the Disarmament Conference and the League of Nations.[130] That evening Eden noted in his diary:

> The Conference was becoming a sham so that it is perhaps just as well now. All the same, I should not like Simon's conscience about the earlier part of the last year when Bruning was still in power. We missed the bus then and could never overtake it.[131]

Despite the failure to break the deadlock at Geneva, Eden's work behind the scenes had not gone unnoticed. On 28 September 1933 the British Ambassador to Paris, Lord Tyrrell, wrote to Stanley Baldwin that Arthur Henderson had praised Eden's work at Geneva. Tyrrell added:

> As I consider him your official child I thought that you would like to have this tribute.
>
> You may soon have to protect him against possible jealousies his success may arouse![132]

Three days later Baldwin received a letter from W. Ormsby-Gore at Geneva stating:

> The man who really has the international position here is Anthony Eden. Somehow or other Anthony has got the confidence — nay the admiration of all these strange animals that live in this zoo. Simon can never get it. If there is a disarmament convention at all — and if there isn't Europe is back in the jungle not merely over armament but over everything else whatsoever — it will be Anthony who will have got it.[133]

On 13 October 1933 Eden had written to Baldwin suggesting that it was time German opposition to the British proposals was put to the test: 'The conference is becoming such a sham through these endless postponements that its fate must be decided one way or the other, or it will fade away ingloriously to death.'[134]

Benes had already informed Eden that he was convinced Germany had no intention of signing a disarmament treaty and that the Germans had already begun a programme of extensive rearmament.[135] This opinion seemed to be confirmed when Germany left the Disarmament Conference on 14 October 1933 and ten days later Hitler announced his intention to establish an army of 300,000 men equipped with what he termed 'defensive' weapons.[136] Although Hitler added that German ambitions were limited to Eastern Europe, the whole tenor of his speech reinforced the points made in a memorandum submitted to Sir John Simon on 28 August 1933 by Sir Robert Vansittart emphasising that German ambitions in Austria and Poland were only a prelude to an assault on Western Europe.[137] On 12 October 1933 the Chiefs-of-Staff Annual Review had concluded that the 'international situation is steadily deteriorating' and advocated a steady build-up in the armed services. The Cabinet had been sufficiently alarmed to agree to the establishment of a Defence Requirements Committee (DRC) whose terms of reference were to: 'prepare a programme for meeting our worst deficiencies for translation to the Cabinet.'[138]

On 29 November 1933 the DRC reported that the German demands would give Hitler, within a few years, a military force capable of re-drawing the German borders with Poland and Czechoslovakia.[139] This assessment was supported by reports from the Berlin Embassy throughout 1933 and the increasing anxiety that was generated by reports of the activities of pro-German political factions in Austria.[140]

Following the German decision to withdraw from the Disarmament Conference, the French Government adopted the stance that Hitler had at last shown his true colours and his determination to pursue a policy of rearmament. On 16 November 1933 the French Foreign Minister, Paul-Boncour, informed the British Ambassador in Paris that he saw no point in making further concessions to Germany. He recommended that the Disarmament Conference should continue and attempt to conclude a disarmament convention as Germany was already bound to disarm by the terms of the Versailles Treaty. Furthermore, to counteract the stream of propaganda emanating from Germany concerning the failure of the major powers to agree to disarmament, the French urged the opening of immediate Anglo-French discussion to assemble a dossier of German breaches of the Versailles Treaty military provisions which would be made public. It appeared that the French Government had now taken up an implacable stance based on complete opposition to any measure of German rearmament or any further discussions with Germany outside the confines of the Disarmament Conference.[141]

Despite a great deal of sympathy with the French position and a growing exasperation with the escalation of German demands, the British Government decided once again to attempt to play the role of honest broker between Germany and France. On 23 October 1933 the Cabinet endorsed Simon's recommendation that there was little point in continuing with the Disarmament Conference while Germany was absent. Therefore Britain was to press for an adjournment of the Conference while seeking to bring France, Italy and Germany together to find a compromise.[142] This proposal was put to the French Ambassador, Corbin, by Eden on 31 October 1933 and on 10 November 1933 — with little success as Corbin remained adamant that France would insist on continuing the proceedings at Geneva.[143] It was, therefore, with some trepidation that Simon and Eden travelled to Geneva on 17 November 1933. In a conversation with a member of the French delegation, Massigli, Eden outlined the British position:

> I explained that it must seem to us of little use to draft, in convention form, an offer which Germany had already refused when we knew quite well that the Italian government would not agree to co-operate in such work.

Eden continued that any advance must be based on a further offer to Germany avoiding the mention of an initial trial period and including a commitment to begin the destruction of French heavy material after two years. He was convinced that the French insistence on an initial four-year trial period and their reluctance to outline the material they were prepared to destroy had led to the failure of the previous negotiations.[144] After two days of discussions Eden could only conclude that the French stance had not weakened and an Anglo-French rift appeared imminent. Eden reported to London: 'The consequences of such disagreement upon the state of Europe might prove deplorable indeed.'[145]

It appeared that the Conference was heading rapidly towards a breakdown, until a compromise was devised by Arthur Henderson at a series of private meetings of the delegates drawn from Britain, France, Italy and the USA, held between 19 November and 22 November 1933. It was agreed that the General Commission of the Conference would not be recalled until the new year, although the various working committees would continue their proceedings under the direction of the President until the Christmas adjournment. Paul-Boncour remained adamant, however, that France would not agree to any attempt to modify the proposals presented to the Conference on 14 October 1933.[146]

As outlined by Sir John Simon at Geneva, the British position was that the draft convention was only a basis for discussion and was open to development and modification.[147] Therefore, despite extensive reports of German rearmament in contravention of the Versailles Treaty and increasing pro-German activity in Austria, Britain remained determined to pursue an agreement with Germany.[148] The rationale behind this decision had been suggested by Baldwin in the House of Commons on 27 November 1933, when he outlined the options facing Britain as being either the conclusion of a disarmament convention or a major arms race. In the pursuit of such an agreement it was apparent that both Baldwin and Eden were coming to the conclusion that German rearmament was inevitable and, indeed, already underway. Their main task, therefore, was to gain agreement on levels of re-armament before the German programme advanced any further.[149] The conviction that some form of agreement was necessary, even if it involved concessions to Germany, was reinforced by a despatch from Sir Eric Phipps on 21 November 1933:

> His [Hitler's] signature under even a not altogether satisfactory agreement only partially agreeable to Great Britain and France and not too distasteful to Italy, might prevent for a time any further German shots among the international ducks.

Years might then pass and even Hitler might grow old and reason might come to this side and fear leave that.[150]

Therefore, while opposing Hitler's demands for an army of 300,000, an air force of approximately 25 per cent of the combined strength of Germany's neighbours and the possession of tanks and heavy artillery, Sir John Simon, in the later months of 1933, had decided that Britain must attempt once again to devise an agreement which would satisfy both France and Germany.[151] This task was largely entrusted to the Foreign Office and supervised by Sir Robert Vansittart. In this work the Foreign Office was encouraged by declarations from Hitler that if granted equality of rights Germany would return to the Disarmament Conference.[152] Furthermore Lord Tyrrell reported, on 15 December 1933, that despite its outward hostility to further concessions, the French Government would be prepared to consider a British initiative incorporating an element of limited German rearmament.[153]

In preparing the ground for the British initiative, Simon visited Paris on 22 December 1933 and Rome on 3 January 1934. Although the French remained defensive, the results were encouraging. The Foreign Secretary was particularly pleased at Mussolini's apparent dedication to disarmament and his determination to impose some form of limitation on German rearmament.[154] The British Memorandum on Disarmament was finally completed on 25 January 1934 and presented to Germany four days later, in a deliberate attempt to force Hitler into adopting a conciliatory line in a major speech he was to make before the Reichstag on 30 January 1934. The Memorandum attempted to satisfy French security fears by linking the disarmament convention to the Pact of Paris. If the Pact was infringed or irregularities were identified by the Permanent Disarmament Commission, the signatories of the Pact would be obliged to consult on possible courses of action. In response to Mussolini's conviction that Germany would have to be granted an element of rearmament, the Germans were offered the opportunity to construct tanks up to six tons in weight and to commence the building of an air force if no further agreement on air disarmament had been reached after two years. The treaty was to be phased over a period of ten years, with the major powers commencing the immediate destruction of the heaviest classes of tanks and artillery and reaching a parity level with Germany after seven years. Naval disarmament was to be regulated by the naval conference scheduled for 1935 while German land forces, though open to negotiation, were to be restricted to 200,000 men.[155]

The Disarmament Committee of the Cabinet were anxious that the proposals should not be merely submitted to Berlin, Rome and Paris but should be followed by the visit of a British Minister to ascertain at first hand the general reaction to the British Memorandum. It was decided that Eden should undertake this delicate task.[156] Once again this was indicative of the trust placed in his ability by Simon, Baldwin and MacDonald. In December 1933 Eden had been appointed Lord Privy Seal, a post that had been held by Baldwin for a year following the resignation of Snowden over the issue of tariffs raised at the Ottawa Imperial Economic Conference of July—August 1932. Eden appeared to have been sceptical as to the value of accepting the post. It would seem that he was already considering his claim for full Cabinet status for he noted at the time: 'although it brings the appearance of more authority it actually gives none. I shall not even be a member of the Cabinet Committee that decides the policy I shall be expected to carry out.'[157]

It would seem that Eden only accepted the post after Baldwin had outlined the benefits that would accompany his new status. In particular Eden's elevation to the Privy Council would greatly enhance his future claim for a Cabinet position, while his ministerial rank would also entitle him to appoint a Parliamentary Private Secretary. This post was subsequently filled by Lord Cranborne and, with the addition of Robin Hankey as his Private Secretary, Eden for the first time began to gather around himself the nucleus of a team of advisers and assistants, which further underlined his growing stature within the Conservative Party.[158]

Throughout this period Eden appears to have been in general agreement with the course of action adopted by the Foreign Secretary. At Geneva he had urged the French delegation to adopt a more flexible stance and had emphasised the futility of continuing without Germany. He was also aware that Henderson was toying with the possibility of proposing a scheme for the implementation of economic sanctions to reinforce the British draft convention and appreciated that open discussion of this subject at Geneva was to be avoided at all costs.[159] Therefore the only solution appeared to be an adjournment of the Conference and a further resort to informal negotiations. On 9 December 1933 Eden noted:

> No French Government could be expected to agree to negotiate with Germany on the basis of rearmament for the latter. The only course, and I have felt this strongly for a fortnight, is for us to do that work of unmasking the German batteries. Tell the French what we are doing, but not ask them to participate. The weaker the French Government the less it can do. If, on the other hand, we tackle Hitler skilfully as Phipps can be trusted to do, we shall discover whether the German demands are in truth

exorbitant, as I anticipate, or reasonable. If the former, the sooner British public opinion wakes up to the fact the better. If the latter we shall then have something definite upon which to work.[160]

The visits to Paris, Rome and Berlin were of central importance to the British disarmament proposals. It has been suggested that the Germans were anxious for Baldwin to undertake the task, but his general distaste for foreign affairs and official visits never seriously led to this proposal being considered.[161] Eden, however, had no doubt that Baldwin was behind the decision to entrust him with such an important and prestigious mission. Before leaving for Paris he wrote to Baldwin:

> I want to say 'thank you'. The Cabinet Committee today could not have been more encouraging and I know how much of that help I owe to you. This Pilgrimage is an outside chance but I do feel that it is worth taking.[162]

Eden's brief was outwardly straightforward. He was simply to explain the format of the British Memorandum and then to elicit the comments and suggestions of the Italian, French and German governments. He was not empowered to enter into negotiations or make any commitments other than those contained in the Memorandum. However, on arrival in Paris on 17 February 1934, the mission got off to an inauspicious beginning when, in a preliminary discussion with Massigli,[163] the French official outlined the problems presented by the existence of extensive paramilitary formations in Germany and adopted an attitude which Eden described as 'almost reconciled to failure'.[164] The following day Eden met the new French Prime Minister, Doumergue, and his Foreign Minister, Barthou. Once again Eden was dismayed to discover that the French Government had been almost completely preoccupied with the internal crisis surrounding the Stavisky affair. The suggestion that the Finance Minister and Minister of Justice had contributed through negligence to the embezzlement of several million francs had both brought down the Chautemps government and prevented full consideration being given to the British proposals. The French officials therefore urged Eden to return to Paris after visiting Berlin and Rome in order to give them time to examine the British Memorandum. What comments they did make were not encouraging. Doumergue raised the problem of controlling the German paramilitary formations which he numbered as some 1,200,000 men, while Barthou roundly attacked the proposal to begin the immediate rearmament of German land forces while delaying the rearmament of naval and air forces, the restrictions on which were of

46

primary interest to British security. Furthermore Barthou noted that the Memorandum made no mention of security being guaranteed by the imposition of sanctions on an aggressor. Although Eden attempted to counter the charge that the proposals were based on preserving British security interests and pointed out that the scheme would give France military superiority over Germany for ten years, he was forced to admit that the British Government would not commit itself to automatic sanctions against a state which infringed the disarmament agreement. In reporting to London, Eden could only conclude that the French Government seemed less disposed than its predecessors to make concessions and, as part of any agreement, would demand further security guarantees.[165]

From Paris, Eden travelled to Berlin. After a preliminary interview with Von Neurath in which the Foreign Minister evinced extreme scepticism as to the possibility of Germany accepting the British proposals,[166] Eden had two extended interviews with Hitler.[167] The interviews made an extremely favourable impression on Eden, as he recorded in a letter to Baldwin from Berlin:

> We had our first interview with Hitler yesterday afternoon. We were given a grand salute on arrival by a very fine guard of S.S. (illegal) armed to the teeth (illegal). Having thus condoned breaches of the Treaty of Versailles we march through passages greeted by salutes by everyone, even the typists! More like G.H.Q. in war time than anything else. Eventually we are shown into a vast almost (. . .) room and Hitler came forward to greet us.
>
> He is a surprise. In conversation quiet, almost shy with a pleasant smile. Without doubt the man has charm.

Eden was convinced that he had established an immediate *rapport* with Hitler on the basis of their war-time experiences:

> The war seems to have left an indelible impression upon Hitler . . . .
>
> . . . he likes to talk about the war, seems to feel friendly to anyone who was in it on whichever side, 'Frontkampfer' i.e. one who fought at the front, seems to be as favourite a phrase here as it is extinct at home.[168]

Hitler maintained that Germany wanted peace in order to concentrate on solving its internal problems but that it must be permitted an element of defensive security. To insure itself against an attack by neighbouring states, Germany would require an army of 300,000 men and an air force of short-range aircraft numbering approximately 30 per cent of the combined strength of its neighbours or 50 per cent of French air strength. In exchange Hitler was prepared to agree to participate in a disarmament convention spanning ten years, within which the French would not be obliged to disarm until after the completion of the first five-year period. Furthermore Germany would accept a system of supervision and inspection that would include examination of the SS and SA to ensure that they were not armed or undergoing any form of military training. As a final expansive gesture Hitler offered to reduce the paramilitary Green Police from 140,000 to 90,000, pointing out that these proposals would generate a great deal of criticism within Germany and, therefore, could best be attained if presented as being requested by the British Government. [169] Eden was privately elated at Hitler's proposals which he considered as going a long way towards satisfying the French demand for a trial period of disarmament and control over the various paramilitary formations in Germany. To Baldwin he wrote:

> Whatever the outcome of the disarmament conversations I am glad that we came here. Our hosts are clearly pleased. They have taken an immense amount of trouble to make themselves agreeable and if the result is as exhausting for them as for their victims they must be weary.

> I find it very hard to believe that the man himself [Hitler] wants war. My impression is much more that this country has plenty to do internally to be thus pre-occupied for five years to come.[170]

Before leaving Berlin, Eden agreed to keep the terms of Hitler's proposals confidential until he had reported back to London.[171] However, on arrival in Rome, an initial cloud had already appeared on the horizon in that the Germans had leaked Hitler's proposals to Mussolini.[172] Eden did not appear at all deterred:

> Drummond's view is that Italians will jump at them. Mussolini wants an agreement soon, every month that passes Hitler asks for more.

> I am far from advocating Hitler's proposals but they are better for France than anything I had expected him to offer. This is also Phipps view.

> They may not be [showy?] for our public opinion but must not we lead and educate them to face the realities, if they are as stark as they seem?[173]

The possibility of luring Germany and Italy into a network of controlled rearmament was sufficient for Eden to urge Baldwin to persuade the Cabinet to await his return before pronouncing on the German proposals.

It was soon apparent that Eden's thoughts were not attuned to those of his colleagues in London. MacDonald minuted on Eden's despatch from Berlin: 'We should not allow Germany to dump its confidences upon us in order to use us for its own policy. Hitler should know at once that his proposals in substance and in method of handling are unacceptable.'[174] More specifically Eden was firmly rebuked by the Foreign Secretary: 'Your telegram *No. 78* puts us in a position of great embarrassment. The proposals contained in it are such as we could not possibly ourselves put forward and sponsor.' Referring specifically to Hitler's demand for the immediate legalisation of a German air force, Simon continued that the Government:

> could not moreover consider a proposal which would destroy the whole character of their draft, entailing a rearmament race rather than disarmament and a rejection of our proposal by our own people.
>
> This position would be untenable and unacceptable to us.[175]

The first part of this despatch was immediately countered by a telegram from Sir Eric Phipps in Berlin to the Foreign Office pointing out that Germany had now released its terms to Italy and France and, therefore, there was no question of them being sponsored by Britain.[176] Eden immediately wrote to Phipps from Rome, thanking him for coming to his defence.[177] In reply to Sir John Simon, Eden stressed that he had in no way accepted Hitler's proposals and had only agreed to communicate them to London.[178] This appeared to satisfy the immediate question of procedure and Simon replied on 26 February 1934: 'Your mission is so important and at the same time so difficult that we should like to send you the assurance of our full confidence and we are looking forward to your personal report as soon as possible.'[179]

This message, though, did little to disguise the divergence of opinion that appeared to exist between Eden and the Cabinet. It is difficult to assess just how this situation arose. Certainly Eden could justifiably complain that the failure of the Foreign Secretary to provide a consistent lead in the direction of British foreign policy had allowed an element of confusion and doubt to accumulate. This was an assessment that was supported by several of Simon's senior colleagues. On 3 October 1932 Sir Maurice Hankey recorded in his diary:

The Prime Minister has a low opinion of his Foreign Minister, which he does not conceal from his intimates, including myself. He thinks also that Simon bags his ideas and takes the credit for them himself, without acknowledgement — in which there is a certain amount of truth.

. . . Simon though great at presentation of a case has few ideas and will always eat out of the hand of a more fertile mind like MacDonald.[180]

In January 1934 the Chancellor of the Exchequer, Neville Chamberlain, noted:

Simon's weakness has given rise to much criticism both in the Press and the Cabinet.

. . . he seems temperamentally unable to make up his mind to action when a difficult situation arises.[181]

In relation to the British Memorandum on disarmament, Chamberlain went so far as to claim that, during a Cabinet discussion on the course of action, Simon 'played a rather pitiable part being unable apparently to give us a lead and always asking the Cabinet to give him instructions, the Cabinet eventually agreed on the course I had suggested'.[182] Certainly Simon's problems were compounded by recurring bouts of ill-health for Eden had complained to Baldwin in June 1933 that: 'no work is harder than that of carrying a sick man.'[183]

By January 1934 Neville Chamberlain was privately speculating that Simon was to be replaced at the Foreign Office, and perhaps an awareness of this had encouraged Eden, in December 1933, to hold out for a post of more responsibility than Lord Privy Seal. However, although in February 1934 Baldwin seemed to have been considering a Cabinet reshuffle, there is no evidence to suggest that he had considered promoting Eden to a position within the Cabinet.[184]

It could be suggested, therefore, that the absence of a clear lead in the format of foreign policy from Simon contributed to the existence of a position where Eden found himself markedly adrift from Cabinet opinion on German armament policy. However, Eden had been at the heart of British disarmament negotiations for over twelve months. Throughout this period Britain had maintained that the Reichswehr must be limited to a short-term service force of, at the most, 200,000 men. Furthermore Germany was to be denied an air force until further attempts at air disarmament had been tried. However unrealistic this stance may seem in the light of experience, it is difficult to account for the fact that someone intimately connected with the conduct of

British disarmament policy thought British and French opinion could be re-educated overnight to accept the reality of German rearmament and, particularly, the immediate creation of a German air force. Such a reorientation of policy would have entailed a major shift in stance and attitudes in relation to the whole question of disarmament and the balance of military forces in Europe which neither government, at that time, was either prepared or willing to undertake. It can only be assumed that by February 1934 Eden was so sceptical as to the probable outcome of the Disarmament Conference that he was prepared to accept the limited rearmament of Germany as preferable to a complete breakdown of negotiations and a possible arms race.[185]

It was in pursuit of this goal that Eden met Mussolini on 26 February 1934.[186] In essence the Italian dictator supported Hitler's demand for equality of status and the immediate recognition of the right to possess defensive weapons, including a short-range air force. Eden noted with satisfaction, however, that Mussolini was adamant that once these concessions had been granted Italy would join Britain and France in adopting a 'firm attitude' towards future German demands and in insisting that Germany rejoin the League of Nations. Finally Mussolini expressed his willingness to participate in further four-power discussions on disarmament. The tenor of his remarks was all that Eden had hoped for, as was indicated in his report to the Foreign Secretary:

> Throughout the conversation Signor Mussolini emphasised the need for speedy agreement and I think we could count upon his support for any reasonable compromise upon any terms ranging from those of the British Memorandum to those of Italian Memorandum.[187]

Eden later maintained that the interview 'was lively, friendly, vigorous, and entertaining' and strenuously denied that an element of acrimony had been generated between Mussolini and himself.[188] However, Lord Strang, who attended the meeting, has recorded that the personal relationship between the two men was 'neither successful or agreeable'. It certainly seems that Eden and Mussolini did not establish any sort of *rapport* and subsequent meetings were to be marked by a distinct hostility and distaste on both sides.[189]

Despite an element of personal discord, the two men were basically in agreement that Hitler had made an offer which could possibly form the basis of a compromise.[190] The remaining obstacle to success now appeared to be France and Eden elected to cut short his visit and return immediately to Paris to assess the attitude of the French Government.[191] In outlining Hitler's proposals to Doumergue and

Barthou on 1 March 1934, Eden emphasised that they would guarantee French military supremacy over Germany for a decade. In reply the French Premier maintained that France wished to see the German paramilitary formations not just demilitarised but completely disbanded, while he placed little faith in any German pledge to construct a short-range air force only without the inclusion of bombers. Barthou once again returned to the question of guarantees concerning the implementation of sanctions. When Eden could only repeat his inability to provide such guarantees, Barthou maintained that the French Government would have to give the matter further consideration before stating its position. In rejecting the German initiative while refusing to offer an alternative, the French Government had once again proved an intractable barrier to Eden's work.[192] He concluded that Barthou and Doumergue were timid and hesitant due to the fear of a public backlash against any concessions to Germany and he reported to Sir John Simon:

> Try as I would I could get no more out of them than a promise to let us have their views as soon as possible.

> I was quite unable to make them face realities today . . . .[193]

It was apparent, though, that the realities of the situation, as identified by Eden and as seen by his senior colleagues in London, did not coincide on several points. Eden had come to the conclusion that limited German rearmament was inevitable. Therefore on returning to London he recommended to the Foreign Secretary:

(i) We stand by Convention as amended by our Memorandum.
(ii) We are prepared to accept Hitler's amendments, or something like them, on condition Germany returns to League.
(iii) If France can accept above we are prepared to help her by accepting guarantees of execution or something analogous.[194]

The key to Eden's suggestions lay in the need to pacify French security fears by providing a British guarantee that a disarmament convention would be effectively enforced. It would seem that the Foreign Office was thinking along similar lines for on 21 March 1934 a memorandum was produced for the Cabinet, pointing out that German rearmament 'in both the aeronautical and military spheres . . . may soon become a menace to the balance of power in Europe'. The memorandum continued that, as Hitler desired formal recognition of Germany's illegal armaments, Britain was now in a position to extract qualitative and quantitative armament restrictions from Germany in exchange for recognition of limited German rearmament. An agreement along these lines might also remove the thorny problem of the revision of the Versailles Treaty military clauses: 'Part V is, for practical purposes, dead, and it would become a putrefying corpse which, if left unburned, would soon poison the political atmosphere of all Europe.' The central problem was to gain French agreement and, if future British security was to be identified in terms of Anglo-French interests, the only solution was to offer France the security guarantees demanded by the French Government.[195]

The memorandum was considered by the Cabinet the following day. While agreeing that British interests were inextricably linked to France and rejecting the growing lobby for a purely Anglo-German agreement, the Cabinet refused to commit itself to further guarantees towards French security. This conclusion was based covertly on the Cabinet's persistent refusal to expand Britain's commitments to Western Europe and overtly on the assertion that France had failed to clarify the form of guarantee that it desired. By declining to enter into further discussions until France outlined its demands, the ball was firmly thrown back into the French court.[196] The decision to surrender the initiative to France clearly indicated the lack of clear purpose in British policy following the apparent rejection of the British Disarmament Memorandum. Neville Chamberlain was openly advocating the creation of an international military force to police a European disarmament convention, while Simon appeared unprepared to go any further than the discussion of possible economic and financial sanctions, and only then with the tacit approval of the USA.[197]

While the British Government adopted what Neville Chamberlain termed a 'wait and see' attitude, Eden's hands were effectively tied at Geneva and he could do little but propose further adjournment until the French attitude was made clear.[198] On 10 April 1934 he expressed the hope to Arthur Henderson that the French would agree to a convention based on limited rearmament.[199] This hope was rudely shattered the following week when Barthou, referring to the recently announced increase in the German defence estimates, declared: 'in present circumstances France would not be justified in proceeding with negotiations for a convention legalising rearmament of Germany.'[200] Eden could only conclude that for the present time nothing could be achieved at Geneva,[201] an assessment that Neville Chamberlain underlined in his comments to the Cabinet Committee on Disarmament on 3 May 1934.[202]

The remaining danger was that the French would utilise the Conference as a vehicle to push through further security guarantees directed against Germany. It seemed that British interests would be best served by an adjournment of the Conference while the gulf between France and Germany remained unbridged. To continue the Conference would only have further alienated Germany and exacerbated Anglo-French differences.[203] The task of engineering an adjournment without completely undermining the future credibility of the Conference was entrusted to Eden. It was a delicate task compounded by increasing co-operation between France and the Soviet Union with the aim of gaining acceptance of a series of European security pacts designed to contain Germany. Eden was aware of the dangers inherent in the Franco-Soviet scheme which he saw as designed 'to create "Locarnos" in various parts of Europe but the real purpose would be the encirclement of Germany.'[204]

Eden's brief from London was to go no further than reaffirming Britain's commitment to the Treaty of Locarno and to maintain that little more could be achieved at Geneva until Germany returned to the Conference. With the support of the USA and most of the smaller European states this goal was achieved on 8 June 1934, when it was agreed that the General Commission of the Disarmament Conference would adjourn until a date to be specified by the Bureau.[205] To all intents and purposes the Conference was dead. In July 1934 Eden participated in Anglo-French discussions concerning British approval of the proposed East-European Mutual Guarantee Pact, at which Simon attempted to revive the Conference by linking British support for the Pact to French acceptance of a guarantee for Germany against Soviet aggression.[206] However, this initiative was short-lived as Germany rejected the Franco-Soviet sponsored scheme.[207]

Any hope of success at the Disarmament Conference in 1934 had been effectively stifled by the steady escalation of German demands and Anglo-French differences over the extent of the British commitment to European security.[208] Given these fundamental divergences in attitude there is much to be said for Temperley's assessment: 'We began at the wrong end; it was international relations that needed disarming first, the rest might have followed.'[209] Vansittart later commented: 'We paddled in a puree of words and hoped to catch a formula.'[210]

For his part Eden, while acknowledging the basic problem of reconciling France and Germany, had clung to the conviction that the active participation of the USA in any disarmament convention held the key to the solution. Perhaps, given the extent of French security fears, this presented the only solution that could have satisfied the French and circumvented the British Cabinet's distaste for further European commitments.[211] Therefore, for Eden, the death knell of the Conference was presented in a declaration made by Norman Davis to the General Commission on 29 May 1934. The delegate of the USA stated that his country:

would not participate in European political negotiations and settlements and would not make any commitment whatever to use its armed forces for the settlement of any dispute anywhere. In other words, the policy of the United States is to keep out of war, but to help in every possible way to discourage and prevent war.[212]

This barely concealed rejection of the concept of collective security caused Eden to comment: 'This contradiction in terms was more discouraging than we had expected, even in our pessimistic moments.'[213] Any last chance of engineering a compromise had evaporated with Davis's statement, which was to be followed by Barthou's caustic rejection of any form of German rearmament.

The history of the Disarmament Conference is one of failure, but through his conduct of the British case Anthony Eden was to make his reputation in the field of international affairs. Vansittart later noted:

The Disarmament Conference at Geneva ground on and on. Eden spoke truly of its 'long-drawn agony'. I swallowed more print on this subject than on any other. It was all dreary, all ingenious, its vain details deserve no chronicle, but helped Eden to make a name.[214]

Eden's colleague at Geneva, Temperley, concluded that Eden:

won his spurs at the Conference. His handling of difficult situations gained him a great reputation for sincerity and diplomatic skill. Foreigners liked him and responded to the enthusiasm for the League and for world peace which inspired him.[215]

The significance of Eden's role in the Disarmament Conference was that for the first time he was projected into the public eye both in Britain and internationally. On 1 March 1933 the *Manchester Guardian* noted of Eden after his opposition to a unilateral embargo on the sale of arms to China and Japan had been over-ruled by Simon:

Nobody blames Mr. Eden, who has won the esteem of everybody, and whose sincerity and good faith nobody doubts for a moment. Next to Mr. Henderson, he is the best representative that Great Britain has had in Geneva for years.[216]

There were several, however, who were not quite so enthusiastic about Eden's growing prestige. The following year Randolph Churchill observed:

The latest political fad is the cult of Mr. Anthony Eden. He first leapt into international fame last summer when a French newspaper decided he was the best dressed Englishman. Since then the political prophets and wiseacres have been tipping him as the next Leader of the Conservative Party.

Mr. Anthony Eden is what the Americans call a 'stuffed shirt politician'. He has a fine presence, a deferential manner, a courteous word for everybody, and unlimited patience and docility towards his elders.

We are told how remarkable it is that such a young man should have attained such high office. Considering his limited abilities it is remarkable . . . . Mr. Anthony Eden has none of the qualities of youth. He is sedate, not fiery, respectable, not dashing. That is why he has been successful — but only by kind permission of the older men. His success will continue so long as he continues to serve them.[217]

It is possible, however, that this rather cutting assault on Eden may have been partly inspired by an element of pique, for in March 1934 Eden had been a party, in the House of Commons, to an attack upon Randolph's father, Winston Churchill, and indeed had referred to Churchill's criticism of Baldwin as a 'mischievous absurdity'.[218] Furthermore Randolph Churchill was an associate of Duff Cooper[219] and openly expressed his opinion that Eden's rise within the party ranks had deprived Duff Cooper of the promotion his abilities deserved.[220] A more impartial assessment of Eden's standing is, therefore, to be found in Harold Laski's[221] article for the *Daily Herald* in August 1933:

Mr. Anthony Eden has been one of the few definite successes among the members of the 'National' Government. He has tact and charm . . . . Except Mr. Stanley there is none of the younger Tories whose future appears more certain.

At Geneva I think it is true to say that he is the only representative of the present Government who had won the respect of foreign delegates there. Mr. Eden does appear to recognise that, if Geneva fails, there is no hope for an organised defence for peace; and he has had the courage to make his faith apparent even in the face of something very like the contemptuous disbelief of his leaders.

In domestic politics Mr. Eden had done little to define an attitude . . . Young Tories in a vague and inchoate way would like to do the decent thing if they only knew what is the decent thing to do.

In a word Mr. Eden is the English gentleman at his best. He is a pragmatist to his fingertips. He does not dig into foundations because he knows that it is a dangerous adventure.[222]

Although Laski was using Eden to launch a thinly veiled attack on the National Government, the article indicates quite firmly that Eden was not popularly seen simply as a dapper young man or a 'stuffed shirt' politician. Through his role at Geneva, Eden was increasingly linked with the campaign to overthrow traditional alliance diplomacy and replace it with international collaboration under the aegis of the League of Nations. Whether or not this label was justified is open to question. Certainly Eden had displayed little sympathy for the internationalist cause while serving Sir Austen Chamberlain[223] and he had been amongst those who opposed the imposition of sanctions against Japan following the invasion of Manchuria. In adopting this stance he had made the candid assessment that while the Soviet Union and the USA remained outside the League of Nations, Britain and France were not capable of performing the role of an international police force.[224] This was a realistic assessment of British military capabilities and it could be contended that it was this same sense of pragmatism which led Eden to work so assiduously for an armament agreement at Geneva. While he never embraced the Utopian ideals of complete disarmament and the elevation of the League of Nations to the position of an international forum for the settlement of disputes, he did appreciate the advantages to be secured for British interests from a European agreement on armament limitation. Yet in his approach to the negotiations he was at times naive and insensitive to the political climate. To expect the French in this period to accept both a reduction in their security demands and the recognition of German rearmament represented a radical misassessment of the political climate in Paris. In addition it was apparent that the British Cabinet, while prepared to concede an element of rearmament to Germany, was in no mood to expand its commitments and encompass a guarantee to enforce a disarmament agreement. Perhaps most surprising, however, were Eden's references to possible participation by the USA in a general armament agreement. The record of the USA in this field since its rejection of the League of Nations surely suggested that there was little prospect of it guaranteeing an essentially European settlement.

Given the complexities of the armament negotiations at Geneva, Eden's failure to engineer an agreement impaired neither his public standing nor his emergence as an influential figure in the formulation of British foreign policy. His growing stature was confirmed by his role at the Disarmament Conference and as special envoy to the French, German and Italian governments. In undertaking these difficult assignments he furthered his claim for future advancement, a claim that had already been partially recognised by his promotion to the fringe of the Cabinet as Lord Privy Seal. As always his mentor within the Government was Baldwin and it was to the Lord President of the Council that he looked when his thoughts on foreign policy did not coincide with those of his colleagues.[225] Eden discovered at first hand the problems to be confronted in pursuing a line of policy that was not widely accepted by the Cabinet. The Service Ministers and, particularly, Lord Londonderry on several occasions successfully checked Eden's attempts to reduce British preconditions for an armament agreement, while Simon's cautious and, at times, hesitant approach to the armament negotiations was a source of increasing frustration to Eden. Whatever his doubts about Simon's leadership, Eden elected not to challenge the Foreign Secretary openly. This decision was based, perhaps, on the fact that he occupied a relatively junior position within the Party hierarchy, but more likely upon the knowledge that several Cabinet members were already questioning the Foreign Secretary's conduct of British foreign policy. It did not take a crystal ball to foresee that the next twelve months would be a taxing time for the Foreign Secretary.[226]

References

1   Eden's appointment was finalised on 1 September 1931.
2   For details of the circumstances surrounding Eden's appointment see Eden's diary entries for 27 and 28 August 1931, quoted in Avon, *Memoirs, Volume 1: Facing the Dictators* (London, 1962), p. 19.
3   Eden had lunched with Sir Austen Chamberlain on 27 August 1931. Chamberlain admitted that, with Baldwin's approval, he had strongly recommended Eden's appointment to Lord Reading. See Eden diary entry for 27 August 1931, Avon, p. 19. See also H. Montgomery Hyde, *Lord Reading* (London, 1967), pp. 406–9.
4   *Baldwin Papers* held at Churchill College, Cambridge, vol. 44, f. 14, Eden to Baldwin, 1 September 1931.
5   Lord Vansittart, *The Mist Procession* (London, 1958), pp. 428–9.
6   In later years distance was certainly put between the two by what Vansittart saw as Eden's increasing gravitation towards the 'Cliveden set' centred on Lady Astor, which Vansittart saw as a web of intrigue aiming to influence foreign policy and, in particular, working against the policy of the Permanent Under Secretary. It would seem that on at least one occasion Vansittart attempted to warn Eden of the dangers of his association with the Cliveden set. See Vansittart, pp. 482–3. Also Ian Colvin, *Vansittart in Office* (London, 1965), p. 49.
7   L.S. Amery, *My Political Life*, vol. III (London, 1955), p. 154.

8   Avon, pp. 241–2.

9   Sir John Simon (later Viscount Simon) was Home Secretary 1915–16, Foreign Secretary 1931–5, Home Secretary 1935–7, Chancellor of the Exchequer 1939–40 and Lord Chancellor 1940–5. Sir John Simon was appointed Foreign Secretary on 5 November 1931.

10   Avon, p. 220. For observations on Sir John Simon by Sir Maurice Hankey (Secretary to the Cabinet and CID 1916–38), Ramsay MacDonald (Prime Minister 1931–5), Sir Robert Vansittart and Neville Chamberlain (Chancellor of the Exchequer 1931–7) see: *Hankey Papers* held at Churchill College, Cambridge, HNKY 1/7, diary entry for 3 October 1932; Vansittart, pp. 427–8 and 437; *Neville Chamberlain Papers* held at Birmingham University, NC2/23A, diary entry for 28 February 1934. Interesting sidelights on Baldwin's attitude are thrown up by R. Rhodes James, *Memoirs of a Conservative* (London, 1969), pp. 379–81 and K. Middlemas and J. Barnes, *Baldwin, A Biography* (London, 1969), p. 807.

11   Viscount Simon, *Retrospect* (London, 1952), p. 177.

12   A thorough account of the conduct of British foreign policy during the Manchurian crisis can be found in C. Thorne, *The Limits of Foreign Policy* (London, 1972).

13   *DBFP*, 2nd ser., vol. 8, no. 672, 21 October 1931.

14   *DBFP*, 2nd ser., vol. 8, no. 664, Geneva, 19 October 1931.

15   *DBFP*, 2nd ser., vol. 8, no. 685, 27 October 1931.

16   *DBFP*, 2nd ser., vol. 8, no. 720. Minute by Sir John Simon of 14 November 1931 on a report by Sir R. Vansittart of 10 November 1931.

17   Cabinet meeting of 11 November 1931. See *CAB* 23/66, Cabinet Conclusion (hereafter cited as CC) 73(31)1.

18   See Thorne, pp. 203–10. For Sir J. Simon's assessment of the validity of the Japanese case in Manchuria in November 1931 see *DBFP*, 2nd ser., vol. 8, no. 769, Paris, 23 November 1931.

19   *DBFP*, 2nd ser., vol. 9, no. 238. Minute by Sir R. Vansittart of 3 February 1932 on a memorandum by Sir J. Pratt dated 1 February 1932. See also Sir Victor Wellesley's memorandum of 1 February 1932, *DBFP*, 2nd ser., vol. 9, no. 239.

20   *DBFP*, 2nd ser., vol. 9, no. 636, note 8.

21   At the Cabinet meetings held on 9, 17 and 23 March 1932 it was agreed that Britain was not militarily, economically or financially prepared for a war in the Far East without the support of the United States. See *CAB* 23/70. The extent of Japan's economic interests in Manchuria had been emphasised by Sir J. Simon on 23 November 1931 and reaffirmed by Sir V. Wellesley on 1 February 1932. See *DBFP*, 2nd ser., vol. 8, no. 769 and vol. 9, no. 239.

22   The Cabinet Committee on the Far East consisted of Baldwin, Sir Maurice Hankey (Secretary to the Cabinet), Eyres-Monsell (First Lord of the Admiralty), Viscount Hailsham (Secretary of State for War), Lord Londonderry (Secretary of State for Air), Sir John Simon and Eden. Its proceedings can be found in *CAB* 27/482.

23   A summary of its conclusions was provided by Sir R. Vansittart in his despatch to Geneva of 8 March 1932. *DBFP*, 2nd ser., vol. 10, no. 34.

24   *CAB* 23/70, CC 17(32)1, 9 March 1932.

25   Avon, p. 40. Certainly some of Eden's pronouncements in 1933 suggested that he would have supported a more active role by the League of Nations. See *H of C*, Debs, 5's, vol. 281, cols 150–5, 7 November 1933 and *DBFP*, 2nd ser., vol. 11, no. 270, 1 February 1933. In addition, Eden's minute of 28 March 1933 on a despatch from Tokyo dated 24 February 1933, *DBFP*, 2nd ser., vol. 11, no. 371.

26   For example Eden initialled without comment Sir J. Pratt's memorandum of 31 January 1932, *DBFP*, 2nd ser., vol. 9, no. 216. See also memoranda by Vansittart and Wellesley, *DBFP*, 2nd ser., vol. 9, no. 239 (1 February 1932) and no. 238 (1 February 1932).
27   See Eden's minute of 6 September 1932 on Lindley's despatch from Tokyo of 21 July 1932, *DBFP*, 2nd ser., vol. 10, no. 545.
28   See Avon, p. 523 and Thorne, 210—12.
29   Eden's speech delivered in the House of Commons on 24 November 1927 clearly indicated the limitations that he identified in the British commitment to the League of Nations. *H of C*, Debs, 5's, vol. 210, cols 2160—5, 24 November 1927.
30   On 10 February 1933 Eden wrote to Baldwin concerning his recent involvement in attempts by the League of Nations to solve the Manchurian problem: 'I have never known anything more exhausting or more exasperating'. *Baldwin Papers*, vol. 129, ff. 124—7, Eden to Baldwin, Geneva, 22 February 1933.
31   Foreign Office memorandum 'Germany and the Disarmament Conference' dated 8 April 1931 and transmitted to the British Ambassador in Berlin by the Foreign Secretary on 23 April 1931. See *DBFP*, 2nd ser., vol. 3, no. 208, (no. 425 (C2531/136/18)), Foreign Office, 23 April 1931.
32   Ibid.
33   This discussion, which also recognised the problem of satisfying French security demands, was a result of an interim report of the Cabinet Committee on the Disarmament Conference and memoranda submitted to the Cabinet by Sir R. Vansittart and the COS subcommittee of the CID. See *CAB* 23/69 CC91 (31) 2, 15 December 1931 and CP 317 (31) and CP 213 (31).
34   *CAB* 23/69 CC 91 (31) 2, 15 December 1931.
35   This committee was set up as a result of a Cabinet decision on 4 March 1931. Its format as a subcommittee of the CID was to accommodate Baldwin's refusal to provide Conservative representation on a Cabinet Committee. *CAB* 23/66, CC 16(31) 6, 4 March 1931.
36   *H of C*, Debs, 5th ser., vol. 254, cols 905—18, 29 June 1931. Eden later noted of the committee that it:

> . . . did not get very far or move very fast, there was so much else to vex harassed Ministers in that second Labour Government, nor did its proceedings determine my views.

However his conviction that an international arms agreement was the central goal largely followed the broad conclusions of the committee. See Avon, pp. 18—19. For the proceedings of the committee which Eden attended between 18 March 1931 and 15 July 1931, see *CAB* 16/102.
37   In fact it was not until 7 July 1932 when Baldwin addressed the House of Commons that an attempt was made to formulate a comprehensive set of British proposals that could be submitted to the Disarmament Conference. *H of C*, Debs, 5th ser., vol. 268, cols 624—9.
38   Major-General A.C. Temperley, *The Whispering Gallery of Europe* (London, 1939), p. 174.
39   Ibid., p. 173.
40   Chronological Summary of the Proceedings of the Disarmament Conference, 2 February—23 July 1932. *DBFP*, 2nd ser., vol. 3, pp. 506—7.
41   Temperley, p. 192.
42   Baldwin's declaration of 7 July 1932 candidly admitted that 'Having regard to the widely scattered responsibilities of the British Navy, it is not practicable for us to cut down the number of naval units beyond a certain point'. *H of C*, Debs,

5th ser., vol. 268, cols 624—9. See also Temperley, pp. 193—6.

43   Viscount Cecil, *A Great Experiment* (London, 1941), pp. 237—8.

44   It was apparent, in Cabinet, that the terms outlined by Baldwin on 7 July 1932 represented the furthest extent to which the three Service Ministers were prepared to move towards disarmament. On 24 June 1932 Viscount Hailsham described the British Army as 'little more than an armed police force' while on 6 July 1932 Sir Bolton Eyres-Monsell was supported by the Cabinet when he refused to commit the Royal Navy to the abandonment of shipbuilding after 1937. Furthermore on 12 July 1932 Lord Londonderry energetically defended the need to retain bombers which he argued 'would prove our best defence'. See *CAB* 23/71, CC 38 (32)2, *CAB* 23/72, CC 43(32)1 and CC 44(32)2.

45   *DBFP*, 2nd ser., vol. 3, no. 270. Declaration by Herr Nadolny to the General Commission of the Disarmament Conference, 22 July 1932.

46   *Baldwin Papers*, vol. 118, ff. 177—8, Eden to Baldwin, Geneva, 9 May 1932.

47   See *CAB* 23/71, CC 26(32)2, 4 May 1932.

48   This proposal was to form the basis of the Declaration on British Disarmament Policy made by Baldwin on 7 July 1932. *H of C*, Debs, 5th ser., vol. 268, cols 624—6.

49   CP 176(32) presented to Cabinet on 8 November 1932 in response to a request by the Cabinet on 31 October 1932 that a reply be prepared to Germany's claim of equality of rights in armaments. See *CAB* 23/72, CC 57(32)1 and CC 59 (32)1.

50   Report of Subcommittee of CID on Air Disarmament Policy presented to the Cabinet on 11 May 1932 as CP 152(32). See *CAB* 23/71 CC 27(32)5. This report was accepted reluctantly by the Cabinet which maintained its determination to continue to examine the possibility of the abolition of military aircraft.

51   Yet it was apparent that Londonderry was opposed by both Simon and Baldwin who appreciated the implications raised by President Hoover's call for the abolition of bombing made on 22 June 1932. The Cabinet, therefore, agreed to continue to explore the possibility of aerial disarmament. See *CAB* 23/72, CC 44 (32)2, 12 July 1932. See also *DBFP*, 2nd ser., vol. 3, appendix 5, President Hoover's instructions to the American delegation at the Disarmament Conference 22 June 1932.

52   R.A. Geo. V.K. 2353/1, quoted in S. Roskill, *Hankey Man of Secrets*, vol. III (London, 1974), p. 42.

53   *DBFP*, 2nd ser., vol. 3, appendix 5.

54   Temperley later concluded:

> The President of the United States could hardly have failed to appreciate the opportuneness of launching a disarmament plan which attracted world wide interest, while he was in the middle of an election campaign. A great coup in Geneva might turn the scale in the U.S.A.

Temperley, p. 208.

55   *DBFP*, 2nd ser., vol. 3, appendix 6.

56   See *CAB* 23/71, CC 38(32)2, 24 June 1932.

57   Chamberlain was apparently anxious that the proposed British statement on Disarmament Policy should not cut across the Hoover Declaration, *CAB* 23/72, CC 41(32)4, 30 June 1932.

58   The Lausanne Conference on reparations settlement opened in June 1932.

59   *DBFP*, 2nd ser., vol. 4, no. 92, statement of views of HMG on questions arising out of notes exchanged between the German Government (29 August 1932) and the French Government (11 September 1932) regarding the work of the Disarmament Conference. Foreign Office, 15 September 1932, published 19 September 1932.

60   It would appear that Simon was prepared to over-rule Service Ministry objections to international supervision of armaments in order to draw Germany back to the Disarmament Conference. See *CAB* 23/72 CC 49(32), 30 September 1932. See also Cabinet Papers circulated by Simon, CP 826(32) and CP 323(32).
61   See *CAB* 23/72, CC 50(32)5, 11 October 1932.
62   *H of C*, Debs, 5th ser., vol. 270, cols 545−8, 10 November 1932. This statement, which was agreed by the Cabinet on 9 November 1932, was essentially a compromise devised following the failure to lure Germany and France to a four power meeting at either London or Geneva. The original draft had been prepared by Eden and Vansittart and, in merely asking Germany to provide a guarantee that it would not upset the tranquillity of Europe if Britain and France agreed, in principle, to the German right to possess equality of armament, went as far as Eden thought it possible for Britain to go in engineering a Franco-German compromise formula:

> The policy is as good as can be expected in the circumstances and it now only remains for Simon to go for it. Any way the inkwells at the FO are dry and if Cabinet will not have it Simon should ask them to send someone else to Geneva. I told him this but that he must not ask me to go.

See Avon, p. 26. The Cabinet accepted the formula, in principle, although, following protests from Hankey and Hailsham it was agreed that the declaration should include a commitment to full German equality of armaments only at the end of a trial period. See *CAB* 23/72 CC 57(32)1, 31 October 1932, CC 59(32)1, 8 November 1932, CC 60(32)1, 9 November 1932. Also *Hankey Papers*, HNKY 1/7, diary entries for 23 October and 12 November 1932.
63   A series of meetings between representatives of Britain, Germany, Italy, France and the USA was held at Geneva from 6 December 1932 until 11 December 1932. See *DBFP*, 2nd ser., vol. 4, nos 211−20.
64   The declaration was engineered to satisfy German aspirations for equality of armaments and French demands for a system of security in principle as a broad formula to draw both back to the Conference table at Geneva without either having made significant concessions. *DBFP*, 2nd ser., vol. 4, no. 220, 11 December 1932.
65   On 3 December 1932 MacDonald wrote to Baldwin '. . . there is no doubt a great deterioration in the disarmament position . . . .'. *Baldwin Papers*, vol. 118, JF 239−40, MacDonald to Baldwin, 3 December 1932.
66   *CAB* 23/75, CC 1(33)3, 19 January 1933.
67   *CAB* 23/73, CC 66(32)1, 13 December 1932.
68   It would seem that it was Simon who was largely instrumental in proposing Eden for the task. See *Simon Papers* FO 800/287, Simon to MacDonald, 30 December 1932 (PRO).
69   *Baldwin Papers*, vol. 118, ff. 209−13, Eden to Baldwin, 20 October 1932.
70   *DBFP*, 2nd ser., vol. 4, no. 278. Draft proposals by the United Kingdom Delegation to the General Commission of the Disarmament Conference, 30 January 1933.
71   Temperley, pp. 225−6.
72   As early as March 1932 the War Office had circulated a memorandum to the Foreign Office chronicling Germany's widespread breaches of the military provisions of the Treaty of Versailles. See *DBFP*, 2nd ser., vol. 3, appendix 4, 1 March 1932.
73   Report of the British military attaché in Berlin, dated 9 December 1931, submitted to the Foreign Secretary on 12 December 1931. See *DBFP*, 2nd ser., vol. 2, appendix 4.

74   Eden had been encouraged by the British Ambassador in Paris, Lord Tyrrell, on 17—18 January 1933 to work for a reduction in French demands but later appreciated that the replacement of Herriot by Daladier, at the end of January 1933, had made the task far more difficult. See Avon, pp. 28—9.

75   *Baldwin Papers*, vol. 129, ff. 104—9, Eden to Baldwin, Geneva, 10 February 1933. In making this assertion Eden had undoubtedly been encouraged by a series of meetings with the French Foreign Secretary at which Paul-Boncour had indicated his willingness to proceed to an early discussion of air disarmament. See *DBFP*, 2nd ser., vol. 4, nos 280 (6 February 1933) and 281 (16 February 1933).

76   In particular Eden later argues that he was attempting to circumvent the Foreign Secretary's apparent reluctance to tackle the disarmament problem. See Avon, pp. 28—9.

77   On 4 May 1932 Baldwin had strongly advocated to the Cabinet the destruction of all military aviation and limitations on civil aviation as a goal to be promoted at the Disarmament Conference. *CAB* 23/71, CC 26(32)2, 4 May 1932. Hankey later claimed that he had first suggested the scheme to Baldwin and MacDonald but, while Baldwin 'was badly smitten with the scheme . . . ', MacDonald who had, 'a very soft place for the Air Force' inclined towards supporting Lord Londonderry's opposition to total disarmament. *Hankey Papers*, HNKY 1/7, diary entry for 12 November 1932.

78   *H of C*, Debs, 5th ser., vol. 170, cols 630—8, 10 November 1932. To appease Londonderry, Baldwin had not advocated a British commitment to air disarmament but only called for an enquiry into the feasibility of such measures. Once again Baldwin's text had been primarily drafted by Hankey. See *Hankey Papers*, HNKY 1/7, diary entry for 12 November 1932.

79   *CAB* 23/72, CC 60(32)1, appendix 1, 9 November 1932.

80   The difference of opinion between Eden and Simon on the question of air disarmament is illustrated by an extract from Eden's diary dated 9 February 1933:

> Lunched with Dutchman. While I was there Sir John Simon dragged me to telephone box and tried to dictate sentences of my speech *re* air disarmament.
>
> They [Simon and Londonderry] both wanted to make explicitly a statement about bombing for police purposes. I said right time was Air Committee, if set up. Working Committee would be staggered. Simon unhelpful, but I eventually convinced Charlie far enough for him to ring off. On return to Hotel found telephone message from Simon that I 'must' specifically mention police bombing. Decided not to.

See Avon, p. 30. On 22 February 1933 Eden wrote to Baldwin that the British advocation of air disarmament while insisting on the retention of police bombing was 'cutting an inglorious figure on the Air Committee . . . .', *Baldwin Papers*, vol. 129, ff. 124—7, Eden to Baldwin, Geneva, 22 February 1933.

81   Report of the Ministerial Committee on Disarmament presented to Cabinet on 8 March 1933. *CAB* 23/75, CC 15(33), Appendix, 8 March 1933.

82   Eden also argued that the need for a British initiative had been accelerated by reports that Arthur Henderson was preparing a draft convention which 'would prove unacceptable to us. We should then be on the defensive, the victim and not the hero!', *Baldwin Papers*, vol. 129, ff. 71—3, Eden to Baldwin, Geneva, 24 February 1933.

83   Eden later claimed that he and Cadogan had been working on the format of a draft convention since January 1933 but that Cadogan's efforts to enlist Simon's support had failed. It was Cadogan who had insisted, initially, that only a British initiative could save the Conference in 1933. See Avon, pp. 27—8.

84   Avon, pp. 34–5.
85   See Avon, p. 32 and Temperley, pp. 234–8. Sir Alec Cadogan was Chief Adviser to the British Delegation at Geneva. Sir William Malkin was Legal Adviser to the Foreign Office.
86   In a memorandum to Sir J. Simon dated 24 February 1933 Eden argued that the Conference was likely to collapse within weeks:

> There seems to me to be only one course left to us which might save the Conference and would at least, whatever the consequence of failure, mark plainly to the world that we have done our utmost to achieve success. When, as I fear is inevitable in the course of the next ten days, it becomes clear that the Conference can make no more progress, if we were in a position to lay before the Conference a complete convention, it is just possible that it would be accepted.

See Avon, pp. 31–2.
87   See DC (M) 32, 12th Conclusion. *CAB* 21/379. It would appear that Eden was far more successful than he subsequently admitted, Avon, pp. 32–3.
88   See Temperley, p. 238 and *CAB* 23/75, CC 15(33), Appendix, Wednesday, 8 March 1933.
89   Simon had admitted to the Cabinet on 19 January 1933 that at the Disarmament Conference 'A new programme, firmly promoted and boldly pursued, was the sole hope', *CAB* 23/75, CC 1(33)3, 19 January 1933. However, privately, both he and MacDonald had admitted to Baldwin that they saw little chance of success at Geneva. See *Baldwin Papers*, vol. 118, ff. 239–40, MacDonald to Baldwin, 3 December 1932, vol. 121, ff. 40–6, Simon to Baldwin, 9 March 1933.
90   *DBFP*, 2nd ser., vol. 4, no. 290, record of meeting in Paris between British and French Ministers (W 2792/2792/17), 10 March 1933.
91   In two meetings on 13 March 1933 the Cabinet agreed that the time was no longer suitable to present the draft convention at Geneva. This conclusion was prompted by reports that agreement could only be engineered if Britain reduced its tank requirements and also, that Mussolini was requesting Anglo-Italian negotiations in Rome. The minutes of these meetings were despatched to Simon in Geneva. See *CAB* 23/75, CC 17(33)2 and CC 18(33)1, 13 March 1933.
92   Temperley, p. 240.
93   *DBFP*, 2nd ser., vol. 4, nos 301, 302 and 310. See also extract from Eden's diary, 14 March 1933, Avon, p. 34.
94   See Avon, p. 35 and Temperley, pp. 240–2. This was certainly a generous assertion, for even prior to the adjournment on 28 March 1933 Daladier had restated French insistence on maintaining a three-year military lead on German military development, while Nadolny, the Head of the German Delegation, had reported to Berlin that the proposals were 'unacceptable'. See *DBFP*, 2nd ser., vol. 4, no. 310 and *Documents on German Foreign Policy* (hereafter cited as *DGFP*), ser. C, vol. 1, no. 103.
95   *DBFP*, 2nd ser., vol. 5, no. 104, Mr Patterson (Geneva) to Sir J. Simon (no. 208 LN (W4671/40/98) Geneva, 30 April 1933.
96   For the text of Hitler's speech of 17 May 1933 see *DGFP*, ser. C, vol. 1, no. 246. Also see *DBFP*, 2nd ser., vol. 5, no. 99 (28 April 1933), 110 (3 May 1933) and 123 (9 May 1933).
97   *DBFP*, 2nd ser., vol. 5, no. 133.
98   *CAB* 23/76, CC 35(33)1, 17 May 1933.
99   The telegram was drafted as a result of the conclusions of the Cabinet Committee on Disarmament which met on 12 May 1933. See *DBFP*, 2nd ser., vol. 5, no. 141.

100 *DBFP*, 2nd ser., vol. 5, no. 110, 3 May 1933.
101 *Baldwin Papers*, vol. 121, ff. 27—8, Eden to Baldwin, Geneva, 1 May 1933.
102 *DBFP*, 2nd ser., vol. 5, no. 127, 10 May 1933. See also Temperley, p. 249.
103 *DBFP*, 2nd ser., vol. 5, no. 146, Telegram from President of the United States to His Majesty the King (W 5514/40/98), 16 May 1933.
104 The text of sections of the speech delivered by Norman Davis to the General Commission is quoted in Temperley, p. 251. See also *DBFP*, 2nd ser., vol. 5, no. 170.
105 Eden's reports from Geneva in April and May of 1933 indicated that he was increasingly exasperated by the unaligned nature of the American stance. On 27 April 1933, in reporting the failure of the USA to give anything more than a vague gesture of support for disarmament, Eden noted 'At present though we always hear of the carrot we never see it.' On 9 May 1933, as the Conference headed towards deadlock, Eden reported 'United States delegate took no definite line; he certainly did not give me wholehearted support.' See *DBFP*, 2nd ser., vol. 5, nos 93 and 119. Vansittart later noted 'At the Disarmament Conference the Americans seemed about to make a contribution which came to nothing. Eden was irked by them at Geneva.' Vansittart, p. 466.
106 On 5 May 1933 Eden told the Cabinet that the recent increase in British troop requirements 'was calculated to place him in an embarrassing position', (*CAB* 23/76, CC 33(33)5). See also a despatch from Geneva, dated 1 May 1933, and memorandum by Mr A.W.A. Leeper, dated 29 May 1933, noting the problems created for Eden by the submission to Geneva of military levels actually in excess of existing British strength in 1933. See *DBFP*, 2nd ser., vol. 5, nos 105 and 179.
107 On 29 May 1933 the Secretary of State for Air reminded Baldwin that Eden was bound by Cabinet decisions to maintain the reservation on police bombing. *Baldwin Papers*, vol. 121, ff. 35—7, Londonderry to Baldwin, 29 May 1933. A memorandum drawn up by the Deputy Chief of the Air Staff, Group-Captain Babington, on 29 May 1933, clearly indicated that the Air Ministry saw no effective prospect of air disarmament being achieved at Geneva. (*DBFP*, 2nd ser., vol. 5, no. 177).
108 *Baldwin Papers*, vol. 121, Eden to Baldwin, ff. 29—32, Geneva, 1 May 1933.
109 *DBFP*, 2nd ser., vol. 5, no. 176, Mr Patterson (Geneva) to Sir J. Simon (no. 272 LN (W 6020/117/98)), 27 May 1933.
110 On 19 June 1933 the Cabinet Disarmament Committee emphasised that Britain would make no concessions towards disarmament other than those already outlined in the British draft convention. See DC(M) (32) 17th Meeting, 19 June 1933, *CAB* 21/379.
111 *DBFP*, 2nd ser., vol. 5, no. 172 (26 May 1933) and 188 (31 May 1933).
112 'Memorandum on the Foreign Policy of His Majesty's Government in the United Kingdom', 19 May 1933. See *Vansittart Papers*, 1/7, Churchill College, Cambridge.
113 In the same month Vansittart reiterated his growing conviction that the Hitler regime was determined 'to loose off another European war as soon as it feels strong enough'. Vansittart minute, dated 6 May 1933 on *DBFP*, no. 425, Rumbold despatch from Berlin, 26 April 1933 (C 3990/319/18), *Vansittart Papers*, 2/3.
114 Avon, p. 35.
115 *Baldwin Papers*, vol. 121, ff. 27—8, Eden to Baldwin, Geneva, 1 May 1933.
116 For a record of Ramsay MacDonald and Sir J. Simon's negotiations in Rome, 18—20 March 1933, and Paris, 21 March 1933, see *DBFP*, 2nd ser., vol. 5, nos 44 and 46.

117 For details of the Four Power Pact initialled by Britain on 7 June 1933, see *DBFP*, 2nd ser., vol. 5, no. 216.

118 *DBFP*, 2nd ser., vol. 5, no. 53, 25 March 1933.

119 *DBFP*, 2nd ser., vol. 5, no. 188, 31 May 1933. On 20 May 1933 Nadolny reported that Eden had admitted to him 'the main problems would not be solved in official proceedings of the Conference, it would be necessary instead to adopt the method of private discussions'. However, the German Foreign Ministry rejected any suggestion of Von Neurath attending the Geneva proceedings in person. *DGFP*, ser. C, vol. 1, no. 255.

120 *DBFP*, 2nd ser., vol. 5, nos 207 and 208, 8 June 1933. At these meetings Eden was accompanied by the Secretary of State for Air, Lord Londonderry.

121 This report was presented to the Cabinet by Eden on 9 June 1933. Its tenor, along with the report submitted to Cabinet on 31 May 1933, indicated that the Lord Privy Seal had come to the conclusion that German intransigence meant that the only form of compromise lay in agreeing to French security demands. See *CAB* 23/76, CC 38(33)3, 31 May 1933 and CC 39(33)1, 9 June 1933.

122 *DBFP*, 2nd ser., vol. 5, no. 220, 26 June 1933.

123 *CAB* 23/76, CC 48(33)3, 26 July 1933. In essence MacDonald was confirming a previous decision of the Cabinet Committee on Disarmament to go no further than the concessions outlined in the British draft convention, DC (M) (32), 17th Meeting, *CAB* 21/379, 19 June 1933.

124 In these discussions Eden was hamstrung by the absence of authority to commit Britain to a system of disarmament supervision or to state the British reaction to a German infringement of an armament agreement, *DBFP*, 2nd ser., vol. 5, no. 399, 19 September 1933.

125 *CAB* 23/77, CC 51(33)2, 20 September 1933. On considering Eden's report, presented as CP 220(33), it was apparent that while the French wanted an infringement of the treaty punished by 'definite action' the British viewpoint was that the infringement would merely cancel the agreement to disarm.

126 *DBFP*, 2nd ser., vol. 5, no. 406, 22 September 1933.

127 *DBFP*, 2nd ser., vol. 5, no. 411, 27 September 1933.

128 This remark was made by Eden to the French delegate, Massigli, Assistant Director of Political and Commercial Department and Head of League of Nations in French Ministry of Foreign Affairs, on 29 September 1933. Eden added 'I told M. Massigli . . . that I must leave him in no doubt of the fact that English opinion would today accept no new commitment'. *DBFP*, 2nd ser., vol. 5, no. 420.

129 For Simon's speech of 14 October 1933 see *DBFP*, 2nd ser., vol. 5, no. 455.

130 *DBFP*, 2nd ser., vol. 5, no. 682. Hitler was convinced that the Western powers were so disunited that the only response would be a further attempt at conciliation and concessions to the German viewpoint. *DGFP*, ser. C, vol. 2, no. 9, 17 October 1933.

131 Avon, p. 47, diary entry for 14 October 1933.

132 *Baldwin Papers*, vol. 121, ff. 53—5, Lord Tyrrell to Baldwin, Paris, 28 September 1933.

133 *Baldwin Papers*, vol. 121, ff. 74—6, W. Ormsby-Gore to Baldwin, Geneva, 1 October 1933.

134 *Baldwin Papers*, vol. 121, ff. 91, Eden to Baldwin, Geneva, 13 October 1933.

135 Ibid., loc. cit. Record of conversation with Benes at Geneva on 11 October 1933.

136 *DBFP*, 2nd ser., vol. 5, no. 486, 24 October 1933.

137 The central premise in Vansittart's reasoning was the assumption that Germany could only be stopped by a resolute Anglo-Italian-French alliance. His determination to court Anglo-Italian relations was to have specific consequences during the course of the Abyssinian crisis. *DBFP*, 2nd ser., vol. 5, no. 371. Memorandum on the Present and Future Position in Europe, C 7736/2092/3, 28 August 1933.

138 The Chiefs of Staff report, which had been drawn up on 12 October 1933 and approved by the CID on 9 November 1933, was presented as CP 264(33) to the Cabinet on 15 November 1933. The establishment of the Defence Requirement Committee was an acknowledgement of the abandonment of the Ten Year Rule and the need to remedy deficiencies in British defences. See *CAB 16/109*, CID 1113B and *CAB 23/77*, CC 62(33)5.

139 The DRC was composed of Hankey, Vansittart, Warren Fisher and the Chiefs of Staff. The paper submitted by the DRC on 29 November 1933 had been requested by the Cabinet Committee on Disarmament. *CAB 21/387*, DC(M) (32) 61, 29 November 1933.

140 German activity in Austria had been discussed by the Cabinet on 26 July 1933 and 5 September 1933. See *CAB 23/76*, CC 48(33)4 and *CAB 23/77*, CC 50(33)1.

141 For the French attitude see despatches from the Paris Embassy dated 9 November and 16 November 1933, *DBFP*, 2nd ser., vol. 6, nos 27 and 40.

142 At the Cabinet meeting on 23 October 1933 it was agreed to follow Simon's recommendation that British policy be based on the continued pursuit of an armament agreement and that any agreement must involve Germany. *CAB 23/77* CC 54(33)1.

143 At these meetings Eden urged Corbin to consider a less 'rigid' attitude to the German demands in order to facilitate further negotiations with Germany. *DBFP*, 2nd ser., vol. 5, no. 509 and vol. 6, no. 32.

144 *DBFP*, 2nd ser., vol. 6, no. 54, 19 November 1933.

145 Ibid. Following a discussion on the same day with Vienot, a French delegation member, Eden concluded that the French were not prepared to open negotiations with Germany but might associate themselves with a British scheme if it incorporated concessions to the French stance. *DBFP*, 2nd ser., vol. 6, no. 57, 19 November 1933.

146 For a record of the series of meetings that engineered this compromise, see *DBFP*, 2nd ser., vol. 6, nos. 64 and 66.

147 *DBFP*, 2nd ser., vol. 6, no. 64, 22 November 1933. Simon emphasised to the French, Italian and American delegates at this meeting that he was anxious to promote contacts between Paris, Berlin, London and Rome.

148 The conclusions of the DRC report of 29 November 1933 on the German Disarmament proposals had, in essence, supported a memorandum summarising information received by the Service Ministries on German rearmament and collated by Sir R. Vansittart on 14 July 1933. See *CAB 21/387*, DC(M) (32) (61), 29 November 1933 and *DBFP*, 2nd ser., vol. 5, no. 253, 14 July 1933. For Cabinet reaction to Vansittart's report see *CAB 23/76*, CC 48(33)5, 26 July 1933.

149 In relation to an arms race Baldwin declared 'in no circumstances must that . . . alternative be reached'. *H of C*, Debs, 5's, vol. 284, 27 November 1933.

150 *DBFP*, 2nd ser., vol. 6, no. 60, 21 November 1933.

151 On 7 December 1933 Sir E. Phipps was told by Simon to inform Hitler that HMG agreed in principle to Hitler's suggestion of political assurances between Germany and its neighbours but German armament level demands were still 'excessive'. *DBFP*, 2nd ser., vol. 6, no. 105, 7 December 1933.

152 *DBFP*, 2nd ser., vol. 6, no. 132, 12 December 1933.

153 *DBFP*, 2nd ser., vol. 6, no. 134, 15 December 1933.

154 For an account of Simon's conversations in Paris and Rome see *DBFP*, 2nd ser., vol. 6, nos 144 and 161. Simon was also encouraged by Mussolini's apparent dedication to oppose any attempt at a German putsch in Austria.

155 *DBFP*, 2nd ser., vol. 6, no. 206, Memorandum on Disarmament, W871/1/98, 25 January 1934. In a Foreign Office minute dated 6 December 1933, Vansittart had expressed his view of the strategy surrounding the Disarmament Memorandum:

> We are agreed that we must go on with our explorations at Berlin in the hope of reaching a point where agreement may be possible. We shall not reach it. We shall then try to put forward another plan of our own. We must hope for the best and do all we can to ensure its acceptance but there is no use in disguising the fact that the odds are against us . . . .

Minute on Paris despatch no. 1687, 6 December 1933. See *Vansittart Papers*, 2/13. Vansittart appreciated that the reluctance of British public opinion to accept rearmament forced the government to seek a negotiated arms limitation agreement with Germany. *Vansittart Papers*, 2/10, 1 December 1933.

156 For an account of the decision to despatch Eden on this delicate mission see Avon, p. 55. See also Middlemas and Barnes, p. 751.

157 Avon, p. 51.

158 Eden had been offered the post of Lord Privy Seal in December 1933 by Ramsay MacDonald as a means of placing a Foreign Office representative in the House of Lords. The Prime Minister had, however, stressed that the post would not bring with it a seat in the Cabinet. It appeared that Eden only accepted the post after consulting Baldwin and gaining his assurance that it would be accompanied by a Privy Councillorship. Avon, pp. 51 and 57.

159 On 23 February 1934 Eden wrote to Baldwin that he was in favour of re-opening the Disarmament Conference at Geneva on the basis of agreeing to an element of German rearmament rather than face the prospect of no agreement at all. The task, therefore, was to lure Germany back to Geneva, *Baldwin Papers*, vol. 122, ff. 35—6, Eden to Baldwin, 23 February 1934. See also *DBFP*, 2nd ser., vol. 6, no. 6 (6 November 1933) and 32 (10 November 1933).

160 Avon, pp. 50—1.

161 See Middlemas and Barnes, p. 751. Also Joachim von Ribbentrop, *The Ribbentrop Memoirs* (London, 1954), pp. 36—7.

162 *Baldwin Papers*, vol. 122, Eden to Baldwin, February 1934. Eden was to be assisted by Lord Strang, Lord Cranbourne and Robin Hankey. Avon, p. 131.

163 Massigli was Assistant Director of the Political and Commercial Department and Head of the League of Nations Division in the French Foreign Ministry.

164 For an account of this conversation see *DBFP*, 2nd ser., vol. 6, no. 287, Lord Tyrrell to Sir J. Simon (no. 55 (W1689/1/98)), Paris, 17 February 1934. No mention is made of this interview in Avon, *Facing the Dictators*.

165 For a full account of the discussions, see Avon, pp. 57—60 and *DBFP*, 2nd ser., vol. 6, nos 291 and 297, 17—18 February 1934.

166 Only a cursory account of this interview, at which General von Blomberg, Chief of Staff and Bernhard von Bulow, State Secretary of the German Foreign Ministry, were also present, was provided by Eden (Avon, p. 61). A full account is to be found in *DBFP*, 2nd ser., vol. 6, no. 302 and *DGFP*, ser. C, vol. 2, no. 270.

167 See *DBFP*, 2nd ser., vol. 6, nos 302, 303, 304 and 305. Also *DGFP*, ser. C, vol. 2, nos 271 and 273; and Avon, pp. 61—71.

168 *Baldwin Papers*, vol. 122, ff. 31—3, Eden to Baldwin, 21 February 1934. A sidelight on the relationship between Eden and Hitler is also provided by the accounts of Lord Strang and Joachim von Ribbentrop who were both present at the interviews. Strang later described Hitler's manner as 'cordial and attentive' (Lord Strang, *Home and Abroad* (London, 1956), p. 66), while Ribbentrop referred to the meeting as being 'held in a harmonious atmosphere' (*Ribbentrop Memoirs*, p. 39). This appears to confirm Eden's report to London on 21 February 1934 that Hitler's 'attitude was friendly and an appeal based on war experiences found a ready response'. (*DBFP*, 2nd ser., vol. 6, no. 302).

169 This package involving statements on air strength and para-military formations had undoubtedly been conditioned by a report from the German Ambassador in Paris that Eden's negotiations in Paris had not resulted in Anglo-French unanimity. Von Neurath argued that the British willingness to adopt a more flexible and conciliatory stance than the French could be utilised to isolate France from Britain and Italy. It was, therefore, important to appear reasonable and be prepared to give concessions without surrendering the principle of armament equality in order to exacerbate Anglo-French differences. Von Neurath rightly deduced that the salient areas were the French preoccupation with para-military formations and British concern for an air pact. *DGFP*, ser. C, vol. 2, nos 245, 268 and 270.

170 *Baldwin Papers*, vol. 122, ff. 31—3, Eden to Baldwin, 21 February 1934.

171 The German Foreign Ministry record claims that Eden agreed to abandon his proposed return to Paris and report immediately to London after concluding his negotiations in Rome. No mention of this intention is found in either Eden's account or his reports to London, *DGFP*, ser. C, vol. 2, no. 273.

172 Mussolini had certainly been informed of the course of the Anglo-German discussions before Eden's arrival in Rome. The German Ambassador in Rome had been given specific instructions to take such action on 22 February 1934. See *DGFP*, ser. C, vol. 2, no. 277.

173 *Baldwin Papers*, vol. 122, ff. 35—6, Eden to Baldwin, Rome, 24 February 1934.

174 Foreign Office Minute by Ramsay MacDonald dated 22 February 1934 on Eden's despatch from Berlin of 21 February 1934. *DBFP*, 2nd ser., vol. 6, no. 303.

175 *DBFP*, 2nd ser., vol. 6, no. 308, Sir J. Simon to Sir E. Phipps (no. 51 (W1913/1/98)). FO, 23 February 1934.

176 Phipps also pointed out that Germany's air demands had been repeated quite openly on previous occasions. *DBFP*, 2nd ser., vol. 6, no. 312.

177 *Sir Eric Phipps Papers*, PHPP I 3/2, Eden to Phipps, 24 February 1934, Rome. Ormsby-Gore also came to Eden's defence in a letter to Baldwin dated 26 February 1934:

> Anthony is not responsible for Hitler's new suggestions and he was bound to report them when made to him having personally witnessed how Anthony was ticked off by Simon at Geneva last autumn and being conscious that any success or an advance . . . has been due to Anthony's conviction, faith and energy, I do resent most passionately the way he is treated.

(*Baldwin Papers*, vol. 122, f. 37.).

178 *DBFP*, 2nd ser., vol. 6, no. 316, Sir E. Drummond to Sir J. Simon (no. 76 (W1947/1/98)), Rome, 24 February 1934.

179 *DBFP*, 2nd ser., vol. 6, no. 319, Sir J. Simon and Sir E. Drummond (no. 77 (W1997/1/98), FO, 26 February 1934. This sudden reversal directly suggested

that the Cabinet did not endorse Simon's initial rebuke of Eden's actions in Berlin.

180   *Hankey Papers*, 1/7, diary entry for 3 October 1932.

181   *Neville Chamberlain Papers*, diary entry for January 1934. NC2/23A.

182   Ibid., loc. cit. Chamberlain's suggestion was that a further attempt should be made to engineer a direct Franco-German agreement on armament limitation outside the confines of the Disarmament Conference.

    Chamberlain's concern for Simon's conduct of British policy was apparently shared by his half brother, Sir Austen Chamberlain, who wrote to his sister, Ida, on 3 February 1934 describing Simon as a 'very bad Foreign Secretary' and claiming that this opinion was shared by Ormsby-Gore, Walter Elliot and Hankey. *Austen Chamberlain Papers*, AC 5/1/650.

183   *Baldwin Papers*, vol. 121, f. 50, Eden to Baldwin, 22 June 1933.

184   Chamberlain refers to the prospect of Sir J. Simon being replaced at the Foreign Office on several occasions during 1934 but discounted any suggestion that he wanted the position of Foreign Secretary. *Neville Chamberlain Papers*, NC 2/2 3A, diary entries for January 1934 and 4 and 5 December 1934.

    On 27 February 1934 Baldwin told Tom Jones that, although Eden was amongst the small group of back-benchers whom he considered to have 'ability', none of them could be described as 'outstanding'. Thomas Jones, *A Diary with Letters, 1931–1950* (London,1954), pp. 122–4.

185   It was unlikely that any such reorientation of public opinion could be undertaken at a time when the Cabinet was also preoccupied with the apparent growing German threat to Austria. See Cabinet Minutes for 24 January 1934, 31 January 1934 and 7 February 1934. (*CAB 23/78*.)

186   An account of the meeting is found in *DBFP*, 2nd ser., vol. 6, nos 320 and 322. See also Avon, pp. 73–9.

187   *DBFP*, 2nd ser., vol. 6, no. 320.

188   Avon, pp. 76–8.

189   Strang, p. 67.

190   The German Ambassador to Rome, Von Hassell, who met Eden on two occasions during his visit to Rome, was so encouraged that he reported on 27 February 1934 that Eden 'indicated that the sole point on which he essentially differed with us was the question of air armament with respect to which German demands went very far'. However, both were agreed that France would create the main obstacle to agreement. See *DGFP*, ser. C, vol. 2, no. 283. Eden appears to have been satisfied, following his discussions in Berlin and Rome, that both Hitler and Mussolini sincerely wanted a disarmament convention. *DBFP*, 2nd ser., vol. 6, no. 322.

191   See Avon, p. 78 and *DBFP*, 2nd ser., vol. 6, no. 322. However, Von Hassell claimed that despite the satisfactory nature of the talks in Rome and Berlin, Eden left Rome 'without any great optimism' as to the prospects of gaining French acceptance of the proposals. *DGFP*, ser. C, vol. 2, no. 283.

192   An account of the Paris conversations is found in *DBFP*, 2nd ser., vol. 6, no. 323.

193   Ibid., loc. cit. The failure to impress upon Barthou the importance of the German proposals, as Eden saw them, was confirmed by an interview between Barthou and the German Ambassador in France, Koster, on 7 March 1934. Barthou told Koster:

> Eden was a young, intelligent man with an attractive outlook on life and good manners whom one gladly listened to. This did not alter the fact, however, that the English memorandum demanded disarmament of France at

the same time that rearmament was conceded to Germany. On this point there was a basic difference of opinion between France and England. Eden had not brought with him anything tangible from Rome.

DGFP, ser. C, vol. 2, no. 301, Ambassador in France to the Foreign Ministry, Paris, 7 March 1934.

194   *Avon*, p. 87. Eden appeared convinced that the only solution lay in a further attempt at engineering a disarmament convention accepting controlled German rearmament and offering security guarantees to France. *Avon*, pp. 84–7.

195   *DBFP*, 2nd ser., vol. 6, no. 363. Memorandum on Germany's Illegal Rearmament and its effects on British policy (C1961/20/18), FO, 21 March 1934. Presented to Cabinet on 22 March 1934.

196   At this Cabinet meeting Simon's proposal that French intransigence be bypassed and an attempt be made to settle on the most favourable terms available with Germany was roundly rejected on the grounds that it would create adverse reaction in France and amongst the Dominions. There was also some doubt as to Germany's trustworthiness. See *CAB* 23/78, CC 12(34)1, 22 March 1934.

However, Simon was not alone in his willingness to negotiate directly with Germany. Following the French rejection on 19 March 1934 of the British Memorandum, both Thomas Jones and Sir Maurice Hankey continued to urge their political masters to deal directly with Germany. See Jones, *A Diary with Letters* and Roskill, *Vol. III*, p. 97.

197   Simon had proposed a system of economic and financial sanctions to Chamberlain in March 1934 which Chamberlain considered would be 'difficult if not impossible to discover a way of applying'. *Neville Chamberlain Papers*, NC 2/23A, diary entry for 25 March 1934.

198   See *Neville Chamberlain Papers*, NC 2/23A, diary entries for 3 and 9 May 1934.

199   *DBFP*, 2nd ser., vol. 6, no. 390.

200   *DBFP*, 2nd ser., vol. 6, no. 394, Mr Campbell (Paris) to Sir J. Simon (no. 75 (W3630/1/98)), Paris, 17 April 1934. Barthou justified this stance with reference to the recent increases in German defence expenditure and the failure to return to the League of Nations.

201   *DBFP*, 2nd ser., vol. 6, nos 400, 414, 419 and 426.

202   Chamberlain informed the committee, 'I thought that we should declare our conviction that the Disarmament Conference had failed'. *Chamberlain Papers*, NC 2/23A, diary entry for 3 May 1934. The committee recommended to the Cabinet on 9 May 1934 that Britain go no further than reaffirming its Locarno obligations and tacitly admit the failure of the Conference by concentrating its efforts on drawing Germany, France and Italy into direct discussions (*CAB* 23/79, CC 20(34)2, Wednesday, 9 May 1934).

203   The position was further exacerbated by the French refusal to inform Britain of the line that it proposed to take at Geneva at the meeting of the General Commission of the Disarmament Conference, scheduled for 30 May 1934. See *DBFP*, 2nd ser., vol. 6, no. 426, 15 May 1934.

204   *Baldwin Papers*, vol. 122, ff. 100–1, Eden to Baldwin, Geneva, 3 June 1934.

205   On 5 June 1934 Eden reported that the Bureau of the Disarmament Conference had failed to reach agreement on the format of a scheme to bridge Franco-German differences and that France and the Soviet Union appeared determined to conclude an agreement without Germany (see *DBFP*, 2nd ser., vol. 6, no. 441). Accordingly on 6 June 1934, the Cabinet accepted Simon's recommendation that French security demands had effectively destroyed the

prospects of advancement at Geneva and, therefore, to seek adjournment of the Conference rather than allow the French proposals to divide Europe into armed camps. *CAB* 23/79, CC 23(34)1, 6 June 1934.

206 See *DBFP*, 2nd ser., vol. 6, nos 487, 488 and 489.

207 *DBFP*, 2nd ser., vol. 6, no. 787. See also *DGFP*, ser. C, vol. 3, no. 120, Ambassador in Britain to Foreign Ministry, 26 July 1934. It is interesting to note that in a report to the Foreign Ministry dated 26 July 1934, the German Ambassador to London considered Eden as the leading exponent of a minority group prepared to link equality of armaments with German acceptance of the Eastern Pact.

208 Simon, who certainly felt that the French had actively obstructed the possibility of a compromise, told the Cabinet on 6 June 1934:

> The French did not want a Disarmament Agreement. In no circumstances would they agree to a convention which would allow of any rearmament to Germany.

> To France security meant an alliance to encircle Germany.

See *CAB* 23/79, CC 23(34)1, 6 June 1934.

209 Temperley, p. 275.

210 Vansittart, *The Mist Procession*, p. 487.

211 Eden later stated, 'All through the 1930's I took every opportunity to work closely with the Americans . . . I was convinced that the presence of the United States deliberating in Europe would steady the climate of opinion there and induce caution amongst the most hot headed'. Avon, p. 87.

212 Avon, p. 92.

213 Ibid., p. 92.

214 Vansittart, p. 486.

215 Temperley, pp. 280—1.

216 *Manchester Guardian*, 1 March 1933.

217 Quoted in Randolph S. Churchill, *The Rise and Fall of Sir Anthony Eden* (London, 1959), pp. 72—5.

218 Campbell-Johnson, p. 83.

219 Alfred Duff Cooper (Viscount Norwich after 1952). Although Duff Cooper was to become Secretary of State for War in 1935, in 1934 he was Financial Secretary to the War Office.

220 Churchill, p. 74.

221 Harold J. Laski was Professor of Political Science 1926—50, Member of the Executive Committee of the Fabian Society 1922—36 and Member of the Executive Committee of the Labour Party 1936—9.

222 *Daily Herald*, August 1933.

223 See Chapter 1.

224 See Eden's comment on Sir F. Lindley's despatch from Tokyo of 21 July 1932, *DBFP*, 2nd ser., vol. 10, no. 545.

225 For example see Eden's letters to Baldwin of 9 May 1932 and 10 February 1933, *Baldwin Papers*, vol. 118, ff. 177—8 and vol. 129, ff. 104—9.

226 For example see *Neville Chamberlain Papers*, NC 2/23A, diary entry for January 1934 and *Hankey Papers*, 1/7, diary entry for 3 October 1932.

3 Meeting the dictators
June 1934 — June 1935

On 29 October 1934 the Foreign Secretary reported to the Cabinet: 'The prospect of securing at the present time a Disarmament Convention, i.e. a world-wide agreement limiting and reducing by number and definition the maximum armaments of every country in the world, does not exist.'[1] In this context a period of limited rearmament was inevitable. A response to this situation had been formulated as early as March 1934 when the Defence Requirements Committee (DRC) of the CID had produced a report to meet the worst deficiencies in British defence preparations.[2] The report identified Japan as the most immediate threat to British security in the short term but continued: 'we take Germany as the ultimate potential enemy against whom our "long range" defence policy must be directed'.[3]

In order to remedy immediate shortcomings in British defences, the Committee recommended that an expeditionary force of four divisions be prepared to fight at short notice on the continent and that further funds be allocated to the Royal Navy to increase the rate of construction of Far Eastern naval bases and refit outdated ships. In the air it was proposed that 16 squadrons be added to the Fleet Air Arm and a further 20 squadrons be allocated to Home Defence, boosting the Home Defence target from 52 to 62 squadrons.[4] The format of the report was largely determined by Sir Maurice Hankey and the three Chiefs-of-Staff. Vansittart and Sir Warren Fisher had wanted an even bigger increase in the size of the Home Air Force but were forced to accede to the majority view.[5]

The report was received by the Cabinet on 7 March 1934 and referred to the Cabinet Committee on Disarmament for examination.[6] Eden was a member of this Committee and attended most of the 13 meetings that took place between May and July 1934 before an official pronouncement was made, despite a recommendation by the Chiefs-of-Staff, in April 1934, that an early decision was imperative. The main opposition to the report was provided by the Chancellor of the Exchequer, Neville Chamberlain. Chamberlain wished to scale down the cost of the programme from £70 million to £50 million. Furthermore he was convinced that Britain had not the resources to prepare for possible confrontations with both Japan and Germany. In an attempt to reshape the format of the report he proposed to identify Germany as the primary threat and, therefore, to channel resources away from the Army and the Royal Navy into a rapid expansion of the Royal Air Force by 18 squadrons more than envisaged by the DRC.[7] The eventual amended report, as agreed by the Cabinet, largely reflected Chamberlain's influence, with the original proposals for Army expenditure cut by half and an expansion of the Home Air Force by 13 squadrons more than the target originally established. The thorny problem of naval construction and the future of the Far Eastern bases was left for further discussion between the Treasury and the Admiralty as part of the on-going preparations for the forthcoming naval conference.[8]

The prolonged debate over the report cannot be solely attributed to Chamberlain's determination to amend the provisions formulated by the DRC. It was also indicative of the embarrassment that the British Government felt at announcing a programme of rearmament while the Disarmament Conference had not been formally declared as a failure. The absence, however, of an agreement on armament limitation and the mounting evidence of German rearmament had forced the British Government to reassess its defence strategy and many had come to the same conclusion as Neville Chamberlain, that Germany presented the most immediate threat to British security.[9] Even Baldwin, who had consistently feared a widespread domestic opposition to rearmament, felt sufficiently alarmed to speak out in favour of the increase in the RAF. On 30 July 1934 he told the House of Commons: 'The old frontiers have gone. When you think of the defence of England you no longer think of the chalk cliffs of Dover; you think of the Rhine. That is where our frontier lies.'[10]

Eden's personal contribution and thoughts on the conduct of British defence policy are difficult to assess. Even before the failure of the Disarmament Conference, he had come to the conclusion that an element of German rearmament was inevitable. Therefore if Britain was not to lose ground to its European rivals, a modest programme of rearmament was unavoidable. He almost certainly supported the broad outlines of the DRC report and, in particular, followed Chamberlain and Baldwin in voicing anxiety over the strength of the RAF.[11] In an address at Stoke-on-Trent on 5 July 1934 he stated:

> if there is anxiety at all in respect of our armaments it is rather a doubt lest, having reduced them so far in a world which has been increasing its armaments, we should not be in a position to fulfil the commitments which we have undertaken.

> Britain is essentially a stabilizing and not an unsettling influence in world affairs. An undue weakness in her defence, if over-long maintained in a world that is increasing its armaments, would be no aid to peace.[12]

Although to the public Eden's support for a rapid expansion of the armed forces might have seemed inconsistent with his role at the Disarmament Conference, in reality he was only re-emphasising a concern for British security, particularly in relation to the size of the Home Air Force, that had been a feature of his parliamentary pronouncements since 1924.[13]

In the autumn of 1934 Eden once again undertook the task of representing Britain at the League of Nations. The French and Italian delegates were particularly concerned to orchestrate efforts to ensure Austrian independence following the murder of the Austrian Chancellor, Dolfuss, on 25 July 1934. On 18 September 1934 Baron Aloisi proposed to Eden that Britain join with Italy and other European states in the conclusion of a pact guaranteeing Austrian independence. In his report to Simon, Eden noted:

> I repeated to Baron Aloisi that we could in no circumstances agree to be parties to a pact which involved new commitments for us in Central Europe.

> It is clear to me that we are likely to be hard pressed by Italy in respect of this projected pact in the course of the next few days.[14]

The problem was clearly identified as one of attempting to avoid further European commitments without seriously alienating the French or Italian governments. Given that the Cabinet was insistent that Britain would not participate in any pact of guarantee to Austria, Sir John Simon could do little but suggest that Eden pursue 'delaying tactics' and go no further than reaffirming the joint declaration on Austrian independence made on 17 February 1934.[15] Therefore on 22 September 1934 Eden, in conversation with the French delegate

Massigli, indicated that Britain was anxious to see all of Austria's neighbours drawn into a pact of guarantee and that the scheme should be agreed between Italy and France before being referred to Britain. By these means Eden successfully extricated Britain from the Austrian debate and was ensured of a prolonged respite while Italy and France haggled over the format of an agreement.[16]

At this same session of the League of Nations a more immediate problem was beginning to emerge in the form of the forthcoming plebiscite on the future status of the Saar.[17] The immediate fear was that the existing police force would be unable to maintain control during the period before the plebiscite and that British and French forces might be requested to intervene. The British Government's view was that the Saar would inevitably elect to return to German sovereignty and, while not being averse to the use of French troops in a police role, any postponement of the plebiscite or extension of the League of Nations mandate was only likely to exacerbate Franco-German relations.[18] Eden was, therefore, disturbed by reports from Sir Geoffrey Knox, President of the Governing Commission of the Territory, in the latter months of 1934 that pro-German elements were infiltrating into the Saar and that there was a possibility of a putsch being staged before the plebiscite could be completed.[19] Furthermore, while Barthou had stated that French troops would be available to act as a police force in an emergency, his successor, Pierre Laval, informed Eden in the latter half of November that the French army would only act in concert with British forces.[20]

On 23 November 1934 Eden met with Knox at Geneva and the President of the Governing Commission re-emphasised his fear of an imminent pro-German putsch which he would be unable to quell.[21] Eden later recorded that as a result of this conversation he formulated a report to Simon on 30 November 1934, advocating that Britain sponsor an international police force to maintain order in the Saar throughout the period of the plebiscite. He further claimed that Simon, Hailsham and Neville Chamberlain shunned the scheme and that it was only finally accepted after Baldwin's intervention on 3 December 1934.[22] This account is open to question, for the Cabinet minutes reveal that Sir John Simon raised the question of the creation of an international police force on 28 November 1934. At this meeting it was agreed in principle that Britain would be prepared to contribute troops to an international force as long as the scheme was approved by both France and Germany. The launching of the project, however, was to be delayed until MacDonald, Baldwin and Chamberlain had received further reports from the Foreign Office and the War Office.[23] Eden had already written from Geneva urging the Cabinet to take the initiative and authorise him to place the scheme before the Council of the League of Nations, but it was apparent that Sir John Simon and Lord Hailsham still held reservations about the commitment of British forces to the operation.[24] In an attempt to break the deadlock, Eden returned to London and, in an interview on 3 December 1934, convinced Baldwin that the international force was the only means of defusing a potentially explosive situation.[25] His intervention was probably decisive, for on the same afternoon Baldwin over-rode all objections and the Lord Privy Seal returned to Geneva with a mandate to unveil the scheme provided that it was sanctioned by Germany and France and at least four nations — including Italy but excluding Germany, France and the Soviet Union — agreed to participate alongside Britain.[26]

On his return to Geneva a further obstacle was created when it became apparent that, if the operation was to be launched immediately while German, French and Italian approval could be quickly secured, there was little or no time to gain guarantees of participation by Dutch, Belgian or Swiss contingents.[27] Although Simon telegraphed Eden that such guarantees must be obtained before the scheme was announced, Eden elected to ignore this proviso and on 5 December 1934 informed the Council of the League of Nations that Britain would be prepared to contribute troops to an international force.[28] In so doing he effectively exceeded the guidelines established by the Cabinet. He was aware, however, that having gained Italian support, the participation of further nations would not be too difficult to obtain. The proposals were unanimously accepted by the Council and it was an indication of the relief felt in Paris that the French Government offered to transport the force through its territory free of charge.[29]

Eden further suggested that as Knox was British and the scheme had been a British initiative, Britain ought to insist on appointing the force commander. Italy was to be compensated by being granted the chairmanship of the international committee which would be established to supervise the running of the force. Both of these proposals were accepted by Simon and, after some negotiation, by Mussolini on 7 December 1934.[30]

The entire scheme was approved by the League of Nations on 8 December 1934 and subsequently an international force of 3300 men drawn from Britain, Italy, Sweden and Holland ensured that the Saar plebiscite passed off without incident. It appeared that a potentially dangerous situation had been defused and a victory gained for collective action and the League of Nations. More significantly Simon's handling of the situation was described by Chamberlain as 'timid and half-hearted all through'.[31] It could not have gone unnoticed that Eden had played a conspicuous part in pushing the agreement through and had effectively by-passed the Foreign Secretary in chivying the Cabinet into action. While there is no suggestion that the incident significantly affected Eden's relationship with Simon, it was indicative of his growing influence in the direction of foreign policy.

In the same month Eden was involved in a further crisis at Geneva which, for a time, threatened to engulf Europe in a major war. The assassination of the French Foreign Minister, Louis Barthou, and King Alexander of Yugoslavia at Marseilles on 9 October 1934 by a Croatian terrorist allegedly based in Hungary, threatened to revive deep-seated Balkan rivalries.[32] As Eden later commented:

> The Yugoslav's were indignant, the Hungarians defensive. Behind Hungary stood Italy, behind Yugoslavia, France. Italy's relations with Yugoslavia had been bad since the quarrel over Trieste and her friendship with Hungary was a useful makeweight. The Little Entente, Czechoslovakia, Roumania and Yugoslavia, was in ferment. There was at least suspicion that Mussolini had known what was afoot and, in general terms, he had. The danger of war mounted and the League Council had to be summoned.[33]

The problem was to gain some form of compensation for the Yugoslavs without unduly humiliating Hungary. Furthermore, as Eden pointed out to Benes, to allow the affair to escalate would have strained Franco-Italian relations at a time when their co-operation in the pursuit of European security was vital. In an attempt to find a compromise, Eden agreed to undertake the role of *rapporteur*. It was a measure of his increasing international standing that his selection was agreed upon by all the parties concerned, although the Yugoslavs were disturbed that Eden had already indirectly criticised their decision to expel thousands of Hungarian refugees. After a series of separate interviews with the Yugoslavian Foreign Minister, Yevtitch, and his Hungarian counterpart, De Kanya, an acceptable formula was devised. The solution presented to the League Council enabled both nations to save face by virtue of a veiled condemnation of the Yugoslavian expulsion of Hungarian refugees and a request that the Hungarian Government take appropriate action against any of its officials who had been negligent in their supervision of the Croatian refugees.[34] Observing Eden's work as *rapporteur* at Geneva, Temperley was later to comment:

> Too much praise cannot be given to Mr. Eden for what he accomplished; and every statesman at Geneva was well aware that there was no other man in Europe who could have done it. War could hardly have been avoided if there had been a breakdown.[35]

Temperley's assessment is probably correct in identifying Eden's primary aim as the avoidance of a 'breakdown' and particularly the prevention of an incident which might have damaged Franco-Italian relations, but this task was not particularly difficult for neither Yugoslavia and Hungary nor their powerful allies wanted war and readily accepted a compromise.[36] Eden, therefore, produced a rather bland solution and pointedly ignored the allegation that the Croatian terrorists had far firmer connections with Italy than with Hungary. In this sense the formula was satisfactory to all concerned. In the public eye Eden had proved himself an able negotiator on a world stage and had added a further feather to his cap.

In the latter half of 1934, following the adjournment of the Disarmament Conference and the refusal of Germany and Poland to adhere to the Franco-Soviet sponsored pact of mutual guarantee in Eastern Europe, the problem of European security was still uppermost in the consideration of the British Cabinet. On 12 November 1934 Eden held an interview with Von Ribbentrop in London.[37] The German minister attempted to reassure the Lord Privy Seal that Germany did not hold any aggressive intentions and was anxious to reopen discussions with Britain on disarmament. Eden emphasised that escalating German demands and the rejection of the East-European mutual guarantee pact had created several problems but agreed that further contacts would be of use. The interview had an unfortunate consequence for Eden in that two days later *The Times* published an article, apparently inspired by the German Embassy, claiming that Von Ribbentrop had informed Eden of the extent of German rearmament and that the Lord Privy Seal had indicated British acceptance of the German right to exceed the Versailles limitations.[38] This statement was vehemently denied by Eden in the House of Commons on 14 November 1934 and so annoyed the British Government that MacDonald brusquely rejected Von Ribbentrop's overtures for a personal interview.[39] The Foreign Office record of the interview and Von Ribbentrop's own report to Berlin both support Eden's version of the discussion. It can only be surmised that the German Embassy sought to embarrass Britain and perhaps disrupt Anglo-French relations.[40] If so, the plan was both clumsy and inept and only succeeded in souring Anglo-German relations and in harming Von Ribbentrop's credibility. Not surprisingly Eden's future dealings with the Germans were to be far from cordial.[41]

Such was the concern at the pace and extent of German rearmament that on 21 November 1934 the Cabinet established a Cabinet Committee on German Rearmament to examine the whole question, following the submission of four papers by the CID which indicated that the Reichswehr had a total strength of 300,000 men and that, by the autumn of 1935, Germany was likely to possess 1300 first-line aircraft.[42] The Committee, chaired by MacDonald, reported to the Cabinet on 26 November 1934:

> That the evidence of German rearmament is now so formidable that we feel it can no longer be officially ignored, and that, if the situation in Germany is allowed to develop without let or hindrance on present lines, the German forces may ultimately become a menace to the peace of Europe.

It was suggested that, in response, a statement be issued pointing out that German forces were in excess of their treaty limitations and announcing the acceleration of British rearmament, with the provision of 22 squadrons for home defence within 2 years rather than the previous target of 4 years.[43] The same week Sir Eric Phipps, the British Ambassador in Berlin, was recalled to London to discuss the problem presented by Germany. Phipps concluded that German rearmament was rapidly gaining pace but that Germany was still prepared to accept a European arms-limitation agreement and a return to the League of Nations in exchange for the abrogation of the military limitation sections of the Versailles Treaty. The main obstacles to this agreement remained the French refusal to condone any element of German rearmament and the recently raised problem of Polish and German participation in an East European pact of mutual guarantee. It appeared that only further British pledges of military support for France in the event of a European war would sufficiently alleviate French security fears to allow a compromise solution to be achieved with Germany.[44] However, as the response to feelers by both the Turkish and Belgian Governments in the latter half of 1934 indicated, the British Government was in no mood to expand its military commitments in Europe.[45]

On 27 November 1934 the German Foreign Minister, Von Neurath, admitted to Phipps that Germany was already building up its forces to the levels proposed to Eden by Hitler in February 1934 and, in addition, had commenced the construction of bomber aircraft. He stressed, however, that Germany was still prepared to enter into disarmament negotiations once the question of the future status of the Saar had been resolved.[46] The following day Eden minuted on a further despatch from Phipps:

> The next step is clearly to talk to the French but before doing so we should decide upon our course of action. Time presses for we must not lose control of the situation which we have assisted to develop.[47]

Simon was also aware that the probable reunification of the Saar with Germany, in January 1934, offered an opportunity for a re-opening of the disarmament discussions that ought not to be ignored. On 29 November 1934 he recommended to the Cabinet Committee on German Rearmament that a settlement be sought on the basis of the abrogation of Part V of the Versailles Treaty and official recognition of German rearmament be given in exchange for Germany's return to the League of Nations and the Disarmament Conference. He proposed that French security fears be allayed by the establishment of a net-work of bilateral non-aggression pacts in Eastern Europe, along the lines of the format suggested by Hitler in September 1934 in response to the proposed multilateral East European pact. The whole tenor of the memorandum implied that British patience with French intransigence was growing short and that the possibility of an Anglo-German agreement should be considered if the French continued to reject a settlement based on the German offer of 16 April 1934.[48]

However, when the Cabinet Committee on German Rearmament reported to the Cabinet on 12 December 1934 it was apparent that the majority feeling was firmly in favour of maintaining a common front with the French.[49] It was accepted that Anglo-French dis-cussions were essential before attempting a further initiative on armament limitation. It was, therefore, agreed that the French Premier and Foreign Minister be invited to London for immediate negotiations:

It is desirable to give the forthcoming French visit publicity. The stronger we make the common front between ourselves France and Italy, the more likely it is that Germany will listen to reason. She is frightened at the idea of being isolated.[50]

The British Cabinet had undoubtedly been encouraged by reports from the Paris Embassy that the French Foreign Minister, Laval, was anxious to co-ordinate his work closely with that of Britain. It was all the more disappointing, therefore, when the French rejected the suggestion of a visit to London before the New Year.[51] It appeared that the opportunity of capitalising on the probable transfer of the Saar to Germany was slipping away and, on 19 December 1934, the Cabinet agreed that the Foreign Secretary should travel to Paris to make it plain that Britain could not tolerate a policy of further drift.[52] At a meeting held at the Quai d'Orsay on 22 December 1934, Simon succeeded in eliciting a pledge from Flandin to visit London in the latter half of January following the conclusion of further Franco-Italian discussions in Rome on the maintenance of Austrian independence. It was evident that Laval was determined to gain Italian agreement on the format of a Central European multilateral security pact before engaging in further negotiations with Britain on disarmament and security.[53]

The British Government had, therefore, to be satisfied with the promise of Anglo-French negotiations in the latter half of January 1935. In the intervening period attempts were made to impress upon the French the need for an early settlement with Germany. In London Vansittart, in an interview with the French Ambassador, argued that by the latter half of 1935 German military strength would have reached a level which would allow it to ignore Anglo-French pressure for armament limitation.[54] In January Simon and Eden travelled to Geneva to attend the League of Nations. Despite the failure to lure Germany back to the League of Nations to participate in the negotiations concerning the Saar, Eden and Simon took the opportunity to urge Massigli and Laval that an agreement with Germany on armament limitation was of paramount importance.[55] As a result of these conversations Eden was particularly disturbed at the general lack of direction in French policy. On 11 January 1935 he wrote to Baldwin:

> As to the future of Anglo-French talks, this is not simple. Laval has only just arrived but I had a talk with Massigli, at present in charge for French government, this afternoon. I have known Massigli for some years now and we are firm friends and can talk frankly. It is clear to me that the French are puzzled as to what to do. They want to maintain their firm relations with us and are nervous lest talks with Germany re arms should jeopardise these. They think, I suspect, that German rearmament has already gone so far that agreement at any reasonable level is past paying for.[56]

In his report to London, Eden concluded that France was likely to maintain its demand for rigorous supervision measures and guarantees of execution as part of any disarmament agreement.[57] However, a ray of hope was provided by Laval's account of the Franco-Italian negotiations. It was evident that the French sought to restrain German ambitions by the promotion of a multilateral security pact in Central Europe, based upon the defence of Austrian independence.[58] On 14 January 1935 the Cabinet seized on this report and agreed that, while any attempt to redefine the Locarno commitments would be resisted, concessions could be made to France on the establishment of a scheme of disarmament supervision and a general endorsement of the Central European pact. This general line was subsequently endorsed by the Cabinet on 24 January 1935, with the addition that it should be impressed upon the French that the network of bilateral pacts of non-aggression proposed by Hitler would also be of value in the promotion of European security. However, the Cabinet remained insistent that no further British pledges could be given to the French and, indeed, went so far as to warn Laval that they would not participate in any negotiation on the co-ordination of Anglo-French military forces.[59]

In order to obtain an agreement with Germany the British Government was prepared to consider generous concessions to German rearmament. On 21 January 1935 the Foreign Secretary conceded: 'The object of our present policy is of course to bring the Germans back to Geneva . . . .'[60] To this end the three Service Ministers were prepared to grant Germany an army of 300,000 men equipped with tanks up to 16 tons and guns up to 155 mm. German naval tonnage was to be permitted a 75 per cent increase, while air parity with the French Metropolitan Air Force was accepted as a realistic level of forces.[61] Despite these generous concessions, the weakness of the British position was noted by Eden following a conversation with the Czechoslovak Foreign Minister, Benes, on 24 January 1935:

> Perhaps this is the appropriate moment to set down my personal impression gleaned from all conversations I have had at Geneva, that it would not be possible for any French Government to agree to legalize German rearmament unless as part of that agreement Germany adhered to the Eastern Pact and undertook to return to Geneva.[62]

The British stance hinged on using the East- and Central-European pacts to satisfy French security fears, which was perhaps somewhat surprising given that as recently as 23 January 1935 Hitler had restated his determination not to participate in multilateral security pacts.[63] This point was taken up by Orme Sargent of the Foreign Office on 28 January 1935. He argued that the only solution was to look for an alternative method of guaranteeing East-European security. Eden minuted: 'I agree that the position would be changed if we could make any "security" offer, but what are the chances of that?'[64]

The weakness of the British position was immediately indicated when the Anglo-French conversations opened in London on 1 February 1935. Eden was included in the British delegation and listened to the Foreign Secretary open the negotiations by outlining the main problems of armament reduction and European security. Simon emphasised the need to replace the Versailles restrictions on Germany with a general armament agreement which would incorporate the return of Germany to the League of Nations. Laval immediately countered with the insistence that Germany join the proposed East- and Central-European pacts of mutual guarantee.

The French Premier, Flandin, added that his country's security requirements necessitated the establishment of a network of regional pacts of collective security, supported by an armament limitation agreement incorporating guarantees of execution and the maintenance of French military superiority over Germany. He further proposed that a pact of mutual assistance from aerial attack be concluded by the West-European states to strengthen the bonds of collective security.[65]

It was this last suggestion that the British delegation sought to explore. Vansittart had previously advocated such a scheme which Simon had approved in principle, but he had rejected the proposal that it be incorporated within Locarno.[66] On 2 February 1935 the Cabinet examined a memorandum on the proposed air pact submitted by Simon.[67] It was agreed that the proposal should be followed up as it presented an opportunity to allay French security fears without enlarging upon existing commitments under Locarno. However, while endorsing the recommendation that British participation be subject to German acceptance, the Cabinet rejected Simon's proposal that the air pact should not be dependent on the attainment of an overall agreement on security and armament levels. The air pact was clearly seen as an opportunity to draw France and Germany into a general agreement rather than the beginning of an attempt to come to agreement with Germany in a piecemeal fashion.[68]

On this basis an agreement was reached whereby Britain welcomed the Rome Agreement and, in particular, the proposed regional pacts in East and Central Europe. The French, in return, accepted the principle of German equality of status and the eventual abrogation of the military restrictions, imposed on Germany by the Versailles Treaty, which were to be replaced by a general European armament agreement. Finally the two nations agreed to invite Germany, Italy and Belgium to participate in a pact of mutual assistance directed against unprovoked aerial aggression. It appeared that the agreement satisfied French security fears and provided a platform from which Germany could be approached. However, not all of the British delegation were satisfied with the outcome.[69] On 10 February 1935 Hankey recorded: 'It was the worst conducted negotiation I have ever assisted at, and the French Ministers (to whom I take off my hat!) just made rings with us.'[70]

Hankey's annoyance was almost certainly based on the fact that the air pact had been designed and launched by the Foreign Office without prior consultation with Chiefs-of-Staff:

Thus in 24 hours, or 25 hours, without any proper examination of the proposal; without waiting for the report of the Chiefs of

84

Staff Committee; without giving me an opportunity to be heard, the Cabinet and their representatives at the Conference had virtually pledged us to the most serious military commitment that we have entered into for centuries, if at all. And, as it now transpires, the military advisers (the Chiefs of Staff and myself) are bitterly opposed to it.[71]

Indeed the Chiefs-of-Staff were to point out the absurdity of attempting to make provisions with both Germany and France to co-operate with one against the other, to which the Foreign Office countered: 'The answer is that such a question must be considered in a spirit of realism, and realism renders it obvious that there will be no question of joining Germany against France and Belgium.'[72]

It was apparent that the Foreign Office was determined to override all preliminary objections to the pact in an attempt to reconcile France to the British viewpoint on German armament limitation. It was considered that the offer of an air pact, which could be provided at little further material cost to Britain, was the one factor that could possibly lure Germany into negotiations. If a Franco-German consensus of opinion could be established on the format of an air pact, it was possible that further agreements could be reached in Eastern Europe and on armament levels.

The German reply to the London communiqué was encouraging, for although Von Neurath restated German objections to the East-European pact, he expressed great interest in the proposed air pact and suggested the opening of preliminary Anglo-German negotiations.[73] This proposal was accepted by the Government, with the Foreign Secretary adding that the meeting should be held in Berlin to ensure that Hitler personally took an active part in the discussions.[74] On 28 February 1935 Simon visited Paris to reassure the French that the Berlin visit would be purely exploratory in nature and would cover all of the various questions raised by the London communiqué. He also revealed that further visits to Moscow, Warsaw and Prague were being considered and that these missions would probably be undertaken by Anthony Eden.[75] The extension of the Berlin visit to include the East-European capitals had been actively canvassed by Sir Robert Vansittart, who was anxious to reassure the Soviet Union and Czechoslovakia that the Berlin talks did not signify a British intention to give Germany a free hand in Eastern Europe.[76] The inclusion of Moscow had been opposed by MacDonald but the fact that the proposed Eastern Pact was likely to be a central feature in a European settlement emphasised the usefulness of gaining a first-hand impression of the climate of opinion in the Soviet Union.[77] The secondary role of these missions was indicated by the fact that the

Foreign Secretary did not intend to undertake the visits personally. Given this precondition and having established his credentials at Geneva where he had worked extensively with Benes and Litvinov, Anthony Eden was the natural choice. It was apparent that as early as December 1934, following the successful establishment of the international police force in the Saar, Baldwin had earmarked Eden for a central role in future negotiations. Thomas Jones noted on 16 December 1934: 'S.B. thinks of using Anthony Eden for this as he is doing well in similar negotiations elsewhere.'[78]

However, the opportunity to enhance his reputation as an international negotiator appeared to have been snatched from Eden when on 5 March 1935 the German Foreign Minister informed the British Ambassador that Hitler had a heavy cold and that the visit to Berlin, scheduled for 7 March 1935, would have to be postponed.[79] This sudden reversal of attitude was almost certainly prompted by the publication on 4 March 1935 of the British Defence White Paper which pointedly criticised the increasing militarisation of German youth and the growing rearmament campaign in Germany. The paper, which had largely been engineered by Hankey, concluded: 'An additional expenditure on the armaments of the three Defence Services can, therefore, no longer be postponed.'[80] Hitler's annoyance at this report was confirmed by Sir Eric Phipps who noted: 'my first impression was that the illness was a diplomatic one.'[81]

In Cabinet Neville Chamberlain urged Simon to request an alternative date and to declare that the visits to Moscow and Warsaw would go ahead.[82] In response to this suggestion a reply was elicited from Berlin agreeing to the negotiations being held from 24 to 30 March 1935.[83] Eden saw the German tactics as a further manoeuvre designed to justify an increase in armament demands. While emphasising the need to avoid British entanglement in the details of the Eastern Pact, which would focus attention away from what he identified as the central problem of armament limitation, Eden was quite specific about the goals of the Berlin visit. It was necessary to obtain a definite statement of German armament requirements and a pledge to enter into an international conference to discuss the London communiqué. Finally Germany must agree on the commencement of immediate legal consultations on the drafting of the air pact: 'If Germany accepts these three, then the Berlin visit has indeed been worth while. If she refuses them equally her attitude is made clear to the British Public.'[84] The situation was further complicated when on 11 March 1935 Göring openly admitted to a reporter from the *Daily Mail* that Germany possessed an Air Force that: 'was now so strong in the air that she could repulse any air attack, no matter by whom it was delivered.'[85] In addition on 16 March 1935 it was announced that the

German Army was to introduce universal military conscription, with the object of raising the strength of the Reichswehr to 500,000 men.[86]

In the face of these two blatant infringements of the Versailles Treaty, on 18 March 1935 Sir Eric Phipps delivered a note to the German Foreign Ministry which had been drafted by Simon and approved by the Cabinet. The note condemned the German rearmament announcements but enquired whether the proposed visit to Berlin would still be welcomed by the Germans.[87] The decision to act without consulting France or Italy was later defended by the Foreign Secretary on the grounds that the delay involved would have seriously damaged the prospect of the Berlin visit going ahead.[88] Simon undoubtedly feared that discussion with Rome and Paris could only have led to demands for a vehement condemnation of German remilitarisation and a possible attempt to arraign Germany before the League of Nations. Such action would have destroyed the chance of securing an agreement with Germany and, therefore, the Foreign Secretary was prepared to risk the storm of criticism that his decision would provoke in Italy and France.[89] However, there was disquiet within the Foreign Office at the lengths to which the Foreign Secretary appeared prepared to travel to accommodate German sensibilities. On 19 March Sir R. Vansittart minuted:

In my view we went too fast and too far yesterday.

I feel bound to express my very grave apprehension that unless we are extremely careful, *more* careful indeed, in future, we may find that the German Jack o' Lantern has led us into a deep and irretrievable bog in which we will have sacrificed everything for nothing.[90]

Eden initialled this minute two days later but refrained from comment. Simon's decision to press ahead with the visit to Berlin and the subsequent storm of protest raised in Paris and Rome was to involve the Lord Privy Seal closely, for it was decided by the Cabinet on 20 March 1935 that Eden would undertake a visit to Paris on 23 March 1935 to reassure the French and Italian governments that Britain intended to go no further in Berlin than exploratory talks.[91] This decision was warmly welcomed by Sir Eric Phipps in Berlin:

His Majesty's Government have now, I think, a unique and perhaps a last chance of concluding a comprehensive European agreement and making France and Germany see reason.

If Lord Privy Seal can obtain some idea of minimum requirements from French Government and if these are within reason,

I feel that prospects of your visit will be greatly improved particularly as Herr Hitler and German opinion are favourably impressed by our latest show of moderation and impartiality.[92]

Eden was less sanguine about the prospects for this delicate mission, as he later recorded:

My visit to Paris was most unenviable. The French and Italian press were indignant at our lonely action and on March 20th the French Government addressed an official protest to Geneva against Germany's violation of a treaty by introducing conscription.[93]

The discussions held in Paris with Laval and Suvich, the Under-Secretary of State in the Italian Foreign Ministry, were dominated by Eden's assurances that Britain would go no further in Berlin than exploratory discussions ranging over the entire extent of the London communiqué and that a full report would be given to France and Italy at a three-power meeting in April. Eden was particularly struck by the close unity displayed by the Italian and French Ministers in their insistence that Germany participate in the proposed Eastern- and Central-European pacts. Eden could only reply that Germany could not be forced to enter into any agreement and warned that an alternative to the suggested schemes might have to be examined at a later date. Rather than finding any suggestion that France was prepared to make further concessions to Germany, it was evident that recent events had hardened the French stance and Flandin warned Eden that he expected Britain in future to adopt a much firmer stance towards German infringements of its treaty commitments. In particular he wanted a clear statement of British intentions if the demilitarised Rhineland zone was infringed by Germany and France attempted to invoke the Treaty of Locarno.[94]

As Eden travelled to Berlin he could not but be aware that he had succeeded only in temporarily smoothing the course of Anglo-French relations. Simon and Eden met with Hitler on 25 and 26 March 1935 in a series of four separate interviews, of which Eden subsequently declared:

Hitler was definitely more authoritative and less anxious to please than a year before.

At this second interview, I was most unfavourably impressed by Hitler's personality.[95]

This assessment of Hitler was corroborated by Lord Strang who attended Eden's interviews with the German Chancellor in both February 1934 and March 1935:

> At the meeting in 1934 Hitler had been out to please. By the time that Sir John Simon and Mr. Eden visited him in 1935 his mood had changed. Though he still did not rave or rant, his manner was abrupt and his tone at times verging on the truculent while his voice took on a strident or guttural note and his gestures betrayed an ill-concealed exasperation.[96]

Although Eden took the lead in stating the British attitude to questions on armament limitation and Austrian independence, the interviews were largely dominated by exchanges between Hitler and Simon.[97] In reply to Simon's opening statement on the need for German co-operation in the preservation of peace, Hitler declared that German policy was entirely defensive and that there was no intention of attempting to export the National Socialist revolution. Hitler informed the Foreign Secretary: 'Annexation of territory would merely add to the political and economic difficulties with which he was faced.'[98]

He emphasised that Austria and the East-European nations need not have any fear of German aggression. He was prepared to underline this statement by entering into bilateral non-aggression pacts with neighbouring states, but refused categorically to consider participation in a pact of mutual assistance on the grounds that it might draw Germany into conflicts to which it did not wish to be a party. The German Chancellor was particularly vehement in his denunciation of the tactics employed by the Soviet Union which he saw as aggressive and expansionist. In response to Eden's retort that the Eastern-European pact would assist Germany by stabilising the situation in that area, Hitler stated that the problem of defining an act of aggression was open to such wide interpretation that Germany would not enter into an agreement under which any of the signatories were linked by pacts of mutual assistance, but he would consider a general pact of non-aggression with the obligation to consult and not to aid an aggressor. In relation to the League of Nations, Hitler referred to the link between the Covenant of the League of Nations and the Versailles Treaty which he described as an imposed treaty and, therefore, unacceptable to the German people. In particular Hitler noted that Germany was not permitted to administer a colony and indicated that this was symbolic of the general inequality of rights which would have to be rectified before Germany could re-enter the League of Nations.

At the end of the first day Eden could only conclude:

> Results very bad . . . whole tone and temper very different to a
> year ago, rearmed and rearming with the old Prussian spirit very
> much in evidence. Russia is now the bogey.[99]

The same evening, as Eden dined at the Reich President's House, the
French Ambassador to Berlin, François-Poncet, discovered that Hitler
and Eden had fought on the same area of the Western Front in the
war and observed to Eden:

> 'It is true you were opposite Hitler?'
> I replied it seemed so.
> 'Et vous l'avez manqué. Vous devriez etre fusillé.'[100]

The following day was taken up with negotiations on armament
levels and the air pact.[101] Simon noted that the German suggestion
that its navy be allowed to build up to 35 per cent of the total
strength of the Royal Navy was so excessive as to make a 'general
agreement almost impossible'.[102] Undeterred Hitler outlined the
German demand for an army of 550,000 men in order to counter the
strength of its neighbours. Furthermore he refused to include paramilitary formations in his estimates on the grounds that they were
merely equivalent to officer training-corps schemes operated at British
public schools.[103] In terms of air strength Germany required parity
with the total strength of the French Metropolitan and North-African
air forces. Finally, while Germany would be willing to observe an
armament limitation agreement, Hitler demanded that Germany must
be permitted the possession of all types of weapon held by other
states.

The final interview was concerned with the proposed air pact. Hitler
welcomed the scheme in principle but was disappointed that the
British ministers were adamant that it must be linked to a settlement
of all the questions outlined in the London communiqué. At the close
of the negotiations Sir John Simon candidly admitted to Hitler that:
'the British Ministers did feel somewhat disappointed that it had not
been possible in these two days to get a larger measure of agreement.'[104] While travelling to Moscow, Eden set down his impression
of the Berlin negotiations: 'The essential question seems to be does a
basis now exist for a general European settlement? A year ago I
believe there was such a basis, but it is exceedingly difficult to maintain that it exists now.'

It was apparent that Germany would only return to Geneva following the return of colonies and Eden was opposed to what would be
identified as a bribe:

is there elsewhere any basis of agreement? Germany's demands on land and sea, in respect of neither of which is there any sign of abatement, seem to make an agreement impossible, while her attitude to Eastern Pact and Danubian Pact makes any security agreement extremely doubtful, to say the least.

Eden could only recommend one course of policy now that the role of honest broker appeared to have failed:

> to join with those powers who are members of the League of Nations in reaffirming our faith in that institution and our determination to uphold the principle of the Covenant. It may be that the spectacle of the Great Powers of the League reaffirming their intention to collaborate more closely than ever is not only the sole means of bringing home to Germany that the inevitable effect of persisting in her present policy will be to consolidate against her all those nations which believe in collective system, but will also tend to give confidence to those less powerful nations which through fear of Germany's growing strength might otherwise be drawn into orbit.[105]

A significant factor in the creation of a concerted front to oppose German ambitions was inevitably the attitude of the Soviet Union. In February 1935 Sir Robert Vansittart had declared his belief that the accession of the Soviet Union to the League of Nations in September 1934 had strengthened the forces of collective security, but if further links were not forged with the Soviet Union there was a significant danger that it would seek an understanding with Germany which would considerably undermine any further attempts to limit German ambitions in Europe.[106] However, his opinion was not shared by many leading figures in Britain who continued to regard the Soviet Union with the utmost suspicion and, at times, outright hostility.[107] This stance was underlined when Simon, in briefing Eden before his departure for Moscow, warned the Lord Privy Seal neither to inform the Soviet Union of the possibility of future Anglo-German naval discussions nor offer the prospect of similar Anglo-Soviet negotiations. It was evident that Simon was determined to exclude the Soviet Union from participation in the European armament discussions.[108]

On 29 March 1935 Eden met with the Soviet Commissar for Foreign Affairs, Maxim Litvinov.[109] It was apparent that Litvinov was primarily concerned with gleaning information about potential German expansion in Eastern Europe and Japanese ambitions in the Far East. While the Lord Privy Seal admitted that Hitler had identified the Soviet Union as a 'serious menace', he stressed that the German

Chancellor had emphasised that he had no intention of attacking the Soviet Union. Litvinov was not convinced and declared that, despite frequent protestations of goodwill, German ambitions were now directed primarily eastwards. As evidence of this situation Litvinov pointed to the German refusal to participate in a Soviet-German guarantee of the Baltic States and the recent decision to reject the East-European Pact of mutual guarantee. Litvinov stressed the need for the major powers to enlist in further security measures:

> I do not regard mutual assistance as a real guarantee of defence but rather as a deterrent; as a last resort the Soviet Union has to rely upon her own forces. But if Germany knew that she would find ranged against her a coalition composed of a number of states she might hesitate to risk her fate.[110]

Eden was in full agreement but stressed that this must be achieved through the League of Nations and that Britain would be unlikely to contemplate a guarantee to areas of Eastern Europe which were not of strategic importance to Britain. Such a move, Eden argued, would appear as if Britain were intent upon dividing Europe into rival camps.[111] However, he did hint that perhaps, as a result of the Berlin conversations, Britain could not continue to play the role of honest broker indefinitely:

> The British public was not anti-German at present. But it would be opposed to any country which showed the intention of breaking the peace. A great many people in England thought that French rigidity had helped Hitler's rise. People in England were neither pro-French nor anti-German. If they were finally convinced that Germany intended to break the peace they would align themselves accordingly.[112]

The following day Eden was scheduled to meet Stalin. He obviously approached the interview with some trepidation and, despite Stalin's objections, insisted that Viscount Chilston, the British Ambassador to Moscow, be a party to the discussion. As he later noted he thought it wise to have an 'authoritative witness' to the interview.[113] His fears, however, turned out to be largely groundless. The same suspicion of German ambitions in Eastern Europe and Japanese expansion in the Far East was the main theme of their discussion, although Stalin was more pessimistic than Litvinov and at one juncture described the international situation as 'alarming', comparing it to the tension that existed in 1913. In reply to Eden's remark that the creation of the League of Nations had been a step forward in international relations, Stalin declared:

while he agreed as to the value of the League, he thought international situation was nevertheless fundamentally worse. In 1913 there was only one potential aggressor — Germany — today there were two, Germany and Japan.[114]

While Eden noted that the sale of the Chinese Eastern Railway had stabilised the position in the Far East, Stalin replied that it would only stem Japanese ambitions temporarily. With reference to Germany he argued that the desire to redress the settlement imposed on Germany by the Treaty of Versailles would almost certainly lead Germany to acts of aggression. The League of Nations was too weak to contain Germany and, therefore, it was necessary to work towards the establishment of a network of regional pacts of mutual assistance: 'Germany must be made to realise that if she attacked any other nation she would have Europe against her.'[115] Stalin emphasised the central role that Britain could play in a system of collective security: 'that little island if she chooses can stop Germany by refusing those raw materials without which she cannot pursue aggressive designs.'[116] With reference to the German offer of bilateral non-aggression pacts, Stalin noted: 'that rather than help to keep the peace Hitler might prefer to make a profit out of the differences of others.'[117]

Stalin expressed particular disappointment at British foreign policy which he claimed was hesitant and undecided. Eden replied that perhaps such an outward impression was inevitable given that British policy-makers were constantly forced to take account of a variety of conflicting factors, ranging from public opinion to global defence commitments.

In his report to London, Eden registered his impressions of Stalin:

Stalin showed in the course of this conversation a remarkable knowledge and understanding of international affairs.

Impression left upon us was of a man of strong oriental traits of character with unshakeable assurance and control, whose courtesy in no way hid from us an implacable ruthlessness.[118]

Eden could not conceal a grudging admiration for the Soviet dictator during the two days of discussions and official engagements in Moscow. Lord Strang appears to have been similarly impressed:

Of all the dictators, Stalin was, in personal intercourse seemingly most like a normal human being. Since his power rested, not on the spell binding of the masses but on the manipulation of an all pervading, inquisitional and fear producing regime, he could dispense with the exercise of that sense of the theatre to which Hitler and Mussolini so consistently had recourse . . . .[119]

Eden was also pleased to note that both Stalin and Litvinov continually stressed the desire of the Soviet Union to co-operate actively in collective security, although he appreciated that a major gulf still existed between Hitler and Stalin on the format of an East-European security pact. If his mission had achieved nothing else, Eden considered that it had made a major contribution to the reduction of the suspicion surrounding Stalin's analysis of British policy goals.[120] This appeared to be confirmed by a report from the British Ambassador to Moscow on 5 April 1935:

> A very good impression here had undoubtedly been made by Mr. Eden's visit. Great cordiality was shown to him; and it is clear that Soviet Government regard the visit as of great importance in establishing closer contacts and full exchange of view.

> . . . Soviet Government appear to have got rid of the bogey in their minds, that we were encouraging Germany against Soviet plans for Eastern security and that a considerable section of British public opinion would even view without disfavour German expansionist adventures in Eastern Europe.[121]

Eden's schedule took him from Moscow to Warsaw and an interview with the Polish Foreign Minister, Colonel Beck, on 2 April 1935.[122] As in Moscow the conversation centred on the proposed East-European pact. Eden attempted to assuage Polish fears of Soviet expansionism by explaining that Litvinov had agreed that the provision of military assistance would not be automatic and would be strictly conditional on a request being made by the country being subject to aggression. Beck stoically defended his country's decision only to participate in a security agreement to which the Soviet Union and Germany were both a party:

> Poland was not opposed to mutual assistance as such, her policy was based upon good relations with her two great neighbours and she would not therefore enter into any arrangement which was liable to endanger those relations with either.[123]

The following day Eden reported to Sir John Simon: 'My impression is that while present regime lasts in Poland there is no likelihood of any material modification of this attitude.'[124]

The sole ray of hope was that while Beck had followed Hitler's lead in rejecting a pact of mutual assistance, he had not ruled out the possibility of Poland adhering to a multilateral pact of non-aggression under which some but not all of the signatories would be bound by an agreement of mutual assistance. If Hitler could be brought to accept this, it was possible that a solution could be found which catered for the Soviet-French desire for a mutual assistance agreement and the German—Polish insistence on going no further than pacts of non-aggression.

On 2 April 1935 Eden was granted an audience with the veteran Polish leader, Marshal Pilsudski. It was evident that Eden considered the Marshal was moving rapidly towards senility: 'a great part of the Marshal's remarks, all of which were spoken in French, were unintelligible either to myself or to the two Polish Ministers who were present.' Pilsudski repeatedly alluded to Lloyd George's error in supporting Denikin against the Bolsheviks and declared that Britain should concentrate on its primary interests in areas such as Jamaica, and not interfere in Eastern Europe. Eden concluded: 'I had the impression of a man now very feeble physically who despite his occasional flashes, of which I have given an example, was living completely in the past.'[125]

In Prague, on 4 April 1935, Eden met with the Czechoslovak Foreign Minister, Benes. It was immediately apparent that Benes considered the Polish stance was unrealistic and based upon delusions of great-power status. The Czechoslovak Foreign Minister clearly saw Germany as the immediate menace to stability in Eastern Europe and saw the German refusal of a mutual assistance agreement as indicative of Hitler's determination to regain territory in Poland and the Baltic States. Benes urged the British Government to press for the conclusion of an East-European pact of mutual assistance and emphasised the need to include the Soviet Union in any such agreement. On an ominous note he declared that if an agreement was not established the East-European states would be forced to seek security by coming to terms individually with Germany, which would be playing right into Hitler's hands.[126]

As Eden returned to London he agreed with the conclusion, outlined by Benes, that the key to the situation lay in a concerted course of action being formulated at the Anglo-Italian-French conference to be held at Stresa in the following week. However, while travelling across Germany, Eden's plane was subject to particularly bad weather which forced it to land in Cologne and the remainder of the journey had to be completed by rail and sea. It was discovered that the exertion of the flight had strained Eden's heart and on arrival in London the Lord Privy Seal was ordered to rest for six weeks.[127] His absence from the political scene during this period had important repercussions in that Eden was not able to attend the Stresa Conference with Sir John Simon as had been planned. He was particularly anxious that the Foreign Secretary should not be solely responsible for the determination of the British line and was, therefore, somewhat mollified when it was announced that Ramsay MacDonald was to be added to the British delegation.[128] The second consequence of his sudden illness was that Eden was unable to present a personal report to the Cabinet of the conclusions drawn from his discussions in Berlin, Moscow, Warsaw and Prague. Eden, therefore, had to be content with the presentation of a written summary. This report, dated 7 April 1935, commenced with the assertion that British policy should be based on a 'steady course in support of the League of Nations and of the collective peace system'. He argued that it was important to make this point clear as many of the European states were uncertain of British intentions. Much of this confusion was created by *The Times* which persistently took a line that was at variance with the policy of the British Government. Eden was particularly annoyed at an article published on 4 April 1935 which described Hitler's military demands as 'constructive proposals' and had been interpreted in many European capitals as indicative of an official government reaction:

> It is of little use for members of the Government to make long journeys if a part of the confidence they have striven to create is thus to be destroyed. If we are to pursue an effective foreign policy in Europe, it is essential that it should be made clear that *The Times*, with its defeatist leaders, does not represent His Majesty's Government.[129]

In relation to the forthcoming international conference at Stresa, Eden urged that the opportunity be taken to reaffirm Britain's dedication to upholding the Covenant of the League of Nations and to encouraging France and Italy to press on with the drafting of the Central-European pact so that it could be presented to Germany. In Eastern Europe Eden proposed that use should be made of Colonel Beck's acceptance of a multilateral non-aggression pact, within which states were given the option of concluding a network of mutual assistance agreements:

> If Germany then still persists in her refusal, the world will be the better able to judge Germany's motives.

> The greatest care should be taken to avoid any suggestion that Germany's proposed non aggression pacts are enough, since they are less in fact than the obligations all members of the League undertook towards each other and also less than the obligations which we have undertaken under Locarno.[129]

Eden hoped that the threat of diplomatic isolation would force

Germany to fall into line, but considered that a further British contribution to European security might have to be examined:

> I believe that the most fruitful line of study would be that of a European pact of mutual assistance which would be open to all nations. This might be something in the nature of the protocol of 1924,[130] but limited to Europe.

Finally he described his assessment of the European situation as 'anxious' rather than 'alarming':

> If we refuse to be scared or weakened by Germany's growing demands, if we resist the temptation to accept everything that Germany asks for as a basis of discussion between us, if for a moment we can cease to be an honest broker and become the honest facer of truths, then I am confident that there is no call to view the future with alarm. If on the other hand, we appear to the outside world to be weak and vacillating, if we allow *The Times* to continue to preach defeatism . . . then we shall encourage Germany's demands and, no less serious, encourage the weaker powers to take refuge with her in the belief that the collective peace system can never be effective because England will never play her part in its support.[129]

Eden's memorandum touched two sensitive nerve points in British foreign policy. Firstly he firmly suggested that Britain could no longer successfully pursue the role of honest broker between Germany and France. Eden was convinced that the continual escalation of German demands could only be contained if Germany was confronted with a united and determined front based upon agreement between Britain, France and Italy. The Lord Privy Seal was clearly suggesting that Britain, at the forthcoming Stresa Conference, should seek to establish a common approach to the German problem with France and Italy. Secondly Eden proposed that such a front could be constructed around a simple reaffirmation of the common dedication to uphold the Covenant of the League of Nations. However, he was aware that France in particular might consider this as insufficient and demand something further. If this proved to be the case Eden was convinced that Britain should abandon its opposition to further European commitments and, in the form of a European mutual assistance pact, be prepared to pay the price for creating a common front with France and Italy.[131]

The tentative suggestion of undertaking further military commitments to European security was a delicate subject which was not well received when Eden's report was examined by the Cabinet on 8 April

1935.[132] MacDonald expressed his fear that the establishment of a close union with France and Italy would closely resemble the alliance-building in Europe which had contributed to the outbreak of war in 1914. Neville Chamberlain, while advocating the establishment of an East-European pact of mutual assistance, was just as firm in his conviction that there was no question of Britain extending a guarantee to an area of Europe that he saw as being primarily of interest to Germany and the Soviet Union.[133] Chamberlain recorded the dilemma which confronted the Government in discerning the correct path to take:

> It is a bad situation. Simon is completely at odds with Vansittart. Eden says he and S are on the verge of breaking point, the P.M. is tired and incapable of decision or clear thought. S.B. takes no part in discussion and does not seem to be setting his mind to the problems.[134]

However, while Vansittart broadly supported Eden's conclusions, the balancing factor within the Cabinet lay primarily with the Foreign Secretary. On returning from Berlin, Simon had noted:

> The practical result of our Berlin visit is to establish that Germany greatly desires a good understanding with Britain, but that she is determined to go her own course in rearmament; that she expects in time to get all Germans within her borders, including Austria; that she does not fear isolation and has no intention of joining in collective security . . . .[135]

Simon therefore concluded that Hitler had certain fixed goals and that, short of war, there was little point in attempting to bully or cajole Germany into a system of collective security. Rather than dividing Europe into two armed camps, the Foreign Secretary was in favour of attempting to continue the search for agreement with Germany in areas of mutual interest to reinforce the general format of collective security. Simon, therefore, firmly advocated further approaches to Germany on the subject of an air pact and also a possible naval agreement.[136] This attitude, which incorporated the general aversion to further European commitments, was reflected in the Cabinet debate on the line to be adopted at the Stresa Conference. It was agreed that the British delegation would go no further than reaffirming its obligations under the Treaty of Locarno and would seek to promote further examination of German participation in an air pact and the creation of an East-European non-aggression agreement, possibly supported by treaties of mutual assistance.[137] Therefore, at the Stresa Conference of 11–14 April 1935, MacDonald resolutely declined to endorse any suggestion of a European security agreement being established without German participation and confined himself merely to supporting a proposed French resolution to the Council of the League of Nations which condemned Germany's unilateral repudiation of the armament limitation levels established under the Treaty of Versailles.[138]

With the British refusal to expand upon its Locarno commitments in Europe or even to give any sort of positive indication how this commitment was to be carried out, the Stresa front was, from the outset, little more than a facade. In the following months the course of the Anglo-German naval conversations and further exploration of the format of an air pact firmly indicated that the British Government chose to continue its attempts to act as a mediator between Germany and France rather than commit itself firmly to a policy of alliance with France and Italy directed against Germany.[139] Reporting to the Cabinet on 17 April 1935, MacDonald declared:

> The main problem at Stresa had been to renew the confidence of the French and Italians in this country, which had been somewhat impaired. This had been successfully accomplished.

> In the end the French and Italian representatives had agreed to everything previously declared, and to get that result we had not to undertake any new commitment.[140]

However, whatever initial impact the Stresa front may have had on German perceptions of British policy even before the front overtly began to crumble with the signing of the Franco-Soviet Treaty and the growing tension with Italy over Abyssinia, it was evident that the problem presented by the British determination to keep open the channels of conciliation with Germany had undermined the front from its conception.

Eden's report to the Cabinet of 7 April 1935 is of significance in that it suggests he was undergoing a reassessment of his approach to the problem of European security.[141] During the course of the Disarmament Conference he had largely adopted what he saw as a pragmatic approach and had argued that an element of German rearmament was both reasonable and probably inevitable. In this sense he saw the French stance as unrealistic and a positive barrier to the attainment of an agreement. Although he spoke warmly of the French Foreign Minister, Barthou, in his memoirs, he almost certainly was relieved to see Barthou replaced by Laval in October 1934 in that the incoming Foreign Minister was known to be far more favourable to the improvement of Franco-German relations.[142]

The mounting evidence of German rearmament and the tenor of

Hitler's remarks in March 1935 seem to have convinced Eden, however, that German demands were no longer within the bounds of reason and probably heralded the opening of a campaign to increase German influence in Eastern and Central Europe. The Lord Privy Seal, therefore, appeared to be moving to the conclusion that the German military build-up could only be limited if the three major European powers, Britain, France and Italy, adopted a common front in their dealings with Hitler.[143] It is ironic that while this stance probably brought Eden into line with several of the more senior Foreign Office advisers, particularly Vansittart and Ralph Wigram, it only served to exacerbate his differences with the Foreign Secretary.[144] Sir John Simon still clung to the belief that German demands could be assimilated within a European security agreement and was firmly opposed to the placation of French fears of a revived Germany by expanding the British military commitment to Europe.[145]

Although the differences between the Foreign Secretary and the Lord Privy Seal could not be described as a major rift, Eden indicated, in a letter to Baldwin from Geneva in January 1935, his exasperation at having to work alongside Simon:

> Simon returns to London tomorrow . . . I can hardly tell him without offence, but in truth once he has gone away it is really easier for the man left in charge who has all the threads in his hand to carry on, than to make another change. It is really not easy with the best will in the world to work here double handed.[146]

Eden was particularly disappointed that Simon had not used the Stresa Conference to provide a resolute British lead in the containment of Germany. On 28 April 1935 he recorded in his diary: 'I fear that J.S. is uncertain which way to turn. Vansittart drives him this way, but J.S. is reluctant to travel. Yet he clings to the F.O. It is an unhappy situation for us all.'[147]

The matter, however, was not allowed to fester. Ramsay MacDonald's health had been steadily deteriorating for some time and it was finally decided that he would exchange ministerial positions with Baldwin in June 1935.[148] It was obvious that Baldwin would want to reshuffle the Cabinet and when Simon offered to vacate the Foreign Office in favour of the Home Office, there was great speculation as to the selection of his replacement. Eden's claim to the position was not inconsequential for although he had not achieved full Cabinet status, he had been closely involved in the conduct of foreign affairs throughout the life of the National Government. Certainly few European diplomats could match his record of having met Hitler,

Mussolini and Stalin, while Baldwin must have been aware that Eden's association with the League of Nations might have made his appointment a popular one and perhaps an important electoral asset. Although some had tried to dismiss Eden with unkind tags such as 'the Noel Coward of international politics',[149] it was evident that his candidature for the post was widely supported. In May 1935 *The Spectator* had referred to Eden as the one man 'who has stood out with courage and consistency for the translation of ideals of the post war peace system'.[150] It is conceivable that both Eden's lack of years and his recent bout of ill-health may have mitigated against his appointment but he had a strong following within the younger element of the Conservative Party, several of whom wrote to Baldwin urging his appointment.[151] However, by mid-May it appeared that Baldwin had established a preference for Sir Samuel Hoare, the Secretary of State for India, who had recently enhanced his reputation as a skilful negotiator by piloting the India Bill through the House of Commons.[152] On 16 May 1935 Baldwin asked Eden whether he would consider staying on as second-in-command at the Foreign Office. Eden pointed out that it would create difficulties: 'I held a certain point of view in foreign affairs, the country knew it, foreigners knew it. I could not after all these years, usefully play second to a new chief.'[153]

There is a suggestion that this interview momentarily swung the issue in Eden's favour as Baldwin was determined to retain Eden's expertise at the Foreign Office. However, Hoare had powerful allies the foremost of whom, Neville Chamberlain, noted in his diary on 17 May 1935: 'I suggested S. Hoare, S.B. said he was afraid he was too exhausted by his recent illness following his labours over the India Bill. He thought of giving him a Ministry without portfolio.' To which Chamberlain responded: 'I shouldn't be surprised if he took that very badly and thought you were trying to shelve him. You had better let me sound him out first.'[154]

Following Chamberlain's assurance that Hoare was physically fit and anxious to accept the Foreign Office, Baldwin, although determined to retain Eden at the Foreign Office, decided to offer the post to Hoare.[155] He appreciated that Hoare's greater experience and widespread support amongst the senior echelons of the party provided a far stronger case for his candidature than that of the young and inexperienced Anthony Eden. However, it would seem that Chamberlain had exaggerated his impression of Hoare's determination to obtain the post for when offered the choice between the position of Foreign Secretary and that of Viceroy of India by Baldwin on 2 June 1935, Hoare stated his preference for the latter. This caused Baldwin to reassess the situation before finally offering Hoare the Foreign Office on 4 June 1935.[156] A major factor in this decision was undoubtedly Hoare's willingness for Eden to continue at the Foreign Office with elevated status. Hoare later recorded:

> In the meanwhile the older Conservatives thought Eden either too young or too emotional and wished for someone with a wider experience of the great Departments of State whilst a large section of the Press, particularly *The Times* under Geoffrey Dawson's leadership, hoped that after many years of reconciling Indian differences, I might succeed in bringing France and Germany together in Europe.[157]

Of Eden he noted:

> He had established for himself so notable a position both in Geneva and Westminster that his loss would have been very serious to the world at large as well as to Great Britain. I myself was most anxious that he should not leave the Foreign Office. Baldwin agreed with me . . . .[158]

On the morning of 5 June 1935 Eden was told by Hankey that MacDonald was certain Eden would be the next Foreign Secretary.[159] It therefore came as a bitter pill when, in the afternoon of the same day, Baldwin broke the news that Hoare was to be Foreign Secretary. Eden was to be offered the elevated status of Minister for League of Nations Affairs and a seat in the Cabinet. Baldwin argued that the workload was so heavy in the Foreign Office that two men were needed. Eden immediately objected to the scheme: 'I did not like the plan of two Ministers in the Cabinet each with a responsibility for foreign affairs. I did not believe that it would work, there would be the danger of conflicting advice.'[160] He suggested that he be given one of the Service Ministries but Baldwin was adamant that Eden discuss the matter with Hoare before a further decision was taken. As Eden later noted: 'I did not feel that he had understood my predicament.'[161] Of the meeting between Eden and Hoare, Hoare later recorded:

> Eden and I had a friendly meeting, and all that seemed to be needed was a formula that, while avoiding the creation of a dyarchy within the Foreign Office, gave the assistant Minister a definite sphere of work and an adequate status in the Government.[162]

Eden's account of the interview candidly admits that neither was particularly enamoured by the arrangement and it was agreed to ask Baldwin for a more specific delineation of their relative positions.[163] Baldwin, however, refused to mediate and, on 7 June 1935, publicly announced Eden's appointment as Minister Without Portfolio, although the title was subsequently changed to Minister for League of Nations Affairs.[164] On 10 June 1935 Baldwin declared in a radio broadcast that the post had been created 'in order to give a special emphasis to the importance which H.M.G. attached to our membership of the League of Nations'.[165]

For Eden to have refused the post after this fanfare of publicity would have been a major embarrassment to the Government. He appreciated that there was little alternative but to attempt to establish a working relationship with Hoare. The basis of this relationship was established at a further meeting with Hoare, but Eden subsequently observed:

> I felt that I knew what was needed in British foreign policy and I could not help realising that the Foreign Office would have been glad to see me appointed.
>
> I cannot blame myself for accepting the arrangements. I was relatively very junior and had no taste for blackmailing my colleagues, or even being thought to do so.[166]

In accepting the post Eden was undoubtedly influenced by the fact that Baldwin urged him to accept the compromise and probably both men appreciated that if all went well Eden's future claim to the position of Foreign Secretary was almost indisputable, although neither can have realised that events would lead to Eden gaining the post in little less than seven months' time.

References

1   *CAB* 23/80, CC 37(34)2, 29 October 1934.
2   The Defence Requirements Committee (DRC) was a Subcommittee of the CID, set up by a Cabinet decision of 15 November 1933 on the recommendation of the CID. The body, which consisted of Hankey, Vansittart, Warren Fisher and the Chiefs of Staff, was charged with preparing a programme to meet 'our worst deficiencies' and met eleven times before submitting its report on 7 March 1934. See *CAB* 23/77, CC 62(33)5 and *CAB* 23/78, CC 8(34)3, CC 9(34)13 and CC 10(34)3. For full details of individual meetings of the DRC see *CAB* 16/109.
3   Report of the DRC submitted to Cabinet as CP 64(34). See *CAB* 23/78, CC 10(34)3.
4   Even Hankey was surprised by the enormity of the task and noted in his diary for 4 March 1934 'Our Bill amounts to the staggering figure of £60 million in 5 years (apart from naval construction) and £82 millions over 8 or 9 years'. *Hankey Papers*, 1/7.
5   Hankey resisted their protests on the grounds that the Committee's brief was only to meet 'our worst deficiencies'. See Roskill, vol. 3, pp. 103–4, Vansittart, p. 443 and Ian Colvin, *Vansittart in Office* (London, 1965), p. 116.

6   *CAB* 23/78, CC 8(34)3, 7 March 1934.

7   Chamberlain made his position clear from the outset when, during Cabinet discussion of the DRC report on 19 March 1934 he stressed the need to improve relations with Japan in order to concentrate resources against Germany. On this point he clashed and apparently overcame objections from Simon who argued that the 'German menace, if it developed, was more likely to be to the East and South than to the West'. See *CAB* 23/78, CC 9(34)13 and CC 10(34)3, 19 March 1934. For Chamberlain's account of the Cabinet Subcommittee on Disarmament see *Chamberlain Papers*, NC 2/23A, diary entries for 26 April 1934, 3 May 1934, 6 June 1934 and 31 July 1934. Eden, in his memoirs, makes only a cursory reference to his participation on the Committee and claimed that he was in favour of the final proposals. Avon, pp. 96–7.

8   The report of the Ministerial Committee on Disarmament (CP 205(34)) was approved by the Cabinet on 31 July 1934. See *CAB* 23/79, CC 31(34)1.

9   In a memorandum on 'The present and future position in Europe', submitted to Sir J. Simon on 28 August 1934, Sir R. Vansittart had plainly outlined his belief that Hitler eventually intended to control the European mainland. See *DBFP*, 2nd ser., vol. 5, no. 371.

10   *H of C*, Debs, 5's, vol. 292, cols 2325–2444. With this speech Baldwin tacitly admitted the veracity of Chamberlain's claim that the power of the Air Force forced Britain to take steps to ensure that Belgium and Holland did not come under the control of a hostile power. See Report of the Ministerial Committee on Disarmament (CP 205(34)) and *Chamberlain Papers*, NC/23A, diary entry for 6 June 1934.

11   Avon, pp. 96–7.

12   Ibid., pp. 96–7. See also Eden's speech at Kenilworth on 28 June 1934. Anthony Eden, *Foreign Affairs* (London, 1939), pp. 30–1.

13   Eden's argument was based on the assertion that disarmament had to be a collective measure. Unilateral disarmament would do little but imperil the security of the nation. See Eden's Kenilworth speech, 28 June 1934, *Foreign Affairs*, pp. 30–1.

14   Eden added to this report 'Consultation if it was to have any meaning must pre-suppose readiness to take action'. He was, however, obviously clear in his own mind that the Cabinet had no intention of becoming directly involved in central European affairs. *DBFP*, 2nd ser., vol. 12, no. 97, Mr Patteson (Geneva) to Sir J. Simon (no. 75 LN [R 5129/37/3]), Geneva, 18 September 1934.

15   Simon advised Eden to pursue 'delaying tactics' in a despatch dated 20 September 1934 (*DBFP*, 2nd ser., vol. 12, no. 101). However, the full Cabinet did not discuss the Austrian situation until the first Cabinet following the summer recess on 25 September 1934. At this meeting the Cabinet accepted a recommendation by the Foreign Secretary that Britain refuse to accept any new commitments in respect to Austria and take no part in Franco-Italian discussions on the matter. See *CAB* 23/79, CC 32(34)1 and *DBFP*, 2nd ser., vol. 12, no. 108.

16   As instructed by Simon, Eden urged Aloisi and Massigli to include Yugoslavia in any Franco-Italian discussion on Austria in order to defuse possible Italo-Yugoslavian rivalry. See *DBFP*, 2nd ser., vol. 12, no. 104. It was plain that Britain had no intention of making an advance on the declaration of 17 February 1934 by Britain, France and Italy agreeing 'the necessity of maintaining Austria's independence and integrity in accordance with the relevant treaties'. See *DBFP*, 2nd ser., vol. 6, no. 290.

17   Under the terms of the Treaty of Versailles the Saar territory was surrendered by Germany and placed under the administration of the League of Nations

for 15 years. A plebiscite to be held in January 1935 was designed to determine the future status of the Saar. See F.P. Walters, *A History of the League of Nations* (London,1969), pp. 89—90.

18   See Simon's despatch to Eden of 20 November 1934, *DBFP*, 2nd ser., vol. 12, no. 198 (no. 109 LN [C 7762/74/18]). There were also fears for Sir Geoffrey Knox's life and in October 1934 two officers of the Metropolitan Police Force were despatched to act as a bodyguard. See *DBFP*, 2nd ser., vol. 12, no. 75 (3 September 1934) and no. 77 (5 September 1934).

19   See Avon, p. 101; Temperley, pp. 283—93; and *DBFP*, 2nd ser., vol. 12, no. 103, 21 September 1934.

20   See Cabinet Minutes for 21 November 1934, *CAB* 28/80, CC 41(34)1, also *DBFP*, 2nd ser., vol. 12, no. 137 (12 October 1934) and no. 152 (25 October 1934).

21   For a record of this discussion see *DBFP*, 2nd ser., vol. 12, no. 207 (no. 104 LN [C 7935/74/18]), Geneva, 23 November 1934.

22   Avon, pp. 100—7.

23   *CAB* 23/80, CC 43(34)3, 28 November 1934.

24   Avon, pp. 103—4.

25   Ibid., pp. 103—4.

26   *CAB* 23/80, CC 45(34)2, 5 December 1934. An account of the instructions given to Eden can be found in *DBFP*, 2nd ser., vol. 12, no. 251, 4 December 1934.

27   Eden quickly secured the approval of France, Germany and Italy, *DBFP*, 2nd ser., vol. 12, nos 255, 260 and 262.

28   Avon, pp. 104—5.

29   *DBFP*, 2nd ser., vol. 12, no. 269, Geneva, 7 December 1934.

30   *DBFP*, 2nd ser., vol. 12, nos 270 and 276, 7 December 1934.

31   *Neville Chamberlain Papers*, NC2/23A, diary entry for 9 December 1934.

32   On 10 October 1934 the Cabinet expressed its concern that Italy might attempt to exploit the instability that would be created in Yugoslavia as a result of the King's death. *CAB* 23/80, CC 34(34).

33   Avon, p. 110.

34   For an account of these negotiations see Avon, pp. 111—19 and Temperley, pp. 295—8.

35   Temperley, p. 298.

36   Eden admitted that his role of *rapporteur* was greatly assisted by the work of the French and Italian delegates, Laval and Aloisi, in pressurising their respective allies to 'resolve the more stubborn difficulties', Avon, p. 117; also *DGFP*, ser. C, vol. 3, no. 396, 19 December 1934.

37   Although Joachim von Ribbentrop was not officially given the position of Ambassador to the Reich until 1935, Hitler had used him as a roving ambassador on several occasions in 1934. For an account of his interview with Eden, see *DBFP*, 2nd ser., vol. 12, no. 181, 12 November 1934.

38   *The Times*, 14 November 1934.

39   *H of C*, Debs, 5's, vol. 293, cols 1938—9, 14 November 1934. On 15 November 1934 MacDonald rejected von Ribbentrop's overtures for an interview. See *DBFP*, 2nd ser., vol. 12, no. 197.

40   See *DBFP*, vol. 12, no. 181 and *DGFP*, ser. C, vol. 3, no. 333.

41   Avon, pp. 89—90.

42   CID Papers, nos 1150B, 1151B, 1152B and GR (34)2 submitted to Cabinet on 21 November 1934. See *CAB* 23/80, CC 41(34)2.

43   The Cabinet Committee on German Rearmament consisting of MacDonald, Hailsham, Simon and Hoare met on 22 and 25 November 1934 and submitted its

report to the Cabinet on 26 November 1934, CP 265(34), *CAB* 23/80, CC 42(34)2. See also *DGFP*, ser. C, vol. 3, no. 356.
44   *DBFP*, 2nd ser., vol. 12, no. 208, Memoranda by Sir E. Phipps on German Rearmament (C 80 14/20/18), 23 November 1934.
45   See *DBFP*, 2nd ser., vol. 12, nos 7 and 94.
46   *DBFP*, 2nd ser., vol. 12, nos 216 and 217, Berlin, 27 November 1934.
47   Eden minute dated 28 November 1934 on Phipps despatch of 27 November 1934 warning the Foreign Office that Hitler intended to use the Franco-Soviet *entente* as justification for rearmament. *DBFP*, 2nd ser., vol. 12, no. 222.
48   *DBFP*, 2nd ser., vol. 12, no. 235, Note by Secretary of State for Foreign Affairs, 29 November 1934.
49   Report of Cabinet Committee on Rearmament of Germany (CP 295(34)) submitted to Cabinet on 12 December 1934, *CAB* 23/80, CC 46(34)3.
50   *CAB* 23/80, CC 46(34)3.
51   See *DBFP*, 2nd ser., vol. 12, nos 156 and 288. Laval argued that Anglo-French discussions at that juncture would appear as though France was being pressurised into accepting German rearmament by the British Government.
52   *CAB* 23/80, CC 47(34)4, 19 December 1934.
53   *DBFP*, 2nd ser., vol. 12, no. 311 (R 7279/5311/67). Résumé of a conversation at Quai d'Orsay between M. Flandin, M. Laval and M. Leger and Sir J. Simon, Sir G. Clerk and Mr Campbell, 22 December 1934.
54   Vansittart warned Corbin that the coming months would be the last opportunity to obtain a suitable armament settlement with Germany. *DBFP*, 2nd ser., vol. 12, no. 306, record of Vansittart—Corbin conversation held on 14 December 1934.
55   At this meeting Eden plainly stated the British position: 'If it was possible to secure an agreement which brought a measure of appeasement to Europe while limiting the extent of German rearmament, surely this was highly desirable.' Vansittart endorsed this determination at least to elicit from Germany a statement of demands in a Minute on Eden's report, 'Everyone will at least know then where they are'. *DBFP*, 2nd ser., vol. 12, no. 331, Geneva, 11 January 1935.
56   *Baldwin Papers*, vol. 123, ff. 170—4, Eden to Baldwin, Geneva, 11 January 1935.
57   *DBFP*, 2nd ser., vol. 12, no. 331, Geneva, 11 January 1935. In an interview with Von Hoesch, the German Ambassador to London, on 19 December 1934, Eden had emphasised that if Germany accepted the Eastern pact it would encourage France to grant equality of armaments and neutralise the threat of a Franco-Soviet alignment. By emphasising the extent of Anglo-French co-operation over the Saar issue Eden sought to dispel German suspicions that there were serious divisions in the Anglo-French stance. *DGFP*, ser. C, vol. 3, no. 396.
58   *DBFP*, 2nd ser., vol. 12, no. 335 (no. 6 LN [R318/1/67]), Geneva, 12 January 1935.
59   The essential concessions to France were, therefore, to be:

(1)   A system of armament inspection incorporated in any disarmament convention.
(2)   Endorsement but not participation in the Central European Pact.
(3)   Reaffirmation of the defence of Belgium independence as a primary British interest.

CAB 23/81, CC 3(35)2, report on British contribution to European security, CP 6(35), paragraph 8.
60   *DBFP*, 2nd ser., vol. 12, no. 359, letter from Sir J. Simon to Sir G. Clerk (C 434/55/18), FO, 21 January 1935.

61   This report was compiled by the Foreign Office and the Service Ministries on 25 January 1935 (C 876/55/18) and was submitted to the Cabinet meeting of 30 January 1935 as CP 23(35). *CAB* 23/81, CC 6(35)3.

62   *DBFP*, 2nd ser., vol. 12, no. 367 (C 670/55/18), 24 January 1935.

63   *DBFP*, 2nd ser., vol. 12, no. 362.

64   Foreign Office Minute of 28 January 1935 on a Memorandum by Sargent on the proposed Eastern Pact dated 28 January 1935. *DBFP*, 2nd ser., vol. 12, no. 380. Orme Sargent entered the Foreign Office in 1906. Assistant Under-Secretary of State 1938–9, Deputy Under-Secretary of State, 1939–46, Permanent Under-Secretary, 1946–9.

65   For an account of the first day of the negotiations see *DBFP*, 2nd ser., vol. 12, nos 397 and 398.

66   Vansittart argued that the air convention could satisfy French security fears without expanding on Britain's present security commitments. See *DBFP*, 2nd ser., vol. 12, no. 388. Memorandum on a possible mutual guarantee treaty against air attack (C 1190/55/18), FO, 29 June 1935. Also Sir J. Simon's minute dated 31 January 1935 on Vansittart's memorandum.

67   While Vansittart sought to incorporate the air pact within Locarno, Sir John Simon unsuccessfully urged the Cabinet to accept it as a separate entity which could be used to draw Britain, Germany and France together in an arms agreement which, hopefully, would be the forerunner of land and sea agreements. See *DBFP*, 2nd ser., vol. 12, no. 399, note by Sir J. Simon (C 892/55/18), FO, 1 February 1935. Presented to the Cabinet as CP 34(35).

68   For a record of the Cabinet discussion see *CAB* 23/81, CC 7(35), 2 February 1935.

69   For the second day of the negotiations see *DBFP*, 2nd ser., vol. 12, no. 400. As on the first day the British delegation was composed of Ramsay MacDonald, Stanley Baldwin, Sir John Simon and Anthony Eden. The delegation was assisted by Sir R. Vansittart, Sir Maurice Hankey, Ralph Wigram, Orme Sargent and Oliver Harvey. The text of the final communiqué is also contained in *Baldwin Papers*, vol. 123, ff. 165–8.

70   *Hankey Papers*, diary entry for 10 February 1935. See Hankey Papers 1/7.

71   Ibid., loc. cit. Hankey was particularly annoyed that the Cabinet had accepted a scheme for an air pact on 2 February 1935 without waiting for a report from the Chiefs of Staff.

72   *Hankey Papers*, diary entry for 24 February 1935. At a meeting of Ministerial Committee on Disarmament on 19 February 1935 Hankey condemned the terms of the air pact. The Foreign Office reply to his criticisms was received on 21 February 1935. Although the CID, on 25 February 1935 (268th Meeting, see *CAB* 2/6), did not endorse Hankey's report it appears that the air pact was effectively dismissed as a viable project by the end of the month, largely in response to criticism by the Defence Departments. See Hankey 1/7.

73   *DBFP*, 2nd ser., vol. 12, no. 446, Sir E. Phipps to Sir J. Simon (no. 51 [C 1216/55/18]), Berlin, 14 February 1935.

74   *DBFP*, 2nd ser., vol. 12, nos 477 and 479, FO, 21 February 1935.

75   The mission was particularly important for, by insisting on Anglo-German negotiations, Hitler threatened to drive a wedge between Britain and France. See *DBFP*, 2nd ser., vol. 12, no. 517, record of Anglo-French conversations (C 1657/55/18), Paris, 28 February 1935.

76   Vansittart's views were expressed in a letter to Viscount Chilston at the Moscow Embassy. See *DBFP*, 2nd ser., vol. 12, no. 485, letter by Sir R. Vansittart to Viscount Chilston (C 1339/55/18), FO, 21 February 1935.

77   MacDonald was against the Moscow mission because he considered it would involve Britain in East-European rivalries and diminish the effect of the Berlin negotiations, see *DBFP*, 2nd ser., vol. 12, no. 515 (C 1720/55/18). The Moscow mission was, however, supported by Neville Chamberlain who claimed that it was his suggestion to lighten the workload on the Foreign Secretary by sending Eden to the Soviet Union. See *Neville Chamberlain Papers*, diary entry for 8 March 1935, NC 2/23A.

78   Thomas Jones, *A Diary with Letters 1931–1950* (London, 1954), p. 139.

79   *DBFP*, 2nd ser., vol. 12, no. 524, Sir E. Phipps to Sir J. Simon (no. 86 [C 1759/55/18]), Berlin, 5 March 1935.

80   Defence White Paper dated 1 March 1935, issued as Cmnd 4827 on 4 March 1935 and presented on 11 March 1935 to the House of Commons. Following Cabinet discussion of 25 February 1935 (*CAB* 23/81, CC 11(35)1) the paper was redrafted by MacDonald, Baldwin, Chamberlain and Hankey to move the emphasis away from the question of Continental commitments to the need to remedy defensive deficiencies. The main accent was placed on the need to increase expenditure on all three services. It was suspected that Hitler took exception to the observations on the dramatic increase in German youth organisations which Eden described as 'rougher stuff than anything that had been officially written of German behaviour hitherto' and was probably engineered by Vansittart and Warren Fisher (see Vansittart, pp. 507–12; Avon, p. 126).

81   *DBFP*, 2nd ser., vol. 12, no. 526, Sir E. Phipps to Sir J. Simon (no. 88 [C 1774/55/18]), Berlin, 5 March 1935.

82   See *CAB* 23/81, CC 13(35)2, 6 March 1935, also *Neville Chamberlain Papers*, diary entry for 8 March 1935, NC 2/23A. The Cabinet agreed that the mission to Moscow and Warsaw would continue and be undertaken by Eden. Eden claimed that the details had been settled on 4 March 1935 at a meeting with MacDonald, Simon, Baldwin and Vansittart (Avon, pp. 125–6).

83   *DBFP*, 2nd ser., vol. 12, no. 549, Sir E. Phipps to Sir J. Simon (no. 102 [C 1922/55/18]), Berlin, 9 March 1935.

84   Eden outlined his thoughts in a Minute dated 15 March 1935. See *DBFP*, 2nd ser., vol. 12, no. 568, Minute by Mr Eden (C 1818/55/18), FO, 15 March 1935. Throughout this period Eden held the conviction that Britain had missed its opportunity to forge an agreement the previous year following his visit to Berlin in January 1935. He minuted, 'I have for long past feared that the last chance of an agreement with Germany was on the basis of Hitler's February offer. The French however did not look at it, nor did we endeavour to make them do so — but all that is spilt milk.' Avon, p. 124.

85   *DBFP*, 2nd ser., vol. 12, no. 565, letter from Sir E. Phipps to Mr Sargent (C 2070/55/18), Berlin, 14 March 1935.

86   *DBFP*, 2nd ser., vol. 12, no. 570, Sir E. Phipps to Sir J. Simon (no. 110 [C 2121/55/18]), Berlin, 16 March 1935.

87   The note was drafted by Simon and approved by the Cabinet on 18 March 1935. *CAB* 23/81, CC 15(35), see appendix of the meeting for the text of the note.

88   The French were informed of the contents of the note but were not consulted or asked for their approval. *DBFP*, 2nd ser., vol. 12, no. 600, 18 March 1935. The Paris Embassy reported on 19 March 1935 that Laval was annoyed by this course of action, *DBFP*, 2nd ser., vol. 12, no. 603, similar protest from Rome, *DBFP*, 2nd ser., vol. 12, no. 604.

89   Simon defended his action in a Minute dated 31 March 1935 on a despatch from Rome dated 19 March 1935. See *DBFP*, 2nd ser., vol. 12, no. 604.

90 Minute by Sir R. Vansittart on the above dated 19 March 1935. *DBFP*, 2nd ser., vol. 12, no. 604.

91 It was also decided that in Berlin Eden and Simon should argue that German policy was threatening to divide Europe into two armed camps and that acceptance of the East European pact and arms limitation was necessary to revive an atmosphere of co-operation and stability, *CAB* 23/81, CC 16(35)1, 20 March 1935.

92 *DBFP*, 2nd ser., vol. 12, no. 625, Sir E. Phipps to Sir J. Simon (no. 133 [C 2334/55/18]), Berlin, 21 March 1935. This was a significant reversal of attitude for Phipps had originally opposed the visit on the grounds that Hitler was implacably opposed to the Eastern Pact, *DBFP*, 2nd ser., vol. 12, no. 490.

93 Avon, p. 131.

94 For an account of the meetings with Laval and Suvich, Italian Under-Secretary of State for Foreign Affairs, see *DBFP*, 2nd ser., vol. 12, nos 641, 642 and 643. Eden also had an interview with Flandin and was particularly struck by his concern for the future status of the Rhineland. *DBFP*, 2nd ser., vol. 12, no. 645. Vansittart minuted on this despatch, on 26 March 1935, 'H.M.G. will have to make up their mind on this and very quickly too. It is a most disagreeable necessity . . . .' See also Avon, pp. 132—3.

95 Avon, p. 133.

96 Lord Strang, *Home and Abroad* (London, 1956), p. 66.

97 For an account of these interviews see *DBFP*, 2nd ser., vol. 12, nos 650, 651 and 656. The German version is given in *DGFP*, ser. C, vol. III, no. 555. Eden's account is given in Avon, pp. 133—41.

98 *DBFP*, 2nd ser., vol. 12, no. 651.

99 Diary entry for 25 March 1935, Avon, p. 138.

100 Avon, pp. 138—9.

101 *DBFP*, 2nd ser., vol. 12, no. 651.

102 Ibid.

103 A remark by Hitler to which Eden took particular exception and protested but with little result — 'My protests were disregarded as patriotic deception.' Avon, p. 140.

104 *DBFP*, 2nd ser., vol. 12, no. 651. During the negotiations Eden had been particularly disturbed by the growing evidence that Hitler's ambitions were moving even further ahead. On undertaking the mission to Berlin Eden had expected to encounter difficulties on armament limitation and the Eastern pact, but Hitler had also raised the question of the return of former German colonies as a precondition for Germany's return to the League of Nations. Avon, pp. 137—8.

105 *DBFP*, 2nd ser., vol. 12, no. 656, Viscount Chilston (Moscow) to Sir J. Simon (no. 45 [C 2593/55/18]), Moscow, 28 March 1935. Also included in Avon, pp. 142—3.

106 *DBFP*, 2nd ser., vol. 12, no. 485, 21 February 1935.

107 See Avon, p. 162.

108 *DBFP*, 2nd ser., vol. 12, nos 655 and 659.

109 For an account of this interview see *DBFP*, 2nd ser., vol. 12, no. 673, Viscount Chilston to Sir J. Simon (no. 139 [C 2726/55/18]), Moscow, 30 March 1935. See also Avon, pp. 145—52.

110 Avon, p. 148.

111 This section of the conversation was in response to a suggestion by Litvinov that Britain could assist in the stabilisation of Eastern Europe by guaranteeing the integrity of the Baltic States which the Soviet Commissar for Foreign Affairs identified as Hitler's next target. *DBFP*, 2nd ser., vol. 12, no. 673.

112 Ibid.

113   Avon, p. 152.

114   For an account of the interview with Stalin see Avon, pp. 156–60 and *DBFP*, 2nd ser., vol. 12, nos 669 and 670. The interview took place on 29 March 1935.

115   *DBFP*, 2nd ser., vol. 12, no. 670, Viscount Chilston to Sir J. Simon (no. 49 [C 2690/55/18]), Moscow, 30 March 1935.

116   Ibid.

117   Ibid.

118   *DBFP*, 2nd ser., vol. 12, no. 670, Moscow, 30 March 1935. By the end of the interview his initial apprehension appeared to have been completely overcome. Indeed, in a later report to Sir J. Simon concerning an allegation by Göring that Eden had given an 'unsatisfactory' answer to an enquiry about Britain's determination to assist Germany if it were attacked by France, Eden replied, 'This is a grim warning never to jest with a German but I must warn you that Stalin and I cracked several this afternoon.' *DBFP*, 2nd ser., vol. 12, no. 667 (no. 47 [C 2663/55/18]), Moscow, 29 March 1935.

119   Strang, p. 67.

120   Avon, p. 162. However, in a report to London dated 28 March 1935, Eden conceded that Litvinov 'was clearly in doubt as to what to do next in Eastern Europe'. The only positive contribution was the apparent Soviet commitment to collective security as a means of containing German ambitions. *DBFP*, 2nd ser., vol. 12, no. 656.

121   *DBFP*, 2nd ser., vol. 12, no. 695, Viscount Chilston to Sir J. Simon (no. 55 [C 2892/55/18]), Moscow, 5 April 1935.

122   For a full account of this interview see *DBFP*, 2nd ser., vol. 12, no. 689 (C 2890/55/18), Warsaw, 2–3 April 1935.

123   *DBFP*, 2nd ser., vol. 12, no. 684, Sir H. Hennard to Sir J. Simon (no. 23 [C 2893/55/18]), Warsaw, 3 April 1935.

124   Ibid., loc. cit. See also Avon, pp. 165–8.

125   This interview was a great disappointment to Eden who had thought of the veteran Polish leader as still 'the authority which took the vital decisions', Avon, p. 168. It was obvious that Colonel Beck largely determined Polish foreign policy. *DBFP*, 2nd ser., vol. 12, no. 683 (no. 24 [C 2796/55/18]), Warsaw, 3 April 1935. See also Avon, pp. 168–9.

126   *DBFP*, 2nd ser., vol. 12, no. 693. Record of Anglo-Czechoslovak conversation held at Ministry of Foreign Affairs, Prague, on 4 April 1935 (C 2930/55/18). See also Avon, pp. 172–4.

127   For an account of this journey see Avon, pp. 174–5.

128   Eden seems to have placed little faith in the Foreign Secretary's ability to interpret information and devise a suitable policy. He later stated that Simon 'would certainly try his hardest but he once complained to me that he never knew what people were thinking. In fact, his antennae were weak.' Avon, p. 175.

129   *DBFP*, 2nd ser., vol. 12, no. 701, notes of a statement which the Lord Privy Seal had hoped to make to the Cabinet on 8 April 1935 on his return from Berlin, Moscow, Warsaw and Prague (C 2962/55/18), FO, 7 April 1935. Presented to the Cabinet of 8 April 1935 see *CAB* 23/81, CC 20(35)1, 8 April 1935.

130   A reference to the Geneva Protocol recommended by the Assembly of the League of Nations on 2 October 1924 which sought to impose compulsory arbitration on all disputes and to brand those who rejected arbitration as the aggressors. Walters, pp. 268–94.

131   Eden later claimed that there was a strong element in the Cabinet which 'would not admit that Hitler would only be willing to talk business if the nations who were opposed to Germany's repeated acts of defiance could join in firm

resistance' (Avon, pp. 178–9). There is little doubt that Eden saw Simon as the centre of this caucus. In their assessment of the potential threat posed by Germany, Eden and Vansittart shared common ground but Eden refused to accept Vansittart's conclusion that if the choice was to be made Italian friendship should be put before loyalty to the League of Nations, Vansittart, pp. 512–23.

132 For an account of this meeting see *CAB* 23/81, CC 20(35)1, 8 April 1935.

133 Similarly the Cabinet rejected a suggestion that Britain should join with France and Italy in guaranteeing Austria independence.

134 *Neville Chamberlain Papers*, diary entry for 8 April 1935, NC 2/23A.

135 Viscount Simon, *Retrospect* (London, 1952), pp. 202–3. Simon claimed that this note was composed 'immediately after my return from Berlin'.

136 Simon had taken this line in presenting his report of the Berlin conversations to the Cabinet on 27 March 1935. See *CAB* 23/81, CC 18(35), 27 March 1935.

137 *CAB* 23/81, CC 20(35)1, 8 April 1935.

138 Simon later admitted that the British goal at Stresa was to maintain the appearance of Anglo-French-Italian solidarity while leaving the door open for Germany to return to Geneva and participate in collective security. However, while Britain was unwilling to cement the alliance by admitting and settling its differences with Italy or by agreeing to further continental commitments, the Stresa front was little more than a facade. See Simon, pp. 203–4, Vansittart, pp. 519–21 and *DBFP*, 2nd ser., vol. 12, no. 722, record of Stresa Conversations (C 3289/55/18), 11–14 April 1935.

139 The Anglo-German Naval Treaty was concluded on 18 June 1935. For an analysis of its negotiation and British policy in the first six months of 1935 see Charles Bloch, 'Great Britain, German Rearmament and the Naval Agreement of 1935' in Hans W. Gatzke (ed.), *European Diplomacy between Two Wars 1919–1939* (Chicago, 1972), pp. 125–51.

140 See *CAB* 23/81, CC 24(35)1, 17 April 1935.

141 For the text of Eden's report of 7 April 1935, see *DBFP*, 2nd ser., vol. 12, no. 701 (C 2962/55/18).

142 In *Facing the Dictators* Eden recalled that, on hearing of Barthou's death on 9 October 1934 he noted in his diary, 'Having learnt that Anglo-French co-operation had to be, he had vigour enough to make such co-operation real'. Avon, pp. 108–9. However, Eden's subsequent claim that he and Barthou had established a good working relationship is difficult to substantiate, particularly as Eden had been a vehement opponent of the East-European pact of mutual guarantee and had seen Barthou's promotion of the pact as the main obstacle to a settlement with Germany. For Eden's opinion of the Eastern pact see his letter to Baldwin of 3 June 1934, *Baldwin Papers*, vol. 122, ff. 100–1. For Eden's assessment of Laval see Avon, p. 102.

143 *DBFP*, 2nd ser., vol. 12, no. 701 (C 2962/55/18), 7 April 1935.

144 Sir Robert Vansittart was an outspoken critic of the German Government in this period, referring to the Hitler regime in June 1933 as 'fanatics, hooligans and eccentrics'. On 23 January 1934 he concluded, 'We must be prepared for Germany's refusal to accept even the fairer offers of disarmament'. *Vansittart Papers*, 2/5 and 2/14. On 4 July 1934 Ralph Wigram candidly admitted that Germany had destroyed the principle of European security which Locarno had established, *Vansittart Papers*, 2/16.

145 See Simon's comments at the Cabinet meeting of 8 April 1935. *CAB* 23/81, CC 20(35)1.

146 *Baldwin Papers*, vol. 123, ff. 165–8, Eden's letter to Baldwin, Geneva, 11 January 1935.

147   Quoted in Avon, p. 187.

148   In his diary for 24 February 1935 Hankey recorded that MacDonald had asked his advice as to the advisability of relinquishing the post of Prime Minister after the Silver Jubilee. 'On the whole I thought he would be well advised to do so. The Conservatives supply most of the votes for the National Party, and will consider themselves entitled to the office of Prime Minister. Moreover the P.M. owing to his eyes finds that he does not do well in the House — as he admitted to me. I didn't say so to him, but he is really too tired to continue.' It is interesting to note that in the same week Baldwin expressed to Hankey his doubts as to whether at the age of 68 he was fit enough to continue to lead the Conservative Party. Hankey urged him to continue but largely because as he admitted, 'I don't trust Neville Chamberlain's judgement'. *Hankey Papers*, diary entry for 24 February 1935, Hankey 1/7.

149   A quote attributed to Charles Graves, see Rees-Mogg, p. 55.

150   *The Spectator*, 22 May 1935.

151   For example see the letter from Ormsby-Gore to Baldwin, *Baldwin Papers*, vol. 47, Ormsby-Gore to Baldwin, May 1935.

152   Sir Samuel Hoare (Viscount Templewood) had been Secretary of State for India 1931—5. However, there is some evidence to suggest that Baldwin initially sounded Sir Austen Chamberlain who declined the offer of the post of Foreign Secretary, *Baldwin Papers*, vol. 47, Austen Chamberlain to Baldwin, 21 December 1935.

153   Avon, pp. 216—17.

154   *Neville Chamberlain Papers*, diary entry for 17 May 1935, NC 2/23A.

155   *Neville Chamberlain Papers*, diary entry for 17 May 1935, NC 2/23A.

156   Sir Samuel Hoare's preference for the position of Viceroy of India is noted in Middlemas and Barnes, *Baldwin, A Biography* (London, 1969), p. 822 and confirmed in Hoare's account of this conversation with Baldwin, Viscount Templewood, *Nine Troubled Years* (London, 1954), pp. 107—10 and pp. 135—6. Both sources claim that Geoffrey Dawson urged Baldwin to appoint Hoare. See Templewood, pp. 108—9, Middlemas and Barnes, p. 822, Avon, p. 219.

157   Templewood, p. 108.

158   Ibid., p. 136.

159   See Avon, p. 217 and Middlemas and Barnes, p. 823.

160   Avon, p. 217. Eden had openly stated his distaste for a dyarchy in a letter to Baldwin dated 11 January 1935. *Baldwin Papers*, vol. 123, ff. 170—4, Eden to Baldwin, 11 January 1935.

161   Avon, p. 218.

162   Templewood, p. 136.

163   Avon, p. 218. However, Hoare makes no mention of Eden's claim that 'We agreed that my acceptance of the office was only to be on a temporary basis and that we should both say so to Baldwin'.

164   When asked to further delineate their respective positions Baldwin was recorded as having told Hoare at a Cabinet meeting 'to settle direct with the young man'. Templewood, p. 136. The title of Eden's position had to be changed when the Attorney-General pointed out that a Minister Without Portfolio could not be charged with a portfolio for League of Nations Affairs.

165   Radio broadcast of 10 June 1935.

166   Avon, pp. 217—19. A letter from Austen Chamberlain to Hoare suggests that the Foreign Secretary was also unhappy with the arrangement:

> I can understand and sympathise with your feelings about the rather delicate situation created by Eden's present appointment. I do not like the

arrangement and if it works well it will only be because of the personal characteristics and relationship of Eden and yourself.

Templewood Papers, vol. VIII: 3, Austen Chamberlain to Hoare, 26 July 1935.

4 Minister for League of Nations Affairs

June — December 1935

Although Stanley Baldwin had outwardly created a dyarchy at the Foreign Office, there was little doubt that Sir Samuel Hoare was very much the senior of the two ministers. Eden's new appointment did, however, bring with it several significant improvements in his position within the Foreign Office, particularly *vis à vis* the permanent officials. As an Under-Secretary he had previously been subordinate to the Permanent Under-Secretary, Sir R. Vansittart. Their positions were now reversed and Eden was allowed to promote his own Parliamentary Private Secretary, Cranborne, to the position of Under-Secretary. Furthermore Eden's ministerial status ensured that he was privy to all official departmental despatches and memoranda. The real prize, however, was his Cabinet seat. Eden's departure from the back benches represented his acceptance within the inner circles of the Conservative Party not simply as Baldwin's protégé but as an influential figure in his own right.

Ministerial status, however, also brought with it further demands upon Eden's time. As a roving envoy for the Cabinet he had spent much of the previous two years abroad and it was only as a result of his illness, in April 1935, that he was able to take a complete break from politics. The two weeks of his convalescence with his wife and two small children at Trent Park, the home of Philip Sassoon, provided a rare opportunity to compensate for the considerable amount of time he had been forced to spend away from home.[1] For relaxation Eden turned to his passion for art and, indeed, had taken the opportunity while in Berlin and Moscow to visit several important collections of paintings.[2] It would also seem that he availed himself of the Foreign Office custom of leaving early one afternoon each week in order to play tennis.[3] The darkening international climate, however, was soon severely to curtail even this small luxury.

One of the most immediate problems confronting the Foreign Office in this period was to attempt to defuse the growing tension in Italo-Abyssinian relations. The long-standing rivalry between Abyssinia and the Italian colony of Somaliland for the control of the Ogaden province of Abyssinia had flared out into the open on 5 December 1934, with an armed clash between forces from the two nations at the Wal Wal oasis.[4] The situation was further exacerbated when, as a result of this confrontation, Italy demanded a formal Abyssinian apology, punishment of the Abyssinian officials involved and a $2000 indemnity as compensation.[5] Although by an agreement of 1906 Britain was committed, alongside France and Italy, to maintain Abyssinian territorial and political independence, from the outset the policy of the British Government was to avoid direct involvement in what was seen as a dispute over a largely barren area of territory.[6] The entire tone of British policy was set by the British Minister in Addis Ababa on 10 December 1934:

> I am quite prepared to agree that Italian policy of forceful penetration into Ethiopia is open to gravest criticism. One can also have the utmost sympathy for the Abyssinians. But on general political grounds it is essential for us to avoid a squabble with the Italians over the boundaries of Ethiopia which is why I am against dragging in the 1906 Treaty.

> It seems to me that we have two objectives, namely (1) to safeguard the watering and grazing rights of our tribes in what is admittedly an Italian zone of influence, and (2) to bring about a *détente* between Italy and Ethiopia without allowing our existing relations with either to be affected.[7]

The only point of dispute was how this *détente* was to be engineered. Sir Robert Vansittart was in favour of passing the problem to the League of Nations where it 'belongs and where it will cause least trouble to us *vis à vis* the Italians', but the Foreign Secretary appreciated the danger of laying the case before the full glare of international publicity and scrutiny at Geneva.[8] Sir John Simon, therefore, sought to mediate directly between Mussolini and the Emperor of Abyssinia,[9] but his initiative was blocked by Mussolini's insistence that the proposed $2000 indemnity be paid into a bank on Italian territory. This stipulation was unacceptable to the Emperor who now appeared determined to submit his country's case to Geneva.[10] Once again the British Government, in co-operation with France, sought to sidetrack the Abyssinians by reference to the Italo-Abyssinian agreement of 1928 to refer all disputes to arbitration. The only stumbling-block to this procedure was to ensure Italian participation and Eden was largely instrumental in pressuring Aloisi, the Italian delegate at the League of Nations, to accept the principle of direct negotiation.[11] On the basis of this agreement the Council of the League of Nations was able to defer discussion of the problem until the outcome of the arbitration was known. Although this ploy had achieved its short-term goal of confining the dispute to a purely Italo-Abyssinian affair, in a Foreign Office minute dated 30 January 1935 Eden expressed his disquiet at the long-term consequences: 'I am not quite so cheerfully confident about this and I am sure that if we do not maintain a firm front towards the Italians about this incident, it will only be the fore-runner of others.'[12]

The events of the following three weeks did little to reassure Eden. Amid increasing reports of Italian troop movements to reinforce the garrisons in Eritrea and Somaliland, the British Ministers in both Rome and Addis Ababa voiced their concern that Italy was preparing for a military campaign against Abyssinia.[13] In a Foreign Office minute dated 26 February 1935, on a despatch from the Rome Embassy, Eden recorded his growing concern at events in Abyssinia. The Minister for League of Nations Affairs noted that the Italians had not taken steps to initiate the arbitration process and, by the build-up of forces in the Italian colonies, appeared prepared to ignore the League Council resolution calling on both parties to refrain from provoking further incidents:

> Personally, I have for some time past been anxious at the drift of events in Ethiopia. It is hard to believe that Italian ambitions are limited to a few wells. It would seem now that Italy aims at no less than the absorption of Ethiopia morsel by morsel.
>
> The impression that is left on my mind by all this is, I confess, that unless some hint — and a pretty strong hint — is given to the Italians that we should not view with indifference the dismemberment of Ethiopia, then this dismemberment will take place. It may be argued that such a process is inevitable and that nothing we can say will stop it. I doubt myself whether our influence with Italy is so slight as this.[14]

As a direct result of this minute, Sir John Simon authorised a despatch to Mussolini, via the Rome Embassy, indicating Britain's concern at the build-up of Italian military forces and the recent escalation in Italian demands to Abyssinia.[15] Furthermore Vansittart, in an interview with the Italian Ambassador, Grandi, on 27 February 1935, reminded the Ambassador of his Government's agreement to seek a solution to the problem by conciliation and emphasised that adverse criticism would be provoked in Britain if Italy failed to respect its obligations under the Covenant of the League of Nations. Vansittart went on to observe that, if the Covenant was not upheld in Africa, it would severely undermine the prospect of utilising it to contain German expansion in Europe.[16] This interview was seen by Eden as being particularly important for he was convinced that the British Ambassador in Rome, Sir Eric Drummond, was far too conciliatory in his interviews with Mussolini and was failing to bring home to the Italian government the gravity of the situation.[17]

An ideal opportunity to resolve the problem appeared to be presented by the Stresa Conference of April 1935. Eden was anxious that the dispute be raised at the Conference but due to ill-health was unable to attend in person.[18] However, in the build-up to the Conference the Foreign Office reported that the Italians seemed extremely reluctant to include the Abyssinian dispute on the agenda, insisting that it was a matter for direct Italo-Abyssinian negotiations.[19] It was, perhaps, as a result of this that the Abyssinian question was not raised by the British delegation to the Conference, although Sir John Simon and Sir Robert Vansittart had certainly been well briefed on the Abyssinian question prior to the Conference and an entry in MacDonald's diary for 21 February 1935 indicated that he was alive to the danger of Italian aggression in Abyssinia:

> Italian attack on Abyssinia becomes more and more a wolf and the lamb tale.
>
> It is an irredeemable tale of calculated aggression with a plentiful adornment of assumed innocence and lies.[20]

A possible solution to the strange omission of the Abyssinian question may be found in the suggestion that the British preoccupation with the need to form a united front to contain German ambitions encouraged the British delegation to avoid discussion of a topic likely to inflame Anglo-French relations with Italy.[21] Sir Robert Vansittart's comments in a Foreign Office minute dated 23 April 1935 certainly suggest that the topic was only to be raised, at best, in an informal manner.[22] To have adopted such a stance suggests that the British Ministers either underestimated the problems and issues raised by the Abyssinian dispute, or were bent on what could be described as a Europe first strategy. Whichever was the case, it was very much at odds with Eden's perception of the situation which stressed the need for an outward display of Anglo-

French solidarity in order to deter further Italian aggression against Abyssinia.[23]

The Abyssinian issue was, however, discussed at Stresa by officials from the British and Italian Foreign Ministries.[24] A report filed by Thompson,[25] an Abyssinian affairs specialist from the Foreign Office, of his negotiations with Guarnaschelli[26] left little doubt as to Italian intentions. Thompson noted:

> On my telling him that we were rather disturbed by the widespread rumours of a possible forward military movement by the Italians against Abyssinia in September when the rains are over and that I hoped these rumours were baseless, he replied that the possibility of an offensive could not be entirely ruled out.

Thompson then informed the Italian official:

> Italy could expect no co-operation from the United Kingdom in any attack on Ethiopia; and a forward policy might be found to be inordinately expensive in blood and money, but might well react adversely upon Anglo-Italian relations.[27]

These comments were later endorsed and commended by Sir Robert Vansittart[28] and perhaps explain the toughening of the British attitude towards Italy that was perceptible in the following month.[29] The Foreign Secretary had also been disturbed by an interview with the Italian Ambassador, Grandi, on 3 May 1935:

> Grandi spoke of the situation as a cancer which had to be cut out and he conveyed in veiled though unmistakable terms that Signor Mussolini was contemplating a forward policy of the most serious dimensions.

> I expressed to him my gravest anxiety as to what would be the effect of Italy's contemplated action upon British public opinion.[30]

Eden was appalled at the weakness of the Foreign Secretary's response and registered his dismay in his diary:

> Even from his own account nothing like stiff enough. Italy's request was a diplomatically phrased demand for a free hand in Abyssinia. This should have been strenuously resisted, emphasis laid on our support of the League etc. It is useless to ask Musso how he thinks that Simon can answer questions on the subject in the House.[31]

The point of contention was the attitude to be adopted by Britain at the next meeting of the League Council, scheduled for 20 May 1935. On 11 May 1935 the Foreign Secretary submitted a memorandum to the Cabinet which, while conceding that the Italians were likely to undertake a military campaign against Abyssinia in September or October, argued that any British-sponsored action directed against Italy at the League of Nations would result in Italy leaving the organisation: 'it would in fact be hard to imagine a state of affairs which would be more welcome to Germany.'

Consequently Simon recommended that Britain continue to urge both parties to come to an amicable settlement, while privately warning Italy of the dangers of its existing policy.[32] This course of action was not wholly supported by Eden and it would appear that the Cabinet accepted his recommendation, on 15 May 1935, that Britain must also be seen to be giving full support to the authority of the League of Nations. As a result of the Cabinet meeting the Minister for League of Nations Affairs was given 'a wide discretion as to the best course to be taken' to ensure that the League of Nations took action before September to prevent the commencement of hostilities. It was also decided to recall Drummond to London 'as an indication to Signor Mussolini of how seriously His Majesty's Government was concerned with the course of events'.[33]

Eden, therefore, travelled to Geneva with Cabinet backing to insist that the League of Nations take an active interest in monitoring the Italo-Abyssinian conciliation negotiations. However, Eden's initial meeting with Aloisi on 20 May 1935 only emphasised the problems that existed:

Trend of our talk was one of ever deepening gloom.

I viewed the future with the utmost concern if Italian government were really engaged in a policy of military aggression in Ethiopia. British public opinion was really stirred on this matter already and would become more so.[34]

In a letter to Sir John Simon dated 21 May 1935 Eden gave further details of his discussion with Aloisi:

At one moment he said that we had swallowed *la couleuvre* of Manchuria; why was Abyssinia creating such difficulties? In addition to this there is of course Italy's sense of resentment that she lacks the colonies and mandated territories that others possess and her feeling that now she has an opportunity, perhaps the last, to seize the territory the possession of which would place her definitely among the Great Powers with important colonial possessions.

At the moment it is hard indeed to see any daylight in this dark business.[35]

The following day Eden felt forced to protest to Sir John Simon at Sir Eric Drummond's weak response to Mussolini's most recent demand for recognition of an Italian interest in Abyssinia comparable to that of Britain in Egypt and France in Morocco. Furthermore Mussolini had expressed his resolve to defy the League of Nations if necessary and resort to war against Abyssinia.[36] Eden telegraphed to London:

> It seems to me impossible for us to allow this statement to go unchallenged and I suggest that as a first step Mussolini should be reminded of these treaties and of obligations which we share under them.[37]

This message provoked a further angry response from Drummond, warning the Foreign Secretary that the suggested course of action by Eden would destroy the last vestiges of the Anglo-Italian relationship and propel Italy into Germany's arms.[38] Faced with these two contrasting viewpoints, Sir John Simon elected to back Eden[39] and, in an interview with the Italian Ambassador on 24 May 1935, the Foreign Secretary expressed his full support for Eden's work at Geneva and his recent attempts, in co-operation with the French, to insist that Italy accept arbitration for all Italo-Abyssinian incidents since November 1934. In addition Simon backed Eden's proposal that arbitration must be monitored by the League of Nations and be reviewed automatically at the next meeting of the League Council. In the intervening period Italy was to accept that it would not resort to arms.[40] Faced for the first time by a firm Anglo-French front the Italians capitulated and agreed to the terms.[41] In a despatch to the Foreign Secretary, Eden noted the outcome with satisfaction:

> Italian delegates, who came to Geneva with intention of tiding over immediate difficulty by persuading Council to postpone the issue and content itself with taking note of their appointments to Conciliation Committee, have been compelled to acknowledge the right of the Council to keep in touch with arbitration and to intervene should it be necessary.[42]

However, Eden was to concede that the battle was far from won: 'we have done little more than make it harder for Mussolini, in the eyes of the world at least, to proceed to extreme measures against Abyssinia.'[43]

With the accession of Sir Samuel Hoare to the position of Foreign Secretary, a thorough review was made of British policy towards the

120

Italo-Abyssinian dispute. It was increasingly apparent that Sir Robert Vansittart and Anthony Eden were at odds in relation to how the problem should be approached.[44] Eden maintained stoically that Britain must stand by its international obligations and, as he noted in a Foreign Office minute dated 13 June 1935, not 'assist the Italian government to tear up treaties'.[45] Vansittart, on the other hand, was increasingly preoccupied with the damage being done to Anglo-Italian relations and in particular the consequences for the future of Austrian independence if the Stresa front was broken. A minute drawn up by the Permanent Under-Secretary on 8 June 1935 clearly indicated that Vansittart was in favour of making 'some extensive concession' to Italy in Abyssinia as a price for restoring Anglo-Italian relations.[46] Vansittart later referred to this problem in his memoirs:

> Eden came to us as Minister for League of Nations Affairs, with Cranborne as his Parliamentary Secretary. This was a shade harder for me, because Anthony was even more S.B.'s favourite than Tom Jones; and he and I from the start had our differences, amicable but defined. Anthony and Cranborne were not only correct but straight-forward in pinning faith on the League. That was our rightful policy but I could never see the League's components tackling an aggressor of weight. So I laboured under a certain dualism which might look like duplicity.

> My real trouble was that we should all have to choose between Austria and Abyssinia, if Mussolini stuck to his mania for fame and sand.

> Mussolini soon showed that he would force just that choice on us. I hated it and him for driving a wedge between me and Eden since I necessarily appeared less whole-hearted than he for justice.[47]

Hoare appeared to stand between the two men[48] but, at a weekend meeting of the three, finally agreed to a scheme drawn up by Sir Robert Vansittart which revived a former Foreign Office plan to offer Abyssinia a corridor to the sea and a port in British Somaliland in exchange for the cession of Abyssinian territory in the Ogaden Province. The scheme was adapted so that this territory would be ceded to Italy and, it was hoped, could form the basis of a compromise solution between Italy and Abyssinia. Vansittart proposed that the plan be presented to Mussolini by Eden.[49] Although Eden was sceptical as to the reception the scheme would receive in Rome, he agreed to undertake the mission after an encouraging response from Drummond and subject to it leading to a complete settlement of the dispute.[50] Following Cabinet approval on 19 June 1935, it was announced that Eden would visit Rome for negotiations on the proposed air pact and the implications of the Anglo-German Naval Agreement.[51]

While in Rome, Eden held two interviews with Mussolini on 24 June and 25 June 1935.[52] As far as the Minister for League of Nations Affairs was concerned these meetings were extremely disappointing. Mussolini demanded direct control of all but the central provinces of Abyssinia, and even these were to be subject to Italian direction along the lines of the British position in Egypt and the French in Morocco. When Eden reminded the Italian leader of his obligations under the Covenant of the League of Nations, Mussolini roundly declared that he would leave the League of Nations if it attempted to stand in his path. In his report to Sir John Simon, Eden noted of the discussions with Mussolini: 'There was a gloomy fatality about his temper which I fear it may be beyond the power of reasoning to modify.'[53]

Eden was at pains to emphasise that the meeting had not been marred by any personal ill-feelings between Mussolini and himself. In the official record of the conversation Eden noted: 'The tone of the conversation was at all times friendly and Signor Mussolini spoke quietly and even resignedly; there was no attempt at bluster of any kind . . . .'[54] Following widespread suggestions that Mussolini had been less than polite at each of the meetings, Eden again denied this assertion in a Foreign Office minute dated 27 November 1935: 'Mussolini was definitely cordial throughout — our final interview was of course gloomy — it had to be — but sad rather than bad, and there was no personal feeling whatever.'[55] However, it does appear that following Eden's mission to Rome an element of personal acrimony crept into the relationship between Eden and Mussolini, which was continually inflamed by the vitriolic campaign conducted in the Italian Press against the British Minister.[56]

Following the apparent failure of the Rome negotiations, Vansittart argued that the British initiative had been undermined by the leakage of the terms prior to Eden's arrival in Rome and advocated a further approach to the Italian government.[57] Eden, however, felt that the negotiations vindicated his previous assertions that Mussolini could only be blocked by the presentation of a firm front at the League of Nations and that Abyssinia was assuming the role of a test case with respect to the future credibility of that organisation. In this context his immediate concern was to establish the semblance of firm Anglo-French opposition to Italian ambitions in Abyssinia.[58] On his outward journey to Rome, Eden had visited Paris in order to attempt to repair the damage inflicted on Anglo-French relations by the signing of the

Anglo-German Naval Agreement. As Sir Samuel Hoare later recorded, Eden strenuously defended the agreement in conversation with Leger:

> Did M. Leger think that Part V of the Versailles Treaty that restricted German armaments was now worth anything as a bargaining counter? Our case was that we circumscribed Germany's powers and did not give Germany any new powers. [59]

The French, however, were far from happy with an agreement which apparently not only infringed the Versailles Treaty but also the Anglo-French Memorandum of 3 February 1935.[60] Eden could only reply that Britain adhered in principle to the goals of the Anglo-French Memorandum and that the Naval Agreement contributed towards these goals.[61] On 21 June 1935 Eden reported to London:

> The Anglo-German Naval Agreement is regarded here as having struck a blow at the communiqué of 3 February. Nothing we can say will modify that judgement. None the less Monsieur Laval is himself not unduly disposed to cry over spilt milk. He is, however, determined to preserve what is left in the can of 3 February.[62]

Unfortunately by purposely not informing the French of the terms of the Zeila compromise, even this minimal restoration of relations between London and Paris was undermined on Eden's return to Paris following the negotiations with Mussolini.[63] Laval was dismayed that Eden had been less than frank with him and the Minister for League of Nations Affairs was reminded that any alteration of the status quo in Abyssinia would have infringed the Tripartite Agreement of 1906. Eden countered by observing that he had been particularly disturbed by Mussolini's claim that Laval, in January 1935 during his visit to Rome, had agreed to give Italy a completely free hand in Abyssinia. In particular Eden reported to Laval Mussolini's assertion that, although formally the French had only agreed to Italian economic dominance of Abyssinia, informally they had reached an understanding that France would not oppose the Italian absorption of Abyssinia in its entirety.[64] Laval's response to Eden's question only served to reinforce the growing conviction that more had passed between Laval and Mussolini in Rome than had been publicly admitted:

> If Signor Mussolini thought that France had left Italy a free hand this was true, but it all depended on the use which Italy made of it. He only gave up what France had a right to give up. He had agreed not to obstruct.

123

. . . French policy was to refrain from doing anything which would disturb or make less intimate existing Franco-Italian relations.

Therefore Laval, to Eden's surprise, was prepared to consider the Italian claim for the status of a protectorate over Abyssinia similar to the French position in Morocco and the British in Egypt.[65] As Eden returned to London he could only conclude that support for firm opposition to Italian expansion in Abyssinia was wavering certainly in Paris and also, to an extent, in Britain at a time when it was most likely to be put to a severe test.[66]

In reporting to the Cabinet on 3 July 1935, Eden pointed out that an Italian invasion of Abyssinia would violate the Covenant of the League of Nations and the Kellogg-Briand Pact. Eden attempted to underline the gravity of the situation: 'If these obligations were ignored or evaded, a heavy blow would be struck at the whole of the Pacts and Agreements on which the post war system of Europe had been built up.'

The Cabinet decision to set up a Subcommittee of the CID to consider the possible application of sanctions against Italy appeared to represent a significant move towards the adoption of a determined approach to the containment of Italian ambitions.[67] However, in reality it merely postponed the taking of a decision and reflected the divisions that existed within the Cabinet. While Ministers such as Neville Chamberlain and Anthony Eden appeared prepared to oppose Italy through the mobilisation of opinion at Geneva, several of the Service Ministers were already expressing concern at the possibility of a war in the Mediterranean with Italy. A further group, centred on MacDonald, repeated Vansittart's warnings that to risk a confrontation with Italy would break the Stresa front and the efforts to contain German expansionism in Europe.[68]

It appeared in July 1935 that despite Eden's conviction that Britain must stand firm and cajole France into a similar stance, the Foreign Secretary was reluctant to undertake such a course. His reasoning was undoubtedly influenced by reports from the Paris Embassy that the French Foreign Minister 'was not predisposed to do anything that would mean Italy leaving the League of Nations or that would impair the present harmony between Italy and France'.[69]

In addition Drummond repeatedly warned Hoare that increased pressure on Italy would only result in further alienating Mussolini rather than achieving a compromise solution.[70] In this light Hoare saw the most attractive alternative as lying in an effort to by-pass Geneva and engineer a compromise solution endorsed by both France and Italy.[71] Therefore, in discussion with Eden and Vansittart on

2 and 5 July 1935, the Foreign Secretary promoted the idea of calling a meeting of the signatories to the 1906 Tripartite Agreement on Abyssinia.[72] Vansittart welcomed the initiative which appeared to present a reasonable prospect of defusing the situation. It would appear that the Permanent Under-Secretary was already willing to consider the possibility of an Italian mandate over Abyssinia.[73] Eden, however, would only agree to a compromise attempt that might result in a settlement acceptable not only to the three powers but also to Abyssinia and the League of Nations.[74] Therefore, when Drummond reported that Mussolini would agree to discussions on the assumption that they would lead to an endorsement of his proposal for an effective Italian protectorate over Abyssinia, Eden assumed that the initiative was no longer viable. In a Foreign Office Minute dated 17 July 1935, he concluded:

> We should not in my view give Italy any promise of any kind in advance of support of her case at Geneva. We cannot in decency do this, and any attempt, however hedged about, will only encourage the Italians to think that they can blackmail us as they have blackmailed the French. Our moral position will then be destroyed.[75]

In a memorandum intended for the Cabinet, Eden clearly indicated his view of the line Britain should now take at Geneva if Italy resorted to force in Abyssinia:

> I suggest that I should be empowered to reply in negotiation that if such a situation should arise, and if the case were clear beyond dispute, His Majesty's Government would be prepared to fulfil their obligations under the Covenant, if others would do the same.
>
> If . . . I am able to give a firm reply to this question in private to M. Laval and others, this more than anything else, will bring M. Laval face to face with the realities of the situation and will make him realize that if his Government is not to be placed in the almost intolerable position at Geneva of ignoring the obligations of the Covenant, then he must really exert himself to bring pressure upon Signor Mussolini.[76]

The Foreign Secretary, however, was reluctant to abandon the goal of direct negotiations and in a Cabinet meeting on 24 July 1935 gained approval of his proposal that: 'it was necessary to give the Minister for League of Nations Affairs very wide authority to put all possible pressure on the French to join us in inducing Signor Mussolini to modify his present attitude.'

However, more significantly Eden was not empowered to declare to the French government or to the League of Nations that, if the Abyssinian issue resulted in war, Britain would be prepared to fulfil all of its obligations under the Covenant of the League of Nations.[77] In his desire to keep the opportunity for direct negotiations open, Hoare was assisted by reports from the Treasury that Germany was borrowing £1000 million a year to finance its rearmament. The growing menace presented by Germany in Europe and, therefore, the need to cultivate Anglo-Italian relations was continually to handicap Eden's attempts to take a firm line with Italy and France over Abyssinia.[78]

In an attempt to co-ordinate an Anglo-French front for the forthcoming meeting of the League Council in Geneva, Eden travelled to Paris to meet with Laval on 30 July 1935. The weakness of the British position was immediately apparent when, in response to Laval's inquiry as to the British stance if Italy went to war against Abyssinia, Eden could do no more than refer to a speech made in the House of Commons on 11 July 1935 by Sir Austen Chamberlain, outlining the importance of the Abyssinian question for the future of collective security in Europe and the need for Britain to reaffirm its willingness to fulfil its obligations under the Covenant.[79] In the face of such equivocation Laval was reluctant to risk open condemnation of Italy at the League Council meeting. While the Anglo-French relationship was in such covert, if not overt, disarray, Eden appreciated that the best that could be achieved at Geneva would be a further attempt to set the formal arbitration process in motion alongside a further initiative to promote a three-power meeting.[80] This much the British and French governments were prepared to accept and on 1 August 1935 the League Council accepted an Anglo-French sponsored scheme to defer further scrutiny of the Abyssinian issue until 4 September 1935 while attempts at conciliation proceeded.[81]

On 6 August 1935 Eden, Hankey, Baldwin, Vansittart and Hoare met at Downing Street to discuss the stance to be taken by Eden and Vansittart at the proposed discussions with France and Italy at Paris in mid-August. While accepting that the maintenance of the Anglo-French relationship played a leading role in policy deliberation, the Ministers accepted Eden's proposal that if Italy refused to accept a compromise solution along the lines of recent Anglo-French proposals to the League of Nations, then the Italian delegates must be informed clearly that Britain would expect the League of Nations to carry out its obligations under the Covenant. However, this apparent hardening of the British stance was qualified by the proviso that Eden must not enter into immediate discussion of the nature of the sanctions that were envisaged. A decision was taken to request the

Chiefs of Staff to examine the position that would be created by a war with Italy. This reflected the increasing gravity with which the situation was viewed.[82] Within three weeks, at a meeting on 22 August 1935, the Cabinet had retreated from the minimal advance made on 6 August 1935 and had instructed Eden to take no further initiatives at Geneva on the subject of sanctions without full French support.[83] It was evident that several factors had further fuelled the growing concern over the threat to British interests posed by the steady deterioration in Italo-Abyssinian relations. On 8 August 1935 the First Sea Lord, Admiral Chatfield, informed Vansittart that the COS had concluded: 'that everything possible should be done to avoid precipitating hostilities with Italy until we are more ready.'[84] Vansittart, therefore, recommended to the Foreign Secretary that the risk of war necessitated Britain adopting a very cautious approach to the forthcoming conversations in Paris: 'We are in no position to take a strong line in the Mediterranean — anyhow not for some time.'[85]

With this inauspicious background the British position at the Paris negotiations was handicapped from the outset. The Minister for League of Nations Affairs was unable to give firm guarantees of British military support for sanctions and found Laval still undecided: 'Laval is still pinning all his hopes on a deal, and has not yet cared to face the full consequences if the deal fails.'[86] Faced by an Anglo-French front that seemed preoccupied with conciliation and compromise rather than any determined attempt to restrain Mussolini, the Italian delegate, Aloisi, contemptuously rejected the Anglo-French scheme to guarantee Italian economic predominance in Abyssinia under the auspices of the League of Nations and added that Mussolini now saw little option but to destroy the Abyssinian 'menace'.[87] With the break-up of the final meeting on 18 August 1935 Eden reported pessimistically: 'We are therefore in the presence of the breakdown which we have always foreseen.'[88] Eden could only suggest that the Cabinet be called for a meeting within the next ten days and that immediate measures be taken to improve the anti-aircraft defences in Malta now that war seemed almost inevitable.[89]

In London the Foreign Secretary was complaining bitterly to Neville Chamberlain of the indecision that existed within the Government:

> As you may imagine I have received little or no help from other quarters. Stanley would think about nothing but his holiday and the necessity of keeping out of the whole business almost at any cost. Ramsay has written me a curious and almost unintelligible letter warning me of all the dangers that surround us . . . .

On the one hand I was anxious to suggest no action which would even give the impression of provocation to the Italians or of war to the British public. On the other hand I have been very nervous of leaving undone anything that might make a mad dog act more dangerous. In the circumstances it seemed to me that I could do no more than get the Chiefs of Staff and the Planning Committee to investigate the position and to leave it to the Cabinet to decide upon what action should be taken.

Our line I am sure is to keep in step with the French and whether now or at Geneva, to act with them.[90]

In an effort to assess the political climate in Britain Hoare and Eden, on 20 and 21 August 1935, held meetings with most of the major parliamentary figures not within the Government, including Winston Churchill, Austen Chamberlain, Herbert Samuel, Lansbury and Lloyd George. Despite a variation in emphasis their advice was remarkably similar, being based on the need to support the League of Nations but emphasising that any attempt to exercise sanctions must be truly collective in nature.[91] This broadly confirmed the soundings that were being received from the Dominions[92] and when the Cabinet convened on 21 August 1935 it appeared that, as long as the other members of the League of Nations would render support for sanctions, Britain had no option but to follow suit even if it led to a war with Italy.[93] It was a conclusion that Baldwin, who habitually played a secondary role in foreign affairs, was unhappy about but one to which he could see no alternative. Baldwin, as always sensitive to public opinion, was aware that results of the Peace Ballot indicated there would be little popular support for a war with Italy and most people did not understand that collective security could probably only be enforced by the adoption of military sanctions.[94] He appreciated, however, that support for the League of Nations was likely to be a key factor in an electoral campaign and, therefore, the League could not be openly deserted, even if the chances of achieving a satisfactory solution of the Abyssinian affair through the imposition of sanctions were greatly reduced by the absence of committed support from Germany and the USA.[95] Yet while Baldwin appeared prepared to press on with sanctions on 21 August 1935, at its meeting the following day the Cabinet virtually reversed this policy and instructed Eden to go no further than reaffirming Britain's commitment to the League of Nations and to take no initiative on the question of sanctions without prior support from France.[96]

This policy of extreme caution was prompted by a report from the Chiefs-of-Staff which stated that the Services needed two months to prepare for war with Italy and that these preparations would have to be accompanied by an explicit pledge of military support from France. In view of the Anglo-French discussions recently held in Paris, Eden was the first to concede that the French position remained ambiguous and uncertain. Despite ordering elements of the Home Fleet to sail for Gibraltar on 29 August 1935 and reinforcing the anti-aircraft defences at Malta and Egypt, such was the threat perceived to Britain's worldwide military commitments by a war in the Mediterranean that the Cabinet saw no alternative but to adopt a cautious approach.[97]

While Eden agreed broadly with the assumption that French support for economic or military action against Italy was far from assured, he was largely unhappy with some of the conclusions reached by the Cabinet. By linking British policy firmly to French action, Eden argued that Britain had effectively surrendered the initiative to Paris at a time when the Foreign Office should have been striving to direct French opinion towards the acceptance of the possible need to impose sanctions against Italy.[98] The weakness of this position was illustrated when Eden met with Laval on 2 September 1935 in Paris, in preparation for the scheduled meeting of the League Council at Geneva. Laval was plainly preoccupied with eliciting pledges of British support for measures of collective security in Europe as well as Africa. When Eden could not provide firm assurances, the French Foreign Minister declared that France would go no further than a moral condemnation of Italian policy and a possible trade embargo on war materials following the opening of Italo-Abyssinian hostilities.[99]

When the League Council convened on 4 September 1935, the Italian delegation showed no sign of being willing to accept any form of compromise. Indeed Italy tabled a memorandum at the meeting, adding to its charges against Abyssinia the assertion that the Abyssinian government was uncivilised and not worthy of membership of the League of Nations. When the Abyssinian delegate rose to answer the charges the following day, the Italian delegation promptly left the meeting.[100] As the situation moved rapidly towards deadlock it was decided to set up a Committee of Five, including Eden and Laval, to search for a solution. It was apparent that Eden was still hoping to promote a solution based upon the Zeila compromise and economic predominance for Italy in Abyssinia under a scheme administered by the League of Nations.[101] However, when Hoare arrived in Geneva for the forthcoming meeting of the League Assembly, Eden could only conclude that Italian intransigence and French wavering, following Mussolini's threat to withdraw troops from the Brenner Pass, significantly reduced the prospects of forging a compromise.[102]

The Minister for League of Nations Affairs had not expected a great deal of assistance from Hoare in attempting to stiffen the French stance towards Italy and, therefore, was surprised when, on 10 September 1935, the Foreign Secretary informed Laval that British public opinion would demand that collective security be upheld and that Abyssinia was a vital test case: 'The question whether or not such a policy was possible did not very much matter. The public would insist on it being tried even though it might be found to fail.'[103] Eden was even more surprised to read the text of Hoare's proposed speech to the General Assembly. He later described his and Cranborne's impression of the speech:

> We were both considerably surprised by its strength, which surpassed anything that the tone of discussions with our colleagues had revealed up to the time when I left London a fortnight before.[104]

It is ironic that Eden, who had previously urged Hoare to be more positive in his warnings to Italy, now felt obliged to point out that the speech might be, perhaps, a too-sweeping endorsement of the worldwide role of the organisation and might commit Britain to action in areas of the world, such as the Far East, which were beyond British military resources and capability.[105] Apparently Hoare agreed to a few minor alterations but delivered the speech, which he claimed had been endorsed by Baldwin and Neville Chamberlain, basically unaltered.[106] As Eden expected, international opinion focused on one particular paragraph of the Foreign Secretary's words:

> In conformity with its precise and explicit obligations the League stands, and my country stands with it, for the collective maintenance of the Covenant in its entirety, and particularly for steady and collective resistance to all acts of unprovoked aggression.[107]

With the news that the British Mediterranean Fleet was to be reinforced with two battle-cruisers, it appeared that Britain was at last warning Mussolini it would be ready to respond militarily to an Italian infringement of the Covenant.[108] Eden later recorded that he was also taken in by this speech:

> I remained puzzled that Ministers should have supported such firm language, particularly in the light of their refusal to allow me to give warning to Laval earlier of our intention to fulfil the Covenant. I could only suppose that, while Cranborne and I had been at Geneva, they had been brought up against the character of the obstacle which faced them and had decided to make a clean leap over it.[109]

Eden's apparent surprise at the tenor of Hoare's speech and his apparent acceptance of the sincerity of the Foreign Secretary's words is difficult to explain in that Hoare had given a broad indication that he intended to make a major speech at Geneva as early as 24 August 1935. In a despatch to the Paris Embassy he had outlined the theme of his thoughts:

> it is essential that we should play out the League hand in September. If it is then found that there is no collective basis for sanctions, that is to say in particular that the French are not prepared to give their full co-operation or that the action of the non-member states, for example Germany, the United States and Japan, is so unhelpful as to make economic sanctions futile, the world will have to face the fact that sanctions are impracticable.

> It must be the League and not the British Government that declares that sanctions are impracticable and the British Government must on no account lay itself open to the charge that we have not done our utmost to make them practicable.

> The British Government will certainly have to make its position clear in public at a suitable time in Geneva.[110]

The purpose of Hoare's Geneva speech was therefore three-fold. Firstly it was an attempt to tighten the Anglo-French alliance with reference to the 'maintenance of the Covenant in its entirety', which was aimed specifically at reassuring the French Government that Britain appreciated the dangers posed in Europe by Germany as well as those that existed in Africa. Secondly the speech was part of a major initiative to apply pressure on Mussolini in the hope that the facade of a resolute Anglo-French front might force the Italians to come to terms over Abyssinia. Lastly it was important that Britain be seen by domestic and international public opinion to have exhausted all available avenues before resorting to other means of settling the dispute. In approving the Foreign Secretary's speech neither Baldwin nor Neville Chamberlain were optimistic of success being achieved through the League of Nations but saw an attempt to use such channels as a prerequisite for gaining popular backing for any future alternative forms of action. Hoare certainly shared the general scepticism as to the prospects of success at Geneva but privately differed with the Prime Minister and the Chancellor of the Exchequer in his estimation of the possibility of using a regenerated Anglo-French alliance to forge a compromise with Italy.[111]

For Eden to claim that he was not aware that behind his bold words the Foreign Secretary had little faith in the League machinery and, indeed, had little or no intention of entering into a sanctions policy that might lead to war with Italy is difficult to explain, given Eden's presence at two meetings between Hoare and Laval on 10 September 1935.[112] In these discussions Hoare repeatedly alluded to Germany as the real threat to international stability, the need to strengthen Anglo-French relations and the capability of the League of Nations to resist the German challenge. He therefore saw Abyssinia not as a test case, where Italy must be brought into line, but rather as a hurdle to be circumvented. The Foreign Secretary thought that this could be achieved by the semblance of Anglo-French unity at Geneva and perhaps, if unavoidable, by the utilisation of mild economic pressure:

> They ought therefore to contemplate an examination of the possible application of the kind of pressure which would be effective in stopping war or reducing its duration, but which would not raise the question of belligerent rights. If they failed in any attempt to reach agreement on these lines with other states, they could at least make it clear to the world that an honest attempt had been made to face the situation.[113]

However, the real thrust of Hoare's policy lay in his suggestion that perhaps a solution could still be engineered in negotiation with Italy without involving a confrontation at Geneva. The theme of this discussion was taken up and expanded by Laval in his speech before the League Assembly two days later, on 13 September 1935. While admitting that France would remain loyal to the League of Nations, Laval emphasised the conciliatory rather than the coercive elements of the Covenant in the dispute. Laval informed the Assembly: 'we are studying every proposal likely to satisfy Italy's legitimate aspirations so far as is compatible with respect for the sovereignty of another State Member of the League.'[114]

It would seem, therefore, that Eden was not led to assume the Foreign Secretary's speech on 11 September 1935 represented a shift in his attitude to the role Britain should adopt at Geneva.[115] In essence Hoare remained faithful to the Cabinet resolution of 22 August 1935, that Britain should restrict its initiatives to those which were firmly in step with the French. In this sense the division of opinion between Eden and Hoare was not as wide as Eden later suggested. Certainly they were in agreement that Italy must be warned that an invasion of Abyssinia would not be condoned at Geneva. However, while Eden remained optimistic that such a course of action might be sufficient to deter Mussolini, Hoare was openly sceptical and was already assessing possible alternative solutions to the problem. The central issue with both Ministers was the attitude of the French.

Hoare had obviously heeded the warnings of his military advisers and was unprepared to take any steps that might alienate Paris. Eden, on the other hand, continued to argue that only by bullying the French into adopting a more resolute line could Abyssinia be saved. It is not all that surprising, therefore, that within two weeks of the Foreign Secretary's speech at Geneva Eden was once again complaining that the policy being followed was allowing France to dictate the pace and course of action at Geneva, which Laval was manipulating to the full to avoid a Franco-Italian rift whatever the cost to Abyssinia.[116] On 23 September 1935 Eden reported to Hoare, describing the situation as he saw it unfolding:

> If . . . we are to leave it to Laval to tell Signor Mussolini how these obligations are to be interpreted, then we may be sure that M. Laval, in his anxiety to escape from the dilemma in which he is placed will indicate to Signor Mussolini that the action to be taken by France will be of the mildest and this being so the attitude of His Majesty's Government will be determined by M. Laval and Signor Mussolini will be free from any further anxiety.[117]

The following day Eden telegraphed London once again in response to a suggestion by Laval that Britain might reduce its military forces in the Mediterranean in order to ease the tension with Italy. The Minister for League of Nations Affairs declared:

> it would be fatal in any way to reduce pressure on Signor Mussolini.

> . . . to relax pressure upon him could only restore his confidence and undo good work that has been done.

Once again the equivocal stance of the French Government was identified as the main stumbling-block to progress at Geneva:

> They are driven therefore to a series of manoeuvres object of which is not to antagonise Italy while keeping League alive for another crisis when it may be of value to them.

Eden strongly recommended that Britain should throw its weight firmly behind the League of Nations in the belief that the threat of economic and, possibly, military sanctions would be sufficient to force the Italian leadership, which was already confronted by severe economic problems, into reconsidering its attitude. Therefore he argued that the French could not be allowed to restrain the League of Nations over the Abyssinian affair and Britain must take the lead in forcing Laval to acknowledge his obligation to carry out the terms of the Covenant.[118] However, the Cabinet minutes for the meetings on 24 September 1935 and 2 October 1935 reveal that Eden's opinions were not generally accepted and that the general consensus was to continue avoiding discussion of the thorny problem of sanctions, and concentrating on further efforts to find a compromise acceptable to Italy and Abyssinia.[119]

There was little time for conciliation for in the first week of October reports were received of Italian aerial bombardment of Addis Ababa and the rapid movement of Italian military forces into Abyssinia.[120] Eden was at the hub of the activity at Geneva which sought to deliberate on the nature of these new developments. On 7 October 1935 a Committee of Six, appointed by the League Council to investigate an apparent breach of the Covenant by Italy, reported that Italy had resorted to war and had, therefore, violated Article 12 of the League Covenant. Following the acceptance of this report by 50 out of the total of 54 members of the League of Nations, a General Assembly Committee was established to examine the question of the imposition of sanctions against Italy, in accordance with Article 16 of the League Covenant. It was at this committee, which was soon reduced to a Co-ordination Committee of Eighteen, that Eden, as the chief British delegate, on 12 October 1935 pledged immediate British support for the lifting of the arms embargo on Abyssinia and a general ban on the import of Italian goods. In addition it was proposed that the League orchestrate a campaign to prohibit the export of certain war materials to Italy.[121]

Eden's pronouncement was broadly in line with the British Cabinet decision of 9 October 1935 which gave full approval to the policy of sanctions advocated by the Committee of Eighteen.[122] This was outwardly a bold statement but within a week there were indications that the Cabinet was reconsidering its position.[123] Undoubtedly the need for caution had been emphasised by the French Ambassador in London, Corbin, and Laval in Paris. Both Ministers had indicated that French military support for Britain, in the event of an attack by Italian forces on British positions in the Mediterranean, was by no means certain.[124] Although Eden's reports from Geneva continued to declare that, despite initial hesitations, the French would join in the imposition of sanctions, senior Foreign Office officials did not share his optimism.[125] On 11 October 1935 Ralph Wigram, Head of the Central Department, minuted on a report from Paris in which the French had declined British attempts to initiate Anglo-French naval discussions: 'The French in my opinion are *not* going to give us naval or military or air help against Italy . . . .'[126]

While rejecting Wigram's conclusion that further pressure applied to Laval for a declaration of military support would only result in adding 'poison to our relations with France and leave us without one real friend in Europe', Vansittart agreed that the sanctions policy would have to be delayed until the French declared their position:

> Mr. Eden's instructions were to discuss no sanctions until we were sure of material support. Now we are in the thick of sanctions, with no such assurance from anyone and constantly represented — by no one more than the French — as playing the lead. It must surely be clear that this cannot continue.[127]

There were also those outside the Foreign Office who considered that Eden was attempting to push things along too quickly at Geneva. On 13 October 1935 the Foreign Secretary received a letter from Lord Wigram, Private Secretary to George V, which stated the King's concern at events at Geneva:

> Eden appears to be taking the lead to too great an extent and the League, from reading the papers, would appear to be a 'one man show', and Eden to be justifying Mussolini's contention that the quarrel is really one between Great Britain and Italy and not between the latter country and the League . . . .

In his reply to Lord Wigram, on 14 October 1935, Sir Samuel Hoare rejected the charge that Eden was moulding and propelling the events at Geneva towards a confrontation with Italy.[128] The Cabinet meeting of 16 October 1935 decided, however, that there could be no discussion of further sanctions until the French reservation on military support was withdrawn.[129] The same day Hoare wrote to Eden informing him of the deliberations of the Cabinet: 'it was held in an atmosphere of great perturbation. Our strongest supporters were seriously shaken by Laval's reservation and our critics, of course, immensely strengthened.' Hoare warned Eden that there was 'a considerable feeling that you had recently taken the initiative too much at Geneva', and concluded:

> I feel myself that it is essential that we should go slow until we have the withdrawal and if Laval is recalcitrant, the reason for our going slow will have to come out both in Geneva and in London. I cannot overestimate the urgent importance that the Cabinet attach to this recommendation.[130]

Although, following a strongly worded British protest, the French reservation was withdrawn on 18 October 1935,[131] the element of caution established by the Cabinet meeting of 16 October 1935 was to place British policy in a form of limbo for over a month as the nation was plunged into a General Election and the Abyssinian issue was not discussed again by the Cabinet until 27 November 1935. In an election platform based upon support for the League of Nations and a general policy of rearmament, Eden was an influential and popular figure in the Government's campaign. A central part of Baldwin's platform was contained in a bold reaffirmation of Britain's commitment to the League of Nations and, particularly, the determination to uphold the Covenant of the League of Nations in the Italo-Abyssinian dispute.[132] As a result of his work at Geneva, Eden was popularly portrayed as a champion of the League of Nations and successfully capitalised on this image during the course of the campaign. In Coventry, on 28 October 1935, he emphasised his commitment to his work at Geneva:

> It is fashionable for politicians to look forward to retirement — to pigs, poultry and a pot of ale by the fireside. I promise to allow myself no such indulgence . . . I am convinced that we are all moving into an era when nations will strive to understand one another.[133]

On election day, 14 November 1935, although the Government lost 85 seats from the almost unprecedented number gained in 1931, the overall result was seen as a vote of confidence in Baldwin. The result, however, by no means clarified the problems confronting the Government for although elected on a clear mandate to support the League of Nations, it was evident that any action against Italy would have to be in concert with the other members of the League of Nations and that there would be little popular support for a purely Anglo-Italian confrontation.

While doubts persisted as to the intention of France to commit itself fully to a policy of sanctions against Italy, it appeared logical to investigate further the possibility of arriving at a directly negotiated solution with Mussolini. Following the outbreak of hostilities, the Italian Foreign Office had continued to broadcast its willingness to accept a settlement based on an Italian mandate over what were defined as the Non-Amharic areas of Abyssinia, coupled with direct cession to Italy of the areas controlled by Italy before 1896.[134] While the Foreign Office was unable to accept the extent of the area defined by the Italians as Non-Amharic and insisted that any scheme of assistance must be supervised by the League of Nations, it was decided that the proposals were encouraging and it was worth sending Mr Peterson, Head of the Abyssinian Department of the Foreign Office, to Paris to gauge the French reaction.[135] The Foreign Secretary argued that this initiative was compatible with the programme of sanctions being pursued in Geneva for it was merely a

136

continuation of the attempts at conciliation engineered by Britain and France in August 1935 and the Committee of Five in September 1935, all of which had been endorsed by the League of Nations. As Eden testified in March 1936, he was in complete agreement with this assessment:

> It has always been clearly understood that the functions of the League in dealing with this dispute must be twofold. While the members of the League continue to apply such measures of economic and financial pressure as they are able to impose by common agreement, the organs of the League must neglect no opportunity of trying to find a settlement of the dispute by agreement between the parties.[136]

Peterson later argued that although the news of Italian military successes in Abyssinia added to the urgency of achieving agreement with Italy, the general tenor of his discussions was far from encouraging.[137] On 26 October 1935 he reported that Italy would probably insist upon all the areas of Abyssinia south of the eighth parallel being put under direct Italian administration.[138] At a Foreign Office meeting on 28 October 1935, Hoare, Vansittart and Eden were agreed that such a settlement would be unacceptable.[139] Eden had previously advocated a solution based upon the cession to Abyssinia of an outlet to the sea in exchange for a territorial adjustment in favour of Italy in the province of Bale, subject to approval by the League of Nations, and the Foreign Secretary now suggested that Peterson attempt to pursue a solution along the lines of Eden's proposal.[140] The Paris negotiations soon ended in deadlock, with the Foreign Office rejecting an Italian suggestion of a comprehensive settlement akin to the Anglo-French *entente* of 1904 whereby Abyssinia would be effectively recognised as lying within the Italian sphere of interest. Eden appreciated that such an agreement would be blatantly incompatible with the electoral commitment to support the League of Nations. It appeared, therefore, that little further progress could be made.[141] A new urgency was given to the proceedings, however, by the suggestion of the Committee of Eighteen that oil, coal, iron and steel be added to the list of materials whose export to Italy was to be prohibited. A decision was to be made on this matter on 29 November 1935 and reports from the Rome Embassy clearly indicated that Mussolini would view the imposition of an oil sanction as tantamount to a declaration of war.[142]

While Eden viewed the progress at Geneva as a natural and necessary measure in the campaign to maintain the Covenant of the League of Nations, there were many who placed more faith in traditional diplomacy rather than the vague insurance policy provided by the League of Nations. Vansittart now became the foremost advocate of a negotiated solution with Italy, in the belief that an oil sanction would lead to a war with Italy in which French military support was uncertain. Furthermore such a conflict was likely to destroy the Stresa front and, with it, the main hope of containing German ambitions in Europe.[143] In a Foreign Office note dated 23 November, Vansittart reported of his interview with the Italian General, Garibaldi:

> the General has told me definitely that he fears Signor Mussolini — of whom he has seen much lately — will go to war if oil goes on the list.
>
> . . . he thinks Mussolini is in despair and has lost his head.

The Permanent Under-Secretary, therefore, urged Hoare to avoid a confrontation by postponing the consideration of the oil sanction at Geneva.[144] It was evident that Vansittart was determined to steer the matter away from the League of Nations and on 8 November 1935 the German Ambassador in London, Von Hoesch, reported after a discussion with Vansittart on the Abyssinian crisis:

> things had started to move. Vansittart does not reckon with the possibility of a solution before sanctions against Italy come into effect on November 18th but he did mention the second half of December as a possible date when prospects of a solution might eventuate.[145]

While outwardly Eden and Vansittart appeared to be working in perfect unison, the growing rift in their interpretation of the issues at stake was suggested in their reactions to Sir Maurice Peterson's report from Paris on 25 November 1935. Peterson had reopened discussions with the French Government on 22 November 1935, with instructions from Eden that a solution was to be sought on the basis of adding Adowa and Adigrat to the area to be offered to Italy, with a proportionate reduction of the area offered in southern Abyssinia.[146] In return Abyssinia was to be offered the Italian port of Assab with a connecting corridor and a programme of economic assistance supervised by the League of Nations. Peterson, who was aware that Laval was in close touch with Mussolini, reported that the Italians would probably accept the suggested territorial exchange with the addition of the province of Danokil and most of the Ogaden but would expect effective control of the areas to be ceded, even if formal administrative authority was vested in the League of Nations.[147] Vansittart immediately welcomed the scheme which promised to satisfy the Italians and defuse the crisis: 'I am entirely

138

in favour of Mr. Peterson's proposals (I think they are the best we can hope for: we should be very happy if the Italians accepted).' Eden was far more guarded in his reaction and expressed his concern that any scheme must fulfil the requirements of the League Council:

> I agree with Mr. Peterson's (1) and (2) subject of course to the proviso we have always made and must always maintain that a settlement must be acceptable to the three parties Italy, Abyssinia and the League. How large the area might be for the Italian chartered company would have to be a matter of bargaining. The Emperor would never agree to one third of his territory, or more, being so dealt with, and such a proposal would certainly have to be combined with non-Italian League control as suggested by Mr. Peterson in (3).[148]

Despite Eden's reservations, the Foreign Secretary was sufficiently encouraged to seek further exploration of Peterson's proposals.[149] Certainly, as a telegram to the British Ambassador in Washington dated 29 November 1935 indicated, Sir Samuel Hoare shared Vansittart's concern that the imposition of an oil sanction would be met with a violent reaction by Mussolini and, therefore, destroy any hopes that existed of an early settlement. Hoare readily agreed to Laval's request for a postponement of the oil debate at Geneva until 12 December 1935 and the proposal that the intervening period be used to search for a further solution to the problem. The Foreign Secretary candidly admitted to Sir R. Lindsay: 'we intend to use the next weeks for a serious attempt to bring about a settlement.'[150]

On 28 November 1935 M. Leger of the French Foreign Office had proposed that Hoare and Laval meet to discuss the Abyssinian question[151] and Hoare now decided to use his impending journey to Switzerland for a Christmas holiday to meet Laval in Paris on 7 December 1935.[152] Hoare was anxious that Vansittart accompany him and the letter to the King's Private Secretary, concerning their absence from the country, leaves little doubt that Hoare saw the Paris meeting as of central importance:

> if I leave at the end of the week, I shall be passing through Paris and can accept M. Laval's urgent invitation to have a talk with him on Saturday (7th December). If I postpone my departure, this talk will be impossible before the important meeting of the League (Committee of Eighteen) on 12th December.

> If as I hope, M. Laval and I agree upon a basis for a peace negotiation, Vansittart will stop on in Paris for a day or two in order to clinch the details.

So far as the Abyssinian controversy is concerned it looks to me as though the next few weeks are going to be a period of intensive negotiation for a settlement. We intend to go all out for bringing the conflict to an end.[153]

Although Eden, Simon, Runciman and Neville Chamberlain agreed on 29 November 1935 that the oil sanction must be delayed to allow further discussions with the French, there was no indication that they realised Hoare was expecting to do anything more than sound French opinion and the general consensus was that the oil sanction would have to be applied on 12 December 1935.[154] The main factor in the Paris discussions, therefore, appeared to be the pursuit of a firm reassurance of French military support in the event of an armed conflict with Italy.

The last Cabinet meeting before Hoare left for Paris was held on 2 December 1935. Not surprisingly it was dominated by discussion of the Abyssinian crisis. The reports submitted by the Subcommittee of the CID on Defence Policy and Requirements, dated 26 November 1935,[155] and by the individual Service Ministers were discouraging and clearly outlined the threat posed by the Italian Air Force to the British Mediterranean Fleet and the danger to the British position in the Far East that would be precipitated if the Royal Navy were embroiled in a Mediterranean conflict. While the Foreign Secretary did not side with those Ministers who thought the imposition of an oil sanction was too great a risk to run, he did urge that steps be taken to elicit firm military assurances from France and moral support from the USA. The Cabinet, therefore, sanctioned further discussions in Paris and also a possible further postponement of the oil sanction if the negotiations promised a reasonable prospect of success. With the instruction that the Foreign Secretary need only refer back to the Cabinet if a military assurance from France was not forthcoming or if there were no prospect of a settlement, Hoare was later able to contend that he had been given a mandate to pursue a full settlement in Paris.[156] Indeed the Cabinet minutes specifically authorised the Foreign Secretary to press 'on by every useful means with discussions with the countries concerned with a view, if possible, to a peaceful settlement'.[157]

Baldwin, who had no taste for a war with Italy, was apparently satisfied with the outcome of the Cabinet as were Anthony Eden and Neville Chamberlain, both of whom, while supporting a policy of sanctions at the League of Nations, saw no inconsistency in engineering a compromise solution if acceptable to Abyssinia, Italy and the League of Nations. However, all three subsequently claimed that Hoare gave no indication that the Paris negotiations would lead to a comprehensive settlement proposal.[158] Chamberlain wrote to his sister on 15 December 1935:

> when Sam left for Paris on Saturday the 7th we had no idea that he would be invited to consider detailed peace proposals. I believed, and so far as I know my colleagues believed also, that he was going to stop off at Paris for a few hours on his way to Switzerland to get the discussions with the French into such a condition that we could say to the League 'Don't prejudice the chances of a favourable issue by thrusting in a particularly provocative extra sanction at this moment'. Instead of that a set of proposals was agreed to . . . .[159]

Furthermore Eden discussed the Paris negotiations with Hoare on two occasions before his departure. In particular Eden stressed the need to implement the oil sanction if the credibility of the League of Nations was not to be undermined and supported Chamberlain in arguing that Mussolini would stop short of war with Britain.[160] In a minute presented to the Foreign Secretary, Eden argued that the danger of war was 'remote':

> Moreover Signor Mussolini has never struck me as the kind of person who would commit suicide. He has been ill-informed about our attitude to this dispute and while he may well be exasperated there is a considerable gap between that condition and insanity.[161]

Of their final conversation before Hoare left for Paris, Eden later recorded:

> I warned him against Laval and added more lightly remembering our August negotiations: 'Don't forget that in Paris, Van can be more French than the French.' 'Don't worry' came the confident reply, 'I shall not commit you to anything. It wouldn't be fair on my way through to my holiday.'[162]

Hoare, however, left for Paris with the conviction that an oil sanction might lead to the opening of hostilities with Italy. It was apparent that the Cabinet and its military advisers did not relish the prospect of a Mediterranean war and were insistent that before such a situation could be allowed to develop, firm guarantees must be obtained of French military assistance against Italy. In this context Hoare was confronted in Paris by Laval, who made no secret of his country's reluctance and lack of preparation for a war with Italy. Therefore, when he was presented with a scheme that appeared to represent a reasonable expansion of the terms outlined by the Committee of Five, Hoare agreed to an extension of his visit and eventually recommended the amended proposals to the British Cabinet. In that the scheme was to be referred to the Committee of Five, the principle that the solution be sponsored by the League of Nations appeared to have been maintained.[163] The scheme was fully endorsed by Vansittart who had been in close contact with Grandi, the Italian Ambassador in London, for three days prior to his journey to Paris and whose complicity in engineering the Hoare—Laval plan was later suggested by both Grandi and Rex Leeper, Head of the Press Department of the Foreign Office. Grandi was later to claim that the plan was in fact the 'Grandi—Vansittart plan', while Leeper had been informed by Vansittart immediately before his departure to Paris that a press campaign to re-educate public opinion on the Abyssinian issue would be needed within three days.[164]

The first suggestion that Eden received of the developments in Paris was the announcement that the Foreign Secretary would be extending his visit for a further day. Although there was nothing in the report of the conversations to cause inordinate disquiet, the news that following the conclusion of the second day of negotiations the Foreign Secretary had asked that the Cabinet be summoned immediately convinced Eden something was afoot.[165] Although his attempts to contact Hoare and Vansittart were unsuccessful, he was informed that Sir Maurice Peterson would be returning to London with a full record of the conversations while Hoare continued his journey to Switzerland.[166]

Upon Peterson's arrival in London, Eden was presented not only with a text of the initialled proposals but also a letter from Sir Samuel Hoare. It was apparent that Hoare fully endorsed the compromise formula: 'I strongly recommend the action that I have described to the Cabinet and that it should be taken at once.'[167]

Eden's first impression, however, was that the proposals were far more favourable to Italy than either those suggested by the Committee of Five or the guidelines established by the Foreign Office for Peterson's negotiations in Paris during the last week of November.[168] The Hoare—Laval proposals outwardly followed the format of the scheme drawn up by the Committee of Five in September 1935, which recommended that Abyssinia be given an outlet to the sea through British and French territory. In exchange the Abyssinians were to cede a certain amount of territory to Italy and agree to Italian participation on a commission to be established by the League of Nations for supervising Abyssinian economic development. The Paris negotiations, however, greatly expanded the concessions to be made to Italy with the recommendation that three provinces, totalling some 60,000 square miles, be ceded to Italy and, in addition, 160,000 square miles in Southern Abyssinia were to be placed under effective Italian administration as a zone of economic expansion. Eden's immediate reaction was to consult Baldwin and when they met the same morning he outlined to the Prime Minister the essence of the Hoare–Laval scheme. Eden subsequently claimed that he warned the Prime Minister the proposals would be condemned by world opinion and firmly rejected by both Abyssinia and the League of Nations. To this assertion Baldwin is alleged to have replied 'That lets us out, doesn't it?'[169] The veracity of this account is open to debate, for at the Cabinet meeting summoned that night there was little or no criticism of the Hoare–Laval proposals and it was not seen as necessary to recall the Foreign Secretary from Switzerland to defend or further explain the scheme.[170] Although the decision not to recall Hoare was later defended on the grounds of his poor health, it was apparent that the Cabinet did not foresee the crisis that was to erupt in the following week.[171]

While Eden made no overt move to condemn the proposals, it was apparent that he held reservations as to the general reception that they would be afforded. He therefore warned the Cabinet that:

> while supporting the Foreign Secretary's proposals, [he] felt bound to warn his colleagues that some features of the proposals were likely to prove very distasteful to some States, Members of the League of Nations, including States represented on the Committee of Five.[172]

Furthermore, in order to woo Abyssinian agreement, he insisted that the terms be presented simultaneously to Rome and Addis Ababa[173] and that there could be no suggestion that an Abyssinian rejection of the plan would be a signal for the lifting of sanctions against Italy.[174] It would appear that at this juncture Eden believed the proposals might possibly provide a solution to the Italo-Abyssinian issue, although he was convinced that any overall solution must be sponsored and accepted by the League of Nations.[175] It was, therefore, a major blow when the terms of the Hoare–Laval plan were leaked to the French Press on the evening of 9 December 1935.[176] Given that there had been no time to present the proposals to the Committee of Five, it was apparent that the scheme would be seen as a purely Anglo-French initiative arrived at independently from the machinations at Geneva.

The fate of the Hoare–Laval proposals was decided in the course of two Cabinet meetings held on 10 and 11 December 1935. At the first meeting Eden continued loyally to support the Foreign Secretary with the proviso that Abyssinia be similarly informed of the terms of the scheme. In accordance with this line he suggested that Laval be informed:

> that should Italy accept the proposed basis of settlement and Abyssinia refuse, His Majesty's Government would neither propose nor support the imposition of further sanctions upon Italy unless further developments had modified the situation.

Furthermore Eden was prepared to support this action with a message to the British Minister in Addis Ababa, urging him 'to use your utmost influence to induce Emperor to give careful and favourable consideration to these proposals and on no account lightly to reject them'. In general the Cabinet supported this approach, although, in deference to Neville Chamberlain who had persistently been one of the foremost advocates of implementing a policy of sanctions, it was agreed that Laval be informed that the British pledge not to impose further sanctions was strictly limited to the immediate situation. However, despite this amendment, the Cabinet appeared firm in its resolve to postpone the oil sanction and champion the Hoare—Laval proposals at Geneva.[177] In discussing this meeting with Eden by telephone the Foreign Secretary claimed that Eden:

> did not seem much worried. The only part of the scheme he disliked was the big economic area in the South. I told him to repudiate me (on the extent of the area) if he wished and that I fully agreed with the Cabinet decision to inform Abyssinia and Italy simultaneously.[178]

The following day the mood of the Cabinet was to undergo a radical transformation, as the Cabinet minutes record: 'The Minister for League of Nations Affairs expressed the hope that he would not be expected to champion the proposals made to Italy and Abyssinia in detail at Geneva.'

Eden stressed that the reaction to the Anglo-French proposals, both in Britain and abroad, was likely to be severely critical and that there was little possibility of the scheme being accepted. He therefore argued that the only solution was to insist the scheme was no more than a set of points which were to be presented for scrutiny by the League of Nations.[179] This approach was endorsed by the Cabinet. There was no longer any suggestion of the British Government urging the Abyssinians to accept the proposals and effectively the meeting heralded the first indication of the Cabinet's intention to renounce the Hoare—Laval plan.[180] This sudden about-turn was a result of several factors, not the least being a report by MacDonald that the Dominion High Commissioners had been severely critical of the extent of the

144

concession apparently being granted to the aggressor.[181] Furthermore the scheme, since its leakage in Paris, had received a great amount of adverse comment in the British Press. It was probably, however, the hostility to the scheme evinced by the Opposition benches and the evident growing disquiet on the Government benches during the debate in the House of Commons on the afternoon of 10 December 1935 that were the deciding factors.[182] The gravity of the situation was recorded by Neville Chamberlain in a letter to his sister on 15 December 1935:

> nothing could be worse than our position. Our whole prestige in foreign affairs at home and abroad has tumbled to pieces like a house of cards. If we had to fight the election over again we should probably be beaten . . . .[183]

Although the Foreign Secretary probably did not appreciate the full gravity of the situation, he was sufficiently alarmed to return to London on 15 December 1935. He was not able, however, to attend any Cabinet meetings because of a skating accident in Switzerland that kept him confined to his house.[184] The Foreign Secretary's return, however, was probably too late to enable him to extricate himself from the invidious position which he now occupied.[185] Eden had already departed for Geneva[186] and, following a preliminary meeting with M. Vasconcellos, Chairman of the Committee of Eighteen, he reported: 'Impression which Paris proposals have made upon opinion here is even worse than I had anticipated.'[187]

It was evident that, despite French reluctance, the existing sanctions against Italy would have to be maintained in order to appease opinion at Geneva and Eden's address to the Committee of Eighteen clearly indicated that he saw no alternative but to attempt to play down the significance of the Hoare—Laval scheme and reject the suggestions of Anglo-French connivance to appease Italy. In his report to the Foreign Office, following his speech, the Minister for League of Nations Affairs stated:

> I explained that what we had done was to work proposals out that might be submitted to both sides and that neither we nor the French Government had at any time any other intention than to bring the outcome of our work to the League for the League's information and judgement. I emphasised the fact that the suggestions we had made were not sacrosanct and that if the League did not agree with them we should make no complaint. We would in fact welcome any proposals for their improvement.[188]

Eden's speech was the first public indication that the British Government had decided to reverse its initial endorsement of the Hoare—Laval plan. Upon his return to London, the Cabinet fully supported the tenor of Eden's speech. Furthermore it was decided that there was now no alternative but to repudiate formally the Hoare—Laval plan. This task was to be performed by Eden on 18 December 1935 at Geneva. The text of Eden's speech, as accepted by the Cabinet, left no doubt that the British Government was no longer willing to support the Hoare—Laval proposals:

> It must be emphasised that the Paris proposals which were put forward last week were not advanced as proposals to be insisted on in any event.

> It was proper that the attempt should be made, however invidious the task of those who had to make it. Even if this attempt had been unsuccessful the essential importance of conciliation remains, as the League has frequently recognised. The principle was right, even if its application in this instance has not availed.

> If, therefore, it transpired that these proposals do not satisfy the essential condition of agreement by the two parties and the League, His Majesty's Government could not continue to recommend or support them.[189]

With the formal endorsement of this text it appeared that the Cabinet had almost to a man deserted Hoare and there were already rumours that several members, including Simon, Elliot and Stanley, were calling for his resignation.[190] Only Vansittart and Hoare continued to support the scheme. Neville Chamberlain reported on 17 December 1935 that the Foreign Secretary remained insistent 'there was no chance of getting anything much better than the Paris terms'.[191] The same day Chamberlain, Eden and Baldwin visited Hoare who was still confined to his house. It appeared that a compromise had been forged when the Foreign Secretary agreed that it had been his intention to submit the scheme to the League of Nations for consideration and, therefore, he could agree in principle with the theme of Eden's proposed speech in Geneva.[192] When Eden left for Geneva on 17 December 1935 it, therefore, appeared that Hoare might still withstand the mounting pressure for his resignation.[193] When the Cabinet met on the following day, however, their mood had undoubtedly been influenced by an open rebellion against the Hoare—Laval scheme, staged at a meeting of the Conservative back-bench Foreign Affairs Committee on the afternoon of

17 December 1935.[194] It was now no longer sufficient for the Government quietly to drop the scheme and there was an increasing demand that Hoare admit the plan had been a mistake from the outset. When the Foreign Secretary reported to the Cabinet that he intended to defend the proposals before the House of Commons, only one member, Zetland, spoke in his defence.[195] The general feeling was that Hoare could only make such a speech from the back benches, as Neville Chamberlain recorded:

> It had a very bad reception. There was no support except from Zetland. J.H. Thomas was the first to say that Sam could not really justify himself unless he first resigned for otherwise his speech would commit the Cabinet to views which they did not share.[196]

Chamberlain's account of the meeting only served to confirm what Hoare had already heard from the Government Chief Whip. As Hoare later recorded:

> I told him at once that I was not prepared to make any such recantation. I was convinced that nothing short of the proposals would save Abyssinia and prevent Mussolini from joining the Hitler front. This being so, resignation, not recantation, was the only course open to me.[197]

It appeared that following the Cabinet meeting of 18 December 1935 the gulf between the Foreign Secretary and his colleagues was unbridgeable.[198] On 19 December 1935 the House of Commons was scheduled to receive a motion on the Order Paper which denounced the Hoare—Laval scheme as an attempt to 'reward the declared aggressor at the expense of the victim, destroy collective security and conflict with the expressed will of the country and the Covenant of the League of Nations'. Sir John Simon candidly warned Stanley Baldwin that 'this was very nearly what the Cabinet felt'.[199] The Foreign Secretary's resignation was announced on the evening of 18 December 1935 and the following day he made his defence of the Paris proposals from the back benches of the House of Commons. Hoare maintained that the scheme represented: 'the only basis upon which it was even remotely likely that we could at least start a peace discussion.'[200] He was followed by Baldwin who, although he sympathised with the thrust of the Hoare—Laval scheme which he argued was to avoid an Anglo-Italian war,[201] now bowed to the widespread pressure for recantation and retreat.[202] The Prime Minister effectively renounced any further intention of promoting the Paris proposals:

I felt that there could not be that volume of popular opinion which it is necessary to have in a democracy behind the Government in a matter so important as this. It is perfectly obvious now that the proposals are absolutely and completely dead.[203]

Although somewhat mollified by the Government's formal rejection of the Hoare—Laval scheme, such had been the consternation displayed by the Conservative Party rank and file at the events of the past two weeks that there was still the distinct possibility of an open rebellion. Sir Austen Chamberlain later recorded of the debate: 'Had I thought it compatible with the public interest I believe that after S.B.'s miserably inadequate speech and the initial blunder, I could have so reduced his majority as to force his resignation.'[204] Chamberlain's decision to support the Government was probably decisive in eliminating any suggestion of a back-bench revolt. However, there is a suggestion that this decision was influenced not only by party loyalty but also by a prior conversation with Baldwin at which the Prime Minister had suggested that Chamberlain might be asked to reassume the post of Foreign Secretary.[205] If Austen Chamberlain indeed entertained such hopes, they were rudely shattered when Baldwin dismissed him as too old for the position and indicated that Eden was to be his choice.[206] Suspecting that he had been used by Baldwin to suppress any possibility of rebellion within the party ranks, Chamberlain rejected Baldwin's offer of a seat in the Cabinet without departmental responsibilities:

I could perceive no prospect of public usefulness in the acceptance of such an offer so conveyed and I came to the conclusion that what he wanted was not my advice or experience but the use of my name to help patch up the damaged prestige of his Government.[207]

Although Chamberlain was 73 years of age, there were many who would have welcomed the reinstatement of the Party's senior statesman in the field of foreign affairs at a time when Britain's international prestige had taken a severe blow.[208] Eden was later to record that, until being summoned to 10 Downing Street immediately on his return from Geneva, he had assumed that Chamberlain would be offered the post of Foreign Secretary.[209] At the resulting interview with Baldwin, the Prime Minister rejected Eden's suggestion of Sir Austen Chamberlain and Lord Halifax as suitable candidates for the post on the grounds that the former was too old and the latter was a member of the House of Lords. Baldwin stated that to have a Foreign Secretary in the House of Lords was 'not the answer just now'. Eden later recorded of the interview:

Another silence followed. I had no more names to suggest, nor apparently had Baldwin. Eventually he turned to me and said: 'It looks as if it will have to be you'. Feeling by this time somewhat hurt at this eliminative method of being appointed I replied that six months before I would have been very grateful for the chance to be Foreign Secretary but that now I felt quite differently about it. Baldwin nodded understanding at this, and so this strange interview ended with my words being taken as tacit acceptance.[210]

As heir-apparent since May 1935, Eden's appointment appeared the logical result of Sir Samuel Hoare's resignation. However, the disapproval surrounding the Paris peace-proposals had not been directed solely towards Sir Samuel Hoare. Sir Henry Pownall, Assistant Secretary to the Committee of Imperial Defence, noted in his diary for 12 December 1935:

A devil of a row has boiled up over the 'peace proposals' put up by ourselves and the French.

I don't see how Hoare, Eden and Van can all remain in their jobs.[211]

Four days later he added:

A good deal of mud is sticking to Eden who has had a rough passage over the 'corridor of camels' telegram to Addis.

I gather Eden has got pretty rattled over it all. Moreover I should put Van's chances as about 50/50; he must be at the back of much of this. I should not be surprised to see him moved on somewhere before long.[212]

Vansittart's complicity in the Paris negotiations was undeniable and both Baldwin and Neville Chamberlain were convinced that Vansittart had played a major role in persuading Hoare to accept Laval's proposals.[213] Although, upon assuming the post of Foreign Secretary, Eden was to consider the possibility of taking action against the Permanent Under-Secretary, he eventually bowed to the convention that a civil servant was not accountable for a political decision taken by a Minister.[214] Vansittart did not, however, escape unscathed. He later admitted that his meeting with Baldwin, upon returning from Paris, was like leaving 'one cauldron for another',[215] while Eden's decision to recall Alec Cadogan from China to take up the post of Deputy Under-Secretary suggested that he was considering the possibility of replacing Vansittart in the not-too-distant future.[216]

If the principle of ministerial responsibility had saved Vansittart and condemned Hoare, once the Cabinet had elected to withdraw the protective cloak of collective responsibility, then by the same principle there were certainly some observers who saw the Minister for League of Nations Affairs as sharing a degree of responsibility for the Hoare–Laval affair.[217] Eden, however, largely escaped widespread criticism, not because he disagreed with the Foreign Secretary as to the need to avoid a war with Italy unless assured of French military support but because he had not been a direct party to the discussions in France. Certainly it can be contended that Eden would not have agreed to such sweeping concessions to Italy but he undoubtedly supported Hoare's quest for an Anglo-French compromise that might draw Italy and Abyssinia into an agreement. Where he had differed with the Foreign Secretary was on the urgency of the matter. While Hoare, following Laval's indication that France would be reluctant to take up arms against Italy, saw no alternative but to accede to the French terms, Eden remained optimistic that the threat of further sanctions would be sufficient to force Mussolini to scale down his demands.[218] In this sense Eden would probably have seen little immediate need to accept a formula that was likely to be repudiated by both Abyssinia and the League of Nations. Therefore, while initially supporting the Foreign Secretary's attempt to establish an Italo-Abyssinian settlement, Eden expressed his concern with the format from the outset and felt fully justified in distancing himself from the proposals when it became apparent that they were unacceptable to public opinion both in Britain and abroad.[219]

Eden's appointment to the position of Foreign Secretary was confirmed on 22 December 1935. At the age of 38 he had climbed to the pinnacle of the Foreign Office, although the fact that his main rival was Sir Austen Chamberlain certainly suggests that Baldwin had little faith in Eden's contemporaries within the House of Commons.[220] While Austen Chamberlain commanded the respect of the Conservative Party and could be expected to repair the Anglo-French relationship, Eden had the advantage of both youth and a reputation as a firm advocate of the League of Nations. Confronted with the arduous task of rebuilding British prestige in the aftermath of the Hoare–Laval affair, Baldwin elected to appoint the younger man whose career he had nurtured for over a decade. As might have been expected Eden's appointment was enthusiastically received, being described as 'the most appropriate and reassuring choice' by the *Daily Telegraph*,[221] while the *Daily Herald* declared that 'Any other choice than that of Mr. Eden as Foreign Secretary would have been a blunder of the first magnitude'.[222] Baldwin's decision was also warmly applauded in Washington, Paris and Berlin,[223] although significantly the *Giornale d'Italia* condemned Eden as the man who had destroyed the Hoare—Laval proposals and who sought to pillory the Italian people.[224] While Eden must have been elated at his elevation, he was also aware that, compared to the situation in June 1935, the task before him was both complex and fraught with dangers.[225] The *New Statesman* had described his appointment as 'Mr. Baldwin's Christmas present to the nation'[226] but, as Vansittart was later to note, it was not to be all plain sailing for the new Foreign Secretary:

> Anthony Eden got a lovely Christmas box, bright red and marked F.O. It was full of trouble.[227]

References

1   Avon, pp. 186—7.
2   Avon, p. 130 and p. 158.
3   Avon, p. 187.
4   For an account of this incident and the immediate period beforehand from the Foreign Office's point of view, see *DBFP*, 2nd ser., vol. 14, document nos 24 (2 December 1934), 28 (4 December 1934) and 30 (6 December 1934).
5   *DBFP*, 2nd ser., vol. 14, no. 43, Sir E. Drummond to Sir J. Simon (no. 53 Saving : Telegraphic [J 3028/18/1]).
6   Refers to the Anglo-French-Italian Agreement of 13 December 1906 in respect to Ethiopia. The agreement formally divided Ethiopia into spheres of influence. The three powers also pledged to uphold the status quo in Ethiopia. Britain had denounced the agreement in 1923. For text see *British Foreign and State Papers*, vol. XCIX, pp. 486—9.
7   *DBFP*, 2nd ser., vol. 14, no. 41, Sir S. Barton to Sir J. Simon (no. 87 [J 3011/18/1]), Addis Ababa, 10 December 1934.
8   *DBFP*, 2nd ser., vol. 14, no. 41, Minute by Sir R. Vansittart, dated 13 December 1934.
9   See *DBFP*, 2nd ser., vol. 14, nos 47 (13 December 1934), 57 (26 December 1934) and 73 (31 December 1934).
10   See *DBFP*, 2nd ser., vol. 14, nos 82 (4 January 1935), 92 (12 January 1935), 94 (12 January 1935) and 104 (15 January 1935).
11   For Eden's reports to Sir J. Simon from Geneva see *DBFP*, 2nd ser., vol. 14, nos 100 (14 January 1935), 101 (14 January 1935), 109 (16 January 1935), 115 (16 January 1935) and 129 (19 January 1935).
12   *DBFP*, 2nd ser., vol. 14, Minute by Eden dated 30 January 1935 on no. 138, Sir E. Drummond to Sir J. Simon (no. 56 [J 320/1/1]), Rome, 26 January 1935.
13   See reports from Rome and Addis Ababa dated 16 February 1935 and 18 February 1935. *DBFP*, 2nd ser., vol. 14, no. 160, Letter from Sir E. Drummond to Sir J. Simon (J 973/1/1), Rome, 16 February 1935. Drummond referred to the mobilisation of two Italian divisions and despatch of three militia battalions and numerous technical officers and munitions. Sir J. Simon minuted 'A very grave letter. The P.M. should see it at once.' *DBFP*, 2nd ser., vol. 14, no. 163, Sir S. Barton to Sir J. Simon (no. 50 [J 643/1/1]), Addis Ababa, 18 February 1935.

14 Minute by Eden dated 26 February 1935 on telegram from Rome of 23 February 1935. Sir E. Drummond reported a conversation with Signor Suvich on 22 February 1935 in which Suvich stated that the Italian government would not open negotiations with Abyssinia until the Emperor agreed to the establishment of a 'neutral zone'. See also Avon, p. 199 and *DBFP*, 2nd ser., vol. 14, pp. 164–5 and pp. 167–8.

15 *DBFP*, 2nd ser., vol. 14, no. 178, Sir J. Simon to Sir E. Drummond (no. 133 [J 753/1/1]), FO, 26 February 1935. This despatch was drafted by Eden and Vansittart and based on Eden's minute of the same day. The draft, which was not altered by the Foreign Secretary, was accompanied by a minute from R.I. Campbell (Head of the Egyptian Department) stating that the proposed telegrams to Rome and Paris:

> are an urgent attempt to persuade Italy to use moderation and honour her undertaking to the Council and they provide cover for H.M.G. in case of accident. It is important in the opinion of Mr. Eden and Sir R. Vansittart that our representations should be made at Rome at the earliest possible moment.

The following day Sir J. Simon informed the Cabinet of the telegrams which were designed: 'to put on record, in the friendliest manner, our misgivings at the present turn of events.' See *CAB* 23/81. Twelfth meeting of Cabinet in 1935, Wednesday, 27 February 1935.

16 *DBFP*, 2nd ser., vol. 14, no. 195, Sir J. Simon to Sir E. Drummond (no. 171 [J 808/1/1]), FO, 7 March 1935. The text of Vansittart's interview was transmitted to Drummond to ensure that Mussolini would be under no illusion as to the British stance.

17 Eden claimed that the decision to underline the British attitude by having Drummond re-emphasise the main points of the Vansittart–Grandi discussions was based on his complaint that Drummond had been far too conciliatory in presenting the British telegram of 26 February 1935 to Mussolini (see Avon, pp. 200–1). See also minute by R.I. Campbell, dated 2 March 1935, on Drummond's report of interview with Mussolini, 28 February 1935. (*DBFP*, 2nd ser., vol. 14, no. 187.)

18 For an account of Eden's return from Prague which led to his ill health, see Avon, pp. 174–5. Eden was ordered to rest for six weeks. He was, therefore, unable to participate in the Stresa Conference or attend the vital Cabinet meeting on 8 April 1935 when the British delegation received its instructions for the Conference. Significantly no mention was made in these instructions of the Abyssinian question. See *CAB* 23/81, CC 20(35)1, 8 April 1935.

19 *DBFP*, 2nd ser., vol. 14, no. 225, record of conversation with Signor Fracassi (J 1396/1/1), FO, 5 April 1935. Signor Fracassi informed Mr G.H. Thompson (First Secretary in the Foreign Office and a member of the Egyptian Department): 'the Embassy had received no instructions from Rome and had no reason to suppose that any discussion at Stresa of the Italo-Ethiopian dispute was in contemplation.' Sir R. Vansittart minuted, however, on 8 April 1935 that Mr Thompson would accompany the British delegation at the request of the Italian Ambassador. 'I trust some good may come out of it.' Fracassi (First Secretary of the Italian Embassy in London).

20 MacDonald Diary, 21 February 1935. Quoted in D. Marquand, *Ramsay MacDonald* (London, 1977), p. 773.

21 An account of the proceedings at Stresa is given in *DBFP*, 2nd ser., vol. 12, no. 722.

22   Minute by Sir R. Vansittart, dated 23 April 1935, on a report by Thompson (see note 25 below), dated 12 April 1935, of meeting with Guarnaschelli (see note 26 below) at Stresa. See *DBFP*, 2nd ser., vol. 14, no. 232.

23   A report on the Stresa Conference was given to the Cabinet on 17 April 1935 by Ramsay MacDonald. No mention was made of Abyssinia. MacDonald declared: 'The main thrust at Stresa had been to renew the confidence of the French and Italians in this country which had been somewhat impaired. This had been successfully accomplished.' (See *CAB* 23/81, CC 24(35)1, 17 April 1935.) The preoccupation with Europe and general satisfaction with Stresa can also be seen in the Conclusions of Neville Chamberlain — diary entry for 14 April 1935 (*Chamberlain Papers*, NC 2/23A). Also a memorandum by MacDonald on the European situation in April 1935 (*Baldwin Papers*, vol. 122, ff. 188—90).

24   Discussions held between Mr G.H. Thompson and Signor Guarnaschelli on 11 and 12 April 1935 at Stresa. Negotiations centred on protection of grazing rights for British Somali tribesmen in southern Abyssinia but also covered the possibility of Italo-Abyssinian military conflict. See *DBFP*, 2nd ser., vol. 14, nos 230—4.

25   Mr G.H. Thompson, First Secretary in the Foreign Office and member of the Egyptian Department.

26   Signor Guarnaschelli, Head of the African Department at the Italian Ministry of Foreign Affairs.

27   *DBFP*, 2nd ser., vol. 14, no. 230, record by Mr Thompson of conversation at Stresa with Signor Guarnaschelli (J 1488/1/1), Stresa, 12 April 1935.

28   Minute by Sir R. Vansittart, dated 23 April 1935, on a report by Mr Thompson, dated 12 April 1935. See *DBFP*, 2nd ser., vol. 14, no. 232.

29   *DBFP*, 2nd ser., vol. 14, no. 235, Mr Patteson to Mr Baldwin (no. 68 LN [J 1485/1/1]), Geneva, 16 April 1935. In this report the Foreign Secretary stated that he had informed the Italian representative to the League Council: 'that it is essential that when Council assembles in May it should not be to find that the two parties had in the interval done nothing positive to implement their undertakings.'

30   *DBFP*, 2nd ser., vol. 14, no. 244, Sir J. Simon to Sir E. Drummond (no. 548 [J 1711/1/1]), FO, 3 May 1935.

31   Avon, p. 204.

32   *DBFP*, 2nd ser., vol. 14, no. 253, Memorandum by Sir J. Simon on Italo-Ethiopian situation (J 1850/1/1), FO, 11 May 1935. Presented to the Cabinet as CP 98(35) and drafted in conjunction with Mr Thompson.

33   *CAB* 23/81, CC 27(35)5, 15 May 1935.

34   *DBFP*, 2nd ser., vol. 14, no. 278, Mr Patteson to Sir J. Simon (no. 78 LN [J 1972/1/1]), Geneva, 21 May 1935.

35   *Baldwin Papers*, vol. 122, ff. 202—5, Eden to Simon, Geneva, 21 May 1935. See also Avon, pp. 207—8.

36   *DBFP*, 2nd ser., vol. 14, no. 281, Sir E. Drummond to Sir J. Simon (no. 41 [J 2016/1/1]), Rome, 21 May 1935.

37   *DBFP*, 2nd ser., vol. 14, no. 282, Mr Patteson to Sir J. Simon (no. 81 LN [J 199/1/1]), Geneva, 22 May 1935. Eden proposed that Mussolini be warned that Italian military action against Abyssinia would be in violation of the Covenant of the League, Kellogg-Briand Pact and the Tripartite Agreement of 1906. Eden spoke in this sense to Baron Aloisi at Geneva on the evening of 22 May 1935.

38   *DBFP*, 2nd ser., vol. 14, no. 284, Sir E. Drummond to Sir J. Simon (no. 325 Telephone [J 1996/1/1]), Rome, 23 May 1935. Drummond claimed that Eden's course of action would 'lead to a serious explosion on Signor Mussolini's part and to anger directed against His Majesty's Government'.

39   On 3 June 1935 Sir John Simon minuted on Drummond's despatch of 23 May 1935: 'One of the effects of dictators is to make H.M.G.'s representative very chary of provoking explosions.' *DBFP*, 2nd ser., vol. 14, no. 284.

40   *DBFP*, 2nd ser., vol. 14, no. 291, Sir J. Simon to Sir E. Drummond (no. 622 [J 2008/1/1]), FO, 24 May 1935.

41   For an account of the negotiations at Geneva see *DBFP*, 2nd ser., vol. 14, nos. 278, 280, 283, 288, 289 and 292.

42   *DBFP*, 2nd ser., vol. 14, no. 292, Mr Patteson to Sir J. Simon (no. 90 LN [J 2026/1/1]), Geneva, 25 May 1935.

43   In conversation with Sir Miles Lampson, High Commissioner in Egypt, see *Avon*, pp. 213—14. Eden paid tribute in particular to the co-operation received from the French in bringing strong pressure on the Italian delegation to accept the terms. After the meeting the Ethiopian delegate thanked Eden and Laval for their efforts to bring about 'a pacific and speedy settlement'. See *DBFP*, 2nd ser., vol. 14, no. 292, note 2.

44   Eden refers to this conflict in *Facing the Dictators*, see *Avon*, pp. 141—2.

45   Minute by Eden, dated 13 June 1935, on report by Drummond, dated 31 May 1935, of a conversation with the Italian Under Secretary of State for Foreign Affairs. Suvich had stated that Italy expected Britain and France to render 'assistance' to the Italian government in solving the Abyssinian affair. See *DBFP*, 2nd ser., vol. 14, no. 295 (no. 637 [J 2144/1/1]), Rome, 31 May 1935.

46   Minute by Vansittart on above Drummond despatch dated 8 June 1935. *DBFP*, 2nd ser., vol. 14, no. 295.

47   Sir R. Vansittart, *The Mist Procession* (London, 1958), pp. 521—3. Eden was also a member of Lady Nancy Astor's Cliveden Set which Vansittart saw as undermining his position, pp. 482—3.

48   In his memoirs Sir Samuel Hoare admits that he placed great reliance on Vansittart and his 'brilliant lieutenant' Ralph Wigram (Head of the Central Department at the Foreign Office) — see Viscount Templewood, *Nine Troubled Years* (London, 1954), p. 138.

49   A series of meetings were held between Eden, Hoare and Vansittart, both formal and informal, on the Abyssinian affair between 6—16 June 1935, culminating in the Trent Park meeting on 16 June 1935. The three had agreed, on 14 June 1935, that Vansittart would prepare a set of recommendations for the Cabinet and it was in response to this invitation that he devised 'the Zeila Proposal'. See Templewood, pp. 152—5, also *DBFP*, 2nd ser., vol. 14, nos 301, 306, 308 and 309.

50   The divergence between Eden and Vansittart was indicated in the first week of June 1935. Vansittart noted on 8 June 1935, 'Italy will have to be bought off . . . in some form or other, or Abyssinia will eventually perish'. On 3 June 1935 Eden had registered his approval of a minute by O'Malley in which he had stated 'we must stick to the League principles and stand the racket'. *DBFP*, 2nd ser., vol. 14, no. 301, Minute by Sir R. Vansittart (J 2389), FO, 8 June 1935. See also *Templewood Papers*, vol. VIII : 3 Drummond to Hoare, 17 June 1935.

51   The Cabinet accepted Vansittart's recommendations as presented by the Foreign Secretary. As it was decided that the proposal should be carried by someone of ministerial rank, Eden was assigned the task. *CAB* 23/81, CC 33(35)4, 19 June 1935.

52   For a full account of these interviews see *DBFP*, 2nd ser., vol. 14, nos 320 and 323, Rome, 24 and 25 June 1935.

53   *DBFP*, 2nd ser., vol. 14, no. 320, 24 June 1935. Drummond later remarked that he and Eden considered Mussolini as 'a man driven by fate' — *Templewood Papers*, vol. VIII : 3 Drummond to Hoare, 31 July 1935.
54   *DBFP*, 2nd ser., vol. 14, no. 320, 24 June 1935. See also Avon, pp. 322–9.
55   Minute of 27 November 1935 by Eden (J 844/1/1). See also *DBFP*, 2nd ser., vol. 14, p. 329.
56   Hoare noted in his memoirs: 'He [Mussolini] and Eden did not conceal the extent of their differences that separated them or the personal dislike that they felt for each other.' Templewood, p. 156. Vansittart also subsequently referred to Mussolini's 'discourteous' attitude to Eden, Vansittart, p. 531. There is no evidence to support the assertion that Mussolini was acrimonious, although Eden was naturally bitterly disappointed by Mussolini's abrupt rejection of the Zeila Plan. See Mario Toscano, 'Eden's Mission to Rome on the Eve of the Italo-Ethiopian Conflict' contained in A.O. Sarkissian (ed.), *Studies in Diplomatic History and Historiography* (Longman, 1961).
57   Vansittart is probably wrong on this point as the first leak was an article in the *News Chronicle* on 24 June 1935, the day of Eden's first interview in Rome. See Vansittart, pp. 530–1, also minute by Vansittart dated 26 June 1935, in *DBFP*, 2nd ser., vol. 14, no. 320, 24 June 1935, in which he states his determination to continue attempts for an agreement with Mussolini.
58   A sentiment apparently shared by Neville Chamberlain. See *Neville Chamberlain Papers*, NC 2/23A, diary entry for 5 July 1935.
59   Templewood, pp. 144–5.
60   The French had in fact been informed of the Anglo-German Naval Treaty proposals eleven days before its conclusion but were not asked for their consent. See Memorandum by Mr Craigie of the Foreign Office, June 1935. *Templewood Papers*, vol. VIII : 1.
61   For an account of this interview see Avon, pp. 230–1.
62   Ibid., p. 231.
63   Ibid., pp. 232–5.
64   *DBFP*, 2nd ser., vol. 14, nos 320–3, Rome, 24–25 June 1935.
65   For an account of this interview see *DBFP*, 2nd ser., vol. 14, no. 327, record of Anglo-French Conversations, (J 2529/1/1), Paris, 27 June 1935.
66   See Minute by Eden dated 3 July, on record of conversation by Mr Strang with Baron Aloisi of 28 June 1935. *DBFP*, 2nd ser., vol. 14, no. 330. Eden's suspicions of the extent of the concessions given to Mussolini by Laval, at their meeting in January 1935, have been largely confirmed. See Geoffrey Warner, *Pierre Laval and the Eclipse of France* (London, 1968), also D.C. Watt, 'Document: The Secret Laval–Mussolini Agreement of 1935 on Ethiopia' contained in E.M. Robertson (ed.), *Origins of the Second World War* (London, 1971).
67   It was also decided that Eden would be a member of the Subcommittee of the CID established at this meeting. *CAB* 23/82, CC 35(35)2, 3 July 1935.
68   See Avon, pp. 237–9. However, the risks of war were now becoming very real. In response to the initiative from the Cabinet, the COS reported on 30 July 1935 that economic sanctions would lead to war with Italy. They therefore recommended that active steps be taken to elicit assurances of support from other naval powers (COS Minutes, 147th Meeting, 30 July 1935, *CAB* 53/5). See also Arthur Marder, 'The Royal Navy and the Ethiopian Crisis of 1935–36', *American Historical Review* (June 1970), LXXV, 5, at pp. 1327–56.
69   *DBFP*, 2nd ser., vol. 14, no. 343, Sir G. Clerk to Sir S. Hoare (no. 133 [J 2646/1/1]), Paris, 4 July 1935.

70   *DBFP*, 2nd ser., vol. 14, no. 339, Sir E. Drummond to Sir S. Hoare (no. 369 [J 2613/1/1]), Rome, 2 July 1935.

71   An assessment that was actively supported by Sir Maurice Hankey and COS who were adamant that defence preparations be completed before sanctions were imposed. See S. Roskill, *Hankey, Man of Secrets, Vol. III* (London, 1974), pp. 178–9.

72   See *DBFP*, 2nd ser., vol. 14, p. 356, note 1 and p. 360, note 3.

73   Minute by Sir R. Vansittart, dated 3 July 1935, on note by Mr Strang of a conversation with Baron Aloisi on 28 June 1935. See *DBFP*, 2nd ser., vol. 14, no. 330.

74   Minute by Eden, dated 9 July 1935, on despatch from Rome of 8 July 1935. See *DBFP*, 2nd ser., vol. 14, no. 351.

75   Minute by Eden, dated 17 July 1935, on despatch from Rome, dated 16 July 1935. See *DBFP*, 2nd ser., vol. 14, no. 366.

76   See Avon, pp. 242–3. This memorandum was presented to the Cabinet on 22 July 1935 as CP 151(35). At this meeting the Foreign Secretary declared that he would go no further than 'publicity and conversations with the French' to pressurise Italy. See *CAB* 23/82, CC 39(35)1, 22 July 1935.

77   For account of this meeting see *CAB* 23/82, CC 40(35)1, CC 40(35)4, CC 40(35)6, 24 July 1935.

78   This Cabinet meeting and the growing pressure on the government is also referred to in Middlemas and Barnes, *Baldwin, A Biography* (London, 1969), pp. 845–6.

79   For an account of this meeting see *DBFP*, 2nd ser., vol. 14, no. 407. Sir G. Clerk to Sir S. Hoare (no. 152 [J 3284/1/1]), Paris, 31 July 1935.

80   As a result of this report the Cabinet agreed that: 'they should be extremely cautious as to any references as to what this country would or would not do in the event of an outbreak of hostilities.' See *CAB* 23/82, CC 41(35)1, 31 July 1935.

81   For Eden's reports from Geneva, see *DBFP*, 2nd ser., vol. 14, nos 411, 415 and 416.

82   For an account of this meeting see *CAB* 23/82 – conclusions of conversation at Downing Street, 6 August 1935.

83   *CAB* 23/82, CC 42(35)1, 22 August 1935.

84   *DBFP*, 2nd ser., vol. 14, no. 431, letter from Admiral Sir A. Ernle Chatfield to Sir R. Vansittart (J 3614/1/1), Admiralty, 8 August 1935. Chatfield was referring to the conclusions of COS, 148th Meeting, 8 August 1935, which were adamant that Britain should not fight Italy without a pledge of French support.

85   *DBFP*, 2nd ser., vol. 14, no. 434, letter from Sir R. Vansittart to Sir S. Hoare (J 3614/1/1), FO, 9 August 1935.

86   *DBFP*, 2nd ser., vol. 14, no. 443, Sir G. Clerk to Sir S. Hoare (no. 182 [J 3774/1/1]), Paris, 14 August 1935.

87   See *DBFP*, 2nd ser., vol. 14, nos 456 and 457.

88   *DBFP*, 2nd ser., vol. 14, no. 465, 18 August 1935.

89   *DBFP*, 2nd ser., vol. 14, no. 467, 18 August 1935. Sir S. Hoare agreed that an early meeting of the Cabinet was necessary and asked Eden to consult Baldwin who was holidaying at Aix-les-Bains. It was agreed that the date of the Cabinet meeting be brought forward from 27 August to 22 August 1935.

90   *Templewood Papers*, vol. VIII : 3, Hoare to Neville Chamberlain, 18 August 1935.

91   Accounts of these meetings can be found in *Templewood Papers*, vol. VIII : 1 and also *DBFP*, 2nd ser., vol. 14, nos 476, 477, 480, 481 and 483.

92 These were informal soundings. The official responses from the Dominions were not received until the first week of September 1935 when they confirmed the impressions gained beforehand. See *DBFP*, 2nd ser., vol. 14, nos 521, 529 and 530.

93 See *CAB* 23/82, meeting at Downing Street on 21 August 1935.

94 Although there is a danger in over-emphasising the significance of the Peace Ballot of June 1935, most Ministers agreed that it created an atmosphere where a war with Italy over Abyssinia would not have been popularly supported in Britain. See Avon, p. 237 and Keith Feiling, *The Life of Neville Chamberlain* (London, 1946), pp. 262–6.

95 Middlemas and Barnes, pp. 835–6 and pp. 852–4.

96 *CAB* 23/82, CC 42(35)1, 22 August 1935.

97 This memorandum presented to the Cabinet as CP 166(35), also recommended that the Home Fleet sail for Gibraltar on 29 August 1935 and that the RAF and anti-aircraft personnel be reinforced in Malta and Egypt. The Cabinet rejected a recommendation that naval reservists be mobilised to bring the fleet up to strength. The memorandum had been requested following the meeting of ministers on 6 August 1935, and was considered under CC 42(35)3, *CAB* 23/82, 22 August 1935. See also Avon, pp. 252–3. For a fuller discussion of the military situation see Marder, pp. 1329–34.

98 Avon, pp. 254–8.

99 For an account of this meeting see *DBFP*, 2nd ser., vol. 14, no. 520, Sir G. Clerk to Sir S. Hoare (no. 213 [J 4364/1/1]), Paris, 2 September 1935.

100 For an account of these opening skirmishes see *DBFP*, 2nd ser., vol. 14, nos 537 and 540.

101 This scheme was unveiled by Eden to the Committee of Five on 17 September 1935, and called 'The Charter of Assistance'. See *DBFP*, 2nd ser., vol. 14, no. 578, Geneva, 17 September 1935.

102 Eden had expressed his concern for the frailness of French support in reports to London from Geneva on 11 and 18 September 1935. See *DBFP*, 2nd ser., vol. 14, nos 554 and 579.

103 An account of this meeting can be found in *DBFP*, 2nd ser., vol. 14, no. 553, Geneva, 11 September 1935.

104 Avon, p. 260.

105 Avon, pp. 260–1.

106 Hoare had consulted Baldwin and Neville Chamberlain at length in the preparation of the speech. See *Chamberlain Papers*, letter to his sister, dated 7 September 1935 (NC 18/1/1932). Also Middlemas and Barnes, p. 855, for meeting of the three on 5 September 1935.

107 *DBFP*, 2nd ser., vol. 14, appendix IV.

108 *HMS Hood* and *HMS Renown* arrived in Gibraltar on 17 September 1935. The COS minutes, 149th Meeting, 6 September 1935, indicate that it was considered that war was imminent and, therefore, all steps should be taken to reinforce the British position in the Mediterranean. Hoare described this build-up to Eden on 16 September 1935 as 'precautionary measures' due to fear of an Italian attack. Avon, p. 262. See also Cabinet decision of 22 August 1935, *CAB* 23/82, CC 42(35)3.

109 Avon, p. 261.

110 *DBFP*, 2nd ser., vol. 14, no. 493, letter from Sir S. Hoare to Sir G. Clerk (J 4077/1/1), FO, 24 August 1935.

111 For an account of Hoare's discussions with Chamberlain see *Neville Chamberlain Papers*, letter to his sister, dated 7 September 1935 (NC 18/1/932). Also entry in Chamberlain's diary for 2 August 1935 on general situation with

Italy (NC 2/23A). For further opinions see Vansittart, p. 532; Templewood, pp. 165—71; and Middlemas and Barnes, pp. 855—7. Vansittart later claimed that Hoare's speech was, in essence, directed at the British public in an attempt to muster support for the forthcoming General Election.

112   For an account of these meetings see *DBFP*, 2nd ser., vol. 14, nos 553 and 554, Geneva, 11 September 1935. These accounts indicate the extreme reluctance with which Hoare and Laval faced the sanction problem. However, there is no evidence of a secret agreement to reject military measures against Italy as not practicable, as suggested by some observers. See Middlemas and Barnes, p. 856.

113   *DBFP*, 2nd ser., vol. 14, no. 553.

114   Quoted in J.A. Cross, *Sir Samuel Hoare, a Political Biography* (London, 1977), p. 221.

115   Indeed Hoare was quite taken aback at the reaction to his speech. In a letter to Lord Wigram, dated 14 September 1935, he stated: 'I felt that it would make an impression. I had no idea however that it would make so big an impression.' *Templewood Papers*, vol. VIII : 4.

116   Eden described Laval's attempts to grant Italy a mandate over Abyssinia under the guise of a scheme run by the League of Nations as 'barefaced cynicism' — *DBFP*, 2nd ser., vol. 14, no. 580, Geneva, 18 September 1935.

117   *DBFP*, 2nd ser., vol. 14, no. 619, Geneva, 23 September 1935. See also Avon, pp. 263—8.

118   *DBFP*, 2nd ser., vol. 14, no. 633, Mr Edmond to Sir S. Hoare (no. 165 LN [J 5163/1/1]), Geneva, 24 September 1935.

119   For an account of the Cabinet meetings see *CAB* 23/82, CC 43(35)1, 24 September 1935, and CC 44(35), 2 October 1935, also *DBFP*, 2nd ser., vol. 15, p. V. On 24 September 1935 the Cabinet approved a recommendation by the Foreign Secretary that no decision be taken on sanctions until the attitude of the League of Nations and also non-member states was established. The same day Hoare informed Eden at Geneva, 'I trust you will not allow any haste on the Council in regard to the discussion of sanctions'. *DBFP*, 2nd ser., vol. 14, no. 636. Vansittart was certainly moving in favour of a negotiated solution to appease Italy and minuted, on 30 September 1935, 'The Council may not like this but the European situation is full of menace'. (*Vansittart Papers*, 2/27.)

120   For reports from Addis Ababa by the British Minister, Sir S. Barton, see *DBFP*, 2nd ser., vol. 15, no. 12 (4 October 1935) and 31 (6 October 1935).

121   For details of Eden's work in this period at Geneva see *DBFP*, 2nd ser., vol. 15, nos 16, 26, 33, 35, 36, 40, 64, 71 and 76. On 10 October 1935 Eden emphasised Britain's determination to uphold the Covenant of the League in a speech to the League Assembly and repeated this assurance on 12 October 1935 to the second meeting of the Committee of Eighteen. In addition he proposed an immediate embargo on the supply of war materials to Italy.

122   This, in effect, meant an embargo on Italian exports and examination of further proposals with the proviso that any action would be 'collective', *CAB* 23/82, CC 45(35)1, 9 October 1935.

123   *CAB* 23/82, CC 47(35)1, 16 October 1935.

124   See *DBFP*, 2nd ser., vol. 15, nos 27 (8 October 1935) and 81 (14 October 1935).

125   See letter from Eden to Hoare, 7 October 1935 (*Templewood Papers*, vol. VIII : 3), and Eden report from Geneva, 14 October 1935 (*DBFP*, 2nd ser., vol. 15, no. 78); Sir R. Vansittart's and Sir S. Hoare's minuted criticism of the latter report clearly indicated their concern that the French were forcing Eden continually to take the lead at Geneva.

126 Minute by R.F. Wigram, dated 11 October 1935, on Paris despatch dated 10 October 1935 – *DBFP*, 2nd ser., vol. 15, no. 61.

127 Minutes by Sir R. Vansittart, dated 15 October 1935, and R.F. Wigram, dated 14 October 1935, on Eden's report from Geneva of 14 October 1935. Eden admitted that he had been unable to get assurances of French military support, *DBFP*, 2nd ser., vol. 15, no. 77.

128 Both letters contained in *Templewood Papers*, vol. VIII : 4. See also FO, 800/295.

129 The Foreign Secretary was instructed to seek 'categorical withdrawal by M. Laval', *CAB* 23/82, CC 47(35)1, 16 October 1935.

130 Hoare to Eden, 16 October 1935 (see FO, 800/295), also *DBFP*, 2nd ser., vol. 15, no. 84, note 2.

131 *DBFP*, 2nd ser., vol. 15, no. 115, translation of note communicated by the French Government to Sir G. Clerk (J6 : 52/1/1), Paris, 18 October 1935. In a minute dated 19 October 1935, Vansittart said of the note, 'We have had to get it out of the French with forceps and biceps . . . .'

132 The commitment 'faithfully to take part in collective action decided upon by the League' was contained in the Government's manifesto. See Churchill, p. 94. In addition, see Bardens, *Portrait of a Statesman* (London, 1955), pp. 62–3; and Campbell-Johnson, pp. 114–16.

133 Eden's speech of 28 October 1935, quoted in Campbell-Johnson, p. 115. At the General Election, held on 14 November 1935, the National Government gained 428 seats and the Labour Party 95 seats. The majority was apparently somewhat to his surprise as, in a letter to Baldwin from Geneva on 3 October 1935, he had expressed 'qualms about my own place which my job out here has compelled me to neglect the last year or two'. *Baldwin Papers*, vol. 122, ff. 236–7.

134 For examples of Italian approaches in this period, see Drummond's report to Hoare, dated 18 October 1935 (*DBFP*, 2nd ser., vol. 15, no. 108) and pressure from Paris in Clerk's report of 24 October 1935 (*DBFP*, 2nd ser., vol. 15, no. 139). There is also a suggestion that the Italians were able to gain access to Foreign Office papers at the Rome Embassy and, therefore, may have been falsely encouraged by the conclusions of the Maffey Report produced on 18 June 1935. This interdepartmental Committee on British interests in Ethiopia concluded that these interests were primarily limited to the supply of water from Lake Tsana and grazing rights in southern Abyssinia (see *DBFP*, 2nd ser., vol. 15, appendix II).

135 See minute by Sir R. Vansittart, dated 18 October 1935, on Drummond despatch from Rome of the same day (*DBFP*, 2nd ser., vol. 15, no. 108). The Abyssinian Department of the Foreign Office had been established in August 1935 when Peterson had been transferred from the Western Department. Prior to January 1935 he had served as Head of the Egyptian Department. In the new Abyssinian Department he was assisted by Mr Scrivener and Mr G.H. Thompson. Mr Peterson's initial visit to Paris was 24–27 October 1935. He returned on 22 November 1935 and transported the Hoare–Laval proposals to Britain on 8 December 1935.

136 Eden to Sir S. Barton (Addis Ababa) (J 2043/1/1), FO, 4 March 1936.

137 Peterson recorded the events of October–December 1935 in his memoirs, *Both Sides of the Curtain* (London, 1950).

138 *DBFP*, 2nd ser., vol. 15, no. 151, Sir G. Clerk to Sir S. Hoare (no. 1499 [J 6885/1/1]), Paris, 26 October 1935.

139 See Avon, pp. 286–7.

140 *DBFP*, 2nd ser., vol. 15, no. 162, 30 October 1935. The Foreign Secretary

was referring to a suggestion put by Eden to Laval on 8 October 1935, see *DBFP*, 2nd ser., vol. 15, no. 44, Geneva, 8 October 1935.

141 For an account of Mussolini's proposal of a Mediterranean *détente*, see despatches from Rome, *DBFP*, 2nd ser., vol. 15, nos 160, 188 and 210. The Cabinet minutes for 9 October 1935 also indicate that the Government feared that an Anglo-Italian agreement at that time would have alienated the support of the USA for the League of Nations. *CAB* 23/82, CC 45(35)1, 9 October 1935.

142 See *DBFP*, 2nd ser., vol. 15, no. 208, Signor Grandi to Sir S. Hoare (J 7701/7214/1), 11 November 1935. Also *DBFP*, 2nd ser., vol. 15, no. 242, 22 November 1935.

143 Vansittart, pp. 522—3.

144 Note written by Sir R. Vansittart to Mr Eden and Sir S. Hoare on 23—24 November 1935. Vansittart was largely convinced that an oil sanction would lead to war with Italy for which Britain was not prepared militarily and did not hold firm pledges of support from the Mediterranean powers. See *DBFP*, 2nd ser., vol. 15, no. 251.

145 *DGFP*, series C, vol. IV, 8 November 1935.

146 These instructions were finalised at a meeting of Peterson, Eden, Sir L. Oliphant, Mr H.J. Seymour and Sir R. Vansittart on 19 November 1935. See *DBFP*, 2nd ser., vol. 15, no. 233 (J 8363/1/1).

147 *DBFP*, 2nd ser., vol. 15, no. 254, Sir G. Clerk to Sir S. Hoare (no. 239 [J 8384/1/1]), Paris, 25 November 1935. The French suggested the creation of an Italian chartered company with the presence of non-Italian League personnel as arbitrators.

148 Minutes by Sir R. Vansittart, dated 26 November 1935, and Eden, dated 26 November 1935, on Peterson's despatch from Paris — *DBFP*, 2nd ser., vol. 15, no. 254.

149 Vansittart's case had been reinforced when Hankey in his capacity as Chairman of the DRC, told Hoare on 25 November 1935 that he considered a war with Italy would dangerously weaken Britain's position in both Europe and the Far East. Hankey urged Hoare to postpone the oil sanction: 'All the official world, outside the F.O. (and many within it) are against sanctions and especially the oil sanction.' Furthermore Hankey reminded Hoare of the Cabinet directive of 16 October 1935 not to involve Britain in a war with Italy without French support. (*Hankey Papers*, diary entry for 25 November 1935, Hankey 1/7.)

150 *DBFP*, 2nd ser., vol. 15, no. 280, Sir S. Hoare to Sir R. Lindsay (no. 369 [J 8648/1/1]), FO, 29 November 1935.

151 *DBFP*, 2nd ser., vol. 15, no. 274, Sir G. Clerk to Sir S. Hoare (no. 243 [J 8629/1/1]), Paris, 28 November 1935.

152 This invitation was accepted by the Foreign Secretary in a telegram to Paris on 28 November 1935, see *DBFP*, 2nd ser., vol. 15, no. 274, note 5. Also Templewood, pp. 177—8.

153 *DBFP*, 2nd ser., vol. 15, no. 293, letter from Sir S. Hoare to Lord Wigram (RA GV K 2506/1), FO, 2 December 1935.

154 For reference to this meeting see *Chamberlain Papers*, diary entry for 29 November 1935 (NC 2/23A). Chamberlain claimed that Eden took the lead in recommending postponement of the oil sanction while discussions continued in Paris. See also Cross, p. 238; and Middlemas and Barnes, p. 877.

155 This committee, on which Eden was the Foreign Office representative, effectively endorsed a report by the Chiefs-of-Staff Subcommittee (DRP Paper no. 59) arguing that Britain should not risk a war with Italy without firm assurances of military support from the Mediterranean powers. Eden was to

seek such assurances at the forthcoming Geneva meetings. See *CAB* 23/82, CC 50(35)2.

156   See Templewood, pp. 177–8.

157   For a full account of the Cabinet meetings, see *CAB* 23/82, CC 50(35)2, 2 December 1935.

158   Neville Chamberlain considered Baldwin's support for the imposition of an oil sanction as extremely dubious and on 29 November 1935 warned Hoare that 'P.M. was in his heart dead against his policy of sanction'. *Neville Chamberlain Papers*, diary entry for 29 November 1935, NC 2/23A. See also Avon, p. 297 and Chamberlain diary entry for 15 December 1935 (NC 2/23A).

159   *Chamberlain Papers*, Chamberlain to his sister on 15 December 1935 (NC 18/1/942).

160   Avon, pp. 295–8. See also *Chamberlain Papers*, letter to his sister Ida, 8 December 1935 (NC 18/1/941).

161   Avon, p. 296.

162   Ibid., p. 298.

163   For an account of the Hoare–Laval negotiations and the eventual scheme initialled by the Foreign Secretary, see *DBFP*, 2nd ser., vol. 15, nos 330, 336, 337 and 338.

164   The role of Sir R. Vansittart in the Hoare–Laval negotiations is not fully illuminated by his own account (Vansittart, pp. 538–49), that of the Foreign Secretary (Templewood, pp. 176–82) or the Foreign Office records of the Paris negotiations. The references to Rex Leeper and Grandi are drawn from an analysis by Ian Colvin, *Vansittart in Office* (London, 1965), pp. 73–80 and reflect a duplicity in the negotiations that Eden was subsequently to suspect.

165   *DBFP*, 2nd ser., vol. 15, nos 330 and 335.

166   Avon, pp. 299–301.

167   The note containing the Foreign Secretary's justification of his action was delivered to Eden by Mr Peterson on the morning of 9 December 1935. See *DBFP*, 2nd ser., vol. 15, no. 337, note by Sir S. Hoare on his conversations in Paris (J 9106/1/1), Paris, 8 December 1935. The actual terms agreed are contained in *DBFP*, 2nd ser., vol. 15, no. 336, recommendations agreed by Sir S. Hoare and M. Laval on 8 December 1935 (J 9154/1/1).

168   Avon, pp. 300–1. Indeed the most recent examination of the Abyssinian issue by the Abyssinian Department of the Foreign Office had come out against the cession of the province of Tigre to Italy. See *DBFP*, 2nd ser., vol. 15, no. 393, 2 December 1935. The recommendations of the Committee of Five are referred to by Eden in Avon, pp. 264–5. See also *DBFP*, 2nd ser., vol. 14, no. 578, 17 September 1935.

169   Avon, pp. 301–2. See also Middlemas and Barnes, pp. 884–5.

170   At this meeting the Cabinet was presented with Hoare's recommendations (CP 235[35]) and a hastily drawn up note by Eden (CP 233[35]) containing his two suggestions of amendment which were subsequently accepted. The only attempted explanation of the Foreign Secretary's action was Eden's observation that he had probably been influenced by the French reluctance to enter into a sanctions scheme. See *CAB* 23/82, CC 52(35), 9 December 1935.

171   Avon, pp. 303–4.

172   *CAB* 23/82, CC 52(35), 9 December 1935.

173   Ibid.

174   Ibid. In addition, for an account of the telephone conversations between Eden and Vansittart on the evening of 9 December and the early morning of 10 December 1935, see Avon, pp. 304–5. Also see *DBFP*, 2nd ser., vol. 15, no. 347, Sir G. Clerk to Mr Eden (no. 257 [J 9083/1]), Paris, 10 December 1935.

175 Avon, p. 304.

176 The first leakage of the terms appeared in the French papers *L'Oeuvre* and *L'Echo de Paris* on the morning of 9 December 1935. It appears that the source of the leakage was probably the French Foreign Office, see F.O. Laurens, *France and the Italo-Ethiopian Crisis 1935–36* (The Hague, 1967), pp. 276–7.

177 For an account of this meeting, see *CAB* 23/82, CC 53(35), 10 December 1935. See also *DBFP*, 2nd ser., vol. 15, no. 353, Mr Eden to Sir S. Barton (no. 434 [J 9154/1/1]), FO, 10 December 1935, and *DBFP*, 2nd ser., vol. 15, no. 352, Mr Eden to Sir G. Clerk (no. 346 [J 9083/1/1]), FO, 10 December 1935. The account later given by Eden (Avon, pp. 305) that he drafted the message to Laval does not tally with the Cabinet minutes which clearly show that it was significantly amended by Neville Chamberlain.

178 *Templewood Papers*, vol. XIX : 6, notes for 'Nine Troubled Years — December 1935 Crisis'.

179 Chamberlain was subsequently to claim that he had suggested this course of action to Eden. *Neville Chamberlain Papers*, NC 2/23A, diary entry for 15 December 1935.

180 For a full account of the meeting see *CAB* 23/82, CC 54(35), 11 December 1935. Once again the ambiguous position of the USA was used as a reason for delaying the oil embargo.

181 See *CAB* 23/82, CC 54(35), 11 December 1935.

182 For hostility to the scheme in the American Press see *DBFP*, 2nd ser., vol. 15, no. 359, British Library of Information (New York) to Foreign Office (no. 45 [J 9223/1/1]), New York, 11 December 1935. For the House of Commons debate on 10 December 1935, see *H of C* Debs, 5's, vol. 307, cols 821–56.

183 *Neville Chamberlain Papers*, letter to his sister, Hilda, 15 December 1935, NC 18/1/942.

184 Templewood, pp. 184–6.

185 Neville Chamberlain acted as the main intermediary between Hoare and the Cabinet. See Templewood, pp. 184–5, Avon, p. 309 and *Neville Chamberlain Papers*, NC 2/23A, diary entries for 17 and 18 December 1935.

186 Eden left for Geneva on 11 December 1935 returning to London on 14 December 1935, Avon, pp. 307–8.

187 *DBFP*, 2nd ser., vol. 15, no. 363, Mr Edmond to Foreign Office (no. 252 LN [J 9250/1/1]), Geneva, 12 December 1935.

188 *DBFP*, 2nd ser., vol. 15, no. 364, Mr Edmond to Foreign Office (no. 132 [J 9321/1/1]), Geneva, 12 December 1935. Neville Chamberlain noted of this report that it 'showed that the feeling at Geneva was even worse than we had anticipated'. *Chamberlain Papers*, diary entry for 15 December 1935, NC 2/23A.

189 For an account of this meeting see *CAB* 23/82, Cabinet meeting in PM's room of H of C on 16 December 1935. The meeting was continued the following day when the text of Eden's proposed speech was finally approved, *CAB* 23/82, CC 55(35)3, 17 December 1935.

190 A rumour apparently communicated to Neville Chamberlain by Duff Cooper (*Chamberlain Papers*, diary entry for 17 December 1935, NC 2/23A).

191 See Cabinet Minutes for 17 December 1935, *CAB* 23/82. Vansittart had returned to London on 12 December 1935 and the Foreign Secretary on 16 December 1935, although he was confined to his house on doctor's orders. Neville Chamberlain acted as intermediary between Hoare and the Cabinet.

192 For an account of this visit see Avon, p. 309; Middlemas and Barnes, pp. 891–2; and Cross, p. 252.

193   For Eden's reports from Geneva see *DBFP*, 2nd ser., vol. 15, nos 394 (18 December), 405 (20 December) and 406 (20 December). Following Eden's address, the League Council merely took note of the Anglo-French proposals but did not express an opinion. See also Avon, pp. 309—10.

194   The controversy centred on Sir Austen Chamberlain, Chairman of the Conservative back-bench Foreign Affairs Committee who, to the Cabinet's consternation, on 17 December 1935 condemned the Hoare—Laval scheme. Chamberlain obviously considered that Party opinion was running so strongly against the proposals that they were no longer defensible. Middlemas and Barnes, p. 894.

195   For an account of the Cabinet discussion see *CAB* 23/82, CC 56(35)2, 18 December 1935. The point of contention was the widespread opposition to the speech in defence of his actions that the Foreign Secretary proposed to make in the House of Commons the following day.

196   *Neville Chamberlain Papers*, diary entry for 18 December 1935.

197   Templewood, p. 185.

198   For an account of the Cabinet discussion see *CAB* 23/82, CC 56(35)2. An interesting side-light on Neville Chamberlain's role as the primary intermediary between the Cabinet and the Foreign Secretary can be found in the *Neville Chamberlain Papers*, diary entries for 17 and 18 December 1935 (NC 2/23A).

199   *CAB* 23/82, CC 56(35)2.

200   *H of C*, Debs, 5's, vol. 307, cols 2007—17, 19 December 1935.

201   Baldwin told Tom Jones, on 7 January 1936, that he had:

> repeatedly told Sam 'Keep us out of war, we are not ready for it.' We could cut Italy's communications but if Mussolini broke out there would be more killed in Valetta in one night than in all the Abyssinian campaign up to date, and until we got agreement with the French we would have to go single-handed fighting Italy for a month or so.

Thomas Jones, *A Diary with Letters, 1931—1950* (London, 1954), pp. 158—9. Neville Chamberlain also noted in his diary on 29 November 1935 that Baldwin feared that the imposition of an oil sanction would pose a serious military threat to Britain's position in the Mediterranean. *Neville Chamberlain Papers*, NC 2/23A.

202   See Harold Nicolson, *Diaries and Letters, 1930—1939* (London, 1966), pp. 230—2; Brian Bond, *Chief of Staff, The Diaries of Lieutenant General Sir Henry Pownall, Volume 1 : 1933—1940* (London, 1972), pp. 92—3. Also see Jones, pp. 159—61.

203   *H of C*, Debs, 5's, vol. 307, cols 2030—9, 19 December 1935.

204   Quoted in Sir Charles Petrie, *The Life and Letters of the Rt Hon. Sir Austen Chamberlain*, vol. 2 (London, 1940), p. 406.

205   It was subsequently claimed that Sir Austen Chamberlain informed Ralph Wigram that Baldwin had confided to him 'when Sam has gone, I shall want to talk to you about the Foreign Office' (see Colvin, p. 83). The suggestion that Baldwin tacitly attempted to buy Chamberlain's support is not referred to by Sir Charles Petrie and cannot be substantiated.

206   Petrie, p. 406. Eden later recorded that Sir Austen Chamberlain had told him Baldwin had, by implication, suggested that he was too old for the post and, in effect, 'ga-ga'. Avon, p. 316.

207   Petrie, pp. 406—7.

208   Feiling, p. 277.

209   Avon, p. 315.

210   Ibid., pp. 315—16.

211   Bond, p. 92, Pownall's diary entry for 16 December 1935.

212 Ibid., p. 93.
213 Baldwin told Tom Jones on 7 January 1936 that he was convinced Hoare had been pushed into the Paris agreement by his senior Foreign Office advisers who had told the Foreign Secretary 'It was the best thing he had done'. Jones, p. 159. In particular Neville Chamberlain noted that Vansittart's account of Laval's reluctance to support Britain militarily against Italy was far more exaggerated than the account submitted by Hoare. *Neville Chamberlain Papers*, diary entry for 15 December 1935, NC 2/23A.
214 *DBFP*, 2nd ser., vol. 15, no. 437 (RA GV K 2506/8), communication from Mr Eden to HM King George V, 8 January 1936. There was also a suggestion that Vansittart was urged by Beaverbrook not to resign on the grounds that the responsibility for the Paris agreement was solely the Foreign Secretary's, see Colvin, p. 84. Only Hankey appears to have come to Vansittart's defence, pointing out to Eden on 26 December 1935 that the Cabinet had every reason to doubt they could expect military assistance from France. Furthermore Hankey wrote to Sir E. Phipps on 2 January 1936 expressing the hope that Vansittart would not be made the scapegoat for 'Sam Hoare's escapade in Paris'. See Roskill, pp. 190–1.
215 Vansittart, p. 541.
216 *DBFP*, 2nd ser., vol. 15, no. 437, 8 January 1936. Cadogan replaced Sir Victor Wellesley and took up his new post on 1 October 1936.
217 Bond, p. 92, diary entry for 16 December 1935.
218 Throughout the crisis Eden was continually more confident than his colleagues that France would eventually give full support to a sanctions policy against Italy. See Eden's report from Geneva, *DBFP*, 2nd ser., vol. 15, no. 78, 14 October 1935.
219 See Cabinet minutes for 9, 10 and 11 December 1935. *CAB* 23/82, CC 52(35), CC 53(35) and CC 54(35). Neville Chamberlain also noted Eden's loyalty to Hoare despite his obvious reservations as to the Hoare–Laval proposals. *Neville Chamberlain Papers*, NC 2/23A, diary entry for 15 December 1935.
220 See Jones, pp. 122–4, diary entry for 27 February 1934. There is no suggestion that Baldwin had altered his opinion by December 1935.
221 *Daily Telegraph*, 23 December 1935.
222 *Daily Herald*, 23 December 1935.
223 For example see comment in *New York Times, Le Temps* and *Deutsche Allgemeine Zeitung* for 23 December 1935.
224 *Giornale d'Italia*, 23 December 1935.
225 Avon, pp. 317–18.
226 *New Statesman*, quoted from Geoffrey McDermott, *The Eden Legacy* (London, 1969), p. 32.
227 Vansittart, p. 543.

5 Foreign Secretary —
Abyssinia and the Rhineland

Eden travelled to Sandringham to be formally appointed by the Monarch on 23 December 1935. He later recorded that his conversation with King George V only served to convince him further that Hoare had dramatically misread the climate of popular opinion:

> The King said that he had talked to Hoare when he surrendered the seals and told him that the Hoare—Laval proposals had been a blunder. 'You cannot drive a train full steam in one direction' he said, 'and then, without warning, suddenly reverse without somebody coming off the rails.' I thought His Majesty's reaction significant, because he had at an earlier audience spoken to me with vehemence about the importance he attached to good relations with Italy. He added: 'I said to your predecessor: "You know what they're all saying, no more coals to Newcastle, no more Hoares to Paris." The fellow didn't even laugh.'[1]

While having few qualms about seizing the opportunity proffered, it was not entirely surprising that Eden viewed the prospect of high office with less relish than he might have in May 1935. His subsequent assessment that he succeeded to 'a wretchedly disordered heritage' was not far from the mark.[2] The intervening six months had witnessed a steady deterioration in relations with Italy which had not been counterbalanced by an improvement in either Anglo-French or Anglo-German relations. The goal of a European security agreement appeared as distant as ever, while the London Naval Conference threatened to exacerbate the rising tension on the subject of armament limitation amongst Japan, the USA and the European nations.[3]

If the problems on the international horizon were not enough, Eden was aware that, as a relatively young and inexperienced senior Minister, his policies would be subject to intense scrutiny both by the Cabinet and the senior civil servants.[4] In a Cabinet containing two former Foreign Secretaries much would depend on Eden gaining their support, given the Prime Minister's uninspiring leadership in the field of foreign affairs.[5] Furthermore, although the post of Minister for League of Nations Affairs was not filled, it was clear that the Lord Privy Seal, Lord Halifax, was designated to assist the Foreign Secretary. Eden later noted of the relationship established with Halifax:

> Lord Halifax, who had then no departmental duties, was Lord Privy Seal, as I had previously been, and stood in for me at the Foreign Office from time to time. He did not have a room, nor a Private Secretary, or any official position, but he eased some of my burden, especially on my brief spells of leave. We had long been friends and I was grateful for an arrangement which never caused me any anxiety, even when we did not agree about the decisions to be taken, as happened later.[6]

Eden could have been under no illusion, however, that Halifax's appointment was a strategic manoeuvre by Baldwin, designed not only to assist his young Foreign Secretary but also to placate certain sections of the Conservative Party which were suspicious of both Eden's youth and his association with the League of Nations.[7] Therefore, while there is no suggestion that Eden was not given a relatively free rein in the conduct of foreign policy, it was clear that his actions would be subject to close and informed scrutiny by his colleagues.

It was quickly apparent that Eden could not expect a period of grace on taking up the reins at the Foreign Office, for the Hoare—Laval affair had left British policy in relation to Abyssinia and the League of Nations in disarray.[8] Although Eden's speech at Geneva on 18 December 1935 had partly restored international confidence in Britain's determination to pursue a solution within the guidelines established by the League of Nations, the events of December 1935 had further exacerbated the problem of maintaining a united Anglo-French front.[9] The equivocation displayed by the British and French governments following the Paris negotiations had, if anything, probably strengthened the Italian resolve to resist any settlement of the Abyssinian issue which did not recognise a predominant Italian economic and political influence in that country.[10] While French preoccupation with European security effectively ruled out the possibility of the further extension of sanctions against Italy and cast a question-mark over the possibility of French military assistance in the event of an Anglo-Italian conflict, the position at Geneva appeared deadlocked.[11]

The Foreign Secretary's first task was to restore confidence at Geneva in the British commitment to the League of Nations and, therefore, to prevent the collapse of the sanctions front against Italy. To this end, in January 1936, Eden assured Turkey, Greece and Yugoslavia that if they were subject to aggression as a result of their participation in sanctions proposed by the League of Nations, Britain would fulfil its obligation to come to their assistance.[12] However, on the central question of Anglo-French relations Eden conceded to the Cabinet, in its first meeting of 1936, that such was the French determination to oppose the extension of further sanctions against Italy, the best that could be hoped for was the establishment of a subcommittee by the Committee of Eighteen to examine the possible effectiveness of an oil embargo.[13]

It was evident in this period that Eden was moving towards the conclusion the oil sanction was the only effective weapon, short of war, that Geneva had left in its armoury against Italy. If the credibility of the League of Nations was to be restored, the employment of this sanction was unavoidable.[14] The problems confronting the Foreign Secretary in attempting to pursue this course of action were, however, manifold. Eden was faced not only with the French reluctance to risk any further deterioration of relations with Italy[15] but also, on 12 February 1936, with a report from the Petroleum Committee which had been established by the Committee of Eighteen. The report concluded that an oil sanction against Italy would only be effective if a similar ban was imposed by the USA.[16] Eden appreciated that recent reports from Washington suggested the Americans were unlikely officially to limit the extent of their oil exports to Italy and were certainly not prepared to consider a total embargo.[17] Therefore, it was, perhaps, surprising that at the Cabinet meetings of 19 and 26 February 1936 Eden continued to insist that the British Government agree in principle to participate in an oil sanction against Italy.[18] This stance was openly attacked by Eyres-Monsell and Runciman whose departments had borne the brunt of sanctions against Italy. The Cabinet minutes record that they urged: 'that the Government should not yield to "left wing" opinion. Gestures and symbols of this kind were dangerous and to adopt a non-effective sanction was to get the worst of both worlds.'[19]

In reply Eden declared that the oil sanction was the only measure likely to break Italian resistance and to avoid the issue would represent a fatal blow to the League of Nations and encourage aggression throughout the world. It also appeared that as a symbol of collective security the Foreign Secretary hoped the oil sanction would play a key role in winning support from the USA for collaboration in sanctions directed against Italy.[20] In essence Eden's reasoning appeared little different from that of his predecessor on the symbolic value of the oil sanction but, whereas Sir Samuel Hoare eventually bowed to the threat of the oil sanction precipitating a war with Italy, Eden argued that the possibility of such an event was receding.[21] Furthermore the Foreign Secretary declared: 'The risk of an alliance between Italy and Germany was also thought to be small owing to the contempt in which Herr Hitler is believed to hold Italy.'[22]

These bold assertions, which were certainly not shared by the Service Ministers, were probably based on the calculation that the oil sanction was unlikely to result in a complete embargo on the supply of oil to Italy. In this context the possibility of Mussolini being driven, in desperation, to an attack on the British positions in the Mediterranean was remote.[23] In addition Eden remained optimistic that, despite the steady deterioration of Anglo-Italian relations, the continuation of Italo-German rivalry and suspicion over predominance in Austria would be sufficient to keep Mussolini and Hitler apart. It was quickly apparent, however, that in adopting such a stance and declaring his willingness to risk a military conflict with Italy while the possibility of French military assistance remained questionable, Eden was exposing himself to an open confrontation with the Service Ministers.[24] The decisive factor in the debate, therefore, was the intervention of Baldwin. The Prime Minister not only saw it as prudent to support Eden in his first major policy clash within the Cabinet, but had also evidently digested the lesson to be learnt from the events of December 1935. Baldwin concluded that: 'a refusal to impose an oil sanction would have a disastrous effect both now and at the next General Election.'[25] Despite dissenting votes from Runciman and Eyres-Monsell, Eden won the day with agreement that he would support the principle of an oil sanction at the forthcoming meeting of the League of Nations.[26]

However, even this step — which, in effect, represented only a modest advance on the position adopted by the Cabinet in November 1935 — was actively opposed by Flandin at Geneva on 2 and 3 March 1936.[27] If Eden had expected the change of government in France to produce a reorientation of attitudes in Paris to the League of Nations and the Abyssinian affair, he was to be sadly disappointed. As he later noted: 'Flandin's attitude was indistinguishable from Laval's but was more skilfully and consistently presented.'[28]

Flandin indicated that his concern lay primarily with European security. Therefore the need to avoid a further deterioration of relations with Italy assumed precedence over attempts to enforce a sanctions policy designed to halt the Italian forces in Abyssinia. In this context he sought to obstruct the imposition of an oil sanction on the grounds that it would cause Italy to leave the League of Nations and also possibly renounce its obligations under the Locarno agreement. Initially the French Foreign Minister demanded that any move to impose an oil sanction be preceded by the Committee of Thirteen undertaking an attempt to engineer a ceasefire in Abyssinia and further Italo-Abyssinian negotiations.[29] In deference to the French position Eden was prepared to agree to this proposal, given the condition that the Committee of Thirteen would be bound to report on its conciliation attempt on 10 March 1936 at the latest. Flandin, however, was not satisfied with this concession and on 3 March 1936 he declared that he could only consider imposing the oil sanction if he held specific assurances that Britain would fulfil its obligations under Locarno, irrespective of the attitudes adopted by Italy and Germany. In response to this blatant attempt to link the sanctions issue with further guarantees of the British determination to assist France militarily in Europe if the Locarno agreement collapsed, Eden could only take note of Flandin's statement and inform him that a reply would be formulated after it had been discussed by the British Cabinet.[30]

The Cabinet decision of 5 March 1936 to establish a Cabinet Committee to examine the position in the event of Germany and Italy renouncing their Locarno commitments and the decision to authorise Eden to make an immediate approach to the German Government for the negotiation of an Air Pact, certainly indicated that Flandin's demands at Geneva had injected an element of urgency into British foreign policy deliberations.[31] It appeared that the central factor in these proceedings was the search for a European security agreement which encompassed an element of armament limitation. This process had been set in motion with the opening of the Disarmament Conference in February 1932 but was no nearer fruition due to Franco-German rivalry and hostility when the Conference was adjourned in June 1934.[32] A further attempt at armament limitation had been made in the form of the Anglo-French communiqué of 3 February 1935 but, given the absence of any semblance of a Franco-German consensus on the extent and equipment of their respective armed forces, the prospect of success was, from the outset, remote.[33] In an attempt to circumvent this apparent *impasse* the British Cabinet had elected on 5 June 1935 to drop their insistence that naval and air limitation agreements could only be accepted as part of a comprehensive settlement on armament levels and European security, as had been suggested by the Anglo-French communiqué.[34] One product of this more flexible interpretation of simultaneity had been the Anglo-German Naval Agreement concluded on 18 June 1935 and also parallel negotiations for a European Air Pact.[35] Eden had been instrumental both in attempting to pacify French concern over the naval agreement and in attempting to gain French and Italian support for the Air Pact. It was soon apparent from his discussions with Laval in June 1935 that while the French were tacitly prepared to admit the value of the naval agreement, the possibility of the establishment of an air agreement was a far more emotive security concern for the French Government. Laval's insistence that an Air Pact could only be part of a general settlement including non-aggression and mutual assistance agreements in Central and Eastern Europe and also underwritten by an Anglo-French military pact, effectively blocked any further progress in the summer of 1935.[36] The project was shelved in the latter half of 1935 when it became apparent that Germany was determined to observe the product of the Anglo-French clash with Italy before committing itself to a European security agreement.[37]

If the prospect of concluding an Air Pact had receded in the latter half of 1935, the whole question of an agreement with Germany was brought sharply back into focus with the submission of the Third Report of the DRC on 21 November 1935. In its assessment of the international climate the report noted: 'we are living in a world more dangerous than it has ever been before, that we can count on no-one but ourselves unless we are strong.'

In particular Germany was seen as 'rearming at full speed and re-joicing at the dissolution of the Stresa front'. In addition the report argued that Japan appeared determined 'to dominate the Far East as Germany means to dominate in Europe'. It was clear that Germany and Japan were singled out as the main threats to international stability. In the long term the report saw 'no alternative to our raising our armaments to a far more effective level than they will attain when existing approved programmes are completed'. However, in the short term, it was advocated that Britain must 'do everything we can in conjunction with France, to promote and maintain friendly relations with Germany'.[38]

On the same day that the DRC report was submitted a Foreign Office memorandum by Wigram and Sargent entitled, 'Britain, France and Germany', squarely reopened the question of whether a settlement of differences with Germany was desirable and examined the areas in which Germany might expect concessions. In referring to the demand for equality of rights contained in Hitler's speech of 21 May 1935, the memorandum argued that to satisfy Germany on this point would necessitate a revision of the Treaty of Versailles and, therefore, a reopening of the various debates surrounding the Rhineland de-militarised zone, the territorial settlement in Eastern and Central Europe and the German claims to a colonial empire: 'It is impossible to suppose that there are not, as Germany gathers strength at an increasing rate of progression, still great changes to be made in the treaty settlement.' While not delineating the exact terms of any future settlement, Wigram and Sargent unequivocally supported the con-clusion that it would be to the advantage of the British Government to engineer an early settlement of its differences with Germany:

> The fundamental idea is of course that the ex-Allied Powers should come to terms with Germany in order to remove grievances by friendly arrangements and by the process of give and take, before Germany once again takes the law into her own hands. This is the only constructive policy open to Europe — the alternatives of drift and encirclement are avowedly policies of negation and despair.[39]

On assuming the post of Foreign Secretary, one of Eden's first tasks had been to take stock of the state of Anglo-German relations. On 17 January 1935 he circulated a collection of reports from the Berlin Embassy and in a covering memorandum entitled 'The German Danger' he attempted to assess the objectives of the recent course of German diplomacy. Eden concluded that Hitler was aiming at:

> the destruction of the peace settlement and the re-establishment of Germany as the dominant power in Europe. The means by which this policy is to be effected are two-fold:
>
> (a) Internally through the militarisation of the whole nation in all its aspects.
>
> (b) Externally by economic and territorial expansion so as to absorb as far as possible all those of German race who are at present citizens of neighbouring states, to acquire new markets for German industry and new fields for German emigration, and to obtain control of some of the sources of those raw materials at present lacking in Germany.
>
> I draw two conclusions from the situation thus presented. The first . . . is that it is vital to hasten and complete our own re-armament.
>
> My second is that . . . it will be well to consider whether it is still possible to come to some *modus vivendi* — to put it no higher — with Hitler's Germany which would be both honourable and safe for this country and which would, at the same time, lessen the

increasing tension in Europe caused by the growth of Germany's strength and ambitions.[40]

This memorandum, which was submitted to the Cabinet on 29 January 1936, was followed by a meeting of the senior Foreign Office policy advisers on 3 February 1936 to consider a memorandum by Sir Robert Vansittart on the possible grounds for a settlement with Germany. Vansittart argued that:

> The Versailles system has broken down and until something else is put in its place general instability and consequent tension will continue and draw nearer to breaking.

> If we wish to achieve a comprehensive settlement, as contrasted with a temporary *détente*, then we must face the fact that this settlement must take the form of a bargain. A bargain can only be achieved at a price.

In essence Vansittart advocated the pursuit of a comprehensive settlement which included the return of Germany to the League of Nations, armament limitation and territorial adjustments. In reply to his critics within the Foreign Office, who argued that Germany could be bought off with British recognition of its economic predominance in East Europe, the Permanent Under-Secretary noted:

> Two points must, however, be made perfectly plain. One is that no commercial facilities alone will ever satisfy 'A People without Room' stoked to fever heat and artificial fertility. The second is that we cannot possibly in the existing state of Europe, make any statements of renunciation in Central Europe, for such action would produce panic and a political landslide.

In coming to the heart of his argument Vansittart strongly recommended that German ambitions be satisfied with the granting of colonial concessions in Africa and Asia:

> I would say definitely that the present rulers of Germany are bent upon eventual adventures that will be almost certain to unleash a European war. What we can do is to gain time . . . .

> Would not a colonial restitution, as part of a reasonable and comprehensive settlement, reached in collaboration with France, and concluded in Geneva, justifiable in any case be doubly so if no other bridging material can be devised?[41]

Eden's doubts as to the timing of a settlement with Germany and particularly as to the advisability of the cession of colonies were reflected in his report to the Cabinet on 5 February 1936:

he had reached the view that the policy of reconditioning the Defence Services must be accompanied by some attempt at an agreement in the political sphere with Germany, although he could not at the moment specify when and in what circumstances.[42]

The Foreign Secretary undertook to circulate a further memorandum on the topic to the Cabinet on 12 February 1936. This report, however, did little more than recommend that any concessions to Germany must be part of a comprehensive settlement:

> I am in favour of making some attempt to come to terms with Germany but upon one indispensable condition: that we offer no sops to Germany. There must be no concession merely to keep Germany quiet, for that process only stimulates the appetite it is intended to satisfy.

Yet in terms of concrete proposals Eden offered little more than a suggestion that the Cabinet establish a subcommittee to examine the possible bases of an agreement with Germany.[43]

The fact that little positive progress had been made after a month of deliberation and consultation was, in effect, indicative that, while Eden and most of his colleagues were in agreement on the need to improve Anglo-German relations, there was no general consensus on either the nature of the concessions that Germany would demand or on what form the general reaction would take, both in Britain and internationally, to a decision to support the granting of colonial mandates to Germany. It would seem, therefore, that the leisurely pace of the discussions was influenced not only by the complexity of the matter but also by the conviction that Germany was unlikely to press the issue in the immediate future. Reports from the Berlin Embassy in December 1935 had reinforced the suggestion that Hitler fully appreciated Britain's desire for a settlement of differences and that he was, therefore, unlikely to take any precipitate action in the foreseeable future that might jeopardise the opening of negotiations.[44] In January and February of 1936 Eden had worked actively to reassure the Germans that Britain was willing to meet several of their demands as part of a wider settlement and to reassure Hitler that neither the Franco-Soviet Pact nor the Mediterranean Pact negotiations were designed to obstruct or infringe legitimate German ambitions.[45] Therefore when the Cabinet Committee on Germany met for its initial session on 17 February 1936, while appreciating the importance of the prospective negotiations with Germany, little sense of urgency was evinced. It appeared that most shared the Foreign Secretary's opinion that any solution would have to involve the League of Nations and Germany would be content to wait until after the settlement of the Abyssinian issue before opening formal negotiations. The meeting was, therefore, adjourned while further reports were prepared for the Committee's examination.[46]

Given the above conclusions, the tone of Eden's report of the Cabinet Committee meeting to Sir E. Phipps on 24 February 1936 is perhaps somewhat surprising. Whereas the meeting had appeared prepared to await the end of the Abyssinian conflict and the completion of the forthcoming French elections before launching an initiative, the Foreign Secretary now warned Phipps that such calculations could no longer govern British policy: 'it seems to be becoming clearer and clearer that before long we shall be making a supreme effort to reach an understanding with Germany.'

Phipps was also warned that the approach to Germany might well be in the form of a unilateral British initiative rather than as part of a broad Anglo-French agreement. Eden concluded: 'I have a feeling . . . that there will eventually be an inclination to use the Air Pact as the means of the first move towards Germany.'[47]

The reason for this sudden change of pace is far from clear, although Eden argued that it was quite logical given the imminent unveiling of the Defence White Paper which in its advocacy of increased expenditure to counter German ambitions was likely to sour Anglo-German relations. In addition he contended that Italian participation in the London Naval Conference indicated that the Abyssinian conflict need not rule out the possibility of Italian co-operation in a European security settlement prior to the settlement of the Abyssinian affairs.[48] This explanation is far from convincing given that Eden had been fully aware of both of these factors for at least a month. It is perhaps more illuminating, therefore, to look at the drafting of the despatch to Sir E. Phipps and to note that it was largely the work of Ralph Wigram. The Foreign Office had been receiving reports from its Berlin and Paris Embassies since February 1935 suggesting that Germany considered the proposed format of the Franco-Soviet Treaty to be incompatible with French obligations under the Treaty of Locarno.[49] Little credence, however, had been placed in Wigram's warnings that Hitler was determined to reoccupy the Rhineland zone and was unlikely to wait until the settlement of the Abyssinian conflict. In particular Wigram emphasised that the Germans were likely to respond to the ratification of the Franco-Soviet Treaty in the latter half of February with the contention that the agreement nullified the Locarno Treaty and, therefore, released Germany from its commitment not to remilitarise the Rhineland.[50]

Although Eden had initially discounted Wigram's warnings, if only on the grounds that Germany had already covertly remilitarised much of the Rhineland zone, he had been sufficiently disturbed to call for appreciations of the military value of the zone from the Ministries of Air and War.[51] Two factors, however, in the latter half of February may have served further to convince Eden of the need to increase the pace of the deliberations on a possible approach to Germany. Firstly Eden received further reports from Phipps which indicated that the German Foreign Ministry was still adamant that the ratification of the Franco-Soviet Treaty would clearly conflict with French commitments under the Treaty of Locarno.[52] It was obvious that a move to reoccupy the Rhineland could not be entirely discounted. Secondly a series of conversations which Wigram had held with Von Hoesch and Bismarck in February 1936 suggested the German officials were sufficiently receptive to the idea of an air agreement to the extent that Von Hoesch requested an interview with Eden, on 27 February 1936, to discuss specifically the prospect of Britain presenting a draft proposal.[53] Given German interest in the Air Pact scheme and a prospective dip in relations following the release of the Defence White Paper, it would seem that Eden accepted Wigram's advice that it would be in Britain's interest not only to open negotiations as soon as possible but also to utilise the Air Pact to initiate discussions which might eventually be expanded to encompass the general issue of European security. As any eventual agreement would have to incorporate the surrender of the Rhineland to full German sovereignty it seemed wise to attempt to extract some form of *quid pro quo* from Germany before Hitler took the matter into his own hands.

While Wigram's arguments probably prompted Eden's despatch of 24 February 1936 to Berlin, it does not automatically follow that he fully accepted Wigram's conviction that a German move against the Rhineland zone was imminent. Indeed in response to Flandin's repeated probing as to what stance Britain would adopt in the event of Germany infringing the demilitarised status of the Rhineland zone, Eden, with Cabinet approval, refused to be drawn and maintained that it was initially a matter for France to declare its position.[54] The British response certainly suggested that the Cabinet remained sceptical of the possibility of Germany openly remilitarising the Rhineland and, therefore, saw no reason to co-ordinate Anglo-French strategy. In addition Eden also suspected that not only were further military commitments to support France probably unnecessary but also that they could be counter-productive, in that they would increase the French reluctance to offer concessions to Germany as part of an overall settlement and undermine German confidence in Britain's sincerity in working for an equitable solution to the problem of European security.[55] The French, however, did hold one trump card in that Flandin linked his support for further sanctions against

Italy to the receipt of assurances of the British determination to maintain its Locarno commitments, irrespective of the attitudes adopted by the other treaty signatories. This move created a particular dilemma for Eden for to give such an assurance, when neither Eden nor the Cabinet wanted to commit Britain to the possibility of having to fight to maintain the demilitarised zone, made little strategic or diplomatic sense given the delicate nature of negotiations with Germany.[56] However, if the French request was ignored or refused, there was a very real prospect of Eden's strategy at Geneva being blocked by the French Government. At the Cabinet meeting on 5 March 1936, Eden sought to sidetrack the French demands, in the short term, by the establishment of a Cabinet Committee to examine the whole question of the situation that would arise if Italy or Germany abrogated or directly infringed the Treaty of Locarno and, in the long term, by opening immediate discussions with Germany for a European security agreement which would also placate French security fears. For this purpose the Air Pact scheme, which tackled the central problems of mutual assistance and armament limitation in Western Europe, appeared to be the most suitable vehicle for a *rapprochement*. Furthermore, given that the pact had been agreed in principle by all of the potential major participants and was not directly subject to the tangled web of either East-European or League of Nations' diplomacy, the prospect of an early agreement seemed promising.[57]

On the basis of these conclusions Eden outlined his proposal for an Air Pact to the German Ambassador on 6 March 1936. This initiative unfortunately was too late to have any significant impact on the course of German foreign policy.[58] Hitler had been carefully observing the political situation in Europe for over twelve months with the express purpose of capitalising on any opportunity that was presented for the reoccupation of the Rhineland zone. On 14 February 1936 a despatch to the Rome Embassy indicated that Hitler was considering the possibility of making a move: 'Until now he had always envisaged the Spring of 1937 as the right moment. Political developments, however, made one wonder whether the psychological moment had not arrived now.'[59]

The political developments referred to were undoubtedly the various rifts generated in relations between France, Britain and Italy by the Abyssinian affair, which suggested that Germany was unlikely to have to face a united and determined front if it chose to denounce the Locarno agreement. In this context a despatch from the German Ambassador in Rome, dated 22 February 1936, was probably decisive in Hitler's calculations. After a discussion with Mussolini, Hassell reported: 'Mussolini would not take part in action by Britain and

France against Germany occasioned by an alleged breach by Germany of the Locarno Treaty.'[60]

Given this tacit assurance of Italian neutrality and Britain's open desire for negotiation rather than confrontation with Germany, an opportunity to reoccupy the Rhineland had been plainly presented. On 2 March 1936 General Von Blomberg issued orders to the Commanders-in-Chief of the three Services to prepare for the movement of units into the demilitarised zone.[61] On 7 March 1936, despite Eden's efforts at the eleventh hour, German military units moved unopposed into the Rhineland.

Although it must be conceded that the British Government's determination to pursue an agreement with Germany encouraged Hitler to take a calculated gamble in reoccupying the Rhineland, it does not necessarily follow that a different line would have deterred the German Chancellor. Hitler was aware that the Abyssinian dispute had eliminated the possibility of Italy fulfilling its pledge to uphold the Treaty of Locarno. In addition the Germans probably suspected that the French army, which was the only military force capable of physically opposing the German occupation of the Rhineland, was completely unprepared for any form of offensive operation in the demilitarised zone.[62] It would appear, however, that the British Foreign Secretary erred in his assessment of two factors. Firstly, while admitting the force of the growing German campaign for full sovereignty over the Rhineland zone, Eden failed to give sufficient weight to the assessments from Berlin, Paris and also from within the Foreign Office which repeated the German contention that the Franco-Soviet Pact was incompatible with French obligations under the Treaty of Locarno. Therefore, right up until 7 March 1936, Eden did not consider that the integrity of the Rhineland zone was under an imminent threat, despite ratification of the Franco-Soviet Treaty by France on 27 February 1936.[63] Secondly, in his desire to engineer an agreement with Germany, the Foreign Secretary rejected any suggestion of an expansion of Anglo-French ties and commitments in the military and diplomatic spheres. This both encouraged Hitler to gamble on the Rhineland operation and was to inhibit a positive Anglo-French response to the German action at a time when the Stresa front was already under extreme pressure with the alienation of Italy.[64]

On 7 March 1936, after a brief initial discussion on the course of negotiations for a further Anglo-German naval agreement, the German Ambassador presented Eden with a memorandum declaring that his government considered the recently ratified Franco-Soviet Treaty contradicted the terms of the Treaty of Locarno. Germany, therefore, no longer felt itself bound by the Treaty and had accordingly taken steps to remilitarise the Rhineland zone 'in accordance with the fundamental right of a nation to secure its frontiers and ensure its possibilities of defence'. This declaration was followed by a pledge that, with the restoration of unrestricted sovereignty in the Rhineland, Germany was prepared to collaborate fully in the pursuit of a European security settlement. To this end it was proposed that a new demilitarised zone be established straddling the Franco-Belgian frontiers with Germany and that discussions be opened in the near future for a European Air Pact and a network of 25-year non-aggression pacts with Germany's neighbours in both Western and Eastern Europe. Finally, now that German equality of rights had been restored, Von Hoesch stated that his country was prepared to resume membership of the League of Nations.[65] While Eden refused to comment on the German memorandum other than to point out that it represented, in his opinion, a clear breach of a treaty that had been freely negotiated and signed by the German Government (and therefore of a distinctly different status from the Treaty of Versailles), his initial reaction was indicated when the French Ambassador, Corbin, was subsequently summoned to the Foreign Office. Although the Foreign Secretary had been assured by Flandin at Geneva on 4 March 1936 that, in the event of Germany infringing the demilitarised status of the Rhineland zone, France would not take any direct military measures against Germany without first consulting both the League of Nations and its Locarno allies,[66] Eden emphasised that the British Government was unlikely to take any immediate military action. Eden stressed that:

> This very important memorandum would require very careful consideration by the Cabinet when it met on Monday morning . . . .

> He felt sure that until consultation had taken place the French Government would not do anything to render the situation more difficult.

In particular the Foreign Secretary emphasised that popular outrage in Britain resulting from the German action would probably be quickly tempered by a determination to explore the terms outlined in the German memorandum: 'we must not close our eyes to the fact that a "contre partie" was offered and that would undoubtedly have a very considerable effect on public opinion.'[67]

While awaiting a reply from Paris, Eden travelled to Chequers to discuss the situation with the Prime Minister. It appeared that Eden's initial assessment of the situation was entirely supported by Baldwin. Of their conversation Eden later recorded: 'Baldwin said little, as was his wont on foreign affairs. Though personally friendly to France he was clear in his mind that there could be no support in Britain for any military action by the French. I could only agree.'[68] Furthermore Eden's warning to Corbin that Britain did not envisage taking immediate military action appeared to have had the desired effect when a despatch from Paris was received advocating a meeting of both the Locarno signatories and the Council of the League of Nations as soon as possible. In the intervening period the French Government agreed to consider 'the situation calmly and steadily and would not do anything to render it more difficult'.[69]

It appeared that an immediate crisis, in the form of a military conflict with Germany, had been avoided. As Eden set about preparing a detailed memorandum on the situation for a Cabinet meeting called for Monday 9 March 1936, it was apparent that, although the German action represented a clear breach of the Treaties of Versailles and Locarno, the Foreign Secretary did not see the end-product as entirely unwelcome and certainly not as a justification for a radical reassessment of the rationale underpinning recent attempts to establish the grounds for a European security agreement with Germany.[70] In attempting to justify this position Eden pointed out that on both strategic and diplomatic grounds the British Government had seen little reason to obstruct the eventual return of the Rhineland zone to Germany and, indeed, had sought positively to avoid a situation where Britain might be required to fight for the maintenance of the zone. A decision, therefore, had already been taken to seek the surrender of the zone as part of solving the central problem of establishing a European security agreement. While the German action had effectively pre-empted the British initiative, the proposals for an Air Pact, treaties of non-aggression and the return of Germany to the League of Nations approximately fulfilled the terms desired of Germany. The Foreign Secretary was, therefore, determined to look to the positive aspects of the situation and to exploit the opportunity for a European settlement which Hitler had presented him with:

> The myth is now exploded that Herr Hitler only repudiates treaties imposed on Germany by force. We must be prepared for him to repudiate any treaty even if freely negotiated (a) when it becomes inconvenient; and (b) when Germany is sufficiently strong and the circumstances are otherwise favourable for doing so.

> On the other hand owing to Germany's material strength and power of mischief in Europe it is in our interest to conclude with her as far-reaching and enduring a settlement as possible whilst Hitler is still in the mood to do so.

The immediate problem was to persuade the French Government to follow the British lead and, rather than alienating Germany further through the imposition of sanctions, to be content with a formal denunciation of the German action and focus attention on a discussion of the terms offered. Eden was forced to concede that the problem of dissuading the French from demanding punitive measures against Germany would be difficult to solve, given that the British Government was unwilling to consider any form of Anglo-French commitment in excess of its existing obligations. The memorandum concluded:

> The essential thing will be to induce or cajole France to accept this mandate. The trouble is that we are in a bad position to browbeat her into what we think reasonableness, because, if she wishes to do so, she can always hold us to join with her in turning the German forces out of the Rhineland. The strength of our position lies in the fact that France is not in the mood for a military adventure of this sort. Unfortunately, between military action on the one hand and friendly negotiation on the other, there lies the policy of sulking and passive obstruction, and it is this policy to which the French government, in their weakness, will be inclined to have recourse and out of which we shall have to persuade them.[71]

A further memorandum of the same date to the Prime Minister, requesting that the Chiefs-of-Staff reassess the advisability of including the Air Pact within a comprehensive settlement and proposing that the Colonial Office examine the possibility of the transfer of Colonial Mandates held by the League of Nations to Germany, only served to emphasise Eden's determination to grasp the opportunity presented by Hitler.[72]

On 9 March 1936 the Cabinet endorsed Eden's proposals. In order to placate the French it was agreed that the Foreign Secretary would reaffirm Britain's commitment to the Treaty of Locarno in the House of Commons that same afternoon.[73] Furthermore it was agreed that Eden and Halifax would travel to Paris for a meeting of the Locarno powers on the following day.[74] It seemed that Eden's assessment of the popular reaction to the German remilitarisation of the Rhineland had been largely vindicated. Of the national newspapers, only the *Daily Telegraph* insisted that Britain should take up the challenge presented by Hitler to the principles of the Treaty of Locarno.[75] At the other end of the spectrum the *Daily Mail*, the *Daily Express* and the *News Chronicle* all patently scorned any suggestion of sanctions while the *Manchester Guardian* and *The Times* focused specifically on the opportunity to rebuild the European security system contained in the German terms.[76] It was apparent that the Press was generally determined to draw a clear distinction between Italian aggression in Abyssinia and Hitler's reoccupation of German territory. The *Manchester Guardian* typified the prevailing mood in its sympathy for the German position:

> If we cannot overlook a repudiation which was as wicked as it was unnecessary, neither can we forget that for Germans to insist on defending their own territory with arms is not the same heinous moral offence, nor deserving the same penalties, as waging war, like Mussolini, on an unoffending country or preparing a base for an actual invasion.[77]

Despite the apparent desire for conciliation with Germany in Britain, Eden's fear that the French Government would not be so flexible was soon confirmed at the meeting of the representatives of the Locarno powers held in Paris on Tuesday 10 March 1936. Flandin opened the discussion by insisting that France would not commence negotiations with Germany until the German Army had been withdrawn from the Rhineland zone. When asked by Eden how the French intended to enforce an evacuation of the German forces, the French Foreign Minister proposed that the German violation of Articles 42 and 43 of the Treaty of Versailles be reported to the Council of the League of Nations and support be sought for the imposition of economic, financial and ultimately military sanctions against Germany. In that the German action had infringed the ruling of the Council of the League of Nations of 17 April 1935 on the sanctity of treaties, Flandin was confident that there would be widespread support for the imposition of sanctions. On this point Eden was openly sceptical, for the League Council ruling only invited members to enforce economic or financial sanctions that would have little immediate impact on the situation. The Foreign Secretary suspected that the only outcome of economic sanctions would be the creation of a military confrontation with Germany, for which Britain, France and Belgium would receive little tangible support from either their Locarno ally, Italy, or the League of Nations.[78] When, at a subsequent private meeting of the Foreign Minister, Flandin and Van Zeeland confirmed their determination to pursue a policy of sanctions to restore the demilitarised status of the Rhineland, Eden was sufficiently disturbed to break off not only from the Paris negotiations but also his planned journey to Geneva in order to report back to the Cabinet in London.[79]

As Eden reported to the Cabinet on the evening of 11 March 1936, the possibility of war appeared to be very real given the outward determination of France and Belgium to enforce sanctions against

Germany. Eden's belief that economic and financial sanctions would not be sufficient to force Germany to retreat from the Rhineland was supported by a despatch from the British Ambassador in Berlin commenting on the Paris negotiations:

> I do not share M. Van Zeeland's optimism that the chances of war would be only 1 in 10.
>
> Germany is ruled by bold and determined adventurers . . . . If as a consequence of sanctions or similar measures the water rises to Herr Hitler's neck he . . . will take the plunge into war rather than submit lamely to be drowned.[80]

Yet the policy of conciliation supported by the Cabinet on 9 March 1936 had gained little response from either France or Belgium. Eden reported of the Paris negotiations that he 'had soon discovered that our policy of condemning the German action and then developing a constructive policy to re-establish the European situation had no chance of acceptance'.[81]

The Foreign Secretary remained convinced that a policy of conciliation was the only viable option. He had undoubtedly been encouraged by a private meeting with Van Zeeland who had indicated that the replacement of Locarno with some form of similar Anglo-French military understanding, perhaps underwritten by specific assurances incorporating General Staff negotiations, might be sufficient to persuade the French to open discussions with Germany.[82] With the possibility of negotiations not entirely eliminated, Eden's immediate task was to forestall the imposition of sanctions. To this end the Cabinet agreed that, if necessary, the Foreign Secretary would warn the French that Britain had neither the military capability nor the popular domestic support necessary to mount a military operation against Germany. It was appreciated, however, that France could only be drawn into negotiation if some form of reciprocal concession were forthcoming from Germany. The Cabinet, therefore, endorsed Eden's proposal that he act upon Van Zeeland's recommendation that the Germans accede to the withdrawal of all but a symbolic number of troops from the zone and agree not to construct fortifications while negotiations for the settlement of the issue were set in motion.[83]

It seemed that Van Zeeland's estimation of Flandin's willingness to compromise had been vindicated when on 12 March 1936 the French Foreign Secretary, while continuing to insist upon the redefinition of Britain's Locarno commitments and the right to demand British collaboration in sanctions organised by the League of Nations against Germany, agreed to Eden's suggestion that if the

German Forces moved into the Rhineland on 7 March 1936 were withdrawn, France would be prepared to open negotiations with Germany for a European security settlement incorporating the surrender of the zone to Germany.[84] Even this modest advance was overturned the following day, however, with the addition to the French delegation of M. Paul-Boncour, Minister for League of Nations Affairs. As Eden noted in a despatch to the Paris Embassy, Paul-Boncour claimed that he 'was staggered to find how far we had drifted already from the point of view of the French public'.[85] His presence was certainly instrumental in forcing Flandin to retreat from the modest concessions that he had made and to insist once again that a full German military evacuation was a prerequisite to the opening of negotiations. Faced with an apparent *impasse*, Eden acted on the Cabinet instructions of 11 March 1936:

> We told M. Paul-Boncour that in our view the policy which he put forward might well result in war.
>
> . . . we were convinced that British public opinion was not prepared to go to war in order that the Germans should be compelled to go out of the Rhineland one week and be allowed to come into it the next.[86]

The French response was disappointing in that Flandin, while admitting to Eden his sympathy for the British position, insisted that his Government would not consider any further concessions. A breakdown in the negotiations appeared imminent in that the French Minister could only suggest that an early adjournment would assist him in attempting to gain support for a more moderate set of proposals from his colleagues.[87]

As Eden reviewed the situation on 15 March 1936, the prospect of achieving a compromise settlement must have seemed remote. A further blow had been dealt to Eden's peace initiative the previous day when the Counsellor of the German Embassy, Prince Von Bismarck, had informed the Foreign Office that Hitler felt he could go no further than undertake not to increase the level of troops in the Rhineland above their existing strength.[88] It appeared, however, that Eden still felt the key to the situation lay with France and the establishment of a solution that would placate French security fears. He therefore recommended that Locarno be replaced by a network of non-aggression pacts between France, Germany and Belgium, guaranteed by Britain and Italy. This system would be backed by pacts of mutual assistance between Britain, France and Belgium which would be cemented by contacts between their respective General Staffs. Germany would be invited to participate in the network of pacts but Hitler's acceptance would not be seen as a precondition for the establishment of links between France, Belgium and Britain. It was hoped that the conclusion of the mutual assistance pact would be sufficient to persuade France to accept a compromise over the Rhineland issue. In return the French would be required to accept a ruling by either the Court of International Justice or the Permanent Court of International Arbitration as to whether the Franco-Soviet Treaty was compatible with French commitments under the Treaty of Locarno. Pending the outcome of the case, France, Belgium and Germany would undertake not to fortify their respective frontier zones and accept the imposition of an international military force straddling the Franco-German and Belgian-German frontiers. Finally all parties would agree to take note of the German proposals advanced on 7 March 1936 and participate in negotiations to revise the status of the Rhineland within the format of a European security settlement.[89]

These proposals, which were accepted by the Cabinet on 16 March 1936, once again indicated Eden's conviction that the solution to the problem lay in exploiting the terms offered by Hitler on 7 March 1936 and that, therefore, the initial task was to win the French over to this position.[90] The suspicion that the French Government was by no means as inflexible in its attitude to the situation as Paul-Boncour had suggested had been further reinforced by reports from both Neville Chamberlain and Ralph Wigram of informal conversations with Flandin and Massigli. Both Ministers had hinted that the French Government was willing to consider the establishment of an international force and reference of the dispute to arbitration, particularly as this would delay the prospect of a confrontation with Germany until after the completion of the French elections.[91]

The Foreign Secretary's proposals were approved by the Cabinet on 16 March 1936 and presented to the French and Belgian delegations the following day. It was a great disappointment to Eden when the French Foreign Minister rejected the idea of an international force straddling the frontier and insisted on it either being based on German territory or being composed of an Anglo-Italian force on French soil, as evidence of support by the guarantors of Locarno for the French case. In addition Flandin demanded that Germany agree the ruling of the Court of International Justice be binding on both parties and prior agreement be reached by Britain, France and Belgium on the format of economic and military sanctions to be imposed on Germany in the event of Germany refusing the above terms.[92]

In a private conversation after the meeting Flandin confessed to Eden:

that his mission to London had been a failure.

> M. Flandin further said, without any heat or ill feeling, that the present meeting was a misfortune not only for the League but for Anglo-French relations.

He warned Eden that he would have to return to Paris at the end of the week and that he feared the forthcoming elections would now result in a victory for those who sought a purely Franco-German settlement of the European security question and were hostile to Britain.[93] The prospect of a breakdown in Anglo-French relations was certainly uppermost in Eden's mind when he reported to the Cabinet on the evening of 18 March 1936. While a proposal by Halifax of British participation in an international force to be stationed in the Rhineland and a force drawn from the Locarno powers to be despatched onto French and Belgian territory had closed the gap between the two delegations, Flandin was still demanding a firm commitment of support from Britain, particularly in the co-ordination of possible military action against Germany. In his report to the Cabinet Eden concluded that the French had not budged an inch from their original estimation that a show of Anglo-French resolve would be sufficient to force the Germans to retire from the Rhineland. In addition he added:

> the French and Belgians were actuated by a conviction that unless Germany was brought to reason now, there was a certainty of war in two years time — which the Secretary of State for Foreign Affairs regretted to say was not an improbable forecast.

Eden, therefore, recommended that Britain agree to the opening of military conversations with France and Belgium for the co-ordination of possible military measures against Germany. This proposal was not well received and, as the Cabinet Minutes recorded, the general feeling was that such a step:

> would be very unacceptable to public opinion in this country which was strongly opposed to any forcible action to compel the Germans to evacuate the Demilitarised Zone. Moreover, we were not in a position to give effective military support in any such operation as the French were well aware.[94]

In reaching this conclusion the Cabinet had undoubtedly been influenced by a report from the Chiefs-of-Staff Subcommittee of the CID, which had concluded that the commitment of forces to the Mediterranean had completely undermined Britain's ability to conduct any form of successful military campaign against Germany without a period of two to four months' preparation.[95] Therefore the Cabinet rejected any suggestion that Britain specifically define the format of economic and military sanctions which might be taken against Germany, although it did agree in principle to the opening of Staff talks providing that they were confined purely to technical co-ordination of defence measures resulting from existing agreements. While the Foreign Secretary felt obliged to warn the Cabinet that negotiations on the basis outlined were liable to fail, it was apparent that he shared many of the reservations held by various members of the Cabinet as to the propriety of surrendering to the French position on military sanctions.[96] Although Eden had only tacitly supported Stanley Baldwin's assertion that the outcome of crushing Germany militarily would be to open the door to Communist insurrection in that country,[97] as early as 12 February 1936 the Foreign Secretary had expressed his doubts as to the wisdom of French policy in deciding to ratify the Franco-Soviet Treaty.[98] In particular Eden seemed to consider that the Treaty was indicative of the French determination to continue to play a role in Eastern Europe, which was no longer realistic or practicable given the re-emergence of a powerful German nation. As the main military value of the de-militarised zone was to permit France to move quickly against Germany in the event of aggression against its East-European allies, Eden was not entirely unhappy to see such a potentially explosive commitment effectively liquidated.[99] On the question of military sanctions against Germany, Eden shared the Cabinet's suspicion that the French were far from united in their determination to fight, if necessary, to regain the zone. In his memorandum to the Cabinet Committee on Germany, Eden had noted:

> M. Flandin's surroundings show I think, that the French Govern-ment are themselves uncertain as to what attitude they ought to adopt. They would probably like us to make up their minds for them, and then excuse themselves for not fighting for the Zone on the ground that we would not join them. Although it would be dangerous to be too categorical, it seems unlikely that any French Government would attack Germany merely in order to maintain the demilitarisation of the Rhineland.[100]

In this context there was a strong undercurrent within the Cabinet which felt that the French were merely using the threat of a demand for British assistance in order to lever further military assurances from Britain of such assistance in the event of a clash with Germany. It was felt, therefore, that to provide such assurances would only encourage the French to be even more intransigent in their attitude towards a general security settlement and the acceptance of Germany as a major international power.[101] Therefore, despite the Foreign Secretary's hesitations, the Cabinet on 18 March 1936 effectively decided to call the French bluff. To Eden's relief Flandin acceded to the British terms. The Foreign Secretary accepted the French demand that an international force be stationed solely in the Rhineland and that the dispute be referred to arbitration that was to be binding on both parties. Germany in the intervening period would not be permitted to fortify the zone. In return Flandin withdrew his stipulation that the opening of negotiations with Germany be conditional on the evacuation of German forces from the Rhineland and an agreement on the format of economic and military sanctions in the event of Germany rejecting the Anglo-French-Belgian proposals.[102] Flandin's decision not to press the sanction issue and to accept a simple re-affirmation of Locarno, supported by the promise of technical discussions between the respective General Staffs, appeared to confirm the suspicion that the French Government and its military advisers had privately entertained serious doubts as to the wisdom of employing military sanctions against Germany.[103] This view was supported by a subsequent report from the British Ambassador in Paris:

> In taking up and in maintaining the attitude adopted during the London negotiations, the French Government have undoubtedly been showing themselves far more rigid than their own public opinion or even that of the French press . . . . That they have felt themselves obliged to stiffness is, I think, partly due to electoral considerations.[104]

The settlement was presented on 19 March 1936 to the Cabinet which, as Neville Chamberlain noted, was 'delighted with the final result'.[105] Eden later recorded:

> These results were received by all in Britain with relief and by many with satisfaction.

> There was nowhere a suggestion that we should have been sharper with Hitler, still less that we should have joined in military sanctions in the Rhineland or the Saar.[106]

The settlement seemed to represent a great personal achievement for Eden in that he had apparently succeeded in reassuring France of Britain's commitment to Locarno without pledging the Government to the implementation of sanctions against Germany.[107] More significantly for the modest price of agreeing to military conversations on a technical level, Eden had wrested the initiative away from the French. From this point onwards Eden was aware that, as long as this pledge was fulfilled and negotiations appeared to be progressing with

Germany, he was in a position to dictate the format and pace of the Anglo-French approaches to Germany.

This position was immediately challenged, however, when it became apparent that Hitler was unlikely to accept the three basic premises of the proposals presented to him, namely the placing of the dispute before the Hague Court, acceptance of an international force and an undertaking not to fortify the Rhineland zone.[108] In order to forestall the anticipated French demand for the reconsideration of a sanctions policy, Eden took immediate steps to set the machinery for Staff talks in motion and to explore new avenues in order to keep the process of conciliation with Germany in progress. While on 25 March 1936 the Cabinet approved Eden's recommendation that Britain formally confirm to France and Belgium its willingness to undertake military conversations, it was appreciated that there would be intense opposition to such a move from elements within the Conservative Party and the nation which were opposed to further foreign entanglements. The Cabinet agreed that: 'The great mass of public opinion appeared to assume that we had no commitments on the Continent and did not realise the extent of the obligations we had already assumed under the Treaty of Locarno.'[109]

It was agreed that the Foreign Secretary would undertake to point out to the House of Commons the extent of Britain's commitment to Europe as a forerunner to the announcement of the opening of military conversations.[110] In a Foreign Affairs debate the following day, Eden outlined at length Britain's commitment not only to the principles of the League of Nations but also more specifically to the balance of power in Western Europe:

> It is a vital interest of this country that the integrity of France and Belgium should be maintained and that no hostile force should cross their frontiers. The truth is, and I say it with apologies to my Right Hon. Friend the Member for West Birmingham, there was nothing very new in Locarno.

While emphasising that he did not envisage the acceptance of any new commitments, Eden repeated his determination to fulfil Britain's obligations under the Treaty of Locarno:

> There are some who may regard us as freely and fortunately placed at this anxious moment in European affairs, some who regard us as arbiters with a fortunate destiny. But we are not arbiters in this business; that is not so. We are guarantors of this Treaty, and as guarantors, for good or ill . . . we have certain commitments and they are very definite.

188

I am not prepared to be the first British Foreign Secretary to go back on a British signature.[111]

Although opposed vigorously by Lloyd George, Eden undoubtedly won the day. Neville Chamberlain wrote of Eden's performance in a letter dated 28 March 1936:

> Anthony made the speech of his life, and it was not only a good speech, it showed both courage and statesmanship and more than anything else it brought the House to see the situation in a truer perspective.[112]

In addition *The Times* described Eden's speech as 'an admirable Parliamentary performance — the best, because the most spontaneous, he has given since he became Foreign Secretary'.[113]

The Prime Minister was similarly delighted with Eden's work,[114] in that the Foreign Secretary's speech had established the platform for the announcement of the intention to initiate military conversations following Hitler's formal repudiation of the settlement terms communicated to the British Government on 1 April 1936.[115] Despite open German hostility to the suggestion of Anglo-French-Belgian military discussions, Eden was aware that the negotiations, although restricted in nature, were an important factor in placating French opinion. On 2 April 1936 Eden replied to Sir E. Phipps's report that Germany would welcome the postponement of military negotiations by stating:

> There could be no question of our refusing the French Government that measure of satisfaction to which, in my judgement, they were fully entitled.

> To restore confidence each Government had to make a contribution. Our contribution had been these Staff conversations.[116]

Therefore, despite German protests, the Staff conversations were held in London on 15 and 16 April 1936. Although the negotiations were restricted to the exchange of technical information on the co-ordination of defence measures in the event of unprovoked German aggression, the respective parties appeared satisfied with the outcome.[117]

If the military conversations were seen in Paris as an outward demonstration of Anglo-French determination to deal firmly with Germany, it would appear that in London the negotiations were seen as a concession to France while the primary goal of policy was still seen as the need to establish the basis for a settlement with

Germany.[118] The determination not to allow the London military negotiations to eliminate the possibility of future conversations with Germany had been clearly enunciated by the Chiefs-of-Staff in a memorandum dated 1 April 1936:

> The point arises in connection with preliminary conversations now contemplated with the Locarno Powers, other than Germany, for the reason that such preliminary conversations may prejudice the possibility of usefulness of later negotiations for Military and Air Pacts in which Germany would be included.
>
> We think it clear that full and unrestricted preliminary conversations with France and Belgium are, in these circumstances, out of the question and it is essential that the conversations immediately to be undertaken should be strictly limited in scope in order to prejudice the future as little as possible.[119]

Eden appreciated that the main threat to the progress of further negotiations with Germany lay in Flandin claiming that the German statement of 31 March 1936 signified the breakdown of the process of conciliation and, therefore, in demanding a further meeting of the Locarno Powers with the express purpose of organising the imposition of sanctions. When the French Ambassador approached Eden on this topic on 2 April 1936, the Foreign Secretary reacted firmly in an attempt to scotch any suggestion that conciliation had failed:

> If, for instance, it were in the mind of the French Government to arrange for a meeting in order that we might take note of the breakdown of conciliation and that as a consequence the letter had come into force, then I must make it quite clear to him that it would be impossible for me to agree to any such course. In our view the efforts at conciliation were continuing and there could be no question of my going to Brussels or Paris merely to agree that they were not.[120]

Although Eden deflected this initial approach with the suggestion that the Anglo-French case should first be referred back to the League of Nations before any discussion of sanctions was initiated, it was evident that the Foreign Secretary was already considering embarking on a further attempt at conciliation with Germany.[121] On 30 March 1936 Eden had remarked to the French Ambassador that he:

> had been interested to read the speech made by M. Flandin on 29 March. Would it perhaps be possible for us to consider a number of questions that the Three Powers might agree to put to the German Government on receipt of their answer?

190

These questions might serve both to elucidate the position and impress on German and other opinion the kind of help required if our negotiations were to succeed.[122]

It was apparent that Eden was anticipating Germany rejecting the Anglo-French-Belgian settlement formula and was already moving to establish agreement, on a further approach to Germany designed to elucidate the basis of an agreement that would be acceptable to Hitler. As expected the French reaction to the German memorandum of 31 March 1936 was scathing and declared that its contribution to the cause of peace was 'more apparent than real'. In response the French proposed an immediate meeting of the Locarno Powers to examine the possible imposition of sanctions. It was also proposed that immediate negotiations be opened between the four remaining Locarno Powers for the conclusion of a pact of mutual assistance.[123] While Eden agreed to a meeting of the Locarno Powers, given that the four nations were already scheduled to be in Geneva on 9 April 1936 for a meeting of the Committee of Thirteen on the Abyssinian dispute, he sought to prevent any suggestion of a consensus on the French suggestion that conciliation had broken down. Therefore the Foreign Secretary sought to placate Flandin by referring to the proposed Anglo-French-Belgian military conversations, while proposing that further action be deferred to permit the exploration of the German position. On 10 April 1936 Eden reported of the Locarno meeting: 'We urged that effort of conciliation had not been exhausted: and we suggested that His Majesty's Government should be authorised to clear up ambiguities in German proposals.'[124]

Given Flandin's desire not to damage the prospect of military negotiations, despite their largely symbolic value, Eden's proposals prevailed. It was agreed that the German response had not made a contribution to the restoration of international confidence but that the process of conciliation had not completely broken down. The British Government was, therefore, authorised to approach Germany with the objective of achieving 'the elucidation of a certain number of points'.[125]

The Geneva meeting was undoubtedly a further success for Eden but it was apparent that his attempts to pursue a policy of negotiation with Germany had been seriously hampered by the German memorandum of 31 March 1936. In a memorandum to the Cabinet on 29 April 1936, Eden was forced to admit that in his opinion Germany: 'had no intention of respecting the integrity of her smaller neighbours, no matter what papers she may sign.'

Despite the wealth of reports supporting this assertion, the Foreign

Secretary appeared to have no doubt that further conciliation should be attempted:

> These despatches present a gloomy view of the future for Europe. I fear that any rosier view would be illusory. They will not, of course, make any difference to our intention to probe and explore Herr Hitler's offers and to construct if possible, something reliable out of them.[126]

In attempting to account for Eden's determination to continue the search for an agreement with Germany, two factors appear to be significant. Firstly on 22 April 1936 Eden reported to the Cabinet that, in his opinion, it seemed wise to await the completion of the forthcoming French election before holding a further meeting of the Locarno Powers.[127] Along with several of his colleagues he suspected that Flandin's advocacy of a sanctions policy against Germany had been largely forced upon him by the need to win electoral support. It therefore seemed prudent to continue the process of conciliation and avoid any major meetings with the French until the new government was firmly established.[128] Secondly in a memorandum submitted to the Cabinet on 29 April 1936 Eden indicated his desire to obtain from Hitler an unequivocal declaration of the future course of German policy. As Eden declared to the Cabinet: 'to content ourselves with anything less than complete clarity would be a neglect for which we should rightly be held responsible.'[129]

It was evident that the Foreign Secretary still thought an agreement could be achieved with Germany and that he was thinking specifically of offering Hitler colonial or economic concessions in exchange for German participation in a network of non-aggression pacts guaranteeing the European status quo. Furthermore he remained convinced that, given French hostility to any suggestion of granting concessions to Germany, the best chance of initiating negotiations lay in a primarily British approach to Hitler.[130] In this context he proposed to submit to Hitler a set of questions with the aim of establishing the German viewpoint on key areas of armament and security policy. It was to be a purely British project and he informed the French Ambassador in quite explicit terms that he would not brook any interference in the drawing up of the questions, which would be communicated to France and Belgium only at the time when they were presented to Germany.[131] In content the questionnaire was a direct continuation of the policy pursued in the opening months of 1936, in that it sought to explore the proposals put forward by Hitler on 7 and 31 March 1936 and to establish the minimum terms that Germany would accept as the price for participation in a European security system. At the very least it was considered that a negative response would indicate the aggressive nature of Hitler's policy and show that the responsibility for the breakdown of negotiations lay firmly with Germany.[132] The limited and exploratory nature of the document was indicated by Eden's presentation of the initial draft to the Cabinet meeting of 30 April 1936. The Foreign Secretary noted: 'that the difficulty in drafting the questions had been not to give offence to the Germans and not to encourage them to make fresh claims.' The Cabinet were agreed that the overall object was to draw Germany into further negotiations:

> The Document, it was suggested, should be as unsensational as possible in order to bring down the international temperature. The impression it should give should be that we were most anxious to reach a bargain with Germany but as a preliminary step we want to clear up their attitude on certain points.[133]

It was surprising, therefore, that Baldwin insisted on devoting a further two Cabinet Meetings to the questionnaire before a draft was agreed.[134] The main bone of contention was opposition from Simon and Chamberlain to Eden's proposal that Germany be asked whether it would agree not to attempt to alter the political and territorial status quo in Europe except by free negotiation. Although the Foreign Secretary won the battle, he later recorded his disgruntlement at the attempts made by several of his colleagues to dilute the extent of the questionnaire:

> The words 'provocative' and 'pinprick' figured largely in these meetings and reluctantly I had to agree to cut out or modify portions of my draft, depriving it, in my judgement, of some of its usefulness, part of the purpose having been to educate opinion outside Germany, whether Hitler replied or not. In particular, some questions I wished to ask were robbed of much of their point and punch.[135]

However, despite Eden's suggestion that the questionnaire should be followed by the visit of a British Minister to Berlin to open negotiations with Hitler, the prospect of success was from the outset remote.[136] While in the short term the document served the purpose of outwardly keeping the conciliation process in motion and, therefore, restraining any suggestion of being requested to provide further commitments to France, in the long term its success depended entirely on Hitler's willingness to participate in a binding security agreement. As Sir Eric Phipps noted in a despatch from Berlin dated 15 May 1936, Hitler was unlikely to undertake such a commitment while the course of European politics remained fluid. Indeed, while the Abyssinian conflict continued to rupture Anglo-French relations with Italy and generate tension between Paris and London, there appeared to be positive advantages in Germany retaining a free hand in European politics.[137] This conviction was borne out by Hitler's guarded response to the questionnaire, refusing initially to reply until the new French Government had been installed and later linking his response to further clarification of the Anglo-French position on sanctions and the format of collective security.[138] When several weeks had elapsed and there was no indication of a positive response from Germany, it became apparent that the senior Foreign Office advisers were quickly losing patience with Germany. On 15 May 1936 Wigram minuted on a despatch from Berlin: 'It is, of course . . . a matter of gaining time and seeing what happens as between Italy and ourselves, and perhaps launching some new coup before the negotiations can take place . . . .'[139] Thirteen days later Orme Sargent concluded of Hitler:

> as soon as we recognise that the isolation of France is the one and only thing he is working for, all his manoeuvres become quite clear . . . we [are] aiming at a general agreement, including France, and Hitler is striving for an Anglo-German agreement to the exclusion of France.

This opinion was apparently endorsed by Sir R. Vansittart: 'Hitler has never meant business in our sense of the word. The sooner the Cabinet realise that the better for this long misguided country!'[140]

Despite these warnings and a further report from Sir E. Phipps concluding that Hitler 'does not desire any negotiations and that he is merely playing for time', Eden publicly and privately refused to be deflected from his determination to pursue a response from Hitler to the questionnaire.[141] In reply to Wigram he minuted on 18 May 1936 that the Foreign Office must:

> consider the next step, for we cannot leave matters as they are. Personally I see some attraction in the offer of a visit of a Minister, if only because this would make it more difficult for Herr Hitler to take refuge in evasion and would show our public our determination to get on if we can . . . .[142]

In response to increasing concern within the Foreign Office, Eden replied on 3 June 1936 to Sargent's minute of 28 May 1936:

> we must continue to aim at the general agreement that Mr. Sargent refers to in his last paragraph. It may be that it is

unattainable, but it is we who must prove this by making every effort to attain it . . . .[143]

Even when confronted with a report from Berlin indicating that a German reply to the questionnaire was unlikely, the Foreign Secretary maintained that the policy of conciliation could not be considered as having failed until a reply of some sort was forthcoming.[144] Furthermore Eden openly declared in the House of Commons on 18 June 1936 that his goal was still 'nothing less . . . than a European settlement and appeasement'.[145]

In attempting to account for the Foreign Secretary's persistence in pursuing Germany, despite the lack of response from Berlin, Eden later recorded that he was following the broad guidelines of policy that had been established by Stanley Baldwin. In support of this assertion he quoted from his diary for 20 May 1936:

> Talk with S.B. in evening. Did not get much out of it save that he wants better relations with Hitler than with Musso — we must get nearer to Germany. 'How?' I asked. 'I have no idea, that is your job.'[146]

While Eden's record of this discussion cannot be substantiated, it is probably accurate in identifying the main threads that ran through his handling of the Rhineland crisis. Undoubtedly the Foreign Secretary was motivated by the desire not to split Europe into two armed camps, which might have resulted from a decision to reaffirm the Anglo-French alliance and apply sanctions against Germany. Eden, therefore, chose the alternative course of attempting to mediate between France and Germany in the pursuit of the settlement of outstanding issues surrounding armament limitation and mutual guarantees of security. In this context it can be argued that he failed completely, for by June 1936 he was no nearer an agreement with Germany. In addition the weakness of the Anglo-French response to Hitler's blatant infringement of Germany's international commitments had probably encouraged the German leader to expand his territorial ambitions further. In his memoirs Eden was certainly quite critical of his own handling of the crisis:

> If, as Clemencau tells us, politics is the art of the possible, Hitler's occupation of the Rhineland was an occasion when the British and French Governments should have attempted the impossible. Academically speaking there is little dispute that Hitler should have been called to order, if need be forcibly, at his first breach of an accepted international agreement.[147]

This judgement would seem rather harsh in that the options available to the Foreign Secretary in March 1936 were severely limited. The suggestion of an attempt to force a German withdrawal by the imposition of financial, economic or ultimately military sanctions was unanimously rejected by the Cabinet, the Foreign Office and the Service Ministers.[148] Not only were the Locarno Powers in disarray and Britain militarily unprepared for a European war, but the whole tenor of public opinion saw the German action as not entirely unreasonable and certainly not comparable to Italian aggression in Abyssinia.[149] Given this position it was quite natural that the Cabinet should expect the Foreign Secretary to seize the opportunity provided by Hitler's declaration of 7 March 1936 to establish a settlement of the European security problem. Although the overall results were disappointing, Eden handled the negotiations with skill and ultimately forced the French to accept the British stance. It can be argued that Flandin's admission that France could not be inflexible in its dealings with Germany and the British Cabinet's decision to reaffirm its Locarno commitments brought Britain and France closer together than they had been for several years and more than repaired the damage inflicted by the Hoare—Laval negotiations on the Anglo-French relationship.[150] The main obstacle was the indeterminate nature of the German demands. It was not surprising, however, that having overcome the immediate French objections to the use of the Rhineland crisis to forge an agreement with Germany and given the unattractive nature of the alternatives, Eden was reluctant to abandon all hope of initiating negotiations; by the last week of May the Foreign Secretary was forced to concede that the prospect of an early settlement was increasingly remote.[151]

While Eden awaited the reply to the British questionnaire, attention was once more focused on the Italo-Abyssinian dispute. Anglo-French co-ordination at Geneva, which had taken a severe knock in December 1935, had been further exacerbated in March 1936 when Eden rejected the French suggestion that the possibility of using the League of Nations to impose sanctions on Germany be examined. In response Flandin clearly indicated his unwillingness to take any action that might provoke Italian retaliation in the Mediterranean at a time when the situation in Western Europe was unclear.[152] Therefore, with the open reluctance of the French to consider the imposition of further sanctions against Italy and increasing pressure from the British Chiefs-of-Staff to transfer naval strength from the Mediterranean to Home waters, Eden was forced to concede to the Cabinet, on 6 April 1936, that the existing sanctions were unlikely to force Mussolini to reconsider his position.[153] The Foreign Secretary admitted that the closure of the Suez Canal to Italian shipping would significantly hinder the Italian military campaign but concluded that such action was likely to provoke a war with Italy. As the Cabinet minutes noted, the Prime Minister responded to Eden's allusion to war with a firm declaration that he 'was unwilling to envisage in the present state of Europe' the possibility of Britain provoking an open conflict with Italy. Therefore, while Eden was authorised to continue his campaign to press for the expansion of sanctions if Italy gave no indication of a willingness to compromise, it was apparent that he saw little hope of success.[154] The events at Geneva during the following two weeks only served to confirm this suspicion. Despite reports of the rapid disintegration of the Abyssinian military position, Flandin continued to resist Eden's attempts to force an open admission that conciliation had failed. On 9 April 1936 Eden reported:

> Today's meetings of the Committee of 13 were very difficult. M. Flandin argued the Italian case with confident cynicism and did what he could to obstruct any action of the Committee either against the use of gas by Italians or in favour of pressure for cessation of hostilities.[155]

Following a report to the Committee of Thirteen on 17 April 1936 that the Abyssinians had once again rejected the conditions for direct negotiation demanded by the Italians, Eden was finally able to formulate a compromise with the French.[156] In exchange for a French admission that the conciliation process had failed, Eden bowed to pressure from Paul-Boncour to delay consideration of the possible imposition of further sanctions until after the completion of the French elections.[157] Reporting to the Foreign Office on 18 April 1936, the Foreign Secretary concluded: 'The result seems on the whole as satisfactory as we could have hoped to obtain in the existing difficult circumstance.'[158]

Four days later, in a report to the Cabinet, Eden stressed the difficulty of making progress at Geneva while international attention was focused on German ambitions in Europe. Eden declared that he had discovered 'hardly anyone had been thinking of Abyssinia and Africa at all'. He argued that the best that could be done was to prevent the immediate break-up of the sanctions front and to continue to work for the restoration of Anglo-French relations.[159] This conclusion was supported by Sir R. Vansittart, although there was a growing suspicion within the Foreign Office that the Foreign Secretary was considering the abandonment of the Abyssinian cause.[160] On 9 April 1936 Mr Thompson of the Abyssinian Department minuted:

> Are we not misleading British public opinion and incidentally

making things worse for Abyssinia by giving, or seeming to give, the impression that the Committee of Thirteen are in a position to exert effective pressure on the Italians. The facts are indeed beginning to speak for themselves.[161]

Eleven days later, following Eden's compromise with the French, Thompson again warned that to delay further action through the League of Nations was courting disaster:

> I find it very difficult to exact any satisfaction from this situation. We are confronted with the gravest blow the League has ever received *plus* the failure of the policy pursued by H.M. Govt. The effects on British prestige are bound to be serious.[162]

Indeed there was force in Thompson's arguments, given that the avowed goal of British policy was to assist the League of Nations in restoring the sovereignty of the Abyssinian Government over its territory. By 19 April 1936 Eden was in possession of reports from Sir S. Barton in Addis Ababa, arguing that the position of the Abyssinian military campaign was desperate and that an Italian victory could only be halted by immediate assistance to the Abyssinians.[163] In response to Eden's remarks that the Italian campaign would soon be halted by the summer rain, even Sir R. Vansittart had been moved to note on 17 April 1936: 'It has got to rain *very* hard — and very *quick* — and very *long*.'[164]

Yet despite the evidence of an imminent Italian victory in Abyssinia, Eden continued to insist that Britain would participate only in collective action to assist Abyssinia organised by the League of Nations.[165] Given his own admission that the existing network of sanctions was unlikely to be effective, it appeared that the fate of Abyssinia had been sealed. The best that the Foreign Secretary could offer was the promise of a further debate of the issue at Geneva during which 'the Italians will once more have to undergo the ordeal of a world expression of opinion at their conduct and methods of warfare'.[166]

In defending the decision not to push for further measures against Italy, Eden — at the Cabinet meetings of 22 and 29 April 1936 — referred to the difficulty of promoting action against Italy at a time when attention was focused on German ambitions in Europe. In particular the Foreign Secretary alluded to the growing concern over the future of Austria: 'There was some evidence that Herr Hitler was turning over in his mind the possibility of a "Putsch" against Austria in order to take advantage of Mussolini's preoccupation elsewhere.'[167]

It would appear, however, that the conclusions which Eden drew from the deadlock at Geneva went far further than the immediate fate of the Abyssinian and Austrian regimes. The Foreign Secretary's faith in the effectiveness of the machinery of collective security had undoubtedly been severely shaken by the Abyssinian and Rhineland crises. On 22 April 1936 he candidly admitted to the Cabinet that he doubted whether the League of Nations could successfully prevent a German 'putsch' in Austria.[168] In the following week a discussion with Neville Chamberlain indicated that Eden was prepared to admit the League of Nations was not, in its existing form, able to maintain international stability and peace. Prompted by Neville Chamberlain it seemed that Eden was moving towards a conviction that the League of Nations should be downgraded to the level of 'a moral force and focus of opinion', while international security was best controlled by a network of regional pacts.[169] In response to what was, in effect, a significant reorientation of policy, the Cabinet agreed to Eden's request of 29 April 1936 for the establishment of a Cabinet Committee to consider the future direction and format of British foreign policy.[170]

While Eden seemed to be considering the negotiation of a Mediterranean security pact and a radical restructuring of the Covenant of the League of Nations as a means of liquidating the confrontation with Italy, he realised that in the short term British and international opinion would not accept the abandonment of the sanctions front against Italy. Therefore the Cabinet supported the Foreign Secretary when, on 29 April 1936, he rejected the suggestion that the British naval presence in the Mediterranean be relaxed. As the Cabinet minutes recorded: 'It was suggested that the dangers from public opinion at home and abroad outweighed the very real difficulties of the Admiralty.'[171] Any hopes, however, that the Foreign Secretary may have entertained as to the continuation of pressure forcing Italy into negotiations with Abyssinia at the League of Nations, were rudely shattered on 5 May 1936 by reports of Italian forces entering Addis Ababa.[172]

The following day Eden tacitly admitted to the Cabinet that the consideration of further sanctions against Italy was pointless. While refusing formally to acknowledge the Italian victory, the Foreign Secretary was already looking to liquidate the issue with a proposal that the September meeting of the Assembly of the League of Nations be invited to consider the redrafting of the League Covenant.[173] In attempting to maintain the sanctions front until the autumn of 1936 it was apparent that the Foreign Secretary still considered a negotiated solution was possible. His goal was, therefore, to placate international and domestic opinion with a solution incorporating a restructuring of the role of the League of Nations alongside the creation of a network of regional security agreements.[174] In addition Eden hoped that the defeat over the Abyssinian issue might be offset by Germany rejoining the League of Nations as a result of Anglo-German negotiations in the summer of 1936 and the redrafting of the Covenant of the League of Nations. Throughout the month of May, however, the domestic and international movement for the removal of what was patently an ineffective sanctions campaign gathered momentum.[175] French reluctance to maintain sanctions against Italy was reinforced by reports from Berlin that Hitler was unlikely to accept any European commitments while still able to exploit the continuing rift in Anglo-French relations with Italy.[176] Within the Foreign Office Vansittart openly voiced the opinion that a satisfactory agreement with Germany was only possible if relations were first re-established with Italy. On 21 May 1936 the Permanent Under-Secretary noted:

> Compromise is always disagreeable, but our condition necessitates it in the case of *both* Dictators if possible. We shall, however, certainly have to compromise with Mussolini, for we can never compromise or even live safely with 'Dictator Major' if we are at lasting loggerheads with 'Dictator Minor'.[177]

Vansittart's words were reinforced a week later in a minute by Ralph Wigram on a despatch from Berlin: 'I find it difficult to regard the negotiations with Germany as a serious proposition as long as the present state of our relations with Italy continues.'

Eden's response indicated his reluctance to retreat from a policy with which he was personally identified:

> All this may be true, but it is not we who have broken the Covenant, and the British public is not prepared to sit around the table on friendly terms with the aggressor for many a long day — nor can I blame them.[178]

Therefore, when Sir R. Vansittart reported on 21 May 1936 that the Italian Ambassador had expressed Mussolini's desire to collaborate on a Mediterranean security agreement in exchange for the lifting of sanctions, Eden replied:

> There is a touch of blackmail about this, and we are not in a mood to be blackmailed by Italy. Some constructive contribution by her is also called for and there is no evidence of it here. If Mussolini thinks he has only to beckon and we will open our arms, he is vastly mistaken.[179]

Despite the complaints voiced by the First Lord of the Admiralty and the President of the Board of Trade, it was apparent that the

Cabinet largely supported Eden's attempts to extract some form of *quid pro quo* from Mussolini in exchange for the lifting of sanctions.[180] In response to a speech by his brother suggesting that sanctions should be abandoned, Neville Chamberlain wrote to his sister on 10 May 1936:

> I believe that public opinion here would be greatly shocked if we showed ourselves in too great a hurry to throw up the sponge. But all we need to do is to avoid an announcement of policy and adopt a waiting attitude.[181]

By the last week of May, however, the force of the arguments in favour of lifting sanctions against Italy was all but irresistible. The situation was discussed by the Cabinet on 27 and 29 May 1936. While defending his policy the Foreign Secretary admitted that the removal of sanctions would be of great assistance in repairing relations with Italy and reducing tension over the future of Austria.[182] Eden went on to concede that the existing measures were unlikely to force Italy to retreat from Abyssinia, but that he still hoped that Mussolini could be induced to guarantee economic access for all nations to Abyssinia and agree not to raise a native army as part of a general settlement. With a report that the Dominions were in favour of lifting sanctions and an admission from Eden that the French were unlikely to support the continuation of sanctions at the forthcoming meeting at Geneva, the issue hung in the balance. The deciding factor was apparently Eden's report that the Italians had expressed a desire to improve relations with Britain with the negotiation of a Mediterranean Pact.[183] The Foreign Secretary commented on this offer:

> As to Italy's goodwill, he thought that Signor Mussolini's approach was genuine and that he wanted a *détente*. He had no confidence in the duration once it had ceased to suit Signor Mussolini. We should have to keep a watchful eye on Italy for a long time to come.[184]

In essence Eden opposed the exploration of the Italian initiative on the grounds that the Abyssinian issue was a matter for Italy and the League of Nations to resolve and not for Anglo-Italian negotiations. However, with the Cabinet decision to instruct the Foreign Secretary to contact the Italian Ambassador in order to discuss the basis of a possible settlement and to circulate a memorandum on the results to be derived from continuing sanctions, it was obvious that the Cabinet was moving firmly in favour of removing sanctions against Italy. On this issue Baldwin admitted to the Cabinet:

Keeping them on was not likely to have any effect on Signor Mussolini except to make matters worse. The difficulty was one of face-saving and public opinion in this country, the United States, Canada, etc.[185]

While finding such a course personally distasteful, it was evident that Eden appreciated the alternatives were rapidly being eliminated. On 10 June 1936 the Foreign Secretary reported to the Cabinet that, as a result of his negotiations with the Italian Ambassador, he was 'personally not optimistic as to Signor Mussolini's probable reply. The announcement that morning of the appointment of Count Ciano as Italian Foreign Secretary did not inspire confidence'. Eden, however, conceded that: 'He himself was rather veering towards the view that if sanctions were to be removed there was something to be said for our taking the initiative.'

Therefore, while agreeing in principle to the removal of sanctions, the point of contention was still Eden's determination to obtain some form of declaration of future intent from Mussolini as a *quid pro quo*. To this end the Cabinet agreed to await the outcome of further negotiations with the Italian Ambassador.[186] The very same day, however, Neville Chamberlain, obviously tired of what he had called a 'waiting game', chose to force the Foreign Secretary's hand. In a speech to the 1900 Club, which was reported in *The Times* the following day, Chamberlain claimed that collective security 'has been tried out and it has failed to prevent war, failed to stop war, failed to save the victim of the aggression'. Chamberlain attacked, in particular, those who still maintained:

> the idea that if we were to pursue the policy of sanctions and even to intensify it, it was still possible to preserve the independence of Abyssinia. This seems to me the very midsummer of madness.[187]

Although Baldwin immediately denied that Chamberlain spoke for the Government and later rebuked the Chancellor of the Exchequer for not consulting either himself or Eden before making the speech, the damage had been done.[188] Eden subsequently recorded of Chamberlain's speech:

> In the disintegrating atmosphere, Neville Chamberlain's speech on 10th June was to me unexpected, not least because his support of my arguments for maintaining sanctions had been so consistent and firm.

> Whatever the merit of his argument, its timing was explosive.

Despite Baldwin's truthful denial of Government responsibility, the sanctions front was now out of joint. There was no dispute that sanctions would have to be called off soon, the question was where and when.[189]

Yet the distance between Chamberlain and Eden was not as great as Eden suggested. Certainly Chamberlain did not think so, as he noted in a letter to his sister on 14 June 1936:

> The only person I actually consulted was Sam who strongly approved. I did not consult Eden between ourselves because although I believed that he was entirely in favour of what I was going to say, I knew that if I asked him he was bound to bid me not to say it.[190]

In his diary for 17 June 1936 Chamberlain clearly outlined his motive in making the speech:

> I did it deliberately because I felt that the Party and the country needed a lead and an indication that the Government was not wavering and drifting without a policy and I am satisfied that I was right.

> He [Eden] . . . has been as nice as possible about it though it is of course true that to some extent he has had to suffer in the public interest. However, in the long run I believe it will have helped him by preparing public opinion.[191]

Although the Foreign Secretary had every reason to feel aggrieved that a member of the Cabinet had made such a major incursion into the field of foreign affairs without prior consultation, there was certainly an element of truth in Chamberlain's assertion that the thrust of his speech was in line with the Foreign Secretary's own thinking. Indeed in a memorandum for the Cabinet dated 11 June 1936 Eden had finally admitted that it was no longer possible to insist that an Italian declaration of intent must precede the raising of sanctions. The Foreign Secretary, therefore, recommended that while the League of Nations should be urged to continue its condemnation of the Italian act in Abyssinia, the British Government should be prepared to abandon a sanctions policy which no longer served any purpose following the Italian military victory.[192] It would, therefore, appear that Chamberlain's speech did not provoke a significant reassessment of British policy towards Italy but perhaps contributed to a marginal acceleration of the reorientation of attitudes to the policy of sanctions which was already in progress.

Eden's recommendations were accepted by the Cabinet on 17 June

1936 and the following day the Foreign Secretary admitted to the House of Commons that he had 'come to the conclusion that there is no longer any utility in continuing these measures as a means of pressure upon Italy'.[193] The one condition that Eden insisted upon was that Britain reaffirm its commitment to assist any Mediterranean nation which was subject to aggression as a result of its participation in sanctions against Italy.[194] Whilst this stipulation was seen as an indication that Britain was not intending to renege its commitment to the League of Nations, the complete collapse of the front against Italy was clearly displayed when only Abyssinia of the 49 nations represented at the General Assembly of the League of Nations on 4 July 1936, opposed the lifting of sanctions against Italy.[195]

The dissolution of the sanctions front appeared to represent a severe blow to the prestige and policy of the Foreign Secretary. Harold Nicolson noted of Eden's speech in the House of Commons on 18 June 1936 announcing the intention to lift sanctions against Italy: 'Anthony Eden adopts a tone of regretful frankness which, however, rather suggests an embarrassed apology.'[196]

Given Eden's role in the imposition of sanctions, both as Foreign Secretary and Minister for League of Nations Affairs, subsequent commentators have suggested that with the collapse of collective action against Italy Eden should have resigned.[197] Even before July there were some who questioned the wisdom of the Foreign Secretary's course of action. Following the fall of Addis Ababa, Tom Jones noted:

> We are all defeated and depressed and hardly know what to do.
>
> The League is discredited and Lothian is talking of going back to the alliances and the balance of power. Eden has played his hand out. It has been magnificently consistent but was it diplomacy? Did he fail to foresee the débâcle or did he prefer to be consistent?[198]

Neville Chamberlain was representative of those within the Cabinet who considered that the events at Geneva had left British policy without any positive direction.[199] On 6 July 1936 Eden conceded to the Cabinet that his attempt to achieve the appeasement of Europe had patently failed and that tension in Europe had increased:

> He himself felt that the international situation was so serious that from day to day there was the risk of some dangerous incident arising and even an outbreak of war could not be excluded.
>
> . . . he could give no guarantee of the certainty of peace even during the present year.

The Cabinet Minutes, however, give no indication of any suggestion of the possibility of resignation even being raised and little or no criticism of the Foreign Secretary's course of action was recorded.[200] In his own defence Eden noted:

I did not feel called upon to resign, for I had not had control of policy, either in the earlier stages of the dispute, or during the critical first period in the imposition of sanctions, when my own decisions would have been more persistent and far-reaching than those which were taken. Nor would the Abyssinians have remained unarmed if I had had my way.[201]

This is a curious defence given that Eden and the Cabinet were in broad agreement that the failure of the sanctions front had not been due to any lack of British resolve but rather the reluctance of the French to support the British initiatives at Geneva.[202]

The root of Eden's disappointment at the failure of sanctions would, therefore, seem to lie not so much in the consequences for the Abyssinian people or the prestige of the League of Nations but rather in the failure of a policy with which he was personally associated. In fact the Rhineland affair had clearly indicated that the Foreign Secretary was not completely committed to the use of Geneva as a body for international arbitration and law enforcement. While Eden had accepted the League Council ruling that Germany was in breach of its international undertakings, it was evident that the Foreign Secretary had no intention of allowing the League of Nations to take any further action in a matter that he saw as primarily an affair for Britain, France and Germany to resolve.

The Italian invasion of Abyssinia, however, was seen by Eden in a very different perspective. His promotion of a sanctions policy under the auspices of the League of Nations was based on the assessment that the mobilisation of world opinion against Italy provided a possible path to the achievement of a satisfactory solution. Certainly such a policy ran a risk of provoking an Italian attack on the British outposts in the Mediterranean but Eden remained confident that evidence of a broad international alliance against the Italian action would be sufficient to deter Mussolini.[203] Yet at no time did he restrict his options to simplify the enforcement of sanctions and he was as prepared as Hoare and Vansittart to endorse a privately negotiated settlement if the terms were acceptable to Geneva. The Hoare—Laval pact, however, and Eden's role in its abandonment at Geneva was to cast him firmly in the mould of a champion of the League of Nations. It was not a role that he accepted unwillingly for it brought with it a certain amount of kudos, but it also further soured his personal standing in Rome and was to place limitations on the policy options available in the pursuit of an Italo-Abyssinian settlement.[204] While he was able effectively to exclude the League of Nations from the Rhineland deliberations, the expectations of popular opinion forced him to continue the sanctions policy against Italy despite the mounting evidence of its ineffectiveness.[205]

By May 1936 Eden concurred with his Cabinet colleagues that continuation of the sanctions policy was pointless following the fall of Addis Ababa and that given the need to seek a settlement with Germany there was a positive need to improve Anglo-Italian relations. While conceding these points Eden still sought, however, to devise a face-saving formula whereby Italy would outwardly make some form of concession in exchange for the lifting of sanctions.[206] Mussolini, however, remained unmoved and as the situation approached an *impasse* it could be argued that Chamberlain actually rendered the Foreign Secretary a service by bringing the issue to a head and by creating the appearance of the Foreign Secretary reluctantly bowing to pressure from his colleagues to abandon sanctions. If Chamberlain, therefore, provided a belated escape route for a somewhat embarrassed Foreign Secretary, Eden's determination not to be similarly trapped in the future was clearly indicated by his proposal that the League of Nations be completely restructured and effectively devolved to the role of a focus for world opinion. It was evident that by the summer of 1936 the Foreign Secretary was already considering the utilisation of a re-vamped League of Nations, stripped of its coercive powers, as a forum to draw Italy — and ultimately Germany — back into negotiations for the solution of the overriding problem of a European security agreement.[207]

References

1   Avon, p. 317.
2   Ibid., p. 316.
3   The first plenary session of the London Naval Conference was held on 9 December 1935. The conference finally closed on 25 March 1936. The Japanese delegation withdrew on 15 January 1936. For details see *DBFP*, 2nd ser., vol. 13, chapters 7 and 8. Also *Documents of the London Naval Conference 1935* (HMSO, 1936).
4   See Avon, pp. 319–20. Eden describes an initial clash with Sir Warren Fisher over the procedure for the appointment of Ambassadors. Eden told Baldwin that he 'would rather resign than give way'. Eden eventually won his case after explaining the position to Neville Chamberlain and it was agreed that Eden did not have to submit his proposed appointments to Fisher.
5   The two former Foreign Secretaries were Ramsay MacDonald and Sir John Simon. They were subsequently to be joined by Sir Samuel Hoare. Of Baldwin's leadership in this period Neville Chamberlain noted on 12 January 1936: 'I saw

the P.M. last night but was totally unable to extract any opinion from him on any of the questions I wished to discuss. I never knew him worse.' On 1 March 1936 he concluded: 'I fear S.B. asks too many for opinions. They contradict one another and then he is left in the air having no opinion of his own.' See *Neville Chamberlain Papers*, NC 2/23A, diary entry for 1 March 1936, and NC 18/1, letter to his sister Hilda, 12 January 1936.

6 Avon, p. 319.

7 For a discussion of this aspect see Broad, p. 65, and Earl of Halifax, *Fulness of Days* (London, 1957), p. 183.

8 Avon, pp. 317–18.

9 Mr Ingram, Counsellor to Rome Embassy reported on 27 December 1935 that the appointment of Eden, who was associated with the League of Nations' sanctions policy against Italy, had not been well received in Rome and that Mussolini was reported as saying that it amounted to: 'shutting the door, for a long time at least, upon any attempt at compromise.' *DBFP*, 2nd ser., vol. 15, no. 417 (no. 510 [J 9983/1/1]), Rome, 27 December 1935. Eden responded to this report by informing the Italian Ambassador, Grandi, on 6 January 1936:

> there was no foundation whatever for the reports . . . that I was anti-Italian or had been in any way actuated in anything I had done in the last few months by antipathy to the Fascist regime or to the Head of the Italian Government. Still less was it true that during my conversations with Signor Mussolini in Rome in the summer there had been any sharp personal differences.

DBFP, 2nd ser., vol. 15, no. 427 (no. 27 [J 212/1/1]), Foreign Office, 6 January 1936.

10 See Ingram's report of 27 December 1935, *DBFP*, 2nd ser., vol. 15, no. 417, Rome.

11 Eden had been informed on 26 December 1935 that Leger, Secretary General of the French Ministry of Foreign Affairs, had expressed the opinion that his government was opposed to any further initiatives towards Italy in the form of either sanctions or mediation. *DBFP*, 2nd ser., vol. 15, no. 414, Mr Lloyd-Thomas (Paris) to Mr Eden (no. 1799 [J 9828/1/1]), Paris, 26 December 1935.

12 See *DBFP*, 2nd ser., vol. 15, nos 438 (8 January 1936) and 445 (10 January 1936).

13 *CAB* 23/83, CC 1(36)4, 15 January 1936.

14 See Avon, pp. 325–9. Also *DBFP*, 2nd ser., vol. 15, no. 442 (J 450/216/1), note by Eden on extension of economic sanctions in the Italo-Ethiopian dispute, 9 January 1936 (forwarded to the Cabinet of 15 January 1936 as CP 5[36]).

15 Eden saw Laval at Geneva on 20 January 1936 and his successor, Flandin, in London on 27 January 1936. Both French Ministers were preoccupied with European security and sternly opposed any further initiatives towards Italy. See *DBFP*, 2nd ser., vol. 15, nos 464 and 484. See also Eden's report to the Cabinet of 5 February 1936, *CAB* 23/82, CC 4(36)2.

16 For the report of the Petroleum Committee on 12 February 1936 which had been requested by the Committee of Eighteen on 22 January 1936, see *DBFP*, 2nd ser., vol. 15, no. 514 (J 1376/757/1), Mr Stevenson (Geneva) to Mr Eden, 12 February 1936.

17 *DBFP*, 2nd ser., vol. 15 (no. 45 [J 1644/136/1]), Sir R. Lindsay to Mr Eden, Washington, 21 February 1936.

18 For full details of these meetings see *CAB* 23/83, CC 8(36)3 and CC 11(36)3.

19   *CAB* 23/83, CC 11(36)3, 26 February 1936.
20   In relation to the USA it was apparent that Eden sought to expand the understanding that he was actively trying to promote at the London Naval Conference. See *Avon Papers*, FO, 954/6B, FE 36/1, Memorandum of discussion with Mr N. Davis, 10 January 1936. See also *DBFP*, 2nd ser., vol. 13, nos 599, 643 and 718.
21   As a result of conversations with Baron Aloisi and Titulesco at Geneva in January of 1936, Eden had concluded that there had been a distinct relaxation of Anglo-Italian tension. See *Avon Papers*, FO, 954/13A, IT/36/1 and IT/36/2.
22   Eden was already aware that without active support from the USA an oil embargo was unlikely to have any immediate impact on the conduct of the Abyssinian campaign. On 21 February 1936 the British Ambassador to Washington had confirmed that isolationist sentiment was strengthening in the USA. See Avon, pp. 326–7, and *DBFP*, 2nd ser., vol. 15, no. 535.
23   *Avon Papers*, FO, 954/13A, IT/36/1 and IT/36/2.
24   Hankey's interview with Hoare on 25 November 1935 at which he stressed the need to avoid a confrontation with Italy and justified his action by reference to the Cabinet decision of 16 October 1935 not to apply further sanctions against Italy without unequivocal guarantees of military support from France, was indicative of the Service Ministries' determination to avoid war with Italy. See *Hankey Papers*, diary entry for 25 November 1935. Hankey Papers 1/7.
25   *CAB* 23/83, CC 11(36)3, 26 February 1936.
26   Ibid.
27   For a record of Eden's discussions at Geneva with Flandin see *DBFP*, 2nd ser., vol. 16, nos 3, 6, 11, 12 and 20.
28   Avon, p. 328.
29   *DBFP*, 2nd ser., vol. 16 (no. 17 [J 1971/757/1]). Mr Edmond to Foreign Office, 2 March 1936.
30   *DBFP*, 2nd ser., vol. 16 (no. 21 [J 1984/587/1]). Mr Edmond to Foreign Office, 4 March 1936.
31   *CAB* 23/83, CC 15(36)1, 5 March 1936. It was evident that Flandin's fears for the future of the Rhineland zone had impressed Eden and therefore action was necessary given Cabinet agreement:

> that neither France nor England was really in a position to take effective military action against Germany in the event of a violation of the Treaty of Locarno.

32   British policy during the course of the Disarmament Conference has been discussed previously, see pp. 26–55.
33   For the text of the Anglo-French communiqué of 3 February 1935 see *DBFP*, 2nd ser., vol. 15, appendix.
34   *CAB* 23/81, CC 32(35), 5 June 1935. At this meeting the Cabinet decided that the question of air limitation be taken up as a separate question from that of the general settlement.
35   For details of both sets of negotiations see *DBFP*, 2nd ser., vol. 13. In particular see documents 289, 290, 304, 305, 311, 318, 337 and 348. Eden was presented with the unenviable task of explaining to the French the rationale behind the decision to conclude a bilateral treaty with Germany for naval limitation. See *DBFP*, 2nd ser., vol. 14, no. 362, and Avon, pp. 230–1.
36   While in the summer of 1935 Eden and Laval often met at Geneva to discuss the Abyssinian situation, their meetings were also used to attempt to convince the French Government that it shared an interest in entering into an air limitation agreement with Germany irrespective of the continuing deadlock over

land armaments. See *DBFP*, 2nd ser., vol. 13, nos 235, 339, 362 and 383. On 27 June 1935, however, Eden could only report that the prospects of French co-operation remained remote unless Britain agree to a further series of Anglo-French bilateral pacts. For Eden's conversation with Mussolini on the Air Pact see *DBFP*, 2nd ser., vol. 13, no. 377, 25 June 1935.

37   See *DGFP*, ser. C, vol. 4, no. 252, Foreign Minister to Von Bulow, 7 August 1935. This was a response to Hoare's message to the German Government of 1 August 1935 urging the opening of Air Pact negotiations, see *DBFP*, 2nd ser., vol. 13, no. 447.

38   DRC 37 of 21 November 1935, quoted in Roskill, pp. 192—4.

39   *DBFP*, 2nd ser., vol. 15, appendix 1, Memorandum by Messrs O.G. Sargent and R.F. Wigram on 'Britain, France and Germany' (C 7752/55/18), 21 November 1935.

40   *DBFP*, 2nd ser., vol. 15, no. 460 (C 454/4/18). Memorandum by Mr Eden on 'The German Danger', 17 January 1936 — see *CAB* 23/83, CC 3(36)4. A sense of urgency was added to the report by Eden's closing remarks to the Cabinet that: 'after recent experiences no one thought that France was likely to move in the matter of collective security except where her own frontier was in danger.' It was agreed that Eden would consult Sir E. Phipps before formulating a positive response to the situation.

41   *DBFP*, 2nd ser., vol. 15, appendix IV, Memorandum by Sir R. Vansittart on 'Britain, France and Germany' (C 997/4/18), 3 February 1936. Circulated to Cabinet as CP 42(36).

42   *CAB* 23/83, CC 4(36)1, 5 February 1936. Concern at the consequences resulting from the cession of colonies to Germany had been further fuelled by a report from Ormsby-Gore outlining the danger to British-African possessions that would result from the German remilitarisation of its former colonies. *Baldwin Papers*, vol. 124, ff. 7—11, Ormsby-Gore to Baldwin (with copy to Eden), January 1936.

43   *DBFP*, 2nd ser., vol. 15, no. 509, Memorandum by Mr Eden on policy towards Germany (C 997/4/18), 11 February 1936. Submitted to Cabinet as CP 42(36). On Eden's recommendation Baldwin established, on 14 February 1936, a Cabinet Committee to examine policy towards Germany. *CAB* 23/83, CC 6(36), 12 February 1936.

44   For the text of Phipps's interview with Hitler of 13 December 1935, see *DBFP*, 2nd ser., vol. 15, no. 383.

45   For example see Eden's interview with Von Neurath of 27 January 1936, *DBFP*, 2nd ser., vol. 15, no. 486, and with Von Hoesch on 4 February 1936, *DBFP*, 2nd ser., vol. 15, no. 510.

46   *DBFP*, 2nd ser., vol. 15, no. 524, draft minutes of 1st meeting of Committee on Germany (C 1028/4/18), 17 February 1936. Indeed it was evident that Eden still felt that French intransigence had contributed greatly to difficulties with Germany: 'if France had shown more wisdom two years ago, our difficulties might not have arisen in their present form.'

47   *DBFP*, 2nd ser., vol. 15, no. 541, letter from Mr Eden to Sir E. Phipps (C 750/4/18), 24 February 1936.

48   Ibid.

49   Warnings as to the impact of the ratification of a Franco-Soviet Treaty on the future status of the Rhineland zone had been sounded by the Paris Embassy as early as 30 April 1935 and were supported by the Foreign Office assessments in the summer of that year. These warnings were repeated by both the Berlin and Paris Embassies in the early months of 1936. See *DBFP*, 2nd ser., vol. 13, nos 149 and 405; *DBFP*, 2nd ser., vol. 15, nos 418, 464 and 486.

50   For Wigram's assessment of the situation see *DBFP*, 2nd ser., vol. 15, no. 455, Memorandum on the Rhineland Demilitarised Zone (C 291/4/18), 16 January 1936. Wigram's conclusions broadly followed those of Orme Sargent who had minuted in May 1935 that Hitler would reoccupy the zone if he felt that the Stresa front was sufficiently at odds to make military retaliation unlikely. (*DBFP*, 2nd ser., vol. 13, no. 149.) Wigram, therefore, advocated the surrender of the zone as part of a great settlement before Hitler took the matter into his own hands.

51   German military penetration of the zone had been admitted by the Foreign Office in July 1935. *DBFP*, 2nd ser., vol. 13, no. 405.

52   *DBFP*, 2nd ser., vol. 15, no. 504, Sir E. Phipps to Mr Eden (no. 35 [C 798/4/18]), Berlin, 10 February 1936.

53   For a record of Wigram's conversations with Von Hoesch and Prince Bismarck, see *DBFP*, 2nd ser., vol. 15, nos 510 and 515. In addition Eden used Lord Cranborne to probe further Bismarck's reaction to a possible improvement of Anglo-German relations. Eden's refusal to be drawn on the matter by Von Hoesch on 27 February 1936, however, was indicative of his appreciation of the need to co-ordinate any initiative with the French. See *DBFP*, 2nd ser., vol. 15, nos 529 and 552.

54   See Eden's despatches to Paris of 12 and 13 February 1936. *DBFP*, 2nd ser., vol. 15, nos 516 and 517. See also *CAB* 23/83, CC 6(36)3, 12 February 1936. As recently as 27 January 1936 Eden had assured Flandin that he was convinced 'It seemed unlikely that they [the German Government] would take any precipitate action in the near future'. *DBFP*, 2nd ser., vol. 15, no. 484.

55   British annoyance at the French pursuit of an agreement with the Soviet Union was indicated by Eden's remarks to the Cabinet on 12 February 1936, following a French enquiry as to whether Britain considered that the Franco-Soviet Treaty violated the Treaty of Locarno: 'he proposed to express no opinion. We had not been consulted before the signature of the pact and there appeared no reason why we should express any opinion now.' *CAB* 23/83, CC 6(36)3.

56   Reports from the Ministries of War and Air in January 1936 indicated that the military value of the Rhineland zone lay primarily in its value as an invasion route for France to fulfil its commitment to its East-European allies. Therefore Eden was quite willing to envisage the surrender of the zone as part of a European security settlement. See *DBFP*, 2nd ser., vol. 15, nos 482, 483 (Air Ministry and War Office reports) and no. 521 (Eden's recommendations for Cabinet Committee on policy towards Germany).

57   While Eden still maintained that he considered a German violation of the demilitarised zone unlikely, he advocated the promotion of the Air Pact as a suitable vehicle to facilitate the surrender of the zone as part of a European security settlement. *CAB* 23/83, CC 15(36)1, 5 March 1936.

58   *DBFP*, 2nd ser., vol. 16, no. 29, Mr Eden to Sir E. Phipps (no. 35 [C 1450/4/18]), 6 March 1936.

59   *DGFP*, ser. C, vol. 4, pp. 1142−4, 701/261360−63, Memorandum by the Ambassador in Italy, Rome, 14 February 1936.

60   *DGFP*, ser. C, vol. 4, pp. 1172−7, 6710/E 506174-81, Ambassador in Italy to Foreign Ministry, Rome, 22 February 1936.

61   *DGFP*, ser. C, vol. 4, p. 1218.

62   See J.T. Emmerson, *The Rhineland Crisis* (London, 1977), pp. 39−71, also John C. Cairns, 'March 7 1936 Again: The View from Paris', printed in Hans Gatzke (ed.), *European Diplomacy between Two Wars, 1919−1939* (Chicago, 1972), pp. 172−92.

63   *DBFP*, 2nd ser., vol. 15, no. 550, 27 February 1936.
64   From the outset of the crisis the Italian representative at the meeting of the Locarno Powers held in Paris on 10 March 1936 made it clear that he was only an observer. Due to the sanctions imposed by the League of Nations on Italy, Cerruti pointed out that his Government would not agree to economic, political or military measures against Germany. See *DBFP*, 2nd ser., vol. 16, no. 63.
65   A similar memorandum was presented to the British Ambassador in Berlin on 7 March 1936 by the German Foreign Minister, Von Neurath. Phipps informed Eden that he believed the army chiefs had been over-ruled after opposing the reoccupation. *DBFP*, 2nd ser., vol. 16, nos 33, 34 and 42.
66   See *DBFP*, 2nd ser., vol. 16, no. 12.
67   *DBFP*, 2nd ser., vol. 16, Mr Eden to Sir G. Clerk (no. 42 [C 1486/4/18]), 7 March 1936.
68   Avon, pp. 343–4.
69   *DBFP*, 2nd ser., vol. 16, no. 39, Sir G. Clerk to Mr Eden (no. 108 [C 1490/4/18]), Paris, 7 March 1936.
70   Although Eden notes that his memorandum was examined by Vansittart, he makes no reference to the meeting with Baldwin and Neville Chamberlain that the latter claimed took place on the morning of Sunday 8 March 1936. *Neville Chamberlain Papers*, Political Diaries, NC 2/23A, diary entry for 8 March 1936.
71   Eden evidently hoped that France would be willing to explore the German terms once its pride had been restored by condemnation of the German action by the League of Nations and the reference of the compatibility of the Franco-Soviet Treaty with the Locarno Pact to the Hague Court. *DBFP*, 2nd ser., vol. 16, no. 48, Memorandum by Mr Eden on Germany and the Locarno Treaty (C 2361/4/18), 8 March 1936. Presented to Cabinet on 9 March 1936 as CP 73(36).
72   *DBFP*, 2nd ser., vol. 16, no. 50, Mr Eden to Mr Baldwin (C 1937/4/18), 8 March 1936.
73   For Eden's speech see *H of C*, Debs, 5's, vol. 309, cols 1808–13, 9 March 1936.
74   *CAB* 23/83, CC 16(36)1, 9 March 1936.
75   *Daily Telegraph*, 9 March 1936.
76   *Daily Mail*, *Daily Express*, *News Chronicle* and *The Times*, 9 March 1936. The article in *The Times*, 'A Chance to Rebuild', is often quoted as indicative of British opinion. It is interesting to note, however, how closely this coincided with the views of the 'popular' daily papers. For example the *Daily Express*: 'The Germans have reoccupied the Rhineland. What does this mean to *us*? The question is *will Britain be involved in war*? The answer is *No*.'
77   *Manchester Guardian*, 9 March 1936. The general rejection of the possibility of war appeared to have influenced most sectors of British society. See Nicolson, p. 248 and Bond, Pownall Diary for 9 March 1936, pp. 105–6. In addition the Foreign Office was receiving reports from the City indicating the danger of Germany repudiating substantial loans owed to British bankers in the event of sanctions being enforced. *DBFP*, 2nd ser., vol. 16, nos 55 and 79.
78   *DBFP*, 2nd ser., vol. 16, no. 63, record of conversation between representatives of the Locarno Powers held at the Quai d'Orsay (C 1673/4/18), Paris, 10 March 1936. For Eden's account see Avon, pp. 347–9.
79   Flandin and Van Zeeland argued that Germany could be effectively isolated if Italy was placated by the lifting of sanctions resulting from the Abyssinian crisis. See *DBFP*, 2nd ser., vol. 16, no. 61, Sir G. Clerk to Foreign Office (no. 122 [C 1614/4/18]), Paris, 10 March 1936. Also Avon, pp. 349–51.

80   *DBFP*, 2nd ser., vol. 16, no. 65, Sir E. Phipps to Mr Eden (no. 74 [C 1670/ 4/18]), Berlin, 11 March 1936.
81   *CAB 23/83*, CC 18(36)1, 11 March 1936.
82   The problem was that to accept Van Zeeland's proposal of a British guarantee to Belgium and France, irrespective of the German stance, would have amounted to a military alliance which would have cut across Eden's attempts to engineer a general settlement with Germany. From the outset Eden appreciated that Britain could do little more than reaffirm its existing obligations under the Treaty of Locarno. The problem, therefore, was to persuade France that this was sufficient. See Avon, pp. 349—50 and *DBFP*, 2nd ser., vol. 16, no. 69.
83   *CAB 23/83*, CC 18(36)1, 11 March 1936. These terms were communicated by Eden to the German Ambassador the same day. *DBFP*, 2nd ser., vol. 16, no. 70.
84   *DBFP*, 2nd ser., vol. 16, no. 82. Eden had no doubt been encouraged by the report of an informal conversation that Flandin had held with Ralph Wigram which indicated his broad agreement with the British proposals. He later noted his surprise that Flandin was ready to negotiate with Germany if the troops moved into the Rhineland since 6 March 1936 were withdrawn. Avon, pp. 355—6 and *DBFP*, 2nd ser., vol. 16, no. 78. Flandin's flexible approach had perhaps been influenced by an informal warning from Neville Chamberlain that British public opinion would not support sanctions of any kind against Germany. *Neville Chamberlain Papers*, NC 2/23A, diary entry for 12 March 1936.
85   *DBFP*, 2nd ser., vol. 16, no. 91, Mr Eden to Sir G. Clerk (no. 63 [C 1861/ 4/18]), 14 March 1936.
86   Ibid. Flandin later attempted to explain this sudden shift of emphasis by referring to the news that opinion in France was demanding nothing less than a complete German evacuation of the Rhineland. To ignore this would have been to play into the hands of the political opposition. *Neville Chamberlain Papers*, NC 2/23A, diary entry for 14 March 1936. This was followed by the suggestion that the French Government could not present a more flexible approach until after the conclusion of the forthcoming elections. *DBFP*, 2nd ser., vol. 16, no. 114, Minute by Mr Wigram (C 2442/4/18), 16 March 1936.
87   For accounts of conversations by Eden and Neville Chamberlain with Flandin, see Avon, pp. 357—8 and *Neville Chamberlain Papers*, NC 2/23A, diary entry for 15 March 1936.
88   *DBFP*, 2nd ser., vol. 16, no. 97.
89   *DBFP*, 2nd ser., vol. 16, no. 110, Memorandum by Mr Eden on Germany and the Locarno Treaty (C 2362/4/18), 15 March 1936.
90   *CAB 23/83*, CC 20(36)1.
91   See *DBFP*, 2nd ser., vol. 16, nos 98 and 114, also *Neville Chamberlain Papers*, NC 2/23A, diary entry for 15 March 1936.
92   *DBFP*, 2nd ser., vol. 16, no. 131. There were certainly those within the Foreign Office, including Sargent and Vansittart, who now saw little option but to delay the negotiations until after the completion of the French elections (see Minutes by Sargent and Vansittart, dated 17 March 1936, on Wigram's Minute of 16 March 1936 — *DBFP*, 2nd ser., vol. 16, no. 114).
93   *DBFP*, 2nd ser., vol. 16, no. 119, Mr Eden to Sir G. Clerk (no. 73 [C 2026/ 4/18]), 17 March 1936.
94   *CAB 23/83*, CC 21(36)3, 18 March 1936. Baldwin had informed the Cabinet, as recently as 12 March 1936, that Britain could not contemplate any form of automatic obligation to respond to an invasion of France or Belgium which he considered would represent 'a dangerous commitment, especially when air action was considered . . . .' *CAB 23/83*, CC 19(36). The desire to avoid

further entanglements in Europe was reinforced four days later when Malcolm MacDonald warned the Cabinet that the Dominions were unlikely to support a British war in fulfilment of its Locarno commitments (*CAB* 23/83, CC 20(36)3, 16 March 1936).

95   The COS advised the Cabinet that it would take two to four months to redeploy its military units from the Mediterranean to Britain. See *DBFP*, 2nd ser., vol. 16, no. 134, report by COS Subcommittee of CID (C 2608/4/18), 18 March 1936.

96   *CAB* 23/83, CC 21(36)3, 18 March 1936. Indeed Neville Chamberlain opposed further concessions to France on the grounds that the present French Government was likely to fall within the near future irrespective of the British stance.

97   On 11 March 1936 Baldwin had informed the Cabinet that he:

> thought that at some stage it would be necessary to point out to the French that the action they proposed would not result in only letting loose another great war in Europe. They might succeed in crushing Germany with the aid of Russia but it would probably only result in Germany going Bolshevik.

CAB 23/83, CC 18(36)1, 11 March 1936. See also Nicolson, pp. 249–50.

98   *CAB* 23/83, CC 6(36)3, 12 February 1936.

99   On 17 March 1936 Lord Cranborne minuted on France's 'very wide obligations in Central and Eastern Europe' which were dependent on the maintenance of the Rhineland zone:

> Without the Demilitarised Zone, France cannot in fact effectively fulfil her obligations in Central and Eastern Europe. We should merely be bolstering up a position which cannot be maintained.

On 18 March 1936, Eden minuted on this memorandum 'there is much force in this'. While agreeing that French commitments in Eastern Europe were over-extended, he refused to follow Cranborne's suggestion that the region be recognised as a German sphere of influence. *DBFP*, 2nd ser., vol. 16, no. 122, Minute by Lord Cranborne on British Commitments in Europe (C 2086/4/18), 17 March 1936.

100   *DBFP*, 2nd ser., vol. 15, no. 521, Memorandum by Mr Eden on The Rhineland Demilitarised Zone (C 1027/4/18), 14 February 1936. Circulated to the Cabinet Committee on Germany as G (36)3.

101   It would appear that Sir John Simon was amongst the most vociferous in opposing the opening of Staff talks with France in any form. Eden later noted that he had to ask Baldwin to speak to Simon on the subject. Kingsley Wood also warned Baldwin that Staff talks would not be well received by the Conservative back-benchers. See Avon, pp. 360–2.

102   *DBFP*, 2nd ser., vol. 16, no. 144, text of proposals drawn up by representatives of Britain, Belgium, France, Northern Ireland and Italy (C 2148/4/18), London, 19 March 1936.

103   See Cairns, 'March 7th 1936 Again', pp. 172–92.

104   *DBFP*, 2nd ser., vol. 16, Sir G. Clerk to Mr Eden (C 2564/4/18), Paris, 28 March 1936.

105   *CAB* 23/83, CC 22(36)3, 19 March 1936. See also *Neville Chamberlain Papers*, NC 18/1, letter to his sister Hilda, 21 March 1936.

106   Avon, p. 361.

107   While Neville Chamberlain considered that he had played the major role in engineering the compromise with France, Vansittart insisted that Eden had played the major role. Yet he warned Eden on 22 March 1936:

What you have accomplished is a skilful survival of the first round — with a good margin of manoeuvre for the second.

You and your colleagues indeed deserve praise.

Quoted in Colvin, pp. 101–2. See also *Neville Chamberlain Papers*, NC 18/1, letter to his sister Hilda, 21 March 1936.

108   For Von Ribbentrop's reaction to the proposals, see *DBFP*, 2nd ser., vol. 16, no. 163, Mr Eden to Sir E. Phipps (no. 370 [C 2274/4/18]), 24 March 1936. See also Avon, pp. 360–2.

109   *CAB* 23/83, CC 24(36)1, 25 March 1936.

110   Ibid. It was agreed that formal notification of the intention to hold Staff talks would be delayed until after the House of Commons debate.

111   For the text of Eden's speech, see *H of C*, Debs, 5's, vol. 310, cols 1439–53, 26 March 1936. See also Avon, pp. 362–6.

112   *Neville Chamberlain Papers*, NC 18/1, letter to his sister Ida, 28 March 1936. Eden later noted: 'The result was better than I had dared to hope; the House was understanding and the majority of members were fervent in support.' Avon, p. 362. See also Nicolson, diary entry for 26 March 1936, p. 254.

113   *The Times*, 27 March 1936.

114   Tom Jones, p. 185.

115   The German reply delivered to Eden by Von Ribbentrop refused any suggestion of German troop withdrawals from the Rhineland, *DBFP*, 2nd ser., vol. 16, no. 193. Mr Eden to Sir E. Phipps (no. 400 [C 2532/4/18]), 1 April 1936.

116   *DBFP*, 2nd ser., vol. 16, no. 198.

117   The guidelines for the Staff Talks had been established by the Cabinet on 8 April 1936 (*CAB* 23/83, CC 28(36)2, 8 April 1936). For the views of the Cabinet and the military advisers see *CAB* 23/84, CC 30(36)1, 22 April 1936 and Pownall Diary entry for 15 April 1936 (Bond, p. 109). See also *DBFP*, 2nd ser., vol. 16, no. 262.

118   In despatches to both the Paris and Berlin Embassies Eden emphasised that the opening of Staff talks did not indicate that the conciliation process had broken down but that Britain was prepared to accept new political or military agreements. *DBFP*, 2nd ser., vol. 16, no. 188 (31 March 1936) and no. 198 (2 April 1936).

119   *DBFP*, 2nd ser., vol. 16, no. 194, Memorandum on Staff Conversations with Locarno Powers (C 2608/4/18), 1 April 1936. Presented to Cabinet on 8 April 1936 as CID 1224-B. The Cabinet accepted the conclusions of the COS on the limitation of discussions, *CAB* 23/83, CC 28(36)3, 8 April 1936.

120   *DBFP*, 2nd ser., vol. 16, no. 199, Mr Eden to Sir G. Clerk (no. 601 [C 2614/4/18]), 2 April 1936.

121   Ibid.

122   *DBFP*, 2nd ser., vol. 16, no. 188.

123   For the text of the French response see *DBFP*, 2nd ser., vol. 16, no. 217, Sir G. Clerk to Foreign Office (no. 194 [C 2804/4/18]), Paris, 8 March 1936.

124   *DBFP*, 2nd ser., vol. 16, no. 234, Mr Edmond to Foreign Office (no. 20 [C 2850/4/18]), Geneva, 10 April 1936. Eden's resolution to resist the French proposals had been underlined by the Cabinet meeting of 8 April 1936 which emphasised that there was no specific agreement within the Locarno Treaty to impose sanctions on an aggressor. *CAB* 23/83, CC 28(36)2, 8 April 1936.

125   *DBFP*, 2nd ser., vol. 16, no. 231, a Minute by Sargent dated 10 April 1936 was indicative of the general suspicion that the French promotion of sanctions

was part of a wider strategy designed to draw Britain into military commitments in Eastern Europe — *DBFP*, 2nd ser., vol. 16, no. 236.

126 *DBFP*, 2nd ser., vol. 16, no. 272. Memorandum by Mr Eden on Germany (C 32974/4/18), 25 April 1936. Submitted to the Cabinet on 29 April 1936 as CP 121(36).

127 *CAB* 23/84, CC 30(36)2, 22 April 1936.

128 Paul-Boncour had warned Eden on 17 April 1936 that the French election was delicately poised but would swing away from the present government if any further excuse for an outburst of Anglophobia was created. *Avon Papers*, FR/36/11, 17 April 1936. See also *Neville Chamberlain Papers*, NC 18/1, letters to his sisters, 4 and 13 April 1936.

129 *CAB* 23/84, CC 31(36)2, 29 April 1936. It was decided to hold a special Cabinet meeting to consider the proposed questionnaire the following day.

130 Avon, pp. 371–2.

131 *DBFP*, 2nd ser., vol. 16, no. 297, Mr Eden to Sir G. Clerk (no. 820 [J 3894/84/1]), 4 May 1936.

132 The initial draft was drawn up by Eden in consultation with Baldwin and Neville Chamberlain and presented to the Cabinet on 30 April 1936. *DBFP*, 2nd ser., vol. 16, no. 277, Memorandum by Mr Eden on questions to be addressed to the German Government (C 3297/4/18), 28 April 1936.

133 *CAB* 23/84, CC 32(36)3, 30 April 1936.

134 Meetings of the Cabinet on 4 and 6 May 1936. *CAB* 23/84, CC 33(36)4 and CC 34(36)1.

135 Avon, p. 372. While Eden was forced to modify the draft in the light of Cabinet opinion, he successfully resisted attempts to alter paragraph eight relating to German assurances not to alter the status quo, except by free negotiation, in Europe. On 4 May 1936 he told the Cabinet:

> all his advisers at the Foreign Office, whatever their general attitude towards Germany, were in favour of including paragraph 8. He wished to place on record that if the Cabinet insisted on omitting it they would be closing their eyes to a matter of great importance.

CAB 23/84, CC 33(36)3, 4 May 1936.

136 Eden had first advocated the visit of a British Minister to Berlin in the Cabinet meeting of 22 April 1936 — *CAB* 23/84, CC 30(36)2, 22 April 1936. See also *DBFP*, 2nd ser., vol. 16, no. 306, 6 May 1936.

137 *DBFP*, 2nd ser., vol. 16, no. 328, Sir E. Phipps to Foreign Office (no. 179 [C 3677/4/18]), Berlin, 15 May 1936.

138 See *DBFP*, 2nd ser., vol. 16, nos 324 (14 May 1936) and 369 (16 June 1936).

139 Minute by Wigram dated 15 May 1936 on a despatch from Sir E. Phipps dated 15 May 1936, see *DBFP*, 2nd ser., vol. 16, no. 328.

140 Minutes by Sargent and Vansittart, dated 28 May 1936 and June 1936 respectively, on a despatch from Sir E. Phipps dated 26 May 1936. Vansittart added that the requirements of the rearmament programme dictated the need to obtain some form of *détente* with Germany but pointed to the long-term danger of letting an Anglo-German understanding impair Anglo-French relations. This point was particularly relevant as Eden admitted to the Cabinet on 20 May 1936 that Hitler had requested that Britain not inform France of the German intention not to agree to refrain from fortifying the Rhineland. See *DBFP*, 2nd ser., vol. 16, no. 339, *Vansittart Papers*, 2/26 and *CAB* 23/84, CC 38(36)2.

141 Sir E. Phipps's despatch from Berlin dated 26 May 1936. See *DBFP*, 2nd ser., vol. 16, no. 340.

142　Minute by Eden dated 18 May 1936 on a despatch from Sir E. Phipps dated 15 May 1936. Vansittart opposed the despatch of a British Minister to Berlin while Germany showed little inclination to respond to the British questions. See *DBFP*, 2nd ser., vol. 16, no. 328 and *Vansittart Papers*, 2/26, 1 June 1936.
143　Eden Minute dated 3 June 1936 on despatch from Berlin dated 26 May 1936. See *DBFP*, 2nd ser., vol. 16, no. 339.
144　In despatches dated 16 and 22 June 1936, Phipps admitted that the German reply would be delayed, at best, until after the resolution of the Italian sanctions issue and it was possible 'that our questions may never be answered'. Eden on 17 June 1936, however, endorsed a Minute by Sargent which concluded: 'Conciliation can *not* break down until Germans have replied and H.M.G. reject German reply.' See *DBFP*, 2nd ser., vol. 16, nos 369 and 374.
145　*H of C*, Debs, 5's, vol. 313, col. 1209, 18 June 1936.
146　Avon diary entry for 20 May 1936, quoted in Avon, p. 374.
147　Avon, pp. 366–7.
148　See in particular the Cabinet meeting of 11 March 1936, *CAB* 23/83, CC 18(36)1, 11 March 1936. For the position of the Service Ministers and the Dominions, see the Cabinet Minutes for 16 and 18 March 1936, *CAB* 23/83, CC 20(36)3 and CC 21(36)3.
149　The articles contained in the *Daily Mail, Daily Express, News Chronicle, The Times* and *Manchester Guardian* on 9 March 1936 all indicated the general sympathy for the re-establishment of German sovereignty over the Rhineland. Further discussion of this point can be found in Franklin Reid Gannon, *The British Press and Germany, 1936–39* (Oxford, 1971).
150　Eden certainly argued that Flandin had been far more inflexible than many of his colleagues and French public opinion in general. He, therefore, contended that France readily accepted the British stance, Avon, p. 361 and *DBFP*, 2nd ser., vol. 16, no. 159, 23 March 1936.
151　On 3 June 1936 Eden admitted that a general settlement was now probably 'unattainable'. Eden Minute dated 3 June 1936 on a despatch from Berlin dated 26 May 1936, *DBFP*, 2nd ser., vol. 16, no. 339.
152　For the Cabinet refusal to consider sanctions, see *CAB* 23/83, CC 21(36)3, 18 March 1936. Evidence of the growing French reluctance to consider the imposition of sanctions is contained in *DBFP*, 2nd ser., vol. 16, nos 159 and 182.
153　Although at a meeting of the CID, held on 3 April 1936, it had been agreed not to request the immediate withdrawal of Royal Navy vessels from the Mediterranean, the COS were firmly in favour of a move to restore relations with Italy. See Roskill, p. 238, also Arthur Marder, 'The Royal Navy and the Ethiopian Crisis of 1935–1936', *American Historical Review*, vol. LXXV, no. 5, June 1970, pp. 1327–56.
154　*CAB* 23/83, CC 27(36)1, 6 April 1936.
155　*DBFP*, 2nd ser., vol. 16, no. 224, Mr Edmond to Foreign Office (no. 31 LN [J 2966/587/1]), Geneva, 9 April 1936.
156　*DBFP*, 2nd ser., vol. 16, no. 246, Mr Edmond to Foreign Office (no. 42 [J 3229/84/1]), Geneva, 17 April 1936.
157　Paul-Boncour candidly warned Eden that the consideration of further sanctions against Italy would have provided a significant boost to anti-British right-wing elements in the French election campaign. See *DBFP*, 2nd ser., vol. 16, nos 248 and 249. In addition *Avon Papers*, FR/36/11, 17 April 1936.
158　Eden argued that to press the sanctions issue would have led to a rift in Anglo-French relations and the eventual collapse of the sanctions front. See *DBFP*, 2nd ser., vol. 16, no. 250. Baldwin was later reported as saying that

Paul-Boncour had warned Eden that further sanctions would have led to the loss of 60 seats to the right-wing opposition at the election. See Tom Jones to Dr Abraham Flexner, 25 April 1936, Jones, p. 187.

159   *CAB* 23/84, CC 30(36)3, 22 April 1936.
160   *DBFP*, 2nd ser., vol. 16, no. 235, Minute on the Italo-Abyssinian conflict by Sir R. Vansittart (J 2973/1000/1), 10 April 1936.
161   Minute by Mr Thompson dated 9 April 1936 on Eden's despatch from Geneva of the same date. *DBFP*, 2nd ser., vol. 16, no. 224.
162   Minute by Mr Thompson dated 20 April 1936 on Eden's despatch from Geneva dated 18 April 1936. *DBFP*, 2nd ser., vol. 16, no. 250.
163   See Sir S. Barton's despatches from Addis Ababa of 8 and 19 April 1936. *DBFP*, 2nd ser., vol. 16, nos 216, 218 and 256. Barton advocated the widening of sanctions against Italy in addition to financial and material support for Abyssinia.
164   Minute by Vansittart dated 17 April 1936 on Eden's despatch from Geneva of the same date. As late as 8 April 1936 Eden was willing to accept projections that an Italian victory in Abyssinia could not be accomplished until after the rainy season and probably not for several years. *DBFP*, 2nd ser., vol. 16, nos 221 and 246.
165   *DBFP*, 2nd ser., vol. 16, no. 264, Mr Eden to Sir S. Barton (no. 172 [J 3253/3249/1]), 21 April 1936.
166   By 18 April 1936 Eden was prepared to concede that the fate of Abyssinia hung on whether the Emperor's forces could survive until the rainy season commenced. *DBFP*, 2nd ser., vol. 16, no. 250.
167   *CAB* 23/84, CC 31(36)4, 29 April 1936.
168   *CAB* 23/84, CC 30(36)3, 22 April 1936.
169   At a meeting on 27 April 1936 Chamberlain told Eden that the League of Nations had patently failed over the Abyssinian issue. He recommended that it be effectively replaced by regional security pacts and some form of international police force, which would be much more attractive to Germany. Chamberlain claimed that Eden agreed but expressed his concern at the timing of such a radical change in policy. *Neville Chamberlain Papers*, NC 2/23A, diary entry for 27 April 1936.
170   *CAB* 23/84, CC 31(36)5, 29 April 1936. The first meeting of the Cabinet Committee on Foreign Policy, chaired by Baldwin, was held the following day. It was agreed that Eden's recommendation should be followed and an investigation be conducted into the future role of the League of Nations and, in particular, the format and imposition of sanctions. The Committee, however, did not meet again until July 1936. See Middlemas and Barnes, *Baldwin, A Biography* (London, 1969), p. 953.
171   *CAB* 23/84, CC 31(36)4, 29 April 1936.
172   *DBFP*, 2nd ser., vol. 16, Sir S. Barton to Mr Eden (J 3898/3249/1), 5 May 1936.
173   The Cabinet, however, supported the Foreign Secretary in showing no inclination for an early capitulation to Italy. It was emphasised that the question of League reform was to be left to the September meeting of the General Assembly, while a French suggestion of immediate Anglo-French-Italian negotiations under the terms of the 1906 Treaty for a solution of the Abyssinian problem was declined. *CAB* 23/84, CC 34(36)4, 6 May 1936.
174   Avon, p. 378. Eden was apparently supported by the Prime Minister who reportedly described Mussolini as 'a savage' and referred to Mussolini and Hitler as 'two lunatics'. See Avon, p. 378 and Jones, diary entry for 30 April 1936; Jones, p. 191.

175 Within the Cabinet support for the abolition of sanctions lay primarily with the Ministries most affected — the Board of Trade and the Service Ministries. It was important to note, however, that in May 1936 Eden was also urged to liquidate the sanctions against Italy by Ramsay MacDonald, Lord Hailsham and Lord Halifax. In addition Malcolm MacDonald warned Eden that only South Africa, of the Dominions, wholeheartedly supported the continuation of sanctions. See Eden correspondence in *Avon Papers*, ETH/36/11, ETH/36/24, ETH/36/25, ETH/36/27, ETH/36/28, ETH/36/42. See also *Baldwin Papers*, vol. 124, Runciman to Baldwin, 27 May 1936.

176 The mood in Paris and Berlin was illustrated by Sir G. Clerk's despatch of 24 May 1936 and Sir E. Phipps's despatch of 27 May 1936. See *DBFP*, 2nd ser., vol. 16, nos 338 and 343.

177 Memorandum by Sir R. Vansittart, 'The future of Anglo-Italian relations and of the League of Nations', 21 May 1936, *Vansittart Papers*, 1/14. Vansittart was convinced that sanctions could not be maintained until September for the sanctions front was already crumbling and they would only further antagonise Mussolini. *Avon Papers*, ETH 36/43.

178 Minutes by Wigram dated 28 May 1936 and Eden dated 31 May 1936 on Sir E. Phipps's despatch of 27 May 1936. See *DBFP*, 2nd ser., vol. 16, no. 343.

179 Minute by Eden dated 27 May 1936. See *DBFP*, 2nd ser., vol. 16, p. 461, note 1.

180 On 18 May 1936 the First Lord of the Admiralty asked the Cabinet either to approve partial mobilisation of naval reservists or place the Mediterranean fleet back on a peace-time footing. The Cabinet followed Eden's suggestion that a Cabinet Committee examine the question of temporary enlistment. *CAB 23/84*, CC 37(36)3, 18 May 1936. On 27 May 1936 the President of the Board of Trade outlined the damage being inflicted on British industry by sanctions, *CAB 23/84*, CC 39(36)8.

181 *Neville Chamberlain Papers*, NC 18/1, letter to his sister Ida, 10 May 1936.

182 See *CAB 23/84*, CC 39(36)8 and CC 40(36)5.

183 In an interview on 28 May 1936 the Italian Ambassador, Grandi, had emphasised to Eden Mussolini's desire for the normalisation of relations in the Mediterranean and also for a reaffirmation of the Stresa front in order to contain German ambitions. *DBFP*, 2nd ser., vol. 16, no. 347.

184 *CAB 23/84*, CC 40(36)5, 29 May 1936.

185 Ibid. An opinion supported by Sir Maurice Hankey who forwarded a memorandum to Eden on 8 June 1936 pointing out the danger of confronting Italy, Germany and Japan simultaneously and urging the Foreign Secretary to: 'grasp the hand held out by Signor Mussolini, however repugnant it may be', *Avon Papers*, FP 36/4.

186 Eden's optimism as to the possibility of a *quid pro quo* being extracted from Mussolini was based on the belief that the Anglo-French sanctions front could at least be maintained until the next designated meeting of the League Council on 26 June 1936. To this end he was reluctant to accede to suggestions that he allow Mussolini to by-pass the League of Nations by simply making a general statement of future Italian intentions. *CAB 23/84*, CC 41(36)1, 10 June 1936.

187 *The Times*, 11 June 1936.

188 *H of C*, Debs, 5's, vol. 313, cols 401—3. See also Avon, p. 385.

189 Avon, pp. 384—5.

190 *Neville Chamberlain Papers*, NC 18/1, letter to his sister Hilda, 14 June 1936.

191 *Neville Chamberlain Papers*, NC 2/23A, diary entry for 17 June 1936.
192 Eden's argument was based on the conclusion that Abyssinia could only be reconstituted by military force. Given the unwillingness of the League of Nations either to initiate or risk an open military conflict with Italy, Eden argued that it would only be a matter of time before the existing sanctions front crumbled. It was also apparent that the Foreign Secretary was moving towards the body of opinion that advocated the need to restore Anglo-Italian relations as a prerequisite to the containment of German ambitions. *DBFP*, 2nd ser., vol. 16, no. 360, Memorandum by Eden on the maintenance of sanctions (J 5345/216/1), 11 June 1936. Presented to Cabinet on 17 June 1936 as CP 159(36).
193 *H of C*, Debs, 5's, vol. 313, cols 1201—5, 18 June 1936.
194 *CAB* 23/84, CC 42(36)1 and CC 42(36)2, 17 June 1936. For Eden's recommendations to the Cabinet on the Mediterranean assurances, see CP 165(36).
195 As Eden had suspected Blum and Delbos were 'in full agreement' with the decision to raise sanctions and he expected that: 'we shall now find it easier to work with France than we have for some time past.' *Avon Papers*, FR/36/13, 26 June 1936.
196 Harold Nicolson, diary entry for 18 June 1936, Nicolson, p. 265.
197 Stephen Roskill, *Hankey, Man of Secrets, Vol. 3, 1931—36* (London,1974), p. 241.
198 Tom Jones to Lady Grigg, 3 May 1936, Jones, pp. 192—3.
199 *Neville Chamberlain Papers*, NC 2/23A, diary entry for 11 July 1936.
200 *CAB* 23/85, CC 50(36)2, 6 July 1936.
201 Avon, pp. 387—8.
202 Avon, pp. 387—8 and *CAB* 23/84, CC 34(36)4, 6 May 1936, and *CAB* 23/84, CC 41(36)1, 10 June 1936.
203 For example see reports of Eden's discussions with Aloisi and Titulescu of Geneva in January 1936. *Avon Papers*, FO, 954/13A, IT/36/1, and IT/36/2.
204 See Italian press comment on Eden's appointment, *Giornale d'Italia*, 23 December 1935 and *DBFP*, 2nd ser., vol. 15, no. 417, 27 December 1935.
205 The extent of Cabinet opinion in support of the removal of sanctions as the first step in a positive attempt to mend fences with Italy had been indicated at the meetings held on 29 May and 23 June 1936. At the latter meeting the Cabinet discussed a memorandum submitted by the Chiefs-of-Staff Subcommittee to the CID which emphasised the value of improving relations with Italy from the standpoint of Imperial Defence. See *CAB* 23/84, CC 40(36)5 and CC 43(36)3. Sir R. Vansittart was the central figure of a group within the Foreign Office which consistently advocated an improvement of relations with Italy as a precondition for a further initiative to Berlin. For example see Minutes by Wigram and Vansittart, dated 28 May 1936, on Sir E. Phipps's despatch from Berlin, dated 27 May 1936. *DBFP*, 2nd ser., vol. 16, no. 343.
206 See in particular the Cabinet discussion of 29 May 1936, *CAB* 23/84, CC 40(36)5.
207 Neville Chamberlain records that on 27 April 1936 Eden, in a private conversation, fully endorsed his suggestion that the League of Nations be divested of the authority to impose sanctions and essentially: 'should be kept in being as a moral force and focus but for peace we should depend on a system of Regional Pacts to be registered and approved by the League.' *Neville Chamberlain Papers*, NC 2/23A, diary entry for 27 April 1936. See also Cabinet Minutes for 6 May 1936. *CAB* 23/84, CC 34(36)4.

6 The Spanish Imbroglio
June 1936 — May 1937

In the General Election held in May 1936, the French Government was defeated by a coalition of left-wing political parties fighting under the banner of the *Front Populaire*. Although the new administration was not technically installed in office until 4 June 1936, Eden took the opportunity to discuss the international situation with the incoming Prime Minister, Leon Blum, while passing through Paris on 15 May 1936. While their discussions were informal and of a very general nature, Eden subsequently claimed that the meeting heralded a distinct improvement in Anglo-French relations:

> The French Prime Minister was very cordial in his welcome and, I considered, sincere in the emphasis he laid upon Anglo-French co-operation. In this respect and in his antipathy to dictatorships wherever they might be, we were at one. I rejoiced at the improvement he would be on his predecessors.
>
> I respected Blum's intelligence, integrity and courage and our friendship was never marred by a serious difference or even a misunderstanding.[1]

The significance of a change of Government in Paris was not immediately apparent. The formulation of a positive Anglo-French approach to the Italo-Abyssinian conflict had been resisted in March and April of 1936 by the French Foreign Minister, Flandin, who had argued that the imposition of more sanctions was only likely to undermine further his Government's standing with the French electorate.[2] Although the defeat of the Sarraut Government and its replacement by an administration which declared its commitment to collective security[3] outwardly augured well for the reassertion of Anglo-French unity at Geneva, the British Cabinet was forced to concede, at meetings held on 27 and 29 May 1936, that the new French Government was unlikely to support further sanctions against Italy.[4]

It was not, therefore, the change of Government in Paris which initiated the improvement in Anglo-French collaboration in the latter half of 1936 but rather it was the Cabinet's decision, in June 1936, to abandon its sanctions policy against Italy which cleared the path for a reassertion of relations between London and Paris.[5] The immediate impact of this decision was indicated by the fact that at the meeting of the League of Nations summoned to witness the formal lifting of sanctions, Eden was approached by Blum and Van Zeeland who expressed their desire to reopen negotiations for a West-European security agreement by calling a meeting of the Locarno Powers. When it became apparent that the purpose of the meeting would be to formulate a constructive set of proposals to be presented to Germany, Eden appreciated the advantages to be derived from both side-stepping the all-but moribund questionnaire and co-ordinating British policy with France, Belgium and also possibly Italy now that the Abyssinian issue was likely to be defused.[6] In addition the Foreign Secretary was aware of the need for a new initiative in order to counter criticism of the apparent failure of his previous overtures to Germany. It was no secret that Baldwin was being urged to take a more active interest in the conduct of Anglo-German relations. In May 1936 Thomas Jones had visited Germany and had held a series of interviews with Von Ribbentrop and Hitler. The express purpose of this mission was to engineer a meeting between Hitler and Stanley Baldwin.[7] That Eden was aware of Jones's intentions and disapproved of them is indicated by an extract from his diary for 3 June 1936:

> Saw S.B. Warned him that object of German foreign policy was to divide us from French. Hence Anglo-German Naval Agreement and Ribbentrop's repeated missions here. At the moment . . . we had asked Hitler a number of perfectly reasonable questions which in fact he could only fail to answer if his intentions were bad. It was therefore most important that he should be given no occasion to cloud the issue, above all that S.B. should not. I think S.B. saw the force and was rather alarmed.[8]

Any suggestion of Baldwin travelling to Germany was eventually scotched when on 16 June 1936 Eden openly declared to the Prime Minister, in the presence of Jones, his opposition to the scheme.[9] Undoubtedly the Foreign Secretary was motivated by a determination to rebuke elements within the Government and Civil Service which sought to manipulate personal contacts with Baldwin in order to influence the course of foreign policy.[10] More specifically, however, the Foreign Secretary did not want Baldwin interfering in the field of Anglo-German relations at a time when he was considering the possibility of a further initiative for a settlement with Germany.

On 6 July 1936, upon his return from Geneva, Eden presented the Cabinet with a review of the international situation.[11] He admitted that his attempts to lower the level of tension had failed: 'He, himself, felt that the international situation was so serious that from day to day there was the risk of some dangerous incident arising and even an outbreak of war could not be excluded.' Pointing to the ineffectiveness of the League of Nations and the evidence of extensive German rearmament, he declared that: 'he could give no guarantee of the certainty of peace even during the present year.' In particular he highlighted the uncertainty as to how the German problem was to be tackled:

> The suggestion was made that the present policy of yielding to Germany on every occasion merely encouraged Herr Hitler to pursue his aggressive policy and the question was raised as to whether Herr Hitler ought not to be told that there was a definite limit beyond which we could not allow him to go otherwise every surrender would bring us nearer to war.

> It was pointed out, however, that at the present moment the country had neither the means — nor the heart — to stop them.

Consequently Eden argued that British policy must accept certain limitations: 'The objects of British policy, it was pointed out were first to secure peace in the world, if possible, and second, to keep this country out of war.'

Eden contended that in order to avoid a European war Britain had to continue to search for an agreement with Germany. Given that Hitler would resist a multilateral security pact covering Eastern Europe and also that Britain had neither the military capacity nor the popular domestic backing for the imposition of an East-European settlement, Eden argued that the only way forward was to concentrate on the maintenance of Britain's immediate interests in Western Europe. He therefore concluded with a plea that the proposal made by Blum and Van Zeeland for a meeting of the Locarno powers to formulate an approach to Germany be accepted. It would seem that the force of Eden's argument was widely accepted by the Cabinet and it was agreed that a meeting of the Locarno Powers be called for 22 July 1936.[12] The need to turn once again to the German problem was unanimously accepted and the timing of such an initiative seemed particularly appropriate given the fillip to Anglo-Italian relations provided by the liquidation of sanctions. Although the Cabinet's decision to support British participation in a meeting of the Locarno Powers was subsequently reviewed, following Italy's decision to decline an invitation to the proposed meeting, the Foreign Secretary's arguments once again prevailed.[13] On the evening of 15 July 1936 Eden declared to the Cabinet Committee on Foreign Policy that to postpone a meeting of the Locarno Powers would both surrender the initiative to Germany and deflate French and Belgian confidence in British leadership.[14]

The resulting meeting of British, Belgian and French Ministers in London on 23 July 1936 was entirely satisfactory from Eden's point of view in that agreement was reached on a joint approach to Germany and Italy to attend a Five Power Conference which would seek, initially, to negotiate an agreement replacing Locarno and also look at other aspects of European security.[15] As Eden informed the German Chargé d'Affaires on 24 July 1936:

> Much dead wood had been cut away and I could see no reason why the five Powers should not meet and collaborate.

> . . . I did not think that the Conference should be unduly delayed since if this was, as it appeared to be, the psychological moment, this moment was not to be missed.[16]

It appeared, however, that Eden's conception of 'the psychological moment' was not shared by the German Government. The German Foreign Minister, Von Neurath, replied on 30 July 1936 that his government was not in favour of a meeting being held until October.[17] While Eden initially accepted this decision, the prospect of a Conference being convened had receded by September with the announcement that the German Government could not accept a provisional date in October on the grounds that such a meeting would require extensive preparation.[18] Of a more ominous nature, reports were received from Paris that the German Minister for Economics, Dr Schacht, had outlined to the French Government Germany's need for both economic assistance and the restoration of its colonial empire as a source of raw materials.[19] The German delaying tactics and the suggestion of concessions in order to entice Germany into negotiation were received with growing exasperation by the Foreign Office. In relation to the German colonial demands as a *quid pro quo* for collaboration in a Five Power Conference, Vansittart wrote to Eden on 21 September 1936: 'We are in fact being asked, as I said to you, to play the ace of spades the very first trick in order to take the two of clubs.'[20]

Ten days later Ralph Wigram went so far as to challenge not only the price to be paid for a Five Power Agreement but, indeed, the value of any such agreement. In a Minute endorsed by Vansittart and Orme Sargent, Wigram argued: 'What tangible advantage, from the point of view of our interests, will the treaty represent to us? I find it difficult to see. Why then not leave the Germans to make the running from now on?'[21] In response Eden reminded his colleagues that he was not prepared to grant colonial concessions to Germany as a precondition for the opening of negotiations and, indeed, he had informed the House of Commons on 27 July 1936 that:

> the question of any transfer of mandated territories would inevitably raise grave difficulties — moral, political and legal — of which His Majesty's Government must frankly say they have been unable to find any solution.[22]

Unlike Wigram and Vansittart, however, he did not see the German tactics as establishing an insuperable barrier and insisted that the Foreign Office must continue to press the German Government to agree to both a date for the opening of the Conference and a suitable agenda.[23] Even Eden's optimism, however, was stretched in the latter half of October. In particular the question of possible exemptions from the commitments to be incorporated within the network of non-aggression pacts was a constant source of irritation. The German suggestion that its involvement in a conflict with France's allies in Eastern Europe, particularly the Soviet Union, would not be sufficient to release France from its non-aggression treaty with Germany generated increasing concern in London.[24] While Eden had gone to great lengths to remind the French that they could not expect Britain to guarantee the status quo in Eastern Europe, he appreciated that the German attempt to nullify the French alliance network would not be accepted in Paris and, indeed, contravened French and British obligations under the Covenant of the League of Nations.[25]

On 19 November 1936 Eden attempted to close the gulf between the French and German standpoints with a proposal that an exception be made to the non-aggression pacts in the event of a non-signatory being attacked by a signatory power. The determination of such an act of aggression was to be placed in the hands of the League of Nations.[26] The Germans, however, appeared to be in no mood for conciliation. On 8 December 1936 Von Ribbentrop informed Eden that the: 'memorandum had been a grievous disappointment to the

Chancellor.'[27] What hopes that remained for the early convening of the Five Power Conference were virtually eliminated three weeks later when Von Neurath warned Sir E. Phipps that Anglo-German relations were unlikely to improve until after the settlement of the conflict in Spain.[28]

While the negotiations for the Five Power Conference had met with little tangible success, they were significant in indicating a growing divergence between Eden and several of his senior Foreign Office advisers on the role and future course of Anglo-German relations. By December 1936 Sir R. Vansittart and Ralph Wigram appeared to have reached the conclusion that Germany would only enter into an agreement at a price, probably in the form of either colonial concessions or recognition of its political and economic supremacy in Eastern Europe. Given the tacit surrender to Germany over the Rhineland issue, Vansittart and Wigram opposed any suggestion of further concessions without a positive *quid pro quo* in addition to a German agreement to enter a Five Power Conference.[29] Given Hitler's reluctance to accede to either of these conditions, they saw little possibility of a settlement being achieved with Germany. In this context they saw the role of the negotiations as primarily a delaying tactic while the British rearmament programme gathered momentum and further strengthened the bargaining position *vis à vis* Germany. They assumed therefore the ambivalent position of seeing little hope for the on-going negotiations meeting with success but at the same time opposing any suggestion of either abandoning the negotiation process or attempting to force the pace of the discussions.[30] Therefore, in response to a suggestion by Eden that Germany should be pressed to respond to the proposals presented for the format of the Five Power Conference, Vansittart minuted on 2 January 1937: 'It would be dangerous to get representatives of the 5 Powers round a table yet awhile. It might mean the premature end of negotiations. Anyhow I don't think the Germans would come.'[31]

This only served to underline Vansittart's general apprehension as to the course of Anglo-German relations in 1937. On 31 December 1936 he concluded:

> on any showing Germany will be ready for big mischief at least a year — and probably more — before we are ready to look after ourselves. To the Foreign Office therefore falls the task of holding the situation at least till 1939, and the foregoing account of the world shows that there is no certainty of our being able to do so, though we are doing our utmost by negotiating with Germany, endeavouring to regain lost ground with Italy, and reducing the demands on our still exiguous strength by a treaty with Egypt.[32]

It was apparent, however, that during the latter half of 1936 the Foreign Secretary still clung to the belief that a mutually acceptable agreement could be engineered with Germany. The basis for this conviction was Eden's faith in reports that the German economic and financial position was steadily deteriorating and that, therefore, Hitler would be forced to seek assistance from Britain and France. [33] While appreciating the significance of the rearmament programme in the long term, Eden argued on 16 November 1936:

> It is becoming increasingly clear that we shall have one more chance, perhaps a final one, of coming to terms with Germany. If we are to have any chance of success, she must be given *nothing* except she change her political ways. To ease Germany's economic difficulties without political return is merely to facilitate her rearmament and make it easier for her to carry on her politico-economic policies in Central and South Eastern Europe. [34]

Eden agreed with Vansittart, therefore, that any agreement must contain a firm German *quid pro quo*, but differed in his appreciation of the prospects of achieving such an agreement. While the Permanent Under-Secretary remained sceptical, the Foreign Secretary displayed his determination to force the pace of negotiations. On 8 December 1936, in response to Minutes by Wigram and Vansittart questioning the decision to apply further pressure for a positive response from Berlin, Eden noted:

> It must be remembered that we are 'in charge' of these negotiations and have ourselves recently sent proposals to the other four powers. It is not good for our position that these proposals should be ignored by all concerned, and therefore I favour a reminder all round next week. [35]

In addition Eden openly challenged the recommendations of the Chiefs-of-Staff to the Cabinet on the question of British commitments to Europe and specifically on the issue of Belgian neutrality. [36] Eden was determined that their reluctance to envisage further military commitments to Europe could not be allowed to hinder the progress of the negotiations. [37] By the turn of the year, however, he was forced to concede that the immediate prospects of success were not bright and that tension was continuing to mount in Europe. In a letter to Baldwin dated 27 December 1936 it was apparent, though, that Eden still entertained the expectation that an agreement could be forged in the coming twelve months:

My own conviction grows that next year is going to be of the greatest importance in Foreign Affairs. It appears increasingly evident that the present administration in Germany cannot face another winter as they now are. Therefore the alternatives confront them. Foreign adventure or a change of methods.[38]

While conceding that Hitler would continue to seek to exploit the outbreak of Civil War in Spain and perhaps also turn his attention towards Czechoslovakia, Eden remained hopeful that economic problems would force the German leadership into a compromise with Britain and France.[39]

If Eden's first twelve months of office had not yielded a positive return in terms of solving the threat posed to European stability by German ambitions, the Foreign Secretary had enjoyed a measure of success in other quarters. On 26 August 1936 a treaty of alliance had been concluded between Britain and Egypt.[40] The Treaty, which was ratified by both parties in December 1936, was the result of several years of tentative negotiations between the two countries. One of Eden's first acts as Foreign Secretary had been to urge the British High Commissioner in Egypt, Sir Miles Lampson, to increase the pace of negotiations. The Italian invasion of Abyssinia had brought home to the Egyptian and British Governments the need to improve both political and military relations if Mussolini's growing stature in the Islamic world was to be countered. In addition the doubts surrounding Britain's future status in Egypt not only inhibited defence planning in the Mediterranean but also exacerbated the British position in Palestine. Any sign of British weakness or uncertainty was only likely to fuel further the demands of the Palestinian Arabs for self-government and a halt to Jewish immigration.[41]

The point of contention in the Anglo-Egyptian negotiations was primarily the question of whether agreement could be reached on the continuation of a British military presence in Egypt. It was apparent that the desire of the War Office to maintain a major presence in Egypt was not acceptable to the Egyptian Government. It was Eden, although undoubtedly ably supported by Lampson, who succeeded in engineering a successful compromise in the summer months of 1936.[42] In a memorandum to the Cabinet dated 8 June 1936, the Foreign Secretary emphasised the danger to Britain's position in the Mediterranean that would result from a failure to consolidate Anglo-Egyptian relations in the face of a growing Italian military challenge. He proposed, therefore, a compromise agreement based upon the British military presence being restricted to the Suez Canal Zone, given an Egyptian undertaking that this did not exclude the possibility of British forces being reintroduced to their former bases at some future date. The position of the Suez Canal base was to be reviewed after the lapse of 20 years. In attempting to overcome significant opposition from the War Office, Eden noted:

> It is for consideration whether in the light of the above, and of the disquieting limitation of our resources during the crucial years immediately ahead, it is wise to risk a breakdown in the discussions when we can apparently secure a treaty giving to us, even if some time after twenty years we were to evacuate the Canal Zone, the right to bring back our forces in unlimited numbers in the event of an apprehended emergency.[43]

This compromise formed the basis of the treaty that was eventually signed in London on 26 August 1936. The agreement was undoubtedly a triumph for Eden in that it secured British communications in the Eastern Mediterranean and allowed attention to be focused more specifically on Italian ambitions in the Western Mediterranean. Furthermore the relinquishment of British bases at Cairo and Alexandria permitted the reallocation of troops to deal with the growing disturbances in Palestine.[44] The Foreign Secretary had successfully capitalised on Egyptian fears of Italian ambitions to negotiate an alliance in perpetuity which, in exchange for scaling down the direct British presence in Egypt, guaranteed Britain's rights to continue to defend its interests in Egypt and the maintenance of Egyptian sovereignty.[45]

Eden later recorded of the Egyptian treaty that it was 'the only event which had given me any satisfaction during these dismal months'.[46] This note of gloom was caused not only by the failure to re-establish relations with Germany but also by the deteriorating military and political situation in the Western Mediterranean. Despite its significance for the maintenance of Britain's global commitments, the conclusion of the Anglo-Egyptian treaty was largely overshadowed by events in Spain. As early as 25 March 1936 the British Ambassador in Madrid had warned the Foreign Office that a military *coup d'état* against the Popular Front Government, elected the previous month, was a distinct possibility.[47] However, although political instability in Spain had generated debate as to the future of British commercial interests in that country, the Foreign Office appeared to have discounted the possibility of a military coup in the summer of 1936.[48] The outbreak of hostilities on 17 and 18 July 1936, therefore, took the Foreign Office by surprise. Eden informed the House of Commons on 22 July 1936 that the situation was unclear but he was sufficiently disturbed to recommend the immediate despatch of British war-ships to the main Spanish ports to evacuate British subjects.[49] Although Tom Jones recorded that Baldwin explicitly informed the Foreign

Secretary 'on no account, French or other, must he bring us into fight on the side of the Russians',[50] it was apparent that from the outset Eden had little personal hesitation in deciding that Britain must pursue a course of strict neutrality. Given the delicate state of negotiations for a Five Power Conference, to risk an open rift with Italy or France over Spain was unthinkable. It was apparent that the immediate problem was to resolve the question of the supply of war materials either to the Spanish Government or the rebel forces.[51] On 29 July 1936, while not advocating a formal embargo on the export of war material to Spain, the Foreign Secretary suggested to the Cabinet that an informal embargo could be applied if the Service Ministries were to lay prior claim to all British armament production under the pretext of accelerating the British rearmament programme.[52] Two days later Eden minuted, in response to reports that the Spanish Government had requested military assistance from France: 'This may mean that we shall be asked now. I hope that we shall be able to avoid supplying, by some means or other.'[53]

Having established the broad guidelines of non-intervention, Eden felt sufficiently confident to travel north to Yorkshire and leave the implementation of policy during the summer recess in the hands of Sir Alexander Cadogan, with reference to the Lord Privy Seal, Lord Halifax, if necessary.[54]

The situation, however, was far more delicate in Paris, with the French Government clearly divided over the question of responding to requests for military assistance from the Spanish Government. The decision taken on 25 July 1936 to suspend the export of war material to Spain was challenged, as reports were received of guns and ammunition being supplied to the rebels by the Italian Government.[55] While the British Admiralty firmly rejected any suggestion of concerted Anglo-French naval action designed to thwart the possibility of Italy and Germany seizing the Balearic and Canary Islands, it was apparent that pressure was growing in France for the provision of military supplies to the Republican forces in Spain.[56] On 7 August 1936 the British Ambassador, Sir G. Clerk, warned the French Foreign Minister, Delbos, of the distinct absence of support in Britain for a policy of assistance to either party in Spain. Clerk recorded of the conversation:

> I felt in so critical a situation I must put before him the danger of any action which might definitely commit the French Government to one side of the conflict and make more difficult the close co-operation between our two countries which was called for by this crisis.

Clerk added that he had undertaken the interview 'without instructions' from London and because: 'I had reason to believe that the extremists in the Government were putting increasing pressure on M. Blum and I felt sure what I said might strengthen the hands of the moderate and sober elements.'[57]

Clerk's interview certainly had the desired effect, with the announcement the following day that the French Government had decided to impose an embargo on the supply of arms to Spain.[58] While Eden was later able to argue that this was purely a French decision and that Clerk had emphasised he was only voicing a personal opinion, it was apparent that the Foreign Office was fully aware of the use that Delbos was likely to make of Clerk's statement to sway the French Cabinet and that the Ambassador's sentiments were fully endorsed in London.[59]

If Clerk's intervention had been partly instrumental in directing the French Government towards a policy of non-intervention, it had not solved the overall question of the format of any such agreement. Halifax had agreed in principle, on 4 August 1936, to a French proposal that non-intervention must be enshrined in a formal agreement amongst the major parties concerned. At the same time, however, he was determined that any such agreement must be endorsed by Italy and Germany.[60] It was evident that the Lord Privy Seal shared the concern evinced by several of the senior Foreign Office officials that a purely Anglo-French alignment would only crystallise the divisions in Europe and exacerbate relations with Hitler and Mussolini. Halifax, therefore, rejected any suggestion of detailed Anglo-French discussions until assurances were received of Italian and German participation.[61] Whilst this policy of caution was attractive to certain elements within the Cabinet and the Foreign Office which were broadly sympathetic to the rebel cause in Spain, Eden had evidently decided by the end of the second week of August that it could not be maintained indefinitely.[62] In a telephone conversation with Sir G. Mounsey he instructed the Assistant Under-Secretary of State to do everything possible in supporting the French attempts to gain agreement on a non-intervention declaration.[63] Eden's intervention, followed by his return to London two days earlier than expected on 16 August 1936, undoubtedly was a cardinal factor in the acceleration of the Anglo-French negotiations and the exchange of notes agreeing, in principle, to the prohibition of the export of arms to Spain on 15 August 1936.[64] The Foreign Secretary's decision was motivated not only by the growing welter of criticism directed at Britain's apparently less than whole-hearted support of the French non-intervention proposals, but also by the growing appreciation that unless positive steps were taken quickly to isolate the Spanish conflict there was a very real possibility that it could develop into a wider European confrontation. The Foreign Secretary therefore saw no alternative but to endorse fully the French non-intervention proposals immediately.[65] Following the decision to impose an embargo on the export of British arms to Spain, Eden wrote to Baldwin: 'I felt it necessary to do this even before we achieved international agreement in order that we might, by setting an example, do our best to induce others, more particularly Germany and Italy, to follow suit.'[66]

Furthermore the Foreign Secretary recommended to the Cabinet Committee on Foreign Policy, on 26 August 1936, that Britain accede to the French request that an international committee be established in London to scrutinise the implementation of the arms embargo and investigate any reported infringements.[67]

The Non-Intervention Committee, which was comprised of some 26 nations, first met in London on 9 September 1936. Britain accepted the responsibility for the organisation and chairing of the Committee and undoubtedly this was indicative of Eden's determination to divorce the Spanish issue from the wider context of European politics. During the fourteen meetings held in the last four months of 1936, the British Government attempted to deal, with strict impartiality, with the various infringements of the arms embargo that were alleged to have been committed by Italy, Germany and the Soviet Union. Furthermore Britain was at the forefront of those nations which sought to reinforce the embargo with the implementation of measures permitting direct control and examination of all materials being imported into Spain.[68]

This policy was apparently motivated by the conviction that non-intervention was a viable policy and also directly served British interests. On 30 August 1936 Eden minuted:

> We must continually bear in mind in relation to this dispute that we are in a particularly strong position to intervene, because we are known to be more neutral than any other great power and because a compromise is in our national interest. The victory of either extreme would be most unwelcome to us so that we must be up and doing in favour of compromise whenever opportunity affords.[69]

The pursuit of compromise was by no means a simple matter. In the face of growing evidence of foreign intervention in Spain, Eden conceded to Litvinov at Geneva on 1 October 1936:

> No one could expect a system of this kind which had been hastily improvised, to be absolutely water-tight.

. . . the important thing to consider from the point of view of the European situation was whether the agreement had resulted in a reduced supply of arms to both sides. This, I was sure, had been the result. [70]

The Foreign Secretary also publicly defended his decision to continue to support a policy of non-intervention:

> Because some who should be firemen take a hand now and again in feeding the flames, that is no reason why the whole fire brigade should leave their posts and join in fanning Europe into a furnace. [71]

Eden, however, was obviously dismayed at the evidence which suggested Italy and Germany were not willing to co-operate with France and Britain in an international exercise of such importance as the Spanish arms embargo. Eden's disillusionment with the tactics pursued by Hitler and Mussolini was hinted at in an entry in his diary for 21 November 1936 relating to the question of the granting of belligerent rights to the rebel regime:

> My own feeling is at present against granting of belligerent rights to Franco for international rather than Spanish reasons. I do not want even to appear to follow Hitler and Mussolini at the moment, but would prefer to 'show a tooth' in the Mediterranean; still less do I want to facilitate an attempt at a blockade that is maybe intended to starve Madrid. [72]

In this light his determination, against the advice of the Admiralty, not to confer belligerent rights on the rebel regime was indicative not only of his intention to continue to pursue a policy of non-intervention but also of his growing exasperation with the blatant disregard evinced for the Non-Intervention Committee by the Italian and German governments. [73]

The Spanish conflict had dealt a major blow to hopes of restoring Anglo-Italian relations, following the liquidation of the sanctions front in the first week of July. Eden had been sufficiently encouraged by the Italian aide-mémoire of 17 July 1936 to announce to the House of Commons, on 27 July 1936, that the Government no longer saw a need to continue the guarantees recently reaffirmed to Greece, Turkey and Yugoslavia. [74] The outbreak of hostilities in Spain, however, significantly altered this position. Reports of Italy providing extensive military assistance to the rebel forces prompted the Southern Department of the Foreign Office to warn the Foreign Secretary that there was every likelihood Italy was seeking to exploit the situation with the intention of establishing military bases on the

Balearic Islands. It was emphasised that the acquisition of such facilities posed a major challenge to the British naval base at Gibraltar and to the maintenance of British communications in the Western Mediterranean.[75] If the Foreign Secretary was reluctant to impair relations with Italy while negotiations for a Five Power Conference were in progress, such was the seriousness of the Italian threat that Eden felt obliged to warn the Italian Government on 3 September 1936 that the British Government would view with the 'closest concern' any alteration in the territorial status quo in the Western Mediterranean.[76] Although assurances were received that Italy had no intention of altering the Mediterranean status quo[77] and both the Italian Ambassador, Grandi, and the Foreign Minister, Ciano, continued to profess their desire for an improvement in Anglo-Italian relations, it was apparent that Eden now saw little hope of any such amelioration of relations being achieved.[78] This scepticism was based not only on the growing evidence of Italian infringements of the non-intervention agreement, but also on reports of Italian-inspired, anti-British propaganda in the Near East and Grandi's suggestion that relations could only be cemented by British recognition of the Italian position in Abyssinia.[79] The problem was compounded on 24 October 1936 by Mussolini's speech at Bologna in which he alluded to Italian military strength and determination and particularly to a 'forest of eight million bayonets well sharpened and wielded by young intrepid hearts'.[80] On 5 November 1936 Eden minuted:

> Does anyone in the Foreign Office really believe that Italy's foreign policy will at any time be other than opportunist? Any agreement with Italy will be kept as long as it suits Italy. Surely nobody can now place any faith in her promises. All this is not argument against seeking to improve Anglo-Italian relations, but against placing an exaggerated valuation on any such improvement if and when we get it.[81]

In this context it was perhaps surprising that Eden was prepared to react so rapidly to Mussolini's speech of 1 November 1936, suggesting that he desired Anglo-Italian agreement covering the Mediterranean which would be 'sincere, swift and complete on the basis of respect for our mutual rights'.[82] In a statement before the House of Commons on 5 November 1936, the Foreign Secretary reminded Italy that the Mediterranean was not simply 'a short cut by which the British Empire reaches its outlying territories more quickly' but represented to Britain a 'main arterial road'. Eden, however, went to great lengths to dispel any suggestion that British and Italian interests in the Mediterranean were not compatible and, therefore, concluded that there:

never has been so far as concerns this country an Anglo-Italian quarrel.

In these conditions it should, in our view, be possible for each country to continue to maintain its vital interests in the Mediterranean not only without conflict with each other, but even with mutual advantage.[83]

As Eden conceded to Drummond the following day his words were: 'definitely intended as an attempt to bring about a *rapprochement* between our two countries.'[84]

In the following week, with the announcement that the guard at the British legation in Addis Ababa was to be withdrawn and that commercial arrangements were to be concluded with Italy, it was apparent that Eden had decided to pursue an agreement with Italy.[85] The remaining question centred on the terms of any such agreement and in a despatch to Rome, dated 14 November 1936, the Foreign Secretary clearly outlined the British *desiderata*. Drummond was instructed to sound Ciano on an agreement guaranteeing the maintenance of the status quo in the Western Mediterranean and the cessation of anti-British propaganda in the Near East. In addition Drummond was to seek assurances that Italy would adhere to the London Naval Treaty and the Montreux Convention, and return to effective membership of the League of Nations. Finally Eden implicitly rejected any suggestion that he would be willing to recognise the Italian position in Abyssinia or limit the British naval presence in the Mediterranean as a *quid pro quo* in order to attain an agreement.[86]

As they stood the terms outwardly represented a reaffirmation of the Foreign Secretary's determination to seek a settlement of outstanding differences with Hitler and Mussolini, but to couple any agreement with concessions to the British position and positive assurances as to the future conduct of the participant states within the framework of international relations. Following reports from Rome that Ciano appeared reluctant to discuss anything other than a Mediterranean declaration,[87] Eden minuted on 10 December 1936:

The Italians are at their old game of getting something for nothing. They are apprehensive of our growing strength in the Mediterranean and would no doubt like to be reassured. But what do we get in return? Anti-British propaganda in the Near East, a redoubling of activity in Majorca and the most cavalier treatment of our representatives or suggestions on any subject. This is not what we want.

An agreement that only adds one more scrap of paper to the world and changes nothing in fundamentals is not worth so much effort.[88]

Eight days later Eden once again pressed Drummond to insist upon the widening of the topics under negotiation: 'You should accordingly press for a real *tour d'horizon* permitting a review of all points of common interest.'[89]

It was perhaps surprising, therefore, that on 2 January 1937 the Anglo-Italian Gentleman's Agreement was signed which limited itself to reaffirming the compatibility of British and Italian interests in the Mediterranean and to a public exchange of notes undertaking not to alter 'the *status quo* as regards national sovereignty of territories in the Mediterranean area'.[90] Despite the absence of any form of positive Italian assurance on the question of anti-British propaganda or Italian accession to either the London Naval Treaty or the Montreux Convention, Eden minuted on 2 January 1937: 'this is very satisfactory . . . . It is particularly satisfactory that we should have obtained our formula regarding Spain and I am glad that we were firm about this.'[91]

The key to this marked relaxation of the conditions demanded of Italy lay perhaps in the pressure exerted by elements within the Cabinet for a restoration of relations with Italy. It was certainly true that the Service Ministries were not alone in believing that the elimination of Italy from the list of nations seen as potential enemies was a vital prerequisite for the strengthening of the British negotiating position *vis à vis* Germany.[92] In reality, however, the reasoning behind Eden's decision to conclude the Gentleman's Agreement had been clearly outlined in a Foreign Office memorandum as early as 13 November 1936:

It may be borne in mind that it's exceedingly doubtful how far any gesture of friendliness by us would induce Fascist Italy fundamentally to alter or modify her policy in the Mediterranean. What is her main aim, constantly reaffirmed? The reconstitution of the Roman Empire. That aim may seem far off, may seem to us utterly fantastic and unreal; but as long as she is moving along these lines, she can hardly enter into sincere collaboration with England, the one great obstacle in her path.

Eden, however, was not prepared to exclude the possibility of an agreement:

To sum up: unless some further reply be made to Signor Mussolini's advances, he will undoubtedly recur to the suspicions and animosities of the last eighteen months and employ with increased energy the numerous methods open to him by which the nuisance value of Italy's policy can be directed to our detriment.

An early, careful and not ungenerous response on the other hand might help to produce a *détente* in the Mediterranean while British rearmament proceeds.[93]

It was apparent that, while discounting the possibility of a long-term understanding with Italy, the Foreign Secretary accepted the logic of establishing a limited *détente*, especially if it could be obtained at little or no cost to Britain. Therefore within the wider context of the creation of a possible platform for the future improvement of Anglo-Italian relations, the Gentleman's Agreement served the specific purpose of effectively neutralising Italian ambitions in the Balearic Islands. The events of the following six months, however, only served to confirm Eden's conviction that the policy of expansion pursued by Mussolini throughout the Mediterranean precluded the establishment of a comprehensive Anglo-Italian *détente*.[94] Within a week of the conclusion of the Gentleman's Agreement Eden was in possession of reports from the British Consul in Naples confirming that a further 8000 Italian volunteers had sailed for Spain.[95] While Sir E. Drummond was instructed to express Eden's disappointment and disquiet at these reports to the Italian Foreign Minister, Ciano, it was evident that Mussolini was unmoved by Eden's suggestion that the cessation of the flow of Italian volunteers to Spain 'would be of the greatest benefit not only to Anglo-Italian relations but to European appeasement'.[96]

There was also increasing evidence that Italian ambitions were not limited solely to Spain but were also seeking to expand Rome's influence in the Eastern Mediterranean. Despite British attempts to dissuade the Yugoslav Government from concluding a pact of non-aggression with Italy, such an agreement — titled the Pact of Belgrade — was signed on 25 March 1937 and the Foreign Office was further disturbed by reports of an Italian initiative for a similar agreement with Turkey.[97] In addition the Italian campaign directed against the British position in the Near East also appeared to gain in momentum following Mussolini's visit to Libya in March of 1937. Before a massed crowd in Tripoli, on 18 March 1937, Mussolini was presented with the Sword of Islam and reaffirmed the pledge, made in Beda Littoria six days previously, that 'Moslems may rest assured that Italy will always be the friend and protector of Islam throughout the world'.[98] Following the Italian seizure of Abyssinia, the implied threat to the British position in the Near East was apparent and in a speech delivered in Liverpool on 12 April 1937, Eden responded with a thinly veiled attack on those nations which sought to expand their power and influence:

> There will be no confidence in peace until this doctrine of live and let live, of non intervention in the affairs of others is both preached and practised. What is delaying the return of confidence is not only actual intervention across the frontiers of other countries, but the fear that such intervention may take place.

> Let the nations rid themselves of the idea that they should strive for a Pax Germanica, a Pax Gallica, a Pax Italica, or even a Pax Britannica. The only sure peace is not a national but an international peace . . . .[99]

In the following two months, however, the debate surrounding the question of *de jure* recognition of the Italian position in Abyssinia and the vitriolic press war conducted between the two countries were indicative of the failure of the Gentleman's Agreement to produce an amelioration of Anglo-Italian relations.[100] In February 1937 the Chiefs-of-Staff, in a review of Imperial Defence, had admitted that the possibility of a military clash with Italy in the Mediterranean could not be discounted and that the consequences of such a confrontation posed a serious threat to Imperial Defence:

> In the Mediterranean, the United Kingdom and Italy each have the power to threaten communications essential to the other and there is reason to assume that Italy, so long as the Fascist regime continues, will show herself more adventurous and aggressive than in the past. We hope, however, that the recent Anglo-Italian declaration will restore a certain degree of Anglo-Italian co-operation, but it would be rash to count on an immediate return to conditions under which Italy could, in all circumstances, be relied upon to follow a friendly policy towards this country. The danger that Italy will attack our interests would only be likely to arise if we were engaged in a war with another Power and Italy considered that her intervention might lead to our defeat.[101]

In essence, the central thread of this report, as accepted by the CID on 25 February 1937,[102] was summed up in the following assertion agreed by the CID on 11 February 1937: 'Italy cannot be counted on as a reliable friend but, in present circumstances, need not be regarded as a probable enemy.'[103]

By June 1937 the Foreign Office was sufficiently alarmed by the deterioration of Anglo-Italian relations to contend that the above assumption could not continue to form the guidelines for defence planning in the Mediterranean and the Red Sea. Following a report from Sir M. Lampson in Cairo expressing his 'grave misgivings' regarding the Italian ambitions in the Arab world,[104] the Foreign Office argued that it was necessary to revise the assumptions on which relations with Italy were based. In a memorandum dated 15 June 1937 it was proposed that:

> Italy cannot be considered as a reliable friend and must for an indefinite period be regarded as a possible enemy, especially if she can count on the goodwill and potential support of Germany or if the United Kingdom were involved in difficulties elsewhere.[105]

Although this formula was resisted by the CID, it was agreed on 21 June 1937 that the Joint Planning Subcommittee would examine and recommend measures to 'ensure the rapid defeat of Italy'.[106]

While Eden had both welcomed Lampson's report and endorsed the Foreign Office memorandum on the probability of war with Italy, his approach to the problem of relations with Italy in this period could be described as firm but essentially low-key.[107] This stance was typified by the debate surrounding the Italian campaign for British recognition of *de jure* Italian sovereignty over Abyssinia. Although the Foreign Secretary maintained that Britain had no immediate intention of affording such recognition, he took several steps in an attempt to pacify Italian opinion on what was identified in Rome as an emotive and key policy area, governing Italian relations with both Britain and the League of Nations.[108] In response to intense Italian criticism of the decision to invite the Emperor of Abyssinia to the coronation of King George VI, Eden used the medium of the Press and the House of Commons to stress that the invitation did not carry any political overtones, was purely a matter of protocol and, therefore, did not affect existing British *de facto* recognition of Italian sovereignty in Abyssinia.[109] Furthermore the Cabinet accepted Eden's proposal, on 24 March 1937, that the Opposition Party leaders be approached with a view to persuading them to reduce the volume of anti-Italian rhetoric in the House of Commons, which the Foreign Secretary argued was a significant factor in exacerbating Anglo-Italian relations.[110]

This almost conciliatory approach in the face of widespread Italian intervention in Spain and the growing challenge to the British position in the Near East was partly conditioned by the body of opinion within the Cabinet and, in particular, the Service Ministers who advocated the adoption of measures to improve relations with Italy. The re-establishment of cordial Anglo-Italian relations was seen not only as of central importance in Imperial defence calculations, which placed emphasis on the need to concentrate resources in the Home theatre and the Far East,[111] but also in the on-going campaign to weaken the Rome—Berlin Axis and, therefore, strengthen the British hand in relations with Germany.[112] The Foreign Secretary, however, did not subscribe to this viewpoint and in a memorandum on relations with Italy, dated 1. April 1937, argued that, in the long term, Mussolini's ambitions precluded any genuine understanding with Britain. In this sense Eden concluded that only British military strength would deter Mussolini from an attempt to extend Italian influence throughout the Mediterranean and the Near East. Therefore while Eden was prepared to pursue a policy of conciliation in the short term, he believed that a lasting settlement could only be achieved if Britain was in a position to dictate terms to Mussolini through the possession of superior military forces.[113] Such a policy was only viable if the balance of power between the two nations was moving in the long term steadily in Britain's favour. Eden argued that this was certainly the case, not only due to the gathering pace of the British rearmament programme but also as a result of the strain being imposed on the Italian economy by the economic and military commitment required to maintain the Italian forces assisting the Nationalist Army in Spain.[114] Eden calculated that, following Franco's failure to capture Madrid in the latter months of 1936 and the reversals suffered at Guadalajara in March 1937, the Nationalist forces were unlikely to win a clear victory within the foreseeable future. Therefore given Mussolini's commitment to the Nationalist cause, it appeared likely that Italian military and economic strength would be increasingly dissipated on the battlefields of Spain while the British rearmament programme steadily gained in pace. On 20 April 1937, in response to a Minute by Sir R. Vansittart arguing that the international situation remained fraught with danger, the Foreign Secretary replied:

> But meanwhile we become daily a little stronger; in this sense time is on our side, for the French become stronger too, not so the Italians who are probably at full stretch already.[115]

Eden's belief in the weakness of the Italian position in the long term had important ramifications for his approach to the whole question of Anglo-Italian relations and particularly the significance to be assigned to the Rome—Berlin axis. In response to a report from the Berlin Embassy arguing that Mussolini was 'not irrevocably committed to the German embrace', the Foreign Secretary minuted on 24 April 1937:

It is interesting to note that the Berlin–Rome axis is only attractive to Germany (1) as a means of intimidation to others, (2) when Italy appeared to be 'getting away with it'. The failure of sanctions, which Germany rightly or wrongly interpreted as our fear of Italy, made Rome an attractive partner, particularly to the politicians. The soldiers probably never believed very much in Italy's military value.

Now the scene is undergoing a change — Italian setbacks in Spain, both political and military, the prolonged strain which Abyssinia is placing upon an Italy economically weak, all these factors have resulted in Italy being able to play less and less part in Central Europe where she is now but a rather poor second fiddle to Berlin. This no doubt has its advantages for German policy in Central Europe but has its disadvantages as an axis, if one end of the axis is thereby shown to be weak. Germany cannot feel comfortable if she has to face the world with only a weakened and untrustworthy Italy as an ally. In this may perhaps be found the explanation of recent German quietude, as also in our re-armament, our close relations with France, and the evidence of U.S. sympathy with two Western democracies.[116]

This Minute encapsulated Eden's approach to the Italian question. In discounting the strength and resilience of the Rome–Berlin axis, the Foreign Secretary was pointing firmly to the conclusion that there was little to be gained from the pursuit of a comprehensive restoration of relations with Italy and, indeed, Mussolini's ambitions in the Mediterranean precluded the attainment of any such understanding. Eden indicated that the focus of European instability lay in Berlin and it was in this direction that he was disposed to concentrate his efforts. The Foreign Secretary's perception of the need to improve Anglo-German relations was clearly established in the first full Cabinet meeting of 1937. In the course of his survey of the international situation Eden expressed his conviction that the German economy was unable to face the prospect of another hard winter: 'It looked, therefore, as though this year would determine Germany in following a policy alternatively of co-operation or foreign adventure.'[117]

The Foreign Secretary placed considerable emphasis on reports from the British Ambassador in Berlin, Sir E. Phipps,[118] who argued that the balance of power in Berlin was delicately balanced between moderates such as Dr Schacht and the Army hierarchy and extremists within the Nazi Party who advocated an aggressive expansionist foreign policy: 'Our object must be to try and restrain the latter. This . . . could best be achieved by our present policy of being firm but always ready to talk.'[119] In particular Eden was concerned at the possible impact of the speech that Hitler was due to deliver to the Reichstag on 30 January 1937. While advocating the value of a statement on the progress of the rearmament programme by Inskip or Baldwin as an indication of British resolution, the Foreign Secretary was determined to offer Hitler a further olive branch in the hope of deterring an outburst by the German Chancellor which would prejudice the chances of improving Anglo-German relations.[120] On 19 January 1937 Eden used the platform of the House of Commons to address a thinly veiled plea for co-operation to Germany:

> The future of Germany and the part she is to play in Europe is today the main preoccupation of all Europe. Here is a great nation of 65,000,000 people in the very heart of our Continent which has exalted race and nationalism into a creed which is practised with the same fervour as it is preached.

> Germany has it in her power to influence a choice which will decide not only her fate but that of Europe. If she chooses co-operation there is nobody in this country who will not assist whole-heartedly to remove misunderstandings and to make the way smooth for peace and prosperity.[121]

The German Chancellor's reply on 30 January 1937, while declaring a willingness to respond to Eden's plea for increased international co-operation, questioned the value of any such co-operation until Germany was accepted as a full and equal member of the international community. In particular Hitler denounced the War Guilt clauses of the Treaty of Versailles and reaffirmed his intention to pursue the return to German administration of its pre-war colonial empire. Coupled with ominous references to the rights and status of national minorities in Eastern Europe and the need to suppress the forces of Bolshevism in Spain, the Chancellor's address clearly indicated that Hitler was still outwardly bent on an expansionist course.[122] The Foreign Secretary's comments on Hitler's speech, addressed to the Cabinet on 3 February 1937, registered particular concern at Hitler's failure to include Czechoslovakia amongst the nations with which he was prepared to restore relations. The German Chancellor's speech represented a major setback to any hopes that might have existed of improving Anglo-German relations. Eden concluded: 'It was, however, to the good that the "era of surprises" was declared at an end, but there was not a statement that the era of collaboration was to begin.'[123]

The events of the following six months supported this assessment, as the preparations for the Five Power Conference continued to be blocked by German intransigence over the questions of possible exceptions to the proposed network of non-aggression pacts and the role of the League of Nations in determining that an act of aggression had been committed.[124] On 18 March 1937 Eden admitted to the Cabinet Committee on Foreign Policy that the chances of an agreement being reached 'were very small indeed'.[125] Four days later, in a memorandum for the same body summing up the German and Italian standpoints, the Foreign Secretary concluded that German policy appeared dedicated to the destruction of the main principles of collective security and, particularly, to the weakening of French ties with its East-European allies and Britain.[126] Indeed the tangled web of diplomacy surrounding the Five Power pact negotiations had been further complicated by a Belgian declaration of 11 February 1937, indicating that Belgium, while prepared to receive guarantees of non-aggression, was not willing to provide reciprocal guarantees to its European neighbours.[127] As Eden noted in a memorandum to the Cabinet Foreign Policy Committee, this decision to return to a position of effective neutrality was indicative of Belgian fears that it would be drawn into any future Franco-German conflict. On a more disturbing level, however, it also opened the path for the possible conclusion of a Belgian—German non-aggression pact which Hitler had openly advocated in his statement of 30 January 1937. Eden argued that such an agreement would:

> mark the invasion by Germany of a sphere of influence which we have made peculiarly our own. Nor is it desirable that Germany should introduce into Western Europe the bilateral method of solving political problems.

Therefore, in order to circumvent the possibility of a Belgian—German alignment, the Foreign Secretary proposed that Belgium be invited to participate in a network of non-aggression pacts with Britain, France and Germany designed to guarantee the maintenance of Belgian neutrality.[128] The frequency of reports suggesting that Hitler was urging the Belgians to open negotiations for a bilateral security pact persuaded Eden that an immediate response was necessary.[129] Following the failure to lure King Leopold to Britain in February 1937, the Cabinet Committee on Foreign Policy, on 6 April 1937, accepted Eden's recommendation that he visit Brussels personally to deliver the proposals to the Belgian Government.[130] This visit, which was undertaken from 25 to 27 April 1937, was overtly far from a success in that the Belgian Government, while agreeing to examine the British proposals, rejected any suggestion of the continuation of formal links and conversations between the General Staffs of Britain, France and Belgium. While Eden had to be content with an assurance that Belgium would continue to keep Britain informed of the state of its defences, the major objective of his visit was, however, achieved in that Van Zeeland emphasised that his Government had no intention of pursuing a bilateral agreement incorporating military co-operation with Germany. The result of this tangled web of negotiations was that by May 1937, while the possibility of engineering a Five Power agreement had receded, Eden had been successful in resisting any suggestion of Belgium being positively detached from the Anglo-French sphere of interest in Western Europe.[131]

Although the negotiations for a Five Power Conference were apparently the central factor in Anglo-German relations in this period Eden was, in fact, increasingly preoccupied with the growing German campaign for the return of its former colonial possessions. The issue centred primarily on a series of informal meetings held by Dr Schacht with the French Premier, Blum, in August 1936, at which the German Minister had indicated the possibility of German expansionist designs being placated by the restoration of its colonial empire as a source of raw materials.[132] Although Eden had initially dismissed this initiative and repeated his determination to adhere to the stance outlined on 26 July 1936,[133] he was under pressure from the Treasury to explore Schacht's proposals further and to support an informal meeting between Schacht and Sir Frederick Leith-Ross, Chief Economic Adviser to the Government.[134] In January 1937 Eden finally agreed to authorise such a meeting, but with the rider that Leith-Ross must adopt a purely passive role:

> We have no proposals to make to Schacht: on the contrary the meeting is to hear Schacht's views and ideas and has been arranged in response to the many feelers he has put out for such a meeting.[135]

It was evident that the Foreign Secretary was prepared to consider the question of colonial restitution but only as part of a general settlement incorporating arms limitation, Germany's return to the League of Nations and participation in multilateral security agreements in Western and Eastern Europe.[136] The outcome of the Schacht-Leith-Ross negotiations was not entirely unsatisfactory in that Schacht suggested that German expectations were limited to the return of Togoland and the Cameroons. Significantly Schacht argued that colonial restitution would clear the path for a comprehensive settlement:

> Hitler was at present open to argument and if he [Schacht] could show that other means were available to give Germany a chance, he was convinced that he would be able to get Hitler to take that chance and to give us the guarantees which we wanted.

Leith-Ross concluded of the conversation:

> Unless we are determined in no circumstances to yield on the colonial question, we surely can lose nothing by defining the precise conditions for any discussion of the question and seeing what comes of it.[137]

The report was the subject of intense debate during the course of the following month.[138] While the Foreign Secretary did not subscribe to the rejection of any suggestion of the return of former German colonies, which was favoured by Ormsby-Gore,[139] he did appreciate the problems presented by such a solution. Not only was the territory in question predominantly under French administration but, also, Schacht appeared to be suggesting that the return of colonies would precede the attainment of a general settlement rather than be inextricably part of any such settlement. Eden, therefore, argued that further progress could only be made if the colonial question was discussed alongside the issues of European security and armament limitation and that this could only be achieved through the medium of formal negotiations with the German Foreign Ministry.[140]

This latter point led to a direct clash between Eden and Neville Chamberlain at the seventh meeting of the Cabinet Committee on Foreign Policy held on 18 March 1937. While agreeing with Eden on the necessity of linking the colonial issue with that of a general settlement, Chamberlain was insistent that further use be made of Schacht as an intermediary between the two governments.[141] It was significant that Chamberlain's view was accepted by the Cabinet Committee and, furthermore, the Chancellor of the Exchequer was allowed to make considerable amendments to Eden's despatch to the French Government, outlining Schacht's references to the return of Togoland and the Cameroons and the political guarantees that would have to be demanded as a suitable *quid pro quo*.[142] Although the debate surrounding the colonial issue turned out to be largely academic following the French Government's rejection of the possible cession of Togoland and the Cameroons,[143] it was significant in indicating not only Chamberlain's increasing influence in the field of foreign affairs but also the absence of unequivocal support within the Cabinet for Eden's direction of British relations with Germany.[144]

The problems encountered in the conduct of relations with Italy and Germany in this period had undoubtedly been severely handicapped, in the latter half of 1936, by the Spanish Civil War. It was evident that by January 1937 the Foreign Secretary was convinced the scale of German and Italian intervention in the Spanish conflict was such that the outcome of the Spanish *imbroglio* would appear to be the main factor in dictating the future format of German and

Italian foreign policy. In a memorandum dated 8 January 1937, Eden expressed his grave concern at events in Spain:

> The Spanish Civil War has ceased to be an internal Spanish issue and has become an international battleground. The character of the future Government of Spain has now become less important to the peace of Europe than that the dictators should not be victorious in that country.

Referring specifically to the impact of a Nationalist victory in Spain on German ambitions in Memel, Danzig and Czechoslovakia the Foreign Secretary argued:

> If German interference is not checked in Spain, there will be no chance of moderating influences in that country checking any similar aggressive tendencies in respect of any of these three danger points. It is therefore my conviction that unless we cry a halt in Spain, we shall have trouble this year in one or other of the danger points I have referred to. It follows that to be firm in Spain is to gain time, and to gain time is what we want.

Eden, therefore, advocated a bold initiative envisaging not only international agreement on the prohibition of the despatch of foreign volunteers to Spain but also a comprehensive network of frontier and sea patrols to supervise the blockade on war materials to Spain. Foreseeing that agreement on such a scheme would take time to engineer, the Foreign Secretary recommended that the Royal Navy be employed to establish an immediate naval patrol while international agreement was sought. In presenting these proposals to a meeting of senior ministers Eden concluded:

> The object of the Foreign Office proposals was to avoid a European war. They thought that if we did not stand up to the Dictator Powers now it would bring war nearer. In addition, we should lose the support of our friends in Europe if war came. [145]

The scheme, however, was widely attacked by Eden's Cabinet colleagues. [146] Sir Samuel Hoare questioned not only the desirability of endorsing a plan which appeared to be designed to prevent a Nationalist victory in Spain but also argued that a naval blockade could not be effective without the utilisation of both the Home and Mediterranean fleets and the mobilisation of reservists. Only Lord Halifax openly supported the scheme, while Wood, Stanhope, Cooper and Inskip were in broad agreement that it was unlikely to shorten the war in Spain and, in fact, would exacerbate the possibility of a direct clash with Italy or Germany. In an effort to gather support for his proposals Eden warned the Cabinet that:

> If Germany and Italy were not checked in their Spanish ambitions we might arrive at a situation in which those two countries would, in effect, conquer Spain.

> He urged on his colleagues the danger that would arise if the situation were allowed to drift.

It was significant, however, that Baldwin made no move to support his Foreign Secretary and when he eventually intervened, his conviction that the difficulties involved in the establishment of a naval blockade were 'insuperable' indicated to Eden that his cause was lost. The resulting decision to limit British action to an announcement of the intention to prohibit the flow of volunteers to Spain from Britain and merely to request other nations to suggest further means of enforcing such measures, represented a severe blow to Eden's hopes of providing a clear lead, not only with regard to the Spanish problem but also in relations with Germany and Italy.[147]

Eden later noted that he 'was bitterly disappointed' at his colleagues' reaction and argued that:

> An arresting British action might have drained the Spanish ulcer of its poison. It could certainly not have weakened Britain's authority and the dictators would have had either to recant or agree. It is my belief that they would have had to accept our offer, or something like it. At the time I more than suspected that the Naval arguments advanced by Hoare were not sound, but I could not prove it. The First Lord's technical objections impressed my colleagues, most of whom had no experience with which to counter them.[148]

This was an odd statement given Eden's own admission to his colleagues on 8 January 1937 that he did not envisage the imposition of 'an effective blockade' but rather measures limited to 'some kind of watch on non intervention'.[149] Given, therefore, that the patrol scheme was not expected to stem the flow of military material to Spain completely, it is difficult to see how it could have significantly drained 'the Spanish ulcer of its poison'.[150] While a patrol scheme imposed by the Royal Navy would probably not have been susceptible to the political pressures that led to the collapse of the scheme sponsored by the Non-Intervention Committee in June 1937,[151] the establishment of a purely British scheme was probably beyond the capability of the Royal Navy without the transfer of significant elements of the Home Fleet to the Mediterranean and the mobilisation of reservists.[152] In that the Cabinet was anxious to minimise the risk of a purely Anglo-Italian military clash, it was hardly surprising that the proposals were seen as over-ambitious and were rejected in favour of continuing to press for the creation of an international naval force.

The significance of Eden's proposals, therefore, seemed to lie in their symbolic value as a possible warning to Hitler and Mussolini of the British determination to oppose the expansion of their influence in Europe and the Mediterranean. The Cabinet, however, obviously considered that the price of such a gesture was far too high in terms of the prospect of provoking a clash with Italy and, furthermore, Hitler's ambitions in Eastern Europe were unlikely to be deterred by a display of British naval strength in the Mediterranean.[153] The naval patrol scheme in fact promised little except to exacerbate relations with Italy and to over-extend further the resources of the Royal Navy. While Eden later defended the scheme as an opportunity that was missed and suggested that he had been baulked by a group of Ministers who were intent on assisting a Nationalist victory in Spain, his arguments are difficult to substantiate and, indeed, could be presented as a scapegoat for his inability to obtain a satisfactory security agreement with Italy and Germany.[154]

Having spent twelve months tentatively exploring the various economic, political and military levers that could be utilised to establish a European security agreement by January 1937, Eden had made little positive progress. It would seem that the rejection of the Spanish patrol scheme forced him to begin a reappraisal of the position. Almost certainly his ideas in this period were influenced by William Strang who had replaced Ralph Wigram as Head of the Central Department in the Foreign Office following the death of Wigram in December 1936. In a Minute dated 1 February 1937, Strang argued that the blows dealt to the League of Nations in recent years had eliminated any possibility that might have existed of that organisation administering an effective scheme of collective security. He, therefore, contended that Britain's immediate policy had to be based on the cultivation of a position of strength centred on a programme of rearmament and close relations with France. While avoiding further foreign commitments, Strang advocated an attempt to keep Germany, Italy and Japan guessing by refusing to clarify the areas of the globe where Britain would fight to maintain the status quo and by seeking to align the Soviet Union and the United States with the forces opposing the aggressor states. In attempting to sum up this approach Strang emphasised that Britain must: 'Use our power of manoeuvre, our still undoubted prestige, and all the imponderables, to the utmost.'

In such a policy was the implicit suggestion that Britain must seek to gain time while it attempted to out-manoeuvre the aggressor states diplomatically and militarily. Furthermore he emphasised the dangers that lay in an attempt to buy German acquiescence at an exorbitant price in terms of economic aid or colonial concessions. In conclusion he noted:

> We should leave the doors open and wait and see what time brings. It may bring war. If so, it will be the end of many things, perhaps of the British Empire. But it may not. I do not think we are sufficiently master of our fate to decide for certain, one way or the other.[155]

It is remarkable to note the similarity between the tone and tenor of this Minute and the content of Eden's address on the international situation to the first meeting of the principal delegates to the Imperial Conference on 19 May 1937. At this meeting the Foreign Secretary identified a 'deterioration' in the international situation since 1930, chronicled the failure of the League of Nations to combat aggression in Manchuria and Abyssinia and concluded that the existing machinery of the League of Nations was unlikely to serve as an effective defender of international law. Eden, therefore, argued that, while continuing to support the concept of the Covenant, British policy had to be based on three principles: firstly the establishment of agreed defence priorities which, despite the maintenance of a facade of British interest in the entire spectrum of international affairs, would, in effect, be limited primarily to the defence of the British Isles, the Low Countries, the Empire and Egypt; secondly a commitment to a programme of extensive rearmament — Eden informed the delegates that:

> He was satisfied that only by our rearmament could we hope ultimately to secure a Disarmament Convention.

> . . . there would be a grave risk that, if we approached other countries for arms limitation before our own programme was nearer completion, our advances would be regarded as mere bluff

and finally the Foreign Secretary clearly saw the need to enlist the co-operation of the USA as a cardinal factor in containing the ambitions of the aggressor states. His optimism in this quarter was plainly indicated to the Conference delegates:

> Whatever our relations with the rest of the world might be, our relations with the United States were excellent, and indeed, had never been better and closer than at the present time. There was

248

no doubt that the United States were ready to help so far as they possibly could and, in particular, were ready to work in agreement with us, and in ways which could be agreeable to us.[156]

It was apparent that Eden and Strang were in broad agreement on the need to pursue an essentially defensive foreign policy in an attempt to negate the German challenge. Although the Foreign Secretary was prepared to admit to the Imperial Conference that British strategic interests centred on the Empire, the Low Countries and Egypt, he followed Strang's advice and publicly continued to declare British interest in the maintenance of the international status quo. In a thinly veiled warning to Hitler over the mounting campaign for the unification of Austria with Germany, the Foreign Secretary informed the House of Commons on 25 June 1937:

> we desire in Central Europe and elsewhere, peace and good understanding. We cannot, even if we would, disinterest ourselves in the course of events there, any more than we can disinterest ourselves in the course of events anywhere else on the earth's surface as conditions are today. Our interest in peace is universal.[157]

Eden's address to the delegates to the Imperial Conference represented a significant shift in his stance on Anglo-German relations. While as recently as December 1936 Eden had viewed the possibility of achieving a European security agreement with Germany with relative optimism, the events of the first half of 1937 had forced him to review this prediction.[158] It was clear that he had come to the conclusion an agreement was unlikely to be secured in the immediate future. Furthermore it appeared that a settlement could only be negotiated from a position of strength and, therefore, steps would have to be taken to identify primary British interests and bolster the nation's military capacity to defend those interests. In reaching these conclusions it was apparent that Eden was now accepting the outlook on the future format of Anglo-German relations forwarded by Wigram, Vansittart and Sargent in the latter months of 1936.[159] It was evident that there was now broad agreement between Eden and his principal advisers that an agreement with either Germany or Italy could only be obtained at an exorbitant price and would only be respected as long as it continued to give advantage to Hitler and Mussolini. They, therefore, advocated a policy of caution which, while continuing to welcome the opening of negotiations with Germany and Italy, demanded that discussions be conducted through formal diplomatic channels and be accompanied by an indication of a willingness to accept a comprehensive security settlement involving multilateral pacts of non-aggression, agreement on disarmament and a restoration of the authority of the League of Nations.[160] The only area of disagreement was to what extent the British Government should attempt to deter Hitler from seeking to expand German influence in Eastern Europe. On this point Sargent and Strang described British policy as a 'poker game' with a 'fair admixture of bluff'.[161] While Sargent and Cadogan appeared prepared to accept the expansion of German influence in Eastern Europe, Eden argued that any attempt to change the status quo by force would contravene the Covenant of the League of Nations and could neither be condoned nor ignored. Eden was, however, moving towards the conclusion that the expansion of German influence in Eastern Europe in some form was all but inevitable. Therefore while he was unwilling to see Czechoslovakia absorbed into the Third Reich he was prepared to admit that the Austrian question was more complex and that there might be grounds for the establishment of close links between Germany and Austria.[162]

While the problems encountered in the first half of 1937 had served to unite the senior figures in the Foreign Office on their approach to the German problem, it was difficult to be optimistic about the future course of Anglo-German relations. It was significant that the Prime Minister, who had habitually given his Foreign Secretary a virtual free rein in the direction of foreign policy, made a point of addressing the opening session of the Imperial Conference on the subject of international relations and chose to emphasise his concern for the future of European stability. In particular he singled out the problem presented by the unpredictability of German and Italian ambitions and concluded that only a programme of extensive rearmament was likely 'to combat the idea in dictator countries that democracy was effete and decadent and never knew its own mind'.[163] Such a rare incursion into the field of foreign affairs was perhaps prompted by the imminence of Baldwin's departure from the political scene and, therefore, represented a testament to the problems that had confronted the administration during his period of office as Lord President and later Prime Minister. Any such summation could not but acknowledge the fact that there had been a failure to defuse the threat to European stability posed by the re-emergence of a strong and discontented German state. This in itself, though, was probably not a direct criticism of Eden's handling of foreign affairs but rather an attempt to outline the difficulties encountered in trying to reconcile British and French differences with the dictator states.

Despite the Prime Minister's obvious disappointment with the state of international relations in May 1937, there was no indication that his faith and confidence in Eden's ability had been reduced. Indeed Baldwin's reluctance to intervene in foreign affairs, other than to establish broad guidelines, meant that throughout the period from January 1936 to May 1937 Eden enjoyed a remarkable degree of latitude in the conduct of foreign policy. At no time had this been more apparent than in the summer of 1936 following the outbreak of hostilities in Spain. Although Baldwin had candidly warned Eden on 26 July 1936 that he was to avoid a direct British commitment to the Republican cause in Spain, the formulation of the format of the British stance on non-intervention was left entirely in the Foreign Secretary's hands.[164] It was not until 19 August 1936 that Eden wrote to Baldwin to inform him of the course of action that he had put into motion.[165] Subsequent suggestions that Baldwin had taken a close interest in the development of the situation were scotched by Eden, who noted in his diary on 26 August 1936:

> The communiqué in the press this morning announcing that S.B. is not coming up to London is a little 'tall', since his 'constant touch' with me has consisted in one letter and one telephone call this month, and these about my spending a weekend with him in South Wales.[166]

Eden was subsequently to claim, however, that although he enjoyed a great deal of freedom in the day-to-day running of foreign affairs, Baldwin's patent lack of involvement in this field was often counter-productive and considerably weakened his hand in attempting to gain Cabinet approval for his policy proposals:

> My difficulties were not only international. I was aware that my appointment was not welcome to all my elders in the Cabinet, where there was no lack of former Foreign Secretaries and other aspirants to the office. I knew that Baldwin's support would be fitful and lethargic. I had also seen the practice . . . of a multiplicity of Ministers taking a hand at drafting a despatch. On one of these occasions about a year later, I began to protest vigorously, when Baldwin passed me a note: 'Don't be too indignant. I once saw Curzon burst into tears when the Cabinet was amending his despatches.' After the meeting he told me I must remember that out of my twenty colleagues, there was probably not more than one who thought he should be Minister of Labour and nineteen who thought they should be Foreign Secretary.

There were those, however, who sympathised with the Foreign Secretary as the victim of too much tutelary zeal. My diary for 20 May 1936 records:

'Cabinet in a.m. Germany fairly satisfactory though Kingsley

[Wood] rather tiresome . . . . Outburst from Duff [Cooper] that Cabinet were always interfering in foreign affairs, result compromise, my policy thwarted. Much better leave matters to me — not interfere so much.'[167]

It can be argued that in this quotation Eden overstated the problems which he encountered, for the Prime Minister almost invariably supported the Foreign Secretary in Cabinet discussions. Furthermore it would seem that Eden positively welcomed the latitude that Baldwin gave him. Eden's disillusionment with the Prime Minister, therefore, probably dates from the Cabinet's rejection of the Spanish naval patrol scheme in January 1937. On this issue Baldwin, for once, sided with the Foreign Secretary's opponents and Eden obviously took the resulting defeat very badly. In the following months little progress was made, either in solving the Spanish situation or in improving relations with Hitler, and Eden increasingly saw Baldwin's apparent lack of interest in foreign affairs as effectively undermining the pursuit of a positive policy and strengthening the hand of those who sought a more conciliatory approach to relations with Germany and Italy. An example of Eden's frustration with Baldwin's attitude was provided by Oliver Harvey in his diary entry for 12 April 1937, at a time when the question of the Bilbao blockade was foremost on the Cabinet Agenda:

Prime Minister sent for A.E. this morning and said he must ask him to stay over Question Time in House of Commons in case Opposition move adjournment when Prime Minister makes his statement on decision regarding Bilbao, as Prime Minister does not feel able to take it. If no adjournment is moved, A.E. can go to Liverpool by aeroplane and yet be in time for his meeting. A.E. very annoyed at this further instance of lack of help given by Prime Minister who, however, confessed to him that he had not been able to take in the question at all.[168]

To have expected more from the Prime Minister in this period, though, was perhaps unreasonable. The deterioration in Baldwin's health, which had enforced his absence from London during the months of July, August and September 1936, would almost certainly have led to his resignation in the last quarter of that year if not for the growing storm surrounding the future of the monarch.[169] On returning to London, Baldwin candidly warned Eden that he could expect little help from him in the direction of foreign affairs. Eden subsequently recorded of this interview:

In the third week of October Baldwin returned to London and I had my first talk with him for three months. Naturally I was impatient to deploy the course of events and to take council with him, particularly about the Spanish civil war, which had become so international a menace since our last talk together. Baldwin listened for a while, but his mind was evidently not on the subject. I thought this unconcern exasperating. At a pause in my dissertation Baldwin astonished me by saying: 'Have you had any letters about the King?' 'No. Not as far as I know' I said, 'Why should I have?' 'Well', Baldwin went on, 'I wish you would inquire. I expect that you have had some. I fear we may have difficulties there.' He added, 'I hope that you will try not to trouble me too much with foreign affairs just now.'[170]

It was apparent that Baldwin saw the remaining term of his office as being devoted to the resolution of the growing storm surrounding the position of the monarch. When, in December 1936, it appeared that abdication was perhaps the only possible course of action, Baldwin saw it as his duty not only to pilot the nation through this difficult period but also to remain in office until the new King was crowned. It was agreed, therefore, that he would surrender the office of Prime Minister on 27 May 1936, 15 days after the coronation of King George VI. Baldwin was both mentally and physically exhausted and wanted nothing more than to escape the hurly-burly of political life.[171] On 15 February 1937 Tom Jones had recorded that Baldwin was 'counting the hours to his release' and told him: 'When I get out of here, I'll sleep for a week. Here I've been for fifteen years, going down to the House to answer fatuous questions.'[172]

The retirement from the political scene of the senior party figure who had guided and moulded Eden's career for over a decade was not as painful for Eden as might have been expected. Undoubtedly his respect and admiration for Baldwin had been tempered by the conviction that the Prime Minister's lack of application to the problems presented by the implementation of a programme of rearmament and the format of relations with Germany had both hindered his own position and produced a general lack of direction in the conduct of British foreign policy. This conviction was still evident four years later when Eden sought to defend Baldwin against the army of critics which had assailed him following his retirement:

I felt sorry for S.B. He has grand things about him. He attempts no self-justification. I believe that history will treat him more kindly than his contemporaries now do. He did much to kill class hatred and to unite the country. He did not understand the storms that raged without, nor did he make Neville's mistake of believing that he did.[173]

It would seem, therefore, that by May 1937 Eden had come to the conclusion that Baldwin's retirement was both inevitable and necessary. While there were doubts surrounding Neville Chamberlain's suitability for the post of Prime Minister given his age and poor health, there was never any serious doubt that the man who had held the post of Chancellor of the Exchequer since 1931 would be Baldwin's successor. The lack of a credible alternative candidate had been discussed by Eden and Harvey on 23 March 1937:

> I lunched with A.E. today and discussed political situation here. He fears for health of Neville Chamberlain and feels it is perhaps a pity that a younger man is not available. He agreed with me that Sam Hoare would be fatal, Walter Elliot not very effective, Inskip a possibility, Duff disappointing at War Office and will probably be shifted, Kingsley Wood very bad influence in foreign affairs and cynical professional politician.[174]

Although Eden insisted that he had no ambition but to retain his post at the Foreign Office, it was apparent that both he and Harvey appreciated that if he wished to claim the post of Prime Minister he would have to wait until 'two or three years' time when Neville Chamberlain goes, if peace is preserved'.[175]

There is no doubt that Eden expected Chamberlain to become Prime Minister and that he fully supported his candidature. In his diary entry for 26 March 1937, Oliver Harvey noted:

> A.E. went to see Chancellor who is in bed with gout, although this is not known. He found him in very good spirits and looking forward to becoming Prime Minister. He told A.E. that he intended to give him much more support at F.O. than he had had hitherto.

> A.E. thought Neville Chamberlain had makings of a really great Prime Minister if only his health held out. I said 'if he isn't too grim': but A.E. thought this need not necessarily matter: he had a grip of affairs which Stanley Baldwin had never had.[176]

The Foreign Secretary's confidence in being able to forge a successful working relationship with Chamberlain was based on the experience of the previous two years when the two had often consulted closely, especially at the height of the Hoare—Laval affair and the Rhineland crisis. Their discussions had indicated a remarkable degree of unanimity on the course of action to be pursued and had generated a significant element of mutual respect, to the extent that Eden was later to note:

Before Chamberlain became Prime Minister, I would think it true that he and I were closer to each other than to any other member of the Government, exchanging opinions on many Cabinet matters without any disagreement. I would sometimes on a Sunday evening, if we were both in London, call in at No. 11 Downing Street, for a quiet talk. A Foreign Secretary and a Chancellor of the Exchequer, the Prime Minister's two principal colleagues, are apt to be thrown together, particularly if the Prime Minister is holding the reins very loosely, as Baldwin was during his last months in office.[177]

While Neville Chamberlain was almost certainly far closer to Sir Samuel Hoare than he was to Eden, there is no question that he had every respect for Eden's ability in the field of foreign affairs.[178] During the early months of 1937 Chamberlain carefully selected his Cabinet. Eden was one of only six ministers who retained their former posts and, indeed, Chamberlain's Private Papers give no indication that he ever considered making a change at the Foreign Office, and intimated as much to Eden as early as March 1937.[179] Of their discussion when Chamberlain officially confirmed the appointment, Eden later recorded:

> One May morning, when I was about to leave for Geneva and we were talking in Chamberlain's beautiful room at the Treasury, I was not at all surprised when he mentioned that he was soon to take over from Baldwin and added the hope that I would continue with my work at the Foreign Office. Nor was I dismayed when he said with a smile: 'I know you won't mind if I take more interest in foreign policy than S.B.' We both knew that no-one could have taken less.[180]

It was surprising, however, that in the same section of his memoirs Eden chose to recount the story of a social meeting between himself, Neville Chamberlain and Austen Chamberlain at which Austen told Neville: 'Neville you must remember you don't know anything about foreign affairs.'[181]

Eden made no comment on the statement except to note that Neville 'smiled wryly'. In fact he must have been aware that Austen Chamberlain's observation was far from being a true reflection of Neville Chamberlain's grasp of the important issues in foreign policy. As a senior Cabinet Minister and close colleague of successive Foreign Secretaries since 1931, Chamberlain was undeniably well-versed in the problems confronting British foreign policy and, in fact, probably had more experience in this field than any of his Cabinet colleagues with the possible exception of Eden who although only a permanent member of the Cabinet since June 1935, had held successive posts with the Foreign Office since August 1931.[182] There was certainly no question of Chamberlain being an amateur in the conduct of foreign policy.[183] Furthermore he was well-versed in the running of the Foreign Office. Not only had he taken a leading role in policy formulation at Cabinet meetings but he had also received several confidential reports from key figures in both the Civil Service and the Cabinet assessing the performance of the Foreign Office and its attempts to manage relations with Germany and Italy. In particular Sir Warren Fisher, Permanent Secretary at the Treasury and Head of the Civil Service, was at the forefront of those who urged Chamberlain to change his senior personnel at the Foreign Office. It was no secret that Eden and Fisher had clashed over the question of whether Fisher, as Head of the Civil Service, was entitled to vet Eden's overseas appointments.[184] In addition Eden had opposed the Treasury's advocation of the use of Dr Schacht as an informal contact with Hitler.[185] It was unlikely, however, that Eden fully appreciated the extent of Fisher's determination to engineer a change of policy at the Foreign Office.[186] Vansittart was the particular object of Fisher's attacks and, following Sir Robert's visit to Germany in the autumn of 1936, Fisher wrote to Chamberlain on 15 September 1936:

> What of course is clear is (1) that after Van's recent outing in Germany and establishment of agreeable personal relations with Hitler and Co., the immediate removal of Van from the F.O. would be interpreted in Germany as disapproval by H.M.G. of this personal improvement; this interpretation would be strengthened by his transfer to Paris in view of Van's previous reputation in Germany as pro-French. (2) Paris is at present of no great importance, whereas Berlin (and Rome) are.

> The fact is that the German visit of Van's must inevitably *postpone* the reform of the F.O., though my views about the need remain unchanged.

> I see in all this the hand of Alec Cadogan who is likely to become Permanent Under Secretary of State himself; and Anthony — who is and always will be very light metal — has been party to the folly of providing us with the worst of every world.

> None of us at present can endorse any change at the F.O. for any appreciable time for the German reason I've already mentioned, but when the time comes Alex Cadogan is out of the question; and if nothing else will prevent it, I shall have to work the Government to put me there though this would mean a step down in rank for me and a loss of £500 a year.[187]

It was Fisher along with Sir Horace Wilson, Industrial Adviser to the Prime Minister, who were the key figures in a curious incident in May 1937 involving J.P.L. Thomas, who had recently been appointed as Eden's Parliamentary Private Secretary. At an informal meeting Fisher and Wilson outlined to Thomas their dissatisfaction with the Foreign Office and 'especially with Vansittart'. Thomas then claimed that they suggested he act as a 'bridge between 10 Downing Street and the Foreign Office' in order to 'lessen the damage which had been done by the Foreign Office in general and by Vansittart in particular'. While there is no evidence to corroborate either Thomas's account of the interview or his claim that he rejected any suggestion of being willing 'to work behind the back of my own chief', the incident does serve to illustrate the growing doubts being expressed within the corridors of Whitehall as to the advisability of the course being pursued by the Foreign Office.[188] These doubts and the air of dissatisfaction with the performance of the Foreign Office were not confined to senior figures in the civil service. On 17 March 1937 Sir Samuel Hoare had written in a similar vein to Chamberlain:

> Do not let anything irrevocable or badly compromising happen in foreign policy until you are in control. I say this because I am convinced that the F.O. is so much biased against Germany (and Italy and Japan) that unconsciously and almost continuously they are making impossible any sort of reconciliation. I believe myself that when once you are Prime Minister it will be possible greatly to change the European atmosphere.[189]

If these reports did succeed in establishing certain question-marks in Chamberlain's mind and, perhaps, hardened his resolve to take an active interest in foreign affairs, there is no evidence that they shook his personal faith in Eden. Indeed the central factor was certainly the role of Vansittart within the Foreign Office and on this subject Eden was in full agreement with his critics that it was time the Permanent Under-Secretary relinquished his post.[190] Though Eden concurred with much of Vansittart's advice, the Permanent Under-Secretary's effectiveness had undoubtedly been impaired by his identification with an anti-German stance and his personal conviction that it was impossible to establish an understanding with Germany while Hitler's policy was based on 'violence and robbery'.[191] Eden had served notice of his resolve to replace Vansittart as early as 10 February 1936 when he declared his intention to appoint Sir Alex Cadogan as Deputy Under-Secretary of State and, furthermore, in December 1936 he had prevailed upon Baldwin to attempt to persuade Vansittart to accept the post of Ambassador to France.[192] Although Vansittart had declined the offer, Eden indicated his determination to pursue the matter in a letter to Baldwin dated 27 December 1936:

> it is vital that our personnel in the F.O. and the diplomatic service should be posted to best advantage and Van's place in that scheme of things is Paris. I am more than ever convinced of this. I should add that all conversations to date with Van have been on the most friendly footing, the difficulty will come if he cannot be persuaded to see his duty as we see it.[193]

On 7 March 1937 Oliver Harvey noted that Eden 'spoke about his lack of confidence in Van's judgement' and expressed his desire to 'find him another job'.[194] It was not until 4 May 1937, however, that Eden openly broached the topic with Chamberlain, who indirectly admitted that Fisher had tackled him on the question of a new appointment at the Foreign Office. Harvey recorded:

> A.E. spoke to Chancellor about Van and necessity of replacing him. Chancellor agreed to such action being taken but said that it would obviously be wise to wait a little. He asked A.E. who he wanted instead. A.E. said 'Alex Cadogan'. Chancellor said Warren Fisher strongly opposed to this and wished to see Findlater Stewart from the India Office appointed. Chancellor added he did not favour A.C. A.E. told me afterwards he could not possibly have an outsider not a trained diplomat and would insist on A.C.[195]

If Eden's willingness to see Vansittart replaced was tempered by his determination to oppose the imposition of an 'outsider', there is no suggestion that he believed either his personal position or the authority of the Foreign Office was likely to be threatened by Chamberlain's elevation to the post of Prime Minister. On the contrary it would appear that in the spring of 1937 Eden was confident that the Foreign Office, far from being under attack, had actually strengthened its position with the acquisition of a Prime Minister with whom he could forge a working relationship in the field of foreign affairs.[196] Indeed the proceedings of the Imperial Conference had reinforced Eden's conviction that he and the Prime Minister were in broad agreement on the basic tenets of British foreign policy. In particular it was apparent that they concurred in the identification of Germany as the focus of discontent in Europe and agreed that the object of British policy must be to continue the search for a comprehensive European security settlement, while the promotion of the rearmament programme was seen as an important factor in strengthening the British bargaining position *vis à vis* Germany.[197] In this context the Prime Minister, while offering to give his Foreign Secretary far more vigorous support in the conduct of foreign affairs, did not appear to be demanding a radical reorientation of policy. Therefore it is, perhaps, not surprising that, as Eden subsequently noted, he was able to view Chamberlain's promotion in May 1937 without alarm and even with a certain degree of optimism:

> While I was always grateful for Baldwin's personal kindness to me, I looked forward to working with a Prime Minister who would give the Foreign Secretary energetic backing.[198]

References

1   Avon, p. 381.
2   See *Avon Papers*, FO, 954, FR/36/11, 17 April 1936. Also *Neville Chamberlain Papers*, NC/18/1, letters to his sisters dated 4 and 13 April 1936. In addition, *DBFP*, 2nd ser., vol. 16, nos 248 and 249.
3   Avon, p. 381.
4   *CAB* 23/84, CC 39(36)8 and CC 40(36)5.
5   *CAB* 28/84, CC 42(36)1, 17 June 1936.
6   For Eden's reports of his discussions with Blum and Van Zeeland at Geneva in the period 30 June–3 July 1937, see *DBFP*, 2nd ser., vol. 16, nos 393, 397, 403 and 407 and also Avon, pp. 389–90. On receiving a report of the Foreign Secretary's initial conversation with Blum and Van Zeeland, the Cabinet decided on 1 July 1936 to defer a firm decision until the Foreign Secretary returned to London to present the proposals personally to his colleagues, *CAB* 23/85, CC 48(36), 1 July 1936.
7   Thomas Jones (1870–1955), Lecturer and Professor of Economics, Glasgow and Belfast; Special Investigator, Poor Law Commission, 1906–9; Secretary of National Health Insurance Commissioners for Wales, 1912–16; Deputy Secretary of the Cabinet, 1916–30; Secretary of the Pilgrim Trust, 1930–45. Jones was a close confidant and adviser to both Lloyd George and Baldwin. For an account of his visit to Berlin see Jones, pp. 195–200. At their meeting on 16 May 1936, Von Ribbentrop openly suggested to Jones that he act as private emissary between Hitler and Baldwin and also urged Jones to engineer a meeting between the two men. Jones repeated this proposal to Baldwin on 20 May 1936, and continued to urge the PM to visit Germany during the following week. Jones, pp. 202–9.
8   Avon, p. 374.
9   Eden had undoubtedly been disturbed by reports that Jones had held a further meeting with Von Ribbentrop in London on 2 June 1936. Furthermore Jones claimed that Baldwin had agreed in principle to visit Berlin if Eden concurred. The Foreign Secretary's objection, registered on 16 June 1936, appeared to have killed the project and two days later Jones could only suggest to Von Ribbentrop that he attempt to persuade Eden to reconsider his stance. See Jones, pp. 214–24.
10   Jones himself admitted that the object of the Baldwin–Hitler meeting was to initiate direct contacts which would by-pass the Foreign Office. Tom Jones, diary entry for 8 June 1936, Jones, pp. 218–19.

11   For a record of this Cabinet meeting see *CAB* 23/85, CC 50(36)2, 6 July 1936.

12   *CAB* 23/85, CC 50(36)2, 6 July 1936. The decision to attempt once again to initiate direct negotiations was supported by the Cabinet and the Foreign Office. Baldwin had addressed the House of Commons in a similar vein on 18 June 1936. (See *H of C*, Debs, 5's, vol. 313, cols 1238—9). Furthermore Orme Sargent had pointed out, on 1 July 1936, that the only alternative was an Anglo-French-Belgian defensive alliance against Germany which was an undertaking that the Belgians were unlikely to accept. See *DBFP*, 2nd ser., vol. 16, no. 393.

13   The invitation to participate in a meeting of the Locarno Powers was rejected by Germany on 7 July 1936 and by Italy on 11 July 1936. See *DBFP*, 2nd ser., vol. 16, nos 417 and 436.

14   Eden reported to the Cabinet, on 16 July 1936, that the Cabinet Committee on Foreign Policy had agreed that Britain should participate in the Locarno meeting despite the absence of Italy and Germany. *CAB* 23/85, CC 53(36)1, 16 July 1936.

15   For the text of this meeting see *DBFP*, 2nd ser., vol. 16, nos 476 and 477.

16   *DBFP*, 2nd ser., vol. 17, no. 15, Mr Eden to Mr B.C. Newton (no. 870 [C 5483/4/18]), 24 July 1936.

17   Von Neurath argued that a meeting was not possible until after the completion of the September meeting of the General Assembly of the League of Nations which was likely to consider the reform of the League of Nations. *DBFP*, 2nd ser., vol. 17, no. 37, Mr Newton to Mr Eden (no. 240 [C 5628/4/18]), Berlin, 30 July 1936.

18   Not surprisingly Eden minuted the same day that this report was 'not very encouraging' but insisted that the Foreign Office continue its preparations for the Conference. *DBFP*, 2nd ser., vol. 17, no. 186, record by Sir R. Vansittart of a conversation with Prince Von Bismarck (C 6431/4/18), 11 September 1936.

19   The Blum—Schacht negotiations were first reported on 28 August 1936 by Sir G. Clerk. Clerk believed that the talks were limited to economic and financial matters. It was not until 20 September 1936 that Clerk was informed by Blum of Schacht's allusion to German colonial demands. See *DBFP*, 2nd ser., vol. 17, nos 145 and 210.

20   *DBFP*, 2nd ser., vol. 17, no. 220, letter from Sir R. Vansittart to Mr Eden (C 6637/97/18), 21 September 1936.

21   Wigram's Minute was in response to a report from Berlin outlining Hitler's continued reluctance to agree to German participation in a Five Power Conference. See Minute by Wigram, dated 1 October 1936, on despatch from Berlin of 30 September 1936. *DBFP*, 2nd ser., vol. 17, no. 248.

22   *H of C*, Debs, 5's, vol. 315, cols 1131—2. This stance was based on the findings of the Plymouth Committee released on 9 June 1936. *DBFP*, 2nd ser., vol. 16, appendix 3 (C 4275/97/18).

23   On 11 September 1936 Eden recommended to the governments of France, Italy and Belgium that the Conference be convened in the latter half of October. *DBFP*, 2nd ser., vol. 17, no. 184.

24   *DBFP*, 2nd ser., vol. 17, no. 321, Memorandum communicated by the German Chargé d'Affaires (C 7247/4/18), 12 October 1936.

25   As recent as 6 July 1936 Eden had admitted to the Cabinet that:

Britain was neither strong enough nor public opinion well enough informed to guarantee peace in West and East Europe.

. . . policy ought to be framed on the basis that we could not help Eastern Europe.

CAB 23/85, CC 50(36)2, 6 July 1936. On 13 August 1936 Vansittart had warned Blum that Britain would not accept a military commitment in Eastern Europe. In a memorandum for the Cabinet dated 23 October 1936, however, Eden admitted that the French were justified, by reference to their obligations under the Covenant of the League of Nations, in demanding exceptions to the proposed network of non-aggression pacts in Western Europe. See *DBFP*, 2nd ser., vol. 17, nos 200 and 321.

26   *DBFP*, 2nd ser., vol. 17, no. 389, Memorandum by H.M.G. regarding the agenda of the Five Power Conference (C 8265/4/18), 19 November 1936.

27   *DBFP*, 2nd ser., vol. 17, no. 455, Mr Eden to Sir E. Phipps (no. 1370 [C 8792/4/18]), 8 December 1936.

28   *DBFP*, 2nd ser., vol. 17, no. 524, Sir E. Phipps to Mr Eden (no. 391 [C 1/1/18]), Berlin, 31 December 1936.

29   In a Minute dated 14 November 1936, Vansittart urged Eden not to consider any further concessions to the German position:

> the essential object is to get a good durable defensive treaty with the Germans. And we shall only get that by firmness. There is nothing of that in all the watery amendments suggested.

DBFP, 2nd ser., vol. 17, no. 389.

30   In Minutes dated 2 and 9 December 1936 respectively, Wigram and Vansittart argued against the despatch of a further reminder to Germany, France, Belgium and Italy on the grounds that such action might precipitate a complete breakdown of negotiations. *DBFP*, 2nd ser., vol. 17, no. 488.

31   Minute by Vansittart dated 2 January 1937, on Eden's despatch to Paris of 21 December 1936 (no. 2176 [C 9106/4/18]). See *DBFP*, 2nd ser., vol. 17, no. 495.

32   *DBFP*, 2nd ser., vol. 17, appendix 2, Memorandum by Sir R. Vansittart, 'The World Situation and British Rearmament' (C 8998/8998/18), 31 December 1936.

33   On 18 October 1936 the Foreign Secretary had minuted on a despatch from Berlin:

> I do not think that we have any illusions as to the difficulties inherent in the Locarno negotiations, but they keep the door open, should it happen that Germany's economic difficulties dispose her to talk. I agree that we have no time to lose in our rearmament and said so in Cabinet again last week.

DBFP, 2nd ser., vol. 17, no. 233.

34   Minute by Eden dated 16 November 1936, on a despatch from Berlin dated 4 November 1936 (no. 1179E [C 7901/99/18]). See *DBFP*, 2nd ser., vol. 17, no. 350.

35   Minute by Eden dated 8 December 1936. See *DBFP*, 2nd ser., vol. 17, no. 488.

36   On 2 September 1936 the Cabinet had examined a report by the COS Subcommittee of the CID on the proposed Five Power Conference which had rejected the suggestion of a military commitment to Eastern Europe and had also questioned the advisability of a West-European Treaty and concluded that: 'the desirability of limiting our commitments in Europe is as insistent as ever.' See CP 218(36), presented to Cabinet on 2 September 1936. *CAB* 23/85, CC 56(36)3. See also *DBFP*, 2nd ser., vol. 17, no. 156 (C 6223/4/18), 1 September 1936.

37   In a memorandum dated 3 December 1936, Eden vigorously challenged the COS assertion that Belgium be allowed to return to a position of neutrality. On

9 December 1936 the Cabinet authorised Eden to approach the Belgian Government in order to ascertain the extent of the commitments that it was willing to accept. See *DBFP*, 2nd ser., vol. 17, no. 433 (C 8744/270/4) and *CAB* 23/86, CC 73(36)2.

38   *Baldwin Papers*, vol. 124, ff. 55—7, Eden to Baldwin, 27 December 1936.

39   On 30 December 1936 Eden minuted that he was in full agreement with Sargent's Minute of the previous day (C 9152/4/18) which had stressed the economic and political pressures that were mounting on the German Government and which Hitler was likely to attempt to counter by seeking an expansion of German influence in Spain and Czechoslovakia. *DBFP*, 2nd ser., vol. 17, no. 521.

40   For the text of the Treaty of Alliance between the United Kingdom and Egypt signed on 26 August 1936, see *Documents on International Affairs 1936*, hereafter cited as *DIA 1936* (London 1937), pp. 478—92.

41   The Palestinian issue was discussed by the Cabinet in this period on 23 June 1936 and 2 September 1936, *CAB* 23/84, CC 43(36)1 and *CAB* 23/85, CC 56(36)8. See also Walters, pp. 746—8.

42   Eden's account of these negotiations is given in Avon, pp. 390—4.

43   *DBFP*, 2nd ser., vol. 16, no. 354, Memorandum by Mr Eden on Anglo-Egyptian Treaty negotiations (J 5401/2/16), 8 June 1936. Presented to Cabinet on 10 June 1936 as CP 156(36). Further considered by the Cabinet Committee on Anglo-Egyptian conversations on 15 and 16 June 1936. See *CAB* 23/84. It was apparent that by 23 June 1936 the Service Ministries were prepared to evacuate Cairo and Alexandria in exchange for alternative facilities in Cyprus and the Canal Zone, *CAB* 23/84, CC 43(36)1.

44   On 2 September 1936 the Cabinet acknowledged the growing unrest in Palestine and decided to reinforce the British Forces with the addition of a further division and the imposition of martial law. *CAB* 23/85, CC 56(36)8.

45   For the text of the Treaty of Alliance between the United Kingdom and Egypt signed on 26 August 1936, see *DIA 1936*, pp. 478—92.

46   Avon, p. 390.

47   *DBFP*, 2nd ser., vol. 16, no. 167, Sir H. Chilton to Mr Eden (no. 72 [W 2678/62/41]), Madrid, 25 March 1936.

48   The British Government was particularly concerned at the possibility of the Rio Tinto Company losing its concessions to mine copper in Spain. The Acting Chargé d'Affaires in Madrid had protested to the Spanish Government on 12 June 1936 about the pressure being applied to British interests in Spain. See *DBFP*, 2nd ser., vol. 17, p. 3, note 10. There was evidence to suggest, however, that by the latter half of June 1936 the Foreign Office was increasingly concerned at the growing internal unrest in Spain. *DBFP*, 2nd ser., vol. 17, nos 1 and 2, 23 and 29 June 1936.

49   *H of C*, Debs, 5's, vol. 315, col. 449, 22 July 1936. The same day Eden reported to the Cabinet that the situation in Spain was still unclear but that he intended to despatch ships to the major Spanish ports to protect British residents. *CAB* 23/85, CC 54(36)5.

50   Tom Jones, diary entry for 27 July 1936. Jones, pp. 230—1.

51   Avon, pp. 395—401.

52   *CAB* 23/85, CC 55(36), 29 July 1936. The decision to pursue a policy of non-intervention was endorsed by the Foreign Office. Sir G. Mounsey, Assistant Under-Secretary of State, minuted on 2 August 1936: 'our main object should, I think, be to be completely impartial and free to pursue the policy of non intervention in Spain.' *DBFP*, 2nd ser., vol. 17, no. 45.

53   Minute by Eden dated 31 July 1936. *DBFP*, 2nd ser., vol. 17, no. 30, note 5. For an assessment of British policy see Jill Edwards, *The British Government and the Spanish Civil War, 1936–1939* (London 1979).

54   Avon, p. 401. The decision to leave Cadogan in charge at the Foreign Office was prompted by the fact that Vansittart was about to undertake an informal visit to Germany. Vansittart later reported of his visit that he had 'not gone into any detailed discussion' but he had 'succeeded in dispelling the idea that the Foreign Office is a nest of anti-German prejudices . . . '. See *DBFP*, 2nd ser., vol. 17, no. 85, letter from Sir R. Vansittart to Mr Eden (Ge/36/17), Berlin, 12 August 1936. See also Colvin, pp. 104—14.

55   There is no evidence to suggest that the French decision to suspend the export of war material to Spain was a result of pressure exerted by Britain at the Anglo-French-Belgian meeting of 23 July 1936. In fact it appears that Spain was not discussed at this meeting. See *DBFP*, 2nd ser., vol. 16, nos 476 and 477. For reports of Italian intervention in Spain, see *The Times*, 31 July 1936. Also J.F. Coverdale, *Italian Intervention in the Spanish Civil War* (Princeton, 1975).

56   On 5 August 1936 Lord Chatfield informed Vice Admiral Darlan and Rear Admiral Decoux that the Royal Navy would not participate in a joint action with the French Navy designed to prevent a possible Italian landing on the Balearic Islands and German intervention in the Canary Islands. *DBFP*, 2nd ser., vol. 17, no. 56 (W 7781/62/41).

57   *DBFP*, 2nd ser., vol. 17, no. 67, Sir G. Clerk to the Foreign Office (no. 252 [W 7964/62/41]), Paris, 7 August 1936.

58   *DBFP*, 2nd ser., vol. 17, no. 72, Sir G. Clerk to the Foreign Office (nos 262 and 263 [W 8055/62/41]), Paris, 8 August 1936.

59   Eden told Arthur Greenwood on 19 August 1936, in reply to a suggestion that the French decision had been prompted by British pressure, 'that there was no truth whatever in this suggestion, that the initiative was entirely French . . . '. It is significant, however, that on 10 August 1936 a Foreign Office despatch concluded of Clerk's conversation with Delbos that the Ambassador's action 'is approved and appears to have had good results'. See *DBFP*, 2nd ser., vol. 17, nos 67 and 81. See also Edwards, pp. 25—8. This issue is also discussed in D. Carlton, 'Eden, Blum and the Origins of Non Intervention', *Journal of Contemporary History*, 6, 1971.

60   *DBFP*, 2nd ser., vol. 17, no. 52, letter from Mr Eden to Cambon (W 7504/62/41), 4 August 1936. Although in Eden's name this letter was almost certainly composed by Halifax after consulting Eden by telephone. See also Minute by Sir G. Mounsey dated 2 August 1936, on a Note from Cambon, Chargé d'Affaires in the French Embassy, of the same date (W 7504/62/41), *DBFP*, 2nd ser., vol. 17, no. 45.

61   It was apparent that while Cadogan and Mounsey shared Sargent's fear that the Spanish conflict was likely to lead to the division of Europe into ideological blocs, Mounsey also appreciated that the proposed Non-Intervention Committee might serve as an opportunity to establish a working arrangement with Germany and Italy. See Edwards, pp. 32—4.

62   The extent of sympathy for the rebel cause was indicated by Hoare's note of 8 August 1936 registering approval of Lord Chatfield's decision not to initiate active co-operation with the French Navy around the Spanish coast. Noting that such action was likely to hinder the rebels, Hoare concluded:

> On no account must we do anything to bolster up Communism in Spain particularly when it is remembered that Communism in Portugal, to which it would probably spread and particularly in Lisbon, would be a grave danger to the British Empire.

Sympathy for the rebels was also fostered by reports from Spain detailing dramatic purges and destruction of church and private property by extreme left-wing elements. See *DBFP*, 2nd ser., vol. 17, nos 38, 46 and 56.

63   *DBFP*, 2nd ser., vol. 17, no. 92, Minute by Sir G. Mounsey of a telephone conversation with Mr Eden (W 8885/62/41), 14 August 1936.

64   See *DBFP*, 2nd ser., vol. 17, no. 94. It was also likely that, as a result of Eden's intervention, the Foreign Office prompted *The Times* to print a statement, on 17 August 1936, emphasising H.M.G.'s support for the French attempts to promote an international agreement on non-intervention.

65   Avon, pp. 401–3.

66   Ibid., p. 403.

67   Edwards, p. 38.

68   For a record of the 1st Meeting of the Non-Intervention Committee, 9 September 1936, see *DBFP*, 2nd ser., vol. 17, no. 178 (W 11115/11115/41). See also Avon, pp. 407–18, and Edwards, pp. 40–9. For an assessment of the scale of intervention in the latter half of 1936, see *DBFP*, 2nd ser., vol. 18, no. 34, 8 January 1937.

69   Minute by Eden dated 30 August 1936. See *DBFP*, 2nd ser., vol. 17, no. 157.

70   *DBFP*, 2nd ser., vol. 17, no. 254 (no. 68 [W 12789/9549/41]), Geneva, 1 October 1936.

71   Avon, p. 416.

72   Ibid., p. 413. The Cabinet agreed to follow Eden's recommendation that belligerent rights would not be conferred on the Nationalist forces unless they were successful in capturing Madrid and, therefore, in gaining an upper hand in the conflict. See *CAB* 23/86, CC 64(36)4, CC 66(36)3 and CC 67(36)2.

73   This exasperation was not limited purely to Italy and France for the Foreign Office had extensive evidence of similar infringements of the Non-Intervention Agreement by the Soviet Union. See *DBFP*, 2nd ser., vol. 17, no. 308 (W 14097/9549/41), 20 October 1936. It was evident, however, that the Foreign Secretary now saw Spain as the central problem in engineering European co-operation and already appreciated that non-intervention could not work without a formal military supervision scheme. See Avon, pp. 411–12 and p. 418. More seriously the Foreign Secretary argued that there was no viable alternative to non-intervention if Europe was to avoid being divided into opposing ideological power blocs. See *Avon Papers*, FO, 954, Memorandum by Eden dated 19 August 1936, SP/36/9.

74   See *DBFP*, 2nd ser., vol. 16, no. 473 (no. 897 [R 4372/294/67]), 21 July 1936. The Italian communiqué was considered by the Cabinet on 22 July 1936 (*CAB* 23/85, CC 54(36)4) and resulted in Eden's announcement to the House of Commons on 27 July 1936 (*H of C*, Debs, 5's vol. 315, cols 1122–3).

75   This note dated 19 August 1936, which was submitted to the Cabinet Committee on Foreign Policy as FP(36)10, was drawn up by Mr O'Malley of the Southern Department. While Eden rejected the proposal that Britain and France guarantee the status quo in the Western Mediterranean, he accepted the danger presented to the British position in Gibraltar. See *DBFP*, 2nd ser., vol. 17, no. 115 (W 9885/9549/41) and no. 126 (W 9708/62/41).

76   *DBFP*, 2nd ser., vol. 17, no. 159 (no. 342 [W 10452/9549/41]), 3 September 1936.

77   *DBFP*, 2nd ser., vol. 17, no. 188 (no. 597 [W 11235/9549/41]), 12 September 1936.

78   *DBFP*, 2nd ser., vol. 17, nos 203, 271, 291, 312 and 314.

79   For an account of Eden's interview with Grandi of 13 October 1936, at which the questions of Abyssinia and Egypt were discussed, see *DBFP*, 2nd ser., vol. 17, no. 291 (no. 1140 [R 6128/226/22]), 13 October 1936.

80   For Eden's reaction to this speech see Avon, p. 424. See also *Avon Papers*, FO, 954, It/36/25, It/36/26 and It/36/27.

81   *DBFP*, 2nd ser., vol. 17, no. 352, Minute by Mr Eden (R 6646/226/22), 5 November 1936.

82   For the text of Mussolini's speech of 1 November 1936 delivered in Milan see *DIA 1936*, pp. 343–7.

83   *H of C*, Debs, 5's, vol. 317, cols 282–3. See also Avon, pp. 425–6. This speech was timed to coincide with a similar declaration made by Halifax in the House of Lords professing that Anglo-Italian interests were 'not divergent but complementary', see *H of L*, Debs, 5's, vol. 103, col. 28, 5 November 1936. It had been agreed at Cabinet the previous day that Eden would make a friendly reference to Italy in his speech following Inskip's reminder that the COS strongly favoured an improvement in Anglo-Italian relations. See *CAB 23/86*, CC 62(36)3, 4 November 1936.

84   *DBFP*, 2nd ser., vol. 17, no. 356, Eden to Sir E. Drummond (no. 1225 [R 6580/226/22]), 6 November 1936.

85   For text of Vansittart's interview with Grandi see *DBFP*, 2nd ser., vol. 17, no. 353 (R 6602/226/22), 6 November 1936.

86   *DBFP*, 2nd ser., vol. 17, no. 376, Eden to Sir E. Drummond (no. 428 [R 6693/226/22]), 14 November 1936.

87   See Sir E. Drummond's reports from Rome of 17 and 27 November 1936. It was in the former interview that Drummond first referred to a 'Gentleman's Agreement'. *DBFP*, 2nd ser., vol. 17, no. 380 (no. 695 [R 6867/226/22]) and no. 415 (no. 717 [R 7187/226/22]).

88   Minute by Eden dated 10 December 1936 on Drummond's despatch from Rome of 6 December 1936 (no. 727 [R 7370/226/22]). *DBFP*, 2nd ser., vol. 17, no. 440.

89   *DBFP*, 2nd ser., vol. 17, no. 482, Eden to Sir E. Drummond (no. 481 [R 7373/226/22]), 18 December 1936.

90   For the text of the agreement and the accompanying exchange of notes, see *Documents on International Affairs 1937* (London 1939), pp. 87–9.

91   Minute by Eden dated 2 January 1937, on a Minute by Sargent on the Anglo-Italian negotiations, dated 1 January 1937 (R 12/1/22). See *DBFP*, 2nd ser., vol. 17, no. 527.

92   For example see the pressure placed on Eden to engineer an amelioration of relations with Italy at the key Cabinet meetings on 4 November 1936 (*CAB 23/86*, CC 62(36)3 and CC 63(36)3). This pressure was probably induced by Count Ciano's visit to Berlin in October 1936 which appeared to indicate that the Rome–Berlin Axis was being strengthened. For the text of the Official Communiqué issued at the conclusion of this visit on 25 October 1936, see *DIA 1936*, p. 341.

93   Quoted in Avon, p. 428.

94   Avon, pp. 432–3.

95   See report from the Rome Embassy, dated 2 January 1937, and a Minute by Mr Sargent on Soviet Policy with regard to Spain, dated 8 January 1937. Both give estimates of the extent of the flow of Italian Volunteers to Spain in the first week of January 1937. *DBFP*, 2nd ser., vol. 18, nos 2 and 34.

96   *DBFP*, 2nd ser., vol. 18, no. 25, Mr Eden to Sir E. Drummond (no. 13 [W 457/7/41]), 7 January 1937. In response Drummond admitted on 8 January 1937 that he was 'not hopeful' that Eden's message would induce Mussolini to

curb the flow of volunteers to Spain unless guarantees were similarly extracted from France and the Soviet Union. *DBFP*, 2nd ser., vol. 18, no. 30.

97 For details of Eden's despatches to Belgrade urging Sir R. Campbell to warn Prince Paul of Britain's 'grave misgivings' at the format of the proposed treaty with Italy, see *DBFP*, 2nd ser., vol. 18, nos 154, 233, 262 and 330. For the text of the treaty see *Documents on International Affairs 1937* (hereafter cited as *DIA 1937*) (London 1939), pp. 302—3. On 3 April 1937 the Foreign Office responded to reports from Turkey that Italy was attempting to initiate similar negotiations with Turkey by instructing Sir P. Lorraine to use his influence to convey to the Turkish Government British opposition to any such negotiations. *DBFP*, 2nd ser., vol. 18, nos 369 and 355.

98 For an assessment by the Rome Embassy of Mussolini's visit to Libya, see *DBFP*, 2nd ser., vol. 18, no. 292, Sir E. Drummond to Mr Eden (no. 153 [R 1789/1/22]), 16 March 1937. See also Drummond's report dated 26 March 1937, *DBFP*, 2nd ser., vol. 18, no. 353, letter of Mussolini's speeches delivered at Beda Littoria (12 March), Benghazi (15 March), Tripoli (17 and 18 March 1937) and given in *DIA 1937*, pp. 267—9.

99 *The Times*, 13 April 1937. Also reprinted in full in Rt Hon. Anthony Eden, *Foreign Affairs* (London 1939), pp. 189—98.

100 The ferocity of the Anglo-Italian press battle was referred to in detail in Sir E. Drummond's despatches from Rome dated 25 March 1937 and 6 April 1937. See *DBFP*, 2nd ser., vol. 18, nos 343 and 378.

101 *DBFP*, 2nd ser., vol. 18, appendix 1. Review of Imperial Defence by the Chiefs-of-Staff Subcommittee of the Committee of Imperial Defence (W 2852/1384/50), 22 February 1937.

102 The Review was finally approved by the CID as 'applicable to the international situation as it exists today' on 25 February 1937, 289th meeting of the CID, *CAB* 2/6.

103 288th Meeting of the CID, *CAB* 2/6. This recommendation was approved by the Cabinet on 24 February 1937 (CID Paper no. 441C). See *CAB* 23/87, CC 9(37)4.

104 *DBFP*, 2nd ser., vol. 18, no. 529, Sir M. Lampson to Mr Eden (no. 52 [R 3795/1/22]), Cairo, 22 May 1937.

105 This memorandum entitled 'The Probability of War with Italy' was drawn up by O'Malley and subject to minor amendments by Sir R. Vansittart and Sir O. Sargent. *DBFP*, 2nd ser., vol. 18, no. 615 (R 3831/1/22), 15 June 1937.

106 212th Meeting of the Chiefs of Staff Subcommittee of the CID, 5 June 1937, quoted in Roskill, vol. 3, pp. 266—8.

107 See Minute by Eden on Lampson's report from Cairo, *DBFP*, 2nd ser., vol. 18, no. 529 and also Roskill, p. 266.

108 See Minute by Eden dated 16 April 1937, on Drummond's despatch from Rome of 6 April 1937. Eden concluded:

> I see little prospect of recognising *de jure* position in Abyssinia in May. But perhaps the recognition that Abyssinia has ceased to exist — a self evident fact — will suffice.
>
> I did my best at Liverpool to preach 'live and let live'; more we cannot do.

DBFP, 2nd ser., vol. 18, no. 378.

109 For details of the debate surrounding this affair, see *DBFP*, 2nd ser., vol. 18, nos 207, 213, 219, 220 and 230. In addition see also *The Times* for 27 February 1937 and Eden's speech in the House of Commons (*H of C*, Debs, 5's, vol. 321, col. 5) of 1 March 1937.

110 *CAB* 23/87, CC 13(37)4, 24 March 1937. It was also significant that in April 1937 Eden chose not to publish the British Consul's report on Italian atrocities in Addis Ababa following the assassination attempt on the Italian Viceroy in Abyssinia, Graziani, in deference to the maintenance of Anglo-Italian relations. See diary entry for 12 April 1937 of Oliver Harvey, Private Secretary to Eden, in John Harvey (ed.), *The Diplomatic Diaries of Oliver Harvey 1937—40* (London 1970), pp. 37—8.

111 The priority allocated by the Chiefs of Staff to the preparations for a possible conflict with either Germany or Japan constantly demanded that an improvement of relations with Italy be engineered in order to safeguard communications through the Mediterranean. As recently as 4 November 1936 Inskip, Cooper and Hoare had emphasised, at Cabinet, their general agreement with the conclusions of the COS Subcommittee to the CID, presented to Cabinet on 2 June 1936, which advocated the need to improve relations with Italy. See CP 174/36, presented to Cabinet on 23 June 1936, CC 43(36)3, *CAB* 23/84. Also CC 62(36)2, *CAB* 23/86, 4 November 1936.

112 The need to improve Anglo-Italian relations as a lever in disrupting the Rome—Berlin axis was a theme frequently reiterated by Sir E. Drummond in his reports from Rome. See *DBFP*, 2nd ser., vol. 18, no. 463, Sir E. Drummond to Mr Eden (no. 364 [R 3123/135/22]), Rome, 4 May 1937.

113 *DBFP*, 2nd ser., vol. 18, no. 365, Minute by Mr Eden on Anglo-Italian relations (R 2258/1/22), 1 April 1937.

114 On 11 January 1937 Eden had minuted, on a despatch from Rome dated 4 December 1936, his agreement with a comment made by Gladwyn Jebb dated 15 December 1936, outlining Italy's deteriorating economic position but opposing any suggestion of British aid to alleviate the Italian position. See *Vansittart Papers*, 2/30.

115 Minute by Eden dated 20 April 1937, on a despatch from Berlin dated 15 April 1937. *DBFP*, 2nd ser., vol. 18, no. 405.

116 Minute by Eden dated 24 April 1937 on a despatch from Berlin dated 13 April 1937. Eden was in essence responding to, and attempting to counter, Sir E. Phipps's conclusion that Britain must look to woo Mussolini away from his alliance with Berlin. *DBFP*, 2nd ser., vol. 18, no. 399.

117 *CAB* 23/87, CC 1(37)2, 13 January 1937.

118 For example see Sir E. Phipps's report from Berlin dated 4 January 1937. *DBFP*, 2nd ser., vol. 18, no. 8.

119 *CAB* 23/87, CC 1(37)2, 13 January 1937.

120 Ibid.

121 *H of C*, Debs, 5's vol. 319, cols 93—108, 19 January 1937.

122 For extracts of Hitler's speech to Reichstag of 30 January 1937, see *DIA 1937*, pp. 161—75.

123 *CAB* 23/87, CC 5(37)3, 3 February 1937. The text of Hitler's speech was particularly disappointing, given Sir E. Phipps's report of 21 January 1937 emphasising his conviction that Germany desired 'to co-operate in the family of nations'. *DBFP*, 2nd ser., vol. 18, no. 99.

124 See the German reply to the British proposals of 19 November 1936 dated 12 March 1937. *DBFP*, 2nd ser., vol. 18, no. 280.

125 For the conclusion of the seventh meeting of the Cabinet Committee on Foreign Policy held on 18 March 1937, see *DBFP*, 2nd ser., vol. 18, no. 307 (C 2303/37/18).

126 *DBFP*, 2nd ser., vol. 18, no. 327, Memorandum by Mr Eden on German and Italian memoranda concerning preparations for a Five Power Conference (C 2311/1/18), 22 March 1937.

127 *DBFP*, 2nd ser., vol. 18, no. 166, note communicated to Sir O. Sargent by the Belgian Ambassador on 12 February 1937. (C 1223/1/18), 11 February 1937.
128 *DBFP*, 2nd ser., vol. 18, no. 259, Memorandum by Mr Eden on the position of Belgium and proposed conversations with the Belgian Government (C 1896/181/4), 8 March 1937. Circulated to the Cabinet Committee on Foreign Policy as FP (36)17.
129 In the last week of February 1937 Eden held meetings with his senior Foreign Office advisers and also with Von Ribbentrop which appeared to confirm his suspicion, voiced to Oliver Harvey on 23 February 1937, that Belgium 'appeared to be slipping into the German camp largely owing to anti-French feeling'. See Harvey diary entries for 23, 24 and 26 February 1937. Harvey, pp. 15–17.
130 See conclusions of the 6th and 8th Meetings of the Cabinet Committee on Foreign Policy held on 11 March 1937 and 6 April 1937 respectively. *DBFP*, 2nd ser., vol. 18, nos 266 and 379.
131 For Eden's reports from Brussels dated 26 and 27 April 1937, see *DBFP*, 2nd ser., vol. 18, nos 440, 441 and 443. On 28 April 1937 the Foreign Secretary described the Belgian Government's attitude as 'most cordial and anxious to cultivate the best possible relations with this country'. See *CAB* 23/88, CC 19(37)1. Harvey, who accompanied Eden to Brussels, described the negotiations as 'an undoubted success' and believed that the Belgians were 'determined not to allow German interference inside Belgium'. See Harvey, diary entry for 28 April 1937, Harvey, pp. 42–3.
132 The Blum–Schacht negotiations were first reported by Sir G. Clerk on 28 August 1936. It was not until 20 September 1936, however, that Clerk discovered the colonial issue had been discussed. *DBFP*, 2nd ser., vol. 17, nos 145 and 210.
133 *H of C*, Debs, 5's, vol. 315, cols 1131–2, 27 July 1937. This speech followed the findings of the Plymouth Committee released on 9 June 1936. *DBFP*, 2nd ser., vol. 16, appendix 3 (C 4275/97/18).
134 At a meeting held on 18 January 1937, Neville Chamberlain urged Eden to support an informal meeting between Dr Schacht and Sir Frederick Leith-Ross, if only to circumvent the possibility of further Franco-German discussions on the colonial issue. *DBFP*, 2nd ser., vol. 18, no. 86, record by Mr Sargent of a meeting of 18 January 1937 (C 475/1/18).
135 In assenting to the meeting between Leith-Ross and Schacht, Eden was undoubtedly influenced by the hope that an indication of British willingness to discuss the colonial question might induce a moderate tone in Hitler's address to the Reichstag scheduled for 30 January 1937. See *DBFP*, 2nd ser., vol. 18, no. 86. For Eden's instructions to Leith-Ross, see *DBFP*, 2nd ser., vol. 18, no. 92 (C 475/1/18), 19 January 1937.
136 *DBFP*, 2nd ser., vol. 18, no. 92, letter from Mr Eden to Sir F. Leith-Ross (C 475/1/18), 19 January 1937.
137 *DBFP*, 2nd ser., vol. 18, no. 148, note by Sir F. Leith-Ross for the Chancellor of the Exchequer (C 1476/78/18), 4 February 1937.
138 In order to verify Schacht's version of his discussion with Blum of August 1936, Eden asked the French Government on 23 February 1937 for a copy of the conversations which had taken place on 26 and 28 August 1936. This was supplied by the French Government the following day. See *DBFP*, 2nd ser., vol. 18, nos 163 and 210.
139 *DBFP*, 2nd ser., vol. 18, no. 296, Memorandum by Mr Ormsby-Gore on Anglo-German relations with particular reference to the Colonial Question

(C 2302/37/18), 16 March 1937. Presented to the Cabinet Committee on Foreign Policy as FP (36)19.

140 Eden's views were expressed in a memorandum to the Cabinet Committee on Foreign Policy entitled 'Memorandum by Mr Eden on conversations between Dr Schacht and French Ministers in August 1936 and between Dr Schacht and Sir F. Leith-Ross in February 1937' (FP (36)18). *DBFP*, 2nd ser., vol. 18, no. 289. The decision to insist on the opening of formal negotiations with the German Foreign Ministry was fully supported by Sir R. Vansittart, Sir O. Sargent and Mr Strang. See *DBFP*, 2nd ser., vol. 18, no. 163. See also Minutes by Strang and Vansittart on Sir G. Clerk's despatch from Paris dated 24 February 1937, *DBFP*, 2nd ser., vol. 18, no. 210.

141 *DBFP*, 2nd ser., vol. 18, no. 307, extracts from conclusions of the seventh meeting of the Cabinet Committee on Foreign Policy (C 2303/37/18), 18 March 1937.

142 At the eighth meeting of the Cabinet Committee on Foreign Policy held on 6 April 1937, Chamberlain forced Eden to agree in principle to the continuation of discussions with Dr Schacht and also to modify his draft despatch to the French Government accordingly. See *DBFP*, 2nd ser., vol. 18, no. 379 (C 2619/270/18), 6 April 1937.

143 For the French response to the tentative suggestion that Germany would require the return of Togoland and the Cameroons, see *DBFP*, 2nd ser., vol. 18, nos 462 and 473, note 3. On 10 May 1937 the tenth meeting of the Cabinet Committee on Foreign Policy concluded that it was unlikely further progress could be made on the colonial issue in the near future. *DBFP*, 2nd ser., vol. 18, no. 485 (C 3590/37/18), 11 May 1937.

144 It was evident at the eighth meeting of the Cabinet Committee on Foreign Policy that, while Chamberlain and Eden were in broad agreement on the need to link the colonial issue with a general settlement, Halifax, Hoare, Inskip and Simon supported the Chancellor of the Exchequer in pressing Eden to continue informal negotiations with Germany. It would appear that Baldwin made no move to defend his Foreign Secretary and, indeed, did not contribute to the discussion. *DBFP*, 2nd ser., vol. 18, no. 379 (C 2619/270/18), 6 April 1937.

145 *DBFP*, 2nd ser., vol. 18, no. 32, Memorandum by Mr Eden on Spain (W 1612/1/41), 8 January 1937.

146 The paper was presented to Cabinet as CP 6(37) on 8 January 1937. See *CAB* 23/87, note of a Meeting of Ministers to discuss the situation in Spain.

147 Ibid., loc. cit. Baldwin's passive role in the debate was particularly galling for Eden in that he subsequently claimed the Prime Minister had examined and fully approved his proposals before the meeting. Avon, p. 435.

148 Avon, pp. 435—7.

149 *CAB* 23/87, note of a Meeting of Ministers to discuss the situation in Spain, 8 January 1937.

150 Avon, pp. 435—7.

151 For a discussion of the collapse of the patrol scheme implemented by the Non-Intervention Committee after the alleged attacks on the German ships *Deutschland* and *Leipzig*, see Jill Edwards, *The British Government and the Spanish Civil War 1936–1939* (London, 1979), pp. 101—31. Also Avon, pp. 438—9 and pp. 446—7. The incidents were discussed by the Cabinet on 2, 21, 23 and 30 June 1937. *CAB* 23/88, CC 23(37)3, CC 25(37)2, CC 26(37)2 and CC 27(37)1.

152 *CAB* 23/87, note of a Meeting of Ministers to discuss the situation in Spain, 8 January 1937.

153 The Review of Imperial Defence by the Chiefs-of-Staff Subcommittee of the CID dated 22 February 1937, had concluded that British military interests in central and Eastern Europe were 'only indirect' and that participation in a war to defend that region could only be contemplated if France took the offensive to fulfil its treaties with Poland and Czechoslovakia, and only then 'if the only alternative was likely to be the domination of Western Europe by Germany'. See *DBFP*, 2nd ser., vol. 18, appendix 1 (W 2852/1384/50).

154 Eden subsequently claimed that Sir Samuel Hoare was the principal spokesman for a group of Ministers who opposed any move likely to prevent a Nationalist victory in Spain and were particularly alarmed at the prospect of a victory for the Republican forces assisted by the Soviet Union, Avon, p. 435. If such a group did exist it is difficult to substantiate Eden's suggestion that it was able to influence Cabinet decisions, particularly given the Cabinet's refusal to grant belligerent rights to the Nationalist Government in March 1937, see *CAB* 23/87, CC 12(37)3. In addition the Cabinet, despite protests from the Admiralty, warned Franco in April 1937 that the Royal Navy would protect British merchantmen on the high seas supplying the Republican regime with food. See Cabinet Minutes for 7, 11, 21 and 28 April 1937. *CAB* 23/88, CC 14(37)3, CC 15(37), CC 18(37) and CC 19(37)2. For the despatches to Franco warning him of the intention to protect British shipping to within three miles of the Spanish coast, see *DBFP*, 2nd ser., vol. 18, no. 393 (11 April 1937) and no. 447 (28 April 1937).

155 *DBFP*, 2nd ser., vol. 18, no. 135 (C 593/3/18), Minute by Mr Strang, Foreign Office, 1 February 1937. In this Minute Strang was replying to an essay by Dr Maxwell Garnet, Secretary of the League of Nations Union, advocating a further attempt to lure Germany back to the League of Nations.

156 *DBFP*, 2nd ser., vol. 18, no. 510 (T 9197/226/384), Minutes of the first meeting of principal delegates to the Imperial Conference 1937, held on 19 May 1937. For full Minutes of the Conference proceedings, see FO, 371/3201−2.

157 *H of C*, Debs, 5's, vol. 325, col. 1603, 25 June 1937.

158 Minute by Eden dated 8 December 1936. See *DBFP*, 2nd ser., vol. 17, no. 488 and *Baldwin Papers*, vol. 124, ff. 55−7, Eden to Baldwin, 27 December 1936.

159 See Minutes by Vansittart and Wigram dated 9 and 2 December 1936 respectively. *DBFP*, 2nd ser., vol. 17, no. 488. In addition see Vansittart's memorandum of 31 December 1936, *DBFP*, 2nd ser., vol. 17, appendix 2.

160 It was apparent that Eden, Vansittart and Strang were in broad agreement with Sargent's assertion, of 10 February 1937, that further negotiations with Germany 'should be carried on through the normal diplomatic channels and not through the intermediary of Dr Schacht'. *DBFP*, 2nd ser., vol. 18, no. 165 (C 958/78/18).

161 The references to a 'poker game' and a 'fair admixture of bluff' were made by Sargent and Strang respectively in Minutes dated 2 July 1937 relating to British policy in Central Europe. *DBFP*, 2nd ser., vol. 18, no. 670, note 6.

162 The debate surrounding the extent of the British commitment to central Europe was exemplified by an exchange of internal Minutes between Strang and Sargent in July 1937. While Sargent agreed with Strang that Britain's interest in events in this area was primarily 'bluff', he rejected Strang's central premise that Britain was 'morally bound to go to war if Germany upsets the status quo in Central Europe'. Eden, however, appeared to favour Strang's analysis, particularly in relation to Czechoslovakia, although he conceded that the Austrian question was more complex. See *DBFP*, 2nd ser., vol. 18, minute by Eden (8 July), Strang (2 July) and Sargent (2 July) on the Record of Conversation between Mr Leeper

and Mde Margerie (C 4757/3/18), FO, 30 June 1937. While Cadogan on 28 May 1937 emphasised the need to explore the German claims in Central Europe, he was apparently in agreement with Vansittart that Britain's obligations under the League of Nations would force it to react to any German attempt to change the status quo by force. See *Vansittart Papers*, 2/31. Minutes by Vansittart and Cadogan on Lord Lothian's interview with Hitler of 10 May 1937 (C 3621/270/18).

163 For the text of Baldwin's speech delivered on 19 May 1937 to the first meeting of the principal delegates to the Imperial Conference, see *DBFP*, 2nd ser., vol. 18, no. 510 (T 9197/226/384).

164 Thomas Jones recorded on 27 July 1936 that Baldwin informed him he 'told Eden yesterday that on no account, French or other, must he bring us in to fight on the side of the Russians'. Jones, pp. 230—1.

165 Baldwin's ill-health forced him to convalesce in South Wales throughout most of August, September and October of 1936. For an account of Eden's activities in this period in relation to Spain, see Avon, pp. 401—10. See also the account in Middlemas and Barnes, p. 962.

166 Avon, p. 404.

167 Ibid., pp. 318—19. The impact of Baldwin's deteriorating health on his leadership was referred to by Thomas Jones who noted on 24 July 1936: 'Downing Street Secretaries are concerned about state of Baldwin's health. It is impossible to get a decision on anything out of him. We conspire with Dawson (Physician in Ordinary to the King) to pack him off for a holiday.' Jones, p. 230.

168 Oliver Harvey, diary entry for 12 April 1937, Harvey, pp. 37—8.

169 For references to Baldwin's ill-health see Thomas Jones, diary entry for 5 November 1936 and letters to Lady Grigg and Dr Flexner on 3 November and 12 December 1936 respectively. See Jones, pp. 279—85 and pp. 294—7.

170 Avon, p. 410.

171 See Thomas Jones, diary entry for 11 January 1937. Jones, pp. 302—3.

172 See Thomas Jones, diary entry for 15 February 1937, Jones, pp. 313—15. See also Middlemas and Barnes, pp. 964 and 1018.

173 Quoted in Avon, p. 446.

174 Oliver Harvey, diary entry for 23 March 1937, Harvey, pp. 31—2.

175 Ibid.

176 Oliver Harvey, diary entry for 26 March 1937, Harvey, pp. 33—4.

177 Avon, p. 445.

178 Although Sir S. Hoare recorded in his memoirs that Eden was 'delighted' with Chamberlain's appointment as Prime Minister, he also noted that while Parliament was in session he and Chamberlain met most mornings to discuss 'Government affairs before going to our offices' and these conferences were continued regularly during the recess at various country houses. Templewood, pp. 257—9.

179 See Oliver Harvey, diary entry for 26 March 1937, Harvey, pp. 33—4. In addition Neville Chamberlain's diary for the period January to May 1937 was concerned almost solely with his plans for the construction of his first Cabinet. There was no suggestion that he ever considered removing Eden from the Foreign Office and David Margesson, the Chief Government Whip, had written to Chamberlain in March 1937, acknowledging that there was not to be a change at the Foreign Office. See *Neville Chamberlain Papers*, NC 2/24A and NC 8/24/1.

180 Avon, p. 445.

181 Ibid., p. 445.

182 Neville Chamberlain's interest and central role in the conduct of Foreign

Affairs prior to May 1937 is chronicled in Keith Feiling, *The Life of Neville Chamberlain* (London, 1961).

183 Indeed on several occasions Eden had acknowledged the assistance rendered by Chamberlain in the conduct of foreign affairs while he was Chancellor of the Exchequer. For example see *Neville Chamberlain Papers*, NC 7/11/29/16, letter from Eden to Chamberlain, 9 November 1936.

184 Avon, pp. 319—20.

185 See Minutes of the Seventh Meeting of the Cabinet Committee on Foreign Policy held on 18 March 1937. *DBFP*, 2nd ser., vol. 18, no. 307.

186 For discussions between the Foreign Office and the Treasury in January 1937 on the advisability of opening informal discussions with Dr Schacht, see *DBFP*, 2nd ser., vol. 18, nos 53, 60, 76, 86 and 92.

187 *Neville Chamberlain Papers*, NC 7/11/29/19, letter from Sir Warren Fisher to Chamberlain, 15 September 1936.

188 J.P.L. Thomas (later Lord Gilcennin), succeeded Roger Lumley as PPS to Eden in May 1937 following Lumley's appointment as Governor of Bombay. The account of Thomas's meeting with Fisher and Wilson is contained in Avon, pp. 447—8.

189 *Neville Chamberlain Papers*, NC 7/11/30/74, letter from Sir S. Hoare to Chamberlain, 17 March 1937.

190 Avon, p. 521.

191 Minute by Sir R. Vansittart dated 20 May 1937, on Henderson's despatch from Berlin of 6 May 1937. See *DBFP*, 2nd ser., vol. 18, no. 466 (no. 445 [C 3428/2/18]).

192 Sir A. Cadogan effectively took up the post of Deputy Under-Secretary of State on 1 October 1936 following the retirement of Sir Victor Wellesley. See *DBFP*, 2nd ser., vol. 15, no. 437, note 2. See also Avon, p. 521 and Vansittart, p. 549.

193 *Baldwin Papers*, vol. 124, pp. 55—7, letter from Eden to Baldwin, 27 December 1936.

194 Oliver Harvey, diary entry for 7 March 1937, Harvey, pp. 22—3.

195 Oliver Harvey, diary entry for 4 May 1937, Harvey, pp. 43—4.

196 Avon, pp. 445—6.

197 For a record of the first meeting of the principal delegates to the Imperial Conference on 19 May 1937 see *DBFP*, 2nd ser., vol. 18, no. 510. A full record of the Conference proceedings is to be found under the classification 226/384 in volumes FO, 371/3201—2. In addition see Eden and Chamberlain's comments at the Cabinet meetings held on 2 and 17 June 1937, *CAB* 23/88, CC 23(37)3 and CC 24(37)2.

198 Avon, p. 445.

7 Chasing the dictators
June — December 1937

On 17 June 1937 Malcolm MacDonald presented to the Cabinet a report on the proceedings of the Imperial Conference which had been held in London between 14 May and 15 June 1937.[1] The Secretary of State for the Dominions concluded:

> Since 1926 the Imperial Conferences had been mainly concerned with constitutional relations and the tendency had been to lay the main stress on the nationhood of the Dominions which had perhaps encouraged an impression abroad of some growing disunity in the British Commonwealth of Nations. . . . the general result of the Conference had been to reassert somewhat the principle of co-operation.

> No doubt we should have our difficulties with the Dominions in the future but the Conference had been a great stride forward in the direction of unity.[2]

Undoubtedly this apparent rekindling of co-operation was seen by the Cabinet as an important factor which signified the determination of Britain and the Dominions to defend their interests throughout the world. While the main thrust of this declaration of unity was probably designed to deter Japanese ambitions in the Far East, Eden was also anxious to impress upon Germany the extent of Imperial ties and commitments. To this end he was aware that during the course of the Conference the Canadian Prime Minister, MacKenzie King, had promised Neville Chamberlain that: 'if he [Hitler] should ever aggress in a way to injure us [Britain], Canadians would swim the Atlantic rather than be prevented from coming to our aid.'[3]

Eden persuaded King to repeat the pledge to Hitler during his forthcoming visit to Berlin.[4] While the Foreign Secretary calculated that such a declaration of Anglo-Canadian solidarity was bound to impress the German leader, he was also aware that it was unlikely to solve the immediate problem of persuading Hitler to enter into negotiations for the conclusion of a European security settlement. Eden had originally intended to use the proposed Five Power Conference for this purpose but interest in the convening of such a Conference had been progressively eroded as the focus of attention in Europe had moved away from the renegotiation of the Locarno Treaty to events in Spain.[5] It appeared, however, that an opportunity had been presented to utilise the Spanish conflict for opening direct negotiations with Germany when, in the last week of May, the German pocket battleship, *Deutschland*, was subject to an aerial attack while participating in the naval patrol scheme around the Spanish coast. As a result of the assault the German Government announced its withdrawal from the Non-Intervention Committee and declared its intention to bombard the Republican-held port of Almeria in retaliation.[6]

At a Cabinet meeting on 2 June 1937 Eden proposed that the opportunity be taken to invite the German Foreign Minister, Von Neurath, to London to discuss the re-establishment of German co-operation in the enforcement of non-intervention. In addition he added that: 'Advantage might also be taken of the visit for a general review of the international situation.'[7] The Foreign Secretary's intention to use the *Deutschland* incident to initiate a broad discussion of European affairs was confirmed in a Minute dated 4 June 1937: 'Nothing could be more beneficial for the interests of H.M.G. than an improvement of Anglo-German relations even if it only proved temporary — Spain is a possible field for our collaboration.'[8]

The format and scope of the proposed discussions with Von Neurath were discussed at a meeting of senior Foreign Office officials on 18 June 1937. At this meeting Strang produced a memorandum clearly outlining the problems that would be encountered:

> The fact, of course, is that there is a fundamental divergence between British and German policy (as at present established) and in their outlook on foreign affairs.
>
> Germany is in favour of change, and of drastic change. She has strengthened herself in order to secure that changes should take

place to her advantage, by peaceful means if possible, by war if necessary. We, on the other hand, though we pay lip service to the idea of peaceful change, have not reached any clear conclusion in our own minds as to what changes we should regard as tolerable. Indeed, our policy is to preserve the 'status quo' even against peaceful change (if the change should be to Germany's benefit) as long as possible and we belong to an international organisation, the object of which (however weakly that object may be achieved in practice) is to prevent the operation of change by other than peaceful means.[9]

Strang was clearly suggesting that it was important for the British Government to ascertain the nature of German ambitions and to be far more precise in determining its probable response to any attempt to change the status quo. In this context he was prepared to draw a distinction between British interests in Western Europe and those in Central and Eastern Europe. While the defence of France and the Low Countries was of key importance in British defence calculations, the maintenance of the status quo in Central and Eastern Europe could not be assigned the same priority. Strang, therefore, suggested that Britain could perhaps be more flexible in accommodating German ambitions in that region but it was necessary first to establish the extent and format of Hitler's demands.[10] Eden was in complete agreement with this approach. At the Imperial Conference the Foreign Secretary and the Prime Minister had admitted that Britain was not in a position to provide a military commitment to uphold the status quo in Central and Eastern Europe. It was, however, in Britain's interest to maintain political stability throughout Europe and to attempt to ensure that any alterations to the status quo in Central and Eastern Europe must be obtained by peaceful negotiation and mutual consent.[11] It was important, therefore, that a dialogue be opened with Germany in order to establish the German *desiderata* and Eden decided that the prospective negotiations with the German Foreign Minister must be widened to include such matters as the situation in Austria, Czechoslovakia and Danzig. Furthermore it was possible that the discussions could be used to reactivate the German proposals of March 1936.[12]

An invitation to visit London had been despatched to Von Neurath on 2 June 1937.[13] Despite the German Government's initial acceptance of the invitation, by the end of the month a firm date had not been agreed. Initially the visit was to be delayed until after the conclusion of Von Neurath's tour of the Balkan nations but a further obstacle was raised in the second week of June, when it was announced that the question of German participation in the Non-

Intervention patrol scheme would have to be satisfactorily settled before the German Minister visited London.[14] By this time Eden was rapidly coming to the conclusion that Hitler was once again seeking to cloud the issue and avoid the opening of Anglo-German negotiations. In a despatch to Henderson dated 11 June 1937, Eden registered his disappointment:

> I am surprised that Herr Von Neurath should now suddenly stipulate that his visit must be made dependent on a previous settlement of the *Deutschland* question. He will remember that my original reason for inviting him was precisely to discuss this particular trouble . . . .

> For your information I would add that I am considering informing Herr Von Neurath if he still feels that he cannot discuss the Spanish problem in any of its aspects, that the original value of the visit will no longer exist, and he will no doubt agree with me that in such circumstances it would perhaps be preferable to postpone the visit altogether until a more favourable opportunity presents itself.[15]

Although the German Government later claimed that it only wished to exclude all references to the discussion of Spain from the official communiqué, any remaining possibility of the visit taking place was effectively eliminated on 21 June 1937 when Hitler informed Henderson that after the alleged torpedo attack on the German cruiser, *Leipzig*, on 19 June 1937 there was no possibility of Von Neurath leaving Berlin at such 'a time of tension'.[16] In the following week Eden's insistence on a full investigation before supporting the German contention that the assault was staged by the Republican navy and, therefore, his refusal to despatch British vessels to participate in a naval demonstration off the Republican port of Valencia, resulted in Germany once again withdrawing from the Spanish naval patrol scheme.[17] An attempt by Eden to restore the position, in a discussion with Von Ribbentrop on 30 June 1937, only served to confirm the gulf between the two parties as the German Ambassador emphasised Hitler's displeasure at the British refusal to support the naval demonstration off Valencia, while the Foreign Secretary maintained that Britain could not sanction any such action until an independent inquiry had ascertained the full facts surrounding the attack on the *Leipzig*.[18]

Eden's exasperation at the evasive nature of the German tactics was reflected in a despatch to Henderson following Von Neurath's decision to postpone his visit to London:

We are astonished at Herr Von Neurath's decision which appears to us to have insufficient justification. Nobody here will understand such a decision, particularly as Spain was one of the objects of the visit.

Herr Von Neurath must obviously take his own decision and we do not wish to influence him but such visits cannot be lightly put on and off and postponement unless fully justified may mean indefinite delay in the opportunity of coming to close quarters. If so, it will not be our fault.[19]

Neville Chamberlain expressed similar, and more candid, sentiments in a letter to his sister, Ida, on 4 July 1937:

The Germans and Italians are as exasperating as they can be and it is rather difficult to reconcile their professions of desire for our friendship with the incredible insolence and licence of their press.

It was apparent, however, that he had not given up all hope of luring the German Foreign Minister to London:

I still get the impression that neither of them wants to go to war and accordingly we have played for time and avoided a break.

. . . I shall not give up hope of seeing him [Von Neurath] later. If only we could get on terms with the Germans I would not give a rap for Musso.[20]

Indeed the Prime Minister declared before the House of Commons that he still entertained the hope Von Neurath would visit London at a later date.[21] The fact that this statement was made by Chamberlain rather than Eden was seen in some quarters as indicating that the Foreign Secretary no longer shared Chamberlain's enthusiasm for the opening of discussions with Germany.[22] This was a suggestion that Eden felt obliged to attempt to dispel. On 16 July 1937 he instructed Henderson to provide the German Foreign Ministry with the text of the Prime Minister's speech and to emphasise that the Prime Minister and the Foreign Secretary were in complete agreement on the need to improve Anglo-German relations.[23] It is evident that throughout this period, despite the obstacles raised by Hitler, Eden continued to work behind the scenes to establish a suitable climate for the launching of Anglo-German negotiations. His efforts were directed primarily towards the defence of the Non-Intervention Committee. Between 19 and 22 June 1937 he chaired four meetings of the respective Ambassadors from Germany, Italy and France in an attempt to avert a complete collapse of the Committee following the *Leipzig* incident.[24] In addition he was able to persuade the Editor of *The Times*, Geoffrey Dawson, to delay publication of a series of articles by Lord Lothian which the Foreign Secretary feared might prejudice the chance of concluding a satisfactory agreement with Germany.[25] His efforts, however, were to no avail and it was an indication of defeat when he finally agreed to adopt Henderson's suggestion that General Göring be approached by the British Ambassador with a view to obtaining an informal review of the various German 'grievances'.[26]

Despite the failure to lure Von Neurath to London the Cabinet concluded, on 7 July 1937, that the search for an agreement with Germany was still the main goal of British policy in Europe.[27] This conviction was based not only on the determination to defuse political tension in Central and Eastern Europe but also on the belief that unless Anglo-German relations could be improved little could be done to counter 'the disquieting attitude of the Italian Government'. The Prime Minister in reviewing Anglo-Italian relations concluded: 'that there was very little that could be done to improve matters. The real counter to Italy's disquieting attitude was to get on better terms with Germany.'[28]

This assertion was based upon the assumption that the failure to establish an Anglo-German dialogue through either the medium of the Five Power Conference or a visit by Von Neurath to London had almost certainly encouraged Mussolini to pursue an aggressive and expansionist policy throughout the Mediterranean. The steady deterioration of Anglo-Italian relations in this period was outlined by a series of reports from Rome which noted that, despite the establishment of the Gentleman's Agreement, the whole tenor of Anglo-Italian relations was still characterised by suspicion and thinly veiled hostility. In that Italian ambitions appeared to be turning increasingly towards the Mediterranean, Sir E. Drummond expressed his concern at the possibility of a future clash of interests with Britain.[29] A Foreign Office memorandum drawn up on 15 June 1937 and entitled 'The Probability of War with Italy' reflected the anxiety generated by successive reports of Italian military expansion in the Mediterranean.[30] The reinforcement of the garrisons in Libya and Abyssinia, coupled with the vitriolic propaganda campaign waged against the British positions in the Near and Middle East, led to the conclusion that:

> from whatever angle one studies the attitude at present adopted by Italy towards the United Kingdom, there is clear evidence of a definite ill-will in the whole trend of Italy's present foreign policy.

. . . as long as it exists we are bound to consider whether, and in what circumstances, it might impel the Italian Government along a line of action leading to war with the United Kingdom.

The Foreign Office, therefore, felt obliged to request that the Chiefs-of-Staff consider a change in the formula governing defence preparations in relation to a possible conflict with Italy from the existing stance which stated that: 'Italy cannot be counted on as a reliable friend, but in present circumstances need not be regarded as a probable enemy.' As an alternative the Foreign Office proposed:

> Italy cannot be considered as a reliable friend and must for an indefinite period be regarded as a possible enemy, especially if she can count on the goodwill and potential support of Germany or if the United Kingdom were involved in difficulties elsewhere.[31]

While this memorandum was successful in generating a review of defence preparations in the Mediterranean and the elimination of Italy from the list of nations against which war preparations were not considered necessary, the expansion of Britain's military presence in the Mediterranean was effectively blocked by the insistence of the CID that priority of defence expenditure in Europe 'should be given to the provision of a deterrent to aggression by Germany'.[32]

If the focus of Anglo-Italian tension was the strategic implication of one power dominating the sea routes of the Mediterranean and the Red Sea, relations were certainly not improved by the continuing wrangle over *de jure* recognition of the Italian administration in Abyssinia and the attempts to engineer a cessation of Italian intervention in the Spanish conflict.[33] On 25 June 1937 Sir E. Drummond could only conclude:

> As I have repeatedly stated, I believe Mussolini still believes that we intend some day to take our revenge on him for his Abyssinian venture. Till we can finally get this idea out of his head . . . I see little chance of getting back to such terms as will lead him to cease his anti-British activities.[34]

In a report dated 2 July 1937, the Ambassador struck an even more alarming note by expressing the fear that the recent tone of Italian propaganda was reminiscent of the technique used in the early months of 1935 to mobilise support for the invasion of Abyssinia.[35]

Given the tone of Drummond's reports from Rome, it was not perhaps entirely surprising that the Foreign Secretary remained sceptical as to the possibility of achieving a comprehensive settlement of Anglo-Italian differences. Eden was prepared, however, to continue to work for an agreement with Italy that would reduce the prevailing air of tension in relations between the two nations. To this end he assured the Italian Ambassador, Grandi, on 14 June 1937 that British policy towards Italy was still based on the agreement of January 1937[36] and underlined his wish to avoid a clash of interests in a speech to the House of Commons on 19 July 1937:

> If the Mediterranean is for us a main arterial road, and it is, yet there is plenty of room for all on such a road. If we intend to maintain our place on it, and we do, we have no intention of seeking to turn anybody else off it. Least of all do we wish to interfere with those who geographically dwell upon it. There is ample room for all. Free traffic through and out of the Mediterranean is the common interest of Great Britain and of all the Mediterranean powers.

Furthermore in direct response to Drummond's reports that Italian belligerence was fostered by fear of British reprisals following the seizure of Abyssinia, Eden declared:

> This country has no intention of pursuing towards any other country a policy either of aggression or of revenge. Such a possibility has never occurred to the British people. The word 'vendetta' has no English equivalent.

> What I have said about the Mediterranean applies equally to the Red Sea. It has always been, and it is today, a major British interest that no great power should establish itself on the eastern shore of the Red Sea. I need hardly add that this applies to ourselves no less than to others.[37]

Drummond had identified formal British recognition of the Italian position in Abyssinia as the key to the improvement of Anglo-Italian relations[38] and there were indications that Eden was prepared to consider supporting such a move at the forthcoming meeting of the League of Nations, scheduled for September, if it was likely to lead to a reduction in tension between the two nations.[39]

Yet while Eden publicly denied that British and Italian interests were incompatible, it was apparent that on the central issues of the cessation of Italian intervention in Spain and the defence of British strategic interests throughout the Mediterranean and the Red Sea the Foreign Secretary entertained little hope of a full settlement of Anglo-Italian differences.[40] In this conviction he was supported by his senior advisers at the Foreign Office and in particular by Sir Robert Vansittart who on 14 June 1937, in reply to Drummond's proposal that Eden agree to *de jure* recognition of Abyssinia, had noted:

if we were to let Mussolini know that we should not hesitate to use our strength in defence of our vital interests, he might be prepared in the future to be more reasonable.

In other words, unless we are strong and show Mussolini that we intend, if necessary, to use our strength, the Italians will continue to *blackmail* us.[41]

In addition the Foreign Secretary was aware that the French Government was in no mood to support British concessions to the Italians in the Mediterranean as part of any attempt to improve Anglo-Italian relations. French exasperation at the escalation of Italian intervention in Spain, both through the supply of men and arms to the Nationalist cause and the employment of covert naval action against merchant shipping supplying the Republican regime, had reached such an extent that any suggestion of relaxing the Anglo-French pressure to halt Italian intervention was likely to result in a reopening of the French border with Spain and the effective collapse of the Non-Intervention Committee.[42]

While French opinion was certainly significant in persuading Eden to continue to pursue a firm line in the conduct of Anglo-Italian relations, it was apparent that the Foreign Secretary was still convinced that the scope and extent of Mussolini's ambitions in the Mediterranean and the Near East precluded the attainment of a full and open settlement of differences. Therefore, while appreciating the advantages to be gained from a short-term amelioration of relations, the Foreign Secretary remained convinced that a long-term *détente* could only be achieved after British military and economic strength had been expanded to a level at which it would effectively deter Italian expansionist ambitions.[43] This stance was reflected at Eden's interview with the Italian Ambassador, Grandi, on 21 July 1937. Grandi emphasised Mussolini's 'desire for permanent friendship with this country' and his willingness 'to discuss any proposals to further the interests of our two countries'.[44] While Eden repeated his determination to work for an improvement of relations, the shallowness of his words was underlined three days later when he minuted on a memorandum submitted by Sir R. Vansittart chronicling the rise of expansionist tendencies in Italy:

Mussolini has the mentality of a gangster, and if he were contemplating an act of aggression against us the procedure he is at present following is clearly the right one for him. He proclaims that he is frightened of being attacked and can thus work up his own people and produce some kind of excuse before the world, if need be. That is why I view with some suspicion Signor

Grandi's approaches to Mr. Hore-Belisha. If necessary they will one day proclaim: 'We did our best to reach an understanding, the British would not meet us. We had to act when we did as the last moment when we had a chance of defending ourselves.'

All these suspicions of mine may be unfounded, they probably are, but they should not be ruled out entirely. Therefore while reciprocating any advances, we should be watchful in the extreme.[45]

This suspicion of Italian motives was also evident in a brief passed to Chamberlain by Eden as background information for an interview requested by Grandi with the Prime Minister. The brief, which was largely the work of Sir R. Vansittart, recommended that the Prime Minister re-emphasise to Grandi the text of Eden's speech of 19 July 1937 which, while declaring the British determination to defend its interests in the Mediterranean, had concluded that the maintenance of this position was not seen as conflicting with Italian interests.[46] If Grandi referred to Italian concern generated by the expansion of British military forces in the Mediterranean, Vansittart recommended that the Prime Minister point out that these measures were not directed against Italy. In addition Chamberlain could allude to the Italian forces in Libya which plainly contravened the spirit of the Gentleman's Agreement. In conclusion Vansittart noted:

We sincerely desire to bring about better relations with Italy, but progress will be difficult indeed so long as our complete sincerity is not recognised as such and so long as wholly groundless suspicions are being worked up into alarms.[47]

Neville Chamberlain's interview with Grandi of 27 July 1937 has been identified as a significant event in the moulding of the subsequent relationship between Eden and the Prime Minister.[48] The importance of the interview lay in the fact that during the course of the discussion Chamberlain elected to write a personal letter to Mussolini, which he passed directly to Grandi without first consulting his Foreign Secretary. Eden subsequently noted of the incident:

I should have had no objection in principle to a message of greeting, though I would have imposed some conditions to the opening of discussions if I had seen the letter before it was sent, and I would have made some suggestions to guard the sender from appearing too gullible to the recipient. I made no difficulty about the incident at the time, thinking that there was no deliberate intent to by-pass me as Foreign Secretary, but that it was merely a slip by a Prime Minister new to international affairs.[49]

Eden's account, however, made no mention of the fact that the idea of transmitting a personal message to Mussolini had been originally suggested to him by Halifax and was very much at the centre of his thoughts in the last two weeks of July. On 16 July 1937, in a letter to Chamberlain, Eden admitted that he had discussed the possibility of writing personally to Mussolini with Sir Ronald Graham, former Ambassador to Rome, who had strongly endorsed the proposal. Eden, therefore, concluded: 'As soon as I get a breathing space, therefore, I shall try my hand at a draft.'[50]

In this light Eden must have felt a certain amount of pique, in that Chamberlain's letter effectively forestalled his own intention to open a direct dialogue with Mussolini. That Chamberlain's action was neither spontaneous nor 'merely a slip' was confirmed in a letter to his sister dated 1 August 1937:

> My interview with Grandi seems to have made a very good impression in Italy and I see they have now 'revealed' that I sent a personal letter to Mussolini. I made it appear that it was a spontaneous idea arriving out of the conversation but of course I had made up my mind to do it beforehand.

> Grandi himself was delighted and reported that Italy and England had been divorced for two years but were now going to be re-married! I believe that the double policy of rearmament and better relations with Germany and Italy will carry us safely through the danger period if only the F.O. will play up. I see indications that they are inclined to be jealous, but though it is natural that they should be annoyed at Press headlines about the 'Chamberlain touch', instead of the 'Eden touch' there is no desire on my part to take credit away from the F.S. and I shall try now to put him in the foreground again.[51]

This passage suggests that, even at this early juncture in their relationship, there were indications that Chamberlain and Eden differed in their respective views of the degree of emphasis which should be placed on the pursuit of a closer understanding with Italy.[52] In his apparent determination to push the Foreign Office into increasing its efforts to establish an improvement of relations with Mussolini, it is conceivable that the Prime Minister had been influenced by the failure to obtain a direct exchange of views with Germany in the previous month.[53] The indefinite postponement of Von Neurath's visit to London had certainly strengthened the hand of the influential bloc of Service Ministers, who wished to see the Foreign Office make a more positive move towards improving relations with Italy in order to permit the concentration of Britain's limited military resources in the Far-Eastern and Home theatres.[54] As recently as 14 July 1937 the Cabinet had supported the recommendation of the CID that priority in European defence be given to the 'provision of a deterrent to aggression by Germany'. This decision, coupled with the cool reception afforded to Eden's proposal — at the same Cabinet meeting — that a show of naval strength in the Eastern Mediterranean might be beneficial in deterring Italian ambitions in that area, was indicative of the determination of the Service Ministries to see Italy eliminated from the list of potential aggressors.[55] During the month of July, Sir Maurice Hankey wrote to Eden, Chamberlain and Inskip urging that: 'it is a matter of the first importance that every possible effort should be made to place our relations with Italy on a friendly footing.'[56] In particular his proposal to Chamberlain that 'some frank interchange of views' with Italy was necessary must have encouraged the Prime Minister to despatch his personal message to Mussolini.[57]

It would appear, however, that Chamberlain did not need a great deal of persuasion to pursue this course of action and was clearly elated at the prompt response from Mussolini reciprocating the desire for the opening of Anglo-Italian discussions.[58] The Italian Ambassador, Grandi, added though, that he feared any such negotiations would be pointless if the League of Nations continued to deny recognition to the Italian position in Abyssinia. In an attempt, therefore, to clear the final obstacle to the opening of negotiations, on 7 August 1937 Chamberlain wrote to Lord Halifax who was temporary head of the Foreign Office while Eden was on vacation:

> the possibility of success turns on *de jure* recognition. I myself feel that (1) we can't go on indefinitely denying it (2) it has now some marketable value which will continually diminish as time goes on (3) we should therefore be prepared to give it now (or say that we will give it) provided we can get something substantial for it.

> It is very necessary to remember that these dictators are men of moods. Catch them in the right mood and they will give you anything you ask for. But if the mood changes they may shut up like an oyster. The moral of which is that we must make Mussolini feel that things are moving all the time.[59]

In a letter to his sister dated 8 August 1937, Chamberlain reaffirmed his determination to force the Foreign Office to take a more active role in relations with Italy:

> I had a second useful talk with Grandi on Monday when he brought me Mussolini's letter and I am now in communication

with Halifax who is taking Eden's place while he is on holiday. He entirely agrees with what I am doing and he reports that the F.O. is coming along very nicely though I can see that if left to themselves there would be a danger of their letting pass the critical moment.

As it is, I can look back with great satisfaction at the extra-ordinary relaxation of tension in Europe since I first saw Grandi. Grandi himself says that it is 90% due to me and it gives one a sense of the wonderful power that the Premiership gives you.[60]

If Chamberlain agreed with Grandi's estimation that the improvement of relations was '90%' his own work, there is no suggestion, however, of any desire on his part to overshadow completely the Foreign Secretary. It would seem, therefore, that after giving a clear lead to the Foreign Office and significantly easing the path to negotiations, Chamberlain was prepared to retire once again to the sidelines.[61] There is little doubt, however, that Eden had not taken kindly to the Prime Minister's decision to adopt a leading role in the direction of relations with Italy without consulting his Foreign Secretary. On 25 July 1937 Oliver Harvey had warned Eden of the problems that would result from Chamberlain opening a direct link with Mussolini: 'there is the idea of a personal letter, if sent by the P.M. (which would be more normal as Mussolini is P.M.) it would, I fear, revive the legend that you alone are intransigent.'[62]

Not only was there a danger of this prophecy being fulfilled but having received a copy of Chamberlain's letter to Halifax of 7 August 1937, Eden could be under no illusion as to the Prime Minister's determination to take advantage of the Italian dictator's present benevolent 'mood' and forge an agreement with Italy.[63]

Despite the encouraging tenor of Mussolini's reply to Chamberlain, it was apparent that Eden still did not relish the prospect of attempting to achieve a settlement of differences with Italy and, indeed, had been positively alarmed at the possibility of an exchange of military information as proposed by Grandi to Hore-Belisha on 22 July 1937.[64] While Chamberlain had been initiating his personal link with Mussolini, the Foreign Secretary had engaged the services of Sir Ronald Graham, a former Ambassador to Rome, to sound the Italian monarch on the conditions that Italy would demand as part of any settlement. Graham's report that the Italians were determined to achieve both recognition of their position in Abyssinia and a Nationalist victory in Spain only served to reaffirm Eden's suspicion that the price of any agreement was prohibitive.[65] In this assessment of the situation he was supported by Sir R. Vansittart. The Permanent Under-Secretary urged Halifax, on 3 August 1937, not to agree to the initiation of negotiations until after Sir E. Drummond had been recalled for consultations.[66] In addition on the following day he wrote to Eden expressing his concern at the prospect of a possible exchange of military information with Italy and outlining the concessions that he considered must be extracted from Mussolini as part of any settlement. Eden replied to this letter the same day:

> I am presuming that there will be no further correspondence between No. 10 and Rome without my seeing it. I naturally attach importance to this.
>
> Meanwhile I think that the French are taking a more realistic view of this Italian move than some of our press. No doubt Mussolini wants recognition of Abyssinia, but so do we want the Italians out of Majorca, mechanized divisions out of Libya, explanation of fortified islands in the Mediterranean and Red Sea etc. It would be the height of folly to concede in fact what the Italians want, in return for mere promises.
>
> I think it important that our press should emphasize the connection in our mind between Italians in Spain and better Anglo-Italian relations . . . . We must not be backward in setting out our *desiderata vis à vis* Italy and there must be an end of giving and of not getting. . . . By all means let us show ourselves ready to talk, but in no scrambling hurry to offer incense on a dictator's altar. . . . We have to remember in all our dealings with Italy that Mussolini's object is to show himself courted, not his only object but an important one. He likes also to point to us as the waning weakling. We must give him no pretext for that, or we shall damage ourselves in the Near and Middle East at a time when our authority is important to us for Palestine, etc. . . . Personally I feel that we have a chance now of bettering conditions in Europe, but this depends on two things:
>
> (1) Our own firmness.
> (2) Maintenance of friendship with France, which alone has maintained peace these last difficult eighteen months.[67]

Given the Foreign Secretary's apparent determination to delay the opening of negotiations with Italy until he was assured that the British *desiderata* could be obtained, he was alarmed to learn that the provisional conclusions of a meeting between Halifax, Drummond and the senior Foreign Office advisers, held on 10 August 1937, had recommended not only that Britain should be prepared to take the initiative at Geneva in raising the question of the recognition of the Italian position in Abyssinia, but also that the Chiefs-of-Staff be asked to consider the necessary preconditions for a military agreement with Italy in the Mediterranean and the Red Sea. Although it was agreed that an Italian withdrawal from Spain and a reduction in the Libyan garrison would have to be part of any settlement, the Foreign Secretary was obviously disturbed at the increasing pace of the British preparations for the opening of negotiations with Italy.[68] Eden responded immediately to the Foreign Office proposals in a letter to Halifax which expressed his reluctance to grant *de jure* recognition to the conquest of Abyssinia, particularly following the brutal reprisals exacted by the Italians on the local population in Addis Ababa after the attempt upon the life of Marshal Graziani. Furthermore he expressed his distaste for a purely Anglo-Italian military agreement covering the Mediterranean:

> Have you thought of the possibility of a Mediterranean pact instead of an Anglo-Italian arrangement? It has many advantages:
>
> (1) Includes our friends.
>
> (2) Consistent with our policy of regional agreements (bi-lateral is what dictators always want).
>
> (3) Would really contribute to pacify a region. All arrangement between us and Italy alone could never do that, for we are not alone concerned.
>
> As to Spain, Franco's manners seem poor, and he appears not even to answer our notes. The time has almost come for us to seize a cargo or two of his and hold them until he behaves! You will see how strong I am feeling after my ten days of sea breezes.[69]

A further letter to Halifax, on 13 August 1937, indicated that Eden was resolved to block Halifax's attempts to engineer an early opening of discussions with Mussolini: 'I have read the office "note" on Anglo-Italian conversations which you sent to me by the same bag and you probably will not be surprised to hear that I disagree with it.'[70]

Although previously Halifax and Eden had apparently been in broad agreement, it was plain that Halifax now favoured a more active exploitation of the opening that Chamberlain's correspondence with Mussolini had produced.[71] On 15 August 1937 he wrote to Vansittart expressing his sympathy with Eden's reluctance to work with 'Machiavellian gangsters' but registering his opposition to any attempt to postpone negotiations indefinitely:

This letter from Anthony disquiets me. I am not saying anything about Anthony's attitude to the P.M. at present. But it is — as I see it — dangerously divergent from what the P.M. contemplated and what he has been trying to do.[72]

When a meeting between Eden and Halifax at Southampton on 18 August 1937 failed fully to reconcile their differences, Halifax wrote to Chamberlain recommending that he break off his holiday to meet Eden and himself in London.[73] This meeting, held in the last week of August and to which Eden made no reference in his memoirs, contained the first suggestion of Chamberlain's impatience with the Foreign Secretary's policy of caution. In a letter to his sister dated 29 August 1937, Chamberlain noted of the meeting:

there were various differing ideas. Not unnaturally there is a great deal of suspicion about Mussolini and a certain apprehension about the reception in 'this' country of any proposal to accord recognition of the Abyssinian conquest.

Coming to the main thrust of his thesis, however, the Prime Minister concluded:

We can't go on for ever refusing recognition in the Abyssinian affair and it seems to me that we had better give it while we can still get something in return for it.

In this context the Prime Minister preferred the advice of Sir E. Drummond who stressed the need to grasp the opportunity presented by Mussolini. Chamberlain noted:

he at any rate believes that if we follow it up we can to a great extent if not entirely restore Anglo-Italian relations to what they were before the Abyssinian adventure.[74]

The difference of opinion between Eden and Chamberlain on the opening of negotiations with Italy was becoming increasingly difficult to conceal and at the Cabinet meeting of 8 September 1937 there was an open rift when the possible recognition of the Italian position in Abyssinia was discussed. Eden was adamant that recognition could not be afforded as part of a purely Anglo-Italian settlement for it would have to be incorporated within a general agreement amongst the major European powers. The Foreign Secretary argued that a bilateral agreement on Abyssinia would be widely portrayed as: 'a nefarious bargain by which Italy gained our assent to her wrong doing in return for material advantages to ourselves.'

The Foreign Secretary, therefore, insisted that recognition could not even be considered until after the conclusion of the proposed international conference at Nyon. Chamberlain, however, adopted a far more pragmatic approach, stating that the Cabinet 'must be realistic and face the facts' and pointing out that the establishment of cordial Anglo-Italian relations was an important factor in determining the future format of relations with Germany. In response to Eden's assertion that an improvement of relations was difficult while 'Italy was unstable and untrustworthy', Chamberlain informed the Cabinet:

> He knew that the Secretary of State for Foreign Affairs found difficulty in going quite so far as he [the P.M.] would like to go, but he hoped that we should be able to do everything we possibly could to recover the better atmosphere of the early summer.

Despite Chamberlain's intervention, Eden appeared to have won the day when the Cabinet agreed that Grandi be warned that recent Italian activities in the Mediterranean had complicated Anglo-Italian relations and that no reference was to be made to the possibility of future recognition of Italian sovereignty in Abyssinia.[75] Undoubtedly the spate of attacks on British shipping in the Mediterranean in the latter half of August had hardened Cabinet opinion against concessions to Italy and, therefore, strengthened Eden's hand.[76] The contents of a letter from Chamberlain to his sister dated 12 September 1937 indicated that, despite this setback, he remained determined to capitalise on the indications of goodwill which had resulted from his letter to Mussolini and particularly that he was not prepared to let the Foreign Office block this policy:

> I am not too happy about the F.O. who seem to me to have no imagination and no courage. I must say A.E. is awfully good in accepting my suggestions without grumbling but it is wearying to have always to begin at the beginning again and sometimes even to rewrite their despatches for them. I am terribly afraid lest we should let the Anglo-Italian situation slip back to where it was before I intervened. The F.O. persist in seeing Musso only as a sort of Machiavelli putting on a false mask of friendship in order to further nefarious ambitions. If we treat him like that we shall get nowhere with him and we shall have to pay for our mistrust by appallingly costly defences in the Mediterranean.[77]

The Foreign Secretary's reluctance to deal with Italy had certainly been reinforced by the increasing reports of attacks on merchant shipping supplying the Republican regime and also the Royal Navy patrols seeking to protect British merchantmen outside Spanish territorial waters. Although it was impossible positively to identify the assailants, given that the vast majority of attacks were reportedly made by submarines, it was widely suspected that the Italian Navy was directly involved.[78] On 12 August 1937 Sir R. Vansittart privately warned the Italian Chargé d'Affaires that the British Government would not tolerate attacks on its shipping.[79] When the attacks continued, Eden called a meeting of Ministers at which it was agreed that a public warning be issued through the press declaring that:

> His Majesty's Government have issued instructions through the Admiralty that, if any British merchantship is attacked by a submarine without warning, His Majesty's ships are authorised to counter attack the submarine.[80]

The problem was, however, one of enforcing this warning, given the Admiralty's open reluctance to commit further forces to expand both the scope and effectiveness of its naval patrols in the Western Mediterranean. Indeed in advocating the granting of belligerent rights to both sides in the Spanish conflict it was apparent that the Admiralty was anxious to absolve itself of the responsibility for the protection of British merchantmen trading with Spain.[81] Therefore despite the public indignation aroused by the reports of attacks by 'pirate' submarines on British merchantmen and Royal Navy patrols, it was only after the production of further evidence of extensive Italian intervention in the fighting on the Spanish mainland that the Foreign Secretary was able to mobilise sufficient support for a further review of the situation. Ironically this evidence was provided quite openly by Mussolini in a message of congratulation to General Franco following the capture of Santander:

> I am particularly glad that during ten days of hard fighting the Italian legionary troops have made a valiant contribution to the splendid victory of Santander.

> This comradeship of arms, now so close, is a guarantee of the final victory which will liberate Spain and the Mediterranean from all threats to the civilisation we share.[82]

This blatant acknowledgement of official support for the Italian volunteers assisting the Nationalist forces produced a wave of public outrage in Britain. More significantly, however, the French Government, which had observed the Italian intervention in Spain with growing exasperation, proposed to Eden on 28 August 1937 that a conference be called of the Mediterranean and Black Sea powers to discuss the provision of measures for the protection of air and sea routes throughout the Mediterranean. The exclusion of Italy from the list of nations to be invited left little doubt as to where the French intended to place the blame for the attacks on shipping in the Mediterranean.[83] While Eden was not greatly attracted to the prospect of a conference designed specifically to pillory Italy, further attacks on British shipping in the last week of August and the reluctance of the Admiralty to consider direct action against Nationalist naval bases forced Eden to request a meeting of Ministers on 2 September 1937 to consider the French proposals.[84] At this meeting, chaired by Sir J. Simon in Chamberlain's absence, it was accepted that action had to be taken and that Britain should support the call for a conference of the Mediterranean powers if the French agreed to the inclusion of Italy. Furthermore the despatch of four destroyers to the Mediterranean was agreed as an indication of British determination to halt the attacks on its shipping.[85]

In the course of the following two days Eden successfully established, with the French Ambassador, the format of an acceptable Mediterranean patrol scheme which involved the restriction of Spanish submarines to territorial waters and an agreement that submarines from the various Mediterranean powers operating outside territorial waters must remain on the surface. Any submarines not observing this code of conduct in the open sea would be liable to attack.[86] The problem of the constitution of the conference was, however, far more protracted and, as Eden reported to the Cabinet on 8 September 1937, was only solved after detailed discussions with Delbos. While conceding that an invitation had to be extended to Italy, the French Foreign Minister insisted that the Soviet Union, which had also suffered attacks on its shipping, be similarly invited. Eden resisted this proposal for the expansion of the conference from a purely Mediterranean constitution because it immediately raised the question of German participation. When, however, Delbos remained insistent on the extension of an invitation to the Soviet Union, it was agreed that there was little alternative but to add Germany to the list of nations to be invited to the conference.[87] On this basis the joint Anglo-French invitations were despatched on 5 September 1937 and Eden's action was approved by the Cabinet on 8 September 1937, although Chamberlain emphasised that he would not accept the participation of the Soviet Union in any Mediterranean naval patrol scheme.[88]

The conference, which opened at Nyon on 10 September 1937, was attended by ten nations. Although Italy and Germany declined to attend, the conference was a remarkable success. Despite an initial wrangle over the possibility of the participation of the Soviet Union in a Mediterranean and Aegean naval patrol scheme, which was strongly opposed by the Eastern Mediterranean powers, it was agreed on 11 September 1937 that the six patrol zones would be policed primarily by Britain and France with assistance, on request, from the Eastern Mediterranean powers.[89] Throughout the conference Eden was aware of Chamberlain's anxiety to avoid alienating Italy and in a letter to the Prime Minister, dated 14 September 1937, the Foreign Secretary stressed that: 'the Italian Government has been kept in touch and has been treated with more courtesy than any other power which refused to attend a Conference in similar circumstances.'[90] More positively, however, the Tyrrhenian patrol zone was not allocated specifically to either Britain or France in the hope that Italy would eventually agree to participate in the naval patrol scheme.[91]

As the Foreign Secretary informed the Cabinet on 29 September 1937, he was delighted with the outcome of the Nyon conference.[92] On 14 September 1937 Eden had written to Winston Churchill:

> I hope that you will agree that the results of the Conference are satisfactory. They seem so as viewed from here. The really important political fact is that we have emphasized that co-operation between Britain and France can be so effective, and that the two Western democracies can still play a decisive part in European affairs.[93]

The lessons to be derived from Nyon were clearly, in Eden's opinion, that Britain must continue to co-ordinate its policy closely with France and that a firm Anglo-French front could be successful in forcing the dictators to modify their stances.[94] It was in this vein that he wrote to the Prime Minister on 14 September 1937:

> It is possible no doubt that the Rome reaction will be violent. All the more so perhaps because for the first twenty-four hours they did not know what to say. But if this is so I am sure that there is no alternative for us but to stand firmly and quietly by our decision.
>
> So far as Mussolini himself is concerned, though he may be very angry for a while, he is likely to respect us all the more in the end. Be that as it may, we could not I am convinced have allowed this conference to end in failure. It was more than time that the democracies should make themselves felt in Europe.[95]

Those conclusions appeared to be borne out when in the following weeks, after initial prevarication and demands from both Berlin and Rome for the revision of the Nyon agreement had received no response from Paris or London, the Italian Government eventually elected to participate in the naval patrol scheme and accept its allotted zone in the Tyrrhenian Sea. Furthermore in the last week of September the Italians indicated informally, to both the British and French Governments, that they were prepared to halt the flow of volunteers to Spain.[96] As a result of this initiative, Eden and Delbos agreed that Rome be approached on the subject of Anglo-French-Italian negotiations which could be utilised to test the recent Italian professions of goodwill and possibly lead to a settlement of outstanding differences.[97] Accordingly Lord Perth informed Count Ciano, on 1 October 1937, that the British Government was prepared to open discussions on issues of mutual interest in the Mediterranean and Red Sea.[98] The Italian response, however, was disappointing in that Ciano rejected the suggestion of negotiations with Britain and France and insisted that the focus of discussion be confined to the Non-Intervention Committee.[99] In effect this decision forced the Cabinet to concede that the prospect of direct negotiations with Italy was now remote.[100]

Although Grandi and Woermann informed the Non-Intervention Committee on 20 October 1937 that they were prepared to accept measures for the assessment of the number of foreign volunteers in Spain and their ultimate withdrawal, their subsequent refusal to be bound by the findings of an independent investigatory commission soon negated any progress that had been achieved.[101] Eden was not unduly disappointed for the Cabinet decision of 3 November 1937 to make 'unobtrusive' improvements to Egyptian defences coupled with the continuing stalemate in Spain — which both suited British political goals in Spain and provided a drain on Italian resources — supported his conviction that Britain was gradually gaining ascendancy over Italy in the Mediterranean.[102] More significantly Eden was convinced that the evidence of Anglo-French resolve displayed at Nyon had made a major contribution to the reinforcement of the British position *vis à vis* Italy. Despite the Foreign Secretary's concern that growing French impatience with Italian prevarication over the issue of intervention in the Spanish conflict — which threatened in October 1937 to lead to the reopening of the French frontier with Spain and the possible collapse of the Non-Intervention Committee — it was evident that the latter months of 1937 represented a period of remarkable Anglo-French unanimity.[103] On 29 and 30 November 1937 Chautemps and Delbos visited London. In discussion with Chamberlain and Eden it was agreed that further negotiations with Italy were pointless unless there was evidence of Italian goodwill in the form of the cessation of hostile propaganda and acceptance that the recognition of the Italian position in Abyssinia was purely a matter for the League of Nations, not a subject for Anglo-French-Italian negotiations. Furthermore Chamberlain assured the French that they would be kept fully informed of any further Anglo-Italian discussions.[104] In a letter to his sister, in the following week, Chamberlain noted:

> The meeting with the French Ministers really was, for once, as successful as the papers reported it. Anthony said it was the best meeting with the French he had ever had.[105]

It was apparent, however, that Chamberlain did not entirely share Eden's confidence in the ultimate success of a policy in regard to Italy based upon restraint and patience. While conceding that Italian belligerence in Spain and the Near East had unavoidably soured relations with Mussolini, it was evident that the Prime Minister still sought to resurrect and build upon the atmosphere of goodwill which he considered his personal message to Mussolini had established in the summer months of 1937.[106] Evidence of his doubts as to the impact of the Nyon conference on Anglo-Italian relations was contained in a letter to his sister dated 19 September 1937:

> Anthony has I am sure done his best to keep Italy quiet though he has never actually believed in Musso's sincerity, but the Italians have been just about as difficult as could be and at the moment I don't know how we can improve the situation.[107]

In the following months Chamberlain sought to prevent any further deterioration in Anglo-Italian relations. Not only did he seek to cultivate a personal relationship with the Italian Ambassador, Grandi, but he also attempted to dissuade Eden from making any further public condemnations of Italian policy.[108] In particular the Prime Minister attempted to discourage the Foreign Secretary from making a major speech on foreign affairs, scheduled to be delivered to an audience of 18,000 at Llandudno on 15 October 1937. Chamberlain suggested that the engagement be cancelled on the grounds that Eden's extensive commitments were overtaxing his health. Eden suspected, however, that Chamberlain's concern was not primarily to protect the health of his Foreign Secretary but rather to leave the field open for his own proposed speech on foreign affairs to be delivered on 12 October 1937.[109] He, therefore, insisted upon going ahead with the Llandudno meeting, although, perhaps, in deference to Chamberlain's sensibilities, while condemning both piracy in the Mediterranean and the cynical disregard for treaty commitments exhibited by certain nations, the Foreign Secretary refrained from specifically naming Italy as the guilty party.[110] Three weeks later, however, following a speech by Mussolini on 28 October 1937 attacking Bolshevism and justifying the right of Germany and Italy to build empires in Africa,[111] the Foreign

Secretary took the opportunity in the House of Commons to attack those nations which sought to divide the world into blocs and use the threat of Communism as a justification for an aggressive foreign policy:

> it follows . . . that we will join no anti-Communist and no anti-Fascist *bloc*. It is nations' foreign policies, not their internal policies, with which we are concerned. We will work whole-heartedly with other nations who are like-minded, with us, and there are many such. We offer co-operation to all, but we will accept dictation from none.[112]

It was evident that Chamberlain was annoyed by this further assault on Italian policy by his Foreign Secretary; on 6 November 1937 he noted in a letter to his sister:

> Anthony's speech in the House of Commons was a great personal triumph for him but it contained some unfortunate passages from my point of view and shows again a characteristic of the F.O. mind which I have frequently noticed before. They never can keep the major objects of foreign policy in mind with the result that they make obstructions for themselves by endeavouring to give smart answers to some provocative foreign statement.

> But Anthony should never have been provoked into an attack which throws Germany and Italy together in self defence when my policy is so obviously to try and divide them. It was perhaps fortunate that Grandi was lunching with us the next day and I found an opportunity of whispering a few words into his ear to show that my attitude was unchanged.[113]

It was apparent, therefore, that in this period Eden and Chamberlain were not in complete harmony. Following the confrontation over Eden's proposed speech at Llandudno, Oliver Harvey noted:

> AE had shortly before this, on his return from holiday, discussed P.M. with me and said that there was no doubt a difference as to methods between them, but he believed P.M. *au fond* had a certain sympathy for dictators whose efficiency appealed to him . . . and that he really believed it would be possible to get an agreement with Muss by running after him. AE disapproved of his precipitate reply to Musso's letter offering conversations . . . .[114]

Almost two months later, on 8 November 1937, Harvey was still writing in the same vein:

AE's conversation with P.M. went very badly. P.M. stiff; never even mentioned AE's speech; complained that F.O. never made genuine effort to get together with the dictators. AE said it was useless and impossible to do so unless and until we were strongly armed . . . .[115]

It would be a mistake, however, to see this divergence as purely one between Eden and Chamberlain. It was quite apparent that they were, in essence, representative of factions within the Cabinet itself which differed in their conceptions of the need to achieve an amelioration of relations with Italy. This point was made quite forcibly by Harvey in his diary entry for 15 October 1937:

There is no doubt that he [Eden] has more appeal than any of his colleagues. He has the H of C behind him as well as the country, but in the Cabinet he is criticised and thwarted by half his colleagues who are jealous of him and would trip him up if they had half a chance.[116]

The real problem lay in the fact that amongst Eden's opponents were the influential Service Ministers and the former Foreign Secretaries, Sir John Simon and Sir Samuel Hoare. The problems presented by this situation were outlined by Harvey on 3 November 1937:

The Cabinet cannot use AE's popularity and sabotage his foreign policy. The majority of the Cabinet are against AE and the Cabinet are too far to the right both of the H of C and the country. His supporters in the Cabinet are flabby and unassertive, i.e. Stanley, MacDonald, Elliott, De La Warr; his opponents, Simon, Sam Hoare, Kingsley Wood, Swinton, Hailsham are important and effective. AE's last speech brought him the greatest ovation he has ever had; it was also his firmest speech; yet the Cabinet would certainly have prevented him making it if he had shown it to them.[117]

While an element of this opposition to the Foreign Secretary can be explained perhaps in terms of personal intrigue — and indeed Hoare certainly appeared to harbour an ambition to reassume the reins at the Foreign Office[118] — the centre of discontent was undoubtedly the Service Ministries which continually maintained that, given the financial constraints imposed upon the rearmament programme, it was impossible to prepare adequately for a war with Germany, Italy and Japan. While the Service Ministries welcomed Eden's firm support for the expansion of the rearmament programme, at the same time they wanted the Foreign Office to act more decisively to reduce the list of potential opponents in any future conflict.[119] Following the conclusion of the Nyon Conference, Eden had attempted to answer their criticism of his policy:

> There are those who say that at all costs we must avoid being brought into opposition with Germany, Japan and Italy. This is certainly true, but it is not true that the best way to avoid such a state of affairs is continually to retreat before all three of them. To do so is to invite their converging upon us. In any retreat there must on occasion be counter-attack, and the correct method of counter-attack is to do so against the weakest member of the three in overwhelming force. That is the justification of Nyon.[120]

It was apparent, however, that rather than confront Italy with 'overwhelming force', which only threatened to result in further Italian military efforts to reinforce their position in the Mediterranean and the Red Sea, the Service Ministries were in favour of a more accommodating approach to the problem of Anglo-Italian relations. In particular, as Inskip informed the Cabinet on 24 November 1937, they opposed the devotion of further expenditure to the defence of the Mediterranean. The Minister for Co-ordination of Defence saw his first task as:

> to provide for the security of the United Kingdom, which would be weakened by the despatch of forces to the Mediterranean. From this point of view the ideal would be a restoration of relations with Italy to the position that existed before 1935: but if this was impossible just now, the next best would be a gradual approach to better relations during which we should exercise great patience. In any case, however, the vital importance of gaining time for the completion of our rearmament should never be lost sight of.[121]

This theme was reaffirmed on 8 December 1937 when the Cabinet was presented with the report of the COS Subcommittee of the CID entitled, 'A Comparison of the Strength of Great Britain with that of certain other nations as at January 1938'. Paragraph forty-two of the report noted:

> it will be seen that our Naval Military and Air Forces in their present stage of development are still far from sufficient to meet our defensive commitments, which now extend from Western Europe, through the Mediterranean to the Far East . . . . Without overlooking assistance which we could hope to obtain from France and possibly other allies, we cannot foresee the time

when our defensive forces will be strong enough to safeguard our territory, trade and vital interests against Germany, Italy and Japan simultaneously. We cannot, therefore, exaggerate the importance, from the point of view of Imperial Defence, of any political or international action that can be taken to reduce the numbers of our political enemies and to gain the support of political allies.[122]

It was interesting to note that while the Prime Minister accepted the main thrust of the report, which was directed towards the improvement of relations with Italy, he pointedly remarked that in terms of defence preparations 'Germany was the real key to the question'. Indeed it was in the identification of Germany as the primary threat to European stability and, therefore, to British security that Eden and Chamberlain were in agreement.[123] They had, however, drawn different conclusions from this basic premise in relation to Italy. Chamberlain was convinced of the necessity of improving Anglo-Italian relations as a means of disrupting the Rome—Berlin Axis and, therefore, strengthening the British hand in future negotiations with Germany. Eden, on the other hand, not only doubted that British concessions would cause Mussolini to deviate in any way from his policy of expansion but also argued that any such concessions would be accepted without reciprocation and would merely be seen as further evidence of weakness and retreat on the part of the Western democracies.[124] In this sense the Foreign Secretary questioned the assumption that an Anglo-Italian agreement could reduce the significance of the Rome—Berlin Axis and had expressed this reservation to the Cabinet on 29 September 1937 when the possibility of opening tripartite discussions was broached. The Foreign Secretary warned the Cabinet that:

> if anything had been concluded in the nature of an agreement under which Germany should have a free hand in Austria in return for supporting Italy in the Mediterranean, it was doubtful if the conversations would serve any useful purpose.[125]

While Eden was prepared to play a waiting game in relations with Italy in the belief that Anglo-German relations held the key to European stability, it was apparent that in the first half of 1937 the Foreign Secretary had significantly failed to improve the tenor of relations between London and Berlin. On 29 September 1937 Eden circulated a series of reports from Henderson following his discussions with the Nazi hierarchy at the National Socialist Party rally held at Nuremberg. In particular Eden highlighted a remark made by Göring to the British Ambassador which emphasised: 'the danger of allowing the German people to continue indefinitely to regard England as the enemy in their path.'[126]

The reports, however, were circulated purely for information and the Foreign Secretary did not present any proposals to the Cabinet. While alive to the danger of allowing relations with Germany to drift without a positive direction, it was apparent that Eden appreciated that the problems to be confronted in engineering an improvement of Anglo-German relations were manifold. The point of dispute between the two nations did not centre solely on the evidence of direct German involvement in the Spanish Civil War for the British Government had also been increasingly disturbed by indications of Germany's desire to increase its political and economic influence in Central Europe, with particular reference to the possible incorporation of Danzig, Austria and the Sudetenland within the German Reich. Furthermore it was evident that the German Government still held hopes of recovering its former colonial empire in Africa.[127] That little or no progress had been made in the resolution of these issues was testimony not only to the complexity and sensitivity of the issues but also to the fact that the German Government had shown no inclination to enter into discussions and, indeed, had positively rebuffed Eden's attempts to persuade Von Neurath to visit London in the summer of 1937.[128] In addition it was apparent that contacts between the two nations were not assisted by the less than cordial relationship established between Eden and the German Ambassador, Joachim Von Ribbentrop.[129]

Despite these obstacles there is little doubt that in the autumn of 1937 the Foreign Secretary would have welcomed the opportunity for direct negotiations with either Hitler or Von Neurath in order to discuss the European and international situation.[130] It must, therefore, have been with mixed feelings that Eden received the news that Lord Halifax had been invited to attend the International Sporting Exhibition in Berlin as a guest of the German Hunting Association. While it was stressed that Halifax had been invited in his capacity as Master of the Middleton Hounds, it was apparent that the invitation had emanated from Göring and offered the possibility of informal discussions with both Göring and Hitler.[131] Although the invitation to Halifax, who had worked closely with Eden at the Foreign Office, was not entirely unwelcome, it was certainly something of a rebuff to the Foreign Secretary and caused him subsequently to remark, 'I more than suspected by this time that Hitler did not like me'.[132] Furthermore Eden suspected that the invitation was partly the product of collaboration between Halifax and Chamberlain, from which he had been excluded.[133] Halifax subsequently denied that there had been any prior collusion with Chamberlain and that the idea of using the visit for political purposes had come from Eden:

> I pooh-poohed the idea, but he stuck to it and said he would speak to the Prime Minister about it, and we could all talk about it together after that. This in due course we did, and it was in consequence of that talk that I ultimately went to Berlin and Berchtesgaden.[134]

This account does not tally with Eden's own version[135] and, indeed, is contradicted by Churchill, who claimed that he was present when Halifax informed Eden of the proposed visit on 14 October 1937:

> Lord Halifax came up and said in a genial way that Goering had invited him to Germany for a sports visit, and the hope was held out that he would certainly be able to see Hitler. He said that he had spoken about it to the Prime Minister, who thought it would be a very good thing, and therefore he had accepted. I had the impression that Eden was surprised and did not like it; but everything passed off pleasantly.[136]

Halifax's account is further undermined by that of Nevile Henderson, the British Ambassador to Berlin, who subsequently noted:

> the visit was described as entirely private and unofficial . . . but the fact remained that it was designed by Mr. Chamberlain to establish that personal contact between a prominent British statesman and the Nazi leaders which Hitler was believed to seek and which, it was hoped, might result in a better understanding.[137]

The matter is, however, clarified by an excerpt from Chamberlain's letter to his sister dated 24 October 1937:

> A little while ago Halifax told me that he had received an invitation to attend an International Sporting Exhibition in Berlin in connection with which there were to be 'hunting' expeditions in the forest.

> As one form of hunting was to shoot foxes Edward was much amused and sent on the invitation to Anthony saying that he was going to select that particular kind of sport for his day out. It seems, however, to have occurred to him that it might possibly be desirable to take it more seriously so he had a talk with Anthony and Van, at which the former said he would be 'quite happy' if he went while the latter strongly argued that he should

not go as he would certainly be asked awkward questions. When Edward told me all this I was horrified. I said another opportunity to be thrown away. I can't allow that. And I appointed a meeting with Edward and Anthony and it is now fixed that E will go.

But really that F.O.! I am only waiting for my opportunity to stir it up with a long pole.[138]

It was apparent, therefore, that there was an element of collusion between Halifax and Chamberlain but that the opposition to the visit emanated primarily from Vansittart. Eden subsequently suggested that his tacit agreement was based, in part, on his desire to avoid further confrontation with the Prime Minister:

I was sure that Lord Halifax wanted to go and thought it probable that the Prime Minister would have the same sentiments. This seemed an instant where I could reasonably meet them and it would be best to do so with a good grace.[139]

Furthermore the Foreign Secretary calculated that Halifax's mission would dovetail neatly with the discussions with Von Neurath which he hoped to engineer at the Brussels Conference in the first week of November.[140] The negotiations were also likely to be of general value in ascertaining Hitler's views on foreign affairs, very much in the vein that Eden had proposed to despatch a Minister to Berlin in the summer of 1936 in order to gauge the German reaction to the British questionnaire of May 1936. The one stipulation that Eden insisted upon was that Halifax was to adopt a primarily passive role in discussions with Hitler, with the intention of allowing the German Chancellor to elucidate his stance on foreign affairs. On this matter Eden minuted:

I have spoken to Lord Halifax and Sir Nevile Henderson together. The former will listen and confine himself to warning comment on Austria and Czechoslovakia. I have impressed on Sir N. Henderson the need for doing all we can to discourage German intervention in these two states. We must keep Germany guessing as to our attitude. It is all we can do until we are strong enough to talk to Germany.[141]

In addition the Foreign Secretary, in the House of Commons on 1 November 1937, served notice that Germany could not expect any immediate move to restore its colonial empire.[142] In a letter to Chamberlain Eden hinted that this had been done not only to counter 'Mussolini's championship of Germany's colonial claims' but also with a weather eye to Halifax's visit, and as an attempt 'to stop some form of ultimatum about the colonies, such as may be, I fear, impending'.[143] In this context the limited role of Halifax's mission was acceptable to Eden when he left London for Brussels on 1 November 1937. The situation had, however, altered upon his return on 14 November 1937. In a despatch from Brussels the Foreign Secretary had contended that the announcement of the conclusion of a Tripartite Pact between Italy, Japan and Germany on 6 November 1937 had significantly altered the balance of Anglo-German relations.[144] Eden argued that: 'from the point of view of our position in Europe and public opinion at home it is essential to avoid giving the impression of our being in pursuit of German Chancellor.'[145] He, therefore, registered his opposition to any change in the format of Halifax's visit to Germany which would involve the abandonment of the envisaged informal discussions in Berlin in favour of the Lord President of the Council requesting an official interview with Hitler, and travelling to Berchtesgaden specifically for that purpose.[146]

While undoubtedly the announcement of the Tripartite Pact influenced Eden's decision to express his concern at the prospect of Halifax departing from the agreed format of his visit to Germany, it was also apparent that the Foreign Secretary had been nettled by the premature leakage to the London Press of the announcement of the Lord President of the Council's prospective interview with Hitler. The resulting magnification of Halifax's mission to the level of a major diplomatic initiative which plainly by-passed the Foreign Office was not only a personal rebuff to Eden but was also a source of official embarrassment, in that the French had not been previously informed of the intention to despatch Halifax to Germany.[147] Although Delbos accepted Eden's apology, he emphasised the importance attached by his Government to the prevention of German interference in Czechoslovakian affairs and expressed his wish that Halifax reaffirm this sentiment in negotiations with the German hierarchy. As Eden subsequently noted, the announcement of the visit before the French had been officially informed was unfortunate in that it came at a time when it was 'imperative to do nothing . . . to weaken the good relations between our two countries', but it was also probable that the Foreign Secretary's hostility to the Halifax mission had been further fuelled by the German decision not to attend the Brussels Conference.[148]

It was apparent that Eden's intention to overshadow the Lord President of the Council's discussions in Germany by direct negotiation with the German Foreign Minister at Brussels had been effectively baulked. This failure, coupled with the added stature being afforded to Halifax's visit by the Press, rekindled Eden's fears of being publicly eclipsed in the foreign policy process by Halifax and Chamberlain. It was not surprising, therefore, that in his despatches from Brussels and upon his return to London the Foreign Secretary sought to reassert his position.[149] While Eden appreciated the value of direct negotiations with Hitler, he was insistent that the British Press moderate its enthusiasm for the visit and acknowledge that the discussions were purely unofficial and informal. When a Press release from the Foreign Office News Department failed to achieve this goal, the Foreign Secretary elected to tackle the Prime Minister directly on the matter.[150] Eden subsequently admitted to Oliver Harvey that his interview with Chamberlain, which was held on 16 November 1937, 'couldn't have gone worse'.[151] Although the Prime Minister agreed to attempt to tone down Press coverage of Halifax's mission, it was apparent that his patience with Eden was close to exhaustion and he attacked both Eden's interpretation of the significance of the Brussels Conference and his views on the pace and format of rearmament. As a parting shot Chamberlain, as Harvey noted, 'advised AE to go to bed and take an aspirin'.[152]

As a result of this interview there was open speculation of a division between Eden and Chamberlain and Harvey observed on 17 November 1937:

> Jim told H.W. how Cartland had told him that Beverley Baxter [Atticus in *Sunday Times*] had been visited by both Simon and Hoare separately to explain that A.E.'s flu was the beginning of the end for A.E., that strain was too great and he would soon go.
>
> H.W. said P.M. was aware of these intrigues.[153]

Indeed Chamberlain had already taken steps to defuse the situation by despatching a letter to Eden 'full of friendly sentiments' and attributing their differences to Eden's ill-health.[154] In addition Horace Wilson[155] informed Thomas on 17 November 1937:

> that P.M. was devoted to A.E. and regarded him as first man in his Cabinet and that there was no question of any personal hostility or jealousy; but at the same time P.M. did think his own policy of using every opportunity of getting together with the dictators was right and that he was determined to go on with it. P.M. genuinely thought A.E. was wrong and that 'he was saving A.E. from himself'.[156]

For his part Eden appeared unrepentant and in a letter to Chamberlain, composed immediately following their interview of 16 November 1937, he repeated his conviction that steps were necessary to moderate Press coverage of Halifax's visit and increase the tempo of the rearmament programme. He, therefore, included the text of a note which he proposed to pass to the Press and, on the subject of rearmament, concluded:

> Papers like that submitted by the Air Ministry recently are, therefore, of profound significance for they show that, despite comforting speeches, we are not in truth getting stronger *vis à vis* Germany at least. Therefore I feel personally that we should in present conditions buy material from everywhere we can get it, because it is the situation during the next eighteen months that may decide the future of Europe.[157]

The relationship was apparently soon restored, for upon Halifax's return to London he reported his impressions to Eden and Chamberlain on 22 November 1937 and Eden held a further interview with the Prime Minister the following day.[158] While disappointed at Hitler's reluctance to consider further negotiations towards the attainment of a general settlement of the European security problem, it was apparent that Eden was generally pleased with Halifax's handling of the sensitive questions of the future format of Central Europe and the possibility of the return of former German colonies. At the Cabinet meeting of 24 November 1937, the Foreign Secretary: 'expressed great satisfaction with the way the Lord President had dealt with each point in his conversations with the Chancellor.'[159] The tone of the Lord President of the Council's report was encouraging in that he considered that 'he had encountered friendliness and a desire for good relations', which led him to conclude: 'that the Germans had no policy of immediate adventure. They were too busy building up their country, which was still in a state of revolution.'[160]

Halifax was forced to concede, however, that while Hitler had assured him that he would not use force to press German claims in Central Europe, it was apparent that the colonial question was the only area upon which the Germans were prepared to open negotiations. In response to this statement Eden expressed his concern at what appeared to be an attempt to separate the colonial issue from that of a general settlement. The Foreign Secretary noted that the Germans:

> had suggested that their policy in Eastern Europe would not give rise to difficulties for other nations, but had given no indication of any *quid pro quo* for any colonial concession. Germany clearly did not wish to connect Central Europe with the Colonial question.

Eden was adamant that there was no possibility of the British

Government considering the colonial question except as part of a general agreement incorporating a settlement of German claims in Central Europe, agreement on an element of qualitative disarmament and Germany's return to the League of Nations. This stance was fully endorsed by Chamberlain who, while welcoming the establishment of direct discussions with the German leadership, agreed that the colonial issue could not be considered separately.[161]

It appeared that Hitler's reluctance to open negotiations on anything other than a colonial settlement had allowed Chamberlain and Eden to patch up their differences in that they were agreed that such negotiations without consideration of the questions of European security and disarmament were not acceptable. This unity was reflected in their discussions with Chautemps and Delbos on 29 and 30 November 1937 in London.[162] While warning the French that there would be little public support in Britain for a war to maintain Czechoslovakian sovereignty and urging the Czechoslovakian Government to defuse the situation by granting further autonomy to its German subjects, the British Ministers assured their French counterparts that Britain would not disinterest itself from events in Eastern Europe and would continue to press for a peaceful settlement of the German claims in that region. Furthermore Chamberlain informed Chautemps that Britain would accept nothing less than a general settlement of differences with Germany and would keep Paris fully informed of the outcome of any future British negotiations with Germany and Italy.[163] It would appear that Eden fully supported this stance and, indeed, Harvey noted on 5 December 1937:

> Events of last ten days — Halifax visit to Berlin and French visit here have much clarified position. Negative results of Halifax mission and fact that it demonstrated that no immediate deal for peace with Germany was possible has evidently impressed P.M. who now admits that no immediate action is possible, but that the colonies issue must next be carefully studied. The French visit left the best impression; the P.M. was very good in the conversations and removed all their suspicions. They saw P.M. and A.E. in close harmony, while they in turn created good impression on the P.M. by their common-sense attitude. Thus I think the P.M. and A.E. are now together again, the former having learnt much from his experience.[164]

This impression was reinforced two days later when Harvey recorded:

> A.E. had a very satisfactory talk with P.M. and they were in absolute agreement about Germany — viz no settlement except a general European settlement.[165]

At this same meeting Chamberlain once again raised the question of Sir R. Vansittart's removal from the post of Permanent Under-Secretary of State at the Foreign Office. Eden accepted his proposal that Vansittart be offered the position of Chief Diplomatic Adviser, on the understanding that his own nominee, Alex Cadogan, would succeed Vansittart as Permanent Under-Secretary. Furthermore it was clear that Vansittart's new post, while technically holding equal status to that of the Permanent Under-Secretary, would effectively restrict his role to that of a diplomatic adviser while the day-to-day running of the Foreign Office would be firmly in the hands of Cadogan.[166] To the surprise of many, Vansittart accepted the appointment which was formally announced on 31 December 1937. It was soon apparent that although Vansittart retained his position on the CID, all matters of policy were to be the direct responsibility of the new Permanent Under-Secretary.[167] It seemed, however, that Vansittart accepted much of this with good grace and, indeed, it would appear that he no longer wished to continue the fight against those who sought to oust him from the influential position of Permanent Under-Secretary. Eden's decision to support his removal appears to have been particularly significant for, as Vansittart later noted: 'Anthony and I were divided and I fully understood his desire for a change.'[168] Ian Colvin suggests, however, that he did not relinquish his position without a parting shot at Eden after Chamberlain had asked him to accept the new appointment: 'I have to go, Anthony. I don't like it. If I go, you won't last long.'[169]

Chamberlain's delight at the removal of Vansittart was expressed in a letter to his sister, Ida, on 12 December 1937:

> it is settled and Van has accepted my proposal. Indeed I did not give him any alternative.

> I think the change will make a great difference in the F.O. and that when Anthony can work out his ideas with a . . . man like Alec Cadogan he will be much steadier. Van had the effect of multiplying the extent of Anthony's natural vibrations and I am afraid his instincts were all against my policy.

> After all the months that S.B. wasted in futile attempts to push Van out of the F.O. it is amusing to record that I have done it in three days.

> I suspect that in Rome and Berlin the rejoicing will be loud and deep.[170]

There is no evidence, however, to suggest that the ousting of

Vansittart was forced upon Eden for, as he subsequently recorded of the incident:

> In the autumn of 1937, however, I felt that the time had come for a change which would strengthen my staff at the Foreign Office. Mr. Chamberlain . . . was insistent, but this of itself would not have been enough if I had not felt that there were other advantages.

> The appointment of Sir Robert Vansittart to this post [Chief Diplomatic Adviser] was well received when it was announced in the New Year 1938. I have no doubt that my team was fortified by the new arrangement.[171]

It would seem, therefore, that Eden welcomed Vansittart's removal and, indeed, had been working to engineer such an event since the early months of 1936 when he had appointed Cadogan as Deputy Under-Secretary. Eden was fully aware that Vansittart had played a major role in the Hoare—Laval episode and although they had been in broad agreement in their suspicion of German and Italian motives, Vansittart's pronounced Germanophobia was a constant source of embarrassment to the Foreign Secretary in the conduct of Anglo-German relations. There was little doubt that Eden considered the task of improving relations with Berlin would be considerably eased once Vansittart had been effectively eclipsed from the foreign policy-making process.[172]

If, however, Eden was confident that he had improved his 'team' at the Foreign Office, there were few indications that he or his advisers saw any solution to the problems generated by the apparent expansionist ambitions of Germany, Italy and Japan. Harold Nicolson[173] recorded that the Foreign Secretary told the Foreign Affairs Committee on 9 December 1937:

> that there is no imminent likelihood of war and a far better prospect of appeasement than ever before.

> As regards Germany . . . we must make every effort to come to an agreement, but that it must be a general agreement and not of 'sops'.[174]

In a memorandum for the CID dated 26 November 1937, in reply to a memorandum by the COS of 12 November 1937 pointing out the inability of Britain to fulfil adequately its global defensive commitments, Eden was far more candid.[175] While conceding that the state of the British rearmament programme denied any assumption 'that we and our potential allies and associates are necessarily in a position to prevent the attainment of the aims of Germany, Italy and Japan', the Foreign Secretary repeated his conviction that it would be:

> a mistake to try to detach any one member of the German–Italian–Japanese bloc by offers of support or acquiescence in the fulfilment of their aims. The aims of all three are in varying degrees inimical to British interests and a surrender to one might well be the signal for further concerted action on the part of all three powers.

Eden, therefore, concluded that until the rearmament programme was complete there was little that could be done to restrain the dictators:

> We may indeed have to acquiesce perforce in more than one *fait accompli.*

> . . . in present circumstances our best course is likely to be the unheroic policy of so called 'cunctation'.[176]

While it was apparent that Eden and the Service Ministries were in broad agreement on the need to accelerate the rearmament programme, the tenor of the Foreign Secretary's memorandum was not well received by the growing element which firmly believed Eden was refusing to pursue a *détente* with the dictator powers which would significantly ease the British defence burden. On 3 November 1937 Hankey had written to Vansittart emphasising the problems facing the Service Ministries:

> We have our danger in the West (Germany) and our danger in the Far East (Japan) and we simply cannot afford to be on bad terms with a nation which has a stranglehold on our shortest line of communication between the two possible theatres of war.[177]

Three weeks later, in a letter to his son, Hankey repeated his exasperation with Eden's reluctance to deal with Hitler and Mussolini following the Foreign Secretary's attempts to tone down the significance of Halifax's visit to Germany:

> Anthony is the real problem.

> He hates dictators so much that he seems to be unwilling to make a real effort.

> . . . at bottom he is vain and doesn't like anyone else to get any credit in Foreign Affairs.[178]

The extent of the dissatisfaction with Eden's stance was indicated at the Cabinet meeting of 22 December 1937 when Inskip, in presenting his interim report on future defence expenditure, concluded:

> That in the long run the provision of adequate defences within the means at our disposal will only be achieved when our long term foreign policy has succeeded in changing the present assumption as to our potential enemies.[179]

It was apparent that until this goal was achieved Inskip saw little alternative but to concentrate primarily on the expansion of British defensive capabilities and, therefore, to channel funds into the Royal Navy and the Royal Air Force. A plea by Eden that consideration be given to the provision of an Expeditionary Force which could assist in the defence of France and Belgium was rejected by the Cabinet.[180]

The fact that Eden's position within the Cabinet seemed to be increasingly linked with his relationship with Chamberlain was suggested by Harvey on 5 December 1937:

> The intrigues in the Cabinet — Simon, Hoare, Swinton — continue actively, however, but I fear them less or indeed not at all, so long as P.M. and A.E. see eye to eye. Halifax, though not an intriguer, is tiresome and a captious critic . . . .

> A.E. complains bitterly of defeatist attitude of all of his older colleagues, including Inskip, in matter of rearmament and attitude towards dictators generally. He says there is little doubt that his policy — now shared by P.M. — is that of a minority within the Cabinet. He wonders whether he could not serve his country better outside the Government. I told him I did not think it had come to this yet — so long as A.E. found himself in agreement on main lines with P.M., but if latter definitely joined dissentients, then he would have to reconsider his position seriously.[181]

Eden's doubts were probably based upon the conviction that the Prime Minister was unlikely to be content for long with a policy of 'cunctation'. In this context Eden had already agreed to Chamberlain's proposal that the possibility of restoring relations with Italy be once again examined.[182] In the latter half of December he admitted to Harvey that any such negotiations would inevitably centre on the sensitive question of Abyssinia, which had been exacerbated by Mussolini's announcement of the Italian intention to withdraw from the League of Nations.[183] The Foreign Secretary indicated, however, that he was prepared to appease Chamberlain by re-examining the Italian question. Harvey noted of his discussion with Eden of 23 December 1937:

He feels we may be in danger of cutting off our nose to spite our face by too negative an attitude.

> . . . he always felt he must be particularly careful to prevent his personal prejudices in regard to Musso from colouring his attitude too much. He said he regarded Musso as anti-Christ! I said I did too. He has now directed the Department to draw up a list of our *desiderata* which we would demand of Musso in return for *de jure* recognition, supposing it were decided to go ahead independently of the League of Nations. He would in any case act only in conjunction with the French.[184]

There was also a suggestion that Chamberlain had not relinquished all hope of engineering a settlement of differences with Germany. On 26 November 1937 he had written to his sister, Ida, describing the Halifax visit as:

> from my point of view a great success, because it achieved its object, that of creating an atmosphere in which it is possible to discuss with Germany the practical questions involved in a European settlement. Both Hitler and Goering said separately and emphatically, that they had no desire or intention of making war, and I think we may take that as correct, at any rate for the present. Of course they want to dominate Europe; they want as close a union with Austria as they can get without incorporating her in the Reich, and they want much the same things for the Sudetendeutsche as we did for the Uitlanders in the Transvaal.

> They want Togoland and Kameruns. I am not sure where they stand about S.W. Africa but they do not insist on Tanganyika, if they can be given some reasonably equivalent territory on the West Coast, possibly to be carved out of Belgian Congo and Angola. I think they would be prepared to come back to the League, if it were shorn of its compulsory powers, now clearly shown to be ineffective, and though Hitler was rather non-committal about disarmament, he did declare himself in favour of the abolition of bombing aeroplanes.

> Now here, it seems to me, is a fair basis of discussion though no doubt all these points bristle with difficulties.

> But I don't see why we shouldn't say to Germany 'Give us satisfactory assurances that you won't use force to deal with the Austrians and Czechoslovakians and we will give you similar assurances that we won't use force to prevent the changes you want, if you can get them by peaceful means'.[185]

310

It was apparent that the Prime Minister was particularly interested in the colonial issue as a possible lever which might be used early in the new year as an inducement to lure the Germans into a general discussion of differences.[186] Chamberlain had secured an agreement with the French at the Anglo-French negotiations of 29 and 30 November 1937 that the colonial issue be reconsidered.[187] In the first week of December he sought to translate this agreement into action by placing the matter before the Foreign Affairs Committee of the Cabinet.[188] Eden warned the Prime Minister that 'he did not at all like the idea of any swapping round of colonies' and emphasised that the colonial issue could not be separated from a general settlement.[189] Eden was confident, however, that the differences between Chamberlain and himself were not sufficient to warrant the postponement of an extended vacation that he intended to take in the West Indies over the Christmas period and into the New Year. The holiday was long overdue and it was evident that he would need to be fully rested in preparation for the further round of negotiations with Hitler and Mussolini that were likely to be launched upon his return.[190]

References

1   The Imperial Conference was held in London between 14 May and 15 June 1937. A full record of the Conference proceedings can be found under the classification 226/384 in vols FO 371/3201–2.
2   *CAB* 23/88, CC 24(37)5, 17 June 1937.
3   *Neville Chamberlain Papers*, NC/18/1/1008, letter to his sister Ida, 20 June 1937.
4   *Avon Papers*, FO 954/10A, GER/37/22, Eden to Henderson, 18 June 1937.
5   Eden had admitted to the Cabinet Committee on Foreign Policy on 18 March 1937 that the chances of a Five Power Agreement being achieved 'were very small indeed'. See *DBFP*, 2nd ser., vol. 18, no. 307 (C 2303/37/18).
6   For accounts of the *Deutschland* attack and the subsequent withdrawal of Germany from the Non-Intervention Committee see Edwards, pp. 58–9; and Gerhard L. Weinberg, *The Foreign Policy of Hitler's Germany, Vol. 2* (Chicago, 1980), pp. 99–100. For admiralty reports on the attack see *DBFP*, 2nd ser., vol. 18, no. 555, 30 May 1937.
7   *CAB* 23/88, CC 23(37)3, 2 June 1937.
8   Minute by Eden dated 4 June 1937 on a Minute by Mr O'Malley on Anglo-Italian relations of 2 June 1937. *DBFP*, 2nd ser., vol. 18, no. 566 (R 3795/1/22).
9   *DBFP*, 2nd ser., vol. 18, no. 623. Minute by Mr Strang for the visit of Baron Von Neurath to London (C 5200/3976/18), 17 June 1937.
10   Ibid.
11   A full record of the Imperial Conference of 1937 can be found under the classification 226/384 in vols FO 371/3201–2. Eden and Chamberlain's respective attitudes to Eastern Europe in this period are discussed by David Carlton, see Carlton, pp. 102–4.
12   This discussion held at the Foreign Office on 18 June 1937 is discussed by

Weinberg, vol. 2, pp. 102–4. A full record is contained in FO 371/20749 (C 5200/3976/18).

13   *DBFP*, 2nd ser., vol. 18, no. 561, Eden to Henderson, 2 June 1937.

14   For details of the German delaying tactics in June 1937, see *DBFP*, 2nd ser., vol. 18, nos 563, 582, 583, 584, 585 and 596.

15   *DBFP*, 2nd ser., vol. 18, no. 600 (no. 104 [C 4196/3976/18]), Eden to Sir N. Henderson, 11 June 1937.

16   See *DBFP*, 2nd ser., vol. 18, nos 603, 630 and 635.

17   The *Leipzig* incident was discussed by the Cabinet on 21 June 1937 at which it was agreed that Eden's recommendation, that Germany be informed that Britain would not take naval action against Republican forces without a prior full investigation, be accepted. See *CAB* 23/88, CC 25(37)2. This decision was communicated to Von Ribbentrop the same day. *DBFP*, 2nd ser., vol. 18, no. 638 (W 12212/7/41). Subsequent Admiralty reports reinforced the suspicion that an attack had not been made on the *Leipzig*. See *DBFP*, 2nd ser., vol. 18, nos 651 and 652. See also Edwards, pp. 151–2 and Weinberg, pp. 100–1.

18   *DBFP*, 2nd ser., vol. 18, no. 669 (no. 882 [W 12642/7/41]), Eden to Sir Nevile Henderson, 30 June 1937.

19   *DBFP*, 2nd ser., vol. 18, no. 631 (no. 111 [C 4458/3976/18]), Eden to Sir N. Henderson, 20 June 1937.

20   *Neville Chamberlain Papers*, NC 18/1, letter to his sister Ida, 4 July 1937.

21   *H of C*, Debs, 5's, vol. 325, cols 1546–9, 25 June 1937.

22   See particularly Henderson's despatch to Eden of 15 July 1937 in which he referred to the exploitation of Chamberlain's speech by 'certain circles' in Germany in order 'to set up the Prime Minister as against yourself'. *Avon Papers*, FO 954/10A, Ger 37/29, Henderson to Eden, Berlin, 15 July 1937.

23   *Avon Papers*, FO 954/10A, Ger 37/30, Eden to Henderson, 16 July 1937.

24   For a record of these meetings conducted at the Foreign Office on 19, 21 and 22 June 1937, see *DBFP*, 2nd ser., vol. 18, nos 628, 636, 638 and 641.

25   *Avon Papers*, FO 954/10A, Ger 37/23, Geoffrey Dawson to Eden, 20 June 1937.

26   This despatch was in response to Henderson's despatch of 8 June 1937, outlining the value of putting the British viewpoint to General Goering in direct negotiations in Berlin. *DBFP*, 2nd ser., vol. 18, no. 593 (no. 551 [C 4185/270/18]).

27   *CAB* 23/88, CC 29(37)3, 7 July 1937.

28   Ibid.

29   Drummond's despatch from Rome of 11 June 1937. *DBFP*, 2nd ser., vol. 18, no. 601 (no. 125 [R 4124/1/22]). See also Drummond's reports of 23 March 1937 and 4 May 1937, *DBFP*, 2nd ser., vol. 18, nos 338 and 463.

30   This memorandum was drafted by Mr O'Malley in response to CID Paper 447C of 4 May 1937 on the defence of Cyprus (R 3215/78/19) which indicated the need to reassess existing assumptions relating to the probability of a war with Italy. Eden had suggested that such a reassessment was necessary as early as 19 April 1937 at the first meeting of the Defence Plans (Policy) Subcommittee of the CID. See *DBFP*, 2nd ser., vol. 18, no. 615 (R 3831/1/22), 15 June 1937 and Roskill, pp. 286–9.

31   *DBFP*, 2nd ser., vol. 18, no. 615. The existing stance on defence in the Mediterranean and the Red Sea had been determined at the 288th Meeting of the CID on 11 February 1937 and had been approved as CID Paper no. 441C by the Cabinet on 24 February 1937. *CAB* 23/86, CC 9(37)4.

32   At the meeting of 14 July 1937 the Cabinet accepted the recommendation that, while the previous decision not to incur expenditure in preparation for an

attack by Italy was to be rescinded, no large expenditure was to be authorised and priority to defence against a German assault was to be maintained. *CAB* 23/89, CC 30(37)5, 14 July 1937. See also Roskill, pp. 266–7.

33 On 4 May 1937 Drummond had warned Eden that Ciano saw the Abyssinian issue as the central point in determining future Italian contacts with the League of Nations and the significance to be assigned to the Rome–Berlin axis. *DBFP*, 2nd ser., vol. 18, no. 463 (no. 364 [R 3123/138/22]), 4 May 1937.

34 *DBFP*, 2nd ser., vol. 18 (no. 658 [R 4488/1/22]), letter from Sir E. Drummond to Sir R. Vansittart, Rome, 25 June 1937.

35 *Avon Papers*, FO 954/13A, It/37/7, see enclosed report by Sir E. Drummond dated 2 July 1937.

36 *DBFP*, 2nd ser., vol. 18, no. 610 (no. 589 [R 4147/1/22]), FO, 14 June 1937.

37 For the full text of this speech see Eden, *Foreign Affairs*, pp. 199–214.

38 See Drummond's report of 20 June 1937, *DBFP*, 2nd ser., vol. 18, no. 629 (no. 352 [R 4261/1/22]).

39 It was apparent that only opposition from the Polish and Mexican delegates on the Committee on Credentials, established by the League of Nations on 26 May 1937, had prevented the status of Abyssinia being discussed at the special session of the Assembly convened on the last week of May. On 2 June 1937 Eden admitted to the Cabinet his regret that the issue had not been discussed, for it was apparent that both Eden and Chamberlain were increasingly of the opinion that recognition of the Italian position could not be denied indefinitely, although the Foreign Secretary insisted that any final decision would have to be part of wider discussions on the future of the League of Nations and European security. See *CAB* 23/88, CC 23(37)2 and *DBFP*, 2nd ser., vol. 18, no. 542. Further information is also provided by David Carlton, *Anthony Eden* (London, 1981), pp. 110–11 and Feiling, pp. 330–1.

40 Avon, pp. 448–58.

41 Letter from Sir R. Vansittart to Sir E. Drummond (R 3795/1/22), 14 June 1937. See *DBFP*, 2nd ser., vol. 18, no. 601, note 2.

42 The possibility of lifting the arms embargo on Spain was discussed by Eden and the French Ambassador on 30 June 1937. Corbin expressed his exasperation at the absence of Italian co-operation in the enforcement of non-intervention and pointed out that the granting of belligerent rights to both parties in Spain 'would be easily defensible', *DBFP*, 2nd ser., vol. 18, no. 668. See also Edwards, pp. 155–6.

43 At the Cabinet meeting of 14 July 1937 Eden had unsuccessfully urged that a show of British military strength in the Mediterranean was the surest way to moderate Italian behaviour and demands. *CAB* 23/89, CC 30(37)6. See also a letter from Oliver Harvey to Eden dated 25 July 1937, urging Eden to avoid a military agreement with an Italian regime which was 'militarist and expansionist' and led by a 'gangster'. Harvey concluded that Mussolini must be 'kept in play, for time is on the side of the democracies', Harvey, pp. 411–15.

44 At this meeting it was agreed that an interview with Chamberlain be arranged for Grandi so that the Ambassador could pass on a personal message from Mussolini expressing his desire for an improvement of Anglo-Italian relations. Eden apparently saw no dangers in such an interview. Avon, p. 450.

45 Avon, p. 451.

46 *H of C*, Debs, 5's, vol. 315, cols 1122–3, 19 July 1937.

47 *Avon Papers*, FO 954/13A, It/37/14, letter from Eden to Chamberlain containing Vansittart's brief dated 24 July 1937.

48 For example see Feiling, pp. 329–31.

49   Avon, p. 452.

50   See *Avon Papers*, FO 954/13A, It/37/11, letter from Eden to Chamberlain, 16 July 1937.

51   *Neville Chamberlain Papers*, NC 18/1, letter to his sister Hilda, 1 August 1937.

52   In a diary entry for 19 February 1938 Chamberlain subsequently admitted 'I did not show my letter to the Foreign Secretary for I had the feeling that he would object to it'. *Neville Chamberlain Papers*, NC 2/23A, diary entry for 19 February 1938.

53   Ibid. In the same entry Chamberlain referred to his disappointment of the cancellation of the Von Neurath visit as one of the factors in influencing his decision to approach Mussolini directly.

54   The review of Imperial Defence conducted by the Chiefs-of-Staff Sub-committee of the CID on 22 February 1937 had emphasised the need to prepare for a possible future conflict with either Germany or Japan, while stressing the need to restore relations with Italy. In particular the committee stressed the need to strengthen the Far-Eastern Fleet and the Singapore base in preference to committing resources to the Mediterranean. *DBFP*, 2nd ser., vol. 18, appendix 1.

55   *CAB* 23/89, CC 30(37)5 and 6, 14 July 1937. It was apparent that Eden was opposed by Inskip, Swinton and Hoare on the subject of reinforcing the Mediterranean, while Chamberlain was reluctant to divert resources away from measures to counter a possible German assault.

56   For the text of the memorandum submitted by Hankey to Eden on Anglo-Italian relations, see *Avon Papers*, FO 954/13A, It/37/12, Hankey to Eden, 23 July 1937.

57   This statement was apparently contained in a covering letter to Chamberlain accompanying the memorandum on Anglo-Italian relations. See Roskill, p. 267.

58   Chamberlain, however, was far more interested in Mussolini's proposal that it might be possible to open negotiations in August with the object of improving Anglo-Italian relations. Avon, p. 454.

59   *Avon Papers*, FO 954/13A, It/37/23, Chamberlain to Halifax, 7 August 1937.

60   *Neville Chamberlain Papers*, NC 18/1, letter to his sister Ida, 8 August 1937.

61   Indeed at the Cabinet meeting of 28 July 1937 Chamberlain had specifically reminded his colleagues of:

> the exceptional pressure of work to which the Foreign Secretary had been subjected more or less continuously for a long time. He paid a tribute to the skill, patience and ability with which he had dealt with the situation and expressed the hope that he would be able to take some holiday.

This tribute was unanimously approved by the Cabinet, *CAB* 23/89, CC 32(37)6, 28 July 1937.

62   Letter from Oliver Harvey to Eden dated 25 July 1937, Harvey, pp. 411–15.

63   For an account of this meeting see Avon, pp. 450–1 and for Oliver Harvey's comments on the meeting in a letter to Eden dated 25 July 1937, see Harvey, pp. 411–15.

64   See *Avon Papers*, FO 954/13A, It/37/11, Eden to Chamberlain, 16 July 1937.

65   *Avon Papers*, FO 954/13A, It/37/16, Sir Ronald Graham to Eden, 31 July 1937.

66   *Avon Papers*, FO 954/13A, It/37/17, Sir R. Vansittart to Lord Halifax, 3 August 1937.

67   For details of this exchange of letters see *Avon Papers*, FO 954/13A, It/37/20 and Avon, pp. 454—5.
68   This meeting of senior Foreign Office advisers was called by Halifax to establish the possible bases for negotiations with Italy which Halifax wished to initiate in the latter half of August or the beginning of September. See *Avon Papers*, FO 954/13A, It/37/19, Halifax to Chamberlain, 4 August 1937 and It/37/24, Halifax to Chamberlain, 11 August 1937.
69   *Avon Papers*, FO 954/13A, It/37/27, Eden to Halifax, 11 August 1937. See also Avon, p. 456.
70   Eden emphasised that he was opposed to rushing into conversations or even giving any impression that Britain was ready to open negotiations. *Avon Papers*, FO 954/13A, It/37/30, Eden to Halifax, 13 August 1937.
71   In a letter to Eden dated 12 August 1937, Halifax had stressed the need to bow to the Italian desire for a formal recognition of its position in Abyssinia in order to improve relations. *Avon Papers*, FO 954/13A, It/37/29, Halifax to Eden, 12 August 1937.
72   *Avon Papers*, FO 954/13A, It/37/31, Halifax to Vansittart, 15 August 1937.
73   *Avon Papers*, FO 954/13A, It/37/34, Halifax to Chamberlain, 19 August 1937. Eden later noted of his conversation with Halifax concerning the possible recognition of Italian sovereignty over Abyssinia:

> I told him we would soon find that our relations with Mussolini were as bad as ever, if we gave him what he most wanted without settling the dominant question of Fascist intervention in Spain.

See Avon, p. 457.
74   *Neville Chamberlain Papers*, NC 18/1, letter to his sister, Hilda, 29 August 1937.
75   *CAB* 23/89, CC 34(37)8, 8 September 1937.
76   A meeting of Ministers held on 17 August 1937 had considered information provided by the Admiralty indicating that Italian aeroplanes and submarines were responsible for recent assaults on British merchantmen trading with the Republican Government. As a private warning by Sir R. Vansittart to the Italian Chargé d'Affaires had not led to the cessation of attacks, it was decided to issue a public warning of the intention to retaliate against submarines attacking merchantmen, Avon, p. 457. The warning, however, had little effect and at the turn of the month there were further attacks on British merchantmen and Royal Navy vessels. See Edwards, pp. 117—22.
77   *Neville Chamberlain Papers*, NC 18/1/1020, letter to his sister Hilda, 12 September 1937.
78   Between August 1936 and September 1937 seven ships of the Royal Navy had suffered attack while on the Spanish patrol. Edwards, p. 118. The incidence of attacks by submarines in the last 3 weeks of August on merchantmen, however, increased dramatically with 26 recorded assaults which resulted in the sinking of 7 British ships. Peter Gretton, 'The Nyon Conference — the Naval Aspect', *English Historical Review*, 90, 354, January 1975, p. 105.
79   Avon, p. 457.
80   Ibid., p. 457.
81   The reluctance of the Admiralty to take any action which might involve the Royal Navy in a clash with the Italian Navy is discussed by Edwards, pp. 112—27. In addition see Lawrence R. Pratt, *East of Malta, West of Suez, Britain's Mediterranean Crisis, 1936—1939* (London, 1975), pp. 87—93.
82   Quoted in Avon, p. 457. Mussolini's speech was made on 23 August 1937.
83   Avon, pp. 459—60.

84 In the last week of August Eden urged the Admiralty to consider the possibility of direct retaliation against the Nationalist navy by sinking its biggest ship, the cruiser *Canaris*. Not surprisingly the Sea Lords rejected this proposal. Pratt, pp. 88–9; and Edwards, p. 120.

85 Avon, pp. 460–1.

86 Ibid., pp. 461–3.

87 Eden gave a full report of his discussions with the French Foreign Minister, Delbos, and his consultations with the Admiralty to the Cabinet on 8 September 1937. *CAB* 23/89, CC 34(37)3 and Appendices 2 and 3.

88 *CAB* 23/89, CC 34(37)3, 8 September 1937.

89 The Nyon Conference opened on 10 September 1937 and agreement was reached on the evening of 11 September 1937 amongst the delegates of the nine attending nations. A full account is given in Avon, pp. 465–8. See also Pratt, pp. 89–92; and Edwards, pp. 123–7.

90 *Avon Papers*, FO 954/2, Con/37/6, Eden to Chamberlain, 14 September 1937.

91 Avon, p. 468.

92 *CAB* 23/89, CC 35(37)2, 29 September 1937.

93 Quoted from Winston S. Churchill, *The Second World War, Vol. 1, The Gathering Storm* (Penguin, 1960), p. 223.

94 See Eden's statement to the Cabinet of 29 September 1937, *CAB* 23/89, CC 35(37)2. In addition it was apparent that Eden had decided that a victory by the Nationalists was not in Britain's interests and would only lead to the establishment of a 'third Dictator State'. *CAB* 23/89, CC 35(37)3.

95 *Avon Papers*, FO 954/2, Con/37/6, Eden to Chamberlain, 14 September 1937.

96 Avon, pp. 470–1 and Edwards, p. 125. In his diary for August and September 1937 the Italian Foreign Minister, Count Ciano, admits that Italian submarines had been assisting the Nationalist Navy and also outlines Mussolini's annoyance at the display of Anglo-French solidarity resulting from Nyon. As a result Mussolini agreed on 21 September 1937 to change from 'pirates to policemen of the Mediterranean'. *Ciano's Diary 1937–38* (translated by Andreas Mayor) (London, 1952); see entries for 28 August, 31 August, 2 September, 11 September, 18 September and 21 September 1937.

97 This approach to Rome was agreed by the Cabinet on 29 September 1937, *CAB* 23/89, CC 35(37)3.

98 Avon, p. 474.

99 See *Ciano Diary*, 4 and 9 October 1937, pp. 17–19.

100 The failure of the initiative was noted by the Cabinet on 13 October 1937, *CAB* 23/89, CC 37(37)1.

101 Count Grandi, the Italian Ambassador to London, and Woermann, Counsellor at the German Embassy. Their manoeuvrings at the Non-Intervention Committee in October 1937 are described in John Harvey (ed.), *The Diplomatic Diaries of Oliver Harvey 1937–1940* (London, 1970), diary entries for 20 and 24 October 1937, pp. 52–3.

102 *CAB* 23/90, CC 40(37)6, 3 November 1937. This decision was a result of Inskip's report of 20 October 1937 indicating the build-up of Italian troops in Libya, *CAB* 23/89, CC 38(37)6.

103 The problem of restraining the French from an attempt to pillory Italy was indicated by Eden's discussion with Corbin, the French Ambassador, on 12 October 1937, *CAB* 23/89, CC 37(37), Appendix.

104 Eden made a full report to the Cabinet on the Anglo-French discussions on 1 December 1937, *CAB* 23/90, CC 45(37)5.

105 *Neville Chamberlain Papers*, NC 18/1, letter to his sister Hilda, 5 December 1937.
106 Following the Nyon Conference, Chamberlain had warned the Cabinet of the danger of a firm Anglo-French front alienating Italy from future co-operation in the Mediterranean, *CAB* 23/89, CC 35(37)3, 29 September 1937.
107 *Neville Chamberlain Papers*, NC 18/1, letter to his sister Ida, 19 September 1937.
108 *Neville Chamberlain Papers*, NC 18/1, letter to his sister Ida, 26 September 1937.
109 This incident is alluded to in Avon, pp. 471–2 and Oliver Harvey, diary entry for 22 September 1937, Harvey, pp. 47–8.
110 Extracts from Eden's speech of 15 October 1937 are given in *DIA 1937*, pp. 49–51.
111 Extracts from Mussolini's speech of 28 October 1937 are given in *DIA 1937*, pp. 289–90.
112 *H of C*, Debs, 5's, vol. 328, cols 578–96, 1 November 1937.
113 *Neville Chamberlain Papers*, NC 18/1/1027, letter to his sister Hilda, 6 November 1937.
114 Oliver Harvey was appointed as Principal Private Secretary to Eden in January 1936. His previous post had been as First Secretary to the Paris Embassy 1931–1936. See Oliver Harvey, diary entry for 22 September 1937, Harvey, pp. 47–8.
115 Ibid., Oliver Harvey, diary entry for 8 November 1937, p. 58.
116 Ibid., Oliver Harvey, diary entry for 15 October 1937, pp. 50–1.
117 Ibid., Oliver Harvey, diary entry for 3 November 1937, pp. 55–6.
118 Harvey noted on 15 October 1937 that Hoare had landed 'his party on the rocks in six months and had never forgiven A.E. for succeeding him'. On 17 November 1937 he noted that he had heard that Hoare was 'prepared to take F.O. again!'. Oliver Harvey, diary entries for 15 October and 17 November 1937, Harvey, pp. 50–1 and p. 61.
119 On 27 October 1937 the Minister for Co-ordination of Defence, Inskip, had warned the Cabinet that it would be difficult to raise the money necessary to finance the proposed rearmament programme, *CAB* 23/90, CC 39(37)29. This was followed by a further report on 24 November 1937 advocating the need to restore relations with Italy in the Mediterranean, *CAB* 23/90, CC 43/37)7.
120 Quoted in Avon, p. 471.
121 *CAB* 23/90, CC 43(37)7, 24 November 1937.
122 This report was submitted to the Cabinet on 8 December 1937, *CAB* 23/90, CC 46(37)10.
123 Ibid.
124 On 8 September 1937 Chamberlain had urged the Foreign Secretary in Cabinet to do everything that he 'possibly could to recover the better atmosphere of the early summer'. Eden had indicated his scepticism of Italian intent and described Italy as 'unstable and untrustworthy', *CAB* 23/89, CC 34(37)8.
125 *CAB* 23/89, CC 35(37)3, 29 September 1937.
126 *CAB* 23/89, CC 35(37)1, 29 September 1937.
127 The need for a colonial empire in order to provide Germany with access to raw materials and the determination to renounce the Versailles Treaty whereby Germany had lost territory to its East-European neighbours was a central factor in Hitler's speeches throughout 1937. For example see his speeches of 7 September 1937 and 21 November 1937. *DIA 1937*, pp. 231–2.
128 Eden heard on 22 June 1937 that Von Neurath's proposed visit to London

had been cancelled by Hitler following the attack on the *Deutschland. Avon Papers*, FO 954/10A, Ger/37/24, Henderson to Eden, 22 June 1937.

129 Joachim Von Ribbentrop succeeded Von Hoesch as German Ambassador to London on 11 August 1936. Eden was not pleased with the appointment, Avon, p. 370; and Von Ribbentrop subsequently admitted that he and Eden 'once or twice . . . had rather rough passages because I had instructions to take Hitler's uncompromising line', Joachim Von Ribbentrop, *The Ribbentrop Memoirs* (London, 1953), pp. 56—7.

130 On 7 November 1937 Harvey noted that Eden was against any further initiative to Italy but favoured an immediate approach to Germany for a 'bi-lateral declaration of policy'. Oliver Harvey, diary entry for 7 November 1937, Harvey, p. 57.

131 The invitation is discussed in Earl of Halifax, *Fulness of Days* (London, 1957), pp. 183—4 and Neville Henderson, *Failure of a Mission* (London, 1941), p. 97.

132 Avon, p. 508.

133 Ibid., p. 509.

134 Halifax, p. 184.

135 Avon, pp. 508—9.

136 Winston S. Churchill, *The Second World War, Volume 1: The Gathering Storm* (Penguin, 1960), pp. 226—7.

137 Henderson, p. 97.

138 *Neville Chamberlain Papers*, NC 18/1, letter to his sister Hilda, 24 October 1937. This account is confirmed by a letter from Halifax to Eden dated 27 October 1937. *Avon Papers*, FO 954/10A, Ger/37/37.

139 Avon, p. 509.

140 The Brussels Conference on the Far East was convened in November 1937 as a result of China's appeal to the League of Nations. The Conference was called to consider the problem of Sino-Japanese conciliation and was attended by the signatories of the Nine Power Pact of 1922. Eden had informed the Cabinet on 27 October 1937 that Von Neurath would travel to Brussels to attend the Conference, *CAB* 23/90, CC 39(37)4.

141 Quoted in Avon, p. 509.

142 *H of C*, Debs, 5's, vol. 328, cols 578—96, 1 November 1937.

143 Quoted in Avon, p. 508.

144 The Tripartite Pact between Germany, Japan and Italy was signed in Rome on 6 November 1937. It further cemented the Anti-Comintern Pact of 26 November 1936 and Ciano saw it as the establishment of 'the most formidable political and military combination which has ever existed'. Ciano, diary entry for 6 November 1937, Mayor, p. 29.

145 Quoted in Avon, p. 510.

146 In making this point, Eden telephoned Lord Cranborne and instructed him to oppose Halifax having to request an interview with Hitler. Vansittart supported the Foreign Secretary but on 11 November 1937 Chamberlain told Cranborne that he considered the attainment of an interview with Hitler as of the utmost importance. See Avon, pp. 510—11 and *Avon Papers*, FO 954/10A, Ger/37/42 and Ger/37/46.

147 Avon, pp. 510—11 and Oliver Harvey, diary entry for 11 November 1937, Harvey, p. 59.

148 Avon, p. 511.

149 Avon, pp. 510—11. Cranborne urged Eden to return to London on 11 November 1937 as soon as possible. *Avon Papers*, FO 954/10A, Ger/37/45.

150 Avon, p. 511. Oliver Harvey, diary entries for 14 and 16 November 1937, Harvey, pp. 60—1.
151 Oliver Harvey, diary entry for 16 November 1937, Harvey, pp. 60—1.
152 Ibid., pp. 60—1. This account is confirmed by Eden, Avon, pp. 511—12. The reference to the aspirin was probably prompted by the fact that Eden had recently suffered an attack of influenza and Chamberlain was suggesting that he still was not thinking straight, Avon, p. 511.
153 Oliver Harvey, diary entry for 17 November 1937, Harvey, p. 61.
154 Ibid., Oliver Harvey, diary entry for 16 November 1937, pp. 60—1.
155 Sir Horace Wilson, Chief Industrial Adviser to HM Government, 1930—39, seconded to the Treasury for service with the Prime Minister 1935. J.P.L. Thomas succeeded Roger Lumley as PPS to Anthony Eden.
156 Oliver Harvey, diary entry for 17 November 1937, Harvey, p. 61. See also Avon, p. 513.
157 See *Avon Papers*, FO 954/10A, Ger/37/51, Eden to Chamberlain, 16 November 1937.
158 See Avon, p. 513 and Oliver Harvey, diary entry for 22 and 23 November 1937, Harvey, pp. 61—2.
159 *CAB* 23/90, CC 43(37)3, 24 November 1937.
160 Ibid. For further accounts of Halifax's discussions with Hitler see Halifax, pp. 184—91 and Dr P. Schmidt, *Hitler's Interpreter* (London, 1950), pp. 75—8.
161 *CAB* 23/90, CC 43(37)3, 24 November 1937.
162 A full report of these discussions was given to the Cabinet by Eden on 1 December 1937, *CAB* 23/90, CC 45(37)5. See also Avon, pp. 516—17 and *Neville Chamberlain Papers*, NC 18/1, letter to his sister Hilda, 5 December 1937.
163 *CAB* 23/90, CC 45(37)5, 1 December 1937.
164 Oliver Harvey, diary entry for 5 December 1937, Harvey, pp. 62—3.
165 Ibid., Oliver Harvey, diary entry for 7 December 1937, pp. 63—4; and Avon, p. 52.
166 Ibid.
167 Ibid., Oliver Harvey, diary entry for 18 December 1937, pp. 64—5. This interpretation of the new relationship between Cadogan and Vansittart was confirmed by Cadogan. D. Dilks (ed.), *The Diaries of Sir Alexander Cadogan* (London, 1971), Cadogan diary entry for 2 January 1938, Dilks, pp. 31—2.
168 Vansittart, p. 549.
169 Ian Colvin, *Vansittart in Office* (London, 1965), p. 172.
170 *Neville Chamberlain Papers*, NC 18/1, letter to his sister Ida, 12 December 1937.
171 Avon, p. 521.
172 Ibid., p. 521. In April 1937 Vansittart had labelled German objectives as 'unreasonable and illegitimate' and on 19 November 1937 likened German policy to conviction that 'might is right'. He remained unconvinced that an agreement could be reached until Britain possessed superior military forces. *Vansittart Papers*, 2/34.
173 Harold Nicolson, National Labour Member for West Leicester 1935—45, Vice-Chairman of the Foreign Affairs Committee of the House of Commons.
174 Nigel Nicolson (ed.), *Harold Nicolson, Diaries and Letters 1930—39* (London, 1966), diary entry for 9 December 1937, pp. 314—15.
175 CID Paper no. 1366B of 12 November 1937 which was presented to Cabinet along with CP 296(37) on 8 December 1937, *CAB* 23/90, CC 43(37)10.
176 This memorandum, dated 26 November 1937, was presented to a meeting of the CID on 2 December 1937. It is referred to in Roskill, vol. 3, p. 295; and Carlton, pp. 115—16.

177 Quoted in Roskill, vol. 3, pp. 270—1.

178 Ibid., p. 265.

179 *CAB* 23/90, CC 48(37)9, 22 December 1937.

180 Ibid. The Secretary of State for War endorsed this position in that he argued that the Maginot Line would prevent a German invasion and therefore negated the need for an Expeditionary Force to be despatched to France immediately on the outbreak of hostilities, *CAB* 23/90, CC 49(37)1, 22 December 1937. See also Avon, pp. 497—501.

181 Oliver Harvey, diary entry for 5 December 1937. Harvey, pp. 62—3.

182 *Neville Chamberlain Papers*, NC 18/1, letter to his sister Ida, 12 December 1937. In a Foreign Office Minute dated 7 December 1937, Eden outlined his wish to explore the possibility of improving Anglo-Italian relations, Avon, p. 475. A meeting to discuss the situation was held on 31 December 1937 attended by Eden, Cadogan, Sargent and Harvey. Oliver Harvey, diary entry for 1—13 January 1938, Harvey, pp. 66—8.

183 For the text of Mussolini's speech of 11 December 1937 see *DIA 1937*, pp. 290—1.

184 Oliver Harvey, diary entry for 19—23 December 1937, Harvey, pp. 65—6.

185 *Neville Chamberlain Papers*, NC 18/1, letter to his sister Ida, 26 November 1937.

186 The Prime Minister insisted before the Cabinet on 22 December 1937 that colonial concessions would have to be accompanied by some equivalent concession by the German Government, *CAB* 23/90, CC 49(37)1.

187 *CAB* 23/90, CC 45(37)5, 1 December 1937.

188 Ibid.

189 Oliver Harvey, diary entry for 7 December 1937, Harvey, pp. 63—4.

190 Oliver Harvey, diary entry for 5 December 1937, Harvey, pp. 62—3.

8 Resignation
January — February 1938

On 9 January 1938 Eden wrote to Chamberlain thanking him both for his assistance and advice and setting out his thoughts on the general tenor of the international situation:

> I do hope that you will never for an instant feel that any interest you take in Foreign Affairs, however close, could ever be resented by me. I know . . . that there will always be some who will seek to pretend that the Foreign Secretary has had his nose put out of joint, but that is of no account beside the very real gain of close collaboration between Foreign Secretary and Prime Minister which I am sure is the only way that Foreign Affairs can be run in our country.
>
> But this is going to be a very difficult year with the three anti-comintern powers doing their best to undermine our position and that of France and even U.S.A. None the less their tactics may have the effect of bringing U.S.A. closer to us and Tokyo and Rome may eventually succeed in embarrassing Berlin considerably. I am sure that Hitler and many other Germans are serious about the racial business. In this they differ from Musso. The more Tokyo preaches the anti-white crusade the less will an important part of Germany like to be associated with the Japs. This is a development we must watch closely for it may facilitate our negotiations with Berlin. It will have no effect in Rome.[1]

The Foreign Secretary's reference to the need to forge close links with the USA was particularly pertinent in that the improvement of Anglo-American relations was a goal that he had actively pursued throughout 1937. Although in November 1936 the United States Ambassador in Berlin, William Dodd, had assured his British counterpart, Sir E. Phipps, that President Roosevelt was considering the summoning of a world peace conference during the course of 1937,[2] the only positive expression of Roosevelt's intention to play a leading role in the cause of collective security was a speech delivered in Chicago, on 5 October 1937, in which the President had spoken of the need to 'quarantine' those members of the international community which threatened the maintenance of peace and stability.[3] The speech, however, was received with a great deal of scepticism in London, given continued reports of the strength and influence of the isolationist lobby in the USA.[4] This scepticism was apparently justified when in the following week Summer Welles, Under-Secretary of State, admitted to the British Chargé d'Affaires that the President had no intention of adopting any immediate measures to 'quarantine' the aggressor states.[5] On 9 October 1937 Neville Chamberlain, in a letter to his sister Hilda, noted of the incident that it:

> confirms my first impression that the President's pronouncement was intended to sound out the ground and see how far his public opinion was prepared to go but that he himself had thought nothing out and in any case had no present intention of doing anything that wasn't perfectly safe.[6]

While Eden shared Chamberlain's suspicion that Roosevelt's international initiatives were often ill-defined and generated very little domestic support, he continued to emphasise the importance of improving Anglo-American relations as a central strand in the containment of not only Japanese ambitions in the Far East but also German expansionism in Europe. In this context, while schemes encompassing the summoning of a world conference and a possible international freeze on armament expenditure seemed both naive and potentially counter-productive to British observers, Eden remained convinced of the sincerity of Roosevelt's motives and sought to harness American economic and military muscle to a more effective means of deterring aggression.[7] The belief that Roosevelt was anxious to improve Anglo-American relations was primarily fuelled by reports relayed to the Foreign Secretary through the medium of the United States Ambassador in London, Robert Bingham. Of a meeting between the two held on 20 March 1937, Eden recorded:

> The Ambassador said that it was quite true that President Roosevelt had been contemplating some initiative to attempt to

better the present international situation. He was, however, determined to take no initiative except in close consultation with us. What, therefore, the Ambassador wished me to know was that President Roosevelt was not only ready but eager to help, that he would be ready to take an initiative if and when we thought the moment right and that he would take none unless we were in accord as to its appropriateness. This message, the Ambassador said, he had been specifically instructed by the President to deliver personally to me.[8]

Although tentative negotiations during the first half of 1937 for an Anglo-American commercial agreement and the possible visit of either Eden or Chamberlain to Washington were not enthusiastically received by the Roosevelt administration, a further outbreak of Sino-Japanese hostilities in July 1937 appeared to have provided an area of mutual interest which could be used to foster Anglo-American collaboration.[9] On 20 July 1937 Eden proposed to Bingham that only a firm Anglo-American initiative could stem the expansion of Japanese influence in China. The Ambassador's response was encouraging in that he considered his government would be anxious to establish a solution to the Sino-Japanese conflict and recommended that Eden examine the possibility of an Anglo-American embargo on trade with Japan.[10] The response from Washington was, however, disappointing in that in the following months it became increasingly clear the State Department was firmly opposed to the imposition of any form of sanction against Japan, whether of an economic or military nature.[11] This position was underlined at the Nine Power Conference held in Brussels in November 1937 to consider the situation in the Far East.[12] In both informal conversations with Eden prior to the opening of the Conference and during the proceedings of the meeting, the United States representative, Norman Davis, emphasised that his Government had no intention of considering the imposition of any form of sanction against Japan if mediation in the dispute was not successful.[13]

Despite the failure of the Brussels Conference either to solve the Sino-Japanese dispute or to cement Anglo-American solidarity, Eden was not unduly pessimistic in that he appreciated economic sanctions against Japan were unlikely to succeed unless they were supported by evidence of Anglo-American military resolve to contain Japanese ambitions in the Far East. In this sense the Foreign Secretary's attention was turning increasingly to the task of persuading Roosevelt to participate in a demonstration of Anglo-American naval strength in the Far East, on a scale sufficient to deter Japanese aggression.[14] With the approval of the Cabinet the British Ambassador in Washington, Sir Ronald Lindsay, proposed to the State Department that Anglo-

American Naval Staff conversations be opened with a view to the establishment of a joint naval task-force to be despatched to the Far East.[15] Once again the response from Washington was disappointing. Welles indicated to the British Ambassador on 27 November 1937 that his Government was not prepared to engage in joint military manoeuvres in the Far East and added that he had been surprised by the British initiative, given that ten days previously the British Government had declared that it 'was not in a position to divert any considerable portion of its naval force from European waters'.[16]

The situation was, however, dramatically altered in the second week of December, following attacks on *HMS Ladybird* and *HMS Bee* and the sinking of the United States naval gunboat, *Panay*, by Japanese aircraft on 12 December 1937.[17] In a telegram to Lindsay dated 13 December 1937, Eden sought to exploit the indignation generated by the *Panay* incident:

> No doubt, the United States Government will be contemplating the presentation of a series of stiffly worded demands and if we could have information as to what they are we should be prepared to send similar intimation. More important is the question whether the United States Government will be taking simultaneous action of a more menacing character such as the mobilisation of their fleet, or a part of it, pending the receipt of the Japanese reply. If anything of the kind were contemplated we should wish to know as soon as possible, as in that case we should probably desire to take similar action, although of course our ships could not reach eastern waters as soon as United States ships.[18]

Although the State Department declined the British suggestion of a co-ordinated Anglo-American *démarche* to Tokyo,[19] Eden refused to let the matter drop and two days later instructed Lindsay to seek a personal interview with Roosevelt, at which he was to emphasise the gravity with which Britain viewed the situation and to urge the President to match the British offer of the despatch of eight or nine capital ships, or at least to place the fleet on a war footing.[20] The Foreign Secretary concluded:

> We are receiving evidence of a loss of prestige in the Far East affecting not only the U.K. but also all democracies and consequently HMG think that some action should be taken to restore the situation. We fully realise difficulties which U.S. Government experience with their public opinion but hope that they might be willing to consider mobilisation as a first step.[21]

The results of Lindsay's interview were well received by Eden for, while Roosevelt talked vaguely about an economic blockade of Japan in response to future acts of aggression, on a more positive note he accepted the principle of Anglo-American Naval Staff conversations to be held in London in the near future.[22] On 20 December 1937 Eden telegraphed Lindsay to urge the President to sanction the immediate opening of naval negotiations and was rewarded with the reply that Captain R.E. Ingersoll, the Head of the United States Navy Department's War Plans Division, was expected to arrive in London on 1 January 1938.[23]

The Foreign Secretary interpreted the decision to despatch Ingersoll to London as indicative of a major breakthrough in Anglo-American relations and immediately rescheduled his Christmas vacation so that he would be able to discuss the situation with Ingersoll. Oliver Harvey noted in his diary for the period 19–23 December 1937:

> A.E. began to doubt the wisdom of going so far away as Madeira in view of forthcoming negotiations with U.S. over joint action in Far East. I felt bound to agree with him that it was essential that he should be in London when U.S. naval representative arrived, i.e. just after Christmas. As he said this development of Anglo-American relations was the most important thing that had happened and what he had been working for for years.[24]

The results of Eden's interview with Ingersoll held on 1 January 1938 were, however, mixed in that Ingersoll's brief was strictly limited to an exchange of technical information on the dispositions of the two fleets. Harvey recorded of the interview:

> A.E. saw Ingersoll, the U.S. Naval representative sent over by Roosevelt on January 1st. He did not turn out to have any definite plans or proposals to submit for moving U.S. ships to the Far East, but he has authority to show us all their dispositions and to discuss plans, but the idea still seems to prevail in the U.S. that we must wait for the next incident before it will be possible to take any action, whereas we would like to take some joint action now by way of demonstration, which we believe would prevent any fresh incident.[25]

The Foreign Secretary was, therefore, disturbed at the absence of any immediate military response to the situation in the Far East and advocated, as a minimum response, the despatch of a token American force on a courtesy visit to the British base at Singapore.[26] This proposal was not taken up, however, until ten days later when, following a further series of assaults on British citizens in Shanghai by

Japanese soldiers, Roosevelt announced that three cruisers would visit Singapore while the American naval manoeuvres, scheduled to be held in March in the Pacific, were to be brought forward by a month.[27] Eden subsequently noted of these measures:

> All this, though not decisive, was helpful and encouraging to me in my pursuit of closer Anglo-American co-operation as the only effective deterrent to Japan in the Pacific. Japan's partners in Europe, Hitler and Mussolini might also note that the power of the democracies was being aligned.[28]

Eden finally departed for the South of France on 3 January 1938. The tranquillity of his vacation was interrupted, however, on 14 January 1938 by a telephone call from Sir Alex Cadogan requesting the Foreign Secretary to return to London immediately.[29] Having failed to receive a diplomatic pouch despatched to Marseilles, it was not until his arrival at Folkestone the following evening that Eden was informed by Cadogan and Harvey as to the reason for his recall.[30] It transpired that on 11 January 1938 Sir Ronald Lindsay had been given a personal message for the Prime Minister from President Roosevelt. The message outlined the President's intention to address the diplomatic corps in Washington on 22 January 1938, expressing his concern at the deterioration in the international situation and urging the need for an agreement on generally accepted principles of international conduct. If the speech was well received Roosevelt proposed to establish a small working-party, composed of a number of the less powerful nations, to draft a set of recommendations on security, disarmament and access to raw materials that might form the basis for a wider international agreement. The President stressed, however, that he would not proceed with the scheme unless assured of Chamberlain's whole-hearted support.[31]

As the deadline for the British reply was given as 17 January 1938, the scheme was first discussed by Sir Alex Cadogan and Sir Horace Wilson, Chief Industrial Adviser to the Government. The latter was entirely opposed to the scheme and advocated its rejection. Cadogan, however, although he had described Roosevelt's initiative as a set of 'wild ideas about formulating a world settlement', was alive to the danger of hastily rebuffing the President's proposals and, therefore, undermining Eden's recent attempts to cultivate closer Anglo-American relations. The Permanent Under-Secretary recommended Roosevelt be informed that the British Government would prefer the President to delay the launching of his scheme until the outcome of the forthcoming negotiations with Italy and Germany were clear. If, however, Roosevelt chose to proceed with his announcement, Cadogan urged that he be assured of full British support.[32] In stressing the need to avoid an outright rejection of the scheme, the Permanent Under-Secretary had undoubtedly been influenced by reports received from Lindsay underlining the importance assigned by the President to the success of his initiative. On 13 January 1938 Lindsay telegraphed:

> I have long held that the best chance of averting disaster is to range not only the United States administration, but also United States public opinion behind the objectives of the democratic governments. We definitely have no anxiety as to the Administration and this present scheme must have a profound effect on the public opinion.
>
> Destructive criticisms, reservations or attempts to define the issues more clearly can only accomplish very little in favour of anything you may wish to put forward while they will create a disproportionate bad impression in the thoughts of the Administration. I therefore urge respectfully but very earnestly that His Majesty's Government give their reply to this invaluable initiative with a very quick and cordial acceptance.[33]

When Chamberlain examined Cadogan's draft reply on the evening of 13 January 1938, he elected to ignore Lindsay's advice and deleted the section expressing full British support if Roosevelt chose to go ahead and launch his scheme. The eventual reply, therefore, urged the President to defer his initiative so as not to hinder the forthcoming negotiations with Italy and Germany:

> My fear is that, if the President's suggestions are put forward at the present time, Germany and Italy may feel constrained to take advantage of them, both to delay the consideration of specific points which must be settled if appeasement is to be achieved and to put forward demands over and above what they would put forward to us if we were in direct negotiation with them.[34]

In essence Chamberlain was determined to block Roosevelt's scheme. He admitted quite openly to Cadogan that he was averse to the President's proposals and referred to them in his diary as 'fantastic and likely to excite the derision of Germany and Italy'.[35]

It was not until the following day, however, that the Foreign Secretary, who knew nothing of these developments, was finally recalled from France. Eden subsequently noted of the incident:

> I was outraged and uneasy at the way in which this opportunity had been handled and agreed with Lindsay that, if we were not careful, we would lose all that we had gained in the last two years

in our relations with the United States, to which he and I had devoted so much effort.

I thought Lindsay's advice absolutely correct and regarded the Prime Minister's telegram as much too chilling and unjustifiably optimistic about the prospects of our own efforts. I also felt that I should have been summoned to London or consulted by telegraph before any reply was sent. Roosevelt had asked for an answer by 17th January. It was now only the 15th.[36]

In Chamberlain's defence it must be noted that his reluctance to recall Eden was conditioned by the importance that he attached to the Foreign Secretary's proposed meeting with the French Foreign Minister, Delbos, on 16 January 1937. The meeting was to be used to discuss the possible recognition of the Italian position in Abyssinia, which the Prime Minister identified as a cardinal factor in restoring relations with Italy.[37] Not surprisingly Chamberlain was reluctant to cancel this meeting but agreed immediately to Eden's recall when, following the fall of the French Government on 14 January 1938, it was apparent that the Anglo-French discussions would have to be postponed. In this sense the Foreign Secretary would have been consulted as to his opinion of Roosevelt's proposals before the final answer was drafted for despatch on 17 January 1938 and, indeed, full details of Chamberlain's initial response to the President's scheme were despatched by air to Eden on the morning of 14 January 1938.[38] Whilst it is possible to contend that the Prime Minister had not intended completely to by-pass his Foreign Secretary, it was apparent that he had every intention of discouraging the President's initiative.[39] Such a course of action ran directly against Eden's views on the necessity of encouraging Roosevelt to take a greater interest in the strengthening of collective security. Oliver Harvey, in his diary entry for 15 January 1938, recorded the Foreign Secretary's immediate reaction to the President's proposals:

> We discussed the proposals in the train and A.E. took the view we expected, viz. that we must accept. He regarded P.M.'s reply as much too chilling and would himself have accepted outright . . . .[40]

On arrival in London the suspicion that Chamberlain's message seriously risked offending Roosevelt was reinforced by a report from Lindsay:

> Under Secretary of State has telephoned to say that the President will send the Prime Minister a written reply on Monday. He will

indicate his willingness to postpone his scheme 'for a while' but Welles says he feels a little disappointed.[41]

Although Eden was due to meet with the Prime Minister the following day, the Foreign Secretary felt that the situation could only be retrieved by immediate action to reassure Roosevelt of British support and, therefore, despatched a reply to Washington on the evening of 15 January 1938:

> I am sure the Prime Minister will be very grateful for the President's message and for his willingness to postpone his scheme for a while. Mention of a written reply makes me fear that the President may be registering disappointment at finding what he considers to be a negative attitude on our part. That, I am convinced, was not the impression which it was intended to convey.
>
> The President will surely understand that we were in some difficulty owing to the very short time given to us for the consideration of his very far-reaching proposals, more particularly in view of the impossibility of consultation between the Prime Minister and myself.[42]

This message was drafted after discussion with Lord Cranborne, Parliamentary Under-Secretary of State for Foreign Affairs, and Sir Alex Cadogan. While the former supported Eden's action there were already signs that Cadogan, although sympathetic to the Foreign Secretary's position, feared that he was over-reacting to the situation. In a diary entry for 15 January 1938 Cadogan noted:

> A. read Washington telegrams. Thinks we have snubbed the President too much. But this I don't believe. He wants to let President go ahead and doesn't believe a bit in P.M.'s initiatives regarding Italy and Germany. I think he exaggerates as much one way as P.M. does on other![43]

It was hardly surprising, therefore, that Eden's interview with Chamberlain at Chequers the following day was far from cordial. The Foreign Secretary protested vigorously at the Prime Minister's decision to reply to Roosevelt without consulting him. He emphasised his conviction that although the American initiative was not certain to succeed, it would perform an invaluable role in involving the USA in the cause of collective security. Eden urged Chamberlain to despatch a further message to Washington endorsing the Foreign Secretary's telegram of the previous evening. For his part Chamberlain made it perfectly clear that he resented Eden's attempt to reverse his decision to discourage the American proposals and refused to support the

Foreign Secretary's action.[44] It was apparent that the Prime Minister had little faith in Roosevelt's determination to contribute positively to the problem of international security and suspected that the President's rhetoric was unlikely to be matched by deeds.[45] Undoubtedly the ambivalent stance adopted by the USA at the Brussels Conference and the subsequent admission that Roosevelt's quarantine speech was unlikely to be followed by measures to implement such a policy had only served to increase Chamberlain's scepticism as to the extent of the contribution that the Roosevelt Administration was able, or willing, to make to the containment of aggression. Following Roosevelt's speech the Prime Minister noted, in a letter to his sister Hilda on 9 October 1937:

> I read Roosevelt's speech with mixed feelings. What did it really mean? It sounded very fierce but when we examined it carefully it was contradictory in parts and very vague in essentials. What did he mean by 'putting them in quarantine'?

> Now in the present state of European affairs with the two dictators in a thoroughly nasty temper we simply cannot afford to quarrel with Japan and I very much fear therefore, that after a lot of ballyhoo the Americans will somehow fade out and leave us to carry all the blame and the odium.[46]

Chamberlain had, therefore, consistently refused during the latter half of 1937 to support Eden's schemes for the imposition of a joint Anglo-American economic sanction directed against Japan. The Americans were plainly unwilling to envisage the employment of military sanctions against Japan. The Prime Minister, therefore, argued that it was pointless to impose economic sanctions which would not force the Japanese to withdraw from China and, furthermore, would only exacerbate Anglo-Japanese relations at a time when Britain was in no position to shoulder the burden of a war in the Far East against Japan. On 6 October 1937 Chamberlain informed the Cabinet:

> He could not imagine anything more suicidal than to pick a quarrel with Japan at the present moment when the European situation had become so serious. If this country were to become involved in the Far East the temptation to the Dictator States to take action, whether in Eastern Europe or in Spain might be irresistible.

Seven days later this conviction was reaffirmed when he declared to the Cabinet that 'economic sanctions were of no use unless backed by overwhelming force'.[47] It was evident that the Prime Minister believed the strength of the isolationist lobby in the USA was still sufficient to prevent the Roosevelt administration from effectively committing the nation to a policy of collective security. This theme was repeated in a letter to an American relative dated 16 January 1938:

> I fully recognise that goodwill on the part of the U.S. Government is not wanting, the trouble is that public opinion in a good part of the States still believes it possible for America to stand outside Europe and watch it disintegrate, without being materially affected itself.[48]

In this respect the inclusion in Roosevelt's message of a clear statement that his Government had no intention of departing from its 'traditional policy of freedom from political involvement'[49] reinforced Chamberlain's conviction that there was little likelihood of the United States Government relinquishing its broad neutralist stance.

In order to resolve the *impasse* that had seemingly been reached, the Foreign Secretary and the Prime Minister agreed that the matter be referred to the Cabinet Committee on Foreign Policy.[50] Eden subsequently noted of the interview that 'for the first time our relations were seriously at odds'.[51] While there had been no suggestion by either party that the distance between the two men was sufficient to justify Eden's resignation, after the Foreign Secretary had discussed the matter with his Private Secretary on the evening of 16 January 1938 Harvey registered his concern at the gravity of the situation:

> I'm afraid the P.M. may have committed a colossal blunder which it is too late to retrieve. A.E. will have to consider his position very carefully, for he obviously cannot remain responsible for foreign policy if the P.M. persists in such a line.
>
> He cannot accept responsibility for a policy which will antagonise America. The P.M. is being advised in this folly by Horace Wilson who knows nothing about foreign affairs. He, the P.M., is temperamentally anti-American, but he is also, I'm afraid, moved by some vanity over his own ventures with Hitler and Mussolini. If Roosevelt's letter isn't too bad, we may still perhaps retrieve situation, but I'm very much afraid the first shock will have been too much for him.[52]

The following day Eden once again restated his position in a letter to Chamberlain:

> it is almost impossible to over-estimate the effect which an indication of United States interest in European affairs may be

calculated to produce. I know that you fear that the dictators would resent the tone of his communication and that there would be in consequence, a blast and counterblast between democracies and dictatorships. I do not myself think that this would be the result, though I agree that neither of the dictators would like Roosevelt's initiative; they would probably, however, be constrained to conceal their dislike and might even become more negotiable as a result of their knowledge of President Roosevelt's attitude.[53]

It appeared that Eden's position had been strengthened when Roosevelt's reply to the British despatches was received on 18 January 1938. The President agreed to delay launching his scheme but pointedly outlined the problems that he perceived in the opening of immediate Anglo-Italian negotiations. In particular he alluded to the danger of granting *de jure* recognition to the Italian position in Abyssinia at a time when Japan was seeking to consolidate its control over Chinese territory. In addition both the Secretary of State and the Under-Secretary of State emphasised to Lindsay their opposition to the premature recognition of Abyssinia. Summer Welles concluded:

> It would rouse a feeling of disgust; would revive and multiply all fear of pulling the chestnuts out of the fire; and it would be represented as a corrupt bargain completed in Europe at the expense of interests in the Far East in which the United States are intimately concerned.[54]

Armed with this information Eden once again tackled the Prime Minister. The Foreign Secretary argued that Roosevelt's response indicated quite clearly that Anglo-American collaboration was likely to be seriously impaired if the Anglo-Italian negotiations were given precedence over the President's proposals for international co-operation. When Chamberlain retorted that while he was willing to re-examine the question of *de jure* recognition of Abyssinia, he was not inclined to give further encouragement to Roosevelt's initiative or delay the opening of Anglo-Italian relations, it appeared that a deadlock had been reached. Eden subsequently noted of the interview:

> After two hours' wrangling, Chamberlain admitted that there was a deep difference between us. I began to think that we would not be able to work together much longer.

> I determined that if the Cabinet Committee would not support Roosevelt's scheme, I must resign.[55]

This account is supported by an entry in Oliver Harvey's diary for

18 January 1938 which recorded that Eden told his Private Secretary the interview 'had gone very badly' and that Chamberlain had 'admitted that there was a fundamental difference between him and A.E. and left the impression that one or other must go'.[56]

The situation was not resolved until after three meetings of the Cabinet Committee on Foreign Policy held during the period 19–21 January 1938.[57] At the initial meeting Eden maintained that the only solution was to endorse fully the President's proposals and that, in view of Roosevelt's comments on *de jure* recognition of Abyssinia, the matter would have to be deleted from any immediate Anglo-Italian negotiations. To his dismay, however, the Foreign Secretary only gained support from Oliver Stanley, Malcolm MacDonald and Ormsby-Gore. Eden's arguments were roundly attacked by the senior members of the Committee, Simon, Inskip and Halifax, who supported the Prime Minister's assertion that the American scheme was so vague as to be of little value and could not be allowed to interfere with the very real prospect of engineering an improvement in Anglo-Italian relations. In this sense there was broad support for a further message to Roosevelt designed to ascertain the extent of his opposition to the recognition of the Italian position in Abyssinia. Certainly Eden was surprised at the strength of the opposition within the Cabinet Committee to his proposals, for there was some suggestion that he had been led to believe that his prestige would enable him to carry the Committee. On 17 January 1938 Harvey had noted:

> A.E. and I lunched alone at the Savoy to discuss the position. He feels himself that he cannot go on like this. 'The old gang' will do him down if they get him to swallow such treatment. He is the most important person in the Cabinet and if he went the Government would fall. It is most important to prevent him being compromised by this gaffe — which he will be if the P.M. gets his way and the Roosevelt initiative is killed and A.E. still stays on. He has a loyalty to his supporters in the country which is of greater importance than that to his colleagues. If he is firm, moreover, I think the P.M. will give way, especially if he insists on a Cabinet.[58]

It was apparent, however, that the majority of the Committee saw the lure of an Anglo-Italian settlement as far more attractive than Eden's advocacy of support for a further round of international negotiation, which offered little except a vague promise of closer Anglo-American collaboration. In addition to this general scepticism of Roosevelt's commitment to the cause of collective security, the situation was compounded by the general reserve with which the

Service Ministries viewed Eden's attempts to promote Anglo-American co-operation in the Far East. While the Admiralty was anxious to strengthen its position in the Far East they remained firmly opposed to the despatch of a task-force unless similar action was promised by the USA.[59] Even with American collaboration the First Sea Lord warned that to undertake such an action threatened seriously to denude British defences in the Mediterranean and ran the danger of provoking a pre-emptive strike by the Japanese on the British base at Singapore. On 25 January 1938 Chatfield warned Inskip:

> Imperially we are exceedingly weak. If at the present time, and for many years to come, we had to send a Fleet to the Far East, even in conjunction with the United States, we should be left so weak in Europe that we should be liable to blackmail or worse.[60]

In this context a strategy designed to eliminate Italy from the list of potential enemies was of greater interest to the Service Ministries than a policy of collective security which ultimately threatened to involve the USA and Britain in the imposition of sanctions against Japan.[61]

The extent of the opposition within the Cabinet Committee to Eden's stance was such that the Foreign Secretary's resignation seemed to be a very real possibility. On the evening of 19 January 1938 Harvey noted that Eden had declared he was prepared to examine Chamberlain's suggestions, 'but he believes it is right to stand firm and refuse any further concession, and resign'.[62] The following day J.P.L. Thomas, Eden's Parliamentary Private Secretary, had what he later described as a 'stormy' interview with Horace Wilson during which he warned Wilson that if Eden did resign Chamberlain would be exposed for turning 'down the help of a democracy in order that he might pursue his flirtations with the dictators untrammelled'.[63] Eden later argued that the suggestion of his possible resignation was a significant factor in forcing the Cabinet Committee on Foreign Policy to be 'noticeably less stiff' during its second meeting and indicated that 'the Prime Minister had been shaken by the support given to me . . . .'[64]

The evidence, however, would appear to suggest that it was the Foreign Secretary who decided to give ground and retreat from the position of confrontation. In agreeing that Roosevelt's attitude towards recognition of Abyssinia required clarification before discussions could be held with either France or the Dominions, Eden tacitly admitted that it was possible to proceed with negotiations for *de jure* recognition of Abyssinia alongside acceptance of the President's initative. On this basis the Foreign Secretary agreed to draft a series of telegrams both endorsing Roosevelt's scheme and indicating that, while still considering the possibility of recognising Abyssinia, an immediate decision would not be taken until further comments were received from the President on the subject of *de jure* recognition of the Italian position in Abyssinia as part of a general Mediterranean settlement. This arrangement allowed the Foreign Secretary to claim a victory, although it was made quite clear at two further meetings of the Committee the following day that although recognition would only be granted as part of a general settlement with Italy, negotiations could not be delayed indefinitely.[65] Therefore, while Cadogan hailed the outcome as a 'great victory' for Eden, the Foreign Secretary admitted, in a despatch to Sir R. Lindsay, that the result was 'a compromise arrived at after long and arduous discussions. If they are not all that I could wish, they are the best I could achieve . . . .'[66] In fact, although the solution enabled both parties to appear reasonably satisfied, it can be contended that only Chamberlain could have been content with the format of the compromise which was finally agreed. While the Prime Minister had outwardly surrendered to Eden's demand that he formally support the American proposals, the manner and timing of the endorsement, coupled with the express intention to initiate Anglo-Italian negotiations, were a clear indication of Chamberlain's determination not to allow the American scheme to disrupt the opening of negotiations with Germany and Italy. Indeed, when Eden presented a full account of the Cabinet Committee's conclusion to the full Cabinet on 24 January 1938, Chamberlain openly referred to Roosevelt's suggestions as:

preposterous proposals to which the Government were asked to give whole-hearted co-operation.

The Cabinet would probably agree that President Roosevelt's scheme contained nothing new and merely set out four old principles that would most likely be unpalatable to the Dictator States.[67]

In essence the Prime Minister's scepticism was largely vindicated by subsequent revelations of the deep divisions that existed within the Roosevelt Administration as to the advisability of making a firm commitment to the maintenance of collective security.[68] Yet having chosen to make a stand on the subject of Anglo-American relations, it was apparent that Eden had been effectively defeated. Certainly Harvey considered that the Foreign Secretary had capitulated too easily and noted on 21 January 1938: 'I dislike this solution; it seems to me to run a grave risk of antagonising R. and I wish A.E. had insisted on his own terms, if necessary resigning.'[69]

Eden later argued that he had not resigned in January 1938 because to have done so would have drawn attention to Roosevelt's proposals which the President had urged the British Government to treat with the utmost secrecy.[70] This, however, seems to be a rather lame excuse given both the Foreign Secretary's defeat upon a policy area which he had identified as a central pillar of his overall strategy and the extent of his isolation within the Cabinet. From this point onwards Eden's credibility within the Cabinet, given his complete misreading of the strength of opinion against giving the improvement of Anglo-American relations priority over the intention of direct negotiations with Italy and Germany, was certainly open to serious question. Furthermore the Prime Minister had openly challenged Eden's judgement in the direction of foreign affairs. While Eden was prepared to concede that the conduct of foreign affairs required an element of co-operation between Prime Minister and Foreign Secretary, there was a distinct suggestion that Chamberlain was determined to play the leading role in the partnership.[71]

There had been ominous signs during the latter half of 1937 that the Prime Minister had been dissatisfied with the attitude of the Foreign Office, not only in relation to the degree of emphasis to be assigned to the promotion of Anglo-American relations but more significantly Chamberlain had expressed concern at the suspicion and mistrust which clouded relations with Italy and Germany. On 12 September 1937 Chamberlain had noted in a letter to his sister Hilda:

> The F.O. persist in seeing Musso only as a sort of Machiavelli putting on a false mask of friendship in order to further nefarious ambitions. If we treat him like that we shall get nowhere with him . . . .[72]

Two months later the Prime Minister's exasperation with the Foreign Office was again displayed when it was suggested that it might not be advisable for Lord Halifax to visit Germany:

> I said another opportunity to be thrown away. I can't allow that.

> But really, the F.O.! I am only waiting for my opportunity to stir it up with a long pole.[73]

The main object of Chamberlain's attacks was undoubtedly Sir Robert Vansittart. If, however, the Prime Minister expected Vansittart's removal from the post of Permanent Under-Secretary in December 1937 to lead to a dramatic re-evaluation of the stance adopted by the Foreign Office in relations with Italy and Germany, there was little or no evidence of any significant change in the first month of 1938.[74] On 16 January 1938 Chamberlain complained to Eden that the failure to improve relations with Italy was due to the fact that the 'F.O. weren't sincere in their efforts'.[75] In addition Sir Horace Wilson, whom both Eden and Cadogan saw as a central figure in forming Chamberlain's attitudes on foreign affairs, made no secret of his conviction that the Foreign Office presented the main obstacle to the attainment of an understanding with Italy and Germany.[76] On 17 January 1938 Wilson had warned Eden that the Foreign Office needed to adopt a more pliable stance in relations with Italy and three days later, when J.P.L. Thomas indicated that Eden was considering resignation, Harvey noted that Wilson in response:

> defended P.M.'s policy of coming to terms with dictators and condemned the F.O. attitude which he presented as obstructing this. He admitted that there was a fundamental difference between P.M.'s and A.E.'s policies and seemed prepared for a break; he let it be known that if A.E. did go there would be an onslaught on him and the F.O. for their attitude.[77]

Furthermore, with the removal of Vansittart, it was apparent that Eden was now seen increasingly as the main obstacle within the Foreign Office to the improvement of relations with Italy and Germany. The Prime Minister's suspicion that Eden personally disliked and distrusted Mussolini and that this antipathy was adversely affecting Anglo-Italian relations had been further fuelled by a series of letters from his sister-in-law, Lady Ivy Chamberlain, who was in Rome and frequently mixed with senior Italian figures including Mussolini and Ciano.[78] On 16 December 1937 Lady Chamberlain wrote that Mussolini had expressed his belief that Chamberlain 'is friendly but that Eden is not'. The letter concluded:

> Every day at every meal I have to combat the feeling against Anthony. Nothing will convince them that it is not he who is preventing the conversations from starting. They believe that you are friendly but that the F.O. is working against . . . .[79]

A similar letter had been sent by Lady Chamberlain to Eden on 15 December 1937 to which he replied, on the last day of the month, thanking her for her efforts to refute the charge that he was opposed to Anglo-Italian negotiations:

> I am most grateful for the way in which you spoke and indeed could gladly endorse every word of the language you used. Unhappily I fear that we have much suspicion to overcome and the task will not prove easy.[80]

Despite the polite format of this response it was evident that Eden was increasingly irked by Lady Chamberlain's activities in Rome which threatened to portray Chamberlain as over-eager for an agreement with Italy and, therefore, possibly weaken his own bargaining position. This annoyance was compounded during the first month of 1938 when the Prime Minister admitted that he had replied to Lady Chamberlain's letter expressing his determination to work for an improvement of Anglo-Italian relations, and that the letter had been passed on by Lady Chamberlain to Count Ciano.[81] Lady Chamberlain had replied that Ciano had been delighted with the tenor of the Prime Minister's letter and added, as a result of her discussions with the Italian Foreign Minister:

> I am convinced that once we start conversations they will be as daring as possible! Hitler is coming to Rome in May and it is essential that we should come to some agreement before then otherwise I fear that two dictators together could do or say something dramatic.[82]

While Eden did not entirely disagree with Lady Chamberlain's reasoning, he was dismayed that the Prime Minister had apparently once again sought to by-pass the Foreign Office in the conduct of relations with Italy and that Chamberlain should openly admit his action when he used Lady Chamberlain's letters at the Cabinet Committee on Foreign Policy on 19 January 1938, in defence of his determination not to allow the Anglo-Italian negotiations to be postponed indefinitely.[83] Therefore it was, perhaps, surprising that it was not until 8 February 1938, when Eden discovered that a further letter from Chamberlain had been passed by Lady Chamberlain to Mussolini, that the Foreign Secretary elected to tackle the Prime Minister directly on the matter.[84] Eden pointed out to Chamberlain that his sister-in-law's activities were a source of acute embarrassment to the Foreign Office and, indeed, hindered Eden's discussions with the Italian Ambassador, Grandi:

> It recreates in Mussolini's mind the impression that he can divide us and he will be the less ready to pay attention to what I have to say to Grandi. Indeed, I can see that whatever Ciano reports from Grandi, Mussolini will say: 'I know that the Prime Minister is determined to open conversations in February, so do not pay any attention to any conditions Eden may be trying to impose.'[85]

However, it is, perhaps, an error to overestimate the extent of the rift that existed between Eden and Chamberlain at the end of January 1938. Certainly they had collided squarely over the issue of

Roosevelt's proposals, and it was this collision which prompted Eden subsequently to claim that the issue: 'was the most clear cut division which had so far arisen between Neville Chamberlain and myself. Nothing could have exposed more sharply our differences of approach.'[86]

It is possible to contend, however, that Eden subsequently exaggerated the rift with the Prime Minister and that in fact at the end of January both men considered a compromise of sorts had been achieved and the differences that still separated them were not insurmountable. Indeed, as late as 13 February 1938, Chamberlain insisted in a letter to his sister Hilda that, despite speculation in the Press of a clash between the Prime Minister and the Foreign Secretary, in fact they 'were in complete agreement, more complete perhaps than we have sometimes been in the past'.[87] Certainly the beginning of the New Year had seen both men in full agreement on the need to work assiduously for the improvement of relations with Germany and Italy.[88] Steps were taken on 24 January 1938 to transform this agreement into action when the Cabinet Committee on Foreign Policy accepted the recommendation that a belt of territory be established in Central Africa, administered by the major European powers, including Germany, along a set of agreed international guidelines. It was hoped that the prospect of colonial restitution in this form would be sufficient to draw Germany back to the negotiating table for a general settlement, including agreement on disarmament and European security pacts.[89] Chamberlain and Eden were apparently in accord on this topic and, on 9 February 1938, the Cabinet agreed that Henderson be instructed to seek a suitable opportunity to broach the matter with the new German Foreign Minister, Von Ribbentrop.[90]

The decision to launch a further approach to Germany had certainly been influenced by discussions which the Foreign Secretary had held with Delbos at Paris on 25 January 1938 and at Geneva on 28 January 1938.[91] At these meetings the French Foreign Minister had emphasised his Government's desire to move quickly towards the attainment of an agreement with Germany. The Foreign Minister's promotion of this subject was almost certainly prompted by the fear that Germany was once again seeking to expand its influence in Central Europe, probably at the expense of Austrian independence. The French approach was, however, not entirely unexpected given that the former French Foreign Minister, Flandin, had warned Simon on 2 January 1938 that in his opinion 'the next objective on the German list is Austria'. Simon recorded of the interview: 'Flandin thought that there would be striking developments in Austria before the end of March at the latest.' Flandin's information was based on a discussion which he had held with the German Foreign Minister, at which Von Neurath had: 'hinted that there might be internal disturbances in Austria in which Germany would find it necessary to come to the aid of her sympathisers.'[92]

In this context it appeared important, both to pacify French concern and possibly to forestall any precipitate action by Germany in Austria, that measures be taken to reopen negotiations with Germany for security agreements covering Western and Eastern Europe. In principle Eden fully supported the reopening of discussions with Germany as long as the end product was a general settlement of the various disputes over colonial restitution, disarmament and multilateral security agreements,[93] while Chamberlain had admitted in a letter to Eden, on 13 January 1938, that his goal was to seek concurrent negotiations with Italy and Germany.[94] On the topic of prospective discussions with Italy, however, Delbos was far more reticent and stressed the preconditions that must be accepted by Mussolini before negotiations could be commenced. Both Foreign Ministers were, in essence, sceptical of the possibility of achieving an agreement with Italy which would successfully solve the problems presented by foreign intervention in the Spanish Civil War, recognition of the Italian position in Abyssinia and the attainment of a general Mediterranean security agreement.[95] On 1 January 1938, in a memorandum to Chamberlain, Eden had grudgingly admitted that the granting of *de jure* recognition of the Italian Government in Abyssinia could not be indefinitely sidestepped,[96] but his distaste for discussions with the Italian Government was clearly indicated in a further memorandum to the Prime Minister eight days later:

> there seems to be a certain difference between Italian and German position in that an agreement with the latter might have some chance of reasonable life, especially if Hitler's own position were engaged, whereas Mussolini is, I fear, the complete gangster and his pledged word means nothing.

> Indeed it seems to me that the big issues of this year are Anglo-American co-operation, the chances of asserting white race authority in the Far East and relations with Germany. To all this Mussolini is really secondary and because he makes more noise we must not, to quieten him, take any step which will create discord among friends.[97]

Therefore, while Eden was prepared to consider the various formats devised by the Foreign Office for a settlement of differences with Italy, it was apparent that he remained firmly of the conviction Mussolini could not be trusted. In view of this the Foreign Secretary advocated that negotiations with Italy would have to be approached with utmost caution and were only likely to be successful if Mussolini was confronted with a display of Anglo-French solidarity and a resolve not to permit the further expansion of Italian influence in the Mediterranean or Near East.[98] If, therefore, Roosevelt's opposition to the recognition of the Italian position in Abyssinia was significant in swaying Eden against the opening of negotiations with Rome on the Abyssinian issue, his negotiations with Delbos were almost certainly decisive in establishing his conception of the preconditions that would have to be extracted from Mussolini before discussions could be opened. It was apparent from his meetings with Delbos that the French Government would not support the initiation of discussion with Italy unless Mussolini agreed that the issue of Italian intervention in Spain was to be fully discussed and that any agreement would incorporate the withdrawal of Italian assistance to the Nationalist forces. With this consideration in mind Eden minuted on his return from Geneva on 30 January 1938:

> As soon as we have received President Roosevelt's reaction, I would . . . favour opening conversations with the Italians making it clear that *de jure* was among the topics to be discussed and Spain also. Our objective in respect of Spain would be no more than the fulfilment of the British plan which the Italian Government accepted several months ago. Once that was carried through *de jure* could be given. A Red Sea agreement in addition would be useful, also agreements about Libya and propaganda . . . .[99]

The Foreign Secretary's determination to gain an agreement on the withdrawal of foreign volunteers from Spain before discussing *de jure* recognition of Abyssinia was indicated in Harvey's diary entry for 31 January 1938.

> A.E. is now convinced that conversations with Italy must include Spain if *de jure* recognition is to be given. If foreign troops could be withdrawn from Spain as part of an agreement, everybody would welcome it as a real appeasement. A purely Anglo-Italian settlement of Anglo-Italian questions would be regarded as a shady bargain and would not be acceptable either to Geneva or to Roosevelt.[100]

Eden's conviction that the Italian bargaining position was becoming increasingly precarious was supported by a report received from Lord Cranborne on 4 February 1938. Cranborne concluded that the mood in Geneva favoured a 'tough British attitude' in relation to the Abyssinian issue and argued that the economic burden resulting from Italian intervention in the Spanish Civil War was steadily tilting the balance of power in the Anglo-Italian relationship towards London. [101] For his own part the Foreign Secretary had noted with satisfaction the Italian decision to follow the British lead in resuming the full Nyon naval patrol following the sinking of merchant shipping off the coast of Spain by unidentified submarines in the latter days of January. [102] Furthermore during the course of two interviews held with the Italian Ambassador on 4 and 5 February 1938, Grandi had indicated his Government's willingness to include the Spanish situation in any future Anglo-Italian negotiations. [103] With these considerations in mind Eden wrote to Chamberlain on 8 February 1938 urging him to approach the topic of Anglo-Italian relations with caution. Eden was fully aware that the Prime Minister was eager to participate personally in the discussions with Grandi and it was evident that the Foreign Secretary feared Chamberlain's desire to force the pace of the negotiations would encourage the Italians to resist any concessions to Eden's formula for the withdrawal of volunteers from Spain.

> As I see it, the position is now this. Mussolini is in an extremely uncomfortable position. He has commitments in Abyssinia and Spain, neither of which is turning out well. He now sees a government in power in Berlin which, it is quite true, is comparatively enthusiastic for the Rome—Berlin axis, but which is also apparently determined to pursue a more active foreign policy in Europe, with Austria as the first item on the list of intended victims. In such a position we have nothing to gain by showing ourselves over-eager. If Mussolini is really anxious to reach a settlement with us, then the opportunity we are affording him of liquidating his commitments in Spain gives him an excellent chance of proving his sincerity. [104]

Eden was further encouraged when, on 10 February 1938, Grandi reported that Mussolini was prepared to open negotiations at an early date on 'as wide a basis as possible' and agreed to transmit to Rome Eden's stipulation that substantial progress on the withdrawal of volunteers from Spain must precede the opening of general Anglo-Italian discussions. [105] It was, therefore, with a general sense of optimism that the Foreign Secretary addressed a meeting in Birmingham on 12 February 1938 and vigorously defended his policy of caution:

> I say especially the 'younger generation' because the Government today must strive in its foreign policy not only for peace in our time but for peace in yours. And if we are to have peace in your time it means that in any agreements we make today there must

be no sacrifice of principles and no shirking of responsibilities merely to obtain quick results that may not be permanent . . . .

We offer friendship to all, but on equal terms. For it is not by seeking to buy temporary goodwill that peace is made, but on a basis of frank reciprocity with mutual respect . . . .[106]

Although Eden was confident in his own mind that his approach to the Anglo-Italian question was the most appropriate, he was also aware that the Prime Minister remained sceptical and, in fact, openly stated at the Cabinet meeting of 9 February 1938 his belief that Mussolini was unlikely to agree to the withdrawal of Italian volunteers from Spain before the question of British recognition of the Italian position in Abyssinia was discussed.[107] In addition the Foreign Secretary appreciated that there was a growing campaign being mounted demanding an increase in the pace of Anglo-Italian negotiations. In addition to the correspondence that passed between the Prime Minister and his sister-in-law,[108] the Foreign Office was convinced that the Prime Minister was behind a series of Press releases that appeared in the second week of February predicting an early and complete agreement with Italy.[109] The articles clearly suggested once again that the Foreign Secretary and the Prime Minister were not in accord over the Italian question. Harvey recorded on 12 February 1938:

Fleet Street is full of rumours of the division in the Cabinet between P.M. and A.E. This is, of course, the inevitable result of Whitehall speaking with two voices — i.e. recent accounts of our negotiations with Italy (whether put out by no. 10 or by some other Cabinet Minister) independently of, and in conflict with those of, the F.O. News Department. Rex has very circumstantial evidence from journalists that they did come from no. 10 at any rate . . . .[110]

Although two days later Harvey recorded his suspicion that Sir Joseph Ball, Director of the Conservative Research Department, was involved in the Press campaign,[111] it would appear that neither he nor Eden had any knowledge of the clandestine link established between Ball and a subordinate official at the Italian Embassy which subsequent commentators have identified as a further channel used by the Italian Ambassador in an attempt both to by-pass Eden and assure Chamberlain as to Mussolini's sincerity in seeking to improve Anglo-Italian relations.[112]

While there was at this time little evidence of an open rift within the Cabinet between Eden and his opponents, it was significant that

Inskip, on 16 February 1938, in presenting a memorandum on Defence Expenditure concluded:

> that it was beyond the resources of this country to make proper provision in peace for the defence of the Empire against three major powers in three different theatres of war. He therefore desired to repeat with fresh emphasis his opinion as to the importance of reducing the scale of our commitments and the number of our potential enemies.[113]

The Cabinet also took note of a comment by Simon in response to Eden's suggestion that the pace of rearmament could be accelerated by the purchase of foreign production. The Chancellor of the Exchequer declared that the existing estimates 'placed a terrible strain on the national finances but could not be increased without financial disorganisation to an extent that would weaken the resistance of the country'. It was quite evident that both Inskip and Simon were of the opinion that a rapid improvement of Anglo-Italian relations was the most immediate goal in the field of foreign affairs and placed little faith in Eden's contention that Britain had powerful allies in France and the USA and, therefore, could negotiate with Italy from a position of comparative strength. It was clear, however, that Chamberlain agreed with Inskip and Simon and was plainly disappointed at the lack of progress in Eden's recent conversations with Grandi.[114] Although the Prime Minister had acceded to the request that the negotiations be conducted entirely by the Foreign Secretary, on 17 February 1938 he elected to take a far more positive role and instructed Eden to summon Grandi to 10 Downing Street the following day.[115] This decision was probably prompted by two factors. Firstly reports received from Sir Ronald Lindsay on 10 and 16 February 1938 indicated that Roosevelt had no intention of launching his peace initiative until after Hitler's speech of 20 February 1938. Furthermore in the intervening period Lindsay admitted that the President had stated he did not specifically oppose the opening of Anglo-Italian negotiations for a general settlement of differences.[116]

While Eden continued to argue that any discussion of *de jure* recognition of Abyssinia was likely to receive a hostile reception in Washington, Chamberlain was insistent that the President's message had released him from his pledge to delay the opening of negotiations until the American stance was clarified.[117] Although this apparently cleared the path for the opening of discussions, the decisive factor in persuading Chamberlain to force the pace of negotiations was probably provided by a series of reports received on 15 and 16 February 1938 suggesting that the Austrian Chancellor, Kurt Von

Schuschnigg, had been bullied by Hitler into surrendering the Ministry of the Interior to the Austrian Nazi, Seyss-Inquart.[118] At the Cabinet meeting of 16 February 1938 it was evident that while Eden and Chamberlain were in broad agreement that Britain was not in a position to oppose the expansion of German influence in Austria, the two Ministers differed markedly in their respective interpretations of the role played by the Italian Government in the affair. The Prime Minister saw Hitler's move as a direct challenge to the traditional Italian interest in the balance of power in Austria. Chamberlain was convinced that Mussolini would be anxious to reach an agreement with Britain both to counter the expansion of German influence in Austria and to bolster his personal prestige amongst the Italian people. In this sense Chamberlain emphasised the importance of seizing this opportunity to push for an Anglo-Italian agreement.[119] In a diary entry for the period 19–27 February 1938, Chamberlain recorded his intention not to allow Eden to delay further the opening of negotiations:

> In my view to intimate now to Grandi that this was not the moment for conversations would be to convince Musso that he must consider talks with us 'off' and act accordingly. I had no doubt at all that in his disappointment and exasperation at having been fooled with, as he would think, so long, Italian public opinion would be raised to a white heat against us.

> There might indeed be some overt act of hostility, and in any case the dictatorships would be driven closer together, the last shred of Austrian independence would be lost, the Balkan countries would feel compelled towards their powerful neighbours, Czechoslovakia would be swallowed, France would either have to submit to German domination or fight, in which case we should almost certainly be drawn in. I could not face the responsibility for allowing such a series of catastrophies.[120]

The Foreign Secretary, however, suspected that Mussolini had tacitly assented to Hitler's campaign to draw Austria firmly within the German sphere of influence and that, in this context, there was little or no possibility of using the Austrian question to disrupt the Rome–Berlin Axis. Eden therefore considered that Mussolini merely sought the initiation of negotiations with Britain to deflect attention from the Austrian issue and that the Italian leader was unlikely to accept any concessions towards the British demand for 'substantial progress' in the withdrawal of Italian volunteers from Spain.[121] On the evening of 17 February 1938, in a letter to Chamberlain, Eden once again urged the Prime Minister to adopt a cautious approach to the Italian question:

> Such information as we have here tends to strengthen the view that there is some kind of arrangement between Rome and Berlin and that Mussolini had, or thinks that he has, some kind of *quid pro quo* from Berlin in return for his acquiescence in Austrian events.

> My petition, therefore, is that whatever Grandi says to us tomorrow we should content ourselves with saying that we will carefully consider it and send for him again.[122]

Chamberlain was, however, apparently unmoved by Eden's analysis of the situation and, indeed, his determination to forge an agreement with Italy was further fuelled, on the evening of 17 February 1938, by a letter from his sister-in-law containing a message from Count Ciano. Lady Ivy Chamberlain noted that Ciano: 'begged me to let you know that time is everything. Today an agreement will be easy but things are happening in Europe which will make it impossible tomorrow.'[123]

The Prime Minister interpreted this message as a thinly veiled hint that if Britain rejected the Italian advances for an agreement, Mussolini would be forced into even closer collusion with Hitler's Germany.[124] In this light he was convinced that his course of action was the correct one and the following day quickly accepted Grandi's assertion that Italy had played no part in the German campaign against Austria. Furthermore he was delighted to hear that Mussolini was prepared to open negotiations on all of the areas previously raised by the British Government. When questioned by Eden, however, it was apparent that Grandi was either unable or unwilling to state what his Government's stance was likely to be on either the future status of Austria or the possibility of an early acceptance of Eden's recent proposals for the withdrawal of foreign volunteers from Spain. As Grandi later noted, it was apparent that Chamberlain and Eden were in disagreement on the course of action to be pursued. It was decided, therefore, that the Italian Ambassador would return to Downing Street on the afternoon of the same day in order to receive a reply.[125] Eden noted in his diary of the conversation that ensued between Chamberlain and himself following Grandi's departure:

> N.C. made it clear that he knew exactly what he wanted to do. He wanted to tell Grandi at 3 o'clock that we would open conversations at once, send for Perth and announce that he was coming home in order to prepare for opening conversations in Rome.

I demurred pointing out that we had still made very little progress with the Spanish affair and that I was frankly suspicious of the 'now or never' attitude or 'last chance' atmosphere of the telegram [reporting Count Ciano's remarks to Lady Chamberlain]. We had been told that so often before.

Upon this N.C. became very vehement, more vehement than I have ever seen him, and strode up and down the room saying with great emphasis, 'Anthony, you have missed chance after chance. You simply cannot go on like this.' I said 'Your methods are right if you have faith in the man you are negotiating with.' N.C. replied, 'I have'.[126]

It appeared that an *impasse* had been reached and it was agreed that Grandi be informed a decision would not be taken until the Cabinet had been consulted. In addition further clarification was required in relation to the Italian position on the withdrawal of volunteers from Spain. Although it seemed possible that a compromise might be achieved if Italy agreed to Eden's formula on the volunteer question, neither party was optimistic. Over lunch Eden told Cadogan that he was 'determined to hold out', while Chamberlain noted in his diary for the period 19 to 27 February 1938 that he had informed Sir Horace Wilson on the morning of 18 February 1938, 'I was determined to stand firm even though it meant losing my Foreign Secretary'.[127]

When the Cabinet met on the afternoon of 19 February 1938 it was soon apparent that neither party had modified his stance.[128] Chamberlain opened the meeting with a detailed *resumé* of the course of Anglo-Italian relations during the previous twelve months. In particular the Prime Minister emphasised his belief that the failure to improve Anglo-Italian relations had been instrumental in forcing the Italians to look increasingly towards Berlin for a political alliance. In this context Chamberlain referred to the significance of the recent events in Austria: 'It would seem that this must be unpalatable to Signor Mussolini and that an opportunity is offered to encourage him to make a more determined stand.'

He had, therefore, been delighted by Grandi's assurance that the Italian Government was anxious to open early and wide-ranging negotiations with the British Government and he urged the Cabinet to support the despatch of a message to Mussolini, agreeing to the initiation of discussions. Chamberlain concluded:

It was an opportunity to show Signor Mussolini that he might have other friends besides Herr Hitler.

If we rejected the present approach it would be taken as a final rebuff and as a confirmation of the suspicions the Italians had long harboured that we were postponing them until we were strong enough to impose our own conditions.

. . . this was an opportunity that might never occur again, and not to embrace it would be not only unwise but criminal.

In response Eden immediately challenged the Prime Minister's assumption that Mussolini was sincere in his expressed desire for an Anglo-Italian agreement. After detailing the frequency with which Italy had disregarded its obligations under both the Covenant of the League of Nations and the Anglo-Italian Gentlemen's Agreement, the Foreign Secretary argued that the Austrian situation had done nothing to suggest Mussolini had undergone 'a change of heart'. Furthermore Eden indicated that there was every possibility Mussolini had secretly agreed to the German absorption of Austria in exchange for recognition of Italian supremacy in the Mediterranean:

From every point of view, it was a bad moment for the conversations. Europe would treat it as though we were running after Rome. Berlin would regard it as proof of the value of Italian friendship, and it would be anticipating President Roosevelt's statement next week . . . .

Eden, therefore, concluded that he could not agree to the opening of formal negotiations without a prior indication of Italian good faith in the form of the commencement of the withdrawal of Italian volunteers from Spain.

At this point the discussion was thrown open and it was quickly apparent that only Malcolm MacDonald and Walter Elliot openly supported Eden. Although Zetland favoured the opening of negotiations with Germany rather than with Italy, it was obvious that the majority of the Cabinet supported the Prime Minister's analysis of the situation. Chamberlain, therefore, announced that Grandi would be informed on 21 February 1938 that Britain was ready to open negotiations in Rome, irrespective of whether the Italian Ambassador signified that his Government was prepared to agree to a formula for the withdrawal of volunteers from Spain. The division between the Prime Minister and the Foreign Secretary was seemingly unbridgeable and when Eden pointed out that he could not recommend Chamberlain's proposals to the House of Commons, the Prime Minister replied that it was unfortunate 'because he himself held the opposite view so strongly that he could not accept any other decision'.

At this point it was agreed that the Cabinet would meet again on the afternoon of the following day.[129] The only suggestion of a possible compromise lay in the further exploration of Lord Halifax's proposal that the formal Anglo-Italian negotiations be opened immediately, but with the proviso that an agreement would not be concluded until the question of the withdrawal of Italian volunteers from Spain was satisfactorily settled.[130] While Eden might at one time have accepted this format, it was evident that the events of the past week had convinced him he could no longer serve as Chamberlain's Foreign Secretary. Although on the evening of 19 February 1938 both Malcolm MacDonald and Alex Cadogan urged Eden to accept Halifax's formula, the Foreign Secretary was adamant that his demand for Italian agreement on the withdrawal of troops from Spain before the opening of formal negotiations was now a matter of principle from which he could not retreat.[131] In his diary entry for 19 February 1938 Oliver Harvey recorded the debate that ensued between Eden and his advisers:

> We had a short talk on his return on the possibility of accepting some such compromise as Halifax suggested. Alec Cadogan, from official point of view, thought this would be good enough. A.E. would safeguard himself from charge of surrender to Muss, but he thought it very doubtful whether Muss would accept. A.E. feels himself that he would rather go as there is really a profound gulf between him and his colleagues. A genuine difference of outlook.[132]

The Foreign Secretary's conviction that his resignation was the only solution to the problem seemed to be confirmed the following morning when Malcolm MacDonald informed Eden that Chamberlain was of the same opinion.[133] At a meeting between Eden and Chamberlain, held shortly after midday, it was agreed that the Foreign Secretary would announce his resignation at the Cabinet meeting due to be held the same afternoon.[134]

When the Cabinet assembled at 3 p.m. the meeting opened with an invitation to Eden to state his position.[135] This the Foreign Secretary did, pointing out that this was not the first time that he and the Prime Minister had differed but emphasising that on the present issue there could be no compromise:

> He could not recommend to Parliament a policy with which he was not in agreement. He could not disguise, also, that there was a difference of outlook on foreign affairs generally between himself and some of his colleagues, including the Prime Minister.

Eden, therefore, proposed that he tender his resignation and added that, as a result of their discussion prior to the Cabinet meeting, the Prime Minister was in full agreement with this decision. Although Eden had anticipated that the meeting would be quickly concluded, it was evident that there was a general feeling that his resignation was not necessary and that a satisfactory compromise could still be engineered. After almost two hours of debate it was agreed that a sub-committee be established to devise a formula that might bridge the gulf between Eden and Chamberlain.[136]

When the Cabinet reassembled at 6.10 p.m. it was proposed that formal negotiations with Italy be opened subject to Italian agreement on the British formula for the withdrawal of foreign volunteers from Spain and an understanding that *de jure* recognition of Abyssinia would be withheld until the Spanish issue was resolved. For the first time Eden wavered and asked for an hour to examine the sub-committee's proposals. His indecision may have been generated by the Prime Minister's announcement that the Italians had accepted in principle the British formula for the withdrawal of volunteers, but in discussion with Harvey and Cadogan at the Foreign Office it was clear that Eden was still adamant negotiations could not be opened until the Italians had not only agreed to the formula but had also commenced the withdrawal of their 'volunteers'.[137] Although MacDonald once again urged the Foreign Secretary to accept the compromise offered, Eden quickly decided that the terms were still inadequate.[138] Harvey noted in his diary entry for 20 February 1938:

> He [A.E.] said he really couldn't agree to a policy which he was absolutely convinced was wrong and would lead nowhere.

> There were only two alternatives in reality either the P.M.'s of immediate formal conversations and no conditions or his own of informal talks while Spain is being cleared up. A *via Media* would be the worst of both and wouldn't be acceptable even to Musso.[139]

Accordingly at a meeting of Ministers, convened at 7.30 p.m., Eden informed his colleagues that he could accept neither the compromise formula nor the present policy of the Prime Minister and, therefore, would submit a formal letter of resignation to the Cabinet that evening.[140] In his letter Eden clearly indicated the divergence that existed between himself and the Prime Minister:

> The events of the last few days have made plain a difference between us on a decision of great importance in itself and far-reaching in its consequences. I cannot recommend to Parliament a policy with which I am not in agreement. Apart from this, I

have become increasingly conscious, as I know you have also, of a difference of outlook between us in respect to the international problems of the day and also as to the methods by which we should seek to resolve them. It cannot be in the country's interest that those who are called upon to direct its affairs should work in an uneasy partnership, fully conscious of differences in outlook yet hoping that they will not recur. This applies with a special force to the relationship between the Prime Minister and the Foreign Secretary. It is for these reasons that with very deep regret I have decided that I must leave you and your colleagues with whom I have been associated during years of great difficulty and stress.

May I end on a personal note? I can never forget the help and counsel that you have always so readily given me, both before and since you became Prime Minister. Our differences, whatever they may be, cannot efface that memory nor influence our friendship.[141]

Although Eden suspected that the Cabinet might insist on a further attempt to devise a compromise, he received a reply from Chamberlain at midnight informing him that his resignation had been accepted.[142]

References

1   *Neville Chamberlain Papers*, NC 7/11/31/100, Eden to Chamberlain, 9 January 1938.
2   In response to Phipps's report of his conversation with Dodd, Eden minuted 'It would clearly be a great error for us to discourage the President . . . .' Avon, p. 525. Speculation as to American intentions was further fuelled when in February 1937 the Secretary to the Treasury, Henry Morgenthau, informed the British Commercial Attaché that he was considering a bid to gain international agreement on limiting armament expenditure. See *DBFP*, 2nd ser., vol. 18, no. 202 (23 February 1937) and no. 250 (5 March 1937). See also J.M. Blum, *From the Morgenthau Diaries* (Boston, 1959), pp. 455–9 and Cordell Hull, *Memoirs of Cordell Hull*, vol. 1 (London, 1948), pp. 524–7.
3   Extracts from this speech are reproduced in *DIA 1937*, pp. 582–7.
4   Neville Chamberlain described the speech as a 'lot of ballyhoo', *Neville Chamberlain Papers*, NC 18/1, letter to his sister Hilda, 9 October 1937. Eden subsequently admitted that the speech aroused a 'storm of criticism' in the USA, Avon, p. 336. See also D.C. Watt, 'Roosevelt and Chamberlain: Two Appeasers', *Journal of Canadian Institute of International Affairs*, 28, 2, Spring 1973, pp. 190–1 and *CAB* 23/89, CC 37(37)5, 13 October 1937.
5   *Foreign Relations of the United States* (hereafter cited as *FRUS*), 1937, vol. 3, Memorandum by the Under-Secretary of State, Welles, 12 October 1937, pp. 600–2.
6   *Neville Chamberlain Papers*, NC 18/1, letter to his sister Hilda, 9 October 1937.

7   On 1 September 1937 Eden told Barney Baruch that he attached utmost importance to Anglo-American relations and that he was ready to listen to any proposals emanating from Washington, *Avon Papers*, FO 954/29, US/37/20, Minute by Eden, 1 September 1937. See also Avon, pp. 523—6.

8   Quoted in Avon, p. 528.

9   See *Avon Papers*, FO 954/29, US/37/1, US/37/2, US/37/14, US/37/16 and US/37/20. Also *DBFP*, 2nd ser., vol. 18, no. 250. For details of the outbreak of Sino-Japanese hostilities in July 1937 see Bradford A. Lee, *Britain and the Sino-Japanese War, 1937—1939* (London, 1973), pp. 23—49.

10   *Avon Papers*, FO 954/29, US/37/17, 21 July 1937.

11   On 29 September 1937 Eden was forced to concede to the Cabinet that there was no sign of any desire in Washington to improve Anglo-American co-operation, *CAB* 23/89, CC 35(37)4. See also Lee, pp. 45—9.

12   The Brussels Conference on the Far East was convened in the first week of November 1937. The use of the Nine Power Pact of 1922, rather than the League of Nations, to approach the Sino-Japanese dispute was intended to ensure that the USA was an active party to the discussions. Lee, pp. 52—78.

13   See Malcolm MacDonald's report to the Cabinet of 24 November 1937, *CAB* 23/90, CC 43(37)6 and appendix. MacDonald concluded that USA would not take measures against Japan. For a record of Eden's discussions with Davis see Oliver Harvey, diary entries for 2, 3 and 5 November 1937, Harvey, pp. 54—7. See also Avon, pp. 536—40.

14   See Eden's report to the Cabinet of 24 November 1937, *CAB* 23/90, CC 43(37)5.

15   Avon, p. 541.

16   *FRUS*, 1937, vol. 3, Memorandum by the Under-Secretary of State, Welles, Washington, 27 November 1937, pp. 724—5.

17   On 12 December 1937 the British ships *HMS Ladybird* and *HMS Bee* had been shelled by the Japanese, killing one seaman. For details of this attack and the sinking of the *Panay* see Lee, pp. 89—93 and Avon, pp. 541—3.

18   Quoted in Avon, pp. 542—3.

19   Eden informed the Cabinet on 15 December 1937 that Washington showed no indication of any desire to take co-ordinated action of any form against the Japanese. *CAB* 23/90, CC 47(37)4, 15 December 1937.

20   *Avon Papers*, FO 954/29, US/37/23, Eden to Lindsay, Ambassador to Washington, 15 December 1937. This action had been approved at the Cabinet meeting of the same date, *CAB* 23/90, CC 47(37)3 and CC 47(37)4.

21   *Avon Papers*, FO 954/29, US/37/23, Eden to Lindsay, 15 December 1937.

22   Roosevelt's reply was discussed by the Cabinet on 22 December 1937. While pleased to see that the President was considering the opening of Anglo-American Naval Staff conversations and advancing the date of naval manoeuvres to January, they were disturbed to note that he refused any further action until Japan created a further incident, *CAB* 23/90, CC 48(37)5.

23   *Avon Papers*, FO 954/29, US/37/26, Eden to Lindsay, 20 December 1937. See also Lawrence Pratt, 'The Anglo-American Naval Conversations on the Far East of January 1938', *International Affairs*, 47, 4, October 1971, pp. 750—4.

24   Oliver Harvey, diary entry for 19—23 December 1937, Harvey, pp. 65—6.

25   Ibid., diary entry for 1—13 January 1938, Harvey, p. 66. On 2 February 1938 Lindsay informed Welles that Eden considered relations between Italy and France were so bad that the two Governments 'were actually not on speaking terms'. *FRUS* 1938, vol. 1, Memorandum of a conversation by the Under-Secretary of State, Washington, 2 February 1938, pp. 122—4.

26   Avon, pp. 545–6 and Pratt, 'Anglo-American Naval Conversations', pp. 754–5.
27   *Avon Papers*, FO 954/29, US/38/1, Cadogan to Lindsay, 7 January 1937, Avon, p. 546 and Pratt, p. 757.
28   Avon, p. 546.
29   Ibid., p. 548. See also D. Dilks, *The Diaries of Sir Alexander Cadogan* (London, 1971), Cadogan diary entry for 14 January 1938, p. 37.
30   Cadogan, diary entry for 15 January 1938, Dilks, pp. 37–8 and Oliver Harvey, diary entry for 15 January 1938, Harvey, p. 70.
31   See *Avon Papers*, FO 954/30, US/43/51. See also *FRUS* 1938, vol. 1, Memorandum by the Under-Secretary of State to President Roosevelt, Washington, 10 January 1938, pp. 115–17.
32   Cadogan, diary entry for 13 January 1938, Dilks, pp. 36–7.
33   Quoted in Avon, p. 550.
34   The text of Chamberlain's message to Washington of 13 January 1938 is contained in *Avon Papers*, FO 954/29, US/43/51 and *FRUS* 1938, vol. 3, message from Prime Minister to the President, 14 January 1938, pp. 118–20.
35   *Neville Chamberlain Papers*, NC 2/24A, diary entry for 19–27 February 1938.
36   Avon, pp. 552–3.
37   In the first week of January 1938 Eden and Chamberlain had exchanged thoughts on the resolution of the Abyssinian situation and Eden had agreed on 9 January 1938 that a decision could not be taken until the French Foreign Minister, Delbos, had been consulted. See *Avon Papers*, FO 954/6A, ETH/38/1–4, also *Neville Chamberlain Papers*, NC 2/24A, diary entry for 19–27 February 1938.
38   Cadogan, diary entry for 14 January 1938, Dilks, p. 37 and Oliver Harvey, diary entry for 14 January 1938, Harvey, pp. 68–9.
39   *Neville Chamberlain Papers*, NC 2/24A, diary entry for 19–27 February 1938.
40   Oliver Harvey, diary entry for 15 January 1938, Harvey, p. 70.
41   Contained in *Avon Papers*, FO 954/30, US/43/2.
42   Ibid.
43   Cadogan, diary entry for 15 January 1938, Dilks, pp. 37–8.
44   Accounts of this interview at Chequers on 16 January 1938 are contained in Avon, pp. 553–5, *Neville Chamberlain Papers*, NC 2/24A, diary entry for 19–27 February 1938 and Oliver Harvey, diary entry for 16 January 1938, Harvey, pp. 70–1.
45   *Neville Chamberlain Papers*, NC 2/24A, diary entry for 19–27 February 1938.
46   Ibid., NC 18/1, letter to his sister Hilda, 9 October 1937.
47   *CAB* 23/89, CC 36(37)5, 6 October 1937 and *CAB* 23/89, CC 37(37)5, 13 October 1937. See also Avon, pp. 534–5 and Oliver Harvey, diary entry for 2 October 1937, Harvey, pp. 48–9.
48   Quoted in Keith Feiling, *The Life of Neville Chamberlain* (London, 1946), p. 322.
49   *FRUS*, 1938, vol. 1, pp. 115–17.
50   Avon, pp. 554–5.
51   Ibid., p. 554.
52   Oliver Harvey, diary entry for 16 January 1938, Harvey, pp. 70–1.
53   *Avon Papers*, FO 954/29, US/38/3, Eden to Chamberlain, 17 January 1938.
54   *Avon Papers*, FO 954/30, US/43/51 and *FRUS*, 1938, vol. 3, Under-Secretary of State to President Roosevelt, Washington, 17 January 1938, pp. 120–2.

55   Avon, pp. 559—60.

56   Oliver Harvey, diary entry for 18 January 1938, Harvey, pp. 72—3.

57   A full report on the three meetings of the Cabinet Committee on Foreign Affairs was presented to the full Cabinet on 24 January 1938, *CAB* 23/92, CC 1(38)1. Further commentary is supplied by Eden (Avon, pp. 560—5), Cadogan (diary entries for 19, 20 and 21 January 1938, Dilks, pp. 39—40), Harvey (diary entries for 19, 20 and 21 January 1938, Harvey, pp. 74—7) and Chamberlain (*Neville Chamberlain Papers*, NC 2/24A, diary entry for 19—27 February 1938).

58   Oliver Harvey, diary entry for 18 January 1938, Harvey, pp. 72—3.

59   At the Cabinet meeting of 15 December 1937 following the *Panay* incident the First Lord of the Admiralty had made it clear that the Royal Navy was not in a position to take action against Japan without assistance from the USA, and even then British naval forces in the Mediterranean would be seriously weakened. *CAB* 23/90, CC 47(37)4.

60   Quoted from Pratt, pp. 757—8.

61   This course of action was clearly suggested in the memorandum 'Comparison of the Strength of Great Britain with that of certain other nations as of January 1938', presented by the COS Subcommittee of the CID to the Cabinet on 8 December 1937 (CID Paper 1366-B), *CAB* 23/90, CC 46(37)10.

62   Oliver Harvey, diary entry for 19 January 1938, Harvey, pp. 74—5.

63   Quoted in Avon, p. 563.

64   Ibid., p. 563.

65   *CAB* 23/92, CC 1(38)1, 24 January 1938. See also Eden's account (Avon, pp. 563—6) and Harvey (diary entries for 20 and 21 January 1938, Harvey, pp. 75—7).

66   Cadogan, diary entry for 21 January 1938, Dilks, pp. 39—40 and *Avon Papers*, FO 954/30, US/43/51, Eden to Lindsay, 22 January 1938.

67   *CAB* 23/92, CC 1(38)1, 24 January 1938.

68   This issue is discussed by Lee, pp. 102—5. See also Pratt, pp. 755—60 and Watt, 'Roosevelt and Chamberlain', pp. 195—7.

69   Oliver Harvey, diary entry for 21 January 1938, Harvey, pp. 76—7.

70   *Neville Chamberlain Papers*, NC 2/24A, diary entry for 19—27 February 1938. See also Avon, p. 565.

71   Carlton, pp. 119—31. See also Roy Douglas, 'Chamberlain and Eden, 1937—1938', *Journal of Contemporary History*, 13, 1978, pp. 97—116.

72   *Neville Chamberlain Papers*, NC 18/1/1020, letter to his sister Hilda, 12 September 1937.

73   Ibid., NC 18/1, letter to his sister Hilda, 24 October 1937.

74   For Chamberlain's hopes of a change in Foreign Office attitudes following Vansittart's removal from the position of Permanent Under-Secretary, see *Neville Chamberlain Papers*, NC 18/1, letter to his sister Ida, 12 December 1937.

75   Oliver Harvey, diary entry for 16 January 1938, Harvey, pp. 70—1.

76   Indications of the influence wielded by Wilson in foreign affairs are given by Cadogan (Dilks, Cadogan diary entry for 10 January 1938, p. 34); Eden (see Avon, p. 556) and Oliver Harvey (diary entry for 17 January 1938, Harvey, pp. 71—2).

77   Oliver Harvey, diary entry for 17 January 1938, Harvey, pp. 71—2.

78   Lady Ivy Chamberlain was the widow of Sir Austen Chamberlain, Neville Chamberlain's half brother. For details of a series of letters despatched to her brother-in-law from Rome in the latter half of 1937 and the early months of 1938 see *Neville Chamberlain Papers*, NC 1/17/1—10.

79 *Neville Chamberlain Papers*, NC 1/17/5, Lady Ivy Chamberlain to Neville Chamberlain,16 December 1937.

80 *Avon Papers*, FO 954/13A, It/37/41 and It/37/42.

81 This admission was made by Chamberlain to Eden on 18 January 1938. Avon, p. 559 and Oliver Harvey, diary entry for 18 January 1938, Harvey, pp. 72—3.

82 *Neville Chamberlain Papers*, NC 1/17/6, Lady Ivy Chamberlain to Neville Chamberlain, 2 January 1938.

83 Avon, p. 561 and Oliver Harvey, diary entry for 19 January 1938, Harvey, pp. 74—5.

84 Neville Chamberlain wrote a further letter to his sister-in-law on 30 January 1938, which she immediately passed on to Mussolini. Eden only heard of the incident through a report from the Rome Embassy. See Avon, p. 573 and *Neville Chamberlain Papers*, NC/1/17, Lady Ivy Chamberlain to Neville Chamberlain, 2 February 1938.

85 Quoted in Avon, pp. 573—4. An account of the interview is also given in Oliver Harvey, diary entry for 8 February 1938, Harvey, pp. 86—7.

86 Avon, p. 567.

87 *Neville Chamberlain Papers*, NC 18/1, letter to his sister Hilda, 13 February 1938.

88 Eden's letter to Chamberlain of 9 January 1938 indicated his perception of the need to improve Anglo-German relations, while the turn of the year had witnessed an extensive exchange of memoranda between the two men on the subject of finding a suitable settlement of the Abyssinian issue which would allow the restoration of Anglo-Italian relations. See *Neville Chamberlain Papers*, NC 7/11/31/100, Eden to Chamberlain, 9 January 1938 and *Avon Papers*, FO 954/6A, ETH/38/1—4.

89 Cadogan, diary entry for 24 January 1938, Dilks, p. 41; and Oliver Harvey, diary entry for 24 January 1938, Harvey, p. 78.

90 *CAB* 23/92, CC 4(38)2, 9 February 1938 and Oliver Harvey, diary entry for 6 February 1938, Harvey, pp. 82—6.

91 A report of these meetings was given by Eden to the Cabinet on 2 February 1938, *CAB* 23/92, CC 3(38)2.

92 *Avon Papers*, FO 954/10A, Ger/38/1, record by Simon of a discussion with Flandin, 2 January 1938.

93 A point that Eden made to Cabinet Committee on Foreign Affairs on 24 January 1938, Oliver Harvey, diary entry for 6 February 1938, Harvey, pp. 82—6.

94 *Avon Papers*, FO 954/6A, ETH/38/4.

95 *CAB* 23/92, CC 3(38)2, 2 February 1938 and Eden's account in Avon, pp. 569—70.

96 *Avon Papers*, FO 954/6A, ETH/38/1, 1 January 1938.

97 Ibid., FO 954/6A, ETH/38/3, 9 January 1938.

98 Ibid.

99 Quoted in Avon, p. 570.

100 Oliver Harvey, diary entry for 31 January 1938, Harvey, pp. 80—1.

101 Cranborne's report is referred to by Eden (Avon, p. 572) and Cadogan (Cadogan diary entry for 4 February 1938, Dilks, p. 44).

102 The decision to resume the full Nyon patrol was taken by the Cabinet on 2 February 1938, following the sinking of the British ship *Endymion*, *CAB* 23/92, CC 3(38)4. Two days later Grandi informed Eden that Italy would resume its part in the naval patrols, Avon, pp. 571—2 and Oliver Harvey, diary entry for 6 February 1938, Harvey, pp. 82—6.

103 A report of these discussions was given by Eden to the Cabinet on 9 February 1938, *CAB* 23/92, CC 4(38)5. See also, Oliver Harvey, diary entry for 6 February 1938, Harvey, pp. 82—6.
104 Quoted in Avon, p. 574 and Dilks, p. 45.
105 Avon, p. 575.
106 Ibid., p. 576.
107 *CAB* 23/92, CC 4(38)5, 9 February 1938.
108 See Eden's letter to Chamberlain of 8 February 1938 quoted in Avon, pp. 573—4.
109 Cadogan was particularly annoyed at an article which appeared in the *Daily Mail* on 9 February 1938. Horace Wilson attempted to placate him by denying that either he or Chamberlain had inspired the article, Cadogan, diary entry for 10 February 1938, Dilks, p. 46.
110 Oliver Harvey, diary entry for 12 February 1938, Harvey, pp. 88—9.
111 Ibid., Oliver Harvey, diary entry for 14 February 1938, pp. 89—90. Apparently Cadogan also received evidence that Ball was involved, Dilks, p. 46.
112 Avon, pp. 575 and 623.
113 The Minister for Co-ordination of Defence's report (CP 24[38]) presented to the Cabinet on 16 February 1938. *CAB* 23/92, CC 5(38)9.
114 *CAB* 23/92, CC 5(38)9, 16 February 1938.
115 Avon, p. 578 and Oliver Harvey, diary entry for 17 February 1938, Harvey, pp. 92—3. There is also a suggestion that Grandi deliberately exacerbated relations between Eden and Chamberlain by avoiding Eden's attempts to arrange an interview to discuss Anglo-Italian relations. See Oliver Harvey, diary entry for 16 and 17 February 1938, Harvey, pp. 92—3 and *Avon Papers*, FO 954/13A, It/38/6, 16 February 1938.
116 For Lindsay's reports of 10 and 16 February 1938 see *Avon Papers*, FO 954/30, US/43/51. See also *FRUS* 1938, vol. 1, Memorandum of Conversation by the Under-Secretary of State (Welles) with the British Ambassador, 9 February 1938, pp. 124—5.
117 Oliver Harvey, diary entry for 11 February 1938, Harvey, p. 88; Avon, pp. 575—6; and *Neville Chamberlain Papers*, NC 2/24A, diary entry for 19—27 February 1938.
118 Oliver Harvey, diary entries for 15, 16 and 17 February 1938, Harvey, pp. 90—3; Cadogan, diary entries for 14, 15, 16 and 17 February 1938, Dilks, pp. 46—9.
119 *CAB* 23/92, CC 5(38)2, 16 February 1938.
120 *Neville Chamberlain Papers*, NC 2/24A, diary entry for 19—27 February 1938.
121 Oliver Harvey, diary entry for 17 February 1938, Harvey, pp. 92—3.
122 *Avon Papers*, FO 954/13A, It/38/10, Eden to Chamberlain, 18 February 1938.
123 *Avon Papers*, FO 954/13A, It/38/8, Lady Ivy Chamberlain to Neville Chamberlain, 17 February 1938.
124 *Neville Chamberlain Papers*, NC 2/24A 1938, diary entry for 19—27 February 1938.
125 For accounts of this interview with Grandi of 18 February 1938, see Avon, pp. 580—3; Oliver Harvey, diary entry for 18 February 1938, Harvey, pp. 93—4; *Neville Chamberlain Papers*, NC 2/24A, diary entry for 19—27 February 1938. An account from the Italian side is given in *Ciano's Diplomatic Papers* (London, 1948), Despatch by Grandi to the Italian Foreign Minister, 19 February 1938.
126 Quoted in Avon, p. 582.

127 Cadogan, diary entry for 18 February 1938, Dilks, pp. 49—50 and *Neville Chamberlain Papers*, NC 2/24, diary entry for 19—27 February 1938.
128 *CAB* 23/92, CC 6(38)1, 19 February 1938.
129 Ibid.
130 Oliver Harvey, diary entry for 19 February 1938, Harvey, pp. 94—5; and Cadogan, diary entry for 19 February 1938, Dilks, pp. 50—1.
131 Avon, p. 591; and Cadogan, diary entry for 19 February 1938, Dilks, pp. 50—1.
132 Oliver Harvey, diary entry for 19 February 1938, Harvey, pp. 94—5.
133 Oliver Harvey, diary entry for 20 February 1938, Harvey, pp. 95—6; Cadogan, diary entry for 20 February 1938, Dilks, pp. 51—2; and Avon, p. 592.
134 *Neville Chamberlain Papers*, NC 2/24A, diary entry for 19—27 February 1938.
135 *CAB* 23/92, CC 7(38), 20 February 1938.
136 Ibid.
137 Oliver Harvey, diary entry for 20 February 1938, Harvey, pp. 95—7; Cadogan, diary entry for 20 February 1938, Dilks, pp. 51—5; and Avon, pp. 594—5.
138 Ibid.
139 Oliver Harvey, diary entry for 20 February 1938, Harvey, pp. 95—7.
140 *CAB* 23/92, CC 7(38), Secretary's Note of a Meeting of Ministers held at 7.30 p.m., 20 February 1938.
141 For the text of Eden's resignation speech see *CAB* 23/92, CC 8(38), Cabinet meeting held at 10 p.m., 20 February 1938.
142 *CAB* 23/92, CC 8(38), 20 February 1938.

9 Conclusion

On 21 February 1938 Lord Cranborne and J.P.L. Thomas followed Eden's lead and submitted letters of resignation. As was customary Eden and Cranborne took up a position on the Government back benches on the afternoon of 21 February 1938 and it was evident that there was general speculation that Eden would use his resignation speech to outline fully his differences with the Cabinet. If, however, there were some who expected him to launch a bitter tirade against the Prime Minister, they were to be sadly disappointed.[1] Eden opened his speech with a concise summary of the course of Anglo-Italian relations since his assumption of the position of Foreign Secretary and argued that Italy's actions in both Spain and Abyssinia had brought him to the conclusion an agreement with Mussolini was worthless unless accompanied by a positive expression of Italian good-will. In this context he stated his conviction that the opening of negotiations must be preceded by the commencement of the withdrawal of Italian volunteers from Spain. In that the Cabinet was unwilling to support this precondition he felt that he had no alternative but to resign:

> In the light — my judgement may well be wrong — of the present international situation this is a moment for this country to stand firm, not to plunge into negotiations unprepared, with the full knowledge that the chief obstacle to their success has not been resolved.

I am conscious . . . that my Right Honourable Friend the Prime Minister and my colleagues take another view. They believe in their policy and they believe in their method, and they may be right. But, if they are right, their chances of success will certainly be enhanced if their policy is pursued by another Foreign Secretary . . . . It may even be that my resignation will facilitate the course of these negotiations. If so, nobody will be more pleased than I.

Although Eden stressed that he was divided from his colleagues by a 'real difference of outlook and method', his speech was remarkable in that his criticism of the Prime Minister's methods and goals was noticeably restrained.[2] It was left to subsequent speakers to lead the assault on the Cabinet. In a speech that was far more aggressive than Eden's, Cranborne declared that the opening of Anglo-Italian negotiations 'would be regarded not as a contribution to peace, but as a surrender to blackmail'.[3] Taking up this theme, Harold Nicolson informed the house:

However weak we might be, however divided, however muddle-headed, we never defended wrong with cool and planned deliberation as we are doing now. I regret that those great principles of our policy should lie tattered at our feet. Above all I regret we should see 'their sire butchered to make a Roman holiday'.[4]

The attack was taken up again the following day when the Opposition moved a vote of censure on the Government. During the course of the debate, Lloyd George sought to embarrass Chamberlain by suggesting that he had deliberately by-passed Eden through the establishment of clandestine links with the Italian Embassy,[5] while Winston Churchill expressed his regret at Eden's departure from the Cabinet:

All over the world, in every land, under every sky and system of government, wherever they may be, the friends of England are dismayed and the foes of England are exultant.[6]

It was significant, however, that Eden's only intervention in the debate was to point out that, even if he had known before the final Cabinet meeting of the Italian acceptance in principle of the formula for the withdrawal of volunteers from Spain, it would not have altered his decision.[7] At the conclusion of the debate, although a sizeable number of the Government's supporters elected to abstain, the vote of censure was comfortably defeated.[8]

Eden's supporters were both confused and disappointed by his resignation speech. In his diary entry for 22 February 1938, Harold Nicolson noted:

> Anthony did not really make a good speech. It was too restrained in parts and then too unrestrained. Either he should have confined himself to the distressed-colleague point of view or launched out into an appeal for decency in foreign policy. He fell between the two stools.[9]

In particular Eden's admission that his differences with Chamberlain were 'not of aim, but of outlook', lent credence to the view that he had resigned over a matter of procedure rather than a major part of policy.[10] In that Eden showed no inclination to lead an assault on the Cabinet, it was hardly surprising that there was a general feeling the Prime Minister should be given the opportunity to prove that he was correct. It is interesting to note that Nicolson, who had been one of Eden's most outspoken supporters in the debate, noted on 28 February 1938:

> Violet Bonham Carter wants me to go all out and oppose the Government. I refuse to do so, saying that it would be egoistic. She says that country comes before party and that I am being unpatriotic. I say that the moment has not arrived and Chamberlain must be given a chance.[11]

The international reaction to Eden's resignation was mixed. In his memoirs Eden quotes letters from Norman Davis, Robert Menzies and the British Ambassadors in Belgrade and Cairo all firmly supporting his decision.[12] It was evident, however, that these letters were not entirely representative of the reception afforded the news of the Foreign Secretary's resignation. As might have been predicted, the announcement was greeted enthusiastically in Rome. In a diary entry for 21 February 1938, Count Ciano noted:

> It was at a party at the Colonnas' that I learnt of Eden's fall last night. There was a general cheer at the news . . . . I gave instructions for the press not to be too triumphant — we don't want to turn Eden into a victim of Fascism.[13]

It is also significant that Eden's removal was not entirely unwelcome in the Dominions. On 28 February 1938 an official of the Office of the Canadian High Commissioner noted of a discussion with MacKenzie King in Ottawa:

> He naturally regretted Mr. Eden's resignation but he said that he had realised when in London last Summer that there would be

little hope of any agreement with Mussolini or Hitler so long as Mr. Eden was at the Foreign Office.[14]

The reaction of the British Press was, in general, favourable to the Prime Minister. Although several of the major provincial papers, in particular the *Manchester Guardian* and the *Yorkshire Post*, supported Eden's stance against the opening of negotiations with Italy, of the London-based daily papers only the *Daily Herald* displayed any sympathy for Eden's position.[15] On 21 February 1938 the *Daily Herald* declared:

> Mr. Chamberlain has come out stark and nakedly on the side of a system of power politics. In furtherance of that policy any concession, however ignoble and however humiliating will be made to the forces of International Fascism in return for their promise to keep their hands off British interests. For make no mistake about it, Mr. Eden has been sacrificed to Mussolini.[16]

The general tenor of the Press comment, however, was typified by *The Times*:

> It may . . . be predicted with some assurance that nothing fundamental to British aims will be changed by Mr. Eden's resignation — which need not mean that there is no substance in the grounds upon which he has offered it — but that the attempt to prove the possibility or otherwise of building stable relations between democracies and dictatorships will be pursued with a confidence and conviction that Mr. Eden felt unable to give it.[17]

The reaction of the British Press was almost certainly conditioned by the apparent unanimity with which the Cabinet had accepted the resignation. The fact that Eden's supporters were hesitant and finally capitulated to the Prime Minister is confirmed by both the Cabinet Minutes and an extract from Chamberlain's diary for the period 19–27 February 1938.[18] Chamberlain recorded of the Cabinet meetings:

> Some members of the Cabinet were very much alarmed at the disastrous effect which his [Eden's] resignation would have. Elliot, always a weak brother in a crisis, talked of its meaning 'the end of the Government'. The most absurd was Oliver Stanley who agreed with me entirely but announced that he considered that Anthony's resignation would have such calamitous results that he must resign too! This characteristic attempt to run away earned him much contempt and ridicule among his stouter hearted colleagues. Morrison on the other hand showed up well declaring that, although he had felt a little

critical of my 'precipitancy' first of all, he considered that all that could be done had been done to keep Anthony and that now we must all stand together. M. MacDonald was equally staunch. He too had his doubts about whether I was going too fast and moreover he was afraid that he might not be able to get the support of his party, but he informed me that . . . no matter what Ministers left he would stay. A crisis like this brings out the best and the worst in men's characters.[19]

Certainly Elliot and MacDonald expressed their sympathy for Eden's position at the meeting held on 19 February 1938 and the following day Stanley opposed any suggestion of Eden's resignation without further efforts at conciliation. The issue, however, was never seriously in doubt, given the Prime Minister's support from the senior Cabinet Ministers, Simon, Hoare, Halifax, Inskip and the three Service Ministers. There is little doubt, however, that most Ministers were genuinely distressed that Eden saw the issue as sufficient to warrant his resignation and were sincere in their attempts to engineer a compromise. When it became apparent that neither Chamberlain nor Eden was willing to give ground, there was never any suggestion of a cabal forming around Eden; indeed the Cabinet, as a body, gave an expression of complete loyalty to the Prime Minister on the night of 20 February 1938. It was evident the general feeling was that the Foreign Secretary was wrong in seeking to establish preconditions for the opening of negotiations with Italy and that, given Eden's refusal to accept a compromise, the only solution was resignation.[20]

It would appear that this interpretation of the situation was widely accepted. On 21 February 1938 Sir Maurice Hankey wrote to Sir Eric Phipps:

> The Foreign Secretary was always chopping and changing, blowing hot one day and cold the next. He went to Paris and Geneva and did good work in preparing the way for recognition as part of a general bargain of reconciliation. When he got back he seemed to have gone back on the whole idea.[21]

Hankey made no secret of the fact that he believed the Austrian situation had provided a unique opportunity to restore Anglo-Italian relations which had to be seized. In that Eden was opposed to the negotiations, Hankey was patently relieved at his resignation: 'Fond as I am of him on personal grounds, I woke this morning with a strange feeling of relief.'[22]

This sense of relief was evidently shared by the Service Ministries in that what seemed to be the last obstacle to the launching of an attempt to delete Italy from the list of potential enemies had been removed. It was significant that the three Service Ministers had all stood staunchly by Chamberlain throughout the crisis.[23] The conviction that it was necessary to take every step possible to improve relations with Italy and Germany and, therefore, avert the possibility of a military clash until the rearmament programme had been completed is clearly suggested in the diaries of Lieutenant-General Sir Henry Pownall.[24] Pownall, who was Director of Military Operations and Intelligence at the War Office, observed on 14 February 1938:

> Inskip concluded by saying that the bare fact was that we could not afford to arm ourselves for the contingencies of possible wars against three major powers in three different parts of the world. A broadish hint that it is up to the F.O. to reduce the number of potential enemies.[25]

A week later he noted:

> Thank goodness all this F.O. policy has at last come to a head.
>
> I make no doubt that from the Army's point of view — which is the nation's — that things have turned out for the best. The League of Nations' ideals, admirable as they are, are indeed a rotten foundation on which to build one's hopes. We are much safer — or at any rate we shall get a much longer breathing space that the Services so badly need — with a realist like Chamberlain and a decent man like Halifax, who has had experience of tempering ideals with realities.[26]

While it was hardly surprising that the War Office welcomed Eden's resignation, it might have been expected that senior officials at the Foreign Office would have been seriously concerned at the loss of their chief. Certainly Vansittart told Harold Nicolson that he was 'with Eden in principle' and was 'in terror of the Chamberlain course'.[27] Vansittart's power and prestige, however, were on the wane and the most influential figure was now Alex Cadogan.[28] Following the announcement of the resignation he wrote to Eden:

> You have had the most awful time any man could have . . . . I am convinced that you have done right because you have remained true to *yourself*.
>
> Personally, your going is a frightful wrench for me; as I hope you know what it meant to me to work for you. I owe you more than I can repay. You know that everyone in the Office who worked

with you was devoted to you, but no-one was as much as myself in your debt.[29]

Yet although Cadogan on a personal level was dismayed at Eden's departure, he clearly disagreed with his decision to make a stand on the volunteer issue. As his diary entry for 4 February 1938 indicates, the Permanent Under-Secretary was convinced that Eden was wrong to try to impose preconditions for the opening of negotiations:

Horace W. rings me up that P.M. wants A. to fix a meeting with Grandi. A. now digs his toes in. This is all wrong — he has agreed in principle to talks with Musso, and nothing has happened to change situation fundamentally. Spend a lot of time arguing with him and Bobbety. Have to tell H.W. it's no use. A. is silly on this question. He doesn't like the medicine and makes no bones about it; but then he seems to agree to it, and uses every excuse — clutches at it — to run out. This makes very bad impression.[30]

During the discussions in between the Cabinet meetings held on 19 and 20 February 1938, Cadogan urged Eden to accept the various compromise formulae that were devised. In the end he admitted that if he refused to compromise there was no alternative to resignation but, while respecting Eden's determination, he was personally convinced that the Foreign Secretary was wrong in making a stand on the volunteer issue.[31]

It was evident, therefore, that while there was widespread sympathy among Eden's colleagues for his decision to resign on what he saw as a matter of principle, the general feeling was that the opportunity must be taken to open negotiations with the Italians without further delay. If Eden felt any rancour at this effective endorsement of the Prime Minister's position, it was not openly displayed. On 25 February 1938 he addressed his constituents at Leamington. The tenor of his speech was very similar to his parliamentary declaration and there was little sign of any bitterness or malice:

The course that the Government have chosen is an indication of the sincerity of their desire to reach an agreement, it is not necessarily an indication of wise judgement in international affairs. I cannot help feeling that it was perfectly possible to stand firm and obtain the same results, if they are to be obtained, without the risks attendant on the present course.[32]

Oliver Harvey described it as a 'very dignified, not a fighting speech'.[33] It was also apparent that Eden's former Cabinet colleagues were relieved that he had not seen fit to attack the Cabinet openly.

Halifax told Harvey that he thought it was 'an awfully good speech'[34] and Chamberlain wrote to Eden to thank him for his restraint:

> After reading your speech to your constituents last night, I should like to send you a few friendly words. You had a very difficult task. You had to say enough to justify your resignation and to vindicate your view, and the easiest, and perhaps the most popular, way would have been to emphasise differences and to call for support . . . Anyhow, whatever the temptations, you have resisted them, and the dignity and restraint of your speech must add further to your reputation.[35]

It seemed that what had threatened to become a major political storm had blown itself out as a minor squall within a week. Eden's supporters within the House of Commons appeared baffled at his decision to resign over an issue which many saw as a technicality in the timing of negotiations rather than a major matter of principle.[36] Certainly the Cabinet was anxious to portray the incident in this context and, as Harold Macmillan subsequently noted, further substance was given to this interpretation by the suggestion that Eden was suffering from a nervous breakdown which had impaired his judgement.[37] This is an avenue of investigation that subsequent biographers have explored further. For example David Carlton, in an interview held with Malcolm MacDonald in January 1980, discussed the contention that Eden was seriously ill in February 1938.[38] The former Secretary of State for the Dominions recalled of his discussion with Eden on the evening of 19 February 1938:

> During our talk I felt increasingly worried about his state of mind. His thoughts seemed to be less clear and reasonably coherent than they usually were, and his statements were occasionally somewhat confused. I began to wonder whether he was well enough to continue performing the difficult tasks of his supremely important office . . . .

MacDonald claimed that he reported this impression to the Prime Minister the following day:

> I said that I thought that he was too mentally and physically exhausted to continue working wisely and well in his high office, and that in the circumstances, however regrettable, it would be better if he did resign.

> Chamberlain smiled and said that he had 'slept on the matter' and had come to the same conclusion.[39]

This account is supported somewhat by the fact that although MacDonald had been sympathetic to Eden's position in the Cabinet meeting held on 19 February 1938, at the meetings held on the following day it was apparent that he no longer resisted Eden's resignation.[40] There is also evidence to suggest that the Chancellor of the Exchequer had expressed concern at the state of Eden's health. J.P.L. Thomas subsequently recorded of a discussion that he held with Simon on 18 February 1938:

> He [Simon] opened by saying that he was as fond of Anthony as if he had been his own son, that he was becoming more and more depressed in watching A.E. at Cabinet meetings and in realising that he was both physically and mentally ill.[41]

It would seem that Thomas strenuously resisted any suggestion that Eden was ill: 'I replied that Anthony had just returned from a good holiday in the South of France and that his health indeed had never been better.'[42]

Eden later recorded that after discussing with Malcolm MacDonald the suggestion that he 'should stay on for a short while and then resign on grounds of ill health' they both agreed that 'nobody would believe this story and that I should only be acting against my own convictions for nothing'.[43] In addition, when he discovered that there was a rumour circulating that his health had influenced his decision to resign, he made a point of attending the debate in the House of Commons on 22 February 1938 in order to scotch any suggestion that he 'had felt the strain of recent events and was far from well'.[44] Three days later, in his speech at Leamington, he returned to this topic: 'You can judge for yourself whether I look like a sick man. You shall be my witnesses that there is no shred of truth in that suggestion.'[45]

There can be little doubt that as a result of the events of the previous two days, when Eden dined with MacDonald on the evening of 19 February 1938 he must have been visibly tired and jaded. There is very little evidence, however, to substantiate the suggestion that he was physically or mentally ill. Indeed his speeches delivered on 21 and 25 February 1938 were succinct and Oliver Harvey — who, with Cranborne, was a close associate of Eden throughout this period — at no time suggests that his health was impaired or that it was a contributory factor in his resignation.[46] A more plausible explanation, therefore, is that certain figures within the Government were genuinely concerned that if the rift between the Prime Minister and the Foreign Secretary were made public, it might adversely affect the stability of the Government. In this context it could be that they hoped to defuse the situation by persuading Eden to explain his resignation through ill-health. This interpretation is supported by subsequent accounts which J.P.L. Thomas has provided of discussions that he held with Simon and Horace Wilson. On 18 February 1938 Simon urged Thomas to persuade Eden to take six months' holiday and told Thomas that:

> resignation would be 'fatal to the Government, the country, nay the peace of the whole world'.

> On my direct negative he popped his hat on his head, walked down the stairs and did not speak to me again until he had become Lord Chancellor in May 1940.[47]

Of a discussion with Horace Wilson two days later Thomas recorded:

> he had telephoned to me that morning to say that he presumed that all was up and that Anthony would resign for reasons of health. I asked why, when Anthony was so thoroughly fit. 'Because it would be better for him' was the reply, 'and what is more, it would be better for you if you persuaded him to do so'. I put the telephone receiver down and did not see Sir Horace again until he spoke to me at Mr. Chamberlain's funeral.[48]

Thomas's testimony to Eden's health is supported by Oliver Harvey who noted, on 21 February 1938, that the rumour Eden was ill had no foundation and had probably been started by Simon.[49]

If Thomas and Harvey are to be believed, the lengths to which Simon and Wilson were prepared to go to persuade Eden to resign on grounds of ill-health would seem to suggest that they anticipated Eden's resignation would create a far greater political storm than in fact materialised. Certainly in his diary entries for the period September 1937—February 1938 Oliver Harvey repeatedly alluded to his conviction that Eden did have the support of a substantial number of Ministers within the Cabinet and that, in particular, he could usually count on Stanley, MacDonald, Elliot and De La Warr to back his policies. Although this group were often in the minority, Harvey considered that they had sufficient influence to prevent Eden's removal by his opponents.[50] Furthermore Harvey told Eden that his standing in both the country and the House of Commons was of such stature that 'whenever he took a firm line the Cabinet gave way because they couldn't face his resignation'.[51] These statements have led to the suggestion that Eden adopted a resolute stance at the Cabinet meetings of 19 and 20 February 1938 because of his conviction that ultimately the Cabinet would capitulate to his demands rather than precipitate a political crisis. The contention was refined further by Sir Samuel Hoare who suggested that the volunteer issue was perhaps used by Eden as a trial of strength with the Prime Minister.[52] Even if Eden lost the battle in the Cabinet it might have been thought that his standing within the Conservative Party would be sufficient to oust Chamberlain if the Anglo-Italian conversations were not successful.[53] In defence of this interpretation it has to be noted that Eden was aware that a meeting of the Conservative Foreign Affairs Committee, in the House of Commons on 17 February 1938, had warmly applauded Harold Nicolson's proposal that negotiations with either Italy or Germany should be preceded by an indication from Hitler or Mussolini of a willingness to moderate their respective ambitions in Austria and Libya.[54] Furthermore Randolph Churchill claimed that immediately after his resignation Eden discussed with Baldwin the possibility of Chamberlain being forced to resign and Baldwin informed Eden that he would advise the monarch to appoint Eden to the post of Prime Minister.[55]

If any credence is to be placed in the assertion that Eden used the volunteer issue in an attempt either to impose his authority on the Prime Minister or ultimately to oust Chamberlain, it would have to be conceded that the pursuit of such a course of action would suggest he grossly misread both the political climate and the extent of his support within the Government. To resign over an issue that appeared to centre on his opposition to the timing, but not the principle, of Anglo-Italian negotiations was hardly the most favourable ground on which to force a confrontation with the Prime Minister. If such was his intention he would have had a far stronger hand had he openly condemned Chamberlain's luke-warm reception of the proposals communicated to the British Government by President Roosevelt in January 1938. If Eden had resigned over the Roosevelt initiative he would probably have gained far greater sympathy, in that it would have been the Prime Minister who was portrayed as the figure obstructing the endorsement of a major scheme to defuse international tension.[56]

The whole manner of Eden's resignation and the low-key nature of his speeches on 21 and 25 February 1938 suggest that while he wanted to make his position clear, he had no intention of leading a rebellion against the Cabinet or of seeking to undermine Chamberlain's position. To have engaged in intrigue or a trial of strength with the Prime Minister would have been completely alien to Eden's nature, in that throughout his career he had built his reputation on the basis of being a loyal supporter of the Conservative Party and its leadership. In addition there is no suggestion that he ever considered conducting a personal vendetta against Chamberlain. Although they had disagreed over the conduct of Anglo-Italian relations, Eden did not see their differences as irrevocable and certainly envisaged the possibility of his return to the Cabinet within a year if the Anglo-Italian negotiations broke down.[57] Therefore although he felt strongly about the volunteer issue, it would appear that he did not consider the possibility of using it to divide the National Government. No doubt he would have considered such a course of action as both a betrayal of the majority of his colleagues and a manoeuvre that was likely to lead to an abrupt end to his Ministerial career. Undoubtedly Churchill's exile to the back benches over the India Bill was a salutary lesson that deterred many would-be rebels in the latter half of the 1930s.

The belief that his departure from the Cabinet would only be temporary was fuelled by several letters from Chamberlain which emphasised that his actions had not been motivated by any sense of enmity. Upon receiving Eden's letter of resignation Chamberlain had replied:

> I should like to thank you very warmly for your loyal and helpful comradeship during all the time we have worked together and to assure you that nothing which has happened has impaired my admiration of your gifts and my affection for yourself.[58]

Furthermore on 26 February 1938 the Prime Minister concluded in a letter to Eden: 'I won't say more now than my personal feelings towards you are unchanged and I hope will always remain so.'[59]

It was evident that Chamberlain was grateful Eden had chosen not to lead a rebellion against the Government and it would also seem that his personal criticism of his former Foreign Secretary was somewhat tempered by the suspicion that Eden had been poorly advised by his senior officials at the Foreign Office. It is noticeable that Chamberlain's complaints throughout the latter half of 1937 were levelled not personally at Eden but rather at the Foreign Office as a unit, with the suggestion that the senior officials were collectively obstructing the improvement of relations with Italy.[60] This is a view that was also adopted by Hankey and it is interesting to note that in a letter to his son Robin, dated 1 March 1938, he argued that the real problem was that Eden had been influenced 'by a lot of sloppy people in the F.O.', and added that Baldwin had admitted 'that he ought to have straightened out the F.O. before he left'. In this context Hankey predicted that Eden would return to the Cabinet 'before long' and would one day become Prime Minister.[61]

Yet to attribute the confrontation between the Prime Minister and the Foreign Secretary largely to Eden's judgement being impaired by 'sloppy people at the F.O.' would be, in effect, to render Eden a disservice. While he naturally worked closely with, and sought the advice of, his senior officials, to suggest that they were able to manipulate or force upon him a certain line of policy would be erroneous. The central figure within this debate was Sir Robert Vansittart who Pownall referred to as 'the real nigger in the wood pile'.[62] Certainly Chamberlain suspected that Vansittart held undue influence over Eden and he thus went to great lengths to get him removed from the position of Permanent Under-Secretary. Yet while Vansittart was not reserved in his condemnation of Italian and German ambitions, he had never advocated the rejection of negotiations with Hitler or Mussolini. Indeed Vansittart and several of the senior Foreign Office advisers, including Leeper and Sargent, had repeatedly urged Eden in the latter months of 1937 to seek a settlement of differences with Italy. It was apparent they believed that although Anglo-Italian interests in the Mediterranean and the Near East were incompatible in the long run, it was important to undermine the Rome—Berlin relationship as a precondition for negotiations, with the real storm-centre of Europe in Berlin. With the growing number of reports received in November and December of 1937 suggesting that a move to absorb Austria within the German Reich could not be discounted, Vansittart contended that the delay of the opening of Anglo-Italian negotiations could only further imperil Austrian independence. This belief in the need to seek a *détente* with Italy, even if only of a temporary nature, was also upheld by Vansittart's successor in January 1938, Alex Cadogan.[63] In fact the only figure within the Foreign Office who persistently advised Eden against negotiations with Italy, except on the most favourable grounds to Britain, was Cranborne. It was Cranborne who had argued vehemently against the granting of *de jure* recognition of Abyssinia in the latter half of 1937 and it was the Under-Secretary for Foreign Affairs who presented Eden with a memorandum, in the first week of February 1938, suggesting that opinion in Geneva was very much against the granting of any concessions designed to lure Italy into negotiation.[64]

In this context it would be difficult to substantiate the assertion that Eden was manoeuvred into a position of confrontation with the Prime Minister by his advisers at the Foreign Office. The majority feeling within the Foreign Office was in favour of the opening of negotiations without extensive preconditions. It would appear, therefore, that the decision to insist upon the commencement of the withdrawal of volunteers from Spain, although supported by Cranborne and Oliver Harvey, was made by Eden against the counsel of most of his advisers and was certainly opposed by Cadogan.[65] While Eden's decision can be partly accounted for in terms of the personal enmity that existed between Mussolini and himself, it was, in fact, far more deeply rooted in his concept of the nature of British interests and the development of Anglo-Italian relations since 1935. In essence

Eden's views on the format and goals of British foreign policy had been formed under the tutelage of Sir Austen Chamberlain. He, therefore, embraced the traditional shibboleths which surrounded the conviction that British interests were best served by a minimum of involvement in European affairs beyond the maintenance of the status quo in Western Europe in order to free British resources for continuing to pursue a global role. The problem confronting both Eden and Sir Austen Chamberlain in the post-war period was that, despite the apparent elimination of German and Russian competition, the British position was being steadily challenged and eroded by the rise of nationalist movements in the Near East and India and the growing rivalry with Japan in the Far East. Sir Austen Chamberlain's response to this threat was to seek to secure the maintenance of the status quo in Western Europe by the conclusion of the Locarno Treaty and to ally Britain firmly with the growing strength of the Dominions.[66] It was this essentially defensive concept of the goals of foreign policy that Eden observed during his apprenticeship at the Foreign Office and which coloured his outlook in subsequent years.

The only significant departure that Eden was to make from the framework of policy established by Sir Austen Chamberlain was his endorsement of the efforts at Geneva both to secure disarmament and to establish the international authority of the League of Nations. Yet it can be clearly seen that he linked both of these goals squarely to the defence of British interests. In that the maintenance of British influence was plainly linked to the continuation of the status quo in Europe, the Mediterranean and the Far East, it was clearly in the British interest to support international agreements which promised to defuse conflict and more particularly to mobilise the international community against any nation which sought to expand unilaterally its influence and possessions. It was evident, therefore, that despite Eden's reputation as a champion of the League of Nations he at all times put British interests first and, as the Abyssinian and Rhineland crises indicated, he had no intention of allowing the League either to dictate British foreign policy or to involve Britain in a military confrontation that was inimical to British interests.[67] It would not be correct to suggest, however, that Eden's concept of international relations was completely inflexible. He was prepared to concede that change in the relative balance of power between nations was inevitable and he saw Geneva as an invaluable forum which could be used to engineer peaceful and controlled alterations in the status quo. In this sense the League of Nations was seen as an important factor in the defence of British interests, particularly in the period 1930–35 when it became clear that Germany, Italy and Japan were intent upon expanding their international status. It was a major setback, therefore, to the British position when, in the period 1932—36, the prestige of the League of Nations received several severe blows. Firstly the Disarmament Conference, which had been dogged throughout by Franco-German rivalry, was effectively disbanded in 1934 when it became clear that Germany was already rearming and was unlikely to accept any further armament limitation. While this represented a serious threat to the balance of power in Europe, which prompted a rapid review of British military capabilities, it was Mussolini who finally smashed the authority of the League of Nations with the launching of the Italo-Abyssinian war in October 1935. The failure of the League of Nations to defend Abyssinian sovereignty destroyed the credibility of Geneva as a major factor in international politics. When in the Summer of 1936 Eden proposed that the sanctions clauses within the Covenant of the League of Nations be deleted, it was, in effect, an admission that any hope which might have existed of using Geneva to defend British interests had evaporated.

In the course of 1936, with the Italian involvement in Abyssinia, Spain, and the fermentation of anti-British propaganda throughout the Mediterranean and the Near East, it was hardly surprising that Eden saw Mussolini as the most immediate threat to British interests. Furthermore the Italian leader's blatant disregard for the Anglo-Italian Agreement, concluded in January 1937, only added fuel to the British Foreign Secretary's belief that Mussolini was a 'gangster' who respected nothing but naked force.[68] In this sense Hitler's reoccupation of the Rhineland and his demand for the return of former German colonies and a closer relationship with Austria appeared almost reasonable alongside Italian activity in the Mediterranean and the Near East. Therefore, while appreciating the logic of obtaining a temporary *détente* with Italy in order to weaken the Rome—Berlin axis, it became apparent that Eden, by February 1938, had come to the conclusion an agreement with Italy would be virtually worthless. Furthermore he was convinced that the Rome—Berlin axis would be most effectively destabilised by a resolute stand against Italian aggression that would diminish Italy's worth in German eyes. In adopting this stance Eden undoubtedly felt that the Nyon Conference had clearly shown how Italy could be brought to heel. Following the conclusion of the Conference, Eden wrote to Winston Churchill on 25 September 1937:

> I thought your summing up of the position at Nyon 'It is only rarely that an opportunity comes when stern and effective measures can be brought to bear upon an evil doer without incurring the risk of war' effectively described the position. Mussolini has been unwise enough to overstep the limits, but

he has had to pay the penalty . . . . From reports which I have received, Germany herself has not been slow to take note of this fact.[69]

The mistake Eden made, perhaps in an attempt to appease his Cabinet colleagues, was that he did not make his attitude fully clear. By agreeing to continue to explore the grounds for an Anglo-Italian settlement, he led his colleagues to believe that he was perfectly willing to work for such an agreement and certainly they were surprised at his decision to insist upon Italian concessions as a pre-condition to negotiations.[70] That such a stance was unacceptable to the majority of his colleagues was clear, given the general belief that French support in the event of a military conflict with Italy was unsure and that Britain was probably not in either a political or military position to impose its wishes upon Italy.[71] In this sense Chamberlain argued that Eden's policy only threatened to exacerbate relations with Italy and further strengthen the Rome—Berlin axis.

It would seem, in fact, that Eden's policy of 'cunctation' was only viable if progress was being made in the isolation of Italy through the improvement of relations with Germany, or the British position *vis à vis* Germany and Italy was steadily improving through the attainment of military superiority or the establishment of alliances with the remaining major world powers. It was apparent, however, that despite strenuous efforts, Eden in February 1938 was no nearer reaching a satisfactory settlement of Anglo-German differences than he had been in January 1936. On the contrary, as German military power grew, Hitler's desire for negotiations with Britain and France seemed to be proportionately reduced and he appeared to relish the diversion of British resources to the Mediterranean. Eden's problems were compounded by the fact that relations with the two unaligned major powers, the USA and the USSR, were still something of an enigma. While the Roosevelt administration continued to profess its interest in international security, there was no suggestion that the USA was willing to give any form of positive commitment to abandon isolationism and to pledge its resources to the maintenance of a system of collective security.[72]

The other unknown quantity was the USSR. Despite its formal entry into the international community, following its acceptance of membership of the League of Nations in September 1934 and its expressed interest in the maintenance of the status quo in Eastern Europe, Anglo-Soviet relations were still characterised by suspicion and thinly veiled hostility. This might be seen as surprising given that Eden was the first British Minister to visit Moscow and considered that he had 'destroyed some Soviet suspicion of British policy'.[73] It would seem, however, that Eden was as suspicious of Soviet intentions as were most of his colleagues in the Conservative Party, many of whom feared Communism far more than Fascism. In this context the alienation of the USSR was based not only on the desire to placate Hitler but also on the very real fear that the USSR still sought to spread communism throughout Europe. It was certainly no part of Eden's calculations to involve the USSR in the negotiations for a European security settlement.[74]

With the failure of diplomacy to improve Britain's position *vis à vis* Germany and Italy, the justification of Eden's policy fell increasingly upon the assumption that by a programme of rapid rearmament British military strength would, in the long run, reach a level that would be sufficient to deter aggression against British interests in Europe, the Mediterranean and the Near East. It was hardly surprising, therefore, that Eden was a vigorous supporter of the rearmament programme. On 20 November 1936 he told his constituents in Leamington:

> Our first task is to equip ourselves as a nation so thoroughly and so strongly that the whole world may see that we mean what we say, and that our conceptions of international order have behind them adequate force.[75]

He made it perfectly clear, however, that Britain had no intention of acting as the policeman of the world, despite its obligations under the Covenant of the League of Nations:

> there is no automatic obligation to take military action. It is, moreover, right that this should be so, for nations cannot be expected to incur automatic military obligations save for areas where their vital interests are concerned.[76]

Yet the ability of Britain to defend its 'vital interests' was open to question. On 3 February 1937 the Cabinet was presented with figures by the Air Ministry which indicated that Germany would have air superiority over Britain by the Autumn of 1938, particularly in the possession of heavy bombers where it would outnumber Britain by a ratio of over three to one.[77] Although the Chiefs-of-Staff reported in the same month that Germany was not yet in a position to launch a European war, the growing menace posed to European stability by German rearmament was implicit.[78] As a member of the DRC, Eden was closely involved in the rearmament programme and although great strides had been made it was evident that the British programme was barely matching the progress of its competitors. The central question revolved around the extent of the resources which the British economy could afford to allocate to war production. In July 1934 Neville Chamberlain, as Chancellor of the Exchequer, had been successful in trimming down the defence budget from £70 million to £50 million.[79] While the immediate consequence of this decision was the need to identify priorities in defence which resulted in the channelling of resources largely into the Royal Air Force, it was also indicative of a wider debate on the format of rearmament.[80] While Eden would have preferred a short-term programme of rapid rearmament which might have had an immediate impact on Britain's international position, Chamberlain adopted a far more cautious approach. In essence Chamberlain supported the Treasury view that the programme must be dictated by Britain's financial capabilities and that it would be unwise to shackle the economy by diverting inordinate resources to rearmament or by the levying of extensive loans to finance rearmament.[81] Chamberlain, therefore, supported both a long-term programme and selective rearmament, concentrating on Britain's immediate interest in defensive rather than offensive capabilities.

Eden could not have been anything but disturbed when, upon assuming the post of Prime Minister, one of Chamberlain's first actions was to request Inskip to prepare a review of proposed defence expenditure.[82] Although the report was not presented until December 1937, the events of the following six months confirmed Eden's fears in that Chamberlain consistently rejected his suggestions that the British programme be boosted by the acquisition of war material from abroad.[83] Inskip's report, presented to the Cabinet on 22 December 1937, outlined a 5-year programme which limited expenditure to £1500 million.[84] In order to keep within this limit the Expeditionary Force to assist France in the event of war was to be pruned to two mechanised divisions, while production for the Royal Air Force was to be concentrated on fighter aircraft rather than bombers. Eden observed:

> In reading the report, he had formed the opinion that we were concentrating too much on the defensive. The Army was to have an entirely defensive role and it was proposed to deprive the Air Force of part of the offensive power advocated by the Secretary of State for Air.[85]

Although Eden was successful in gaining a marginal reconsideration of the distribution of Royal Air Force production between fighter and bomber aircraft and also further resources for the Royal Navy which added another £150 million to the overall programme, the report was a severe blow to his position.[86] The Cabinet had effectively sacrificed Britain's ability to intervene militarily in European affairs. It was clear that the object of the programme was to bolster Britain's defensive capabilities but not to create a military force that would be of sufficient size to threaten Italy and Germany. It was evident that in seeking to husband Britain's economic resources, Chamberlain was placing the burden of improving relations with Italy and Germany on diplomacy. At the Cabinet meeting of 22 December 1938 the Prime Minister pointedly endorsed Inskip's observation that:

> in the long run the provision of adequate defences within the means at our disposal will only be achieved when our long term foreign policy has succeeded in changing the present assumption as to our potential enemies.[87]

Furthermore it was significant that four days before Eden's resignation Inskip returned to this theme:

> it was beyond the resources of this country to make proper provision in peace for the defence of the Empire against three major powers in three different theatres of war. He therefore desired to repeat with fresh emphasis his opinion as to the importance of reducing the scale of our commitments and the number of our potential enemies.[88]

In this context Chamberlain viewed Eden's obstruction of the Anglo-Italian negotiations with rising impatience. Although he had not sought a pretext to remove his Foreign Secretary, the discussions with Italy were now a prime factor in his concept of British foreign policy and he could no longer brook Eden's prevarication. In a letter to his sister, dated 27 February 1938, he commented:

> I had no idea until the 18th that it would come to a break but after the repeated efforts of the F.O. to stave off conversations and to prevent my seeing Grandi, I knew that the time had come when I must make my final stand and that Anthony must yield or go.

> I doubt whether till the last moment he realised that the issue between us was not whether we should have conversations now but whether we should have them at all. I had gradually arrived at the conclusion that at bottom Anthony did not want to talk either with Hitler or Mussolini and as I did, he was right to go.[89]

Eden's resignation, therefore, was not simply a matter of timing or procedure but rather it was a result of a major division between the Prime Minister and the Foreign Secretary on Anglo-Italian policy. The fact that Eden had allowed himself to be manoeuvred into such a confrontation was, however, indicative of his failure to obtain an agreement with the dictators during the course of the previous two years. By February 1938 it was apparent that his colleagues saw his policies as based upon little more than outright hostility to Italy and unreciprocated gestures of friendship to Germany. Certainly this had not been Eden's intention, for in January 1936 he had been foremost amongst those who advocated the pursuit of agreements with Italy and Germany. Given his isolation within the Cabinet, it was perhaps to his credit that he resigned with dignity and no sign of any rancour. As a result, however, Eden's resignation has been misunderstood and misinterpreted by subsequent historians. For instance, Sir John Wheeler-Bennett referred to him as 'the Golden Boy, slim, handsome and charming'. He added:

> My generation looked upon him as typifying the generation who had survived the war to become the champion and defender of our pathetic belief in what proved to be ephemeral Wilsonian shibboleths of 'a war to end war' and 'let us make the world safe for democracy'.[90]

In essence Wheeler-Bennett failed to appreciate that Eden's championship of the League of Nations and disarmament was not as a result of a commitment to 'Wilsonian shibboleths' but rather as a tool to be used in the defence of purely British interests. For Eden was, in effect, a diplomat of the old school, both in his outlook on the goals of foreign policy and the means to be used to attain those goals. At times he displayed an arrogance and stubbornness that betrayed both his aristocratic background and his belief in the importance of Britain's global role. Yet it cannot be denied that he was a successful and respected diplomat with a talent for conducting international negotiations. This aspect of his ability is amply testified to by his work at Geneva, both during the course of the Disarmament Conference and his handling of the crises surrounding the Saar plebiscite, the Abyssinian war and the reoccupation of the Rhineland. Furthermore in his sponsorship of the Non-Intervention Committee and the Nyon Conference he made his reputation as an international statesman. Yet while Eden succeeded in establishing a fairly close *rapport* with successive French Governments following the lifting of sanctions against Italy, he failed completely to establish a similar relationship with either Italy or Germany. Perhaps his failure in this field illuminates his background and his limitations, for Eden came from a world where diplomacy was conducted between gentlemen and agreements, once made, were honoured. Hitler and Mussolini, however, were a new breed who were neither honourable nor gentlemen and Eden could not conceal his perplexity at, and his distaste for, their methods.

The issue surrounding Eden's resignation, however, is not whether he was right in decrying the value of an agreement with Italy but rather that in January 1936 he had committed himself to the attainment of a European security agreement as a means of defusing international tension. By February 1938 his colleagues, probably rightly, believed that such an agreement was no longer possible given his stance over the Italian negotiations and his failure to improve relations with Germany. In his defence it can be contended that in the form of a rapid rearmament programme and the improvement of Anglo-American relations he had identified plausible alternative programmes but he had not succeeded in winning his colleagues over to either of these programmes. It would, therefore, have been more logical if he had resigned in December 1937 following the acceptance of expenditure limitations on defence, or in January 1938 over the Roosevelt initiative. His decision not to take this course can, perhaps, be explained by his loyalty to the party and also his unwillingness to return to the back benches having sampled the power of Ministerial office. More likely, however, he still harboured a belief that progress could be made on Anglo-German relations particularly in the form of a colonial settlement.[91] It was, therefore, left to Neville Chamberlain to force the issue and, as one subsequent observer had noted, Eden 'was no match for the old boy in political cunning'.[92] Therefore, given that Eden had failed to win over his colleagues to his point of view, he saw resignation as the only course open to him.

While in the appeasement debate Eden must stand in the dock alongside Chamberlain and his Cabinet, it has to be conceded, in his defence, that he chose to resign over what he saw as a matter of principle while many of his colleagues shelved their doubts and elected to soldier on with the appeasement of Italy. Although one subsequent observer has seen fit to describe Eden's approach to foreign policy as a *collage* of the type of 'good intentions with which hell is paved',[93] it would perhaps be fairer to describe him as an honourable man pursuing what he considered were honourable policies, but in February 1938 the time was 'out of joint' and Eden had quite clearly played out his hand. As he conceded in his letter of resignation:

> It cannot be in the country's interest that those who are called upon to direct its affairs should work in an uneasy partnership, fully conscious of differences in outlook yet hoping that they will not recur. This applies with a special force to the relationship between the Prime Minister and the Foreign Secretary. It is for

these reasons that with very deep regret I have decided that I must leave you and your colleagues with whom I have been associated during years of great difficulty and stress.[94]

As it turned out, his decision to follow his own judgement rather than submit to the collective authority of the Cabinet has been seen by many subsequent observers as a point in his favour.[95] However, it perhaps also indicated a certain arrogance in his nature that was to figure in a far more tragic episode almost two decades later.

References

1   Harold Macmillan described Eden's resignation as a 'sensation' and recorded that there was 'considerable excitement' at the prospect of his resignation speech. H. Macmillan, *Winds of Change 1914—1939* (London, 1966), pp. 537—8. See also the account of the debate given by Broad, pp. 111—14.
2   *H of C*, Debs, 5th ser., vol. 332, cols 45—50, 21 February 1938.
3   *H of C*, Debs, 5th ser., vol. 332, cols 50—2, 21 February 1938.
4   *H of C*, Debs, 5th ser., vol. 332, cols 99—104, 21 February 1938.
5   *H of C*, Debs, 5th ser., vol. 332, cols 253—62, 22 February 1938.
6   *H of C*, Debs, 5th ser., vol. 332, cols 235—47, 22 February 1938.
7   *H of C*, Debs, 5th ser., vol. 332, col. 257, 22 February 1938.
8   The vote of censure which had been proposed by Arthur Greenwood was defeated by 330 votes to 165. See *H of C*, Debs, 5th ser., vol. 332, cols 321—6, 22 February 1938.
9   N. Nicolson (ed.), *Diaries and Letters of Harold Nicolson 1930—1939* (London, 1966). See Nicolson, diary entry for 22 February 1938, Nicolson, pp. 323—5.
10   *H of C*, 5th ser., vol. 332, cols 45—50, 21 February 1938. The confusion surrounding Eden's resignation is testified to by Oliver Harvey. See Oliver Harvey, diary entry for 21 and 22 February 1938, Harvey, pp. 97—100.
11   Nicolson, diary entry for 28 February 1938, Nicolson, p. 327.
12   Avon, pp. 602—4.
13   Ciano, diary entry for 21 February 1938, Mayor, pp. 78—9.
14   *Avon Papers*, FO 954/4A, F.L.C. Floud (Office of High Commissioner for UK) to Edward Harding, Dominion Office, 28 February 1938.
15   See *Manchester Guardian* and *Yorkshire Post* for 21 February 1938.
16   *Daily Herald*, 21 February 1938.
17   *The Times*, 21 February 1938. See also the *Daily Telegraph* for the same date.
18   For the Cabinet Minutes of the meetings held on 19 and 20 February 1938, see *CAB* 23/92, CC 6(38)1 and CC 7(38).
19   *Neville Chamberlain Papers*, NC 2/23A, diary entry for 19—27 February 1938.
20   *CAB* 23/92, CC 6(38)1 and CC 7(38). See also Templewood, pp. 279—80; Halifax, pp. 193—5; and Duff Cooper, *Old Men Forget* (London, 1954), pp. 210—14.
21   *Phipps Papers*, PHPP 3/3, f. 81, Hankey to Phipps, 21 February 1938.
22   Ibid.

23   The Cabinet minutes clearly indicate that none of the Service Ministers chose to side with Eden, *CAB* 23/92, CC 6(38)1 and CC 7(38). See also Cooper, pp. 210—14.

24   B. Bond (ed.), *Chief of Staff, The Diaries of Lieutenant-General Sir Henry Pownall, Vol. 1 : 1933—1940* (London, 1972).

25   Pownall, diary entry for 14 February 1938, Bond, pp. 133—4.

26   Pownall, diary entry for 21 February 1938, Bond, p. 135.

27   Nicolson, diary entry for 28 February 1938, Nicolson, p. 327.

28   Alex Cadogan had been given the part of Permanent Under-Secretary in January 1938 with Vansittart's acceptance of the position of Chief Diplomatic Adviser. See further details in Chapter 7.

29   Quoted in D. Dilks, *The Diaries of Sir Alexander Cadogan* (London, 1971), pp. 54—5.

30   Cadogan, diary entry for 4 February 1938, Dilks, p. 44.

31   See Cadogan, diary entries for 19 and 20 February 1938, Dilks, pp. 51—5. Also see Avon, pp. 586—95 and Harvey, diary entries for 19 and 20 February 1938, Harvey, pp. 94—7.

32   Quoted in Avon, pp. 604—5.

33   Harvey, diary entry for 26 February 1938, Harvey, pp. 101—2.

34   Ibid., loc. cit.

35   Quoted in Feiling, p. 389.

36   See Macmillan, pp. 536—7. Also Harvey, diary entry for 21 February 1938, Harvey, pp. 97—8 and Nicolson, diary entry for 22 February 1938, Nicolson, pp. 323—5.

37   Macmillan, p. 538.

38   Carlton, pp. 129—30.

39   Ibid., p. 130.

40   *CAB* 23/92, CC 6(38)1 and CC 7(38).

41   Quoted in Avon, p. 585.

42   Ibid., loc. cit.

43   Ibid., p. 591.

44   Ibid., p. 601.

45   Ibid., p. 604.

46   Indeed Harvey bitterly denied, in his diary entry for 21 February 1938, the 'story spread by the Whips that A.E. was ill', Harvey, p. 97.

47   Quoted in Avon, p. 585.

48   Ibid., p. 595.

49   Harvey, diary entry for 21 February 1938, Harvey, p. 97.

50   For example see Oliver Harvey, diary entries for 15 October 1937, 3 November 1937, 17 January 1938, 21 January 1938, 19 February 1938 and 20 February 1938. See also Oliver Harvey, letter to Eden of 7 November 1937, Harvey, pp. 415—17.

51   Oliver Harvey, diary entry for 8 February 1938, pp. 86—7.

52   Templewood, pp. 279—80.

53   Certainly Harvey appeared to hold this view, Oliver Harvey, diary entry for 22 February 1938, Harvey, pp. 98—100.

54   Avon, pp. 579—80.

55   Randolph Churchill, *The Rise and Fall of Sir Anthony Eden* (London, 1959), p. 149.

56   It would appear that Oliver Harvey felt that Eden should have resigned over the Roosevelt initiative and J.P.L. Thomas and Cranborne were probably of the same opinion. Oliver Harvey, diary entry for 20 January 1938, Harvey, pp. 75—6.

57   Oliver Harvey, diary entry for 22 and 27 February 1938, Harvey, pp. 98–104.

58   Avon, p. 597.

59   Quoted in Feiling, p. 389.

60   For example see *Neville Chamberlain Papers*, NC 18/1, letters to his sisters dated 8 August, 12 September, 24 October, 6 November, 12 December 1937 and 27 February 1938.

61   Letter from Hankey to his son Robin, dated 1 March 1938. Quoted in Roskill, vol. 3, pp. 304–5.

62   Pownall, diary entry for 21 February 1938, Bond, p. 135.

63   The discussions surrounding the possible opening of Anglo-Italian negotiations in August 1937 indicate that Vansittart fully concurred with Eden on the need to extract substantial concessions from the Italians as a precondition for the opening of negotiations. See *Avon Papers*, FO 954/13A, It/37/20, It/37/17, It/37/14. By December 1937, however, Vansittart had decided that the most immediate threat was the German absorption of Austria. In this sense it was necessary to get on terms with Italy in order to nullify the German threats. See *Vansittart Papers*, 1/21, December 1937. Vansittart's biographer Ian Colvin noted that Vansittart told Eden in February 1938 that he had made a mistake in resigning over the volunteer issue when the threat to Austria was so great. Colvin, p. 193. It would seem that while wary of Italy, Sargent and Leeper supported Vansittart's assertion that the opening of negotiations could not be delayed. See Oliver Harvey, diary entries for 7 and 8 November 1937, Harvey, pp. 57–8 and Douglas, pp. 104–5. Cadogan certainly had very little sympathy for Eden's avoidance of Anglo-Italian relations, see Cadogan, diary entry for 4 February 1938, Dilks, p. 44; and *Avon Papers*, FO 954/13A, It/38/1.

64   For Eden's comments on Cranborne's Minute of 16 November 1937, see *Avon Papers*, FO 954/10, Eden to Chamberlain, 16 November 1937. For comments on Cranborne's Memorandum of 4 February 1938, see Avon, p. 572 and Oliver Harvey, diary entry for 6 February 1938, Harvey, pp. 82–6. Cranborne's role is also discussed by Roy Douglas, see R. Douglas, 'Chamberlain and Eden 1937–38', *Journal of Contemporary History*, vol. 13, 1978, pp. 105–9.

65   Cadogan had submitted a memorandum to Eden on 12 January 1938 urging him to seek an opportunity to open negotiations with Italy. *Avon Papers*, FO 954/13A, It/38/1.

66   For the formation of Eden's views under Austen Chamberlain see Chapter 1 and particularly pp. 12–24. For an account of Austen Chamberlain's conduct of British foreign policy in this period see Sir Charles Petrie, *The Life and Letters of the Rt Hon. Sir Austen Chamberlain*, vol. 2 (London, 1940) and Sir Austen Chamberlain, *Peace in Our Time: Addresses on Europe and the Empire* (London, 1928).

67   Eden's attitude to the League of Nations has been discussed more fully, pp. 18–19; 40–41; 87–9 and 312–14.

68   The assertion that Mussolini had 'the mentality of a gangster' was made by Eden in a Foreign Office Minute on 24 July 1937, Avon, pp. 450–1.

69   Quoted in W.S. Churchill, *The Second World War, Volume 1: The Gathering Storm* (Penguin, 1960), pp. 224–5.

70   Certainly the Cabinet Minutes support the conclusion that Eden's colleagues were genuinely surprised at his decision to make a stand on the volunteer issue, *CAB* 23/92, CC 6(38)1 and CC 7(38).

71   As recently as 16 February 1938 Inskip had emphasised the need to reduce the number of potential enemies facing Britain, *CAB* 23/92, CC 5(38)9.

72   It was evident that Roosevelt's initiative of January 1938 did not envisage a positive military commitment by the USA to the maintenance of international security. *FRUS* 1938, vol. 1, pp. 115—17. In addition Welles informed Lindsay on 7 March 1938 that the President had no further initiatives under consideration. *Avon Papers*, FO 954/30, US/43/2.

73   Avon, p. 162 and *DBFP*, 2nd ser., vol. 12, no. 656, 28 March 1935.

74   In his memoirs Eden testifies to the fact that most of his colleagues had a greater fear of Communism than Fascism which was underlined by their reaction to the Spanish Civil War, Avon, pp. 162—3. See also Jones, p. 231. Yet Eden's thinly veiled hostility to the Franco-Soviet pact and his efforts to exclude the USSR from the Nyon Conference more than suggest that he too wished to exclude the USSR from European affairs. *DBFP*, 2nd ser., vol. 13, nos 521, 516 and 522. Also, Avon, pp. 461—2.

75   Avon, pp. 477—8.

76   Ibid., pp. 477—8.

77   *CAB* 23/90B, CC 5(37)12, 3 February 1937.

78   *CAB* 23/87, CC 9(37)10, 24 February 1937.

79   See *CAB* 23/78, CC 9(34)13 and CC 10(34)3, 19 March 1934. For the amended report see *CAB* 23/79, CC 31(34)1, 31 July 1934.

80   Further comment on this decision can be found in Avon, pp. 96—7 and Michael Howard, *The Continental Commitment* (Penguin, 1974), pp. 104—16.

81   Howard, pp. 116—22. The debate between Eden and Chamberlain on rearmament is also discussed by Keith Middlemas, *Diplomacy of Illusion* (London, 1972), pp. 116—28.

82   *CAB* 23/88, CC 27(37)2, 30 June 1937.

83   Avon, pp. 491—4.

84   *CAB* 23/90, CC 48(37)9, 22 December 1938.

85   *CAB* 23/90, CC 49(37)1, 22 December 1938.

86   The decision to raise the upper expenditure limit was confirmed by the Cabinet on 16 February 1938, *CAB* 23/92, CC 5(38)9.

87   *CAB* 23/90, CC 48(37)9, 22 December 1938.

88   *CAB* 23/92, CC 5(38)9, 16 February 1938.

89   *Neville Chamberlain Papers*, NC 18/1/1040, letter to his sister Hilda, 27 February 1938.

90   Sir John Wheeler-Bennett, *Knaves, Fools and Heroes: In Europe between the Wars* (London, 1974), pp. 13—14.

91   Eden had discussed the possibility of a further approach to Germany for a colonial settlement with Chamberlain in the first week of February. It was agreed that Henderson would broach the subject in Berlin in the near future, Oliver Harvey, diary entry for 6 February 1938, Harvey, pp. 82—6. In addition it would appear that Eden supported the attempts to lure Goering to Britain in March 1938 as a sequel to Halifax's visit to Berlin. *Avon Papers*, FO 954/10A, Ger/38/3—4.

92   G. McDermott, *The Eden Legacy and the Decline of British Diplomacy* (London, 1969), p. 53.

93   Ibid., p. 230.

94   Quote from Eden's letter of resignation dated 20 February 1938, Avon, p. 596.

95   In particular see Broad, pp. 104—14; Rees-Mogg, pp. 72—7; Winston Churchill, pp. 230—3; and Campbell-Johnson, pp. 144—57.

Bibliography

A.   Manuscript Sources

— Birmingham University Library

    Avon Papers (Private Office Papers of Anthony Eden 1936–1938)
    With particular reference to subject headings:

FO 954/1A	Austria
FO 954/1B	Belgium
FO 954/2	Nyon Conference
FO 954/4A	Defence
FO 954/4A	Dominions
FO 954/6A	Ethiopia
FO 954/6B	Far East
FO 954/7B	Foreign Policy
FO 954/10A	Germany
FO 954/12B	Iraq
FO 954/13A	Italy
FO 954/14B	League of Nations
FO 954/14B	Locarno Treaty
FO 954/24A	Soviet Union
FO 954/27A	Spain
FO 954/29	United States of America
FO 954/30	United States of America

Austen Chamberlain Papers

    AC 5/1   Correspondence

Neville Chamberlain Papers

NC 2/23A	Political Diaries 1933–1936
NC 2/24A	Political Diaries 1937–1940
NC 18/1/931–1045	Letters to his sisters 1935–1938
NC 1/17/1–10	Letters to Lady Ivy Chamberlain 1937–1938
NC 7/11/29/1–46	Miscellaneous Correspondence 1936
NC 7/11/30/1–76	Miscellaneous Correspondence 1937
NC 7/11/31/100	Miscellaneous Correspondence 1938

— Cambridge University Library

Baldwin Papers

Vol. 44	Political and Party Affairs
Vol. 118	Foreign Affairs 1932
Vol. 121	Foreign Affairs 1933
Vol. 122	Foreign Affairs 1934
Vol. 123	Foreign Affairs 1935
Vol. 124	Foreign Affairs 1936–1939
Vol. 129	Disarmament
Vol. 152	Letters

Templewood Papers

VIII	Foreign Secretary 1935–1936
IX	First Lord of the Admiralty 1936–1937
X	Home Secretary 1937–1939
XIX	Background for 'Nine Troubled Years'

— Churchill College Cambridge

Hankey Papers

HNKY 1/7	Diaries 1923–1942
HNKY 1/8	Pages separated from the above diaries
HNKY 4/28–33	General correspondence 1936–1941
HNKY 5/1	Correspondence with W.S. Churchill
HNKY 5/4	Correspondence with Lord Halifax
HNKY 5/5	Correspondence with Sir Eric Phipps

Phipps Papers

PHPP 1/16—19	Correspondence with Eden 1936—1938
PHPP 3/2	Letters to Eden January 1934—June 1939
PHPP 3/3	Correspondence with Hankey 1929—1940
PHPP 5/5—6	Berlin Embassy Papers 1934—1937
PHPP 5/7	Paris Embassy Papers 1937—1939

Vansittart Papers

VNST 1/1—23	Cabinet Papers 1930—1938
VNST 2/1—34	Foreign Office Minutes 1933—1938

— Public Record Office, London

Cabinet

CAB 23	Cabinet Minutes and Conclusions
CAB 27	Cabinet Committees

Committee of Imperial Defence

CAB 2	Minutes and Reports of the Committee of Imperial Defence
CAB 16	Papers for the Committee of Imperial Defence

Foreign Office

FO 371	General Correspondence of the Foreign Office
FO 800	Papers of Sir John Simon
FO 954	Papers of Anthony Eden

B.   Printed Sources

— Primary Sources

Official Papers

Documents on British Foreign Policy 1919—1939, 2nd ser., vols 1—18 (London, 1946—1980)
Documents on German Foreign Policy 1918—1945, ser. C, vols 1—6 and ser. D, vols 1—3 (London, 1949—1983)

Documents of the London Naval Conference 1935 (London, 1936)

Foreign Relations of the United States, 1937, vol. 3 and 1938, vol. 1 (Washington, 1954—1955)

Royal Institute of International Affairs, *Documents on International Affairs 1935, vol. 2* (London, 1937)

Royal Institute of International Affairs, *Documents on International Affairs 1936* (London, 1937)

Royal Institute of International Affairs, *Documents on International Affairs 1937* (London, 1939)

Royal Institute of International Affairs, *Documents on International Affairs 1938, vol. 1* (London, 1942)

Parliamentary Debates

United Kingdom Parliamentary Debates, House of Commons, 5th ser., vols 169—332

United Kingdom Parliamentary Debates, House of Lords, 5th ser., vol. 103.

Speeches, Diaries and Papers

Baldwin, Stanley, *Service of Our Lives: Last Speeches as Prime Minister* (London, 1937)

Cadogan, Sir Alexander, David Dilks (ed.), *The Diplomatic Diaries of Sir Alexander Cadogan* (London, 1971)

Chamberlain, Arthur Neville, *In Search of Peace* (London, 1939)

Chamberlain, Austen, *Peace in Our Time: Addresses on Europe and the Empire* (London, 1928)

Ciano, Count Galeazzo, Malcolm Muggeridge (ed.), *Ciano's Diary 1937—1938* (London, 1952)

Eden, Anthony, *Foreign Affairs* (London, 1939)

Halifax, Earl of, *Speeches on Foreign Policy* (London, 1940)

Harvey, Oliver, John Harvey (ed.), *The Diplomatic Diaries of Oliver Harvey 1937—1940* (London, 1970)

Hore-Belisha, Leslie, R.J. Minney (ed.), *The Private Papers of Hore-Belisha* (London, 1960)

Jones, Thomas, *A Diary with Letters* (London, 1954)

Nicolson, Harold, Nigel Nicolson (ed.), *Diaries and Letters 1930—1939* (London, 1966)

Pownall, Lieutenant-General Sir Henry, Brian Bond (ed.), *The Diaries of Lt-General Sir Henry Pownall, Vol. 1, 1933—1940* (London, 1972)

Newspapers and Periodicals

Extracts for the period 1924—1938 taken primarily from:

Daily Express
Daily Herald
Daily Mail
Daily Telegraph
Manchester Guardian
News Chronicle
The Times
The Spectator

— Secondary Sources

Books

1. By Anthony Eden, Earl of Avon:

Places in the Sun (London, 1926)
Memoirs, Vol. 1, Facing the Dictators (London, 1962)
Another World 1897—1917 (London, 1976)

2. Other sources:

Amery, L.S., *My Political Life*, vol. 3 (London, 1955)
Aster, Sidney, *Anthony Eden* (London, 1976)
Baldwin, A.W., *My Father, The True Story* (London, 1956)
Bardens, Dennis, *Portrait of a Statesman* (London, 1955)
Barnett, Correlli, *The Collapse of British Power* (London, 1972)
Beloff, Max., *The Foreign Policy of Soviet Russia, Vol. 2, 1936—1941* (London, 1949)
Birkenhead, Earl of, *The Life of Lord Halifax* (London, 1965)
Blake, R., *The Conservative Party from Peel to Chamberlain* (London, 1970)
Blum, J.M., *From the Morgenthau Diaries* (Boston, 1959)
Bond, B. and Roy, I. (eds), *War and Society, A Yearbook of Military History* (London, 1975)
Broad, L., *Sir Anthony Eden* (London, 1955)
Bullock, Alan, *Hitler, A Study in Tyranny* (London, 1974)
Campbell-Johnson, Alan, *Eden, The Making of a Statesman* (London, 1955)
Carlton, David, *Anthony Eden* (London, 1981)

Carlton, David, *MacDonald versus Henderson, The Foreign Policy of the Second Labour Government* (London, 1970)

Cecil, Viscount, *A Great Experiment* (London, 1941)

Churchill, Randolph S., *The Rise and Fall of Sir Anthony Eden* (London, 1959)

Churchill, Sir Winston S., *The Second World War, Vol. 1, The Gathering Storm* (London, 1948)

Coffey, T.M., *Lion by the Tail, The Story of the Italian-Ethiopian War* (London, 1974)

Colvin, Ian, *The Chamberlain Cabinet* (London, 1971)

Colvin, Ian, *Vansittart in Office* (London, 1965)

Cooper, Alfred, Duff, *Old Men Forget* (London, 1953)

Coverdale, J.F., *Italian Intervention in the Spanish Civil War* (Princeton, 1975)

Cowling, Maurice, *The Impact of Hitler: British Politics and British Policy, 1933—1940* (London, 1975)

Craig, G. and Gilbert, F. (eds), *The Diplomats, Volumes 1 and 2* (New York, 1972)

Cross, J.A., *Sir Samuel Hoare, A Political Biography* (London, 1977)

Dalton, Hugh, *The Fateful Years, Memoirs 1931—1945* (London, 1957)

Dreifort, J.E., *Yvon Delbos at the Quai d'Orsay, French Foreign Policy during the Popular Front* (Kansas, 1973)

Eden, Timothy, *The Tribulations of a Baronet* (London, 1933)

Edwards, Jill, *The British Government and the Spanish Civil War, 1936—1939* (London, 1979)

Emmerson, J.T., *The Rhineland Crisis* (London, 1977)

Feiling, Keith, *The Life of Neville Chamberlain* (London, 1946)

Francois-Poncet, A., *The Fateful Years* (London, 1949)

Furnia, A.H., *The Diplomacy of Appeasement, Anglo-French Relations and the Prelude to World War II* (Washington, 1960)

Gannon, Franklin Reid, *The British Press and Germany* (Oxford, 1971)

Gilbert, Martin, *Britain and Germany between the Wars* (London, 1964)

Gilbert, Martin, *The Roots of Appeasement* (London, 1966)

Gilbert, M. and Gott, R., *The Appeasers* (London, 1963)

Halifax, Earl of, *Fulness of Days* (London, 1957)

Henderson, Sir Nevile, *Failure of a Mission* (London, 1940)

Howard, Michael, *The Continental Committment, The Dilemma of British Defence Policy in the Era of the Two World Wars* (London, 1972)

Hull, Cordell, *Memoirs, Vol. 1* (London, 1948)

James, Robert Rhodes, *Memoirs of a Conservative. J.C.C. Davidson's Memoirs and Papers 1910–1937* (London, 1969)

James, Robert Rhodes, *Churchill, A Study in Failure, 1900–1939* (London, 1970)

Kleine-Ahlbrandt, W.L., *The Policy of Simmering: A Study of British Policy during the Spanish Civil War, 1936–1939* (The Hague, 1962)

Laurens, F.O., *France and the Italo-Abyssinian Crisis 1935–1936* (The Hague, 1967)

Lee, Bradford A., *Britain and the Sino-Japanese War, 1937–1939* (London, 1973)

Londonderry, Marquess of, *Ourselves and Germany* (London, 1938)

McDermott, Geoffrey, *The Eden Legacy* (London, 1969)

Macleod, Ian, *Neville Chamberlain* (London, 1961)

Macmillan, Harold, *Winds of Change, 1914–1939* (London, 1969)

Marquand, David, *Ramsay MacDonald* (London, 1977)

Medlicott, W.N., *Britain and Germany, The Search for Agreement* (London, 1969)

Medlicott, W.N., *Contemporary England, 1914–1964* (London, 1967)

Menzies, Robert, *Afternoon Light: Some Memories of Men and Events* (London, 1967)

Middlemas, Keith, *Diplomacy of Illusion: The British Government and Germany, 1937–1939* (London, 1972)

Middlemas, Keith and Barnes, John, *Baldwin, A Biography* (London, 1969)

Montgomery Hyde, H., *Lord Reading* (London, 1967)

Mowat, C.L. *Britain between the Wars* (London, 1955)

Naylor, J.F., *Labour's International Policy, The Labour Party in the 1930's* (London, 1969)

Néré, J., *The Foreign Policy of France from 1914–1945* (London, 1975)

Nicolson, Harold, *Curzon, The Last Phase, 1919–1925* (New York, 1939)

Nicolson, Harold, *King George V* (London, 1952)

Northedge, F.S., *The Troubled Giant: Britain among the Great Powers, 1916–1939* (London, 1966)

Ovendale, Ritchie, *'Appeasement' and the English Speaking World. The United States, the Dominions, and the Policy of 'Appeasement', 1937–1939* (Cardiff, 1975)

Peterson, Maurice, *Both Sides of the Curtain* (London, 1950)

Petrie, Sir Charles, *The Life and Letters of the Rt Hon. Sir Austen Chamberlain*, vol. 2 (London, 1940)

Pratt, Laurence R., *East of Malta, West of Suez, Britain's Mediterranean Crisis, 1936–1939* (Cambridge, 1975)

Preston, A. (ed.), *General Staffs and Diplomacy before the Second World War* (London, 1978)

Robbins, Keith, *Munich 1938* (London, 1968)

Robertson, E.M., *Hitler's Pre-War Policy and Military Plans, 1933–1939* (London, 1963)

Roskill, Stephen, *Hankey, Man of Secrets*, vol. 3 (London, 1974)

Schmidt, Dr P., *Hitler's Interpreter* (London, 1951)

Simon, Viscount, *Retrospect* (London, 1952)

Strang, Lord, *Home and Abroad* (London, 1956)

Swinton, Lord, *Sixty Years of Power* (London, 1966)

Taylor, A.J.P., *Beaverbrook* (London, 1972)

Temperley, Major-General A.C., *The Whispering Gallery of Europe* (London, 1939)

Templewood, Viscount, *Nine Troubled Years* (London, 1954)

Thorne, Christopher, *The Limits of Foreign Policy: The West, the League and the Far Eastern Crisis of 1931–1933* (London, 1972)

Vansittart, Lord, *The Mist Procession* (London, 1958)

Waites, Neville (ed.), *Troubled Neighbours: Franco-British Relations in the Twentieth Century* (London, 1971)

Walters, F.P., *A History of the League of Nations* (London, 1969)

Watkins, K.W., *Britain Divided, the Effect of the Spanish Civil War on British Public Opinion* (London, 1963)

Watt, D.C., *Too Serious a Business, European Armed Forces and the Approach of the Second World War* (London, 1975)

Watt, D.C., *Personalities and Policies* (London, 1965)

Waley, D., *British Public Opinion and the Abyssinian War, 1935–1936* (London, 1975)

Wheeler-Bennett, Sir J., *Knaves, Fools and Heroes: In Europe between the Wars* (London, 1974)

Weinberg, G.L., *The Foreign Policy of Hitler's Germany, Volume 1, 1933–1936* (Chicago, 1970)

Weinberg, G.L., *The Foreign Policy of Hitler's Germany, Volume 2, 1937–1939* (Chicago, 1980)

Welles, Sumner, *Time for Decision* (London, 1944)

Wolfers, A., *Britain and France between the Two World Wars* (New York, 1966)

Wrench, J.E., *Geoffrey Dawson and Our Times* (London, 1956)

Young, G.M., *Stanley Baldwin* (London, 1952)

Zetland, Marquis of, *Memoirs* (London, 1956)

Articles

Baumont, Maurice, 'The Rhineland Crisis: March 1936', in Neville Waites (ed.), *Troubled Neighbours. Franco-British Relations in the Twentieth Century* (London, 1971)

Bloch, Charles, 'Great Britain, German Rearmament and the Naval Agreement of 1935', in Hans W. Gatzke (ed.), *European Diplomacy between Two Wars, 1919–1939* (Chicago, 1972), pp. 125–51.

Braddick, Henderson B., 'The Hoare–Laval Plan, A Study in International Diplomacy', in Hans W. Gatzke (ed.), *European Diplomacy between Two Wars, 1919–1939* (Chicago, 1972), pp. 152–71.

Cairns, J.C., '7 March 1936 Again. The View from Paris', in Hans W. Gatzke (ed.), *European Diplomacy between Two Wars, 1919–1939* (Chicago, 1972), pp. 172–92.

Carlton, David, 'Eden, Blum and the Origins of Non-Intervention', *Journal of Contemporary History*, 6 (1971), pp. 40–64.

Craig, G.A., 'The British Foreign Office from Grey to Austen Chamberlain', in G.A. Craig and F. Gilbert (eds), *The Diplomats 1919–1939, Volume 1* (New York, 1972), pp. 15–48.

Dilks, David, 'The Unnecessary War? Military Advice and Foreign Policy in Great Britain, 1931–1939', in A. Preston (ed.), *General Staffs and Diplomacy before the Second World War* (London, 1978), pp. 98–132.

Douglas, Roy, 'Chamberlain and Eden, 1937–1938', *Journal of Contemporary History*, 13 (1978), pp. 97–116.

Goldman, A.L., 'Two Views of Germany. Nevile Henderson versus Vansittart and the Foreign Office, 1937–1939', *British Journal of International Studies*, 6, 3 (October 1980), pp. 247–77.

Gretton, Peter, 'The Nyon Conference — the Naval Aspect', *English Historical Review*, 90, 354 (January 1975).

Kovrig, Bennett, 'Mediation by Obfuscation: The Resolution of the Marseille Crisis, October 1934 to May 1935', *Historical Journal*, 19 (1976), pp. 191–221.

Lammers, D.N., 'Fascism, Communism and the Foreign Office, 1937–1939', *Journal of Contemporary History*, 6 (1971), pp. 66–86.

Marder, A., 'The Royal Navy and the Ethiopian Crisis of 1935–1936', *American Historical Review*, 75, 5 (June 1970), pp. 1327–56.

Parker, R.A.C., 'Great Britain, France and the Ethiopian Crisis, 1935–1936', *English Historical Review*, 89 (1974), pp. 193–332.

Pratt, Lawrence, 'The Anglo-American Naval Conversations on the Far East of January 1938', *International Affairs*, 47, 4 (October 1971), pp. 745–63.

Schwoerer, L.G., 'Lord Halifax's Visit to Germany, November 1937', *The Historian*, 32, 3 (May 1970), pp. 353–75.

Stone, Glyn, 'Britain, Non-Intervention and the Spanish Civil War', *European Studies Review*, 9 (1979), pp. 129–49.

Toscano, Mario, 'Eden's Mission to Rome on the Eve of the Italo-Ethiopian Conflict', in A.O. Sarkissian (ed.), *Studies in Diplomatic History and Histiography* (London, 1961), pp. 126–52.

Watt, D.C., 'Roosevelt and Chamberlain: Two Appeasers', *International Journal of Canadian Institute of International Affairs*, 78, 2 (1973), pp. 185–204.

Watt, D.C., 'Document: The Secret Laval–Mussolini Agreement of 1935 on Ethiopia', in E.M. Robertson (ed.), *Origins of the Second World War* (London, 1971), pp. 69–78.

Index

Eden, Robert Anthony (cont.)
life and career (cont.):

Office 21; has big majority in 1931 election 23; role in Manchurian crisis, 1931–2 25, 26; views on Disarmament Conference, 1932 29; attached to British delegation at Conference 32; work at Disarmament Conference 33–42 *passim*, 45–55 *passim*; appointed Lord Privy Seal, 1933 45, 58; first meetings with Hitler, 1934 47–8; meets Mussolini, 1934 51; accepts idea of German rearmament 74; accepts modest British rearmament, 1934 74–5; represents Britain at League of Nations, 1934 75; refuses guarantee of Austrian independence 75–6; scheme for international supervision of Saar plebiscite, 1934 76–8; deals with crisis caused by murder of King Alexander of Yugoslavia and Louis Barthou, 1934 78–9; sees Von Ribbentrop, 1934 79; Paris visit, 1935 88; unsuccessful Berlin visit, 1935 88–91; meets Soviet foreign minister, 1935 91–2; meets Stalin 92–3; meets Polish foreign minister, 1935 94; meets Marshal Pilsudski, 1935 95; meets Eduard Benes, 1935 95; ordered to rest 95, 96, 114; reports on journeys throughout Europe 96–8, 99; on need for common front against Hitler 100; becomes Minister for League of Nations Affairs, 1935 102–3, 114; faces Italo-Abyssinian problem 116–26 *passim*, 128, 130–1, 133–4, 137; soothes French over Anglo-German Naval Agreement, 1935 123, 170; tries to reach Anglo-French agreement on Abyssinia 126–7, 129; states British policy of sanctions against Italy, 1935 134, 135; portrayed as champion of League of Nations in 1935 election 136; stresses need for oil sanctions against Italy, 1935 141; reservations on Hoare–Laval Pact 142–3, 144, 145–6; becomes Foreign Secretary on British disavowal of Hoare–Laval proposals, 1935 148–9, 150, 151, 165; assisted by Lord Halifax, as Lord Privy Seal 166; needs to restore confidence in Britain's support of League of Nations, 1936 166–7; considers oil embargo against Italy, 1936 167–8; takes stock of Anglo-German relations 171–2, 173–4; proposals for Air Pact, 1936 176, 178, 179, 180; fails to anticipate German reoccupation of Rhineland 177, 178; consults French on Rhineland issue 181–2, 183, 184, 187; proposes military talks with France and Belgium 185–6, 187–90 *passim*; attempts to reach agreement with Germany, 1936 190–6; unwilling to close Suez Canal to Italian shipping 196–7; delays considering further sanctions on Italy 197, 198; fears German 'putsch' in Austria, 1936 198, 199; loses faith in League of Nations and collective security 199; plan to restructure League of Nations 199–200, 206; reluctant to lift sanctions on Italy 200; desire for *quid pro quo* from Mussolini 201, 202; recommends abandonment of sanctions against Italy, 1936

Times, The 79, 96, 102, 180, 189, 278, 361
Tyrrell, Lord 41, 44

United States of America 373: rejects collective security concept, 1934 54–5, 57; question of oil embargo against Italy, 1936 167, 168; opposed to sanctions against Japan, 1937 323; Anglo-American Naval Staff talks, 1937 325
See also Roosevelt, Pres. Franklin D.

Van Zeeland, Paul 181, 182, 221, 222, 243
Vansittart, Sir Robert 26, 41, 44, 55, 73, 82, 84, 85, 85, 87, 91, 98, 100, 114–18 *passim*, 124, 126, 127, 135, 137, 142, 146, 149, 150, 151, 172, 197, 198, 200, 205, 224, 226, 239, 249, 280, 282, 285, 287, 290, 300, 301, 308, 363, 370: *Mist Procession, The* 22; on Eden 22; on Mussolini 281–2
    period as Permanent Under-Secretary at Foreign Office: on Manchurian crisis, 1931–2 25; memo on Disarmament Conference, 1933 38; ready to do a deal with Hitler, 1935 121, 125, 138; suggests colonial concessions to Germany 172; suspicious of German aggressive intentions 225, 257, 336; campaign to

move him from Foreign Office, 1936–7 256–8; loses job, 1937 306–7, 337
Vasconcellos, Mons. 145
Versailles, Treaty of 27, 31, 33, 53, 179, 181
Von Blomberg, Gen. 177
Von Hoesch, Herr 138, 175, 178
Von Neurath, Baron 40, 47, 80, 85, 225, 274–8 *passim*, 283, 299, 301, 339
Von Papen, Franz 33
Von Ribbentrop, Joachim 79, 211, 224, 276, 299, 339
Von Schuschnigg, Kurt 345

Warwick, Countess of 4
Welles, Sumner 322, 332
Wellesley, Sir V. 26
Wheeler-Bennett, Sir John 377
Wigram, Lord 135
Wigram, Ralph 134, 170, 171, 174, 175, 194, 200, 224, 225, 226, 249: death, 1936 247
Wilson, Sir Horace 257, 303, 326, 331, 334, 337, 347, 364, 367
Woermann, Herr 293
Wood, Sir Kingsley 245, 251–2, 254, 296
World Economic Conference 32

Yevtitch, Bogoljub 78
Yorkshire Post 361
Yugoslavia: murder of King Alexander, 1934 78; Pact of Belgrade with Italy, 1937 236

Zetland, Lord 147, 348

402